INSIDERS' GUIDE® TO

AUSTIN

SIXTH EDITION

CAM ROSSIE AND HILARY HYLTON

INSIDERS' GUIDE®

GUILFORD, CONNECTICUT
AN IMPRINT OF THE GLOBE PEQUOT PRESS

The prices and rates in this guidebook were confirmed at press time. We recommend, however, that you call establishments before traveling to obtain current information.

To buy books in quantity for corporate use or incentives, call **(800) 962–0973** or e-mail **premiums@GlobePequot.com**.

INSIDERS' GUIDE®

Text design by Sheryl Kober
Maps created by XNR Productions, Inc. © Morris Book Publishing, LLC

ISSN 1533-5216
ISBN 978-0-7627-4864-8

Printed in the United States of America
10 9 8 7 6 5 4 3 2 1

CONTENTS

CONTENTS

Directory of Maps

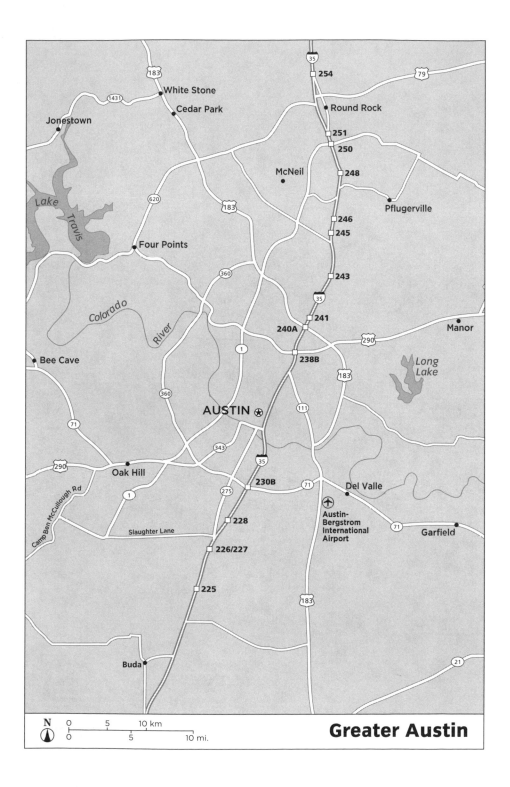

Greater Austin

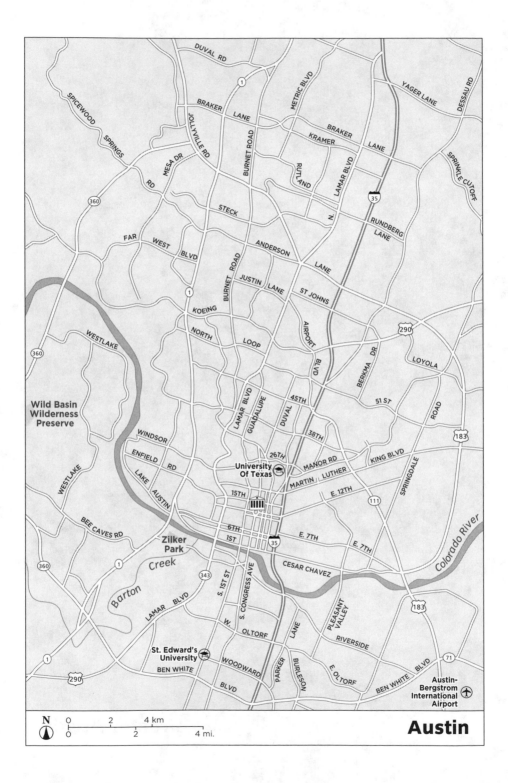

Austin

N

0 2 4 km
0 2 4 mi.

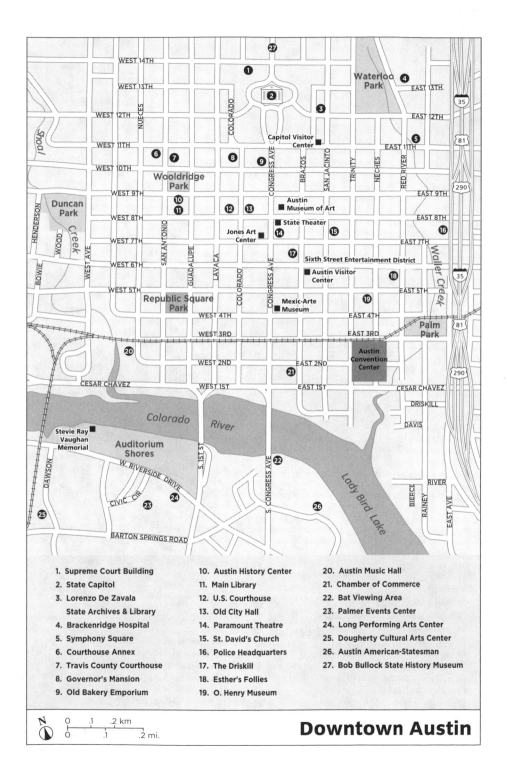

Downtown Austin

1. Supreme Court Building
2. State Capitol
3. Lorenzo De Zavala State Archives & Library
4. Brackenridge Hospital
5. Symphony Square
6. Courthouse Annex
7. Travis County Courthouse
8. Governor's Mansion
9. Old Bakery Emporium
10. Austin History Center
11. Main Library
12. U.S. Courthouse
13. Old City Hall
14. Paramount Theatre
15. St. David's Church
16. Police Headquarters
17. The Driskill
18. Esther's Follies
19. O. Henry Museum
20. Austin Music Hall
21. Chamber of Commerce
22. Bat Viewing Area
23. Palmer Events Center
24. Long Performing Arts Center
25. Dougherty Cultural Arts Center
26. Austin American-Statesman
27. Bob Bullock State History Museum

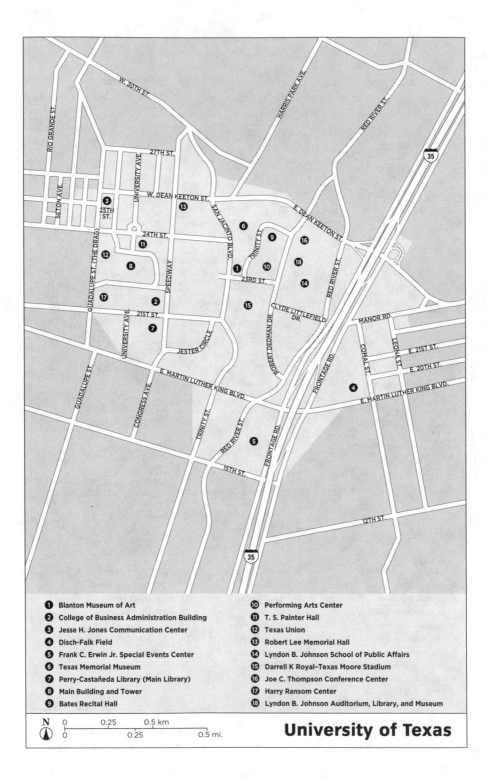

University of Texas

1. Blanton Museum of Art
2. College of Business Administration Building
3. Jesse H. Jones Communication Center
4. Disch-Falk Field
5. Frank C. Erwin Jr. Special Events Center
6. Texas Memorial Museum
7. Perry-Castañeda Library (Main Library)
8. Main Building and Tower
9. Bates Recital Hall
10. Performing Arts Center
11. T. S. Painter Hall
12. Texas Union
13. Robert Lee Memorial Hall
14. Lyndon B. Johnson School of Public Affairs
15. Darrell K Royal–Texas Moore Stadium
16. Joe C. Thompson Conference Center
17. Harry Ransom Center
18. Lyndon B. Johnson Auditorium, Library, and Museum

PREFACE

Austin! Just the name evokes so many images. Music. High Tech. Universities. Government. Movies. Research. The Hills. The Lakes. The Springs. Independence! Opportunity! Austin is all those things and much more, as you'll soon discover.

Riding on nothing more than beauty, its perch on the edge of a wild frontier, and the determination of its citizens, Austin became the capital of the Republic and then of the state of Texas, a vast territory that reaches from the Mexican border almost halfway to Canada. Like other Texans, Austinites who shaped this region developed a kinship with the land and with one another. To be a Texan is a definite distinction. To add Austinite—now that's the shine on the star.

Like many other Austinites, we are not natives, although Austin is one city that quickly becomes your own, no matter where you've lived before. The familiar bumper sticker "I wasn't born in Texas, but I got here as soon as I could" goes double for Austin. We're speaking from experience when we give these words of caution, especially for you who've come for just a visit: Austin sneaks up on you unexpectedly, like a sudden shower on a hot summer day. It will capture your heart as quickly as a dry field blossoms into wildflowers. Once you've gotten swept up in the energy of this city or given in to our peaceful pastimes, it's hard to leave. Austin is clever that way. It's old, and it's new, and every minute it's got something different to offer you. That's part of the Austin mystique.

Perhaps you've come to see for yourself what it is about Austin that causes people to perk up when they hear the name. We hope you'll find this guide useful in that regard. Within these pages we've shared our ideas about the people and places, the sounds and the scenery that contribute to Austin's unique style. We've sought to give you a deeper understanding of who we are by telling you where Austin has been and where it's headed as this booming region endeavors to define its future and preserve its acclaimed quality of life.

It's hard to argue with the national magazines that have rated Austin among the top cities for living and conducting business. Citing Austin's "emergence as a hotbed for high-tech startup firms," the prestigious *Fortune* magazine has listed Austin as "The Best City for Business in North America." "Austin has always been the sort of town where the '60s never really died, where creativity was encouraged, and free spirits were nurtured," *Fortune* praised. In his 2002 book *The Rise of the Creative Class*, economist and author Richard Florida lists Austin as the "No. 2 Creative Hot Spot" in the nation. Indeed, Austinites are warmhearted, outgoing people who tolerate about anything but encroachment on our stunning natural environment or challenge to our way of life. Our music scene is so hot that we call ourselves "The Live Music Capital of the World." Our vibrant film industry, which includes local actors and directors who are making it big, is luring more and more internationally known stars and directors to Austin. At any given time there are a dozen or more stage productions to enjoy as well as art museums and galleries to visit and poetry readings to attend. Our countless sports enthusiasts, the bikers, boaters, runners, golfers, and swimmers, keep Austin humming with their passion.

The University of Texas contributes much more than character and economic drive. UT, along with our other colleges and universities, draws leading scholars and researchers to Austin and offers our students and the public countless educational opportunities and chances to hear world-renowned speakers. Our bookstores and libraries are abuzz day and night. It's no surprise, then, that Austin is considered a literary capital as well as the center of our massive state government. Along with thousands of jobs, the vigorous high-tech industry adds another dimension to Austin's intellectual community. The reward in living and working in Austin comes in knowing that no matter what challenges the day brings, there is a fascinating, fun, beautiful, easygoing city right outside the door.

Austin's amazing ability to combine that vitality—that feeling that anything is possible here—with a sense of tranquility is among its greatest attributes. There's plenty of space to get away: lying on the beach at Lake Travis, strolling along a wooded trail, flying a kite atop breathtaking Mount Bonnell, taking a cool dip in Barton Springs, picnicking at the park, exploring the natural wonders of the Hill Country, canoeing along Lady Bird Lake (formerly Town Lake).

Don't take our word for it, though. Austin is a city that must be experienced firsthand. This book is meant to point you in the right directions. For those of you who've come to live, congratulations, you've chosen well. If you're here as a visitor, enjoy your Austin experience. Like we said, however, beware of its captivating charm.

ACKNOWLEDGMENTS

Working on this latest edition of our guide to Austin reinforced for me, once again, that this is a wonderful place to live. Austin continues to attract creative and interesting people and to nurture those of us who have called the city home for some time. This is a city that resists the cookie-cutter approach to urban life, and there is no shortage of characters, experts, eager amateurs, and cutting-edge professionals in the city's restaurants, stores, galleries, gardens, nightclubs, parks, and boulevards. One fast-growing facet of life in the capital has been the growth of virtual Austin—the city is as dynamic and fascinating in cyberspace as it is in the flesh. Also, the pace of growth in actual Austin is so rapid that changes to the city's cultural and social scene are a constant, giving the city a dynamism that permeates everyday life. Keeping track of those changes means relying on a wealth of resources, friends, neighbors, and those Austinites we interact with every day—the butcher, the baker and the barrista. Thanks to my coauthor, Cam, whose enthusiasm and professionalism are unmatched; and thanks to my husband, Peter Silva, whose insights into our hometown are invaluable.

—Hilary Hylton

One of the perks of working on *Insiders' Guide to Austin* is the opportunity to talk with so many of the fascinating people whose drive and creative energy help make our city so vibrant. Through their eyes I always discover new dimensions of Austin and grow to appreciate the singularity of this region even more than before. Thanks to everyone who took the time to offer their particular Insider information for this sixth edition. I am most appreciative of the editors and staff at The Globe Pequot Press who labor most diligently to make this book happen, and I would like especially to acknowledge my coauthor on this project, Hilary Hylton, an excellent journalist and friend and a true Austin Insider. Of course I am eternally grateful for my daughter, Quint Simon, who always provides pearls of wisdom and outstanding moral support.

—Cam Rossie

HELP US KEEP THIS GUIDE UP TO DATE

Every effort has been made by the authors and editors to make this guide as accurate and useful as possible. However, many changes can occur after a guide is published—establishments close, phone numbers change, facilities come under new management, etc.

We would love to hear from you concerning your experiences with this guide and how you feel it could be improved and be kept up to date. While we may not be able to respond to all comments and suggestions, we'll take them to heart, and we'll make certain to share them with the authors. Please send your comments and suggestions to the following address:

The Globe Pequot Press
Reader Response/Editorial Department
P.O. Box 480
Guilford, CT 06437

Or you may e-mail us at: editorial@GlobePequot.com

Thanks for your input, and happy travels!

HOW TO USE THIS BOOK

Whether you're planning to stay in Austin for a night, a fortnight, or the rest of your life, this book will guide you to, and through, the best the Capital City has to offer in more than two dozen areas of interest. *Insiders' Guide to Austin* is arranged by categories that appeal to both tourists and newcomers and can be useful whether you've just arrived or are only contemplating a visit or a move to Austin. Longtime residents may even discover a new thing or two about our city.

Our challenge in writing this book was to provide solid information and arrange it suitably so that you can map out a tour of Austin according to your own interests. It's up to you whether you take in these pages in one big gulp or choose to savor them slowly, chapter by chapter, as you make your way around town. Whatever your style, *Insiders' Guide to Austin* is meant to be used and used again as you delve deeper into the treasures of our Capital City. More than anything, we've designed this book to answer that age-old question: Where can I go to find . . . ?

Within these pages you'll encounter detailed descriptions of many of our most popular restaurants, attractions, hotels and motels, bed-and-breakfasts, and resorts as well as extensive listings of great places to shop and fun things to do with the kids. The chapter devoted to The Music Scene was a must, as you'll see, and we've dedicated another to Austin Nightlife. We've described our dynamic Literary Scene and given you an introduction to Austin's great Arts community. Nature lovers and outdoor types will discover the best that Austin has to offer in our chapter on Parks and Recreation.

For a wealth of information on our diverse periodicals, and radio and television stations, we've included a chapter on the Media. Newcomers will want to take special note of our chapters on Relocation, The Senior Scene, Worship, and Health Care and Wellness. Our chapter on Schools and Child Care includes information on private schools and all 10 public school districts in and around Austin, including those in our neighboring communities. Of course, no story of Austin would be complete without the Insiders' view of the capital's political personality. Don't miss our Politics and Perspectives chapter to find out what makes Austin tick.

Because much of the subject matter begs to be included in more than one chapter, we've noted where to look in the book for further information on a particular topic. Austin is loaded with resources, and we regret that we could not include every choice available in each chapter. We have, however, provided a solid foundation for you in all our categories and have pointed out additional resource materials that may provide more information. Also look for Insiders' Tips—marked with an ⓘ—that let you in on local secrets.

Finding your way around town will probably be the first challenge you face upon arriving in Austin. While Austin does have some great natural and manufactured boundaries, such as the Colorado River and our main highway arteries, the layout can be confusing due to our unique Hill Country terrain and the fact that Austin isn't too keen on east-west thoroughfares. No two people agree exactly on how to divide Austin into geographic regions, especially now that the city has grown so much. (The area that is still referred to today as West Austin, for example, is now in Central Austin, while a new West Austin is, well, farther west.)

Start your tour of Austin by reading our Getting Here, Getting Around chapter. In this chapter we've explained the boundaries we use in this book to divide the city into 10 regions: Central, South Central, North, South, East, West, Northeast, Northwest, Southeast, and Southwest. In some chapters we've subdivided these regions even further. In the Hotels and Motels chapter, for instance, you will find an extensive listing for accommodations under the Interstate 35 Corridor heading. Because there are so many Attractions in Central Austin, we've divided that region into Downtown, The University of Texas, and Central Austin.

Some chapters will also include an additional listing for Lake Travis, and you'll also find some information on Round Rock, Pflugerville, and Cedar Park. The boundaries we've described may not be universal boundaries, but they seemed the most realistic for us, and convenient for you. Refer to the maps we've provided to get started on your Austin adventure.

We've made every effort to provide you with the most accurate, up-to-date information in all categories. However, if you discover that your opinion differs from ours or that we've missed an important option, please feel free to send your comments or suggestions to us care of The Globe Pequot Press, P.O. Box 480, Guilford, CT 06437.

AREA OVERVIEW

Where do you live?" folks on planes sometimes ask us. "Austin, Texas," we say. Nine times out of 10 the questioner smiles, sighs, and says, "Lucky you."

Austin gets good press. In the past two decades, the city has been touted as a top place to live by numerous magazines. Perhaps the most overused adjective in all this positive coverage is "laid-back." But it fits. After all, this is a city where you can get by with one or two pairs of pantyhose a year or keep your tie rack in the back of the closet.

As former Mayor Kirk Watson once described Austin to us in an interview, "Austin is a city of boots and suits, hippies and nerds, all in the same boardroom . . . a city that allows almost ironic contradictions—at the same time we boast that we are the Live Music Capital of the World, we also boast we are Silicon Hills."

Laid-back, but on the high-tech cutting edge, cherishing the past, but charting the future. That dichotomy makes Austin an exciting, sometimes challenging place to live. We are embracing the future, yet looking longingly at the past, and, as the former mayor told us, so far each new wave of Austinites thinks they got here just in time to enjoy the real Austin.

Austin is a mecca for musicians and moviemakers, software engineers and hardware wizards, entrepreneurs and investors, artists and artisans, intellectuals and teachers, political activists and environmentalists, and lots of hardworking, everyday Texans who labor to make this city flourish. More than a million people call themselves Austinites these days, but there is still a neighborly feel about Austin and a notion that much of what goes on here is authentic.

As Austin has grown in both population and acreage, the pivotal question has been "How can Austin stay Austin, yet flourish?" The answer, so far, has come from within. Homegrown is the key here—whether it is homegrown businesses such as Dell Computer and Whole Foods Markets or homegrown restaurants such as Threadgill's and Jeffrey's, Austin's creative juices flow from the ground up. Franchise and chain operations, national corporations, and international businesses are represented in Austin, and they are growing in number; but, for the most part, they opt to adapt an Austin face, and often are overshadowed when viewed side by side with Austin originals.

This makes Austin a great place to live and to visit. Despite all its attributes, Austin has avoided being labeled a tourist town. Visitors are drawn to Austin not by a single, large attraction, a Disney World or a Fisherman's Wharf, but by the ambience of Austin. Consequently, we also are relatively free of touristy bric-a-brac, restaurants, and other sites that attract only out-of-towners. So whether you're visiting Sixth Street or stopping in for some spicy Tex-Mex food or barbecue, you will find yourself among the locals.

AUSTIN'S MANY FACES

The population of Austin is diverse and growing more so every year as new residents join the Austin melting pot. According to the U.S. Census Bureau, 12.4 percent of the city's residents are African American, 23 percent Hispanic, and 3 percent Asian. Approximately 7 percent of the city's residents are older than 65. About 9 percent of Austin's residents are foreign-born, and 23 percent speak a language other than English at home.

Austin's Vital Statistics

Founded: 1821 by Stephen F. Austin's colonists and named Waterloo; incorporated as Austin December 27, 1839

Mayor/Governor: Mayor Will Wynn; Governor Rick Perry

Population:
>Austin: 750,525
>Austin/Round Rock metropolitan statistical area: 1,557,829
>Texas: 23.5 million

Area:
>Austin: 298 square miles
>Austin/Round Rock metro area: 4,286 square miles

Counties in the Austin area (with major cities and county seats):
>Travis County (Austin is county seat and state capital)
>Williamson County (Round Rock; county seat Georgetown)
>Hays County (county seat San Marcos)
>Bastrop County (county seat Bastrop)
>Caldwell County (county seat Lockhart)

Major airports/interstates: Austin-Bergstrom International Airport; I-35, the Nafta Highway, runs through Austin

Nicknames: "Live Music Capital of the World," "Third Coast," and "City of the Violet Crown"

Average temperatures:
>Mean 68° F
>Mean low 58° F
>Mean high 79° F

Average annual precipitation: 32 inches

Annual days of sunshine: 200+

Major colleges and universities: Austin: University of Texas, Austin Community College, St. Edwards University, Texas State University—San Marcos, Southwestern University Georgetown, Concordia University of Austin, Huston-Tillotson College, Austin Presbyterian Seminary

Major area employers: University of Texas, Dell Computer, City of Austin, Austin Independent School District, Motorola, H-E-B Grocery Company, Seton Healthcare Network, IBM, Internal Revenue Service, Austin Community College, Advanced Micro Devices, Applied Materials

Famous sons and daughters: (Some native; others, as they say in Texas, got here as fast as they could.) Lyndon Baines Johnson, Lady Bird Johnson, O. Henry, Dabney Coleman, Lou Ann Barton, Charles Umlauf, Michael Dell, Stevie Ray Vaughn, Earl Campbell, J. Frank Dobie, James Michener, Lance Armstrong, Ethan Hawke, Zachary Scott, Molly Ivins, Willie Nelson, Karl Rove, Linda Ellerbe, Ben Crenshaw, Nelly, Joe Ely, Roger Clemens, Tom Kite, Bud Schrake, Ann Richards, Steven Fromholz

Public transportation: Capital Metro operates buses and downtown 'Dillo buses, light rail from Cedar Park to downtown Austin opens in the fall of 2008.

Driving laws: Speed limits vary according to the size of the street or highway and its location. Generally, interstate speed limits are 70 mph, city freeways are 55 mph or 65 mph, and most neighborhood speed limits are 30 mph.

Alcohol laws:

- You must be 21 to purchase wine, beer, or liquor in bars, restaurants, and stores.
- Blood alcohol level at which one is presumed to be intoxicated is 0.08.
- Beer and wine may be purchased in grocery and convenience stores seven days a week. Fortified wines like port cannot be sold on Sunday, and liquor stores are closed on Sunday.
- Bars remain open until 2:00 a.m.

Daily newspapers: the *Austin American–Statesman,* the *Daily Texan*

Alternative newspaper: the *Austin Chronicle*

Taxes:

- State sales taxes vary in the Central Texas region but generally range around 8 percent. In the City of Austin the rate is 8.25 percent. Groceries are not taxed.
- Hotel-motel occupancy tax in Austin is 15 percent.

Chamber of commerce: Austin Chamber of Commerce, in the Lakeshore Tower building at 210 Barton Springs Road, Suite 400, Austin, TX 78704; (512) 478-9383; www.austin-chamber.org

Visitor center: Austin Convention and Visitors Bureau, 209 East Sixth Street; (512) 478-0098 or (800) 8660GOAUSTIN; www.austintexas.org

Time and weather:

- KVUE–TV operates a time and temperature service at (512) 451-2424.
- Fox Channel 7 has a live weather cam at www.fox7.com, and Cable Channel 8 has "weather on the eights" throughout the hour.
- National Weather Service: www.srh.noaa.gov/ewx

The percentage of adults with college degrees stands at 35 percent, fourth place among 77 U.S. cities with a population of 200,000 or more. The median income in Austin in 2000 was $42,689, and according to the 2000 census, only 4.5 percent of households received public assistance, ranking 72nd out of those 77 cities. In 2005 the median income was $68,600.

One startling statistic is that the Austin labor force increased 44 percent in the decade from 1980 to 1990, and in recent years, unemployment rates stood at less than 3 percent, dipping to 1.9 percent in mid-2001 and climbing to just under 6 percent in mid-2003. By the spring of 2008, the rate had dipped again to 3.6 percent. Aus-

tin residents are predominantly young, diverse, dynamic, and hardworking; perhaps that is why the Austin lifestyle is characterized by a love for the outdoors and a lively interest in the latest music and art. But there is also a fondness for old Texas traditions; witness the abundance of annual events dedicated to cultural traditions (see our Annual Events and Festivals chapter).

While the past is celebrated, cultural diversity is unfolding at a furious pace in Austin. Restaurants and shops reflecting diverse cultural origins are growing in number. In a city where 25 years ago the choice of restaurants was relatively limited and dominated by Tex-Mex, barbecue, and homestyle cooking, residents and visitors can now choose from a wide variety of cuisines, often presented as "fusion" cuisine by one of the city's hot young chefs. There is a palpable sense of exploration in the air as the city adopts and absorbs a multitude of influences, translating them into an authentic Austin experience.

THE GREAT OUTDOORS

No description of Austin would be complete without an ode to the area's physical surroundings. Forget those clichéd Texas movie images you have seen in the Westerns. Austin is a city where trees and plants abound. Live oaks, pecans, cedar elms, and redbuds shade city streets, and city ordinances make it illegal to cut down trees of a certain diameter. Wildflowers, native plants, and grasses provide a year-round palette for both gardeners and Mother Nature as she paints the wild and natural areas of Central Texas.

Anyone who has visited Austin in the spring when the bluebonnets and Indian paintbrushes are in bloom leaves with a much-changed image of Texas. Hill Country pastures cry out for the brush of Monet, while the grassy banks along city freeways and country roads have been painted with a riot of color thanks to the state highway department's wildflower planting program.

The parade of wildflowers continues to bloom through summer and into fall. Every visitor and resident should make a pilgrimage to the Lady Bird Johnson Wildflower Center in Southwest Austin to take in the beauty, learn about native plants, and pay personal homage to the former First Lady who made saving American wildflowers a personal crusade (see our Attractions chapter).

Other examples of Austin natural wonders include Barton Springs, the spring-fed natural swimming pool that sits in the heart of the city's large downtown greenbelt, Zilker Park (see our Parks and Recreation chapter). Then there are the bats: North America's largest urban colony of Mexican freetail bats lives under the Congress Avenue bridge spring through fall, and their nightly flight in search of bug dinners draws crowds to the shores of Lady Bird Lake in downtown Austin (see our Attractions chapter). To the west of the city are the Highland Lakes, a chain of artificial lakes that stretch more than 150 miles, encompass 56,000 acres of water, and offer 700 miles of shoreline, making up the greatest concentration of fresh water in Texas. A network of lake and state parks, county and city parks, plus nature preserves and greenbelts surround Austin and provide green havens within the city limits (see our Parks and Recreation chapter).

In addition to a beautiful environment, Austinites also enjoy a generally benign climate. There are a few weeks in summer, notably late July and August, when the midday sun can take its toll, but since most buildings and cars in the city are air-conditioned, even those days are bearable. In winter there can be some brief spells of cold weather, but freezes are infrequent and snow is very rare, falling in any measurable amount about once every decade. One local tradition that new residents soon learn is the "plant shuffle"—hauling in all those patio plants that are sensitive to a hard freeze and then hauling them back out again a day or two later, but some winters pass without a single hard freeze.

The so-called blue norther is another Texas phenomenon that quickly becomes part of a newcomer's lexicon. These winter cold fronts often can be seen coming as the wind shifts to the north and the clouds are swept from the sky, allowing temperatures to fall into the 40s and 30s. Visitors often are astounded by how quickly the temperature falls, going from 70-something to 40-something literally in minutes—a good reason to carry a sweater in winter.

Spring is usually the rainy season, but Austin also enjoys spring days that border on the sublime, when residents can keep their windows open night and day. The average yearly rainfall is 32 inches, and there are on average 116 clear days, 114 partly cloudy days, 135 cloudy days, and 84 days with measurable rain. While winters are mild, sudden summer thunderstorms can be threatening. The Hill Country is riddled with what appear to be dry creekbeds, but after a sudden spring or summer rainfall they quickly become dangerous, as flash floods rage along their paths. Never try to drive across a flooded creekbed, and be aware of weather warnings about lightning storms and infrequent tornadoes.

For much of the year, the weather is benevolent and beautiful, allowing Austinites to spend their leisure time outdoors enjoying the many parks and recreational facilities in the area, perhaps a cup of coffee at an outdoor cafe, or a walk along Lady Bird Lake in the heart of downtown. But when the sun goes down they turn to other activities, enjoying the area's casual dining scene (see our Restaurants chapter) and the abundant nightlife.

Notable Events in Austin History:

1730: Spanish explorers establish a temporary mission at Barton Springs.

1821: Stephen F. Austin sends settlers to the banks of the Colorado River near Walnut Creek.

August 1833: The settlers are attacked by Indians.

1835: Jacob Harrell leaves Walnut Creek area and settles near the current site of the Congress Avenue Bridge.

March 2, 1836: Texas declares its independence from Mexico.

1837: William Barton settles on the south bank of the Colorado near artesian springs now named for him.

1838: Mirabeau Lamar, vice president of the Republic of Texas, goes on a buffalo hunt near the Colorado River and declares, "Here should reside the seat of the future empire."

May 1839: A one-story capitol building is erected at what is now Colorado and Eighth Streets.

August 1, 1839: The first city lots are sold.

November 1839: Waterloo is renamed Austin in honor of one of the founders of the Texas Republic.

December 27, 1839: Austin is incorporated.

December 1840: Jean Pierre Isidore Alphonse Dubois de Saligny builds the French Legation mission, Austin's oldest structure still intact.

March 5, 1842: As the Mexican Army takes San Antonio, President Sam Houston orders the Republic's archives moved to Houston.

December 29, 1842: The Archive War begins as Houston moves the capital to Washington-on-the-Brazos east of Austin and city residents refuse to move the archives to the new capital.

Summer 1845: A constitutional convention is held in Austin to ease the Republic's merger into the United States.

February 19, 1846: Texas joins the Union, and Austin is declared the state capital.

1850: A new capitol building is begun on the current site and completed in 1853.

February 1861: Austin and Travis County vote against secession from the Union, 704–450.

December 25, 1871: Houston and Texas Central Railroad reaches Austin, the most western railroad station in Texas, stimulating a decade-long boom.

1874: The first street lamps are placed along Austin's streets.

1876: David T. Lamme Sr. opens a candy store on Congress Avenue; the company is still in business in Austin.

1881: The city charters the University of Texas, which opens two years later. Tillotson Collegiate and Normal Institution opens to provide higher education to African Americans.

1885: St. Edward's College opens.

1886: The Driskill Hotel opens downtown.

May 16, 1888: The new pink granite capitol opens, replacing the first structure, which burned down.

1892: Celebrated European sculptor Elisabet Ney builds Formosa, her home and studio, in Hyde Park.

1893: Austin Dam, 60 feet high, is completed on the Colorado River.

1894: Writer O. Henry dubs Austin "The City of the Violet Crown" in a short story titled "Tictocq."

1895: Thirty-one so-called moonlight towers cast light throughout the night over the city.

April 7, 1900: Austin Dam collapses; eight die and the city is without power for months.

October 11, 1915: The Majestic Theatre opens on Congress Avenue. (Now completely restored and renamed the Paramount Theatre, it's a major performing arts venue.)

1918: Andrew Zilker's land, with iconic Barton Springs, becomes a city park named for its former owner.

1920: Austin's population reaches 34,876, but the city does not grow as fast as other regions of the state and ranks 10th in size.

1923: A major oil find in West Texas on land owned by the University of Texas sets the stage for the establishment of a permanent university fund.

October 14, 1930: Robert Mueller Municipal Airport opens.

December 6, 1933: Travis County Beer License No. 01 is issued to Kenneth Threadgill, whose little saloon would become a major magnet for musicians and help launch the city's modern-day music scene.

1937: The 27-story UT Tower is built, prompting J. Frank Dobie to ask why, with all the space in Texas, does a building here have to look like one in New York City.

1937: Lyndon Baines Johnson is elected to Congress, and his support for New Deal programs, including electrification of the Hill Country, helps Austin through the Great Depression.

July 2, 1939: KTBC–AM radio station opens; some of its notable staffers will include Nellie Connally and Bill Moyers.

1941: Mansfield Dam on Lake Travis is completed.

1942: Dell Valle Air Force Base, later renamed Bergstrom, opens.

Thanksgiving Day 1952: Launched by Lyndon and Lady Bird Johnson, Central Texas's first television station, KTBC, makes its debut.

1956: The University of Texas is the first major Southern school to admit African-American undergraduates.

1963: Football Coach Darrell Royal leads the UT Longhorns to their first national championship.

November 10, 1964: James M. White opens the Broken Spoke, which has become one of the nation's best country music halls.

April 1, 1966: From his perch in the UT Tower, sniper Charles Whitman shoots, killing 14 and wounding 31, after earlier murdering his mother and wife.

1967: IBM locates in Austin.

1968: An African American is elected to the Austin school district; three years later the first African American is elected to the city council. Mexican-American candidates succeed in 1972 and 1975 to the same bodies.

1969: Texas Instruments opens in Austin.

August 7, 1970: The legendary Armadillo World Headquarters opens.

1971: The LBJ Presidential Library opens.

1974: Motorola opens facilities in Austin.

1974: KLRU–TV producer Bill Arhos proposes a new music show, Austin City Limits; Willie Nelson stars in the pilot.

July 15, 1975: Clifford Antone opens his first blues club on Sixth Street. Over the years, Antone's puts Austin blues on the national map.

1982: Lady Bird Johnson opens her wildflower research center.

1983: City political and business leaders push successfully for the MCC high-tech consortium to be located in Austin.

1984: Michael Dell starts his computer company and direct flights, "Nerd Birds," are launched between Austin and Silicon Valley.

1987: Leaders once again make a big catch, luring the Sematech consortium to the city. Dell is the top employer, with annual sales of $12 billion.

1994: A seismic shift takes place in state politics as Republicans dominate both U.S. Senate seats and most of the state's highest offices and judicial posts.

1998: Incumbent Governor George W. Bush leads his party to a sweep of all statewide offices.

November 7, 2000: Thousands of supporters and media stand in a cold downpour on Congress Avenue, watching the presidential election gridlock.

2000: By year-end the dot-com boom has gone bust, with start-ups like living.com and garden.com evaporating.

2001: The year of the lay-offs, with Dell letting 5,700 workers go and some 21,000 lay-offs citywide.

November 2002: The Republican surge continues as the GOP takes all three branches of state government.

May 28, 2003: Signs of life in downtown Austin as the city's newest landmark, the 33-story Frost Bank skyscraper, is topped.

November 2003: More signs of recovery; an estimated 3,000 apartments and lofts are under construction in the downtown area.

October 2004: A record two million yellow "Live strong" bracelets are sold as the legendary cyclist and Austin resident Lance Armstrong rides through the streets of Austin in his annual Ride for the Roses bicycle event, all in support of his cancer-fighting foundation.

March 2005: Austin-born Whole Foods celebrates its 25th anniversary by opening its huge Landmark Store at Sixth and Lamar, just blocks from its first tiny location.

July 2006: *Money* magazine names Austin the "best big city" on its "best places to live" list.

September 2006: Beloved Austin resident, former Governor Ann Richards dies. The Congress Avenue Bridge is renamed in her honor.

July 2007: Another beloved Austin citizen, former First Lady Lady Bird Johnson dies. Austinites line Congress Avenue and the highway all the way to the LBJ Ranch in Johnson City in her honor.

November 2007: A live oak tree is hoisted atop 360 Condominiums, touted as the soon-to-be tallest building in downtown Austin at 563 feet and 44 stories tall. However, plans for the Austonian condo tower downtown outmatch the 360 plan, topping out at 683 feet in 2009.

THE MUSIC SCENE

Boasting the hottest live music scene in the country, Austin rocks day and night with just about any style of music imaginable: blues, country, jazz, folk, funk, punk, bluegrass, Tejano, rock and roll, alternative, and the savory sounds of our true Texas hybrids. Called a mecca for musical mavericks in 1998 by *Billboard* magazine, Austin is world renowned for its unique brands of original music and for attracting top-notch performers who would rather live and play in Austin than bend to the prevailing winds of musical fashion elsewhere. Home to the world's best-known country music outlaw, Willie Nelson, launching stage for the late blues legend Stevie Ray Vaughan, a haven for scores of world-class artists and up-and-comers, Austin is a paradise of live music. Read more about our music haven in The Music Scene chapter, which includes a Close-up on Austin favorites, Willie and Stevie Ray.

THE ARTS

While they haven't earned equal billing with the Live Music Capital of the World, Austin's dynamic arts and literary scenes lend the cultural dimension that makes this city such an inviting place to live. Long known as a haven for artists and intellectuals, more and more talented artists have found inspiration in Austin over the past few decades. Today Austin offers more than 250 theater productions a year, including national touring shows and an excellent variety of local productions. There are numerous annual arts and music events throughout the year, including the SXSW (South-By-Southwest) music and media conference in spring and the Texas Book Festival in fall (see our Annual Events and Festivals chapter). Our art museums, galleries, and bookstores abound with fresh voices in both the visual and literary arts. The city also is home to the Texas Film Commission, the state agency that has been successful in bringing many movie productions to what is affectionately called "The Third Coast." See our chapters on The Literary Scene and The Arts.

THE UNIVERSITY

Sprawling over 357 acres in the very heart of Central Austin, the University of Texas is an omnipresent force throughout this region. UT's contribution to Austin's economy and to its intellectual, political, and artistic development over the past 115-plus years has helped make Austin the envy of Texas and one of the coolest places in the land to live, work, study, and play. With about 50,000 students, UT gives Austin much of its youthful energy while bolstering its reputation as one of the country's hippest small cities. A breeding ground for intellectuals and a renowned research center, UT is one factor driving Austin's knowledge-intensive economy today. What's more, UT rewards Austinites almost daily by offering a rich variety of artistic, educational, and sporting events.

Although it's not considered one of the country's most beautiful campuses, UT nevertheless is a sight to behold. Towering shade trees, sculptures, and fountains by world-class artists, dozens of architectural wonders representing more than a century of development, and the 27-story UT Tower that soars as a landmark for all of Austin give the UT campus its unique flair. UT-Austin, the flagship of the system's 15 campuses spread throughout the state, is a source of pride for all Texans. Read about UT in our Attractions, Spectator Sports, The Arts, and Higher Education chapters and about its libraries in The Literary Scene chapter.

UT's size and importance to the economic development of Central Texas over the past century make UT Austin's most significant institute of higher learning. But our other colleges and universities—St. Edward's University in South Austin, Huston-Tillotson on the east side, Concordia University near UT, Southwestern University north of us in Georgetown, Texas State University south in San Marcos, and Austin Community College's campuses all over the region—combine

i Visitors to Austin are captivated by the flora in Central Texas, particularly the abundant wildflowers. The University of Texas Press publishes a wonderful full-color guide called *Texas Wildflowers* by Campbell and Lynn Loughmiller. The book has a foreword by Lady Bird Johnson.

to give Central Texas its fame as an educational Eden (see our Higher Education chapter).

GOVERNMENT

The Austin economy rests on three sectors: higher education, government, and the high-tech industry. The State of Texas employs approximately 50,000 people in the Austin area. As the state capital, the city is headquarters for many state agencies and, of course, the legislature and high courts.

The Texas legislature is convened on the second Tuesday of January in odd-numbered years for a 120-day regular session. Special sessions are occasionally called at other times by the governor. During the biennial session Austin takes on a little different air as hotels and restaurants fill with politicians, their staffs, and lobbyists. But Austin is also a political city year-round, since many legislative staffers live here, along with those agency heads, judges, and state bureaucrats who live, eat, and breathe the political air of the city.

Austin is also known for its active local political scene where the environment and the fight to keep Austin true to itself are always center stage (see our Politics and Perspectives chapter).

HIGH TECH

The third major pillar of the Austin economy is a relative newcomer. High tech is now an integral part of the picture, and the three largest private-sector employers in Austin are technology companies—Dell Computer Corp., Motorola Inc., and IBM Corp. The vibrant music industry, a burgeoning film scene, and an up-and-coming multimedia sector have added to the diverse economic picture, giving Austin a much wider economic base and ensuring that it is not as subject to the whims of a single economic sector's ups and downs as it was in the past.

Austin's homegrown computer titan, Dell Computer Corp., along with other Fortune 500 companies that established Central Texas branches in the 1980s and 1990s, brought tens of thousands of jobs to become the driving force

Close-Up

Texas Pronunciation Guide

"Texas—It's a whole other country!" Turns out the ad slogan used to promote Texas as a tourist destination is right, at least when it comes to the local lingo. Newcomers and visitors to Austin can be confounded by the local eccentricities in language, so we have developed this handy primer:

Balcones (Bal-CONE-niss) – A geological fault line that runs north-south through the city. This is just the first of several Spanish names that are not pronounced the way you were taught in high school Spanish.

Boerne (BURN-nee, rhymes with Bert and Ernie) – A small town southwest of Austin noted for its dude ranches. Just as many local names have their roots in Mexican culture, many also derive from the German settlers who made their homes in the Hill Country in the last century.

Bowie (BOO!-ee) – As in that buoy in the water. A hero of the Alamo, Jim Bowie gave his name to both a knife and an Austin high school.

Brazos (BRAA-ziss) – A Texas river that runs through Waco and the name of a downtown Austin street. All seven major Texas rivers give their names to downtown, north-south streets in Austin; memorize their names and their respective east-west position on the Texas map and you will know how to find them in downtown Austin (see our Getting Here, Getting Around chapter).

Buchanan (Buck-ANN-un) – Rhymes with buckin' bronco and is one of the Highland Lakes northwest of Austin. We have no explanation for why this Scottish name lost its "Byew" and became "Buck," except, of course, this is Texas.

Buda (BYEW-dah) – Rhymes with phew! This small town just south of Austin is noted for its small antiques and collectibles shops.

Bonnell (Bun-NELL) – That's Mount Bonnell, a popular spot to take in a view of Austin (see our Attractions chapter).

Burnet (BURN-it) – Rhymes with "durn it" and is a road in Austin and a Hill Country community.

Cameron Road (CAM-run) – Drop the middle syllable here, and you'll sound okay.

Coupland (COPE-land) – As in Aaron Copland, a musical connection that is appropriate since this is the home of the famous Coupland Dance Hall (see the Insiders' Tip in our Nightlife chapter).

Dessau (DESS-aw) – Dessau Lane is in North Austin.

Del Valle (Dell Valley) – Another Spanish word that has been anglicized, or Texas-ized, Del Valle is a community southeast of Austin near the Austin-Bergstrom International Airport.

Elgin (ELL-ghin) – No gin here (it rhymes with "kin"), or vermouth, just sausages. This small town east of Austin makes a famous German-style sausage that some barbecue aficionados regard as a mandatory element in any cookout.

Gruene (Green) – The German word for green and the name of a small town south of Austin known for its antiques shops and artists (see our Day Trips and Weekend Getaways chapter).

Govalle (Go Valley) – Another Spanish word corrupted by gringo tongues? Surprise! No, this is derived from a Swedish phrase *go val* meaning "good grazing land," and Swedish settlers gave this name to fertile pastureland east of Austin along the Colorado River. A cabin built there in 1840 by S. M. Swenson, the first Swedish settler in Texas, is now found in the Zilker Park Garden Center (see our Attractions chapter).

Guadalupe (GWA-da-loop) – If you can remember Alley Oop, you will quickly get the hang of this street name. The portion of Gwadaloop that runs through the University of Texas campus is known as "The Drag."

Huston (HYOU-stun) – As in Sam Houston, and part of the name of Huston-Tillotson College (see our Higher Education chapter).

Jager (YAY-gahr) – That's Yeager as in Chuck "The Right Stuff" Yeager and the name of a lane, now a major roadway, in North Austin.

Koenig (KAY-nig) – Another German name that was given to a lane in North Austin and another of those "lanes" that is now a major thoroughfare.

Kreuz (Cry-tzz) – You don't really have to know how to pronounce this name if you have good sense of smell. Simply start sniffing as you approach Lockhart, and your nose will carry you to the famous barbecue spot (see our Annual Events and Festivals chapter).

Lavaca (La-VAH-cah) – One of the few Spanish names pronounced correctly here, it means "the cow" and is also the name of a famous Spanish explorer, an Austin street, and a Texas river.

Llano (LAN-oh) – The name means "plains" in Spanish, but historians believe the county and town of the same name northwest of Austin take their name from the Llano River in the plains west of the Hill Country.

Manchaca (MAN-shack) – Not only has this Spanish word been given the Texas treatment, but the spelling has been changed as well. Legend says a spring south of Austin was named for Colonel Jose Antonio Menchaca, scion of an old San Antonio family. The "e" was changed to an "a" over the years to become Manchaca, the name given the community that grew up around the spring south of Austin. The Manchaca community is now part of the growing Austin, but the elementary school there has been named for Menchaca with the original spelling.

Manor (MAY-ner) – Forget your "to the manor born" accent when pronouncing the name of this community east of Austin and opt for a down-home twang.

New Braunfels (New BRAWN-fells) – This is one of several picturesque Hill Country towns that owe much of their character to German settlers (see our Day Trips chapter).

Nueces (New-AY-sez) – The Spanish word means "nuts," but in Austin the Spanish "nway" becomes "new." It is one of those downtown streets named for a Texas river.

Pedernales (PUR-der-nal-liss) – This "purdy" river runs through the LBJ Ranch near Johnson City (see our Day Trips chapter).

Pflugerville (FLEW-ger-ville) – The "p" is silent here, but this small town northeast of Austin is not a quiet backwater anymore. It is a thriving vibrant community (see our Relocation chapter).

Rio Grande (REE-oh Grand) – If it was good enough for John Wayne, then it's good enough for those Austinites who drop the final syllable here. This is another of those downtown river streets.

San Antonio (San An-TONE) – Not everyone opts for this pronunciation, but it does have a Texas ring to it. Again, a downtown street named for this Texas river.

San Jacinto (San Jah-SIN-tow) – In Spanish it would be "San Hah-seen-toh," but locals opt for the hard "J" here when they pronounce the name of this downtown street, another one of those river streets.

San Marcos (San MAR-kiss) – Round vowels are not the preferred Texas pronunciation, especially when they come at the end of a word, like the name of this college town south of Austin.

Texans (TEX-uns) – It is the round vowel syndrome again.

Texas (TEX-us) – Yet again, flat is better than round.

behind this region's economy. What's more, it didn't take too long for the Texas spirit of adventure to emerge in a big way in the technology field, and venture capital has played a major role.

Oil wildcatters of earlier decades enhanced Texas's mystique as a hotbed of fiercely independent risk-takers, but a new breed of prospectors is leading Austin today. Armed with computer chips rather than drill bits, Austin's modern wildcatters are gambling on start-up technology companies in computers and especially in software development. Some have hit major gushers (see our Politics and Perspectives chapter), while others have gone bust.

GROWTH ISSUES

Long known as a low-growth region, Austin lived out its unique vision for more than 150 years without much concern for policies in then-far-off Round Rock, Cedar Park, Dripping Springs, and other neighboring communities. But as this booming region expands into one big metropolis, Austin now is faced with developing a plan for the future that encompasses all of Central Texas's concerns. Growth has been the No. 1 topic in Austin for the last two decades, and now those once-small, quiet communities like Cedar Park and Dripping Springs are wrestling with the same issue.

Growth has been a two-edged sword for the Austin area. It has brought economic stability and even boom times, but it also has put stress on the environment. It has led to more restaurants, more shops, more donations to the arts, and contributions to the cultural scene, but it also has put pressure on infrastructure and public resources. However, growth also has led to dynamic, creative solutions, has revitalized old neighborhoods, given downtown a new vibrancy, and brought people together in new ways.

AUSTIN OVERLOOK

We called this section Overlook because visitors get many of the grandest views of this city looking down from one of its many hills or from above: the first view of the city from an airplane, a tapestry of lights surrounding two distinctive landmarks, the capitol and the University of Texas tower; a view of the downtown sky line from a scenic lookout point on Capital of Texas Highway west of the city; or the sun shimmering on Lake Travis at sunset, viewed from the deck of a lakeside restaurant; the reflections of the downtown lights in Lady Bird Lake viewed from a high-rise hotel; the view of the city from a picnic site on Mount Bonnell.

But Austin is not a city to be experienced only from above—or from afar. To get the most of this city, walk among the people and the places that have made Austin what it is today. So many of the places visitors find enjoyable are places the locals love to visit also.

By the time you're ready to leave Austin, if you can tear yourself away, you'll really know what it means when the locals bid you farewell with a "Y'all come back." You might even find yourself responding, "Y'all take care!"

Local weather forecasts are available from a variety of sources, including the Web sites of four local television stations: KTBC-TV, Channel 7, www.myfox austin.com; KVUE-TV, Channel 24, www .kvue.com; KXAN-TV, Channel 36, www.kxan .com; and KEYE-TV, Channel 42, www .keyetv.com (see our Media chapter). Time Warner Channel 8, www.news8austin.com, a 24-hour news channel, has weather "on the eights" every hour. The *Austin American–Statesman*, www.statesman.com, and the television stations listed above will send e-mail and cell phone weather alerts to subscribers.

POLITICS AND PERSPECTIVES

"All politics is local," former U.S. Speaker Tip O'Neill reportedly said, and in no place in Texas is that more true than Austin. Not only are city politics hard fought here, but this is also where the state's major parties have their headquarters. Austin is home to political spin doctors and policy wonks, lobbyists of all stripes, political scientists, and ardent grassroots volunteers, consultants, and image-makers.

No description of Austin would be complete without a discussion of politics. It is, after all, an Austin industry and one that flourishes year-round, coming into full bloom every other spring during the biennial sessions of the Texas Legislature. Economic development, business stimulation, and great public works (particularly roads and airports) are viewed as good public policy in Texas by the majority of state legislators. Not all their plans are welcomed by some of the citizens of Austin, and that is at the heart of a long-running love-hate relationship the city has with the legislature. Austin is well known as a "liberal" city, and the majority of voters within the city limits consistently vote for Democratic candidates, although the voter profile in the fast-growing suburbs is tending to be more Republican. However, Austin remains home to progressives and populists, a town where the most active political segment might be labeled the "Greens"—environmentalists, sometimes derided as "no-growthers"—who have been sounding a drumbeat of warnings about the need to limit growth, particularly in the Hill Country (see our Close-up on Barton Springs Pool in the Parks and Recreation chapter).

But the political picture is more complicated than that and, in some ways, getting more blurred as Austin's political profile changes. This is also the city that built the only new international airport in the country in the late 1990s, thanks to the clout of powerful Texas politicians such as the late Democratic Congressman JJ "Jake" Pickle, whose mentor was the biggest Texas politico of them all, President Lyndon B. Johnson. Austin residents can thank Johnson and other Texans with clout in Washington for the Highland Lakes, where so many residents and visitors head for recreation. Of course Austin also was home to President George W. Bush, further strengthening the Austin-Washington ties.

THE PARTNERSHIP

Government is a major employer in Austin, and it is also a major partner in the city's economic development. In the 1960s several visionary leaders in business and at the University of Texas began a campaign to bring industry to Austin. Not only did the city provide a pleasant cultural and social climate for new industry, they argued, but the university's engineering and science programs offered a valuable resource to major research operations. In 1966 the efforts paid off with the announcement that IBM was opening a new plant in Austin.

The move was a catalyst that resulted in Texas Instruments and Motorola opening up plants in the area to link to IBM. The efforts by community leaders had paid off, but they could not know what they had begun.

"IBM was both an end and a beginning—and it was the shape of things to come," Anthony M. Orum wrote in his book *Power, Money & the People: The Making of Modern Austin*. Fast forward to 1983 when William Norris of Control Data Corporation came up with the notion that U.S. companies needed to form a consortium of private technology companies to design the fifth generation of computers. The consortium, which had to turn to the federal government for exemptions from antitrust laws, was named the Microelectronics and Computer Technology Corporation, or MCC for short, and Norris chose Admiral Bobby Ray Inman, a former deputy director of the Central Intelligence Agency, to head up the effort.

Dozens of U.S. cities joined the chase to bring MCC home. Several cities in Texas made the pitch, and Austin ended up on the short list. The city's business leaders, politicians, and the state leadership went into a full-court press.

Austin won the prize. The reasons are disputed, but Orum credits the huge financial package Texas leaders and the university put together. The multimillion-dollar package prompted Atlanta Mayor Andrew Young to sniff that Austin had "bought" MCC.

Austin was on the high-tech map. Hadn't *Megatrends* author John Naisbitt predicted it in his best seller? Suddenly the city was being profiled and touted in national magazines and newspapers. In 1984 Michael Dell began his computer company out of his UT dorm room. Four years later, city and state leaders turned to many of the same team members it had employed in the MCC hunt to lure Sematech, a semiconductor consortium, to town.

Austin was on a roll. At mid-decade the city's population stood at 436,188, a 26 percent gain since 1980. As the *Austin American–Statesman* noted, the city had gained as many people in five years as it had since World War II. In one of those typical Austin dichotomies, growth had fueled a real estate boom, and that had prompted some of the city's most ardent liberals to become lobbyists and lawyers for development interests. Fortunes were being made, savings and loans were being chartered, and "flipping" real estate—buying it and quickly selling it—became the favorite game in town. At the same time, oil prices were sky-high, and since the oil and gas business still accounted for a third of the state's economy, the banks were flush with money to lend.

Then, the bottom fell out of the oil market, inflated land prices began to fall, and the Texas economy fell into recession. Some of the

> **i** There are five state holidays—Martin Luther King's Birthday on the third Monday in January; Texas Independence Day on March 2; San Jacinto Day, marking the defeat of General Santa Anna, on April 21; Emancipation Day, also called Juneteenth, on June 19; and Lyndon Baines Johnson's Birthday on August 27.

most well-known names in Austin declared bankruptcy, and a few went to jail. Texas languished and by all outward appearances was stuck in a rut. But behind the scenes, thanks to public policy and private know-how, the high-tech engines were churning and would soon reach a critical mass that would push both the Austin and Texas economy in a whole new direction.

HIGH-TECH RESCUE

The Austin economy began to turn around, and it became evident the new Austin was not dependent on real estate speculation and government growth for its economic well-being. Michael Dell's company broke the $1 billion mark in 1993, and by the end of 1997, Dell sales stood at $12 billion and the company was the area's largest private employer, with 12,000 people. Along the way, several Dell employees had gone their own way and established their own businesses, plus Dell's success had created hundreds of so-called Dellionaires who were savvy enough to buy Dell stock when it first went public and hang on to it through several stock splits.

In 1994 the daily "Nerd Bird" flights began between Austin and Silicon Valley, California. The city that had called itself the Third Coast in the 1980s now was kicking around the name Silicon Hills. In 1995 Tivoli Systems issued stock, and Lockheed closed its doors in Austin—software was in, military hardware was out.

Samsung broke ground on its memory chip plant in Northeast Austin in 1996. Two years later, the $1.3 billion Samsung plant was in operation. The city had felt some minor bumps on the road as semiconductor prices fell and some ventures failed, but venture capital was being spread around, and new companies were forming weekly. According to the *Austin American–Statesman*, 33 companies raised $164 million in venture capital in 1997, up from $40 million by nine companies in 1995. Those numbers skyrocketed as Austin entered the year 2000. In the first quarter, the newspaper reported, Austin companies had raised and invested $562 million in venture capital—$100 million more than second-place Dallas and a whopping $500 million more than Houston.

The city saw unemployment rates drop to less than 3 percent as the 1990s ended and Austin was enjoying a secure, creative atmosphere for young workers. They flocked to Austin not to sign on for a benefits-loaded package with a traditional employer, but rather to venture forth on their own in Internet and dot-com companies.

For some, the ride was a roller coaster and a few dot-com ventures rode the wave, but overall the high-tech economy continued to grow and feed on burgeoning venture capital.

CHANGING OUTLOOK

By the mid-1990s the empty office towers built during the real estate boom were filling up—in some cases government had come to the rescue again with the state and city buying up the unused towers. The state's coffers were filling up as its economy strengthened, boosted in large part by the emerging high-tech sector and the boom in trade with Mexico, prompted by the signing of the North American Free Trade Agreement (NAFTA) in 1994.

Support of NAFTA had been a bipartisan affair throughout the late 1980s and early '90s. That attitude is rooted in both economic realities and cultural predispositions. Texas leads the states in trade with Mexico with more than $50 billion in annual exports, and the state's cultural,

i **The Texas State Motto is "Friendship," and Texas is said to have been the Spanish pronunciation for a Caddo Indian word meaning "friends" or "allies."**

political, and social history is intertwined with Mexico's.

Sensitivity to Mexico and Hispanic heritage in Texas is a hallmark of both political parties. Governors Richards and Bush both developed diplomatic relations with Mexican leaders and governors south of the border. The political reality is that Hispanic voters have growing clout in Texas and in Austin. From 1980 to 1990, Texas's Hispanic population grew by 45 percent, and Hispanics make up some 25.6 percent of the state's population and 23 percent in Austin. By 2010 Texas is predicted to be a minority majority state, with Hispanics making up the largest sector in that majority. Not only is the Hispanic vote significant in Texas, but so is Hispanic leadership. Texas leads the way nationally in the number of Hispanic officeholders.

POLITICAL CHANGES

In addition to demographic changes, Texas also has undergone significant political realignment, some say because of the influx of new residents, others because of historical changes in the two major political parties. The year 1994 marked a watershed in Texas politics as the Republican Party recorded several landmark achievements. Republican gubernatorial candidate George W. Bush defeated Democratic governor Ann Richards, who had achieved national celebrity status. The pundits opined it would be a tight race, but it was not, and Bush recorded the biggest gubernatorial win in 20 years. He continued to get high ratings from voters throughout his first term.

The Republican Party continued its rise in 1998 as incumbent governor George W. Bush led a historic sweep by his party of all the major statewide races. Bush made major inroads into the traditionally Democratic Hispanic vote, winning almost 50 percent of that electorate. By 2003 Republicans held all major statewide offices and majorities in both the Texas House and Senate.

The battle between the two parties reached a pivotal point in 2004 when the Texas Legislature met in a special session to redraw the state's congressional districts, the one area where

Democrats were clinging to a majority thanks to past redistricting efforts. The session was widely viewed as the work of Congressman Tom DeLay, the Texas Republican who rose from relative obscurity in the state legislature to become Republican Majority Leader in Congress. The new plan gave Republicans an advantage and was, with some adjustments, eventually upheld by the courts. But along the way an epic battle ensued between Congressman DeLay and avowed liberal Democrat Ronnie Earle, the Travis County district attorney. Earle, who has made fighting political corruption a hallmark of his career, sought indictments against DeLay. The legal wrangling has continued; meanwhile DeLay has left Congress and Earle has retired. Life goes on in Austin for both the political junkies and those who simply see the Capitol as a beautiful building in an island of green in the heart of the city.

In local politics, the battle between Republicans and Democrats has not reached the critical mass that it has on the state level. Typically, the political map in Austin looks a little like a doughnut, with the new outer suburbs voting Republican and the inner, older neighborhoods voting Democratic.

City elections are, on the surface, nonpartisan, but many of the political consultants who work state races can be found aligned with various factions in city politics—generally Republicans with pro-business candidates and Democrats with pro-environment groups. The world of city politics can be a Byzantine one for newcomers—one of the most frequent questions longtime residents hear is "Why doesn't Austin have single-member districts?" (That question ranks first, followed by "Why doesn't Austin have any east-west freeways?")

Unlike many other Southern cities where the U.S. Justice Department has required single-member city council districts be drawn to meet voting rights laws, Austin has managed to avoid federal oversight. For years there has been what is openly called "a gentlemen's agreement" that called for one seat on the council to be designated the Hispanic seat and another to be the African-American seat. That agreement has generally held, although there have been criticisms and some changes over the years. As the city grows and more newcomers arrive, more changes are likely.

The battles between newcomers and old-timers, the new suburbs and the older parts of the city continue. Changing demographics, economic diversification, and shifting political tides are altering the power structure in Austin, but there are some common threads that do bind—preserving the authentic Austin experience is one of them.

i One of the best times to see the state Legislature at work is on the final day of the biennial session—usually dubbed sine die, the Latin term meaning the final day—and pronounced with a Texas twang as "sigh–knee dye." The Texas Legislature is convened on the second Tuesday of January in odd-numbered years for a 120-day regular session. Usually, sine die is a hectic day marked with last-minute debate, deal-making, and parties in the halls and offices of the Capitol.

HISTORY

S am Houston rarely lost a fight. Of all the heroes who struggled for Texas's independence from Mexico, General Houston had been the one to lead the decisive bloody conflict. His troops had captured the ruthless Mexican dictator, General Antonio Lopez de Santa Anna, at the Battle of San Jacinto on April 26, 1836. As commander-in-chief of the Texas Army, he had altered the destiny of a continent.

Houston, a towering figure of a man, was born to lead. As a youth he had gone off on his own to live among the Indians and had been accepted as a son by a chief of the Cherokees. His Indian name, Co-lon-neh, meaning the Raven, would add luster to his legend. Houston had served as governor of Tennessee before striking out for the wilds of Texas. He was among the courageous leaders who had signed the Texas Declaration of Independence at Washington-on-the-Brazos on March 2, 1836. And he had already served a term as the first elected president of the fledgling Republic of Texas. In many ways he was the ultimate prototype of the new Texan: tall, independent, fearless, self-assured, every bit the maverick, a hero among heroes.

And he was furious. The year was 1839, and the new president of the Republic, Mirabeau Lamar, was suggesting that Texas's permanent capital be established in the tiny hamlet of Waterloo. What insanity! The hamlet, on the banks of the Colorado River, sat in the middle of nowhere, perched on the edge of a wild frontier. The U.S. border was 250 arduous miles east at the Sabine River, while the disputed Texas-Mexico boundary stood just half that distance away at the Nueces River. Comanche Indians occupied the hills nearby. Mexican marauders could invade at any time. Besides, Houston had already secured a pledge from the Texas government that the capital would remain, at least until 1840, in the town that bore his own name—or so he thought.

Lamar had other ideas. He envisioned a Texas empire that spread far into the west. Moving the capital to the center of the Republic, he believed, would give Texas a launching point from which to carve out its future. Lamar dreamed of the newly adopted Lone Star flag sailing one day over lands still controlled by Mexico and the Indians.

While camping near Waterloo on an excursion with Texas Rangers the year before, Lamar had awakened to shouts that a buffalo herd had been spotted nearby. He rode out and shot the biggest buffalo some had ever seen. As fate would have it, his prey had been standing right on the corner of what would become the heart of downtown Austin at Congress Avenue near Eighth Street. Lamar recalled the beautiful spot when it came time to assign a commission to select Texas's permanent capital.

THE CAPITAL OF TEXAS

The new capital was to be named Austin in honor of the "Father of Texas," Stephen F. Austin, who less than 20 years before had brought the first Anglo settlers to the territory. Citizens of Houston, Washington-on-the-Brazos, Matagorda, and other Texas towns lobbied hard for the capital. But there was something about Waterloo that drew out the romantic in the roughest of men. According to articles published in the *Austin American*, Indian fighter James Jones described the scene in letters to President Lamar in 1839. "We are marching through a beautiful country—

its face presents a scene of grandeur and magnificence rarely, if ever witnessed," Jones wrote. "It is the most beautiful and sublime scene. Rome itself with all its famous hills could not surpass the natural scenery of Waterloo."

Equally infatuated, commissioners investigating potential capital sites filed this report: "The imagination of even the romantic will not be disappointed on viewing the valley of the Colorado, and the fertile and gracefully undulating woodlands and luxuriant prairies at a distance from it. The most skeptical will not doubt its healthiness, and the citizen's bosom must swell with honest pride when, standing in the portico of the capitol of this country, he looks abroad upon a region worthy only of being the home of the brave and free."

Waterloo, renamed Austin, got the nod in April 1839. For the next 33 years Austin would have a precarious grip on the seat of government.

Despite objections from Sam Houston and many others who believed it was madness to venture to the very brink of civilization, Lamar moved quickly to establish the new center of government. He dispatched a veteran of the Texas Revolution, Edwin Waller, to lay out the town and begin construction of its public buildings.

"Convinced that delay would give the opposition an opportunity to crystallize, Waller resolved to have Austin ready when Congress convened in November," Austin historian David C. Humphrey wrote in his book *Austin: An Illustrated History*, "Despite the frenzied pace, Waller planned his infant city in a manner that has pleased its citizens and visitors ever since."

Waller's popularity soared in the town he designed. In January 1840 he won unanimous election as mayor by the town's 187 voters.

As the capitol and other wooden public buildings took shape along Congress Avenue (the capitol was surrounded by stockades to protect it against Indian attack), more and more souls moved to Austin, many to take jobs as public servants in the fledgling government, some to set up private professions and businesses, still others arriving with their owners as slaves. By 1840

Austin's population had grown to 856, according to an informal census taken by a resident, the Reverend Amos Roark. The population, by Roark's count, totaled 711 whites and 145 blacks and included 75 religious people, 35 mechanics, six doctors, four lawyers, and 20 gamblers.

Sam Houston, still seething over the transfer of power to Austin, made plans to end this wild experiment once and for all. Having been reelected president of the Republic, succeeding Lamar in September 1841, Houston was provided the perfect excuse when invading Mexicans briefly recaptured San Antonio in 1842—causing nearly the whole population of Austin to flee. He ordered the official papers be transferred from Austin to Washington-on-the-Brazos, the site Houston had selected for the interim capital. In what has gone down in history as the "Archive War," however, a group of the remaining Austinites fired a cannon at their Texas brethren, and then chased them into the night to recover the papers. The following day, December 31, 1842, the victors returned the archives to Austin. Sam Houston, ever the rebel, continued to conduct his presidential business at Washington-on-the-Brazos. Austin, with no reason for existence, slipped into decline as Comanche raids grew more frequent.

This was the darkness before the dawn, as it turned out. A constitutional convention held in Austin on July 4, 1845, voted to approve the United States' offer to annex Texas. Austin was again chosen the interim capital, this time of the State of Texas. In a poignant ceremony held at high noon on February 19, 1846, Texas President Anson Jones declared, "The Republic of Texas is no more." While the decade-long experiment in frontier democracy had come to an end, its legacy would live on in generations of proud Texans yet to be born.

THE 28TH STATE

With Texas representing the 28th star on the flag of the United States, Austin's tensions could ease somewhat. The Mexican-American War, fought largely on Mexican soil, settled the international boundary far south of Austin along the Rio Grande with the 1848 Treaty of Guadalupe Hidalgo. By 1850, when Austin won another 20-year term as the state capital, the city claimed just 629 residents. Ten years later, the population had grown to 3,494, nearly a third of them slaves, as the number of government jobs grew and the private sector expanded. While the threat of Indian attack remained strong in the new capital during those years, stalwart Austinites moved ahead to build a lasting city. Texas's first permanent state capitol was open for business by 1853, and the city's master builder, Abner Cook, completed the Governor's Mansion (which was extensively damaged by fire in 2008) by 1856. The architecturally magnificent Texas Land Office Building, which today is the Capital Complex Visitors Center, was completed by 1857. The future looked bright. Then came the Civil War—and secession.

Sam Houston had envisioned Texas as part of the United States since the early days of the Republic. Now, as the 70-year-old governor of Texas, "Old Sam" denounced the idea of seceding from the Union, despite the incendiary slavery issue and other grievances about states' rights that increasingly angered the South. In the face of growing revolt against the Union, Houston departed the Austin Governor's Mansion and traveled around the state in an attempt to prevent secession. Houston biographer Marquis James reported in *The Raven* that the aging statesman faced an angry mob in Galveston and still would not back down. "Some of you laugh to scorn the idea of bloodshed as the result of secession," Houston told the throng. "But let me tell you what is coming. You may, after the sacrifice of countless millions of treasure and hundreds of thousands of lives, as a bare possibility, win Southern independence, but I doubt it."

In February 1861, Texas voted overwhelmingly to secede. On March 16, the ever-defiant Houston stepped down as governor rather than take the oath of allegiance to the Confederacy. Despite all his former ill-will toward Austin as the capital, Houston must have taken a small degree of pleasure in learning that Austin and Travis County, as well as neighboring Williamson

County, also voted against secession at first. As historian Humphrey reports so well, Austin was a slave city just as Texas was a slave state, but Austinites, like Sam Houston, "opposed efforts to precipitate Texas 'into revolution.' " After war broke out in April, however, most of tolerant Austin accepted the secession and hundreds of local men and boys marched off to battle. Four years later, Houston's dire prediction came true when the South fell.

While Austin had grown by nearly 3,000 people between 1850 and 1860, the war had taken its toll. By 1870, when Union forces (commanded for a time by General George Armstrong Custer) ended a five-year occupation of Austin, the city claimed just 4,428 residents, not even a thousand more than a decade before. A good portion were freed slaves eager to start new lives. Clarksville, still on the west side of town today, became just one of several thriving black communities that grew up during this period (see our Relocation chapter).

Austin was set to take off. But first it had to battle the city of Houston once again. Austin's 20-year term as interim capital had expired, and the issue again was to be put to a vote. The debate raged across the miles as each side volleyed nasty remarks about its opposition. Houston, according to Austinites, was home to "fetid, green-scum-covered bayous," while Austin was called a "bleak, inhospitable rocky waste," Humphrey reports. In November 1872 Austin won the vote by nearly a 2-to-1 margin over its longtime rival. Four years later, the new state constitution designated Austin the permanent capital. At long last, the issue was settled.

A THRIVING CAPITAL

The years following the Civil War became a time of unprecedented growth for Austin and for Texas as a whole. Despite the enormous suffering brought by the war, the state remained physically undamaged. While much of the South was in shambles, Texas offered huge expanses of open frontier just awaiting settlement. Southern in heritage and yet so Western in character,

Texas became the great Southwestern frontier as immigrants poured in. With the coming of the railroad in 1871, Austin surged full steam ahead. The city more than doubled its 1870 population within 10 years, growing to 11,013. The newcomers arrived largely from the South but also from Europe. Germans, more than any other European ethnic group, forged new lives here, but Swedes, English, Irish, Italians, and Poles came too. Congress Avenue and Pecan Street (now Sixth Street) became the commercial and political center of this thriving region.

The Texas Constitution, which encouraged immigration, certainly contributed to the state's, and Austin's, open attitude toward diversity as both American and foreign-born newcomers discovered a warm climate of acceptance. Great homes and commercial buildings designed to last the ages appeared on the landscape. Scholz Garten, a restaurant and beer garden built by German immigrant August Scholz in 1866, would become a popular gathering spot for Austin citizens of all nationalities during these years—and remains so to this day. Allen Hall, the first building west of the Mississippi River dedicated to the higher education of blacks, rose up on Austin's east side at Tillotson College, chartered in 1877 and opened to students by 1881. Austin, meanwhile, rallied for its next important phase.

Back in 1839, President Lamar had gained recognition as the Father of Education when, at his urging, the Congress of the Republic set aside land in each existing county to be used for public education. In Austin a 40-acre site named College Hill had been designated for a university. But Texas in those early days lacked the resources for such a grand scheme, so education had been left to churches and private schools. In 1854 Governor Elisha Pease had signed a bill establishing the Texas Public School System. Now it was time to do something about a university. The Constitution of 1876 called for establishment of "a university of the first class." The location for the University of Texas was to be decided by a vote of the people.

College Hill had been standing by for nearly four decades. But with the location suddenly up for grabs, town leaders throughout the state quickly moved to claim the university as their own. Ten towns, including Waco, Lampasas, Tyler, and Matagorda, vied with Austin for the honor. But Austin had an ace in the hole in a man by the name of Alexander Penn Woolridge, a New Orleans–born, Yale-educated up-and-comer. As head of the Austin campaign, Woolridge, according to Humphrey, flooded Texas with pro-Austin literature, pointing out the city's beauty, healthfulness, central location, and the fact that Austin already had land ready and waiting. East Texas voters went solidly for Tyler, but Austin triumphed. And Woolridge went on to serve Austin in one capacity or another for four decades. A wonderful downtown city park (see our Parks and Recreation chapter) is named for him. On September 15, 1883, townspeople gathered for an inaugural ceremony in the unfinished Main Building on College Hill, right on the original 40-acre site. In 1885 St. Edward's opened as a Catholic college on Austin's southern edge.

Three years later, on May 16, 1888, the youngest son of Sam Houston dedicated the magnificent new Texas State Capitol with the words, "Here glitters a structure that shall stand as a sentinel of eternity to gaze upon the ages." Presiding majestically over the hill looking down Congress Avenue, the capitol was, indeed, a site to behold.

BUILDING A VIABLE ECONOMY

Seat of government. Center of education. The twin economic pillars for Austin's development stood as solidly as the glorious new structures that served as their symbols. Instead of bringing instant wealth to Austin, however, the University of Texas struggled in its early years. In fact, all of Austin struggled to define its economic future. Early dreams of a commercial center ushered in by the railroad failed to materialize as rail lines spread and shippers found other cities more convenient. The Colorado River proved unnavigable, dashing hopes for lucrative barge traffic. Factories were few and far between. Still, Austin remained the seat of political power in Texas. Along with important government jobs came the prestige of catering to the state's most influential men.

Besides, if jobs didn't come from huge factories or meccas of trade, enterprising Austinites would just invent their own. Retailers, lawyers, doctors, journalists, butchers, bakers, and brewers as well as operators of boardinghouses, brothels, and saloons all found work in Austin. Builders certainly didn't lack work. Some of Austin's finest historic buildings today, including the regal hotel built by cattle baron Jesse Driskill, opened in the latter decades of the 19th century. The distinguished neighborhood of Hyde Park in then far North Austin, which touted electric street car service, got its start during this period and became Austin's first suburb (see our Relocation chapter), while celebrated European sculptor Elizabet Ney set about building her elegant Hyde Park studio. A few blocks west of Congress Avenue, a neighborhood of wealthy merchants and bankers rose up. Churches, hospitals, and a courthouse dotted the Austin landscape, along with two grand opera houses that served the growing population's desire for cultural entertainment. Contributing to that scene were locally formed bands as well as the Austin Saengerrunde, a singing society founded by the city's German immigrants in 1879.

By the late 1880s Austin's growing number of professors and students bestowed a scholarly touch on the region, while the presence of the artist Ney and the short-story writer who would later become famous as O. Henry foreshadowed future artistic and literary communities. O. Henry would later give Austin one of its most endearing nicknames, "the City of the Violet Crown," in honor of the purplish cast that emerges over the city at dusk. (Some say the color comes from the cedar pollen in the air.)

"Austin's diverse population grew like the town itself during these years," historian John Edward Weems wrote in the 1989 *Austin American–Statesman* supplement "Austin 1839–1989." "The diversity helped give the town a degree of tolerance that, however slight at first and however imperfect still today, broadened into an accommodation of people with a remarkable variety of beliefs and lifestyles."

Through it all, dreams of commerce and manufacturing remained strong among some of Austin's leaders. By 1893 Austinites gathered to celebrate the opening of a new million-dollar dam on the Colorado River and the beautiful lake it created. The dam was aimed at producing enough hydroelectric power for both the city and for the manufacturing plants city officials expected would come along to propel Austin to prosperity. Lake McDonald, named for John McDonald, the building contractor-turned-mayor who had championed the dam, quickly became the city's prime recreational center. Accompanied by their dapper escorts, fashionable ladies wearing flower-topped bonnets boarded the great steamers *Ben Hur* and the *Belle of Austin* for relaxing cruises on the lake by day and dances by night. Rowing regattas at the lake attracted sports enthusiasts from around the world. Sunbathers and swimmers relaxed on shore, while the town elite snapped up resort properties along the perimeter.

Despite its increasingly civilized appearance, Austin retained much of its frontier flavor during the last two decades of the 19th century. In 1881 Austinites exhibited a mixture of tolerance and plain common sense by electing Ben Thompson to the job of city marshal. Thompson, considered the best gunfighter in the West by many, was also one of Pecan Street's most notorious gamblers. "During his tenure as marshal, it was claimed that major crime dropped to an all-time low," wrote Larry Willoughby in his book, *Austin: An Historical Portrait.* Unfortunately, the colorful Thompson resigned in 1882 to face murder charges in San Antonio and was killed later in a saloon shootout. Well into the 1890s, according to Humphrey, "Cowboys were familiar figures, and horses tied to hitching posts lined dusty Congress Avenue. Along the east side of the Avenue the saloons, cowmen, and gamblers were so thick in the evenings that 'ladies' would not think of walking there."

Austin's red-light district grew into an enterprise during these years. Located west of Congress Avenue and called Guy Town, "it was not at all an unpopular part of town for many men—Austin residents, male visitors, and legislators," reported Weems. "It was said that additional women were brought in when the state government blossomed into full lawmaking activity."

THE 20TH CENTURY

Austin's Wild West spirit didn't disappear overnight, but the coming of the 20th century marked the beginning of its decline. By New Year's Day 1900 Austin's eyes were clearly focused on the future—and progress. Only one small item appeared on the front page of the local paper that day to indicate anything might be awry in the land of opportunity. "Saturday and yesterday some alarmists were busy circulating the report that there were great leaks in the powerhouse, in the dam, in the lake, and everywhere else out at the power and light plant up the river," the article said. "Superintendent Patterson stated that they were without foundation." Austin got busy with its plans for the new century.

Whether those "alarmist" reports were true at the time mattered little just three months later when the skies unleashed a torrent of rain. On April 7, 1900, dreams of turning Austin into a manufacturing center were literally swept away along with the seven-year-old dam in a devastating flood that cost at least eight lives, destroyed everything in its path, and left Austin without power for several months. When Austin overcame the shock enough to take stock of its situation—no big business, no big industry—city leaders determined to make the best of it. Austin's economic future would be built on the twin pillars of education and government the city had fought so hard to win in the past. Besides, they reasoned, Austin was just a beautiful place to live.

Growth and progress were now the name of the game. Wide and stately, yet made of dirt for more than 60 years, Congress Avenue was finally paved with brick in 1905, while a new concrete bridge replaced a rickety iron bridge across the Colorado River at Congress. "By 1910, Austin had its own skyscrapers, the Scarbrough and Littlefield buildings. The horseless carriage was no longer considered an intrusion into the lives of 'civilized' people, and as early as 1910 the automobile was an invaluable part of Austin's lifestyle and economy. When the first airplane landed in Austin in 1911, the 20th century had really arrived," wrote Willoughby.

COLOR BARRIERS

While Austinites had always made time for leisure and cultural activities, the coming of the industrial age made those pursuits even easier. Austin's new Majestic Theatre (now the Paramount) opened in 1915, hosting major touring acts from around the country. Two years later the Austin Symphony Orchestra presented its first concert. Human habitation at Barton Springs, the jewel in a town endowed by enormous natural beauty, has been traced back several thousand years, but the arrival of the automobile made trips to this glorious swimming hole easier for "modern" Austinites. In 1917 Colonel A. J. Zilker gave the city hundreds of acres around the springs for use as a park. UT football, first played in 1893, became a popular spectator sport in the 1900s, along with the horse races that thrilled the crowds in Hyde Park. Grand balls attended by the city's most fashionable citizens continued at the elegant Driskill Hotel, while the lovely Hyde Park Pavilion hosted other stylish affairs.

Hyde Park, however, was an exclusively Anglo community; its posh gatherings were barred to Austin's minorities, as was Barton Springs, to name just two. Austin's black citizens, who had enjoyed some acceptance during Reconstruction, were now subjected to segregation and discrimination. As far back as 1885 a group of citizens in one ward had formed an "Anti-Colored Movement" to block the reelection of a black city council member, Humphrey reported. During the first decade of the 1900s, Austin's color barrier became as distinct as in many other cities throughout the South. While the white-robed Ku Klux Klan paraded through Austin streets undeterred, blacks sat in a separate section on streetcars, attended separate schools, drank from separate drinking fountains, and used separate public restrooms—when such facilities could be found. They also increasingly congregated on Austin's east side, away from their Anglo oppressors. Austin's many black professionals—doctors, lawyers, dentists, pastors, as well as business owners—found a racially mixed district to work in but remained excluded from Austin "society." Not until 1950 would the first black student be admitted to the UT law school—under order from the U.S. Supreme Court.

Austin's small but growing Mexican-American population also faced treatment that would be considered despicable today. Most of the town's Mexicans had been chased out of town during the 1850s, while those who had followed found themselves still considered foreigners despite their birthright. Even worse, some Austinites counted them as enemies because of the Texas Revolution, forgetting that many Mexicans living in the region during the war had fought—and died—for Texas.

By 1910 Austin claimed not quite 30,000 citizens. Houston, already a railroading and shipping center, witnessed huge industrial development following Texas's first great oil strike in the region in 1901. Its population had surged to nearly 79,000 by 1910. Dallas, enjoying success as a center for insurance, banking, commerce, and the cotton trade, had skyrocketed to 92,000 people. Following World War I, Austin's population had increased by just 5,000, while Houston and Dallas soared to 128,000 and 156,000, respectively.

Although not cash rich at the beginning of the Roaring '20s, the University of Texas did own a great deal of land, including two million acres in West Texas, some of it leased to oil speculators. On Monday morning, May 28, 1923, the Santa Rita oil well blew in a gusher of black gold. The Big Lake Oil Field out west would continue to pump riches into the Permanent University Fund for nearly seven decades. Wealthy for the first time in its 40-year history, UT went on a building spree.

THE "ATHENS OF THE WEST"

Now city officials really had something to brag about. Besides the rapidly growing UT, Austin also claimed St. Edward's University on the south side and two black colleges on the east. Austin was indeed becoming the center of culture, learning, and politics that leaders had envisioned. They began touting Austin as the "Athens of the West," and citizens responded by earmarking funds to develop the city. Parks and playgrounds, wide boulevards, and public buildings rose up. Austin's population more than doubled during the 1920s and 1930s, hitting nearly 88,000 by 1940.

UT's spending binge, coupled with an influx of local and federal funds, staved off the worst of the Great Depression for Austin, according to local historians. One of the city's most treasured landmarks today, the 27-story UT Tower, was among many buildings completed on campus during the 1920s and 1930s. President Roosevelt's New Deal, solidly backed by Austin's ubiquitous new mayor, Tom Miller, brought millions in construction funds to the area through the Works Progress Administration (WPA). Camp Mabry on Austin's west side, home to the Texas Volunteer Guard since 1891, mushroomed with new WPA construction, as did other areas of the city. By late 1936, when *Forbes* magazine reported that Austin was one of the "bright spots in the nation," it appeared the worst of the Depression was over. And yet Miller, along with Austin's newly elected U.S. Representative, Lyndon Johnson, won for Austin the country's first federal housing project, completed in 1939 for the city's rapidly expanding Mexican-American population.

Miller, who would remain at the forefront of Austin business and politics throughout the '30s, '40s, and even well into the '50s, was responsible in many ways for fashioning modern Austin. A liberal among liberal Democrats of the era, Miller was a master politician who worked to gain support from all three sectors of Austin's increasingly tri-racial community. Although he did support racial segregation (not unusual even for liberal Southerners of the era), Miller nonetheless promoted equal civil rights for all.

"Miller was one of those fairly numerous anomalies in the South—the good businessman, the deep Southerner, who also stood strong on behalf of much of Roosevelt's New Deal, and Truman's Fair Deal, civil rights, and the like," according to Anthony M. Orum, author of *Power, Money & the People: The Making of Modern Austin*. Low-income housing extended to blacks and Mexican Americans under his reign, while Miller also saw to it that East Austin's black community received basic city services. The lovely Rosewood Park that remains today was commissioned by Miller. His broader vision, however, remained on the city's future growth.

Among Miller's greatest coups was his success—along with LBJ—in getting federal Depression-era funds to complete the Austin Dam (now named in his honor) by 1940. Two years later, construction of the Mansfield Dam that created Lake Travis wrapped up efforts around these parts to bring the unpredictable Colorado River under control.

SHAPING THE FUTURE

On December 7, 1941, the United States went to war. While Austin's youth waged battle on far-off fronts, loved ones remained at home, sharing with the rest of the country in the hardships of scarcity and rationing—and the fear that a knock on the door would mean a son, husband, brother, or even a daughter had paid the ultimate price. In 1943 Congressman Johnson and his wife, University of Texas graduate Lady Bird Johnson, bought small Austin radio station KTBC. Nine years later, on Thanksgiving Day 1952, KTBC became Central Texas's first television station. What more important event could have been chosen as a first broadcast during the heyday of the postwar years? The station aired the football game between arch rivals UT and Texas A&M. UT, of course, prevailed.

According to Humphrey, the seeds of Austin's eventual blossoming as a high-tech mecca were also planted in the 1940s with the creation of the Austin Area Economic Development Foundation. Established in 1948 with C. B. Smith as president, the council "foreshadowed and helped shape what was to come," Humphrey wrote. "Smith's foundation sought to diversify Austin's economy in a manner compatible with its 'way of life.' Research and development laboratories and high technology companies fit the bill."

Austin would also elect its first woman city council member in 1948. Interestingly, Emma Long was not just a female version of the reigning power elite but "an avowed enemy of the city establishment and a champion of the underdog," as Weems described her.

GAINING NEW SENSIBILITIES

Meanwhile, somewhere during the second half of the 1940s, Austin's population hit 100,000 as the city became one of the fastest growing cities in the Southwest. By 1950 the population had reached 132,459. While nowhere near the size of Houston or Dallas, or even San Antonio, Austin had nevertheless turned into a thriving metropolis.

The time to address some long-ignored social injustices had arrived. Heman Marion Sweatt's victorious Supreme Court battle to gain admission to the UT law school in 1950 opened UT's doors to other black graduate students. Six years later, by decree of the UT Board of Regents, the university admitted its first black undergraduates, while Austin's public schools began the excruciatingly slow process of integration. In 1954 UT graduate and social activist Ronnie Dugger debuted the *Texas Observer* in Austin. Within months the small biweekly magazine had established itself as the liberal voice in Texas media, reporting on lynchings in East Texas. (The *Observer* continues its mission as a liberal voice in Texas media to this day.) As the tide for racial equality swelled across the United States, students at UT and the city's other colleges spearheaded the Austin movement of the 1950s and 1960s.

The movement, however, reached beyond UT and the city's other campuses to extend deep into the community. As a result, Austin experienced nascent political and social enlightenment as established barriers against minorities slowly cracked. Black and Mexican-American communities began taking places in positions of power by the late '60s and into the '70s.

While UT "radical" politics reached back decades, the university boomed during the 1960s as a haven for serious social activists and the hippies who brought their music and their faith in flower power. Austin's antiwar protesters took to the streets throughout the decade as public opinion against the Vietnam War surged. (In May 1970, students led Austin's largest protest of the Vietnam era following the deaths of four students in Ohio during an antiwar demonstration at Kent State University.)

UT enrollment had swelled to more than 25,000 by 1966, although only about half remained on campus for the summer session. The morning of August 1, 1966, dawned like any other hot, lazy summer day in the city. A few hours later, Austin became the site of what was then the largest simultaneous mass murder in American history when a heavily armed 25-year-old UT student and ex-Marine climbed the beloved campus tower and commenced firing. Charles Whitman, who had murdered his mother and his wife the night before, fired round after round at unsuspecting victims below, killing 14 people and wounding 31 more before he was finally shot to death by Austin police. The 19-minute melee would spawn debate across the country over the issue of gun control.

At the epicenter of America's turbulent 1960s stood Lyndon Johnson, the former schoolteacher who had risen to political power from his boyhood home 50 miles southwest of Austin. A century had passed since Sam Houston stared Southern slave owners in the face—and lost. Now another tall Texan was storming the bastion of bigotry. He had already guided two civil rights measures through the Senate and as president was fighting for passage of a landmark civil rights act. Angry Southerners rebuked Johnson and Lady Bird at every turn, but the Texas leader prevailed. Johnson signed the Civil Rights Act of 1964 and the Voting Rights Act a year later. Johnson, however, would be judged at the time not for his efforts on behalf of human rights nor for the dozens of education bills and social reform measures he championed, but for drawing the United States further into the mire of the Vietnam War. Battered by public opinion against the war, Johnson chose not to seek reelection in 1968. He and Lady Bird returned home to their Central Texas ranch.

THE UPS AND DOWNS

While live music concerts had formed part of the Austin lifestyle since its earliest days, the 1960s would see the city boom with musicians of all kinds. Among UT's growing "folkie" music crowd was a shy freshman named Janis Joplin, who performed first on campus and later at a popular beer joint called Threadgill's. Later came the psychedelic sounds, rock and roll, the blues, and the country rock that would eventually turn Austin into the Live Music Capital of the World.

The '60s brought much more than music and social change, however. Attracted by UT's excellent reputation for research and development and by the city's attractive surroundings, high-tech manufacturers moved in. By the end of the decade, Austin claimed three major technology plants: IBM, Texas Instruments, and Tracor. The high-tech revolution had arrived.

By 1970 Austin's population topped a quarter million. UT had mushroomed to more than 40,000 students. The number of city, county, state, and federal government employees reached into the thousands, and high-tech firms had become the city's largest private employers. The Armadillo World Headquarters opened in 1970 and soon earned a nationwide reputation as a hot live music venue. Austin's cultural explosion during this decade extended into the areas of writing, theater, and visual arts as more and more artists found themselves drawn to the city.

In the summer of 1970, just a couple of months after UT students rallied 25,000 people for a march in protest of the Kent State shootings, a group of UT students gathered to map out a plan for Austin's future. Among the students was Jeffrey Friedman, a law school student who had taken a leadership role in the protest march.

Armed with the knowledge that the voting age was about to be lowered from 21 to 18, and realizing that students could register by proclaiming they intended to remain in Austin after graduation, the group determined to register thousands of university students. That accomplished, Friedman and a slate of other liberal candidates decided to challenge the existing power structure.

Friedman, according to Orum, "wanted things to be better in East Austin for the browns and the blacks. He wanted the poor people to have better jobs and better housing. But he also wanted to bring down the forces of the Establishment. He wanted to bring down the rich and the powerful." For his part, Friedman's conservative opponent, Wick Fowler, ran on a platform "that hippies were unfit to hold public office."

While the conservative business sector claimed the majority of seats on the council that year, Friedman won his race to become the first student and youngest council member. Berl Handcox also won election, becoming the first African American to serve on the city council since the 1880s. Five years later Friedman became Austin's youngest mayor in what Orum called "the watershed council election of 1975, in which the majority of those elected were liberals." Among those voted in was John Trevino, Austin's first Mexican-American council member.

TREE HUGGERS UNITE

Apart from the frustration over establishment politics that colored the 1970s, Austin's population explosion became a source of increasing consternation. Longtime residents mourned the good ol' days and expressed fears that Austin's scenic beauty was being bulldozed away to make way for expressways, shopping malls, housing developments, and skyscrapers. The slogan "Keep Austin Austin" became a popular rallying cry during these years. Austin's increasingly powerful environmental protection groups successfully thwarted major development in several environmentally sensitive areas, while helping to keep the protection of Austin's natural endowments

on the minds of old-timers and newcomers alike—as well as on the front burner of local politics. Lady Bird Johnson, who divided her time between Austin and her ranch nearby, spearheaded a project to beautify Town Lake (renamed Lady Bird Lake after her death), which led to the planting of thousands of trees as well as construction of a hike-and-bike trail and gazebos. Austin had indeed changed radically from its days as a small, sleepy town. But of the nearly 94,000 new residents who would move into Austin during the '70s, the majority would still be left breathless by the city's natural appeal—and still are today.

By the mid-1980s nothing appeared to stand in the way of continued growth. The economy boomed as more high-tech industries moved into Central Texas, bringing investment dollars and plenty of jobs. Austinite Michael Dell started his own little computer company in 1984 to add to the high-tech landscape. Housing costs rose, then skyrocketed, as Austin's population continued to expand. Banks made exorbitant loans, with little money down, as real estate speculators and tycoon developers snapped up residential and commercial properties around the region.

Then the bubble burst. Downturns in oil prices—which had already hurt many parts of Texas—contributed to the problem, as did a slump in the technology field, but many economists pointed to the overheated real estate economy as the leading cause of Austin's recession. For a while during the second half of the decade, it appeared that more people were leaving the city than moving in. Real estate prices plummeted, businesses failed, bankruptcies became common, offices closed. By the end of the decade, according to reports, Austin led the country in the percentage of vacant office space and topped all other Texas cities for amount of indebtedness.

THE HIGH-TECH ERA IGNITES

Austin entered 1990 with a gloomy economic forecast. The United States as a whole was in recession, banks remained in turmoil, and another U.S. president who claimed Texas as home, George Bush, was preparing to declare war on Iraq. Despite earlier indications, however, Austin's population had grown by nearly 120,000 people during the past decade. In 1993 Apple Computer bought 129 acres in neighboring Williamson County for a financial services and customer support site. That same year, Motorola announced plans to build a $1 billion chip plant in Northeast Austin. Meanwhile, young Austinites Richard Linklater and Robert Rodriguez had each made a low-budget, wildly successful film (*Slacker* and *El Mariachi,* respectively) that was to skyrocket them to Hollywood—and help put the Austin film scene on the map. All the while, the beat of Austin music pulsated in every corner of the city.

By the end of the decade, Austin was riding the crest of another wave in growth and development as Central Texas solidified its reputation as one of the country's leading high-tech hubs. Dell Computer had grown to become the city's largest private employer and the world's third-largest maker of personal computers, with more than $12 billion in annual sales. Samsung built a $1.3 billion Austin plant. Computer manufacturers and chip makers, however, formed just part of the scene. Local start-up companies focusing on software development and the Internet also swelled during the '90s.

Along with the economic good times came increasing pressures. Rampant growth became the norm as the city expanded by about 1,500 inhabitants each month throughout the decade. Signs of the changing times were clearly visible everywhere as roads jammed, office space diminished, trees were sacrificed to make way for housing and commercial developments, and school districts scrambled to build new facilities to keep up with expanding enrollment.

As a result, a new phrase entered the Austin lexicon in 1998: "Smart Growth." Aiming to develop a city that grew "smart" as it grew fast, the Austin City Council and then-Mayor Kirk Watson presented a series of initiatives designed to protect the environment and to limit sprawl, especially into environmentally sensitive areas, by encouraging development inside the city. Race relations, often ignored in the past, also climbed on the city agenda as more enlightened leaders sought to bring some sense of community to a city that remained fractured in many respects—despite important strides among Austin's minority racial and ethnic groups over the past 40 years.

SINGING THE BLUES

If Austin ever really needed a reason to party, the dawn of the 21st century provided an excellent excuse. Indeed, on December 31, 1999, an estimated 260,000 revelers packed Austin's "A2K" downtown bash. And why not? These were technological boom times, and the venture capital was flowing as freely as the beer. If the U.S. economy was hot, Austin's was red hot. Jobs were plentiful, high-tech salaries soared, and the stock market skyrocketed. Locally, dot-coms glittered among the investment darlings of the "new" Internet economy, while the region's chip makers were selling their goods as fast and furious as Frito-Lay. To the enormous relief of tormented Austin techies, and the partygoers on Sixth Street, the ominously predicted Y2K bug never even hatched.

By March 2000, Austin officials had signed deals with two computer biggies, software manufacturer Computer Sciences Corp. (CSC) and Intel Corp., to build giant complexes downtown—the heart of Smart Growth territory. These were to be the first in a string of computer companies whose presence in the city center would create a "Downtown Digital District" and thus rejuvenate the entire area. The building boom extended even further as the construction of office towers, posh condominiums, and lofts changed the face of downtown forever.

True, Austin's $600 million annual music industry was feeling a pinch as musicians struggled to find affordable housing and clubs faced escalating costs. Austin already had lost three great music venues: Steamboat, the Electric Lounge, and, perhaps worst of all, Liberty Lunch. The Lunch, an Austin leader in live music for nearly a quarter of a century, was demolished to make room for the pending CSC complex and a proposed new City Hall. The city's poor also suffered. Not only had the number of poor increased, but the gap between the lowest- and highest-paid workers in the private sector had doubled. The basic cost of living increased as demands for goods and services by the area's high-salaried consumers—and the droves of new Central Texas residents—drove prices up. In fact, when census figures came in, the Austin Metropolitan Statistical area, which includes Austin's Travis County as well as neighboring Bastrop, Caldwell, Hays, and Williamson Counties, had burgeoned to nearly 1.25 million people—and still the people poured in.

The stock market rollover of April 14, 2000, caused little more than a sprinkle on the long-running Austin parade. By August another computer biggie, Austin's Vignette Corp., announced plans to spend more than $100 million on its new downtown complex. Meanwhile, the man living in the Austin Governor's Mansion, George W. Bush, had clinched the Republican nomination for president and would by year's end become the third U.S. president from Texas.

A year that had started on such a high note, however, then went flat. By the end of 2001, Austin musicians weren't the only ones singing the blues. The Central Texas economy had witnessed its worst downturn in a decade. The stock market plummeted, consumer confidence vanished, venture capital dried up, the chip industry melted, and many developers pulled the plug on downtown plans. To make matters worse, the entire nation was reeling from the September 11 terrorist attacks. The results of Austin's economic downturn included thousands of workers—especially high-wage earners—laid off, foreclosures on expensive homes and office buildings, shrinking retail sales, school districts scrambling to make ends meet, and cutbacks in state and local government budgets. These were the norm well into 2003. CSC did complete its downtown complex, and several other new public and private buildings graced the skyline. Fairly or not, however, Intel's abandoned skeleton of a high-rise stood for years as a grim reminder of better days. In 2003 Mayor Will Wynn and the Austin City Council quietly replaced the Smart Growth plan with a far more extensive economic development policy.

Thanks to its reputation as a tech center and its diverse economy which is no longer reliant on government as a major employer, Austin has weathered recent economic bumps suffered in some sections of the country. Home values have held and even increased in spite of some national trends and the proliferation of cranes downtown is just one visible example of the city's economic strength.

THE BEAUTIFUL AND THE SUBLIME

As the new century builds up steam, debates over Austin's future rage on. Yet the city's heart and soul have managed to survive. Ever true to their eccentric roots, Austinites have embraced a new slogan: "Keep Austin Weird." The phrase, appearing on bumper stickers, T-shirts, event promos, and even on shot glasses, just about says it all. Austin is not the city some old-timers remember; but then again, the generations before them most likely said the same. For the thousands of newcomers who are seeing it for the first time, however, Austin remains one of the prettiest, most vibrant spots on the planet. Austin's once-forlorn downtown is experiencing a renaissance to become a thriving center for culture and entertainment. Live music pours from clubs all over greater downtown as the Live Music Capital of the World continues to attract the young, the restless, and the talented. UT's influence on the arts has helped spawn entire communities of performing and visual artists, writers, and filmmakers. Austin's enduring youthful spirit and creative energy add a luster that is as much a hallmark of this city as the State Capitol and the UT Tower.

The Texas pioneers who first laid eyes on this "beautiful and sublime scene" 165 years ago could not possibly have envisioned the Austin of today. And yet, in countless ways, Austin remains ever so sublime.

GETTING HERE, GETTING AROUND

Xmarks the spot, and smack dab in the middle of Texas is Austin. There is an old saying in the Lone Star State: "The sun has riz and the sun has set, and I ain't outta Texas yet." That says a lot about traversing the state. Austin is about a three-hour drive south of Dallas, a little less than a three-hour drive west of Houston, and a little more than an hour north of San Antonio. It is about a five-hour drive to Nuevo Laredo, Mexico; a five-hour drive to both the Louisiana and Oklahoma borders; and if you are heading west to New Mexico, plan on taking all day for the eight-hours-plus drive.

Interstate 35, often called the Nafta Highway (a reference to the North American Free Trade Agreement), bisects the state from north to south, running from Laredo on the Mexican border up through the middle of the country to the Canadian border. Interstate 10 runs from the Louisiana border through Houston, south of Austin through San Antonio and on to El Paso. U.S. Highway 290 connects Houston to Austin and then joins I-35 for a short stretch, cuts west through the Oak Hill area of Austin and off into the Hill Country.

Austin is literally deep in the heart of Texas. This chapter provides tips on getting here— and getting around once you have arrived.

AIRPORTS/COMMERCIAL

AUSTIN-BERGSTROM INTERNATIONAL AIRPORT
3600 Presidential Boulevard
(512) 530-ABIA: General Information
(512) 530-6358: Travelers with Disabilities
(512) 530-COPS: Airport Police and Lost and Found, 24-hour number
(512) 530-PAGE: Paging, 24-hour number
(512) 530-3300: Parking Information, 24-hour number
www.ci.austin.tx.us/austinairport

Austin was the only city in the United States to embark on a major airport building program as the 20th century drew to a close. In the spring of 1999, the city shut down the municipal airport near downtown Austin, Robert Mueller Municipal Airport, and opened a new international facility in the southeast sector of the city called Austin-Bergstrom International Airport. The airport code remains AUS. The same airlines and rental car companies serve the new $690 million airport, but the facility is much larger with twice as many gates, two runways (as opposed to one) aptly named for two famous Texas politicians, President Lyndon Baines Johnson and Congressman JJ "Jake" Pickle, and a much larger terminal, named in honor of the late Texas congresswoman Barbara Jordan. Austin-Bergstrom has a two-level access road (one level for arrivals, the other for departures) and a three-level parking garage.

The site of the old airport is being developed as a major, mixed-use town center that will be a total community. Already located there are the Austin Film Society's studios and the Dell Children's Medical Center of Central Texas (see our Health Care chapter). There are plans for other health care facilities, plus the University of Texas will build a research campus onsite. Homes, apartments, shops, cafes and open spaces also are planned. For a preview go to www.mueller austin.com.

The designers and builders sought to evoke the spirit of Austin at the new facility by including a stage in the terminal for live music performances and Hill Country landscaping by using water elements, rocks, and native plants. The new terminal includes a business center, 16 restaurants and snack shops (some of them operated by local businesses such as Amy's Ice Cream, Book People, and the Salt Lick barbecue), retail shops, and bookstores. The restaurants and snack bars sell food at "street prices," rather than the inflated prices often found at airports. The retail stores feature regional items, including music by Austin musicians and works by local artists and crafters.

The airport also offers guided tours for groups of adults and children (five years and older). Reservations are necessary; call the program at (512) 530-2242. There is also an outdoor family viewing area (with a parking area and picnic tables) on the west side of Highway 71 East, near the east runway, where one acre has been set aside for visitors to watch planes take off and land.

The parking garage next to the terminal provides 2,419 covered short-term public parking spaces on the first and second levels. Car rental returns are located on the third level. There is a close-in surface parking lot (Lot A) near the terminal and several outlying long-term lots (Lots B, C, D, E, and F), providing 7,733 parking spaces. There are also several privately operated offsite parking facilities. Shuttle buses run every seven to 10 minutes and 24 hours a day from the parking lots. Airport shuttles from all surface parking lots pick up at shuttle stops within the lots and discharge departing passengers in front of the terminal on the lower baggage level. Airport parking shuttles pick up arriving passengers outside the lower baggage level in front of the terminal and take them to surface parking lots.

Wheelchair-accessible parking is available free for up to five days in the parking garage and up to 10 days in all parking lots. Wheelchair-accessible parking spots are located on the first available row in the garage and near the shuttle stops in all surface parking lots. Shuttle buses are equipped with wheelchair lifts.

Airport Transportation

There is a transportation information desk on the ground floor of the terminal. Passengers arriving and departing from the airport have several options, in addition to rental cars and their own personal automobiles. SuperShuttle provides door-to-door minivan service for a fixed fee for one-way rides. Fees are determined by the zip code of destination or pickup. The shuttles also are available for groups at charter rates. Contact SuperShuttle at (512) 258-3826, (800) BLUE-VAN, or make reservations online at www.supershuttle. com. Capital Metro also offers local bus service between downtown Austin and the airport, linking to other bus routes in the city. Call (512) 474-1200, (512) 385-5872 TDD, or 474-1201 (free call from any local telephone booth); or visit www .capmetro.austin.tx.us.

AIRPORTS/GENERAL AVIATION

There are two fixed-base operators at Austin-Bergstrom International Airport. Both provide general aviation terminals, hangars, maintenance, and fuel facilities and access to the adjacent instrumented 9,000-foot runway. They provide 170 spaces, including 50 T-hangar spaces for small aircraft. For general aviation information provided by the airport, visit www.ci.austin.tx.us/austinairport/geninfo.htm.

ATLANTIC AVIATION SERVICES, INC.
4309 General Aviation Avenue
(512) 530-7000
www.atlanticaviation.com

SIGNATURE FLIGHT SUPPORT
4321 General Aviation Avenue
(512) 530-5451
www.signatureflight.com

i A variety of names were suggested for Austin's new international airport, but city officials decided to stick with the name given to the Air Force base that occupied the site. It was named in honor of Austin's first World War II casualty, Captain J. A. Bergstrom.

LAKEWAY
115 Flying Scott Road
(512) 261-4385
www.3r9.com
Operated by Lakeway Airpark Association, a cooperative, this private facility is nonprofit and unattended. There is a 4,000-foot landing strip open from sunrise to sunset plus self-serve gas facilities. Overnight parking is $5, but that is waived with gas purchase. The landing strip is 15.5 statute miles from Austin. The association reminds pilots there is a noise ordinance in place, plus pilots should watch for the deer grazing near the landing strip.

AIR CHARTERS

CAPITOL WINGS
4321 General Aviation Avenue
(512) 530-1700
www.capitolwings.com
Capitol Wings' fleet ranges from a Cessna 414 four-seater to a large Gulfstream III jet. The company, located in the general aviation area of Austin-Bergstrom International Airport, also provides turnkey aircraft management services, flight crews, tie-down services, hangar space, and maintenance management.

McRAE AVIATION
4309 General Aviation Avenue
(512) 385-9615
www.mcraeaviation.com
McRae offers jet charters and light cargo service from its location at the general aviation area of Austin-Bergstrom International Airport.

TRAIN STATIONS

There are several recreational trains for sightseeing in the Austin area. (For more information on recreational trains, see our Attractions chapter.)

AMTRAK
250 North Lamar Boulevard
(512) 476-5684,
(800) 872-7245 reservations
www.amtrak.com

ℹ️ The pink granite on the outer walls of the new Austin-Bergstrom International Airport comes from Marble Falls, west of the city, and is the same type of granite used at the State Capitol.

North/south service is available four times a week on the Amtrak Eagle. Northbound trains leave on Sunday, Tuesday, Wednesday, and Thursday mornings; southbound on Sunday, Wednesday, Friday, and Saturday evenings. The north route goes through Dallas to Chicago, the south route goes to San Antonio. Fares to San Antonio range from $9 to $17, depending on how close to departure time reservations are made; fares to Dallas range from $20 to $40. Children 2 to 15 travel for half price with an adult. East-west service is available from San Antonio; that route connects Los Angeles with Miami.

BUS SERVICES

Bus service within the city of Austin is covered in the Public Transportation section.

GREYHOUND
816 East Koenig Lane
(512) 458-4463, (800) 231-2222
www.greyhound.com
The intercity bus station is near Highland Mall, just west of the intersection of US 290 East and I-35. Greyhound offers service to more than 2,500 U.S. cities and the station is open 24 hours a day.

KERRVILLE BUS CO., INC.
(512) 389-0090, (800) 256-2757
www.iridekbc.com
This Texas-grown bus company is also served by the Greyhound station facility (see previous listing). Kerrville serves several Texas cities and small towns.

ROADWAYS

Austin sits at the crossroads of two major highways: I-35 and US 290. That sounds simple, but as visitors and newcomers to Austin quickly discover, the picture gets muddied first by a local propensity for calling highways by names other than the state highway department designations, and second by the absence of any clear east-west routes in the center of the city.

I-35 runs right through the middle of the city, heading south to San Antonio and on to the Mexican border, heading north to Waco, Dallas–Fort Worth, and points north.

US 290 runs from Houston westward to the northeast section of Austin where it is called US 290 East. It merges with I-35, emerging again in South Austin as US 290 West, where it is called Ben White Boulevard.

Highway 71 merges with US 290 West at I-35 through the southern and southwestern section of the city, separating at what locals call the "Y" in Oak Hill. US 290 West heads west to Johnson City, while Highway 71 heads northwest to Bee Cave and the Highland Lakes.

U.S. Highway 183 runs diagonally through the city from northwest (at Cedar Park) to southeast (near the Austin-Bergstrom International Airport). It has numerous names along its route. In the north, US 183 at intervals is called Research Boulevard, Anderson Lane, Ed Bluestein Boulevard, and Bastrop Highway.

The MoPac Expressway, called Loop 1 on all the highway signs, runs north-south through the western environs of the city. The locals just call it MoPac, as we do throughout this book.

Loop 360, or the Capital of Texas Highway, runs north-south through far West Austin. Businesses along this roadway use Capital of Texas Highway in their addresses, but the locals usually call it "360." We use both in this book.

R.M. 620 is a primarily north-south road that swings around Austin in the Hill Country west of Lake Austin and east of Lake Travis. Usually called just "620." The designation R.M. means Ranch-to-Market road, a leftover from the days when the state built highways so that farmers and ranchers could bring their goods and cattle to town. Some roads are called R.M., while others are F.M. (Farm-to-Market).

Commute times have become longer as the city has grown, but they pale in comparison with commutes in some of America's larger cities. During morning and evening rush hours (6:30 to around 9:00 a.m. and 4:30 to 7:00 p.m.), traffic slows to a crawl on the area's major roadways, notably I-35, MoPac, and US 183. At other times, driving in Austin is relatively easy.

Perhaps the biggest problem in navigating Austin streets is the fact that there is no major east-west freeway in the heart of the city. US 183 has been widened and improved, while in the southern end of the city US 290 West (known as Ben White Boulevard for much of its length) has been widened and turned into a freeway from I-35 to Oak Hill.

As for a midtown freeway, the issue has been a major political football for years as older central city neighborhoods have fought attempts to widen their streets. Another major political battle has been brewing over the increasing use of tollroads. A regional tollroad plan includes a north-south toll road east of the city parallel to the Missouri–Kansas railroad, to be named MoKan, which also will divert some traffic away from I-35. MoPac has been extended north to connect to I-35. Two new tollroads, Highway 130 and Highway 45 North have opened; the first flows from the airport north to Georgetown, the second carries traffic from northwest to northeast, Cedar Park to Pflugerville in the Austin suburbs. Tolls are $1 or less and commuters can buy a TxTag, which allows drivers to fly through tollbooths. The tags issued in Dallas and Houston, Dallas TollTag and Houston's EZTag, also work in the Central Texas area. For information on tags, visit www.txtag.org; for information on tollroads current and planned, visit www.centraltexasturnpike.org.

CAR RENTAL

Rental car counters are located on the ground floor of the airport terminal, with express service available on the third level of the parking garage immediately north of the terminal. In addition to airport-based rental car agencies, several companies offer rental car services in the city.

PARKING

Downtown parking can be hard to find—many meters allow only 30-minute parking, and two-hour meters are located several blocks away from Congress Avenue.

There are several parking garages in the downtown area, which are a good place to park if the weather is hot (shade is invaluable in the hot Texas summer) or at night when street parking can be hard to find. Other lots have attendants, and some have banks of boxes where patrons must deposit their fees. If you don't pay, you will be towed.

Parking around the capitol has improved with the opening of a new visitor parking garage on San Jacinto east of the capitol. There is a large parking garage under the capitol extension, but that is for legislators and their staffs.

Parking meters around the capitol are limited to two-hour stays, which is a hassle for anyone wanting to spend time touring the building or doing business at one of the many state buildings in the area. The idea behind this implementation is to discourage state workers from using street parking.

Generally, the rule is that the farther away from Congress Avenue you are, the longer the meters will allow you to park. The city also sells parking meter debit cards. For prices and locations where the cards may be purchased, go to www.ci.austin.tx.us/help/parking_card.htm.

TAXIS

Taxi cabs line up to serve customers at the western end of the airport terminal. Cabs wait in a holding area at the airport and are dispatched into the pickup lane, which is immediately outside the terminal. Note: There is a $1 surcharge at the airport. Only at very slow times will a passenger have to call for a cab. Austin's taxi services are regulated by the city, which requires companies to operate both smoking and nonsmoking cabs plus wheelchair-accessible vehicles. The flag-drop charge is $1.75, and each mile is $1.75. The charge from the airport to downtown ranges

from around $20 to $30, depending on what part of downtown you need to reach. Taxi service is available throughout the city 24 hours a day, seven days a week. Taxis cruise downtown, particularly around the capitol area. Response time, especially downtown, is very good. Cabbies accept cash and credit cards. There are even pedicabs (roving bicycle cabbies) downtown; their Web site is www.Austinbikecabs.com.

AUSTIN CAB
(512) 478-2222

YELLOW CAB CO.
(512) 452-9999,
(512) 835-7272 TTY

Taxi companies serving the Round Rock area:

ACE TAXI
(512) 244-1133

AUSTIN TAXI CAB SERVICE
(512) 775-7225

ROY'S TAXI OF ROUND ROCK
(512) 218-8200

LIMOUSINES

There are many limousine operators in Austin, and, like taxi cab companies, they are regulated by city ordinances governing safety and business practices. Companies charge hourly rates, starting around $70 for four passengers. Most also add service and gratuity charges, usually 15 percent each, and many also charge more during the peak spring prom season and on holidays such as Halloween and New Year's Eve. Sedan limos used for hotel/airport pickups cost around $120 an hour.

The limo business is highly competitive, and there is frequent turnover. Several large chains also operate in Austin. For a comprehensive listing, check the airport website, www.ci.austin.tx.us/austinairport/limoservice.htm.

PUBLIC TRANSPORTATION

CAPITAL METRO
106 East Eighth Street
(512) 474-1200, (512) 385-5872 TDD,
474-1201, free call from any local
telephone booth
www.capmetro.org
One of the easiest ways to navigate the downtown area is to ride the 'Dillo, the free trolley-style buses that cruise the area from early morning to around 10:00 p.m. Downtown-area bus stops have 'Dillo route maps. A special weekend 'Dillo, Route 470, the "Tour the Town" bus operates from 10:00 a.m. until 6:00 p.m. on Saturday and from 11:00 a.m. to 6:00 p.m. on Sunday, stopping at the major cultural and historical attractions downtown. You can ride the route all day long for just $1. The 'Dillos are just one service of the Capital Metro public transportation service, a publicly funded agency that operates buses and shuttle services in the greater Austin area. Most of the major attractions in Austin are located on bus routes, including the museums and live music spots. Capital Metro also operates an airport-to-downtown bus line and Night Owl routes that carry revelers from the Sixth and Congress area to the suburbs.

In addition to operating bus routes to many of the city's attractions and shopping centers, Capital Metro also runs the UT Shuttle, a bus service that takes students back and forth to the campus for 50 cents a ride—the same fare it charges on its regular city bus routes. The suburbs are served by flyers, which are nonstop buses that operate from park-and-ride stops in the outlying areas. In 2008 light rail service from Leander to downtown was added to the mix.

The Capital Metro bus system serves a 500-square-mile area that encompasses the cities of Austin, Cedar Park, Leander, Lago Vista, Jonestown, Pflugerville, Manor, and San Leanna. Capital Metro offers a comprehensive booklet of its policies and schedules that is available at all area H-E-B, Fiesta, Randall's, and Albertson's grocery stores; Ace Cash Express; major shopping malls; and the agency's offices.

Capital Metro's Customer Information Center has operators on duty from 6:00 a.m. to 10:00 p.m. Monday through Saturday and 7:00 a.m. to 6:00 p.m. on Sunday. The agency operates a local toll-free number, (800) 474-1201, that allows customers to dial free from any local pay phone.

There are several methods of payment on Capital Metro buses. Ticket books are available at previously listed grocery stores and at the Capital Metro Customer Information Center. Each ticket book has 20 tickets valued at 50 cents each for $5, a 50 percent savings on the regular ticket price of 50 cents. Passengers must have tickets or exact change to board the bus.

Seniors and mobility-impaired riders may ride free on city buses by obtaining a free ID at the information center or, in the case of seniors, by showing an ID with a birthdate. There are discounts for individuals who qualify for Special Transit Services, which provide transportation for those who cannot ride public buses. All city buses have bike racks and are equipped with wheelchair lifts.

The agency provides a variety of programs including park-and-ride services, a car-pooling program called Ridefinders, a special van service for seniors called Easyrider, and other programs tailored to the mobility impaired. Capital Metro often provides free public shuttles at major Austin events and festivals, and visitors and downtown workers can avail themselves of the free 'Dillo service.

BICYCLING

Austin is trying its best to be a bike-friendly city. The city even employs a Bicycle & Pedestrian Program Coordinator, who is charged with formulating a bicycle- and pedestrian-friendly transportation plan. The coordinator may be contacted at www.ci.austin.tx.us/bicycle/, by calling (512) 499-7240, or by writing to the Department of Public Works and Transportation, City of Austin, P.O. Box 1088, Austin, TX 78767. The city's Bicycle Planning policy is published by the city, and complimentary copies are available at the above address. There is also a downloadable bike map on the city Web site.

The city currently has approximately 62 miles of roadway with marked bicycle lanes. In the works is the Lance Armstrong Bikeway, named after Austin's famed cyclist who is not the inspiration for the project, but its main planner. The route will take cyclists the 6-mile ride from downtown to the veloway (see our Parks and Recreation chapter). City ordinances also require bicyclists 17 and younger to wear a bicycle helmet. An ordinance to require all bicyclists to wear a helmet was amended after many free-spirited adults complained; however, given the city's busy streets, all riders are advised to wear a helmet in traffic.

We provide more information on recreational biking and cycling, including rentals, in the Austin area in our Parks and Recreation chapter. A great resource Web site is www.bicycleaustin.com.

There are several organizations in Austin that promote bicycle awareness, commuting, and safety. They include:

THE AUSTIN CYCLING ASSOCIATION
P.O. Box 5993, Austin, TX 78763
www.austincycling.org
A recreational riding club. The Web site provides a "map my ride" tool.

AUSTIN RIDGE RIDERS
(512) 835-8411
www.austinridgeriders.com
A recreational mountain-biking club.

AUSTIN/TRAVIS COUNTY SUPERCYCLIST PROGRAM
(512) 708-0513
www.ci.austin.tx.us/bicycle/super.htm
A children's bicycle safety and education program.

AUSTIN TRIATHLETES
(512) 314-5773
A recreational triathlon club.

THE CITY OF AUSTIN BICYCLE PROGRAM
(512) 499-7240
The city's bicycle transportation planning effort.

THE TEXAS BICYCLE COALITION
(512) 476-RIDE
www.biketexas.org
A nonprofit advocacy organization.

THE UNIVERSITY OF TEXAS COLLEGE TRAFFIC SAFETY PROGRAM
(512) 471-4441
A bicycle safety, education, and defensive-cycling course.

THE YELLOW BIKE PROGRAM
(512) 916-3553
www.austinyellowbike.org.
A nonprofit group promoting community free-use bicycles, which are painted yellow and left at various locations, notably around the University of Texas campus.

WALKING

There are areas of Austin where walking can be a pleasure, notably Congress Avenue, the Lady Bird Lake Hike and Bike Trail, and in some of the neighborhood parks. There are also several popular Historic Walking Tours in the city. For more information on these opportunities, see the Attractions and Parks and Recreation chapters.

Walking in downtown Austin is a wonderful way to see the city. Visitors should, of course, always exercise caution. Street crime is not a problem in downtown Austin during daylight hours, but do avoid alleyways after dark. Always exhibit caution when using ATMs, and carry purses and wallets in a secure manner. The Aus-

i Bicyclists 17 and younger must wear helmets in the city of Austin on all streets, on bike trails, and in parks. Violation is a Class C misdemeanor punishable with a $20 fine for the first conviction and $40 for each subsequent conviction.

tin Police Department operates both horseback patrols and bicycle patrols in the city's parks and downtown streets.

HORSE-DRAWN CARRIAGES

One of the most romantic ways to tour downtown Austin is in a horse-drawn carriage. Carriages are not permitted on East Sixth Street, and it's likely the horses would not appreciate the sometimes rowdy atmosphere on that stretch of Sixth between Congress Avenue and I-35, anyway.

AUSTIN CARRIAGE SERVICE
(512) 243-0044
www.austincarriage.com
This service has Belgian and Percheron horses to pull the carriages, which take up positions near the capitol, usually around sunset. Fees are $60 an hour or $30 for a half-hour tour of the downtown area. The drivers are equipped with radios so that they can be summoned to a restaurant, hotel, or nightclub, sometimes for an extra fee if it is far from the capitol. One pleasant ride is a tour of the Bremond Historic District downtown (see the Attractions chapter) or a waterfront tour along Lady Bird Lake. Hours are Sunday through Thursday from just before sunset to around midnight and on Friday and Saturday from sunset to around 2:00 a.m.

DIE GELBE ROSE CARRIAGE
(512) 477-8824
www.diegelberosecarriage.net
Headquartered near the Radisson Hotel at Cesar Chavez Street and Congress Avenue, this carriage company uses Clydesdale horses but also has one Belgian and one Percheron. Rates are $70 an hour or $45 for a half hour. A popular tour is along Congress Avenue to the capitol and past the Governor's Mansion. If he is in the garden, you may get a wave from Governor Rick Perry. Carriages are available from around sunset to midnight during the week and until 2:00 a.m. on weekends.

MOTORCYCLES

Go whole hog and hire a Harley-Davidson motorcycle. Rental operations require a valid motorcycle driver's license, and rates are approximately $150 a day, depending on the day of the week. Longer rental periods also are available. Substantial deposits, charged to your credit card, are required. Roaming the Hill Country on a hog is a popular weekend activity.

AUSTIN HARLEY-DAVIDSON/BUELL
801 East William Cannon Drive
(512) 448-4294
www.austinharley-davidson.com
Rent an Electra Glide Classic, a Buell Blast, or one of eight other models at this South Austin rental agency.

STREET EAGLE
5120 Burnet Road
(512) 250-9010
www.streeteagle.com
This Harley rental business in north Austin offers a membership program for $500 a year that gives members a 50 percent reduction on rental rates.

HOTELS AND MOTELS

Are you the type of traveler who just wants a comfortable, clean, inexpensive place to fling your bags and rest your body so that you can spend all your time getting to know Austin? Or are you looking for a lodging that caters to your every business need? Do you prefer divided space to conduct private meetings or to give you some breathing room from the kids? Perhaps you're looking for accommodations that reflect the history of Austin and transport you back in time. Is luxury the key to your heart? Whether you're looking for a massage and a sauna, a morning jog along Lady Bird Lake, a view, shopping, or nightlife, you've come to the right place!

While Austin offers plenty of accommodations for the traveler who believes the best surprise is no surprise, there also is an ever-increasing number of rooms for those searching for the unique. If you're wishing to be transported, think of us as "OZ-tin," click your heels, make a reservation, and repeat, "There's no place like Texas."

OVERVIEW

Perhaps the most "Austin" of Austin's grand hotels is the Driskill, the Sixth Street landmark that has been treated to a historically accurate restoration valued in the millions of dollars. Another classic Austin landmark, the long-vacant Stephen F. Austin Hotel, has been restored to its earlier splendor and is now part of the luxury Intercontinental chain. An exquisite piece of Austin history, the stately Goodall Wooten Mansion, was rescued in 2003 with the opening of downtown's luxury boutique hotel, the Mansion at Judges' Hill. A hip hotel on trendy South Congress Avenue is the restored World War II–era Hotel San José. These hotels, and a few others scattered around the city, are Austin through and through. Many of the other major chain hotels have also created a Texas ambience, notably the Four Seasons Hotel, where the lobby bar has become a perfect people-watcher spot. Here, high-tech executives from around the world rub shoulders with lobbyists and world-famous musicians, actors, and film executives (see the Nightlife chapter). But travelers don't have to shell out big bucks to get a real Austin experience. Some of our locally owned, older motels are truly Austin—and a lot easier on the pocketbook.

While Austin may never see a return to the days when the grand hotel was the center of community activity, hotels are giving residents more and more reasons to check in. As a result, out-of-towners aren't the only ones to benefit from Austin's hotel industry. For weddings and other festivities, meetings, dining, socializing, or getaway weekends, Austinites are discovering the pleasures of our local hotels.

Whether you've come to live in Austin, or only wish you could, there are a few things you should know before making your hotel or motel reservation in Austin. If this is your first visit to Austin, or you haven't had the pleasure of return-

> **i** Austin is a pretty laid-back city when it comes to dress. Shorts, T-shirts, and sandals are the standard uniform for summer and will get you in just about anywhere. Unless you've come for a gala, casual dress for evening is just perfect. While you can plan on it being hot during the summer, winter can be trickier. We can have 80-degree days and 20-degree days. Mostly, however, Austin's winters are pretty mild, especially compared with those up north. It's best to check the forecast.

ing for a while, allow us to orient you to the lay of the land when it comes to accommodations.

The majority of Austin's full-service and luxury hotels are clustered around downtown. However, you'll also find several noteworthy full-service hotels along the Interstate 35 corridor. Another luxury lodging, the Renaissance Austin Hotel, is in Northwest Austin in the upscale Arboretum area. Northwest Austin, a beautiful area loaded with live oak trees, has seen tremendous growth in limited-service and suite hotels in the past few years, placing it among Austin's chief lodging locations today. Southeast Austin, anchored by the stately Omni Southpark Hotel, is another area that experienced a major boom in the number of hotels and motels with the opening of the new airport. Even Southwest Austin is seeing hotels move in, and more are likely to open in the coming years as business and resort development continues here.

A high concentration of Austin hotels and motels is found along I-35. Because this north-south artery bisects Austin, I-35 hotels and motels can accommodate travelers who want to stay in North, Northeast, East, Central, South, and Southeast Austin. For that reason, we've decided to include sections of I-35 in our geographical listings for those who prefer to stay close to this practical thoroughfare.

We've also tried to point out the best of the other hotels and motels scattered around the city. Although there aren't many of them, they can offer some interesting options and are certainly worth checking out. Of course, there are a number of resorts and bed-and-breakfast establishments in the Lake Travis area. (For information on those see the Resorts Close-up in this chapter and our chapter on Bed-and-Breakfasts and Country Inns.) Our neighboring communities of Round Rock, Cedar Park, and Pflugerville have yet to see construction of a full-service hotel, although they are witnessing a boom in construction of national chain motels and hotels. You'll find some of these properties in the listings of additional addresses we've provided for these chains and in the apartment hotels listings at the end of this chapter.

Austin is bustling, both during the week and often on the weekends, so it's advisable to make advance reservations, especially if you've got a specific hotel in mind. But don't give up the opportunity to stay at the hotel of your choice just because you're late in arriving or making a reservation. There's always a chance. Most often, however, you'll get a better rate with a reservation, as many hotels charge more if they're filling up—the old law of supply and demand. Of course, always ask about discounts or weekend packages the hotel may offer. The annual South by Southwest Music Festival (see the Annual Events and Festivals chapter), sessions of the Legislature, University of Texas football weekends, and other big UT events all draw crowds to Austin, so it's especially important to reserve your room well in advance for these times (check the Annual Events and Festivals chapter).

Are you arriving by air? Travelers who prefer to stay close to the airport have a growing list of choices, including most of the major chain hotels.

Growth in the Austin hotel-motel industry has exploded since we published our first edition of the *Insiders' Guide to Austin* in 1999. Included in that growth are new—or, shall we say, newly restored—Austin originals. For this sixth edition, then, we are focusing primarily on those hotels and motels that are truly unique to Austin or have a particular Austin feel for one reason or another. To offer our readers a range of prices, however, we also have included a few other chain hotels. Other chain-affiliated properties can be found by searching the companies' Internet sites. The listings include a dollar-sign code that will give you an idea of the hotel's rate for a one-night stay for two people in a standard room. Taxes are not included in the rates, so when you're calculating the cost of your stay, make sure to add 15 percent. A portion of the tax goes to support the arts in Austin. The rate information has been provided by the hotels themselves and is subject to change. Unless otherwise noted, all the hotels and motels listed accept major credit cards.

Price Code

The following price code is based on the average room rate for double occupancy during peak business. These prices do not include taxes, which in Austin total 15 percent. Please note that prices may change without notice.

$................. Less than $80
$$ .... $81 to $125
$$$ .... $126 to $170
$$$$.............. $171 to $225
$$$$$......... More than $225

DOWNTOWN

THE DRISKILL HOTEL $$$$$
604 Brazos Street
(512) 474-5911, (800) 252-9367
www.driskillhotel.com

Cattle baron Jesse Driskill opened his stately hotel in downtown Austin on December 20, 1886, offering guests an architectural wonder and such modern conveniences as steam heat and gas lights. More than a century later, The Driskill adds timeless grandeur to the Sixth Street Historic District, where live music pours from the popular nightclubs and packed restaurants of Austin's most-visited strip. Guests leave all that commotion behind when they step into The Driskill's handsome marble-floored lobby. In 1997 and 1998 the hotel underwent a historically accurate multimillion-dollar renovation, and the results are outstanding. Each of the hotel's 180 rooms and suites is unique, designed to reflect the exceptional beauty of the 1880s Driskill. Among the multi-room suites at this hotel are the opulent Cattle Baron Suite, the Lyndon and Lady Bird Johnson Presidential Suite and three distinctive bridal suites. There's also a sitting room named the Maximilian Room, known for its eight gold-leaf mirrors called the Empress Carlota mirrors. These French mirrors were a wedding gift from Maximilian, briefly emperor of Mexico, to his bride Carlota. The story goes that these mirrors were discovered in crates in San Antonio in the 1930s. The two-story side of the hotel is the original

> Don't forget to make The Driskill Hotel part of your walking tour of downtown Austin, even if you're lodging elsewhere. Look for *The Driskill, A Walking Tour* brochures in the hotel lobby, and learn about this historic site.

hotel and features spacious, alluring rooms with nearly 14-foot ceilings. The tower side was built in the 1920s and has nine levels, offering guests better views of downtown Austin. Some rooms feature balconies for an even closer perspective on downtown. The ballroom, upper lobby piano bar, and restaurant also have been remodeled to accentuate the beauty of a bygone era. The piano bar, which features live music in the evenings, is also home to portraits of some of Austin's leading historical figures, including Stephen F. Austin, the Father of Texas (see our History chapter for more on Stephen F. Austin). A captivating Western sculpture called Widow Maker, by the artist Barvo, adorns this lobby—a must see.

The award-winning gourmet restaurant, the Driskill Grill, is open Tuesday through Saturday for dinner, while the meticulously restored 1886 Cafe & Bakery is open seven days a week for breakfast, lunch, dinner and late-night dining. The Driskill also offers a fully equipped fitness center, as well as an executive business center. There is no parking garage on the premises, but valet parking is offered.

EXTENDED STAYAMERICA $$$
600 Guadalupe Street
(512) 457-9994, (800) EXT-STAY
www.exstay.com

Finding a reasonably priced hotel downtown can be difficult, but this national chain offers mid-priced rooms that can be rented by the night or the week. The rooms are small suites with kitchen facilities and desks, making them ideal for business visitors or families on a budget.

FOUR SEASONS HOTEL $$$$$
98 San Jacinto Boulevard
(512) 478-4500, (800) 332-3442
www.fourseasons.com

It doesn't take many steps past the lobby entrance to know you're in one of Austin's premier hotels. Carpeting so thick and plush that your shoes practically disappear leads down the stairs into The Cafe restaurant and terrace, offering a drop-dead-gorgeous view of Lady Bird Lake and of the hotel's own manicured lawns.. The hotel and its 292 exceptionally spacious rooms and suites are designed with a sophisticated Southwestern flair that is both elegant and relaxing. The amenities and services go on and on: 24-hour room service, twice-daily housekeeping service, a heated outdoor pool overlooking Lady Bird Lake, a state-of-the-art health club that includes free weights and features a television on every bike, a spa with massage and body treatments offered, complimentary morning newspaper and overnight shoe shine, and one-hour pressing service. There's even a dock for sunning, splashing your feet in Lady Bird Lake, or, if your rowing team is in town, heading out for training. And while you're outside, you can take advantage of the hotel's direct access to Austin's wonderful Hike and Bike Trail. The Four Seasons will even arrange a bicycle if you want.

LA QUINTA INN $$–$$$
300 East 11th Street
(512) 476-1166, (800) 531-5900
www.laquinta.com
If you want to stay in downtown Austin, but don't need—or can't afford—all the amenities of Austin's upscale hotels, it's hard to beat La Quinta Inn. For comfort, location, and comparative price, La Quinta is an excellent choice. It offers valet parking, a real plus for a motel downtown, where finding parking on the street can be a nightmare. The 145 rooms and suites are spotless and comfortably sized. Nice touches have been added to spruce up the outdoor walkways, such as huge potted flowers and plants. Among the motel's many features are free continental breakfasts, in-room coffeemakers, and Nintendo games. The state capitol is just around the corner, Sixth Street is 5 blocks down the road, and the University of Texas is a mile away. During the week, La Quinta's guests are mostly professionals. Weekends tend to draw a college crowd. Travelers who prefer staying at a La Quinta Inn will be happy to learn there are nine other Austin-area locations, including two in booming Round Rock. The toll-free number for other locations is (800) 687-6667.

THE MANSION AT JUDGES' HILL $$$–$$$$$
1900 Rio Grande Street
(512) 495-1800, (800) 311-1619
www.mansionatjudgeshill.com
Small and ultrachic, the Mansion at Judges' Hill brings one of Austin's historic homes back to splendor—making it, perhaps, even better than during its prime. For more than a century the Goodall Wooten Mansion has stood just a few blocks from the University of Texas in the Judges' Hill neighborhood. But time had taken its toll on this graceful, stone-colonnaded structure. The once-luxurious residence had over the years been used as a dormitory, a sorority house, and finally a drug rehabilitation center. Owner William Gurasich, one of the founders of Austin's well-known GSD&M advertising agency and now a real estate developer, oversaw a complete renovation, paying special attention to the minutest details.

Opened in 2003, this 48-room luxury hotel and gourmet restaurant features rich colors and textures throughout. The large rooms, some with fireplaces, include antique and custom-made furniture, and each is uniquely designed to reflect a timeless quality. Even the spacious bathrooms are gorgeous. Three-room suites also are available. What mansion would be complete without its own private courtyard, library, and covered garage? Amenities include high-speed Internet access, custom bath products, twice-daily housekeeping service, deluxe bathrobes, in-room mini-bars, iron and ironing board, and Egyptian cotton linens. There are separate rates for the Mansion and the North Wing, the latter being somewhat less expensive. This is a perfect place for a wedding or special event. The mansion, built in 1898, was a wedding gift to prominent Austin doctor Goodall Wooten and his bride, Ella Newsome, from their fathers. Ella Wooten, widowed in 1942, sold the house after World War II. The Mansion at Judges' Hill is an exquisite Austin landmark—and an equally exquisite hotel property.

OMNI AUSTIN HOTEL DOWNTOWN $$$$
700 San Jacinto Boulevard
(512) 476-3700, (800) THE-OMNI
www.omnihotels.com

Enormous plate-glass windows supported by steel beams rise from the ground to the towering ceiling in this ultramodern hotel, which features huge abstract paintings and polished granite throughout the atrium-style lobby. Sunlight pours through the tremendous wall of glass and illuminates the sprawling lobby, which is home to Ancho's, the hotel restaurant featuring Southwestern cuisine. The lobby bar next to Ancho's also has that airy look and is a nice place to relax and have a drink or a bite. The hotel has 292 guest rooms, nearly two dozen club rooms and more than 35 one- and two-bedroom suites. The modern, impeccable rooms offer superior comfort and a cozy capital-city feel, with Texas stars scattered here and there throughout the hotel. Guests are treated to the ultimate in comfort in the hotel's large rooms, meeting and convention spaces, and ballroom. The upper floors provide excellent views of downtown Austin and across town. The Omni also offers massage and facial services.

STEPHEN F. AUSTIN HOTEL $$$$$
701 Congress Avenue
(512) 457-8800, (800) 327-0200
www.austin.intercontinental.com

"Austin's Dream Comes True with Brilliant Opening of New Hotel." So read the *Austin American*'s front-page headline on May 20, 1924, the day following the grand opening of the Stephen F. Austin Hotel. Three-quarters of a century later, the hotel reopened as one of Austin's finest luxury hotels. The hotel, vacant for more than a decade, underwent a complete renovation aimed at offering guests the latest in comfort and style while retaining the look and feel of 1920s opulence. A grand staircase of marble and brass beguiles visitors as they enter the lobby and walk up to the Grand Ballroom. The 189 rooms and suites have a truly Texan ambience, with star emblems on some headboards and lots of wrought iron. Facilities include a state-of-the-art fitness center, an indoor swimming pool, a cigar bar, a cafe,

and a restaurant for fine dining. Additionally, the hotel offers 6,000 square feet of meeting and convention space as well as special services for executive travelers, including a business center. Modern amenities, however, are just part of the allure of this hotel. Austin and Texas history wafts through the halls and hangs like tapestries from the walls. Lyndon B. Johnson made this grand hotel his congressional campaign headquarters after World War II, and it seems as if everybody who had a hand in shaping modern Texas walked through its doors at one time or another. In 1984 the *Dallas Morning News* wrote this about the hotel: "To native Austinites and University of Texas Exes, she is known simply as 'the Stephen F.' The name has been adopted for the second story bar which features an outside balcony overlooking Congress Avenue. And if walls could talk, they would relate fascinating tales of oil and cattle deals transacted over breakfast and a handshake, of political intrigue involving state legislators, and of romances begun during World War II." Who knows what tales will be told about the Stephen F. in the 21st century?

SOUTH CENTRAL

AUSTIN MOTEL $$-$$$
1220 South Congress Avenue
(512) 441-1157
www.austinmotel.com

Location, history, personality, and price combine to make the family-owned Austin Motel one of the city's most unique lodgings. As Congress Avenue gentrification spreads south of Lady Bird Lake, this motel is in the right spot at the right time, again. The main buildings were built in 1938 on Austin's central thoroughfare and way before the coming of the highway system. With its now classic red and white neon sign, this motel attracted travelers from near and far. When the traffic moved to the highways, so did much of the Austin Motel's business. South Congress, meanwhile, grew into a popular spot for prostitutes and drug dealers. These days South Congress is hip and happening, and the bad influences are long gone.

Today's Austin Motel, like many other businesses along this funky stretch, is attracting visitors who want to get a distinct feel for Austin. This is not a place for guests who like modern, cookie-cutter accommodations. Artists, musicians, and poets seem especially attracted to the Austin Motel's particular flair, as are others who put character before elegance. This motel has 41 rooms for 41 personalities, from small rooms for those who'd rather spend their time out on the town, to spacious executive suites, to rooms overlooking the large, newly renovated pool. A small, shaded garden just off the pool provides a great place for guests to gather. California wicker, New England dark maple, Florida flamingos, Chinese fans, American red, white, and blue, and Spanish traditional are just a few of the imaginative decor themes that make each visit interesting. Antiques are sprinkled liberally throughout the motel and, while many show their age, all add to the distinctiveness of each room. Owner Dottye Dean, who took over from her mother in 1993, undertook a massive remodeling project that has encompassed every room, including the addition built in the 1960s. Dean and her staff of artists paid special attention to the bathrooms; some feature original fixtures and tile; others have been updated to include marble Jacuzzi bathtubs. One room has a cultured marble shower with two showerheads and seating inside—perfect for a couple. El Sol Y La Luna, the Mexican restaurant next door that is leased from the hotel, is a popular spot for travelers and residents alike (see our Restaurants chapter). This hotel has become so popular with travelers that, beginning in 2008, it asked that guests who want a specific date and room call the hotel directly on the first of the month—three months in advance!

HOTEL SAN JOSÉ $$–$$$$$
1316 South Congress Avenue
(512) 444-7322, (800) 574-8897
www.sanjosehotel.com
Hip is the word most often used to describe this restored Congress Avenue motel, and it suits not only the San José but also the neighborhood. No wonder it is favored by visiting musicians and

artists, since it is just across the street from the famed Continental Club (see our Music Scene chapter) and in the midst of the funky South Congress gallery and retro-shop scene (see our Shopping chapter). The hotel was built in 1939 as a "court hotel," the forerunner of the motel, with rooms built around a central courtyard. Forty rooms and suites in assembled bungalows make up the San José, all decorated in retro-style but with up-to-date conveniences like high-speed Internet service. An additional 18 city-view rooms are being added to the property and the grand opening is scheduled for fall 2009. The courtyards and gardens have been decorated in Texas-style with cactus, aloes and yuccas, gravel pathways, and outdoor seating areas. One public area of the hotel is dedicated to the works of local artists. Prices have increased since the traveling salesmen days, but the hotel offers top-notch services including dry-cleaning, bike rental, access to a music and video library, plus a swimming pool. On First Thursdays (see our Close-up in the Arts chapter), the hotel hosts a live band, while other musical events are held each week on Wednesdays. The popular Jo's Coffeehouse is on the premises. The lower-priced rooms at this hotel are for a shared bath.

HOTEL ST. CECILIA $$$$$
1112 Academy Drive
(512) 852-2400
www.hotelstcecilia.com
We usually don't recommend a hotel we have never experienced for ourselves, but in this case an exception is warranted. The Hotel St. Cecilia opened in late 2008—after our deadline for this sixth edition. However, based on two criteria, we can recommend it for those looking for a luxury boutique hotel that is close to the action on South Congress Avenue. It is owned and operated by the Austinites (Liz Lambert and Bunkhouse Management) who run the Hotel San José (see the previous listing), one of our favorite locally owned establishments, and it is located in the fully restored and expanded former 1888 Miller Crocket House bed-and-breakfast establishment, one of our choice listings in the past.

It also gets a bonus point in our view for its cool, Austin-perfect name. St. Cecilia is the patron saint of music and poetry.

The owners plan to offer 11 guest suites with separate living rooms, and three large rooms with separate seating areas, all decorated luxuriously and surrounded by beautiful landscaping and a swimming pool. Some of the rooms are to have wet bars with small refrigerators and sinks. Five of the rooms are to be inside the main house, built in 1888 and featuring New Orleans-style Victorian architecture. There will also be two new two-story bungalows for a total of six rooms, as well as a new central cottage featuring three more rooms, a central breakfast area and a guest lounge. The hotel did not have a phone number by press time, so check the Web site. For those looking for a quiet, upscale retreat that is close to the bustling SoCo district and downtown, the Hotel St. Cecilia promises to be an excellent choice.

HYATT REGENCY AUSTIN $$$$-$$$$$
208 Barton Springs Road
(512) 477-1234, (800) 233-1234
www.hyatt.com

From the cowhide seat cushions in the lobby to the bed skirts stamped with a boot motif to the reproductions of historic maps and flags of Texas on the walls, this delightful hotel on the south bank of Lady Bird Lake radiates Texas charm. The Branchwater Lounge in the lobby has a stream running through it, and the bar opens out onto an inviting patio that offers an excellent view of the lake. Bat watching is one of the perks for spring and summer guests, although the view of the evening spectacle is not great from the lobby lounge or the lower rooms because the bats take off from the opposite side of the Congress Avenue Bridge (see our Attractions chapter). If you want to catch a glimpse of the bats, be sure to request an appropriate room—perhaps one with a balcony—or take the elevator up to the 17th floor and watch from the huge picture window up there. The hotel underwent a $17 million renovation of its public areas in 2008. This chain also offers business-class hotels in the northwest Arboretum area and in north-central Austin.

> **i** The mall isn't the only place to get your Austin memorabilia or gifts to take home. Many locally owned establishments sell T-shirts and gifts with their own logos, and more. At some you can get locally produced CDs, Austin-made salsas, and other items. When you see a gift section, don't just pass it by. It could have the perfect item for yourself or a loved one who didn't get to come to Austin.

Additionally, it has opened a luxury resort and spa past the airport. See the listing in the Resorts Close-up in this chapter.

SOUTHWEST

THE HEART OF TEXAS MOTEL $
5303 US 290 West
(512) 892-0644
www.heartoftexasmotel.com

This 30-room motel draws a steady stream of regular customers and plenty of newcomers. The attractively decorated, good-size rooms all have microwaves, refrigerators, and coffeemakers. The motel also offers one Jacuzzi-suite room with a king-size four-poster bed. Other rooms have two double beds or a double bed with a sleeper sofa. Upper-level rooms have ceiling fans, a real plus for Austin's long, hot summers. For those who like to spend their spare time outdoors, the Heart of Texas Motel has a putting green, a horseshoe pit, a basketball hoop, and a barbecue grill. On U.S. Highway 290 near the junction with the MoPac Expressway, this motel offers easy access to many parts of town and to Austin-Bergstrom International Airport.

AIRPORT

HILTON AUSTIN AIRPORT $$$-$$$$
9515 New Airport Drive
(512) 385-6767, (800) 774-1500
www.hilton.com

While there are other chain hotels in the Austin-Bergstrom Airport area, this one is the closest—it's on-site. It also is the most "Austin." Housed in the former administration building and officers' headquarters of what was Bergstrom Air Force Base, the round building is affectionately known as "the donut." The hotel offers all the amenities of a full-service hotel, including 262 well-appointed guest rooms, an outdoor swimming pool, state-of-the-art fitness center, jogging trails, a gift shop, lobby bar, and a casual restaurant, "The Creeks." For that really big party, there's also the Bergstrom Grand Ballroom, which holds up to 800 persons. Located two minutes from the passenger terminal, the hotel offers a free airport shuttle. It's 7 miles from downtown Austin and is also located quite conveniently close to the area's high-tech businesses. For those wishing to stay at a full-service Hilton closer to downtown, the high-rise Hilton Austin–Convention Center is at 500 East Fourth Street. For more information, check the Hilton Web site.

LAKE TRAVIS

MOUNTAIN STAR LODGE $$$
3573 Rural Route 620 South
(512) 263-2010, (888) 263-2010
www.mountainstarlodge.com
A great location not far from fabulous Lake Travis and a superb unobstructed view of the Texas Hill Country combine to make the Mountain Star Lodge an excellent choice in accommodations. From its vantage point on Ranch Road 620, the main thoroughfare to an abundance of lakeside recreational spots and restaurants, the lodge offers guests easy access to the community of Lakeway and to fishing, boating, skiing, and other outdoor activities. And yet it's just 1 mile north of Highway 71 in Southwest Austin. The two-story Mountain Star Lodge is locally owned and operated. This lovely building of native limestone offers 20 nonsmoking rooms, each with a private patio or balcony overlooking the large outdoor swimming pool and the vast Canyon Lands Nature Preserve. The rooms, which feature outdoor access and parking just outside the rooms, are decorated in an early Texas theme. Each morning from 7:00 to 9:00 a.m. guests are treated to a complimentary continental breakfast

in the large, inviting lobby, which is designed to reflect the look and feel of a mountain lodge. A large fireplace, a soaring wood-beam ceiling, and huge windows that take advantage of that gorgeous view make this a very cozy spot for relaxing, conducting small business conferences, or hosting parties or weddings.

VINTAGE VILLAS $$$$-$$$$$
4209 Eck Lane
(512) 266-9333
www.vintagevillas.com
The view of Lake Travis is simply stunning from Vintage Villas' hillside perch. It's no wonder this locally owned 43-room hotel is popular for outdoor weddings, parties and business gatherings. But it also is an excellent, meticulously maintained hotel for those who want to escape the hustle and bustle of the city. Divided into three villas, each has its own theme: South Texas, Central Texas and East Texas, and the room decor in each unique room reflects the subtle differences between those regions. The South Texas Villa has more of a western theme; Central Texas has an Austin/Hill Country theme; while the East Texas Villa has a Victorian/antique feel. All of the rooms have a lake view, with patios on the ground floor and balconies on the upper ones, though the view gets better the higher up you are. Each of the villas has its own lounge/common area, while the breakfast room—which serves a reasonably priced complete hot breakfast buffet daily—is located in the South Villa. Additionally, the rooms all feature minifridges, microwaves and coffeemakers. One room in each of the villas is a master suite with a kitchen, living area, king-size bed and more generous bath. The other room choices have either queen-size beds, two queens or a king, though the kings feature the added bonus of a Jacuzzi bathtub. Many of the rooms also have fireplaces. One of the main attractions at this hotel is the great outdoors and the areas for enjoying the lake view. Note, however, that the hotel does not have a beach or direct lake access, though there is lake access for boaters within about three miles. The hotel is less than 1½ miles off of Ranch Road 620, the main thoroughfare to

the lake and the restaurants and clubs in this area. So while the hotel does not serve lunch or dinner, there are many dining choices close by. For weddings and other gatherings, however, there is an in-house executive chef and reception facilities.

INTERSTATE 35 CORRIDOR— NORTH

Hotels in this area are north of the I-35—US 290 East interchange. Because of the high concentration of hotels and motels along I-35, especially in this area, some of the following hotels are only a few blocks north of those listed under I-35 Corridor—Central lodgings.

HABITAT SUITES HOTEL $$$
500 Highland Mall Boulevard
(512) 467-6000, (800) 535-4663
www.habitatsuites.com

For the environmentally conscious traveler—or anyone who wants beautiful environs—the Habitat Suites Hotel is a miniature Eden in the heart of a bustling commercial area. This 96-suite locally owned property in an apartment-like setting has received many major industry awards, including a 2005 Keep Austin Beautiful award. Everything from breakfast to bedtime is planned to protect and honor the earth's bounty. The complimentary full-course breakfast buffet includes healthful alternatives—soy milk, tofu *migas*, stone-ground tortillas, and black beans—as well as an entire range of traditional breakfast dishes. Nontoxic, phosphate-free cleansers are used to maintain the suites and clean the laundry, while the grounds are kept using natural fertilizers and pesticides. Ionizers are used to maintain clean air quality in all the suites, and the hotel uses biodegradable, recycled paper products and returns to the recycling bin all possible items. Habitat is "green" both figuratively and literally. The property is totally surrounded by native foliage and flowering plants that create a lush, inviting atmosphere, while they require the least amount of water. The hotel staff even grows a variety of fruits, vegetables, and herbs on the property. Habitat's outdoor swimming pool, also enveloped

Following the death of Lady Bird Johnson in 2007, Town Lake was renamed in honor of the former first lady who had done so much to make the lake area the Austin gem it is today. Old habits die hard, however, so don't get confused if you hear us call it Town Lake. Even more confusing, it looks more like a river than a lake. It's the body of water that divides north from south in the downtown area.

by greenery, uses ionized water and bromine instead of chlorine, better for the environment and for the skin. What's inside is also inviting. The spacious one- and two-bedroom suites, all with fully equipped kitchens, are tastefully decorated and include, of course, green plants. No smoking is allowed in the rooms, but the hotel has plenty of outdoor benches. The upper-level bedrooms in the two-bedroom units have their own private entrances. The 504-square-foot meeting room provides additional space for gatherings of all kinds. The hotel also treats guests to an evening social hour, with free drinks and snacks. This hotel is within a stone's throw of the Highland Mall shopping center, 16 movie theaters, and several popular restaurants. It's about a 10-minute drive from downtown Austin and offers easy access to all parts of town. This is the only I-35 corridor hotel that's not right on the highway. It's just a few blocks off but worth the extra effort to locate it.

HAWTHORN SUITES—CENTRAL $$–$$$
935 La Posada Drive
(512) 459-3335, (800) 527-1133
www.hawthorn.com

Situated just across I-35 from a major shopping mall, with easy access to downtown and many high-tech industries, and nestled between two of Austin's luxury hotels, Hawthorn Suites can claim a great location as one of its major advantages. But there's much more. Hawthorn's 71 spacious one- and two-bedroom suites all have complete kitchens with full-size appliances, and they all feature patios or balconies, and working fireplaces. A collapsible door separates the sleeping area from the living quarters in the one-bedroom studio unit and on the lower level of the two-bedroom lofts. For the business traveler, Hawthorn Suites offers a meeting room that can accommodate up to 50 people. A second Hawthorn Suites is located near the airport.

MOTEL 6—AUSTIN NORTH $
9420B North I-35
(512) 339-6161, (800) 4-MOTEL 6
www.motel6.com

One of six Motel 6s in Austin for the budget-minded traveler, this North Austin location offers 158 guest rooms on two levels. Guests are treated to free HBO, and the motel's outdoor swimming pool is open from May through September. Complimentary coffee is served in the lobby from 7:00 to 10:00 a.m. This Motel 6 property, Austin's northernmost, offers easy access to I-35, U.S. Highway 183, and US 290. The capitol, University of Texas, and LBJ Library are 6 miles south. Major shopping centers are just a few miles south on I-35. Call the 800 number above for information on other Austin locations, most of them situated along the I-35 corridor.

INTERSTATE 35 CORRIDOR— CENTRAL

This area of I-35 is defined in our book as the area south of the I-35–US 290 East junction and north of Lady Bird Lake. Hotels in this listing can be found on either side of the interstate or just a block or two away.

CLUB HOTEL BY DOUBLETREE $$$–$$$$
1617 North I-35
(512) 479-4000, (800) 444-CLUB
www.doubletreehotels.com

DoubleTree's innovative concept has taken the business traveler's hotel to a new level with its Club Hotel. A self-contained business environment—just like the office back home—has been created right off the lobby area for the use of hotel guests. Two private cubicles complete with reference materials and six well-lighted personal work stations create a functional and comfortable work setting. A private conference room in this space would seat three or four people comfortably. And just a step away guests have access to a copier, a fax machine, and a printer. There is an extra charge for these services. While this area is designed to create an "office-away-from-the-office" setting, the spacious lobby is fashioned to make guests feel as if they are at home. This is all just steps away from Au Bon Pain–The Bakery Cafe, the hotel's delicatessen-style restaurant serving fresh pastries, soups, sandwiches, and more. The limited-service hotel's 152 spacious and immaculate rooms of varying sizes all come equipped with desks, wireless Internet service, and coffeemakers. The hotel offers many other amenities, including an outdoor swimming pool, exercise room, guest laundry facilities, and an evening lounge. A larger meeting room on the premises holds up to 50 people. This hotel is conveniently located just across the interstate from the University of Texas, downtown Austin, and the Frank Erwin Center. The DoubleTree also has a Guest Suites Hotel on 15th Street downtown.

DAYS INN UNIVERSITY $–$$
3105 North I-35
(512) 478-1631, (800) 725-ROOMS
www.daysinn.com

Days Inn University is a reasonable choice for the traveler on a budget who wants to be close to some of Austin's featured attractions. The motel is near the University of Texas and all its sports stadiums. Its location right next to the interstate offers easy access to many parts of town, though there could be some traffic noise. Rates are cheaper during the week. Days Inn operates two other motels in Austin and one in Round Rock. All are on I-35.

HOLIDAY INN—TOWN LAKE $$$–$$$$
20 North I-35
(512) 472-8211, (800) HOLIDAY
www.ichotelsgroup.com

This 320-room property was designed to give guests the best possible view of Lady Bird Lake—and what a view it is. (Last we checked, the hotel was still listed as a Town Lake property, even though the name of the lake has changed). On Austin's central waterway, many of the hotel's sleeping quarters, meeting rooms, common areas, and the outdoor swimming pool provide stunning views of the lake. Large picture windows in the rooms maximize the view. The 14-floor, round "Capitol Tower" portion of this hotel was built in the 1960s, making it one of Austin's oldest full-service hotels. (The newer "Lake Tower" was built in the mid-1980s.) All the facilities are very well maintained, so it's hard to tell when you're in the older part. That, combined with a great location, services, and lower prices than some other full-service properties, make the Holiday Inn comfortable in many aspects. Ask about the hotel's special packages that include tickets to the Austin Children's Museum or Bob Bullock Museum.

INTERSTATE 35 CORRIDOR— SOUTH

The hotels in this area are on I-35 beginning on the south side of Lady Bird Lake and heading south. More national chain hotels are planned for this area, plus along Highway 71 from the Ben White Boulevard interchange on I-35 as it heads east to the airport.

BEST WESTERN AUSTIN SOUTH $$
4323 South I-35
(512) 447-5511, (800) 528-1234
www.bestwestern.com
One of several independently owned Best Western hotels in Austin and Round Rock, the Austin South location offers 95 rooms, most with balconies. A complimentary hot breakfast is served

i If you're coming to Austin for one of our city's major annual events, like SXSW, the Austin City Limits Music Festival, or the Republic of Texas Motorcycle Rally, check the event's Web page or the Austin Visitors Bureau Web site at www.austin texas.org. Often there are special hotel deals available. Don't dally though, as visitors come from far and wide.

daily in the lobby. All rooms have desks, irons, coffeemakers, and Internet access, and the larger rooms come with love seats or recliners. There's also a self-service guest laundry room for those who like to return home with clean clothes.

OMNI AUSTIN HOTEL
AT SOUTHPARK $$$$–$$$$$
4140 Governors Row
(512) 448-2222, (800) THE-OMNI
www.omnihotels.com
An enticing lobby designed with luxurious dark woods, marble, and subdued lighting greets guests upon arrival at the Omni Austin Southpark, I-35's southernmost full-service hotel in Austin, with access to nearby high-tech giant AMD. A unique and inviting horseshoe-shaped gourmet coffee and cocktail bar beckons visitors to "come, relax, unwind." The 313 rooms and suites in this 14-story giant are exceptionally large and comfortable and are well equipped with coffeemakers, hair dryers, irons and ironing boards, desks, and Internet connections. The upper-level floors on the north side offer the best views of downtown Austin and St. Edward's University. There is also a room here called the Kid's Sensory Suite, which is designed with all the amenities children will love. For those who prefer the outdoors, the hotel offers 24 rooms with walk-out balconies. We especially like the huge heated outdoor-indoor swimming pool, a wonderfully original concept. The outdoor portion of the pool is surrounded by a large deck and lovely garden area and then wraps around into the fitness center building. The fully equipped fitness center includes a sauna and a hot tub surrounded by tropical foliage—very relaxing. The Omni's Onion Creek Grille, popular with both travelers and local residents, serves breakfast, lunch, and dinner beginning at 6:30 a.m. Don't miss the made-to-order pasta bar, open for lunch daily. After a full day of work or sightseeing, the Republic of Texas Bar, designed with a Western flair, is a great place to watch a game on television or socialize. For business or social gatherings, the Omni offers 15,000 square feet of space, including a huge ballroom for large groups. The hotel also features

🔍 Close-up

Austin's Resorts

The Texas Hill Country west of Austin and the rolling prairie and woodlands east of the city are conducive to outdoor recreation and relaxation. The lakes and waterways, the natural beauty of the hills, the hospitable climate, and Texas hospitality have been combined to create several top-quality resorts that offer a variety of experiences. Three of the four listed here are noted golf resorts, and they are detailed in our Golf chapter. The fourth is a Hill Country spa that offers not only outdoor recreational activities but also all manner of therapies designed to relax both body and spirit.

Barton Creek Conference Resort and Country Club
8212 Barton Club Drive
(512) 329-4000, (800) 336-6157
www.bartoncreek.com

A topflight resort with four beautiful golf courses designed by the top names in the sport, Barton Creek is on some of the most beautiful land just west of Austin. Barton Creek wends its way through the hills here, creating not only a beautiful setting for golf but also for other activities, including tennis, skeet shooting, jogging on wonderful Hill Country trails, swimming, boating, fishing, and horseback riding. The resort also offers sight-seeing and shopping tours, a spa, and even a Kid's Club where the youngsters can be entertained while Mom and Dad enjoy their own playtime.

The resort has several excellent dining facilities, for both casual meals and special occasions. (It has one of the few restaurants in Austin where a jacket is required.) The resort's spa offers an extensive menu of treatments from facials to salt rubs to aromatic loofah scrubs. There is also a fitness center in the resort complex. The resort maintains recreational facilities, including swimming and tennis, at Barton Creek Lakeside at nearby Lake Travis.

There are a total of 303 rooms at the resort, but despite the size the atmosphere on the 4,000-acre property is private and quiet. The rooms all have views of the golf course or the surrounding Hill Country. The resort offers a number of packages tailored to guest's interests. High season is from March to November; low season is December through February. Packages begin at around $270 per person per night in low season and $330 in high season. Room rates vary from around $230 to $1,000 plus for the large suites.

Lake Austin Spa Resort
1705 South Quinlan Park Road
(512) 372-7300, (800) 847-5637
www.lakeaustin.com

You can ask the concierge to fix you up for a round of golf. Or perhaps a set or two of tennis. A sailboat ride. A little water-skiing. But why would you? Wouldn't you rather just have another massage? This spa on the shores of Lake Austin aims to capture the essence of Austin and rid you of all those uptight urban ills. Readers of *Condé Nast Traveler* and *Travel and Leisure* magazines have named it one of the Top 10 spas in North America. Lake Austin Spa Resort offers a large variety of spa services by the day or week. A three-night refresher package is a little more than $1,500 and includes two spa treatments of your choice, fitness classes and programs, a 30-minute personal fitness consultation, meals, and a deluxe private room. The seven-night ultimate pampering program costs approximately $4,500 to $6,500 depending on room choices, and that includes a monogrammed robe.

Just reading the brochures is enough to make you long for a night or two of pampering. How about a Blue Lagoon massage—a body wrap of blue seaweed. Or a Texas two step—someone rubs your toes while you get an herbal face-lift.

The spa also offers special programs throughout the year on diverse topics, including gardening, cooking, and nutrition. Guest speakers from all walks of life are invited to these presentations. One special package is dubbed "A Gathering of Wise Women" and features experts on women's health issues.

If you really want to get more active, in addition to golf and tennis the spa offers a long list of outdoor activities, including watersports on adjacent Lake Travis and hiking in the hills.

Hyatt Regency Lost Pines Resort
575 Hyatt Lost Pines Road
(512) 308-1234; (888) 591-1234; (800) 228-9548 (TDD)
www.visitlostpines.com

Just 30 miles southeast of Austin sits a piney woodlands called the "Lost Pines"—lost because these loblolly pines are some 100 miles from East Texas where piney woods are ubiquitous. The area is now home to a luxury resort built by Hyatt. The resort attracts golfers to its topflight Wolfdancer Club (see our Golf chapter); families who enjoy outdoor activities, such as horseback riding; seekers of sybaritic pleasures at the hotel's spa; and even movie stars, who sometimes stay here when filming on location in Central Texas. At Spa Django (the name means "I awake") guests can enjoy spiritual awakening treatments like an "herbal spice percussion scrub" that includes a body wrap and rhythmic Austin music for $250. A full day of "awakening" is $650. The resort also features trails for horseback riding, a water park, several outstanding restaurants and quiet corners that reflect the ranch-style atmosphere. There are 492 guest rooms and suites, with rates beginning at $300.

Lakeway Inn
101 Lakeway Drive
(512) 261-6600, (800) LAKEWAY
www.lakewayinn.com

This resort hotel on Lake Travis, west of the city, is a longtime favorite for visitors from around Texas and Mexico. The resort has topflight amenities for golfers and tennis players plus provides the facilities and equipment for a variety of watersports. Prime season is March to November; "value season" runs from December to February. The resort offers a variety of packages ranging in price from approximately $200 a couple per night in value season to $280 in prime season.

In addition to golf packages, the resort also offers romantic getaways, "lake escape" packages, and family packages and is a popular spot for catered events, including weddings and family reunions.

a conference center with tiered seating for 30 people, a gift shop, and a full-service business center. The hotel also is home to the Trinity Spa, which offers massage and facial services.

NORTHWEST

COURTYARD BY MARRIOTT—AUSTIN NORTHWEST $$$
9409 Stonelake Boulevard
(512) 502-8100, (800) 321-2211
www.marriott.com

A view of the indoor pool and the charming breakfast room, complete with fireplace, greets guests at this modern, efficient hotel designed for business travelers. Each of the hotel's 78 rooms features a coffeemaker, iron and ironing board, hair dryer, and two telephones, one conveniently located on a desk. After a hectic business day, guests can flip on the television or work out in the fitness center, which features treadmills, bicycles, and other exercise equipment, or they can take a dip in the pool or a relaxing soak in the hot tub. Courtyard has no outdoor pool on the premises, but guests are allowed to use the pool at Marriott's Residence Inn next door. A small do-it-yourself laundry room and a comfortable meeting room that holds about 25 adults complete the amenities. For guests desiring even more, upgraded rooms that include microwave ovens and small refrigerators are available, as are Executive King rooms that are about 1½ times the size of a normal room.

HAMPTON INN $$
3908 West Braker Lane
(512) 349-9898, (800) HAMPTON
www.hamptoninn.com

Efficient and inviting, the Hampton Inn is one of several hotels in this part of town that cater to professionals, including many who work in the high-tech industries. Each of the hotel's 124 rooms is equipped with a small desk and telephone that features a dataport. The comfortably sized rooms feature coffeemakers and an iron and ironing board. The hotel also offers one-day valet laundry service and provides a fax service. For those who want to unwind after a busy day, there's an outdoor swimming pool and a small fitness center with a treadmill, stationary bike, and stair stepper.

HOMEWOOD SUITES—NORTHWEST $$$
10925 Stonelake Boulevard
(512) 349-9966, (800) CALL-HOM
www.homewoodsuites.com

An exceedingly inviting lobby tastefully designed with a Southwest decor greets guests upon arrival at this all-suites hotel fashioned for both the business traveler and for families. Those traveling with children will especially like the solid door that divides the bedroom—or bedrooms—from the living area, so the children can sleep peacefully while the parents relax, entertain guests, or watch television. The apartment-style suites are stylish and very comfortable with fully equipped, full-size kitchens that even include toaster ovens. Homewood offers one- and two-bedroom suites as well as a choice of bed sizes.

RENAISSANCE AUSTIN HOTEL $$$$
9721 Arboretum Boulevard
(512) 343-2626, (800) 468-3571
www.renaissancehotels.com

Northwest Austin's luxury hotel, the Renaissance Austin pampers each guest as it caters to nearly every whim and any need. Enter through the lobby into the immense pavilion, the airy indoor courtyard that reaches up 10 stories to the skylight. Here among trees and plants, attractive sculptures, and tremendous dangling mobiles, visitors will find Band a Texas bistro that serves breakfast, and lunch, and dinner. The menu features local flavors served tapas style. Across the pavilion is the hotel delicatessen, which is open daily for breakfast, lunch, and dinner and serves lighter fare—sandwiches, snacks, and desserts. Feel like dancing? Drop into Tangerine's, the hotel's nightclub. Need a 2:00 a.m. snack? The hotel also offers 24-hour room service. Swim indoors or outdoors, drop in to the fitness center, or walk next door or across the street to some of Austin's finest shops and a great selection of nearby restaurants. The rooms are ample and tasteful and, for those staying on the Hill Country side, afford excellent views of the trees and hillsides. This hotel, owned by Marriott, is the largest of Austin's luxury hotels, with 478 rooms and suites. The Renaissance, like many other topflight hotels in the area, offers a Club Floor for those guests wanting a little extra space and service. The hotel has an enormous amount of meeting and convention space, including an auditorium with tiered seating for 55 people, an exhibition hall, a 12,000-square-foot ballroom, and many other private rooms and halls. The executive traveler can pop downstairs to the Business Center, which offers copying, faxing, shipping, word processing, and a notary. The Renaissance is one of the farthest hotels from the airport, but its location near the junction of MoPac and US 183 is great for the discriminating traveler who wants to be on the edge of Austin's beautiful Hill Country and yet have easy access to the high-tech industries in the north and other parts of town.

HOSTELS

HOSTELLING INTERNATIONAL $
2200 South Lakeshore Boulevard
(512) 444-2294, (800) 725-2331
www.hi-austin.org

Austin is a mecca for young travelers, especially those fascinated by the city's music scene. Finding a cheap place to stay can be a challenge, but the arrival of Hostelling International on the shores of Lady Bird Lake near the city's Hike and Bike Trail has made Austin affordable for travelers on a budget. There are 39 beds in four dormitories in the facility, and beds are assigned at check-in. Guests must show an ID with an address outside the Austin area, and guests who are members of Hostelling International pay a few dollars less for their accommodations. The central location is not far from the city's entertainment area, and the hostel even offers its own live music two nights a week. The hostel is located on city and University of Texas bus lines and is an easy walk to banks, grocery stores, and restaurants. There is a kitchen on premises, common areas, Internet access, and a laundry, and the hostel is air-conditioned and heated. Visitors also can rent canoes, kayaks, and bicycles. There are some rules—no alcoholic beverages on-site, no smoking inside, and no sleeping bags. Reservations are recommended and can be made with a credit card or a Hostelling International membership card. Groups of up to 20 persons are accepted.

BED-AND-BREAKFASTS AND COUNTRY INNS

For a truly unique Austin experience, spend a night, or longer, in one of our many bed-and-breakfast establishments. The eclectic assortment includes luxury establishments designed to pamper you, restored colonial and Greek Revival homes for stepping back into another era, and plenty of places to just hang out and relax—in town or out by the lake. The common denominator for all our bed-and-breakfasts, however, is the attention to detail paid to each property. The special people who operate these lodgings are, in many cases, sharing their own homes and their lives—not to mention favorite breakfast recipes. Visitors will also find bed-and-breakfasts created for the exclusive use of their guests. There is no better reason to choose a bed-and-breakfast than simply the desire to stay in a one-of-a-kind lodging.

For distinctive special events such as weddings, parties, and business gatherings, several of Austin's bed-and-breakfasts can fulfill all your needs. For that romantic interlude, some offer celebration packages that include champagne and other delights. With all these special services, it's no wonder more and more Austinites are discovering they don't have to leave town to go on vacation.

In this chapter you'll find a wide selection of the bed-and-breakfast establishments in Austin. Unless otherwise noted, the inns listed here accept major credit cards. The Americans with Disabilities Act does not require that these lodgings create wheelchair-accessible rooms, although you will find some with that amenity. Smoking is usually permitted outdoors only at these establishments. Guests should be aware that check-in times and cancellation policies at bed-and-breakfast establishments differ from those at hotels and motels and that some charge a cancellation fee. Please check with the individual establishment regarding the cancellation policy and check-in times when you make your reservation. And if you're planning to stay in Austin for a while, be sure to ask about extended-stay rates.

Price Code

Our rate categories are based on a one-night stay for two people throughout the year. Because some bed-and-breakfasts offer a wide range of room sizes and amenities, their rates can vary greatly. In that case we have given you two dollar codes and you will expect to find rates within those spectrums. These rates do not include the 15 percent total Austin tax on lodgings. Nor do they take into account the extended-stay or other specialty rates available at many establishments.

$	Less than $80
$$	$80 to $125
$$$	$126 to $170
$$$$	More than $170

CENTRAL

1110 CARRIAGE HOUSE INN $$$–$$$$
1110 West 22½ Street
(512) 472-2333
www.carriagehouseinn.org
This well-established, award-winning B&B is unique in that its six guest rooms and suites are housed in three different buildings on-site,

each with its own special features and most with private entrances. The inn's location—on a quiet street yet minutes from downtown and the UT campus—is another pleasant anomaly. The main house, a beautifully restored 100-year-old colonial structure, is the home of proprietors Tressie and Jim Damron. The two lovely guest rooms in this building are upstairs via a private outdoor staircase, which ends at a large deck—perfect for looking down on the gazebo and koi pond below or up at the stars. There's a telescope if you'd like to find Cassiopeia. The rooms here share a kitchen that, like the others at the inn, comes stocked with dishes, crystal, soft drinks, tea, and coffee.

Out back on the property is the Cottage, which houses two spacious suites. The Robinson Suite features a living room/kitchen and a separate bedroom highlighted by a queen-size poster bed. A queen-size sleigh bed is the focal point of the bedroom in the Garden Suite, which also has a comfortable living/kitchen area. Unlike the inn's other rooms, however, this suite has no phone—for those who wish to totally withdraw from the real world. Next door is the Guesthouse, a quaint gem made from lava rock from an inactive volcano near here! In addition to two well-appointed guest rooms, each with a queen-size bed and private bath, this building features a communal living room with extra half bath, microwave, and coffee and tea service. Each of these rooms also has its own private outdoor seating area. The Guesthouse also is home to the B&B's contemporary Western-style breakfast room, accentuated by individual handmade cedar tables. The real treats, however, are the breakfasts Tressie puts on these tables. Homemade waffles with homemade whipped cream and fresh blueberries, rosemary breakfast tacos, chicken sausage, and homemade scones are among her guests' favorites.

The 1110 Carriage House Inn has received several honors from the industry trade publication *Arrington's Bed & Breakfast Journal*, including being listed among the top 15 most elegant inns in the country. Indeed, the inn is long on attributes. We especially like its many private decks,

i The Greater Austin Bed-and-Breakfast Association (GABBA) operates a referral service among members, so if one of the B&Bs you call is booked, the innkeeper likely will be able to refer you to another that suits your tastes and price range. Or you can ask for the name and telephone number of the current GABBA contact.

terraces, and patios—and the large garden itself. Most notable, however, is the warm Texas charm of Tressie herself.

ADAMS HOUSE $$–$$$
4300 Avenue G
(512) 453-7696
www.theadamshouse.com

Adams House opened for business in 1998. And what a house it is. Historic-preservation architect Gregory Free has restored this 1911 home in historic Hyde Park from top to bottom. He installed stylish gray slate floors in some areas and added a gray wash to the original hardwood floors in others. White woodwork, high ceilings, and wraparound sunrooms on two levels give this home a bright and airy look that adds to its beauty. The current resident owner, Sidney Lock, has added her own special touches, which give this old Colonial Revival house the look and feel of a classy modern dwelling—even with the many remarkable antiques throughout. Adams House originally was built as a one-story bungalow. W. T. Adams and his family purchased the home in 1922 and added another level in 1931. The home, however, fell on hard times during the second half of the 20th century and was turned into apartments. Now it looks better than ever before. Original paintings, a baby grand piano, and a designer kitchen with granite counters all contribute to its charm. Adams House offers four rooms on the second floor, accessible only by stairs, as well as a bungalow, a separate house behind the main one. Breakfast on weekdays is a serve-it-yourself continental affair, which includes muffins, croissants, fresh fruit, cereals, juice, and gourmet coffee. On weekends, a full breakfast is specially prepared for guests and served in the dining room. Breakfast tacos, gourmet quiches and other egg dishes, pastries, and homemade breads are just some of the delicacies served.

AUSTIN FOLK HOUSE $$–$$$$
506 West 22nd Street
(512) 472-6700, (866) 472-6700
www.austinfolkhouse.com

Some people stay at this great bed-and-breakfast just to enjoy the eclectic collection of folk art on display throughout the house. But don't come to feast your eyes on the art alone. Young University of Texas grads Sylvia and Chris Mackey have created a classy, Austin-hip inn that invites guests to settle in, relax, and stay awhile. This B&B got its name from the artwork (the collection is from Sylvia's family). The two-story establishment offers nine well-appointed rooms, including one designed for wheelchair accessibility. While all the rooms feature either queen- or king-size beds, each room is quite distinctive. Some are painted in vibrant red or olive tones; others are light and airy. There are sleigh beds, canopy beds, iron beds, and four-poster beds, each with a handmade spread that perfectly accentuates the decor. The romantic Room Seven upstairs is done in crimson and gold and features an exquisite Oriental carpet and an iron canopy draped with elegant fabric. All rooms have private baths, most with tub and shower, phones, TVs, and VCRs. Sylvia serves a full, hot buffet-style breakfast each morning. *Migas*, banana crepes, raspberry waffles, fresh fruit, and fresh-baked breads are among her guests' favorites. A word of warning, though: Her homemade cookies are addictive. The elegant dining room, another showcase for some intriguing paintings, consists of five individual pub tables. Guests also are invited to take their breakfast out to the spacious front porch. The porch, by the way, is a fine hangout any time of the day or night. The kitchen is always open for those who like to make a late-night cup of tea or grab a snack from the fridge.

The Folk House is perfectly located for easy access to downtown or the UT campus, although one trade-off for its central location is a bit of traffic noise. For that, there are soothing sound machines in each room. This B&B also has its own parking lot, a real plus for this neighborhood, and the free 'Dillo people mover stops right across the street. While the establishment does not accept pets, well-behaved children are welcome. Don't forget to ask Sylvia about the Folk House's own T-shirts and the special packages and treats she offers—like mimosas served in your room!

BRAVA HOUSE $$–$$$
1108 Blanco Street
(512) 478-5034, (888) 545-8200
www.bravahouse.com

Blanco Street in downtown Austin is lined with many of Austin's Victorian-era homes, among them Brava House, built in the 1880s and now beautifully restored. The home is within easy walking distance of Austin's central city sights and nightlife. There are two guest rooms, two suites, and a large apartment, each named for the era the decor suggests. The Van Gogh Room on the first floor off the garden has its own private entrance and is completely wheelchair accessible. The room has a lovely bay window and features a queen-size bed with canopy netting. A beautiful four-poster bed is the centerpiece of the Moroccan-style Casablanca Room, which also has a sitting area by the large corner picture windows.

Fireplaces in both the parlor and the bedroom and an antique wooden queen bed add touches of romance to the Garbo Suite, which brings to mind the Hollywood of the 1930s. The spacious Fitzgerald Suite, named for F. Scott of course, has a 1920s Art Deco decor. This room is great for families; there's a sleeper sofa in the parlor, as well as a fireplace. The lovely bedroom has a queen-size bed. The Monroe Suite upstairs is a one-bedroom, fully equipped apartment of about 650 square feet. It features a wood-burning fireplace, full kitchen, and plenty of space in the living room to spread out. All the rooms and suites have private baths, phones, cable TV, coffeemakers, and minifridges.

Sunday morning is special at Brava House—that's when this B&B offers its great champagne brunch, a full hot breakfast complete with mimosas and berries and cream. A hot breakfast buffet is also served on Saturday. On weekdays the breakfasts are continental. Trays are provided so that guests can eat in their rooms if they'd like or enjoy the morning air on the front porch or the exquisite back deck.

CARRINGTON'S BLUFF $$-$$$
1900 David Street
(512) 479-0638, (888) 290-6090
www.carringtonsbluff.com

A 500-year-old native oak is just one of the many trees that shade the one-acre bluff where this attractive bed-and-breakfast stands. Operated by resident owner Phoebe Williams, this English Country–style home is a real Austin original. The Main House, built in 1877, features five guest rooms with elegant king- or queen-size beds, most decorated with floral fabrics and featuring American and English antiques. The large covered porch is a great place to rock and relax while enjoying the view of the garden and gazebo, where many Austin couples have been married. The Writers' Cottage just across the lawn has its own kitchen and living area, as well as three additional guest rooms, including one especially large room that holds two queen-size beds. This cottage is a great place for family retreats or for those who want to feel like they're off on their own, to work or just to unwind. All the rooms have private bathrooms and come with guest bathrobes, irons and ironing boards, TVs, VCRs, and telephones.

Every morning Phoebe serves a complete buffet-style hot breakfast in the dining room of the Main House. The menu always includes one of her specialties, such as a Gouda cheese and bacon frittata, crepes with fresh raspberries, or a green-chile and cheese casserole. Children of all ages are invited to Carrington's Bluff, and so is the family pet. Just give Phoebe a call first.

Carrington's Bluff, part of an original 22-acre homestead of the Republic of Texas, is just above busy Lamar Boulevard, but it's nestled so well amid the lush greenery and flower gardens that it's hard to tell. Guests feel isolated here, even though they're minutes from downtown—and

just 7 blocks from the University of Texas. For those who really want to pamper themselves, Phoebe can arrange on-site spa services, including massages and manicures, but do let her know in advance so that she can accommodate you. She also offers some great special packages, such as candles, flowers and chocolates, and breakfast in bed.

THE INN AT PEARL STREET $$$-$$$$
809 West Martin Luther King Jr.
Boulevard
(512) 478-0051, (800) 494-2261
www.innpearl.com

When the Inn at Pearl Street opened in 1995, it immediately earned a reputation as one of Austin's most luxurious bed-and-breakfast establishments and was selected as the year's Designer Showhouse by the Austin Symphony League. The Inn includes two properties, the five-room Victoria House and the four-room Burton House, as well as two free-standing cottages on the grounds. Each of the rooms and many common areas are luxuriously decorated to reflect Old World radiance. Sumptuous designer fabrics and wallpapers throughout this cozy home add the perfect touch to each room. The French Room, decorated in shades of yellow and gold, features French antique furniture, a stylish four-poster iron bed, a crystal chandelier, and a claw-foot bath. The European Room exudes the utmost in Old World charm, with its king-size bed, billowy-topped floral chintz draperies, and unique furnishings. The Far East Room, decorated in shades of salmon and featuring a beautiful Oriental screen and armoire, offers the perfect escape. Here guests will discover a lovely private balcony and a fabulous private bathroom.

The Gothic Suite, with a separate dayroom and Jacuzzi bath, is perfect for a special occasion, or just a special treat. A glorious cathedral-inspired bed highlights this room, decorated in sage greens, pale reds, and coppery metals. The Gothic Suite includes a refrigerator, coffeemaker, and complimentary toiletries. The common areas also are a feast for the eyes. The music room is especially attractive, with its ivory-lacquered ℹ️ February through June and September through November are the busiest seasons for Austin's bed-and-breakfasts. We highly recommend making your reservations well in advance, especially if your heart is set on one particular establishment. The limited number of rooms in each inn can fill up quickly, especially during special events in Austin.

grand piano, mirrored pedestals, and antique fireplace. The large outdoor deck, surrounded by oak and pecan trees, is perfect for a wedding or a special gathering of any nature. This is one place that begs to be discovered.

The Inn at Pearl Street offers an elaborate European-style self-serve breakfast during the week from as early as you request it until about 10:30 a.m. Cereals, muffins, fruit, bagels, and more are presented along with cold cuts and cheeses to give breakfast that European flair. A full-service breakfast is offered on weekends from 9:00 to 9:30 a.m. While the table service is exquisite every day of the week, the inn pulls out all stops on Sunday with full china and silver service, tantalizing entrees, and mimosas. A house specialty is the wonderful egg soufflé served with smoked ham and fresh bread. For an extra fee and advance notice, you can request breakfast on your private balcony. There is coffee and tea service on both floors. And for those truly special occasions, the Inn at Pearl offers a celebration package, which includes a bottle of champagne on arrival and breakfast in bed. For that special occasion, make arrangements in advance for the Inn's Twilight Dinner: an elegant five- or six-course meal served by candlelight for an extra fee. This bed-and-breakfast is on busy Martin Luther King Boulevard Jr. at Pearl Street, just blocks from the UT campus and close to downtown entertainment of all kinds. Children age 12 and up are invited to stay at this historic inn.

STAR OF TEXAS INN　　　　**$$–$$$$**
611 West 22nd Street
(512) 472-6700, (866) 472-6700
www.staroftexasinn.com

This relative newcomer to the Austin bed-and-breakfast lineup has three unique advantages right from the start: First, it is the site of the former Governors' Inn, which earned a reputation for being one of Austin's finest B&Bs during its long run. Second, it is owned and operated by Sylvia and Chris Mackey, who have won our kudos with their successful (nearby) Austin Folk House bed-and-breakfast. (See listing in this section.) Third, the home itself is a beautifully restored neoclassic Victorian structure—and an Austin treasure—having been built in 1897.

Star of Texas Inn offers 10 guest rooms, ranging from a simple room with a twin-size bed to the larger and more elegantly decorated rooms with king- and queen-size antique beds. Room number 12 (we'll call it the "red" room) on the second floor not only is one of the property's most beautiful guest rooms but also has private access to the large covered balcony, where guests can sit and unwind after a full day—or night—of Austin excitement. The elegant room number 14, which features a four-poster bed and canopy, also has a private door to the balcony and the added advantage of a view of the famous UT Tower (see our Attractions chapter). Room number 10 (the "pink" room) is a large, inviting room with plenty of natural light and a queen-size bed. For those seeking a bit more privacy, this is the only room with an external entrance. There also is an attic room that can accommodate a group of three or four people.

The rest of the house is equally inviting, especially the large, antiques-filled breakfast room, which features individual, elegantly appointed tables, dark wood floors, and artwork depicting the home's era. In addition to the upstairs balcony, this property features a large wraparound porch, a perfect place to while away an Austin afternoon. Several of the rooms feature antique claw-foot bathtubs. Like at Austin Folk House, Sylvia offers a full, hot buffet-style breakfast each morning. See the Austin Folk House listing for details. Star of Texas also has a private parking lot, a real plus in the bustling UT area. If stepping back in time is your idea of a perfect getaway, Star of Texas Inn should not be missed.

ℹ️ The smaller towns in Central Texas claim a growing number of B&Bs and country inns. Check out the Historic Accommodations of Texas Web site at www.hat.org for a listing of some of our favorites.

LAKE TRAVIS/HILL COUNTRY VIEWS

LOST PARROT CABINS $$$$
15116 Storm Drive
(512) 266-8916
www.lostparrotcabins.com

One glance at this property, nestled among the trees in the hills near Lake Travis, and you know this is not your normal bed-and-breakfast. The first impression is the color explosion: six individual cabins painted in bright lavenders, neon oranges and lime greens—Fiesta style. And then there are the large outdoor murals reminiscent of San Miguel de Allende and the Mexican artists Frida Kahlo and Diego Rivera, handpainted by local artist Linda LaPierre. If that isn't enough, take a look at the outdoor b.y.o.b. bar/patio/hot tub area, with its colored lights, Mexican and Guatemalan folk art, and palapa-style tables. And then, standing at the bar, you can look down through the trees upon the crystal-clear swimming pool and large deck area—where musicians perform on Saturday evenings (weather permitting) and at random other times. The urge to mix up a margarita or pop open a Corona is overwhelming. And this is the scene before you even step inside the roomy cabins, each one with its own private deck (complete with hammock) and tasteful, Caribbean-inspired decor. Talavera and Saltillo tiles, more folk art, south-of-the-border textiles, rustic furniture and handpainted detailing on the walls is the common theme, and yet each cabin is so charming it's hard to choose a favorite. And the comfortable queen-size beds and cozy seating areas, some with futons for extra guests, are *muy* inviting. We're not sure what the particular mix of magic is here, but proprietors Cat Flood and Cliff Bennett have managed to create an atmosphere that is both romantic and lively.

Four of the six cabins have complete kitchenettes, with full size refrigerators, stoves, and microwaves, while the other two have mini kitchens with microwaves and small fridges. All have televisions, DVD players and wireless Internet service. Guests also are invited to use the grills and the grass-covered lawns and gazebos for outdoor entertainment. Continental breakfasts at Lost Parrot are served daily on the patio, or baskets of goodies are delivered to the rooms when the weather doesn't cooperate. The 8-acre property is located about 20 minutes from downtown Austin off of Ranch Road 620. That puts it in the vicinity of the lake (and a free place to launch a boat), as well as near several restaurants and clubs—if you can tear yourself away from this adults-only escape. Don't be alarmed when you hit an unpaved, rather bumpy, section of road (and some rather unsightly trailers) as you drive in. The cabins are only about 2/10 mile down this road. Cat and Cliff have created a truly unique, funky Austin, Hill Country escape here.

ROBIN'S NEST $$$–$$$$
1007 Stewart Cove
(512) 266-3413
www.robinsnestlaketravis.com

Resident owner Robin Maisel celebrates the great outdoors with this casual, eclectically furnished bed-and-breakfast on a small Lake Travis cove. She has converted 50-year-old fishing cabins into a fascinating assortment of guest rooms, offering the perfect spot for families traveling with children, couples wanting a little romance, or individuals looking for a peaceful getaway. Offering nine guest rooms and suites, including a cheery three-bedroom cottage with a fully equipped kitchen that can be rented as a whole or by the room, Robin's Nest aims to please. Those looking

ℹ️ No matter which bed-and-breakfast you choose in Austin, you'll be staying close to one of our wonderful lakes or parks. Make sure to ask your host about the nearest outdoor oasis, and check out our Parks and Recreation chapter for details.

for an intimate setting may like the Robin's Perch, which features an antique sleigh bed of burled wood, cozy chairs, cable TV, and a large covered deck overlooking the lake. The private bathroom has a large soaker tub, with plenty of room for placing candles or incense. The compact Biscuit's Room is cheery and light, with a queen-size brass bed, antique school desk, and oak armoire. It has a small private terrace and a bathroom equipped with a double-seated shower. A Western theme prevails in the spacious Windy Lindy's Guesthouse: The drapes are hung on antlers, the antique rockers are done in cowhide, and the king-size bed is made of cedar posts. There's a whirlpool tub in the bath and a 12-foot covered deck. This room is just beautiful. The room, Old Blue Two, has one of the most unique pieces of furniture we've ever seen: an antique table that converts to a love seat. This room also features a small dayroom with a bed, cable television with VCR, and a nice patio just outside.

This waterfront property, located next to the Yacht Harbor Marina, has a huge front lawn, plenty of patios and decks for enjoying the view, a soft hot tub, and its own large dock—a great place to take in some sun or to take a cool dip in the lake. There are telephones in every room.

Four of the rooms are near the water, and five have lake views. Two of the rooms feature working fireplaces for a romantic evening—or a chilly weather stay, when room prices are a bit less. Breakfasts are sit-down family-style affairs. If you prefer more privacy, a breakfast basket can be delivered to your room. Robin offers fresh breads and homemade bran muffins, a daily meat course or smoked salmon with bagels, and fresh fruit. On Sunday she likes to cook up one of her specialties, which include shrimp *migas* and homemade beans, Italian eggs, and blueberry French toast. Breakfast is served at the main house on the outdoor terrace. While Robin's Nest is secluded, it's not far from the Oasis, one of the most popular dining and partying spots in the area (see our Attractions chapter). Downtown and Sixth Street are less than 25 minutes away.

ℹ️ **Migas are a specialty item on the breakfast menu of several Austin B&Bs. For those of you not from these parts, migas are sliced corn tortillas fried up with eggs and cheese and, perhaps, onion, chile-peppers, cilantro, tomatoes—or whatever else inspires the chef.**

RESTAURANTS

If there is one rule of thumb on the Austin restaurant scene it likely is this: You got a shirt, you got shoes or sandals, you got service! There are only a few restaurants in town (maybe a private club or two) where a tie is required. This is a city where dining is supposed to be fun, not an exercise in tailored torture. But as Austin grows, the question being asked is will things stay this way? For years, Austin restaurants were often described as "laid-back," but as the number of "upscale" restaurants increases and more and more restaurants are demanding that diners make reservations, there is a fear that Austin's dining scene will lose some of that wonderful casual flavor. One thing is constant—the Austin dining scene is an exciting one where changes can be swift. Some of the new restaurants are franchises or outlets for a national chain, but many are homegrown. There has been a dramatic increase in the number of Asian restaurants in the city as immigrants from that continent have found a home here. Several long-established local restaurants have opened second, third, and fourth locations, often in the burgeoning northwest and southwest sections of the city. One of the coolest trends has been the emergence of young, dynamic chefs, eager to take advantage of the wide variety of fresh foods in the city and to open up their cafes in what, until now, have been neighborhoods that were not part of the Austin boom, areas like the revived East 11th Street in downtown Austin. Plus, there is a willingness of Austin diners to try new things. (See our Close-up, Texas Cuisine, in this chapter.) There is no such thing as "Austin cuisine." But there are certain signature cuisines that do have a connection to Texas culture. Given the fact that Texas once was part of Mexico and Mexican-American life is vibrant and very much a part of the state's cultural weave, it is only natural that Mexico's culinary influence is felt in a number of ways. There's Tex-Mex, Nuevo Tex-Mex, South Texas/Northern Mexico, New Mexican, Interior Mexican, Latin American, and South American. Even on the menus of so-called fine dining restaurants and in the city's bistros you are likely to detect a hint of Mexican or Southwest influence.

OVERVIEW

Tex-Mex is probably the most prevalent and recognizable cuisine. In our listings we have included a variety of Tex-Mex and other Mexican/Latino restaurants in an effort to give readers a good cross section of that multifaceted cuisine. Not all Mexican food is spicy hot. The chile pepper is a staple of the Mexican kitchen, but not all peppers are hot, and many are served in rich sauces, called moles, that blend the pepper with herbs, spices, even chocolate to create multi-nuanced tastes.

Most Austinites have their favorite Mexican restaurant, particularly when it comes to weekend brunch. A popular traditional dish is *migas*, eggs scrambled with tortilla chips, diced chiles, and tomatoes. Given the city's late nightlife, weekend breakfast is often served into mid-afternoon. During the week, breakfast tacos are the early-morning order of the day, economical and easy to eat—simply flour tortillas stuffed with combinations of eggs, chorizo (sausage), potatoes, bacon, and salsa.

Another star in the Texas culinary pantheon is, of course, barbecue. It's a subject, like religion and politics, that should be discussed carefully and with great consideration for individual beliefs—even the spelling of barbecue promotes debate. Generally speaking, Texas barbecue is slow-cooked with indirect heat over wood coals, often mesquite—a quite delicate-looking tree ℹ️ *Vegetarian Times* magazine named Austin number two on its list of "greenest cities" in 2005. For a green view of the Austin dining scene, visit www.vegoutaustin.com.

with a gnarled trunk that is the bane of ranchers since it spreads like a weed and sucks up water. Brisket is the most popular cut of meat to be slow-cooked, and most cooks "marinate" with a dry rub of spices and sometimes herbs.

(This is treacherous ground, because already some aficionados are saying, "No! No!")

Barbecue is usually served with pinto beans, potato salad, perhaps coleslaw, certainly sliced raw white onions (or sweet 1015 Texas Onions), pickles, plain old white bread, and barbecue sauce—often the ingredient by which a barbecue joint is judged.

Some of the best barbecue can be found in the small towns of Texas, among them five communities just a short drive from Austin. Most barbecue joints are open all day but close around 6:00 p.m.—earlier on Sunday afternoon. We recommend calling ahead to check on hours of operation. Here are just a few of the most famous and popular joints in the area beyond Austin's city limits; other barbecue cafes within the Austin city limits and environs are included in the restaurant listings in this chapter.

Lockhart, which touts itself as the barbecue capital of Texas, is home to several barbecue joints. In 2002, with the death of "Smitty" Schmidt, the fabled owner of Kreuz Market, a family feud erupted. Smitty had left the business to his sons and the building to his daughter. The battle even made national headlines and only quieted when the brothers moved Kreuz Market to a new building nearby at 619 Colorado Street (512-398-2361; www.kreuzmarket.com), while the founder's daughter started selling barbecue in the original building at 208 South Commerce Street (512-398-9344) under the new label, Smitty's (smittysmarket.com). A third popular restaurant is Black's Barbecue, 215 North Main Street (512-398-2712; www.blacksbbq.com).

Luling southeast is famous for its annual Watermelon Thump festival (see the Annual Events chapter), but barbecue aficionados also flock to Luling City Market at 633 East Davis Street (830-875-9019; www.lulingcitymarket.com).

Northeast of Austin, the town of Taylor is home to two Texas barbecue legends: Louie Mueller's at 206 West Second Street (512-352-6206; www.louiemuellerbarbecue.com), and Rudy Mikeska's at 300 West Second Street (512-365-3722; www.mikeska.com).

A fifth Central Texas town, Llano in the Hill Country west of Austin, is home to the "Big Chop," a huge barbecued pork chop that is the highlight on the menu at Cooper's Old Time Pit Bar-B-Que, 505 W. Dallas (325-247-5713; www.coopersbbq.com). Cooper's also barbecues beef and sausage on its old-fashioned pit and you can order from the Web site.

One of the most popular items to toss on the barbecue in Central Texas is Elgin sausage, and the original can be found in the small town of the same name just east of Austin. Visitors can watch the sausage being made just as it has been since 1882 and then sit down to a feast at Elgin Southside Market, 1212 U.S. Highway 290 (512-281-4650; www.southsidemarket.com). The owners also have opened a second location, Meyers Elgin Smokehouse, at 188 US 290 East (512-281-3331).

A word or two about local customs. Smoking is a crime in Austin, as the late Timothy Leary, LSD guru, found out when he lit up in the Austin airport.

Many restaurants are open for major holidays, except Christmas. It is wise to call ahead. Most restaurants do not take reservations except for parties of six or more. We have noted where reservations are advised or required. All restaurants listed accept major credit cards, except where noted. More and more restaurants are staying open later to accommodate Austin's penchant for late-night noshing after the movies or theater, but most close at 10:00 p.m. during the week and 11:00 p.m. on weekends. Some stay open throughout the afternoon to serve late lunch or afternoon snacks, since many Austin businesspeople, particularly the city's large self-employed population, utilize favorite local restaurants as a conference room or an office away from their home office. We have noted restaurants that stay open beyond the usual hours.

Our restaurant listings are arranged by area of town. Where a local restaurant has more than one location, refer to the first listing for menu information.

Price Code

The price key symbol in each listing gives the range for the cost of a meal for two, an entree and beverage, but not including alcoholic beverages, appetizer, or dessert. Since some restaurants serve three meals a day, or have a wide range of entree prices, the range is noted by the symbols.

$................. **Less than $20**
$$ .... **$21 to $40**
$$$ .... **$41 to $60**
$$$$ .... **More than $60**

CENTRAL

1866 BAKERY AND CAFÉ   **$–$$**
116 East Sixth Street
(512) 391-7121
www.1866cafeandbakery.com
Located in the Driskill Hotel, this cafe is famous for its breakfast fare and wonderful baked goods (the Web site even shares some of the recipes). Breakfast here can be simple and healthy, like granola and fruit, or downright Texas-decadent, like the "Austin Eggs Benedict" with poached eggs and smoked bacon atop jalapeño corn biscuits and topped with chorizo gravy. There are crepes and pancakes, plus muffins and croissants from the bakery. Lunchtime features sandwiches and salads and at night there is bistro fare. The cafe serves breakfast, lunch, and dinner daily, and is open until midnight on Friday and Saturday.

34TH STREET CAFÉ   **$–$$**
1005 West. 34th Street
(512) 371-3400
www.34thstreetcafe.com

A popular lunch spot for employees in the nearby hospital and doctors' offices, this neighborhood cafe also attracts a neighborhood crowd that enjoys the commitment to fresh fare, featuring organic vegetables from Austin's popular Boggy Creek Farm (see our Shopping chapter). Pastas, grilled seafood, and meats, plus salads are on the menu, plus light Mexican fare and popular Tuscan pizza. The cafe is open for lunch and dinner Monday through Saturday, late lunch on Saturday.

**AQUARELLE RESTAURANT
FRANÇAIS**   **$$–$$$**
606 Rio Grande Street
(512) 479-8117
www.aquarellerestaurant.com
Austin has seen the proliferation of small boutique restaurants that evoke their European cousins, intimate places where the food is a work of art. The inspiration at this topflight restaurant and wine bar is French with an emphasis on fresh American ingredients. Aquarelle consistently ranks among Austin's best. Dinner only; closed Sunday.

ASTI TRATTORIA   **$$–$$$**
408–C East 43rd Street
(512) 451-1218
www.astiaustin.com
Anyone who is familiar with the Tuscan countryside can't help but see echoes of the Italian landscape in the limestone hills and oak trees of Central Texas. The affinity for things Tuscan doesn't stop there. Rural entrepreneurs producing wine, goat cheese, olive oil, and herbs proliferate in the Hill Country. Emmett and Lisa Fox are longtime fixtures on the Austin culinary scene and key contributors to the successful Texas Hill Country Wine and Food Festival (see our Annual Events and Festivals chapter). They know all about this affinity, and they celebrate it at their neighborhood trattoria in Hyde Park. The trattoria is open Monday through Friday for lunch and dinner, Saturday for dinner only. Closed Sunday.

AUSTIN LAND AND CATTLE COMPANY $$$–$$$$

Enfield Shopping Center,
1205 North Lamar Boulevard
(512) 472-1813
www.austinlandcattlecompany.com

Steakhouse—the term usually brings to mind leather banquettes, red walls, and dark wood paneling—but this locally owned steakhouse in a small, quiet shopping center a few blocks from downtown has a lighter touch. The soft, cool palette acts as a foil to the hearty fare found here. Open daily for dinner.

THE BELMONT $$–$$$

305 West Sixth Street
(512) 457-0300
www.thebelmontaustin.com

With its Sixties–Las Vegas vibe and sink-into leather banquettes, patrons might expect to see the Rat Pack arrive at this downtown bar and restaurant. The menu echoes the surroundings with steaks and seafood, lighter fare at lunch. There is a late-night bar and patio menu featuring sandwiches and salads. The bar also features live music and movies on Monday. Open for lunch on weekdays, dinner and late night dining seven days a week.

BESS BISTRO $$–$$$

500 West Sixth Street
(512) 477-2377
www.bessbistro.com

Some movie stars come to town and fall in love—with Austin that is. Sandra Bullock bought a historic old building, the Stratford Arms, just west of Congress Avenue, and opened a French bistro that gets rave reviews for its traditional fare and comfort food additions like mac and cheese. There is no dress policy, but the Web site urges patrons "just make an effort" and also asks that cameras be left at home. These days, with camera phones, the original no-camera ban is hard to enforce so Bullock wants her customers to "please be considerate." Open for lunch and dinner Monday through Saturday with late night dining and Sunday brunch.

BLUE STAR CAFETERIA $

4800 Burnet Road
(512) 454-STAR (7827)
www.bluestarcafeteria.com

Billed as "uptown comfort food," this hip, modern take on a cafeteria is a far cry from the dull, hot table version of the last century. Along with meatloaf and grilled steak, you will find maple chicken-fried quail, plus pastas, salads (dubbed leafs and oils), sandwiches and burgers. The first Wednesday of the month features wine-tastings. Grown-up fare and a kid-friendly menu make it popular with young families. Open Monday through Saturday for lunch and dinner; Saturday and Sunday for brunch.

BOILING POT $–$$

700 East Sixth Street
(512) 472-0985

The tablecloths are made of butcher paper, the napkins are large rolls of paper towels, and the patrons are swathed in bibs and then armed with mallets, sure signs that dinner will be a messy, finger-sucking affair. A popular item on the menu is the Cajun Combo, made up of boiled crab, shrimp, sausage, corn, and potatoes; or try a platter of snow crab legs. Open Monday through Thursday for dinner, Friday through Sunday for all-day lunch and dinner.

BRICK OVEN $

1209 Red River Street
(512) 447-7006
www.brickovenrestaurant.com

Just east of the capitol on Red River Street is one of Austin's most popular pizza restaurants, noted and named for its wood-fired pies. There are several offshoots around the area. Lunch and dinner are served daily.

CAFE JOSIE $$–$$$

1200–B West Sixth Street
(512) 322-9226
www.cafejosie.com

This is one of those Austin cafes that lie hidden behind unassuming storefronts and in back of other businesses where young chefs are exploring the world of cuisine. The emphasis is on Caribbean flavors described as "cuisine of the American tropics" by chef-owner Charles Mayes. The restaurant is tucked behind Portabla, a gourmet food shop (see our Shopping chapter) in the West Sixth Street shopping district, and has a small indoor dining room plus a comfy outdoor patio. Open for lunch Tuesday through Friday and dinner Tuesday through Saturday.

CARMELO'S $$-$$$
504 East Fifth Street
(512) 477-7497
www.carmelosrestaurant.com
Carmelo's serves large portions of rich Italian-American food with flair and drama inspired by the owner's Sicilian roots. Steak Diane is flambéed tableside, while lobster-stuffed veal is presented with a flourish. The restaurant is housed in an old limestone building that once served as the Depot Hotel. Lunch on weekdays and dinner daily.

CASTLE HILL CAFE $$-$$$
1101 West Fifth Street
(512) 476-0728
www.castlehillcafe.com
Where's the castle? Where's the hill? Old-timers know that this popular cafe began as a tiny, tiny restaurant a few blocks north of its current location near the West Sixth Street shopping district. That spot is now occupied by Wink, see below. West of the original tiny restaurant is a well-known landmark, a home on a hill that looks like a castle—hence the name. Castle Hill outgrew its original location but continues to draw crowds. The food here is a delightful mix of Southwestern, Asian, and Mediterranean with a touch of Caribbean thrown in, created by chef/co-owner David Daley. The restaurant is airy and decorated with Oaxacan folk art, a far cry from the tiny, cramped quarters it once occupied. One thing the larger location does share with the old is the air of culinary excitement. Lunch and dinner daily. Reservations recommended on weekends.

CENTRAL MARKET $
4001 North Lamar Boulevard
(512) 206-1020
www.centralmarket.com
Austin's showcase grocery store and top tourist spot (see our Close-up in the Shopping chapter) is a favorite lunch and early dinner spot, particularly among parents and grandparents. The cafe features a varied menu with homestyle food, bistro fare, sandwiches, pizza, and desserts. Dishes are reasonably priced, and customers can either graze or dig into a hearty meal. There is a large indoor dining room, flanked by a wide wooden deck looking out over the greenbelt. Kids can race around outside, dogs can sit in the shade while their owners nosh, and families can enjoy nightly live music concerts featuring a wide variety of musicians. The eateries are open daily from 7:00 a.m. to 10:00 p.m.

CHEZ NOUS $$-$$$
510 Neches Street
(512) 473-2413
www.cheznous.citysearch.com
Since 1982, Chez Nous has been serving authentic French bistro fare at this cozy restaurant half a block south of Sixth Street. *Bistro* is a word much bandied about these days, but Chez Nous is as close to the real thing as you can get in Austin, with traditional dishes like oven-roasted chicken and homemade pâtés. There is a menu du jour, daily chef's specials, plus lighter fare including crepes. The bistro is open for lunch and dinner Tuesday through Friday; dinner only on the weekends.

CIBO $$-$$$
918 Congress Avenue
(512) 478-3663
www.ciborestaurant.com
Pronounced "chee-bo" as the Italians would, this exquisite restaurant by Chef Will Packwood (*Food & Wine's* best new chef in 2001) is housed in a simple, stone-walled building just a few blocks from the Capitol. Packwood's other Austin efforts in the past have proved to be exciting and popular and he returned to the city to bring this new,

small, elegant-in-an-Austin-way restaurant to life with a menu inspired by the "tri-Veneti" lands of Northern Italy. Simple but artful dishes that use the best naturally raised products to reflect the culinary richness of verdant lands and ocean around Venice are featured on a seasonal menu. Reservations recommended. Open for dinner Tuesday through Saturday.

CIPOLLINA $-$$
1213 West Lynn Street
(512) 477-5211
www.cipollina-austin.com

It looks like a little European sidewalk cafe nestled in the heart of Clarksville (see our Relocation chapter), and it reflects the sensibilities of its owners who also created Jeffrey's, the quintessential Austin fine dining experience across the way. The menu features simple fare, pizzas, salads, small plates, soups, and desserts that can be eaten in-house or taken home or to a picnic. There is an affordable wine menu, also. Open daily for lunch and dinner.

CLAY PIT $$-$$$
1601 Guadalupe Street
(512) 322-5131
www.claypit.com

The Clay Pit occupies a historic stone building not far from the capitol and is a much-praised Indian dining spot, including plaudits from *Bon Appetit* magazine. The owners brought a highly rated chef who had worked at a leading Indian hotel, among other top spots on his résumé. Both vegetarian and meat dishes are on the menu. Open Monday through Friday for lunch and dinner.

DIRTY MARTIN'S PLACE $
2808 Guadalupe Street
(512) 477-3173
www.dirtymartins.com

In this day of image-makers and spin doctors, who would ever name a restaurant "Dirty's"? This is a restaurant that has roots back to the '20s, but the story of the name has been lost in time. Some call this campus-area hamburger joint "Martin's Kumback"—and that is what the sign says—but the majority refer to it as "Dirty's." The

fare is fry-cook simple here: hamburgers off the grill with fries and onions, a cold beer or soda, but Dirty's has entered the Internet age with a Web site and free wi-fi so you can google away while watching the football game on the patio. Dirty's is open daily for lunch and dinner.

DONA EMILIA'S $$
101 San Jacinto Boulevard
(512) 478-2520
www.donaemilias.com

Within three years, Dona Emilia's went from a small cafe on the city's east side to an upscale, downtown venue across from the Four Seasons hotel. The menu also morphed from dishes rooted in Emilia Hurtado's Colombian roots to what she now dubs "new Latin" that get their inspiration from tropical flavors and modern presentations. Open daily for lunch and dinner Monday through Thursday. Open for lunch through dinner Friday and Saturday, Sunday open for lunch through late afternoon.

DRISKILL GRILL $$$-$$$$
Driskill Hotel
604 Brazos Street
(512) 391-7162
www.driskillgrill.com

The Grill, with its polished wooden walls and soft lighting, is one of the best places in Austin for a special dinner—a place where the setting and the food combine to create a wonderful experience. The Grill has been named one of the top 50 hotel restaurants in the country by *Food & Wine* and is noted for seeking out the highest quality ingredients, emploing classic techniques, and adding a touch of Southwestern flavor in an homage to the Driskill Hotel's Texas history. Open for dinner daily.

i Foodies who want to keep up with the latest trends might want to mark their calendars for the Texas Hill Country Wine and Food Festival (see our Annual Events and Festivals chapter). The spring event always attracts some of the top chefs in Texas and the nation.

EDDIE V'S EDGEWATER GRILLE $$$-$$$$
301 East 15th Street
(512) 472-1860
www.eddiev.com

As the Austin culinary scene has matured, seafood has finally taken pride of place at the table in a number of top dining spots. Eddie V's two locations, one downtown and the other northwest, are the creation of two veterans of the local culinary scene, Larry Foles and Guy Villavaso (Z'Tejas creators), and they have chosen to focus on seafood prepared in classic, simple ways. In addition to an oyster bar, Eddie V's also has a relaxing piano bar. Open daily for dinner.

EL ARROYO $
1624 West Fifth Street
(512) 474-1222
www.ditch.com

The hallmark of this West Sixth Street–area restaurant is the large sign out front that offers pithy, scathing, and sometimes self-deprecating comments on a daily basis. The restaurant offers standard Tex-Mex fare, and the owner-humorists have been known to cast aspersions on their own culinary efforts, but that does not stop the crowds from coming. Customers love the funky atmosphere, the cheeky waiters, and the lively bar scene featuring "floaters": margaritas topped with liqueurs. El Arroyo is open daily for lunch and dinner.

EL MERCADO RESTAURANT & CANTINA $-$$
1702 Lavaca Street
(512) 477-7689

One of three El Mercados in the city, this restaurant serves up generous portions of Tex-Mex staples—enchiladas, chimi-changas, and tacos. Some of the dishes have a Texas slant with barbecued meat featured in the brisket tacos and chicken enchiladas. The Mexican background music adds to the fiesta feel. Open daily for lunch and dinner and on weekends for breakfast.

FINN & PORTER $$
500 East Fourth Street
(512) 493-4900
www.finnandporter.com

Austin's downtown hotels can boast some of the city's best restaurants, not always the case in some areas. Located in the Hilton Hotel, Finn & Porter takes the classic seafood and steak fare to new heights. There are several "trios" on the menu, including one featuring a crabcake, petite filet and lobster, the creations of Christopher Bauer who trained at the Culinary Institute of America. There is also a sushi bar in house and the luxurious, clubby surroundings make the restaurant's bar a popular spot. Open daily for dinner and late night dining at the sushi bar.

FINO $$-$$$
2905 San Gabriel Street
(512) 474-2905
www.astiaustin.com

This sister restaurant to Asti Trattoria , described earlier in this chapter, Fino focuses on other areas of the Meditteranean for its inspiration, including Spain, Greece, and northern Africa. Its location upstairs in a small, brick shopping center gives it a "treehouse" feel and the wrap-around outdoor patio is a favorite spot for enjoying tapas and small plates with a glass of wine. Paella is a menu favorite and Tuesday patrons get a discount on the dish. Open daily for lunch and dinner. Closed Sunday.

FLEMING'S $$-$$$$
320 East Second Street
(512) 457-1500
www.flemingssteakhouse.com

Part of a national chain founded in California and with a heavy presence on the East Coast, Fleming's has opened in a restored warehouse near the convention center and offers prime beef, lamb, veal, and top-quality seafood dishes. The restaurant features an exhibition kitchen in a sophisticated setting. One thoughtful touch is an extensive wine-by-the-glass menu, 100 offerings that also can be ordered by flight (three small selections in one serving). Open daily for dinner.

FONDA SAN MIGUEL $$$-$$$$
2330 West North Loop Boulevard
(512) 459-4121
www.fondasanmiguel.com

Some of Austin's finest restaurants are found in unexpected places. Fonda San Miguel is situated in an everyday neighborhood, but once you step over the threshold it is easy to assume you are in Old Mexico. This is an accurate rendition of both Mexican architectural style and food under the direction of Chef Miguel Ravago. Designed to evoke the atmosphere of an old hacienda, the entrance to the restaurant, the bar area, is a small courtyard complete with fountain and plants. Inside, the walls are decorated with antiques and ceramics representative of Colonial Mexico. This is the place to come to understand the complexities and nuances of classic Mexican cuisine. The menu features regional specialties from throughout the country. The doyenne of Mexican cooking, Diana Kennedy, has held cooking classes here. The menu features seafood and grilled meats served in Yucatecan and Veracruzano styles, some spicy, others more Spanish in flavor. And there are several moles, the rich, complex sauces usually called by their color—verde (green) and negro (black)—or by their geographical origin, such as poblano (from Puebla). A good way to sample a variety of fare is to make a reservation for Sunday brunch. This meal evokes the Sunday custom in Mexico, where families sit down for a long, leisurely meal comprising snacks, entrees, desserts, coffee, and long conversation. The restaurant is open daily for dinner and on Sunday for brunch. Reservations are recommended.

GUMBO'S $$-$$$$
710 Colorado Street
(512) 480-8053
www.gumbosaustin.com

The trend in Austin usually follows a pattern—a restaurant becomes a hit in downtown Austin and then takes that success to the suburbs. Gumbo's has bucked that trend by first finding success in Round Rock and then moving downtown. The restaurant chose to move into one of the most interesting buildings downtown, the Brown Building.

It was built in 1938 by Herman Brown, one of the founders of Brown & Root, the legendary Houston construction company that parlayed its close political ties to President Lyndon B. Johnson and others into worldwide ventures. In 1998 the owners, the LBJ Company (guess which prominent Texas political family owns the company), transformed the building into a loft project. Gumbo's occupies a ground-floor space where it serves up a menu with a Louisiana flair. Open weekdays for lunch, daily for dinner. Closed Sunday.

HUT'S HAMBURGERS $
807 West Sixth Street
(512) 472-0693
www.hutshamburgers.citysearch.com

There are 20 types of burgers on the menu here, plus chicken-fried steak, fried chicken, and meat loaf—in a word, all the stuff you want to eat, and you did back when cholesterol was just a gleam in the surgeon general's eye. The daily blue plate specials attract a faithful crowd. The decor here is '50s diner, and the walls are decorated with college sports memorabilia. Hut's is open for lunch and dinner daily.

HYDE PARK BAR & GRILL $-$$
4206 Duval Street
(512) 458-3168
www.hydeparkbarandgrill.com

Look for the two-story giant fork out front and the potato truck parked out back in the historic Hyde Park neighborhood. According to local lore, the grill goes through one and a quarter tons of potatoes a week making its famous spicy, battered fries. But not all the fare is hearty—grilled fish and salads are also offered. The restaurant is open daily for lunch and dinner, with late-night hours on Friday and Saturday. It occupies a large, old home in the Hyde Park neighborhood, the historic heart of Austin just north of the university campus.

III FORKS $$$-$$$$
111 Lavaca Street
(512) 474-1776
www.iiiforks.com

With sister restaurants in Dallas and Palm Beach

Gardens, no wonder this Second Street District restaurant is described as elegant. The black mahogany and Italian marble decor matches the European flair given to the traditional steakhouse menu. There is a fish market menu also and a huge wine list, plus walk-in wine room. The restaurant's piano bar is very popular. Open for dinner Monday through Saturday.

IMPERIA $$-$$$
310 Colorado Street
(512) 472-6770
www.imperia-austin.com

The menu is inspired by Asian flavors and the decor has a luxurious but modern Eastern ambience. This location in the Warehouse District, which is just north of the Second Street District, has been home to several restaurants, evolving from Northern Italian to bistro to nouvelle Asian, reflecting the evolution of this part of downtown that has become increasingly more "upscale." Some of the bars and clubs in the area have reflected this trend, also. Imperia features dim sum and small plates, plus luscious interpretations of classics like Peking Duck. Open for dinner until midnight Monday through Thursday and on Sunday; open until 1:00 a.m. on Friday and Saturday.

IRON WORKS BARBECUE $$
100 Red River Street
(512) 478-4855
www.ironworksbbq.com

Home to the Weigl Iron Works for years, this converted workshop just east of the city's convention center is now a popular barbecue spot, particularly during weekday lunch hours. The Weigl family's ironwork can be seen on several buildings around town, including the History Center at 810 Guadalupe Street. Diners can sit inside or on an outdoor deck. Lunch and dinner are served daily.

JEFFREY'S $$$-$$$$
1204 West Lynn Street
(512) 477-5584
www.jeffreysofaustin.com

This is perhaps the quintessential (and one of the best) Austin restaurant—a longtime favorite of Austinites and the place where President George W. Bush and First Lady Laura Bush loved to take friends when they occupied the Governor's Mansion. Founded in the 1970s by three University of Texas friends (one of them a childhood friend of the First Lady), Jeffrey's was creating topflight cuisine in an unassuming, quiet atmosphere when most Austin restaurants were serving up everyday fare. The restaurant's home is a restored house in Clarksville, one of the city's revered central city neighborhoods (see our Relocation chapter). The founders took over a space occupied by a small wine shop, put up an inconspicuous sign outside and the work of local artists inside, and embarked on a culinary journey that draws on the world's cuisines but has Hill Country roots. A procession of creative chefs has ruled the range here, some going on to spread the Jeffrey's vibe and values to other notable Austin dining spots, but while they each add their own touches to the menu, some items have become signature dishes, like the classic Jeffrey's crispy oysters on yucca root chips with habañero aioli. In addition to a dinner menu fueled by local ingredients and regional flavors, Jeffrey's offers a small plates bar menu. Open nightly except Sunday.

KATZ'S $-$$
618 West Sixth Street
(512) 472-2037
www.katznevercloses.com

The slogan is "Katz's never Kloses"—and it doesn't, making this New York–style downtown deli a very popular late-night spot. In the wee hours, customers are likely to look around and think they may have fallen into an intergalactic bar, since the clientele is so varied—country music fans, heavy metal types, boomers, Gen-Xers, you name it. Katz's also delivers via Yellow Cab to areas close to downtown.

KENICHI $$-$$$$
419 Colorado Street
(512) 320-9993
www.kenichiaustin.com

Who would have thought that Austin would ever

Close-up

Texas Cuisine

Clichés abound when it comes to Texas, perhaps because the state has been celebrated and spoofed, caricatured and lauded in movies and books, magazine articles and newspaper stories around the world. So no wonder that when it comes to eating, most people think a typical Texas meal features a big slab of beef and not much else.

But Texas beef (and it is good) is just one tiny part of the true picture, and while this is a place where cattle do roam, the food picture is much more complex and growing more diverse every day. Agribusiness is 12 percent of Texas's gross state product. Texas farmers and ranchers produce rice, citrus, nuts, pears, peaches, apricots, strawberries, blackberries, avocados, chile peppers, onions, spinach, and herbs; they raise pigs, cattle, goats, sheep, turkeys, and fish; and food processors are engaged in developing a multitude of products that tout their Texas origins—everything from axis deer venison to zucchini blossoms.

In addition to a variety of ingredients, the state also draws inspiration from several cultures and countries: Spain and Mexico, of course, and Germany, as evidenced in Hill Country towns like Fredericksburg and New Braunfels (see our Day Trips chapter). African-American cooks have left their mark, and in the east of the state, Cajuns and Creoles have tossed their contributions into the pot. The culture of the Mexican *vaquero* (cowboy) influenced Texas trail riders, and small towns settled by Czechs, Wends, and Alsatians brought new elements into the mix. Waves of immigrants from Italy and the Mediterranean countries have brought their flavors west (see our Worship chapter for a good tip on where to experience Middle Eastern cooking in Austin in October). More recently, Asian immigrants have left their mark with Chinese, Vietnamese, and Indian cooking introducing new flavors.

With each wave of immigrants, Texas cuisine has grown, and adapted, and old favorites are constantly being re-created. How about shrimp fajitas, pizza topped with chorizo, sushi garnished with goat cheese, chocolate pie with a dash of chile powder?

This cornucopia of food products inspires both the home cook and the state's chefs. Austin's top culinary magicians draw on Texas products for inspiration. If you want to experience that fusion of talent and local produce, check out the work of Tyson Cole at Uchi, Jeff Blank at Hudson's on the Bend, David Garrido formerly with Jeffrey's, Will Packwood at Cibo, Stewart Scruggs and Mark Paul at Wink, and Miguel Ravago at Fonda San Miguel. These are just some of the star names in the Austin culinary pantheon, but other top-quality chefs are celebrating homegrown produce and feeding off each other's inspirations in what has become a very dynamic foodie town.

Some of Austin's most creative chefs also offer cooking classes—Hudson's on the Bend and Fonda San Miguel are just two top picks, and Central Market (listed in this chapter and featured in a Close-up in our Shopping chapter) has an on-site cooking school where top Texas talent and visiting stars teach the culinary arts.

Another good way to get the flavor of the Austin food scene is to read books by some of the city's chefs. Miguel Ravago is coauthor of *Fonda San Miguel: Thirty Years of Food and Art*. Jeff Blank has authored *Cooking Fearlessly: Recipes and Adventures from Hudson's on the Bend,* and David Garrido is coauthor of a fun cookbook, *Nuevo Tex-Mex.*

Not all the food stars are chefs at Austin's top restaurants. Others create in their own whimsical way, working in small commercial kitchens to produce favorite food products. David Ansel followed a girlfriend (now an ex-girlfriend) to Austin and began delivering homemade soups on his yellow bike to a small group of neighborhood clients. His client base grew, he made headlines beyond Austin, and now his business is celebrated in his first cookbook, *The Soup Peddler's Slow and Difficult Soups.* From his Web site, www.souppeddler.com, he now delivers soups and entrees to a large part of the city.

The Soup Peddler is emblematic of what Austin foodies love, something unique that speaks to the Austin heritage of homegrown, individual, and just a little eccentric.

The areas farmers' markets speak to this same theme (see our Shopping chapter), and one of the most beloved is Boggy Creek Farm (again, see the Shopping chapter), an organic farm in East Austin that provides fresh produce to several Austin restaurants. Be sure to sign up for the farm's e-mail list for not just news of what is ready for the market but also wonderful soul-nourishing tales of what is going on at the farm with the workers and animals who live there; www.boggycreekfarm.com.

Another eccentricity turned leitmotif for the city are the street vendors, notably "Airstream Cuisine," featured in *Food & Wine* magazine. These restored Airstream camping trailers serve as kitchens on wheels, setting up in vacant lots and parking areas in the city's busy nightlife districts. Look for Flip Happy Crepes on Jessie Street, just 2 blocks west of South Lamar Boulevard and 1 block north of Barton Springs Road in South Central Austin. Torchy's Tacos has roving kitchens on Sixth Street and South First Street and Hey! Cupcakes (look for the giant cupcake) sells sweet treats in the 1600 block of South Congress Avenue. On a much humbler scale—and one that speaks to Austin's multi-culti vibe—look for the *paleta* man (paleta is a Mexican popsicle) plying his trade from his small freezer mounted on his bicycle in the South Central neighborhoods.

The Texas Department of Agriculture has developed several programs to help small producers market their wares and guide consumers to homegrown products. Look for products labeled "Taste of Texas" and you know you are helping a Lone Star farmer, rancher, or food producer. Products marked "Naturally Texas" have been created by the state's cotton, wool, mohair, and leather producers. Texas grows one-third of the cotton in the United States, and there are approximately two million angora goats in the Hill Country southwest of San Antonio producing 15 million pounds of mohair per year.

The Hill Country also is home to cheese-making ventures, and Texas goat cheese is found in grocery stores and on menus in Austin. Pure Luck Goat Cheese is an award-winning favorite; www.purelucktexas.com. There are also herb and lavender farms west of the city, and early summer is a popular time to harvest lavender and buy Hill Country peaches; www.hillcountry lavender.com and www.texaspeaches.com. There is a lavender festival in Blanco every summer; see our Annual Events and Festivals chapter.

And then there are the state's wineries. Some visitors look askance when a local offers them a glass of Texas wine, but the established industry has won recognition in knowledgeable wine circles. There are several microclimates within the state that are conducive to grape production, including some in the Hill Country and some out in West Texas around Lubbock. There are many producers, but three of the most widely known and marketed are Fall Creek (www.fcv.com), Slaughter Leftwich (www.slaughterleftwich.com), and Llano Estacado (www .llanowine.com).

The Spanish settlers planted the first wine grapes in Texas during the 17th century, and some of the now wild descendants, Mustang grapes, can be found in hedgerows along country roads and even in overrun urban lots. Mustang grapes make a great jam, but be careful if you pick them since snakes like to hang around the bushes and go after the wild birds that feed on the vines. Also, do not eat the raw grapes—they are very tannic.

Information about the state's wineries can be found at www.agr.state.tx.us/wine. (For information about the Hill Country wine trail, see our Close-up in the Day Trips and Weekend Getaways chapter.) To find other Texas products, go to www.gotexan.org.

have a restaurant that attracted the "beautiful people"? Yet that's how one local critic described the clientele when this Japanese-American import from Aspen arrived in Austin. The minimalist setting outside gives way to a high-fashion black-on-black interior. The menu offers beautifully presented sushi, plus American specialties such as steak, lamb, ribs, and seafood for heartier appetites. Dinner daily.

KERBEY LANE CAFE $-$$
3704 Kerbey Lane
(512) 451-1436
www.kerbeylanecafe.com

The original Kerbey Lane Cafe now has three sister restaurants, one south and another northwest, another on the "Drag" Guadalupe Street near the UT campus, testimony to the concept that homemade, healthful food is a necessity 24 hours a day. Many of the cafe's dishes are Tex-Mex in origin, but the emphasis is on fresh local ingredients. The menu also features vegan cuisine, burgers, sandwiches, omelets, pancakes, and desserts. You can buy the famous pancake mix online.

KYOTO $$-$$$
315 Congress Avenue
(512) 482-9010
www.kyotodowntown.com

Kyoto is tucked away in a narrow, stone building on Congress Avenue. There are two dining rooms upstairs: one a sushi bar with counter seating and western-style tables, the second a traditional area with tatami mats and low Japanese tables. In addition to sushi, the restaurant serves *yakitori* and *kushiyaki* dishes plus noodle dishes, tempura, and other traditional Japanese offerings. The restaurant offers lunch Tuesday through Saturday and dinner Monday through Saturday.

LA MADELEINE $
3418 North Lamar Boulevard
(512) 302-1485
www.lamadeleine.com

There are four La Madeleine restaurants in Austin, one in a converted bookstore (northwest), another in a new shopping mall (west), a third in a shopping center in Southwest Austin, and this one in a building that has housed several restaurants over the years. Inside, all three share the atmosphere of a French bakery and bistro, so don't be discouraged when you read that service is cafeteria-style. The restaurants serve breakfast, lunch, dinner, midmorning and midafternoon coffee, and snacks (heavenly French baked pastries) daily.

LAMBERTS $$$-$$$$
401 West Second Street
(512) 494-1500
www.lambertsaustin.com

It had to happen. "Fancy barbecue" is on the menu in this downtown restaurant, the kind of grilled fare we would all like to master on our backyard grills: grilled asparagus, brown sugar, coffee-rubbed brisket, pan-seared French beans, crispy wild boar ribs, and cold-smoked rainbow trout. Lambert's also features live music. Lunch Monday through Friday, weekend brunch and dinner nightly.

LA TRAVIATA ITALIAN BISTRO $$-$$$
314 Congress Avenue
(512) 479-8131

Chef Marion Gillcrist, who learned her profession under Stephen Pyles and was the winner of the *Austin Chronicle* Readers' Poll "best female chef" in 2001, opened this small, intimate restaurant determined to produce authentic Italian cuisine. La Traviata, a romantic spot, consistently gets high marks. Open for lunch Monday through Friday and for dinner nightly, except Sunday.

i **A great way to integrate into the local foodie scene is to join the Dai Due Supper Club. Founded by former Vespaio chef Jesse Griffiths and experienced organic farmer Tamara Mayfield, the club is a roving banquet that offers unique dining experiences often on local farms and always featuring local produce and products. The duo also offers cooking classes. Visit their Web site and blog at www.daidueaustin.com or call (512) 769-7261 for details.**

LOUIE'S 106 $$$$
106 Sixth Street
(512) 476-1997
www.louies106.net

Housed in the historic Littlefield Building at the busy northwest corner of Sixth Street and Congress Avenue, Louie's has the aura of a grand old restaurant in a European capital. The menu leans toward classical Spanish with lots of Mediterranean and European touches. Patrons can simply drop into the bar or a booth for a round of tapas (Spanish snacks). There is a cigar room plus an extensive wine, single-malt whisky, and brandy list. Open weekdays for lunch and daily for dinner. Given its busy downtown location, Louie's offers curbside valet parking.

MANDOLA'S ITALIAN MARKET $
4700 West Guadalupe Street
(512) 419-9700
www.mandolasmarket.com

The creation of Houston restaurateur-turned Hill Country winemaker, Damian Mandola and his wife Trina, this Italian market is a valuable resource for Austin cooks, but it also serves as a family-style cafe serving pizza, panini, antipasto and salads in a light and airy setting at The Triangle, a mixed-use, town center-like development just north of the UT campus. Open daily for breakfast, lunch, and dinner.

MANSION AT JUDGES' HILL $$-$$$
1900 Rio Grande Street
(512) 495-1800
www.mansionatjudgeshill.com

The dining room at this restored mansion not far from the capitol and the University of Texas campus is one of the most sophisticated and refined in Austin. The restaurant echoes the elegant decor of the boutique hotel (see listing in our Hotels and Motels chapter). The mansion has taken the freshest of ingredients—some local, others like lobster and imported foie gras—and created sophisticated dishes that are described as "modern American cuisine with classical French influences."

> **i** Several of Austin's brew houses offer hearty pub grub fare. If you are hungry for fish 'n' chips or Irish stew, check out our listings in the Nightlife chapter. If you are looking for a "hangout"—a place to sip something, nosh, and watch the sunset; or wash those nachos down with margaritas at a bridal shower; perhaps a place where Dad can have a beer while the kids play in a sandbox, check out our Hangouts Close-up in that same chapter.

MANUEL'S $-$$$
310 Congress Avenue
(512) 472-7555
www.manuels.com

The setting is sleek and modern, with black booths, neon signs, and hip jazz music at this downtown restaurant, but the food is light, saucy, and evocative of interior Mexican classics. Chile rellenos are made as they are in Mexico, stuffed with spicy and fruit-studded meat filling then topped with almond sauce. Fish is served Veracruzano-style with tomatoes and peppers, and enchiladas banderas reflect the red, green, and white of the Mexican flag. Manuel's is open for lunch and dinner and has a jazz brunch on Sunday. There is a late-night snack menu. A second location has been opened in Northwest Austin.

McCORMICK & SCHMICK'S $$-$$$
401 Congress Avenue
(512) 236-9600
www.mccormickandschmicks.com

Part of a national chain, this seafood restaurant is housed in Frost Bank Tower, a fitting setting for the sophisticated menu that focuses on fresh seafood. Open daily for lunch and dinner.

MOONSHINE $$-$$$
303 Red River Street
(512) 236-9599
www.moonshinegrill.com

Corn dog shrimp and high-class mac and cheese are just two of the dishes on the menu at Moonshine, where all-American comfort food is taken to new heights in a setting that is both cozy and historic, a small stone house and carriage house just east of the convention center. Open daily for lunch and dinner, open Sunday for brunch.

MOTHER'S CAFE AND GARDEN $-$$
4215 Duval Street
(512) 451-3994
www.motherscafeaustin.com
Vegetarian food with international inspiration is served at this neighborhood cafe. The menu has low-fat and vegan options, and local beers and Texas wines are featured. The cafe is in the heart of the Hyde Park neighborhood and features a large outdoor patio. Open daily for lunch and dinner and serves weekend brunch.

NAU ENFIELD DRUG $
1115 West Lynn Street
(512) 476-1221
An old-fashioned drugstore in the historic Clarksville neighborhood, Nau's serves up sandwiches, burgers, malts, and breakfast dishes daily (see our Attractions chapter). The atmosphere here is authentic and draws customers from both the neighborhood and downtown to the booths and bar daily for breakfast and lunch.

P. F. CHANG'S CHINA BISTRO $$-$$$
201 San Jacinto Boulevard
(512) 457-8300
www.pfchangs.com
Chang's, part of a national chain, is popular for both its sophisticated atmosphere and its menu of fresh Chinese dishes. Vegetarians and lovers of spicy food will appreciate the variety on the menu. P. F. Chang's offers a wide selection of wines. Open for lunch and dinner.

ROARING FORK $$-$$$
701 Congress Avenue
(512) 583-0000
www.eddiev.com
The focus at the Southwestern-themed restaurant is on wood-fire cooking to produce those smokey, spicy flavors of the region. Dishes like green chile pork stew, fish tacos and Dr Pepper-braised short ribs are featured. Open for lunch weekdays, dinner daily.

ROY'S AUSTIN $$-$$$
340 East Second Street
(512) 391-1500
www.roysrestaurant.com
This Austin branch of Chef Roy Yamaguchi's Hawaiian Fusion group of restaurants is one of the new faces around the city's convention center. Yamaguchi has won accolades from *Condé Nast Traveler* magazine and others for his blending of Asian and Hawaiian cuisines, and foodies will also know him from his appearance on the Food-TV Network's *Iron Chef* series. The decor is sophisticated, with a splash of island motifs. Open daily for dinner.

RUTH'S CHRIS $$$
107 West Sixth Street
(512) 477-RUTH
www.ruthchris.com
When it comes to steakhouses, the national Ruth's Chris chain is noted as one of the best. The restaurant is housed in the historic Scarbrough Building, 1 block west of Congress Avenue, and offers valet parking for patrons. The menu features thick-cut steaks simmered in butter made famous by Ruth Fartel, founder of the restaurant chain. Reservations are recommended, particularly when the legislature is in session—in the odd years from January to May, except for specially called sessions.

SABA BLUE WATER CAFE $-$$$
212 West Fourth Street
(512) 478-7222
www.sabacafe.com
Saba's is a combination bar-restaurant, an Austin munchie and meet spot. The menu here reflects Yucatecan–Caribbean–Pacific Rim influences. Housed in a 1907 building but decorated with modern art, including a wonderful blue glass wall, the design was created by Austin's noted urban artist Sinclair Black. Open daily for lunch,

dinner, and late-night snacks, with special prices during happy hour.

SAMPAIO $$–$$$
4800 Burnet Road
(512) 469-9988
www.sampaiosrestaurant.com
The food here dances to a Brazilian samba. Owner Magna Sampaio, a native of Brazil, has brought her country's flavors to Austin in dishes like pastry pastels filled with savory-sweet chicken, paella, *churrasco* (Brazilian barbecue) and, of course, cocktails made from the signature liquor, *chachaca*. The restaurant is uptown on the outer edge of Central Austin. Open daily for lunch and dinner.

SANTA RITA CANTINA $$
26 Doors, 1206 West 38th Street
(512) 419-7482
www.santaritacantina.com
Owner Eddie Bernal has created a mythical culinary saint, Santa Margarita, who looked over the kitchens of South Texas and created a wonderful Tex-Mex cuisine that is a far cry from the standard fare with gloppy yellow cheese and soggy enchiladas that unfortunately passes for the real thing in some restaurants. Bernal gets top marks for his fare. Open from lunch to dinner daily. Brunch on weekends.

SCHOLZ GARTEN $
1607 San Jacinto Boulevard
(512) 474-1958
www.scholzgarten.com
Political junkies regard this old German beer garden as something of a shrine, a place that serves as a favorite watering hole and meeting place for political types, their staffers, and supporters (particularly Democrats). Hillary and Bill Clinton hung out here during their days as workers for the George McGovern presidential campaign. The beer garden is also featured in the 1962 novel about Texas politics, *The Gay Place*, by Billy Lee Brammer. The beer hall, which dates back to

1866, is east of the capitol and is owned by the Austin Saengerrunde, a German-American fraternal organization. The tree-shaded beer garden is a favorite gathering spot for state workers, politicians, and pre- and postgame fans of UT football and basketball. The restaurant features German food and typical American down-home fare: burgers, chicken, sandwiches, Tex-Mex specials, and beer, of course. Scholz's is open for lunch and dinner. Closed Sunday.

SERRANO'S CAFE & CANTINA $$
Symphony Square, 1105 Red River Street
(512) 322-9080
www.serranos.com
There are six (and growing) Serrano's cafes in various regions of the city, but this one has the best setting—in the small historic complex saved by the Austin Symphony (see our Attractions chapter). Tex-Mex plates, grilled meat and chicken, plus fajita platters are popular fare here. Open daily for lunch and dinner.

SHORELINE GRILL $$$$
98 San Jacinto Boulevard
(512) 477-3300
www.shorelinegrill.com
Tucked into a prime location on Lady Bird Lake, just west of the Four Seasons, the Shoreline is known for its sophisticated fish and seafood creations and the great view of the nightly summer evening exodus of Austin's famous bat colony. The best bat viewing is on the restaurant's patio, but seating is first-come, first-served there. Reservations can be made for the indoor rooms. Open daily for lunch and dinner.

i **Want to eat out in? Call EatOutIn, (512) 346-9990, www.eatoutin.com, a local delivery company that brings the food of some 20 local restaurants to your door for a fee. The service will fax you a menu, you can ask them to mail you a brochure, or they can brief you on your choices.**

STARLITE $$–$$$

407 Colorado Street
(512) 374-9012
www.starliteaustin.net

Born in a small bungalow near the University of Texas campus, this top flight bistro took the plunge and moved into the downtown Warehouse District. The menu still focuses on fresh meat and seafood, prepared with a modern, light touch and, occasionally, a touch of whimsy like the s'mores crème brûlée. Open Monday through Saturday for lunch and dinner.

STUBB'S BAR-B-Q $–$$

801 Red River Street
(512) 480-8341
www.stubbsaustin.com

The late C. B. Stubblefield is the soul of this restaurant, and his portrait hangs here as homage to his vision of barbecue and home cooking plus the blues. Barbecue—beef, sausage, brisket, chicken, ribs, turkey—is served with old-fashioned potatoes, beans, and greens. (Stubb's barbecue sauce is used in-house and can be found in Austin grocery stores.) In addition to serving lunch and dinner and offering live music nightly except

ℹ️ **Fast food even has an Austin flair. The creators of P. Terry's, the hamburger drive-in at the corner of South Lamar Boulevard and Barton Springs Road (512-473-2217; www.pterrys.com), read *Fast Food Nation* and vowed to create "anti-fast food." Their burgers are all-natural, their potatoes fresh, the veggie burger tasty, and whether you drive up or drop by you can get a free dog biscuit for your sidekick. Leaf (www.leafsalad.com) is a foodie's dream of a salad bar downtown at 419 West Second Street (512-474-5323). Then there is Zen (www.eatzen.com), which has grown from one location to several across the city selling healthy fast noodles and salads, sushi, and teriyaki. One branch is located at 1300 South Congress Avenue (512-444-8081).**

Sunday (see The Music Scene chapter), Stubb's also serves a Sunday Gospel Brunch with typical Southern breakfast fare and a live gospel band.

SULLIVAN'S $$$–$$$$

300 Colorado Street
(512) 495-6504
www.sullivansteakhouse.com

Just when you think you have Austin figured out as a town where the hallmark is natural and laid-back, you walk into Sullivan's, where the menu is red meat, red meat, red meat, and the atmosphere reeks of confidence and power. Stand in the lobby during the legislative session and you could get a quorum. Chat with the parking valet, and you will hear tales of movie stars and directors who love to eat here. Sullivan's is in the heart of the downtown warehouse district and it touts itself as a "Chicago-style steakhouse." The atmosphere is clubby and definitely alpha male. Reservations are recommended. Dinner is served daily.

SWEETISH HILL BAKERY $

1120 West Sixth Street
(512) 472-1347
www.sweetishhill.com

The lemon bars are addictive, but since no one can live by sweets alone, Sweetish Hill also serves up a popular breakfast and lunch menu that finds inspiration in several quarters—France, Italy, and just plain wholesome. The bakery is in the middle of the West Sixth Street district and is usually busy all morning and into late afternoon as Austinites move to their own internal clocks, eating breakfast and lunch at their own pace. Food can be enjoyed on the premises, inside or on the small sidewalk cafe area, or it can be packed for an afternoon picnic.

TEXAS CHILI PARLOR $

1409 Lavaca Street
(512) 472-2828
www.cactushill.com

The Texas equivalent of a neighborhood pub, this bar and restaurant attracts a loyal clientele, many of them state workers, attorneys, and political types from the nearby capitol. The ambience is funky bar meets roadhouse. The highlight of the menu is, of course, chili, served at varying degrees of heat and completely without beans (beans are a Yankee aberration). Sandwiches, tacos, and burgers are also on the menu, plus something called a Frito Pie, a Texas original—the recipe begins, "Take one bag of Fritos . . . " Open for lunch and dinner daily.

TEXAS FRENCH BREAD $
2900 Rio Grande Street
(512) 499-0544

3213 Red River Street
(512) 478-8796

1722 South Congress Avenue
(512) 440-1122
www.texasfrenchbread.com
This popular Austin bakery and coffee shop chain is expanding quickly in the city. The bakery serves a variety of sandwiches, including the Niçoise sandwich that reflects Mediterranean flavors—tuna is melded with capers, olives, tomatoes, and onions on French bread. Customers can order any sandwich on the bread of their choice. The menu also features a variety of soups. Of course, the bakery also features a large selection of pastries and cookies. Coffee, herbal tea, and a pile of free newspapers make this a favorite spot for an early-morning stop on the way to work or school. Open daily for breakfast and lunch.

THE HOFFBRAU $-$$
613 West Sixth Street
(512) 472-0822
www.originalhofbraueats.com
Since 1934 they have been serving meat off the grill at this West Sixth Street no-frills restaurant. The founder's granddaughter now runs the joint. The decor here has been minimalist before minimalist got a name. The tables are simple orange Formica, and the wall decorations include a print of the Alamo, an old photograph or two, and a proclamation from former state representative Sarah Weddington (attorney in the Roe v. Wade case) praising the joint. In 1934 a T-bone steak was 35 cents, and a bottle of beer was a dime. Prices have risen, but the menu has remained the same—steak or, in a concession to modern times, grilled chicken breast. Salad is extra, but don't expect field greens. On the side there is white bread and saltines. Open weekdays for lunch; early dinner Monday through Saturday.

TRIO AT THE FOUR SEASONS $$$$
98 San Jacinto Boulevard
(512) 478-4500
www.fourseasons.com/austin
Elegant is the word most critics apply to this hotel restaurant, where the menu is a tribute to the best European traditions touched by Southwestern flair as divined by Chef Elmar Prambs. This is the place for a power lunch, power dinner, or divine brunch. The hotel is a favorite among visiting movie stars, high-tech wunderkinder in town for networking, and politicians and lobbyists. The menu is a wondrous combination of elegant dishes, some of them with Texas connections, bistro fare, and healthy, low-fat choices, all concocted in high style. One of the best and most affordable ways to experience the cafe is to sample brunch at the Four Seasons. Lunch and dinner are served daily, plus a prix-fixe brunch. Reservations are recommended.

TRULUCKS $$-$$$
400 Colorado Street
(512) 482-9000
www.trulucks.com
It is all about seafood at Trulucks, one of four restaurants that share the name in Texas. The ingredients are flown in from both coasts and the Gulf, ensuring high quality. Some dishes have a distinctive Texas touch, like the jalapeño salmon béarnaise. Texas Gulf snapper, another regional star, also is featured on the menu. Trulucks offers valet parking. Open for lunch Monday through Friday and for dinner nightly.

UPPER CRUST BAKERY $
4508 Burnet Road
(512) 467-0102
www.theuppercrustbakery.com
The city has several neighborhood bakeries that serve as gathering places for friends and a comfy spot to enjoy a breakfast croissant or midmorning break. In addition to sandwiches, soups, and breads, Upper Crust has a selection of croissants, both sweet and savory, that can be enjoyed while perusing the morning papers. Open daily for breakfast, lunch, and afternoon snacks.

VIN BISTRO $$–$$$
1601 West 38th Street, Suite 1
(512) 377-5252
www.vinbistro.com
A cozy restaurant and wine bar that aims to help diners match bistro-style food with wine. The menu offers suggestions along with descriptions of the dishes. Chef Sean Fulford was named one of the best new chefs in Austin in 2005 by *XLent* magazine. Wines by the glass and tastings are also offered. There is a bar and popular patio. Open Monday through Saturday.

WATERLOO ICE HOUSE $
600 North Lamar Boulevard
(512) 472-5400
This hamburger joint serves a variety of American fare. In addition to burgers, customers can order tacos and chicken-fried steaks. The Lamar Boulevard Waterloo is next door to one of the city's most noted record stores, Waterloo Records, in the West Sixth Street shopping district (see The Music Scene chapter).

WHOLE FOODS LANDMARK STORE
525 North Lamar Boulevard
(512) 476-1206
www.wholefoods.com
The headquarters of homegrown Whole Foods Market is a veritable movable feast. Much more than a grocery store (see our Close-up in the Shopping chapter), the new landmark store houses a vast array of possibilities for diners from 8:00 a.m. until closing at 10:00 p.m. daily. There are several intimate food counters within the store where diners can watch and chat with the cook. There is also a cafe with free wi-fi, plus a rooftop garden where shoppers can picnic with a view of the city. North Side Trattoria offers half a dozen pasta dishes. Fifth Street Seafood features a "catch of the day," and diners can choose not only which fresh fish they want but also how it is cooked and dressed. Lamar Street Greens is a salad heaven with fresh, hot and cold soups. There is also a sandwich bar, pizza and calzone oven, a sushi counter, ethnic food bars, and a favorite spot for the health conscious, the Raw and Living Food counters. Open daily from breakfast to dinner.

WINK $$$–$$$$
1014 North Lamar Boulevard
(512) 482-8868
www.winkrestaurant.com
Blink and you might miss Wink, but you would be missing a small jewel of a restaurant that has wowed locals. The small 15-table restaurant is located in an inconspicuous small shopping center. Austin chefs Stewart Scruggs and Mark Paul have created a popular, if crowded, foodie hotspot. The aim is to create a degustation menu—simply put, several smaller portions to allow diners to sample a variety of delicacies. The chefs and their staff shop daily for the best ingredients they can find. Chef Paul's desserts have won raves—his Chocolate Zin is a play on words to describe a sinfully rich dessert made from cherries soaked in chocolate and Zinfandel and then layered in phyllo pastry. The food is the focus here, and the tiny restaurant bubbles with enthusiasm. Reservations are accepted and recommended, given its size and popularity. Open daily for dinner; closed Sunday.

Close-Up

A Word about Ice Cream

It's hard to beat a cold cup of ice cream on a balmy night as a fitting end to an evening out. Several Austin small businesses offer "handmade" ice cream. Perhaps the most famous is Amy's, which began as a single store but now has nine outlets and growing and also packs ice cream for sale in local shops and restaurants. There is also an Amy's at Austin's airport. Patrons pick their flavor and toppings and watch as they are hand-beaten to a yummy, creamy, but cold consistency on marble counters. For a complete list of all Amy's ice cream shops, check out their Web site, www.amysicecream.com.

All locations are open late; the downtown Sixth Street store is open until 1:00 a.m. on weekends. Look for the big moving cows on the outer wall of Amy's at 1012 West Sixth Street, (512) 480-0673. Other favorite locations are the small, walkup store at 1301 South Congress Avenue and the new Amy's in a remodeled gas station at 5624 Burnet Road, (512) 538-2697, next door to Amy's production plant. On Sunday nights there are "Mooovies" shown on site. The Hyde Park neighborhood in Central Austin is home to the Dolce Vita Gelato and Espresso Bar, 4222 Duval Street, (512) 323-2686, www.dolcevitagelato.com. This neighborhood coffee shop and Italian-style gelateria opens early for breakfast and stays open late for gelato.

Dolce Vita also is a great spot for an after-dinner drink, perhaps coffee and a liqueur, or one of the 35 grappas the cafe has on hand. In addition to gelato, the menu includes wonderful tarts with traditional Italian flavors like hazelnut and walnut. The cafe has a small indoor space plus an outdoor area with tables and chairs.

Another addition to the ice cream scene in Austin is Teo in the 26 Doors Shopping Center in Central Austin. Teo's features authentic Italian ices and gelatos. The shop, which also houses a small coffee shop featuring Italian beans, opens early—around 6:00 a.m. on weekdays, a little later on weekends—and stays open until late evening daily except Sunday, when the cafe shuts down around 9:00 p.m. Teo's is located at 1206 West 38th Street, Suite 1204-B, (512) 451-9555, www.caffeteo.com.

Ice cream stirs passions, as noted above, and Cristina and Vincenzo Ginatta, natives of Turin, Italy, have taken their gelato dreams from one store in Dallas to over 20 in the U.S. and Mexico City. Their latest is Paciugo, 241 West Second Street, (512) 474-7600, www.paciugo.com, a great way to finish a night on the town.

ZOCALO CAFE $–$$

1110 West Lynn Street
(512) 472-TACO
www.zocalocafe.com

This is a "taqueria fresca" in the style of Mexico City, a place where fresh ingredients are used to make a variety of tacos and salads, served along with *agua frescas*, those fresh fruit drinks popular south of the border, and Mexican sodas and beer. This is an expression of Austin's love for our Mexican neighbors and the menu also includes an homage to Mexican vegetarian dishes, all served in the heart of one of Austin's oldest neighborhoods, Clarksville. Open for lunch and dinner, weekend brunch.

ZOOT $$$–$$$$

506 Hearn Street
(512) 477-6535
www.zootrestaurant.com

Gourmet magazine has praised Zoot executive chef John Maxwell for creating some of the "most exciting food" in Austin. Zoot has consistently ranked as one of the city's best restaurants. Located just west of MoPac, strictly speaking Zoot should be listed in our West section, but it is so close to downtown that we have listed it here in the Central section. The small restaurant, housed in a converted bungalow, also captures the spirit of Austin with its relaxed atmosphere and emphasis on the best ingredients, many of them produced in Texas. The menu changes with the seasons, and a vegetarian entree is usually on the menu, perhaps eggplant prepared osso buco-style. The restaurant also offers a prix-fixe pretheater menu for early diners. Given the restaurant's size and popularity, reservations are recommended. Open daily for dinner.

Z'TEJAS GRILL $$–$$$
1110 West Sixth Street
(512) 478-5355
www.ztejas.com
There are two Z'Tejas restaurants in Austin—the original in the West Sixth Street shopping/restaurant district and a second in Northwest Austin near the Arboretum—and perhaps a visit to both is the best way to get a quick fix on old Austin and new Austin. Both serve much the same menu, but the original Z'Tejas is housed in a converted home where the garage doors can be opened, exposing diners to the elements. The interior of the West Sixth Street location is decorated in the bright colors of the Southwest, and the outdoor patio serves as a lazy-day refuge just a few blocks from downtown or a place to relax during rush hour and enjoy the restaurant's "appetizer happy hour." The menu is sometimes described as Santa Fe meets Texas, with a dash of Louisiana thrown in. Don't pass on the restaurant's most famous dessert, Ancho chile fudge pie. Open daily for lunch through dinner, plus Sunday brunch.

SOUTH CENTRAL

ARTZ RIB HOUSE $
2230 South Lamar Boulevard
(512) 442-8283
www.artzribhouse.com
Live music and Texas barbecue are on the menu at this South Austin restaurant, but just to make sure no one feels left out, the menu also offers vegetarian dishes, including a grilled vegetable platter. There is live music seven nights a week. The restaurant has both indoor dining and a screened-in porch with ceiling fans. Open daily for lunch and dinner.

BABY ACAPULCO $–$$
1628 Barton Springs Road
(512) 474-8774
www.babyacapulco.com
A favorite with young, downtown workers, this restaurant on the Barton Springs strip is usually packed on weekends, especially when the weather conjures up margarita fantasies. The Tex-Mex menu offers the usual fare, including 14 types of enchiladas. The outdoor patio is the heart of the action on balmy days, and inside there is a casual, colorful atmosphere. Open for lunch and dinner daily.

CASA DE LUZ $–$$$
1701 Toomey Road
(512) 476-2535
www.casadeluz.org
This is a gathering place where the principles of macrobiotic diets, yoga, taichi, massage and music come together in a quiet retreat not far from downtown Austin. The restaurant features macrobiotic and vegan dishes, a raw food bar with sushi, and Mexican food featured on Wednesdays and Indian on Fridays. Open daily for breakfast, lunch and dinner. The campus also is home to a culinary arts program, The National Epicurean Academy of Culinary Arts (512 476-2276; www.naturalepicurean.com). The students present meals on the second Sunday of every month.

CHUY'S $–$$
1728 Barton Springs Road
(512) 474-4452
www.chuys.com
Chuy's is perhaps the most famous restaurant on the Barton Springs Road strip and one of the most colorful in Austin. Where else would you find a shrine to Elvis? The decor is a mixture of fantasy and kitsch, with iguanas and lava lamps setting the theme. The food is a mixture of Tex-Mex and New Mexico. When the harvest comes in, New Mexico chiles are grilled out front on a large metal barbecue rig. There are now three Chuy's in Austin: this one, one in North Austin, and another in Northwest Austin (see below). The lively atmo-

sphere makes this a popular family spot. The restaurant also sponsors a Christmas Parade (see our Annual Events and Festivals chapter). Chuy's is open for lunch and dinner daily.

CURRA'S GRILL $-$$
614 East Oltorf Street
(512) 444-0012
www.currasgrill.com

Austin abounds in small family restaurants that bring the flavors of Mexico home in a variety of ways. Curra's signature is a variety of authentic salsas. The menu features all-day breakfast tacos, enchiladas and carne guisada, a slow-simmered stew, and other traditional Mexican dishes, including several delicious Yucatecan offerings. Open daily for breakfast, lunch, and dinner, and you can buy the restaurant's tamales online.

EL MERCADO RESTAURANT
AND CANTINA $-$$
1302 South First Street
(512) 447-7445
www.elmercadorestaurant.com

This South Central location, one of three El Mercados in Austin (see the others under Central and North), serves up the same generous proportions of Tex-Mex favorites in a lively, colorful setting. The restaurant is open daily for breakfast, lunch, and dinner.

EL NOPALITO $
2809 South First Street
(512) 326-2026

This typical Mexican cafe near St. Edward's University is popular with the working-class neighbors, students, and foodies who love homemade Mexican food. The small restaurant—its name means "little cactus"—serves breakfast and lunch only. Popular dishes include tacos and *migas* (eggs scrambled with tomatoes, onions, chiles, and strips of corn tortillas), the homemade flan, and, on weekends, *menudo*. Touted as a hangover cure, menudo is a tripe and hominy stew that is an acquired taste. No credit cards.

EL SOL Y LA LUNA $-$$
600 East Sixth Street
(512) 444-7770
www.elsolylalunaaustin.com

What began as an old motel coffee shop in SoCo as a neuvo Mexican cantina, El Sol fast became part of the changing face of South Congress Avenue. It has moved now to the Sixth Street District. A favorite place to have a late breakfast, the menu also features Latin American and Central American dishes and the restaurant showcases the work of local artists and musicians. Open daily for breakfast, lunch, and dinner.

GREEN MESQUITE $-$$
1400 Barton Springs Road
(512) 479-0485
www.greenmesquite.com

Texas barbecue and Louisiana Cajun fare are the specialties here. But there are also chicken-fried steaks, hamburgers, and sandwiches. On the Cajun side, the spicy gumbo jambalaya and catfish are favorites. The pies are homemade, and there is live music on weekends. A second location is found in Southwest Austin (see below). Green Mesquite is open daily for lunch and dinner.

GREEN PASTURES $$$-$$$$
811 West Live Oak Road
(512) 444-1888
www.greenpastures.citysearch.com

In 1945 the Koock family decided to turn their

 Can't afford to splurge for one of those top flight restaurants? Then head to the Texas Culinary Academy, an Austin insider secret where the students serve classical French cuisine at bargain prices. Located in north Austin, the academy serves lunch and dinner at La Ventana, the school's showcase restaurant, 11400 Burnet Road, (512) 339-3850. The menus are featured online at www.tca.edu/our restaurants.asp.

family mansion into a restaurant, and ever since Green Pastures has been a quiet, elegant place to celebrate special events and family gatherings. The mansion was built in 1894 and has been in the Koock family since 1916. Surrounded by a large garden with more than 200 live oak trees, the mansion is hidden away in an everyday South Austin neighborhood. Patrons can begin their dining experience with a glass of milk punch out on the veranda, watch the peacocks stroll on the lawn, and listen to music being played on the restaurant's grand piano. The goal at Green Pastures is to re-create the hospitality of the Old South while offering continental cuisine with touches of Texas. The restaurant serves lunch and dinner daily, but one highlight of the week is the Sunday brunch, when Green Pastures sets a table that astounds both the eye and the palate. Reservations are recommended for brunch and for lunch and dinner on weekends.

GÜERO'S TACO BAR $-$$
1412 South Congress Avenue
(512) 447-7688
www.guerostacobar.com
Architectural ingenuity has turned an old feed store on the avenue into Güero's, where the food reflects both Tex-Mex and Mexican influences. The interior has been decorated with Mexican tiles, old photographs from the Mexican Revolution, and a picture of former President Bill Clinton, who has eaten here when visiting Austin. First Lady Laura Bush sometimes drops by. Breakfast tacos are a bargain here and are served all day, although the restaurant is not open for breakfast during the week. On weekends Güero's opens early for breakfast, featuring tacos, *migas*, huevos rancheros, and other popular Tex-Mex favorites. There is usually live music on Sunday afternoon.

GYPSY $$
1025 Barton Spring Road
(512) 499-0200
www.go2gypsy.com
We admit it, small Austin restaurants are still our favorites—intimate, friendly cafes, bistros,

and trattorias like Gypsy. Gypsy was created in a revived building in a neighborhood sure to benefit from patrons attending the nearby redesigned Long Center for the Performing Arts (see our Arts chapter). Shawn Gamble, trained at the Cordon Bleu and in Italy, has opened his trattoria where the menu has a northern Italian flavor. Maybe it's the oak trees and the limestone, but the Hill Country and Northern Italy are simpatico. Open for dinner Tuesday through Saturday.

KERBEY LANE CAFE $-$$
2700 South Lamar Boulevard
(512) 445-4451
This is the South Austin location of a very popular local cafe that serves homemade, healthful food 24 hours a day.

LA REYNA MEXICAN BAKERY $-$$
1816 South First Street
(512) 443-6369
When the owners of the original bakery, La Reyna (named for the picture of the Virgin Mary whose image hangs on a wall of the bakery), retired, they sold the business to one of their longtime bakers, Jesus Becerra, who still gets to work at midnight. The bakery and cafe is in the heart of one of Austin's predominantly Mexican-American neighborhoods, but it's a neighborhood that, like much of Austin, is changing and trying to hold on to its authentic atmosphere. The cafe is a meeting place for neighbors, local politicians, artists, and those who appreciate the homey atmosphere of the long-established South Austin restaurant. More than 70 different kinds of Mexican sweet breads are offered, and the staff will help you learn their names. Coffee and Mexican hot chocolate are good accompaniments. Be sure to take home a bag of Mexican pastries and cookies—the conchas, a sweet bread with a whirled shell design in sugar, are a favorite. But eat them the same day: Mexican pastries have no preservatives and little salt, so they do not stay fresh for long. The cafe is open daily from 6:00 a.m. to 8:30 p.m.

MAGNOLIA CAFE SOUTH $

1920 South Congress Avenue
(512) 445-0000

There are two Magnolia Cafes, this one in South Austin and the original in West Austin. The cafe is open 24 hours a day, seven days a week, and serves a homestyle menu featuring breakfast dishes no matter the hour.

MARS $$-$$$

1400 South Congress Avenue
(512) 472-3901
www.marsaustin.com

Fusion cuisine is a much-used term these days, but it fits the picture at Mars. Lovers of spicy food congregate here to celebrate a world of flavors. Dishes and techniques are borrowed from the Middle East, Africa, India, Thailand, the Caribbean, and Mexico. The food is spicy, the walls red, the lights dim, except out on the patio under the live oaks in the heart of SoCo. Mars is open for dinner daily. Reservations are recommended for large parties.

MATT'S FAMOUS EL RANCHO $$

2613 South Lamar Boulevard
(512) 462-9333
www.mattselrancho.com

In 2002 Matt's celebrated its 50th anniversary. The Martinez family has been in the restaurant business for longer than that, but in 1952 Matt Martinez opened up the first El Rancho, now operating in a new, large building south of downtown. President Lyndon B. Johnson ate here before he was president, and lots of other Austin notables have come here for a regular Tex-Mex fix. The menu includes all the old faithful standbys: enchiladas, fajitas, tacos, chile rellenos, and grilled shrimp. The hacienda-style restaurant can seat 500, but there is always a line on weekends at peak dining hours. Open for lunch and dinner daily, except Tuesday.

ROMEO'S $$

1500 Barton Springs Road
(512) 476-1090
www.austinromeos.com

From the concrete stone swan planters in front to the plastic grapevines inside, the owners of Romeo's have managed to re-create the kitschy atmosphere of a neighborhood Italian-American cafe with a menu to match. The atmosphere and the prices make this a great date restaurant. Open daily for lunch and dinner plus a Sunday brunch featuring vegetarian and meat fritattas, Italian eggs Benedict, and, of course, migas, the Tex-Mex breakfast must.

SCHLOTZSKY'S MARKETPLACE/
BREAD ALONE BAKERY $

218 South Lamar Boulevard
(512) 476-2867
www.schlotzskys.com

Schlotzsky's is a chain sandwich shop that was founded in Austin and has grown worldwide, including an outpost in Beijing. There are almost two dozen outlets in Austin, but this special branch just south of Lady Bird Lake is notable for its breezy atmosphere, airy architecture, and its on-site partner, Bread Alone Bakery. The famous sandwiches are sold here—the Original is made with special bread (grilled sourdough buns) stuffed with salami, ham, several cheeses, olives, onions, lettuce, and tomato—plus soups, salads, and small pizzas. The bakery offers whole loaves of specialty bread, cakes, cookies, desserts, and coffees. This is a good place to put together lunch or afternoon snacks for an impromptu picnic on the shores of Lady Bird Lake. Open daily for breakfast, lunch, and dinner and offers wireless connections and computer access.

SHADY GROVE $-$$

1624 Barton Springs Road
(512) 474-9991
www.theshadygrove.com

This Texas roadhouse–style restaurant takes its name from the pecan grove that shades the patio and the parking lot. There is seating inside, but many patrons prefer to sit outside and enjoy the sort of food served in roadhouses across America back in the days before interstate highways. Hamburgers are a staple, or try a Frito pie (Fritos topped with chili and cheese). For vegetarians there is a variety of salads and a Hippie Sandwich made with grilled eggplant and other vegetables. The Airstream Chili is hot and named for the Airstream trailer that sits in the garden. During summer, Shady Grove features live music evenings and even movies on the patio. Open daily for lunch and dinner.

TACO XPRESS $

2529 South Lamar Boulevard
(512) 444-0261
www.tacoxpress.com

The bumper stickers in this part of Austin often say "Keep Austin Weird," and funkiness is a point of pride in South Austin. At this—what else—funky cafe the patio features a shrine to Santa Taqueria Austin del Sur, and the menu has literally dozens of taco combos. Owner and chef Maria Corbalon is noted for her roasted meats, which evoke memories of those tacos savored by travelers in the Yucatan and other regions of Mexico. The cafe is open daily for breakfast and lunch, closes midafternoon on Monday and Sunday, and stays open until midevening on other nights.

THREADGILL'S WORLD HEADQUARTERS RESTAURANT $$

301 West Riverside Drive
(512) 472-9304
www.threadgills.com

Eddie Wilson founded the Armadillo World Headquarters (see The Music Scene chapter) and now owns Threadgill's, the two Austin restaurants that cherish home-cooking and celebrate the Austin music scene. The original Threadgill's is in North Austin (see the North section), but this downtown restaurant has carried the Threadgill's banner back to the block where the legendary Armadillo stood. The restaurant celebrates the past by decorat ing the walls with Armadillo memorabilia. Much larger than the original Threadgill's, the downtown venue is nevertheless packed, especially at lunchtime. The food here is down-home diner-style with entrees like meat loaf, chicken-fried steak, fried chicken, and sandwiches. There is live music here and a Sunday gospel brunch. Open daily for lunch and dinner.

i Two local writers are indispensable when it comes to understanding vital ingredients in Texas food. Jean Andrews, often called the "Pepper Lady," has written a couple of books on the genus *Capsicum* and her text, recipes, and beautiful drawings of peppers are invaluable to food fans and cooks. Another local expert with several books in print is herb and tequila expert Lucinda Hutson.

UCHI $$-$$$

801 South Lamar Boulevard
(512) 916-4808
www.uchiaustin.com

Tyson Cole was named one of *Food & Wine's* best new chefs in 2005, and his restaurant housed in a small home (uchi means "house" in Japanese) has become something of a shrine for visiting foodies. But don't be intimidated by all the accolades. The food is lovingly prepared here in a setting that is so reflective of Austin, a humble, converted South Austin cottage. The sushi is inspired by both tradition and inspiration from other culinary realms—chiles, goat cheese, and other nontraditional ingredients make appearances. Foodies know that Cole took his knives to Kitchen Stadium on the Food Network's *Iron Chef* show where he challenged Masaharu Morimoto, someone he admired, to a battle. Cole did not win, but won praise for his efforts. The Web site, which is as beautiful as the food, offers a tour of the menu and the surroundings. Open Monday through Saturday for dinner.

VESPAIO $$-$$$$

1610 South Congress Avenue
(512) 441-6100
www.austinvespaio.com

This Italian-inspired restaurant in the heart of the hot South Congress Avenue corridor (see our Shopping chapter) represents all that is both good and bad about the Austin restaurant scene these days. The food is inspired, the atmosphere lively, but the wait can be long! A small restaurant, Vespaio rocketed to fame soon after it opened. Created by Chef Alan Lazurus, the menu here allows patrons to dine in a small dining area with a view of the kitchen or to sit in the bar area and simply nosh for an hour or two on a wide selection of antipasti. Many of the dishes reflect Italian classics like Tuscan grilled steak and mussels in wine sauce; others are inspirations that draw on top Texas food products prepared in the Italian manner and in tune with the seasons. Next door is Vespaio's country cousin, Enoteca Vespaio which offers casual meals and take away.

Vespaio is open Tuesday through Sunday for dinner.

SOUTH

EL GALLO $-$$
2910 South Congress Avenue
(512) 444-2205
www.elgallorestaurant.com
A popular Tex-Mex eatery that offers servings of enchiladas, tacos, chalupa, and fajitas so generous that no one leaves hungry. The dinner menu also features several dishes that are typical of South Texas cookery, including *cabrito* (roasted baby goat) and chicken mole, the rich, complex chocolate and chile-based sauce that legend says was created by nuns in Puebla, Mexico. The restaurant is located in a colorful building across the street from St. Edward's University. Open daily from lunch through dinner.

EVITA'S BOTANITAS MEXICAN RESTAURANT $-$$
6400 South First Street
(512) 441-2424
www.evitasbotanitas.com
Tex-Mex eateries abound in Austin, but this far-south Austin cafe serves the sort of food you might encounter south of the border at family restaurants. The salsas are the stars here, and four small containers arrive with a preliminary basket of tortilla chips, a typical "botanita," or appetizer. Evita's also opts for authentic ingredients like Mexican queso, the white, mozzarella-like cheese that is used traditionally in Mexico. Evita's is open all day, breakfast through dinner.

HABANA $$
2728 South Congress Avenue
(512) 443-4252
www.habana.com
Roast pork, *tostones*, Cuban sandwiches, mojitos—all the Cuban classics are on the menu here. The restaurant even serves Havana Cola, imported from Florida, this is a pure cane sugar cola that expats yearn for. There is a second location at 709 East Sixth Street (512-443-4252). Open daily for lunch and dinner.

SOUTHWEST

AUSTIN PIZZA GARDEN $-$$
6266 US 290 West
(512) 891-9980
www.austinpizzagarden.com
It took 19 years for James Patton to finish the Old Rock Store in Oak Hill; chances are it won't take much more than 19 minutes for you to get your pizza in the restaurant now housed in the historic building. Patton (the local elementary school is named for him) finished the store in 1898. Now Oak Hill is a suburb of Austin, and a major freeway has wiped out many of the small stores that once lined the old highway. But Patton's stone structure is a registered historic building, and even the highway had to shift south to preserve history. The restaurant also offers take-out service. Open daily for lunch and dinner.

CENTRAL MARKET AT WESTGATE $-$$
4477 South Lamar Boulevard,
Westgate Mall
(512) 899-4300
www.centralmarket.com
Just as the cafe at the original Central Market (see Central Austin) is a popular spot for family dining, this second location has proved to be a favorite place to take the whole family. The varied menu offers sandwiches, home-style entrees, gourmet salads, pizza, burgers, soups, and sandwiches, ensuring that everyone in the group will find something to suit his or her fancy. The cafe also opens early for breakfast, and there is free live music on

the patio at night. Open daily 7:00 a.m. to 10:00 p.m., until 11:00 p.m. on Friday and Saturday.

CHUYS $
4301 West William Cannon Drive
(512) 899-2489
www.chuys.com
The southwest branch of an ever-expanding Austin original. See South Central listings. Open daily for lunch and dinner.

ESTANCIA CHURRASCIA $$
4894 US Highway 290 West
(512) 892-1225
www.estanciachurrascia.com
Tucked away on the side of a freeway access road in Sunset Valley (see our Relocation chapter), the outside of this Brazilian steakhouse looks like another limestone-clad restaurant. But inside the atmosphere is South American home-on-the-range, as gaucho-style cuisine with its heavy emphasis on grilled meat is served—beef, lamb, chicken, and pork ribs cooked the way the south of the equator cowboys do it. Open Monday through Saturday for lunch and dinner, Sunday dinner only.

GREEN MESQUITE $-$$
7010 Highway 71 West
(512) 288-8300
www.greenmesquite.com
Fortunately for residents of Southwest Austin, they don't have to go down to "restaurant row" on Barton Springs Road (see South Central) to enjoy Green Mesquite's barbecue. Open daily for lunch and dinner.

HYDE PARK BAR AND GRILL $-$$
4521 Westgate Boulevard
(512) 899-2700
www.hydeparkbarandgrill.com
See Central listing for description. Open daily for lunch and dinner.

LA MADELEINE BAKERY $
5493 Brodie Lane
(512) 287-4081
www.lamadeleine.com

See our Central listings. Open for breakfast, lunch, and dinner daily.

NUNZIA'S $$-$$$
7720 Highway 71 West
(512) 394-0220
www.nunzias.com
This restaurant in Southwest Austin is just beyond what is locally known as the Y because it is where US 290 West and Highway 71 West part company, one heading west to the hills, the other northwest to the lakes. The menu is contemporary American. Patrons can drop by for a glass of wine and a snack on the outdoor patio. Open daily for lunch and dinner; brunch served on Sunday.

NUEVO LEON $-$$
5900 West Slaughter Lane
(512) 288-4550
www.nuevoleoninaustin.com
The menu at this modern neighborhood cafe pays homage to the cooking of Northern Mexico and the state of Nuevo Leon. The original "mother" restaurant is located in East Austin. The dishes make it plain that Texas once was part of Old Mexico, and many of the featured items are found on South Texas Mexican cafe menus— beef and vegetable *caldo* (soup), fajitas, rib-eye steak with ranchero sauce, and a burrito dressed with chili. Open daily for lunch and dinner, open for breakfast Sunday.

NUTTY BROWN CAFE $-$$$
12225 US 290 West
(512) 301-4648
www.nuttybrown.com
One of the hottest growth areas of Austin has been the southwest region and the once-sleepy community of Dripping Springs down the road from what the locals call the Y at Oak Hill. This is a popular family restaurant, especially on the weekends, when there is live music on the patio. The menu features Mexican food, salads, and sandwiches. On Friday night there is a free taco bar, and on Sunday morning breakfast is served, which makes it a good stop on the way to a Hill

Country day trip. Open daily from lunch through dinner; open earlier on Sunday.

THE SALT LICK $$
Rural Route 1826,
Camp Ben McCullough Road, Driftwood
(512) 858-4959
www.saltlickbbq.com

One of the most atmospheric barbecue restaurants in the area, the Salt Lick occupies a rural site about 12 miles south of US 290 West on R.R. 1826, known as Camp Ben McCullough Road. Set in a Hill Country pasture, the Salt Lick has garnered a worldwide reputation, thanks to its mail-order food shipments, corporate parties by some of Austin's top employers, and coverage in national and international publications. To get there, take R.R. 1826, just past the Y in Oak Hill, and head south for 12 miles—or until you smell the smoke from the smokehouse. There are picnic tables inside and out, and the place is always busy. In winter a large fireplace inside warms diners. The menu includes brisket, chicken, ribs, sausage, homemade pickles, and peach and berry cobblers. Open daily for lunch and dinner. Reservations are suggested for large groups. The Salt Lick is located in a dry area of Hays County, so no beer, wine, or liquor is served; however, patrons can bring their own alcoholic beverages. No credit cards. There is an ATM machine on site, but watch out for those fees.

TRATTORIA LISINA $$-$$$$
13308 FM 150 West, Driftwood
(512) 894-3111
www.trattorialisina.com

Damian Mandola (see Mandola's Italian Market under Central Austin) has made Driftwood, near the famous Salt Lick barbecue, a center for his

> **i** Austin abounds with bakeries where a last-minute picnic can be put together for outdoor (or indoor) munching. Several are listed here in the Restaurants chapter, but also check out the Food/Gourmet/Kitchenware section of our Shopping chapter.

culinary adventures that include a rural trattoria and a winery. The menu is classic Italian with pastas, main course meat dishes including osso buco and rabbit, and dessert includes light fruits and cheeses. Open for dinner Tuesday through Sunday, lunch on Saturday and Sunday.

WEST

BACKSTAGE STEAKHOUSE $$
21814 West Texas Highway 71
Spicewood
(512) 264-2223

Longtime Austin foodies know that Raymond Tatum was the first chef at Jeffrey's, what we describe as the quintessential Austin restaurant. Now he is the conjurer at this relaxed steakhouse west of Austin on the road to the lakes. The food is inspired Texas fare with smoked meats, succulent beef, and seafood touched with the magic of chiles and other favorite Texas ingredients. The patio is a favorite place to dine. Open daily for dinner.

BISTRO 88 $$-$$$
2712 Bee Caves Road
(512) 328-8888
www.bistro88.com

Touted as Pacific Rim cuisine with Euro-Asian flair, the menu here is the creation of three partners who have operated top restaurants in Mexico and China. *Austin Chronicle* readers lauded this West Austin restaurant with its sophisticated menu and decor as "The Best New Restaurant in 2000." Dishes include such fusion creations as hot-and-sour seafood gumbo, roast lamb with a curried Asian pasta, mussels with a black bean sauce, plus entrees featuring top-quality seafood and Texas game. Open for lunch Sunday through Friday, dinner daily.

CHINATOWN $$
3300 Bee Caves Road
(512) 327-6588
www.chinatownaustincom

Among the most popular items on the menu at this West Lake Hills restaurant are several searing dishes, Thai pepper basil shrimp, and jalapeño chicken with black bean sauce—a reflection of the spicy Szechuwan-style Chinese cuisine featured at Chinatown. Of course not all the dishes are spicy, but diners with a taste for the fiery can turn up the heat on request. Chinatown is open daily for lunch and dinner.

CIOLA'S $$–$$$
1310 Rural Route 620 South, Suite C–2
Lakeway Plaza
(512) 263-9936
www.ciolas.com
Finding the kind of traditional Italian dishes that used to be featured in small cafes with checkered tablecloths and Chianti-bottle candles can be hard. Dan and LeAnne Ciola watch over Ciola's, where patrons hungry after a day of waterskiing or sightseeing in the Highland Lakes can find those evergreen favorites. Uncle Dominick opened the first Ciola's in Virginia Beach back in 1949, his dishes based on family recipes from Abruzzi, Italy. Many dishes can be ordered family-style on large platters to be shared by everyone at the table. Open weekdays for lunch and dinner, weekends for dinner only.

COUNTY LINE ON THE HILL $$–$$$
6500 Bee Caves Road
(512) 327-1742
www.countyline.com
Upscale barbecue is the order of the day at this hillside restaurant. Over the years, the view from the hilltop patio has changed as Austin has grown and homeowners have headed for the hills. One of the highlights of the menu is the smoked prime rib, served with baked potato, coleslaw, and beans. Barbecued ribs, brisket, chicken, sausage, pork, and baby back ribs are available by the plate or by the pound. The restaurant is open for lunch during the week and for dinner daily.

HILL COUNTRY PASTA HOUSE $$–$$$
3519 Rural Route 620 North
(512) 266-9445
www.hillcountrypasta.com

This Lake Travis–area restaurant offers a variety of pastas and Italian-inspired entrees. The wood-fired oven produces pizza and focaccia, and there are grilled offerings, including steaks. The restaurant is kid-friendly, and crayons come with the menu so that the kiddies can be occupied while parents ruminate on the choices. Because it is close to the lake, many patrons come in after a day of boating or swimming, so the dress code is relaxed. Open daily for lunch and dinner.

HUDSON'S-ON-THE-BEND $$$$
3509 Rural Route 620
(512) 266-1369
www.hudsonsonthebend.com
Chef/owner Jeff Blank and executive chef Becky Barsch Fischer have built a wide-ranging reputation as innovators in Texas cuisine from their base near the shores of Lake Travis. *Condé Nast Traveler* magazine has named it one of the best 50 restaurants in the United States. The restaurant is housed in and around a small Hill Country cottage. On the grounds are a smokehouse and an herb garden that offers a hint of what Hudson's has to offer. Much of the menu is devoted to showcasing exotic game and ingredients—one of the popular appetizers is Diamond Back Rattlesnake Cakes with chipotle cream sauce. Other dishes utilize venison, javelina (a South Texas wild boar), and Axis antelope raised on Hill Country ranches. For the less adventurous there are top-quality steaks, veal, seafood, and pasta dishes. The restaurant's sauces, both savory and sweet, garnered such a devoted following they are now sold on specialty food store shelves and by mail order. (Look for them at Central Market, and look for Central Market in our Shopping chapter.) Diners can eat or wait for a table on a balmy evening in the garden decorated with twinkling lights. Weekends are especially busy, so reservations are recommended. The restaurant is open daily for dinner but closes a little earlier in winter, so it is wise to call ahead. Hudson's also offers cooking classes.

i As Austin grows, the list of restaurants is beginning to look like a Russian novel. One way to view the Cliff's Notes version is to check in with local food blogs like www.urbanspoon.com or www.chowhound.com where the "locals" give their views and tips.

LA MADELEINE $
701 South Loop 360 (Capital of
Texas Highway)
(512) 306-1998
www.lamadeleine.com
See the Central Austin listing for details on the menu. Open daily for breakfast, lunch, and dinner.

LAS PALOMAS $$
3201 Bee Caves Road
(512) 327-9889
www.laspalomasrestaurant.com
Tucked away in the corner of a fairly nondescript strip shopping center, this Mexican restaurant serves delicious interior food in a light, airy setting. Specialties from various Mexican states are featured, including pork pibil, inspired by Yucatecan cuisine, shrimp a la Veracruzana (green olives, tomatoes, and capers), and the much-praised mole poblano, a complex sauce made from chiles, chocolate, spice, and herbs. The restaurant features live Latino trio music on Friday and jazz midweek to add to the ambience. Las Palomas is open for lunch and dinner daily.

MAGNOLIA CAFE $
2304 Lake Austin Boulevard
(512) 478-8645
www.cafemagnolia.com
This is a homey, comfortable diner where gingerbread pancakes rank as comfort food 24 hours a day, seven days a week. The cafe is not far from downtown, just west of MoPac, and serves breakfast dishes, sandwiches, even fajitas whenever you want them, no matter the hour.

RUDY'S BAR-B-Q $–$$$
2451 Capital of Texas Highway
(Loop 360)
(512) 329-5554
www.rudys.com
You can gas up your car and grab a grocery bag of barbecue at this popular small Texas chain. Rudy's touts itself as serving "the worst barbecue in Texas," but obviously that's a gimmick, judging from the crowd. The gas station is not one of those small-town stations; this is an up-to-date copy that simply reminds patrons that good barbecue originated in small-town country stores. Patrons can eat in or get food to go, and Rudy's opens early to serve breakfast tacos. Open daily for breakfast, lunch, and dinner.

THE EMERALD RESTAURANT $$$–$$$$
13614 Highway 71 West
(512) 263-2147
Step inside this Hill Country cottage and you will think you have crossed the threshold of an Irish country cottage. The walls are decorated with shamrock wallpaper, the tablecloths and curtains are lace, and there are cozy nooks and crannies where diners can enjoy an intimate dinner. The Kinsella family, whose matriarch hailed from County Mayo, runs this little Irish gem near Lake Travis. The evening begins here with orders of Irish soda bread and English treacle loaf (made with molasses) served with whipped strawberry butter and goes on from there to embrace roast pork in puff pastry, chateaubriand for two, roast lamb, grilled salmon inspired by Irish and continental influences. The desserts are rich, and Irish coffee is almost an obligatory end to dinner. The Emerald is open daily for dinner.

TRES AMIGOS $$
1801 South Loop 360
(Capital of Texas Highway)
(512) 327-1776
www.tresamigos.com
A longtime fixture on the Westlake Hills scene, Tres Amigos serves familiar Tex-Mex favorites

such as enchiladas and tacos, fajitas, and Mexican plates. Some of the waitresses have been on the job for years and have watched as families grew up, nourished by the kind of food all Texans hanker for regularly. The setting is a pleasant evocation of Old Mexico. Try the homemade mango ice cream. Tres Amigos is open for lunch and dinner daily.

NORTHWEST

BELLAGIO $$–$$$
6507 Jester Boulevard
(512) 346-8228
www.bellagioitalianbistro.com
This family-owned restaurant, named for a picturesque small town in Lombardy, northern Italy, draws big crowds, especially on the weekends. The Loiacono family is dedicated to serving Italian classics in a sophisticated setting. All the pasta is handmade at the restaurant. The menu features classics like osso buco, calamari, and pasta dishes reflecting many different regions of Italy. Dinner served daily except Sunday.

CHEZ ZEE $$–$$$
5406 Balcones Drive
(512) 454-2666
www.chez-zee.com
This stylish bistro, with a large outdoor patio, art-studded walls, and a baby grand where customers can work a jigsaw puzzle while listening to cafe music, is a fixture on the Austin scene. The

i While some folks have a hankerin' for those national-brand donuts, locals know to look for Round Rock donuts. At first there was only one place to get them— Lone Star Bakery in Round Rock at 106 Liberty Avenue (512-255-3629)—but now the word has spread, and those secret-recipe donuts are being delivered to gas stations and convenience stores around the area, where their presence is proclaimed in big letters on street signs. Check out www.roundrock donuts.com.

menu features both American and continental specialties, including sandwiches, pastas, salads, and grilled entrees, but it is the breakfast and weekend brunch menus that get rave reviews, particularly the crème brûlée French toast. Brunch is served into midafternoon on weekends, breakfast begins early during the week, and lunch and dinner are served daily, plus there is a late-night dessert menu.

CHINATOWN $$
3407 Greystone Drive
(512) 343-9307
www.chinatownaustin.com
The original Chinatown opened in Westlake Hills, see West listing, but this branch in Northwest Austin is equally popular. Open daily for lunch and dinner.

CHUY'S $–$$
11680 Research Boulevard
(512) 342-0011
www.chuys.com
The Northwest branch of the popular downtown favorite, see South Central Austin. Open daily for lunch and dinner.

COUNTY LINE ON THE LAKE $$–$$$
5204 F.M. 2222
(512) 346-3664
www.countyline.com
This Northwest branch of a popular upscale barbecue restaurant (see West Austin) is situated along a creekbed. Diners can wait for a table or enjoy a drink on the outdoor deck under the trees. One word of warning: F.M. 2222 is a wide, winding road that leads to Highland Lakes, making it very busy on weekends. There have been serious accidents here, many involving alcohol; visitors should designate a driver if they plan to drink with dinner. Open daily for lunch and dinner.

EDDIE V'S EDGEWATER GRILLE $$$–$$$$
9400-B Arboretum Boulevard
(512) 342-2642
www.eddiev.com

This is the Northwest branch of the downtown restaurant of the same name where seafood reigns. See our Central listing for details.

EL ARROYO $
7032 Wood Hollow Drive
(512) 345-8226
www.ditch.com
The Northwest branch of the popular downtown Tex-Mex joint. See our Central listing for details.

HOOVER'S $-$$
13376 Research Boulevard
(512) 335-0300
www.hooverscooking.com
The original Hoover's is in East Austin and this homestyle restaurant is a wonderful example of how a humble neighborhood spot finds a place in Austin's heart and grows. The menu is described by founder Hoover Alexander as "smoke, fire and icehouse" cooking that has its roots in Central Texas. A fifth generation Texan, Alexander is inspired by his Mexican-American classmates in Catholic school, his grandmother's homestyle cooking, and barbecue bosses of old. Open daily for lunch and dinner; open for breakfast on weekends.

JASPER'S $$
11506 Century Oaks Terrace
(512) 834-4111
wwww.jaspers-restaurant.com
Jasper's is located in the upscale (there's that word again!) shopping center, The Domain (see our Shopping chapter), and is a sister restaurant to Kent Rathbun's acclaimed Dallas and Houston restaurants. The decor is modern, natural, minimalist cool while the menu features "gourmet backyard cuisine." Open daily for lunch and dinner.

KENOBI $$
10000 Research Boulevard
(512) 241-0119
www.kenobiaustin.com
This Arboretum restaurant (see our Shopping chapter) takes Southwestern flavors and melds them with Asian cuisine all served up amid a decor that evokes the Far East in a stylish way. In addition to sushi, the menu features items like an Asian-marinated rib-eye, a five-spice pork chop and miso-chipotle chile salmon. Extensive sake menu. Open for lunch and dinner.

KERBEY LANE CAFE $-$$
12602 Research Boulevard
(512) 258-7757
Kerbey Lane Cafe operates a branch of its popular Central Austin cafe in this fast-growing section of Austin. The same old-faithful staples are on the menu, including Tex-Mex, burgers, sandwiches, salads, and breakfast dishes. The cafe is open seven days a week, 24 hours a day.

LA MADELEINE $
9828 Great Hills Trail
(512) 502-2474
www.lamadeleine.com
You would never guess this French cafe once was a bookstore. The bakery is open daily for breakfast, lunch, and dinner plus midmorning and midafternoon breaks. (See our Central listing for details.)

MANNY HATTANS NEW YORK DELI $
9503 Research Boulevard, Gateway Shopping Center
(512) 794-0088
www.mannyhattans.com
Manny came to Texas to play college football, but decided to open a New York deli reflecting his family's roots. Traditional deli fare and huge portions. Open daily for breakfast, lunch and dinner, closes midevening Monday through Thursday.

MANUEL'S $-$$$
10201 Jollyville Road
(512) 345-1042
www.manuels.com
The same great Mexican food, inspired by interior Mexican classics, found at the original downtown location (see Central listings) is found at this newer location. Open daily for lunch and dinner.

MIRABELLE $$–$$$
8127 Mesa Drive
(512) 346-7900
www.mirabellerestaurant

Don't be fooled by the location; Mirabelle is one of Austin's best restaurants. Located in Northwest Austin, a neighborhood of town homes and innocuous, small strip shopping centers, Mirabelle consistently ranks as one of Austin's most creative places to dine. The restaurant is the creation of Michael Vilim and Cathe Dailey, two restaurateurs with credits at some of the city's favorite places. Chef David Apthorpe also has been touted in populous polls by the *Austin Chronicle*. The goal of the kitchen here is to take top-quality regional ingredients and concentrate the flavor using time-honored techniques—for example, the espresso-rubbed venison. While the restaurant evokes the name of Provence in its pitches, it also relies on Southwestern touches and emphasizes the role of wine in its cuisine. Open weekdays for lunch, daily for dinner; closed Sunday.

MUSASHINO SUSHI DOKORO $$–$$$
3407 Greystone Drive
(512) 795-8593

The extensive menu at this Northwest Austin sushi bar (housed in the same building as Chinatown) features traditional offerings and some hybrid American takes on Japanese classics. The atmosphere is quietly elegant. Open daily except Monday for dinner only.

NORTH BY NORTHWEST $$–$$$
10010 Capital of Texas Highway
(512) 467-6969
www.nxnwbrew.com

This classy brewpub and restaurant was hailed by the locals as a much-needed addition to what some dub the Silicon Hills region of Austin. The building is sleek and modern, with that "Hill Country" look derived from local limestone and lots of natural light. There is a large bar inside, plus a dining area overlooking the brewery rooms where the House beers are concocted. The menu features grilled meats, fish, salads, sandwiches, and wood-fired pizzas. Open daily for lunch through dinner.

P. F. CHANG'S CHINA BISTRO $$–$$$
10114 Jollyville Road
(512) 231-0208
www.pfchangs.com

The Northwest location of this sophisticated, popular Chinese restaurant. See Central listings for details.

POK-E-JO'S SMOKEHOUSE $–$$
9828 Great Hills Trail
(512) 338-1990
www.pokejos.com

One of four Pok-E-Jo's in Austin, this one helps satisfy cravings for Texas mesquite-smoked barbecue in Northwest Austin. Take-out is popular here. Open daily for lunch and dinner.

RUDY'S BAR-B-Q $$
11570 Research Boulevard
(512) 418-9898
www.rudys.com

With so many barbecue restaurants it can be hard to stand out. Rudy's makes the effort by calling itself "the worst barbecue in Texas," but that belies the packed parking lot. The atmosphere is old country store with gas pumps outside and picnic tables inside. Rudy's opens early to serve breakfast tacos and offers lunch and dinner daily.

SIENA $$$–$$$$
6203 North Capital of Texas Highway
(Loop 360)
(512) 349-7667
www.sienarestaurant.com

The goal here was to create a restaurant evocative of grand dining in Italy, notably northern Italy and the Tuscan countryside, and place it at one of Austin's busiest intersections, Loop 360 and R.R. 2222. Judging from local reviews, Siena has fulfilled that mission. The decor is enough to make patrons imagine they are dining in an Italian villa, and the menu with its extensive wine list enhances that feeling. A popular restaurant, reservations are recommended. Open Monday through Saturday for lunch and nightly for dinner.

Z'TEJAS GRILL $$–$$$
9400 Arboretum Boulevard
(512) 346-3506
www.ztejas.com
The original Z is on West Sixth Street and captures with its menu and atmosphere the much-touted, laid-back Austin lifestyle. The second Z'Tejas is in a new Santa Fe–style building near the Arboretum, and its atmosphere reflects the lively, booming lifestyle of Northwest Austin, where many of the newer city residents and high-tech businesses have located. The menu is almost the same—a mix of Southwestern meets European, with a touch of Asian. Open daily for lunch and dinner, late nights on Friday and Saturday.

NORTH

ANDIAMO $$
2521 Rutland Drive
(512) 719-3377
www.andiamoitaliano.com
Unfortunately some patrons judge a restaurant by its surroundings or by the decor. While the setting is important to enjoying food, don't let a location in a strip shopping center turn you off. Despite its ritzier neighborhoods in this part of the city, Andiamo's serves up great Italian seasonal food in a charming interior. The menu features locally grown products and the restaurant has received plaudits from local critics and customers. Open Monday through Friday for lunch and dinner. Dinner only on Saturday. Closed Sunday.

CHUY'S $–$$
10520 North Lamar Boulevard
(512) 836-3218
www.chuys.com
Chuy's is Tex-Mex with attitude, see original location in our South Central listings. Open daily for lunch and dinner.

KIM PHUNG $
7601 North Lamar Boulevard
(512) 451-2464
www.kplamar.com
Asian noodle aficionados tout this humble-looking cafe as one of the best places in town to sample a wide variety of the Vietnamese specialty. There are more than 40 varieties of noodle dishes on the menu. The restaurant is in a strip shopping center, and the surroundings are plain. Open from midmorning to evening daily.

KIM SON $
10901 North Lamar Boulevard
(512) 832-0500
www.kimsonaustin.com
The first Kim Son was in Houston, a humble noodle house built by Vietnamese refugees, who worked hard and created a big, popular restaurant that got rave reviews in *Baghdad on the Bayou*. The family has now opened an Austin branch in the heart of the city's Asian market district (see Shopping chapter) and the crowds are equally enthusiastic. Dim sum is served every day from lunchtime to midafternoon. Open daily for lunch and dinner.

KOREANA GRILL AND SUSHI BAR $–$$
12196 North MoPac
(512) 835-8888
The shopping mall exterior of this popular restaurant belies the friendly, gracious restaurant inside, where the dining rooms include a sushi bar and a tearoom. Korean specialties, notably the national barbecue dubbed *bulgogi* here, are on the menu, plus *gimbab*, the Korean equivalent of sushi. Open daily for lunch and dinner.

KOREA HOUSE $–$$
Village Shopping Center,
2700 West Anderson Lane, #501
(512) 458-2477
Garlic, sesame, ginger, and peppers are key ingredients in Korean cuisine. Dishes such as Bul Go Ki (different spelling, but same dish as served above at Koreana Grill), a national favorite, is made with

beef, chicken, or pork, thinly sliced and marinated in a sauce made from onions, soy sauce, garlic, sesame, pepper, sake, and grated fruit. The dish is sautéed quickly and served with a variety of garnishes, including kim chee, the potent Korean pickle. Located in the Village Shopping Center east of MoPac on Anderson Lane, the small restaurant has a view of an inner courtyard, which adds to the Oriental design. In addition to Korean specialties, the restaurant serves sushi. Open daily for lunch and dinner.

POK-E-JO'S SMOKEHOUSE $-$$
2121 West Parmer Lane
(512) 491-0434
www.pokejos.com
One of four Pok-E-Jo's in Austin, this one helps satisfy cravings for Texas barbecue in North Austin. Take-out is popular here. Open daily for lunch and nightly for dinner.

SATAY $$
Shoal Creek Plaza,
3202 West Anderson Lane
(512) 467-6731
www.satayusa.com
The spice trade was a two-way affair, bringing spices from the countries in South Asia to Europe and importing Dutch, British, Spanish, and Portuguese customs to the region. Satay celebrates that trade with a menu that reflects Indonesian, Thai, Vietnamese, and Malaysian dishes. Dutch traders adopted the Indonesian custom of serving a variety of dishes at one course, dubbing it "rijsttafel," or rice table. At Satay it is a great way to share a meal with several friends. Another regional specialty is celebrated in the restaurant's name—satay is a Malaysian shish kebab. The menu also features curries, both Thai and Indian-inspired. Satay is well known not only for its diverse menu but also its food products, including a peanut sauce served with satay, which are sold in local food stores. The restaurant is in the Shoal Creek Plaza shopping center, but inside the decor is exotic and features artwork from the South China Seas region.

Satay's sauces and food products are sold in local grocery stores and online at their Web site. Open daily for lunch and dinner.

TAJ PALACE $$
6700 Middle Fiskville Road
(512) 452-9959
www.tajpalaceaustin.com
Both vegetarians and meat-eaters will find an abundant selection at this traditional Indian restaurant near Highland Mall. The vegetarian specialties include *saag paneer*, a homemade cheese and spinach sauté, and *malai kofta*, cheese and vegetable dumplings simmered in a cream and almond sauce. Carnivores can dig into tandoori dishes such as *barra kabab*, lamb marinated in spiced yogurt and then grilled. The menu also features a variety of curries with varying degrees of heat, and the tandoor oven-baked breads are not to be missed. There is an all-you-can-eat daily lunch buffet. Open for dinner daily.

TEXAS FRENCH BREAD $
7719 Burnet Road
(512) 419-0184
Austinites love their bakeries, and this multi-branched bakery ranks among Austin's favorite restaurants. On the menu for breakfast, muffins, croissants, and pastries, while lunch features a variety of sandwiches showcasing the bakery's French, Italian, and American breads. Open daily for breakfast and lunch.

THREADGILL'S RESTAURANT $$
6416 North Lamar Boulevard
(512) 451-5440
www.threadgills.com
Janis Joplin sang here at the legendary (a much overused word, but justified) restaurant and club founded by Kenneth Threadgill on a mundane section of North Lamar Boulevard. Of course, back when Threadgill got a liquor license for the former Gulf gas station, this was the far northern reaches of Austin, practically a rural outpost. "There's music on the menu" is the boast these days, and the mix of Southern hospitality, music,

and homestyle cooking packs 'em in. A second Threadgill's has opened near downtown (see our South Central listings), and both locations offer similar food: old-fashioned favorites such as chicken-fried steak, fried chicken, meat loaf, hamburgers, and lots of veggies. Open daily for lunch and dinner and until midnight on Friday and Saturday. (Read more about the Threadgill's legacy in The Music Scene chapter.)

TIEN HONG   **$$**
8301 Burnet Road
(512) 459-2263
www.tienhong.net
Dim sum is Chinese for brunch, and every Saturday and Sunday this North Austin restaurant is packed as patrons enjoy a variety of what might be called Asian noshes. Waiters roam the dining room with steam carts filled with a variety of dumplings, steamed buns, savory tidbits, deep-fried nuggets of meat and seafood, and tiny sweet creations. Most patrons, and many hail from Austin's growing Asian community, simply look over the carts and point to their choice, but that can be risky for those unfamiliar with dim sum—one delicacy is fried chicken feet. Tien Hong also serves a familiar Chinese menu at lunch and dinner daily. Dim sum is served usually from midmorning to midafternoon on the weekend.

WATERLOO ICE HOUSE   **$**
8600 Burnet Road
(512) 458-6544
www.waterlooicehouse.com
This is another homegrown restaurant chain with four locations in the Austin area. This branch of Waterloo features the same all-American menu of burgers, chicken-fried steak, and tacos. Open daily for lunch and dinner.

NORTHEAST

LA PALAPA   **$–$$**
6640 U.S. 290 East
(512) 459-8729
www.lapalapaaustin.com

ℹ A favorite late-night dining spot among Austin chefs is T&S Seafood, a Chinese restaurant located in north Austin, 10014 North Lamar Boulevard, (512) 339-8434. Open until 1:00 a.m., except on Tuesday.

The thatched roof is a reminder of La Palapa's roots south of the border—a *palapa* is a thatched shelter in Mexico. The restaurant has ties to two La Palapas, one in Laredo, the other in Nuevo Laredo, Mexico. Under the thatch, patrons will find several variations on the fajita theme plus enchiladas and Tex-Mex fare. On Saturday night the restaurant features an all-you-can-eat fajita bar, and Sunday there is an all-you-can-eat lunch buffet. The restaurant's cantina has live music and karaoke on Wednesday, Friday, and Saturday nights. La Palapa is open daily for lunch and dinner

TRES AMIGOS   **$$**
7535 US 290 East
(512) 926-4441
www.tresamigos.com
The name means "three friends," and the original restaurant at this four -restaurant, home-grown chain was opened by three friends 30 years ago. All locations are touted by longtime Austin residents as friendly restaurants where both the menu and the staff are familiar. Tex-Mex is the theme here. Open daily for lunch and dinner.

EAST

ARKIE'S GRILL   **$**
4827 East Cesar Chavez Street
(512) 385-2986
This old-fashioned diner in a working-class neighborhood on the edge of East Austin serves breakfast and lunch. The cooking is homestyle with generous servings, especially those luncheon side dishes of home-cooked vegetables. The cooking attracts a wide variety of faithful customers. No credit cards.

BEN'S LONG BRANCH BARBECUE $
900 East 11th Street
(512) 477-2516
www.benslongbranchbarb.ypgs.net
"We ain't pizza" the owners boast and after 31 years in the neighborhood Ben's has proved it. There is a restaurant rennaissance in this old Austin neighborhood, but Ben's still serves up old-style Texas barbecue from lunchtime until midafternoon every day except Sunday.

CALABASH $$
2015 Manor Road
(512) 478-4857
Just east of the university campus and I-35, this neighborhood cafe offers customers a chance to sample Caribbean fare. Dishes include jerk chicken and Jamaican-style patties (turnovers), served with such island staples as fried plantains and pigeon peas. Open for dinner Monday through Saturday.

CISCO'S $
1511 East Sixth Street
(512) 478-2420
Rudy "Cisco" Cisneros is no longer with us, but his east-side cafe where the likes of President Lyndon B. Johnson took breakfast is still a fixture. The small bakery and restaurant continues to attract the powerful for breakfast or lunch, and the walls are plastered with photos of both current and former politicos. The menu is not extensive; simple Tex-Mex fare is offered along with sweet rolls and cookies from the bakery. Cisco was something of a humorist, so the walls are covered with cartoons, jokes, and even a sign hung on an old gasoline pump that says: OUT OF GASOLINE, WE SELL BEANS. Cisco's is open for breakfast and lunch only.

EASTSIDE CAFE $-$$
2113 Manor Road
(512) 476-5858
www.eastsidecafeaustin.com
Those looking for ways to revive older neighborhoods should visit this cafe east of the interstate in an area of the city that is a mix of economically depressed businesses and urban pioneers. A small, homey cottage has been turned into a thriving enterprise that includes a large kitchen and herb garden plus a cooking and garden shop. Visitors can stroll through the kitchen garden before or after brunch, lunch, or dinner. The menu is a variety of pastas, enchiladas, grilled fish and chicken dinners, and sandwiches and salads. Brunch begins with mimosas (champagne and orange juice) or poinsettias (champagne and cranberry juice), and then patrons can choose from rich waffle dishes or classics such as eggs Florentine. After dining here, wander through the on-site store, where the house salad dressings are sold plus cookware and garden tools. Eastside is open daily for lunch and dinner, brunch on the weekends.

EL AZTECA $-$$
2600 East Seventh Street
(512) 477-4701
Wander the Mexican-American neighborhoods of South Texas and you will find family-owned restaurants like El Azteca, where the menu goes beyond the familiar Tex-Mex as served up by many chain restaurants. The Guerra family has run El Azteca for 40 years. *Cabrito*, spit-roasted baby goat, is a house specialty at this East Austin restaurant, about a mile and a half east of the interstate. Another popular dish is the *barbacoa de cabeza* (barbecued beef head), but don't wince until you have sampled the meat; the moist and tender cheek meat is touted as the best for folding inside a soft flour tortilla. El Azteca also serves *carne guisada*, a slow-simmered stew that is served with flour tortillas for a lick-your-fingers meal, and chicken mole enchiladas, dressed in the rich chocolate-chile mole sauce. The menu also features vegetarian dishes. The walls are hung with portraits honoring Mexican president Benito Juarez and American presidents Abraham Lincoln and John F. Kennedy plus Senator Robert F. Kennedy. The cafe is open for lunch and dinner every day except Sunday.

EL CHILE CAFE $-$$
1809 Manor Road
(512) 457-9900
www.elchilecafe.com

Created by a couple of sous-chefs from Austin's top flight restaurant Jeffrey's (see Central listing), this cafe serves foods flavored and inspired by interior Mexican fare. The brunch on weekends features dishes like the Yucatecan Huevos Motulenos, a Chihuahua-inspired steak and eggs, while dinner might offer a Oaxacan mole or an achiote roasted pork. Open daily for lunch and dinner, brunch on the weekends.

GENE'S $
1209 East 11th Street
(512) 477-6600
www.eatatgenes.com

Gene Tumbs, the son of Arkansas sharecroppers, has created a soul food haven with touches of New Orleans (thanks to his wife Claudia, a Big Easy native) in the heart of Austin's African-American old neighborhood, an area of the city undergoing an economic and cultural revival. The cafe serves po'boys, red beans and rice, smothered pork chops and collards, and there are "soul food Wednesdays." Open for lunch and early dinner daily.

HOOVER'S COOKING $–$$
2002 Manor Road
(512) 479-5006
www.hooverscooking.com

When you can't get home to Mom and you need a comfort food fix, Hoover's is the place. Hoover's doesn't look like much inside or out—it occupies a storefront in a neighborhood where working folks live—but the food is down-home good. Chicken-fried steak is a specialty, as it should be since it occupies a special place in the pantheon of Texas homestyle cooking, plus pork roast, macaroni and cheese, catfish, and barbecued ribs. There is a new Northwest location, also. Open Monday through Friday for lunch and dinner, weekends for breakfast, lunch, and dinner.

NUEVO LEON $–$$
1209 East Seventh Street
(512) 479-0097
www.nuevoleonaustin.com

Dishes inspired by the family's Northern Mexican roots are served at this colorfully decorated restaurant that has found success in a second Southwest location. . Lunch and dinner are served weekdays; breakfast, lunch, and dinner on weekends.

PRIMIZIE OSTERIA ITALIAN CAFÉ $
1000 East 11th Street
(512) 236-0088
www.primizieaustin.com

What's the difference between an "osteria" and a "trattoria?" Well, roughly translated "osteria" might be what we call a "hangout," a neighborhood cafe where the wine flows and atmosphere is—dare we say it—"laid-back." This wine bar and cafe serves pizzas, roman-style pastas, and grills and is yet another example of urban revival in a dynamic part of the city. Open daily for lunch and dinner.

SAM'S BAR-B-CUE $
2000 East 12th Street
(512) 478-0378

Sam's biggest fan was famed guitarist Stevie Ray Vaughan, and the walls of this authentic barbecue joint offer homage to the late musician with pictures and newspaper clippings. The menu is simple: brisket, chicken, sausage, and ribs plus spicy beans and potato salad. Take-out is available at this humble neighborhood cafe. Lunch and dinner are served daily. Open to 3:00 a.m. on Friday and Saturday. No credit cards.

SOUTHEAST

CATFISH PARLOUR $$
4705 East Ben White Boulevard
(512) 443-1698

For more than two decades Catfish Parlour has been pulling in the crowds for all-you-can-eat catfish and more. Both baked and fried catfish are served, plus fried shrimp and chicken. The menu has Cajun touches with hush puppies and gumbo, plus there is a large salad bar. Open daily for lunch and dinner.

MARISCO'S SEAFOOD $
1504 Town Creek Drive
(512) 462-9119

In search of an authentic neighborhood restaurant? Marisco's is housed in an A-frame building east of I-35 on a busy street. The food here is very cheap and simple; seafood entrees are simply prepared, either boiled, fried, or broiled, but there are Mexican touches such as the *vuelve la vida* (back to the good life) seafood cocktail, ceviche, and seafood soup. Marisco's is open daily for lunch and dinner.

ROUND ROCK

GUMBO'S $$-$$$$
901 Round Rock Avenue
(512) 671-7925
www.gumbosroundrock.com

As noted in the Central listings, Gumbo's originated in Round Rock and moved into downtown Austin, contrary to most restaurant trends in the city. The original Round Rock serves the same Louisiana-inspired dishes in a more intimate setting. Unlike the classy, brassy downtown Austin restaurant in the Brown Building loft development, Gumbo's in Round Rock is decorated in white and light colors, with natural stone walls offering a cozy feel. Both locations offer take-out. Open daily for lunch and dinner; closed Sunday.

MAIN STREET GRILL $$-$$$
118 East Main Street
(512) 244-7525

Residents of Round Rock have lovingly restored many of the old homes and businesses in their community, particularly the small downtown buildings that stand at the heart of what was once a small Texas town. (See our Relocation chapter.) The Grill occupies an old bank building on Main Street, and private parties can even reserve the vault dining room. Self-described as "American Continental Grill," the Grill features prime rib, grilled fish, steaks, pastas, and salads. The Grill's salad dressings—maple balsamic vinaigrette and creamy cilantro pumpkinseed—have become so popular the restaurant sells them on-site and at Central Market, Austin's hip grocery store (see Close-up in our Shopping chapter). Main Street also offers "jazz on the patio" on certain nights and special wine-tasting evenings. Open for lunch and dinner during the week; dinner on Saturday. Closed Sunday.

NIGHTLIFE

Austin's nightlife is so vibrant we had to divide it into two chapters: The second, The Music Scene, is a comprehensive look at the musicians and clubs that have made it possible for Austin to claim the title Live Music Capital of the World. This chapter also lists a great many music and dance venues and takes a look at some of the other spots where residents and visitors gather after the sun goes down.

Some places are swanky, some are funky, others reflect old Texas traditions, and still others swing to a Latin beat. Austin after dark can be a quiet glass of wine in a subdued, sophisticated setting; or a cold brew among friends at a cheery pub; perhaps a shot of tequila and a salsa dance; a glass of sherry with tapas; a beach blanket bingo movie with Coke and pizza; or an evening of satire with Austin's favorite comedy troupe, Esther's Follies.

One thing that is constant about the Austin nightlife scene is it is evolving and growing by leaps and bounds. Every month there are new faces on the evening scene as the menu of choices grows. The historic center of the city's night scene is, of course, Sixth Street, sometimes called Austin's Bourbon Street. The scene there has evolved over the past three decades (check the Close-up in this chapter). The liveliest nightlife is to be found downtown around Sixth Street; in the Warehouse District just west of Congress Avenue; and south of the river in SoCo, the South Congress Avenue neighborhood, which is a mix of restaurants, bars, cafes, shops, and street theater. SoCo is particularly lively on the first Thursday of every month (www.firstthursday.info), when stores stay open late and street vendors and performers make the wide avenue a very popular place for a stroll, leisurely shopping, a late night latte, or a festive dinner.

Two of the best places to keep track of the city's evolving nightlife are the *Austin Chronicle,* the city's popular alternative newspaper, and the XLent section of the *Austin American–Statesman,* which appears in the daily paper every Thursday (see our Media chapter). We have divided this chapter into Bars; Brewpubs and Pubs; Wine Bars; Coffeehouses; Comedy Clubs; Dance Clubs and Nightclubs; The Gay Nightlife Scene; and Movie Houses. In addition, the Close-up in this chapter is dubbed "Hangouts" and offers a look at the places that Austinites , well, hang out—be it a beer garden where Fido is welcome; a place to watch the sunset; or a party spot where the gang from the office can plot a management coup over nachos and 'ritas.

Austin swings every night, and most clubs and bars are open every day, except where we have noted in the listings. Where there is music, either live or electronic, there is likely to be a cover charge of a few dollars, but rarely do those covers top $10. Bars must stop serving alcohol at 2:00 a.m. by Texas law, and no one younger than 21 can be served, though some clubs do admit them. Some upscale clubs have a "no one under 25" rule in a bid to keep college students at bay. Driving-while-intoxicated laws are very strict, and bar owners are also held responsible under the state's liquor licensing laws for making sure customers do not overindulge. Taxis cruise the city's major nightlife areas, and patrons who overindulge are wise to take a ride home.

(Q) Close-up

Hangouts

The dilemma: It is a restaurant with a great view or vibe, but the food is not really that great. It is a bar, but kids are welcome. And where do you go to find the "real" Austin.

Solution: Check out these hangouts.

That's what we are calling this potpourri of popular Austin spots where the locals gather to wind down the day and sometimes party into the night, places that do not quite fit either the bar and pub categories in this chapter or recommend themselves to our restaurants chapter (hey, it's food, but you wouldn't crawl over mountains to get there). Places we might go more for the ambience than the menu. Somewhere we could take the kids, the dog; have a 'rita or two or three and recall our youth. And somewhere we could find Austin as it was. . . .

KIDS AND DOGS

The Austin climate with its high number of balmy days makes outdoor dining and sipping popular, so many of the pubs and bars listed in this chapter do have outdoor spaces. But in a city with a relatively young population—among the "creative cities" Austin has the largest population of 24- to 35-year-olds according to one study—some of these spaces are just not kid-friendly. How does dad enjoy a brewski while junior munches on chicken fingers?

South Austin, a popular settling spot for upwardly mobile young families, boasts a few solutions for the couple caught in the parent trap who long for happy hour out on the deck as the sun sets. Freddie's Place, 1703 South First Street, (512) 445-9197, www.freddiesplaceaustin. com, is where we saw a table of rugrats munching on hot dogs while a decidedly hot dog, a pug, sat two tables away being fed off a fork by his "mom." The dads, meanwhile, were sipping one of the 20 or so brands of cold beers offered on the menu. Freddie's has a washer-pitching ring so it's almost a sports bar, but the playscape and sandpit make this a kid-friendly spot. It is packed with families dining under the live oaks at wooden picnic tables on food that is simply burgerlicious and better for dad's soul than nightly chicken. On Sunday there is a stupid pet tricks contest and all the dogs get a Freddie's treat, but most of them prefer the fries. There is free brisket during happy hour on Tuesday, Wednesday, and Thursday, which brings in two-legged and four-legged meat eaters, and there is live music to drown out the squeals of the kids as they fall off the slide. Simply said—a hangout.

Another kid-friendly/Dad-and-Mom-can-be-a-grownup-again place is Doc's Motorworks, 1123 South Congress Avenue, (512) 448-9181, www.docsaustin.com. This SoCo bar and restaurant is always packed and noisy. The video games, shuffleboard and washer pit keep the youngsters and not so youngsters busy. The old metal porch chairs out front on the patio give the place that laid-back, South Austin vibe. Lots of beer varieties on the menu, plus fish tacos, burgers,

BARS

THE APPLE BAR

120 West Fifth Street

(512) 322-9291

There's a whiff of the cosmopolitan Big City about this place, but its size (small) and the ambience (sophisticated, subdued) make it friendly and relaxing. The apple martini is, of course, a favorite.

THE BELMONT CLUB

305 West Sixth Street

(12) 457-0300

www.thebelmontaustin.com

The inspiration here is Las Vegas/Palm Springs/Rat Pack—leather banquettes, dark wood and dim lights. The restaurant serves a full menu, but the bar offers snacks late into the night and the patio features live music midweek, plus movies on Mondays.

and finger foods for the young 'uns. No wonder the place is popular with young families from the neighborhood.

POST-SORORITY BLUES

Remember that Cancun spring break and the wet t-shirt contest? No, oh well, who does remember those tequila-induced hazes of yesteryear? But there are a couple of spots in Austin where the ambience hits a memory nerve. Carlos 'N Charlies is "proud" to be the first north-of-the-border branch of the famous Mexican restaurants created by Carlos Anderson. Located on Lake Austin, 5973 Hiline Road, (512) 266-1683, www.cncaustin.com, this lively party spot boasts a dock so patrons can drop in after a day on the water. There's music, margaritas, parrots, margaritas, bikini tops, margaritas. You get the picture. The food is Mexican-themed and the drinks menu acknowledges local customs—there is an orange-colored "Bevo" tequila shot, named in honor of the University of Texas mascot. Other drinks include Pusser's Painkiller and a "Skip and Go Naked" drink. Definitely a hangout.

Closer to downtown Austin, but also on the water, Chuy's Hula Hut, 3825 Lake Austin Boulevard, (512) 476-4852, www.hulahut.com, touts its "Mexonesian" menu, Polynesian meets Mexico. A typical fusion dish is the shrimp pipeline enchilada. The vibe here is also a mix of South Seas and South of the Border with tiki torches and a *palapa*-covered bar. Popular for group celebrations, the Hula Hut is a casual bar and restaurant where the menu apologizes for requiring shoes and shirts for "health, sanitation and safety" reasons. It also requests that groups designate a driver, a nod to the reality that this is a party hangout.

THE REAL AUSTIN HANGOUT

For those of us who have watched and been excited by Austin's growth, by the vast array of restaurants and nightspots that have flourished here, and the number of choices in off-duty hours funspots that have multiplied, there is always one little nagging regret. What happened to the old Austin? Does it still exist? Can we go home again? The answer is, yes if you like dark, dingy bars with cheap beer and a great jukebox. The Deep Eddy Cabaret (cabaret—that's a joke worthy of the old Austin!) has one of the best jukeboxes in town, featuring Elvis, Otis Reading, even Edith Piaf. The beer is downright cheap and always very cold, brands like Lone Star, Shiner and yes, even Pearl. No liquor. No wine. No cigarettes (thanks to the new Austin), although the walls are a rich brown with years of tobacco smoke. The patrons now have to wrap their nicotine-stained fingers around a longneck on the small patio. A former grocery store, turned bait shop, then neighborhood bar, this hallowed hangout is near Deep Eddy Pool just west of downtown, 2315 Lake Austin Boulevard, (512) 472-0961. Although the lofts are marching westward and change is barking at the gates, strangers are still welcome here. But don't dress up.

THE BROWN BAR

201 West Eighth Street

(512) 480-8330

The renovation of the historic Brown Building in downtown Austin has created not only an architectural gem where lucky loft owners can hang their hat but also has given birth to one of the city's best bars. The Brown Bar with its, yes, brown walls, brown ceilings, and dark furnishings has a comfy, yet sophisticated feel. The clientele is a mix of hip 20-somethings and downtown powerbrokers, lobbyists, and lawyers.

CEDAR DOOR

Second and Brazos Streets

(512) 473-3712

www.cedardooraustin.com

When they built the Cedar Door, they should have put wheels on the building. That would have saved this cherished neighborhood-style bar some money. The Door has moved, literally, several times—the first location is now occupied by a high-rise on 12th Street downtown. Originally a typical Austin cottage-turned-bar, it now lives west of the city's convention center. A popular watering hole for bureaucrats, courthouse lawyers politicos, and journalists, it has all the hallmarks of an old favorite with mismatched chairs and tables, old prints and posters, a munchie menu, plus bartenders who know their regulars well. Its signature drink is the Mexican martini, a hybrid margarita-martini.

CEDAR STREET COURTYARD
208 West Fourth Street
(512) 495-9669
www.cedarstreetaustin.com
The patio of this hip bar, dubbed "the king of gin joints," is a few steps down from the elevated sidewalks that once served as loading docks in the Warehouse District, east of Congress Avenue. Live music fills the air most nights, often jazz music, and the patio is flanked by two dark, cool indoor bars that make a nice retreat on steamy nights. The renovated buildings were designed by one of Austin's most noted architects, Sinclair Black, who still has his offices on the second floor.

CLUB DEVILLE
900 Red River Street
(512) 457-0900
The exterior of Club DeVille looks vaguely 1950s, definitely funky, and is certainly Austin, with its mix of patrons, some dressed up for a posh night on the town, others in jeans and sandals. The guys who founded this Sixth Street–district club did so because they needed a place to hold their regular weekend cocktail parties. One of the owners is Mark McKinnon, a former *Daily Texan* editor and former Democratic political consultant who amazed his friends and political cohorts when he signed on with then Governor George W. Bush as a media consultant. One newspaper critic has described the decor as "hanging out in Grandma's basement while she's in Florida." There is a large outdoor deck equipped with funky furniture and blankets for chilly nights.

> **i** One way to give new meaning to the term "pub crawl" is to take one of Austin's pedicabs from nightspot to nightspot. Austin Bicycle Cabs operate in the downtown area; (512) 930-8791, www.austinbicyclecabs.com. There is also a Web site, www.austinpedicabs.com, devoted to the pedicab community.

The bar does get busy on the weekends, but the relaxed atmosphere is constant.

CUBA LIBRE
401 Colorado Street
(512) 472-2822
www.cubalibreaustin.com
Touted as a chic spot down in the Warehouse District, this bar is so chic female customers can get a manicure with their martini on Thursday night. The menu of tapas has a Caribbean flair.

DONA EMILIA'S
101 San Jacinto Boulevard
(512) 478-2520
www.donaemilias.com
This downtown Latin American restaurant has an upstairs bar, The Atrium, a light-filled airy space where the musical beat is decidedly intoxicating and the drinks made with Brazilian *cachaca* or island rum transport the customer to a laid-back, balmy place.

DRISKILL HOTEL LOBBY BAR
604 Brazos Street
(512) 474-5911
www.driskillhotel.com
The venerable Driskill Hotel (see our Hotels chapter) is like an island of style amid the cacophony of Sixth Street. The lobby's cool marble floors and pillars, ornate gilt mirrors, and chairs a person can sink into make for a plush surrounding for the hotel's piano bar. Happy hour draws people in, and they often stay to unwind to the sounds of classic lounge hits played on the grand piano. Later in the evening, folks gather around and even join in as the old romantic hits are played.

THE ELEPHANT ROOM
315 Congress Avenue
(512) 473-2279
www.natespace.com/elephant
This smoky, dark basement bar in the heart of downtown is a longtime gathering spot for jazz aficionados. For more information about the jazz scene at the Elephant Room, see The Music Scene chapter.

FINN & PORTER
500 East Fourth Street
(512) 493-4900
www.finnandporter.com
This clublike, comfy bar in the Hilton, upstairs from the restaurant of the same name, is a great place for a quiet drink and conversation. Sophisticated, and if you get the munchies there is a sushi bar downstairs.

FIREHOUSE LOUNGE
605 Brazos Street
(512) 478-3473
www.thefirehouselounge.com
You might spot a celebrity in this comfortable, but classy lounge built in a restored firehouse; however, the management boasts that everyone is a VIP. Quiet in the early evening, a little more lively as the night progresses with a DJ.

FOUR SEASONS LOBBY BAR
98 San Jacinto Boulevard
(512) 478-4500
www.fourseasons.com
The lobby bar of this downtown luxury hotel (see our Hotels chapter) is a great place to people-watch. The patrons here might be top Texas businesspeople, foreign investors, high-tech wizards, top-name musicians and movie stars, politicians, or media personalities. The bar offers an extensive list of single malt whiskey and cognac plus wine and snacks, none of them inexpensive. In the afternoons, tea and sandwiches are available.

HOTEL SAN JOSÉ
1316 South Congress Avenue
(512) 444-7322
www.sanjosehotel.com
The interior garden courtyard of the restored Hotel San José in SoCo is an oasis of calm and inspiration. A wonderful place for an end of the day glass of wine and bite of cheese, perhaps with someone you care about, or simply alone for a moment of reflection.

LIGHT BAR
408 Congress Avenue
(512) 473-8544
www.lightbaraustin.com
In Style magazine loved it, as did Forbes: Perhaps it is the patio that looks out over downtown, or the ever-changing mood lighting. Great couches for snuggling, but the vibe gets livelier as the evening progresses with DJs and salsa nights.

LOUIE'S 106
106 East Sixth Street
(512) 476-2010
Unlike many of the other bars on Sixth Street, which appeal to the shots and longnecks crowd, the bar at Louie's 106 is as sophisticated as the restaurant (see our Restaurants chapter). Like its neighbor, the Driskill Hotel, Louie's 106 is a classy haven far from the rowdy spirit of Sixth Street. In addition to being a popular, top-notch restaurant, Louie's is also home to a cigar room and a tapas bar.

MALAGA'S WINE AND TAPAS BAR
440 West Second Street
(512) 236-8020
www.malagatapasbar.com
A fixture in the Warehouse District scene, this wine and tapas bar moved 2 blocks south into the Second Street District. The food is inspired by the wonderful Spanish tradition of nibbling on savories while drinking sherry or wine. There is a full bar, and noshes can be ordered until 2:00 a.m. on weekends and midnight during the week and Sunday.

MOLOTOV
719 West Sixth Street
(512) 499-0600
www.molotovlounge.com
The decor as this quasi-neighborhood bar in the loft-sprouting neighborhood near Whole Foods Landmark Store is retro-Communist with hammers and sickles, splashes of red, even a pointer on the Web site that turns into a flaming Molotov cocktail (the handmade gasoline bombs were contemptuously named after a Russian official by the Finns after Stalin invaded their country in 1939). But the atmosphere is much more pleasant with the literally open-to-the-street walls and the upstairs deck decorated with some very non-Commie, large comic-style portraits of bikini-wearing girls. There is also a karaoke night where it is doubtful you will hear the *Internationale*, the Communist workers' anthem.

PANGAEA
409 Colorado Street
(512) 472-8882
www.pangaea-austin.com
In late December 2007, Austin critic and observer of the city's cultural scene Michael Barnes noted that the "lounge revival" had hit Austin and he named four newcomers—The Belmont Club, Qua, Imperia and Pangaea—as heralds of the Austin "ultra-lounge." Safari-themed Pangaea is the brainchild of Michael Ault whose London and New York clubs have made headlines, notably in gossip columns like "Page Six." The atmosphere is classy, the price tag not cheap and don't even think about showing up in scruffy jeans and flip-flops.

QUA BOTTLE LOUNGE
213 West Fourth Street
(512) 472-2782
www.quaaustin.com
The signature drink at this "ultra-lounge" is premium champagne; the age limit is 25 or over; and don't show up in tennis shoes. There is even a velvet rope line where the judgment is made whether you make the cut. Luxurious surroundings include a shark tank under the glass floor, something that the owners defend on their Web site, while acknowledging that some in Austin have expressed disapproval. Like it or not, it's a sure sign that some things have changed in the city.

STAR BAR
600 West Sixth Street
(512) 477-8550
Just beyond the downtown Warehouse District, West Sixth Street is developing into the hottest spot in town for new restaurants and bars. Star Bar once was a paint shop, but the '50s-style building is now a very hip place to be seen and to watch Austin's 20-something set at play. The store's big plate-glass window looks out on a small street-side patio, while inside the low ceiling and retro furnishings give the place an intimate, jazzy sort of feel.

SPORTS BARS

In addition to the sports bars listed here, check the Brewpub section, since many local pubs also turn on the TV when there is a hot sports event.

AUSSIE'S VOLLEYBAR AND GRILL
306 Barton Springs Road
(512) 480-0952
www.aussiebar.com
Volleyball takes center stage at this South Central Austin bar and grill (see our Restaurants chapter), but sports enthusiasts also gather at the bar to watch sporting events on several television sets. A favorite drink is, of course, Foster's—the national beer of Australia, mate.

BW-3
218 East Sixth Street
(512) 472-7227
Buffalo wings and football; buffalo wings and baseball; buffalo wings and basketball. You get the picture. (Hence the name BW-3.) BW-3 is popular at lunch and crowded in the evenings.

JOE'S BAR AND GRILL
605 West Street
(512) 423-0885
www.joesbargrill.com

A sports bar aimed at the sophisticated, who knew? Joe's has flat screen televisions, pool tables, shuffleboard, and a menu created by the owner and former chef of Louie's 106, the classy Sixth Street restaurant. There is even a wine list and that makes this sports bar just west of downtown a great place for a date and a football game!

LEGEND'S
8901 Business Park Drive
(512) 343-0888

Housed in the Holiday Inn in Northwest Austin, Legend's focus is simply sports, cold beer, and all-American fare. This is the quintessential sports bar: The 22 televisions are always tuned to sports, and the menu features food like hamburgers and steaks. Occasionally there is a cover charge when special sports broadcasts are scheduled.

RINGERS SPORTS LOUNGE
415 Colorado Street
(512) 495-1558
www.ringerssportslounge.com

An addition to the Warehouse District, this sports lounge has 20 plasma television sets and two big screens, bar, and food service. University of Texas teams are prominently featured, but hockey, soccer, pro football, and basketball fans will find their teams on the big screens also. The bar also sponsors Texas Hold 'Em poker tournaments. Open daily from late afternoon to bar closing.

SHOAL CREEK SALOON AND SPORTS PARLOR
909 North Lamar Boulevard
(512) 477-0600

New Orleans Saints fans are drawn to this Central Austin sports bar, perhaps because the pub's menu features Cajun dishes like gumbo and fried catfish.

THE TAVERN
922 West 12th Street
(512) 320-8377
www.austintavern.com

Opened in 1916 as a grocery store on what was then the edge of the city, the building has had several incarnations including, legend has it, serving as home to a brothel. After Prohibition, the Tavern came into its current life and is now a popular place for friends to gather for a burger, a game of pool, or a beer or two during a football game on the big screen.

TEXAS SPORTS PALACE
9504 North I-35
(512) 837-1671

Housed inside Showplace Lanes, a North Austin bowling alley, the Texas Sports Palace offers patrons the next best thing to being at the game. Several big-screen televisions and a state-of-the-art sound system add to your experience of the event, be it a regularly scheduled game or a pay-for-view event, all in cool, dark surroundings.

WAREHOUSE SALOON & BILLIARDS
509 East Ben White Boulevard
(512) 443-8799
www.warehousesaloon.com

This large pool hall is also home to a sports bar where patrons can watch regularly televised events or pay-for-view specials. In addition to 25 tables, the Warehouse also offers video games, pinball, and shuffleboard.

BREWPUBS AND PUBS

In 1993 the Texas Legislature permitted homemade brew products to be sold in public bars, despite the opposition of the big breweries and beer distributors. Microbreweries are as fashionable as coffeehouses these days.

B.D. RILEY'S PUB
204 East Sixth Street
(512) 494-1335
www.bdrileys.com

ℹ️ The Southwest Brewing News (512-443-3607 or 800-474-7291) publishes the latest brew news in the Southwest. Features on new pubs, awards, and taste tests are included in the paper, which can be found in several Austin pubs.

This is a real Irish pub that was built in Dublin and shipped over to Austin by owner John Erwin, whose grandmother, Bessie D. Riley, gave her name to the joint. Beer here is served in Imperial pints for two-fisted drinkers, and the pub grub is some of the best in Texas. In addition to being home of the Austin branch of the Notre Dame club, Riley's offers music, football nights, and pub quiz nights, a popular tradition in the old country.

THE BLIND PIG PUB
317 East Sixth Street
(512) 472-0809
www.blindpigpub.com
Thirty varieties of beer and ale are offered at this pub-cum-sports bar on Sixth Street. The pub has a small beer garden, Foosball, and pool tables, plus big-screen televisions for watching sports events.

COPPER TANK BREWING COMPANY
514 Trinity Street
(512) 478-8444
www.coppertank.com
This Sixth Street brewpub attracts a diverse crowd, including a large college contingent and sports fans, drawn by the bank of big-screen televisions. Local brewery critics give Copper Tank high marks for its brews like Big Dog Brown Ale and Firehouse Stout. Happy hour on Wednesday draws a large crowd, and the bar is popular among downtown workers who want a cold one on hot days.

THE CROWN & ANCHOR
2911 San Jacinto Boulevard
(512) 322-9168
This UT campus–area pub is popular among students and perennial campus habitués. The aim here is to re-create an English pub, hence

the dartboards and the wide selection of beers. Patrons can play pinball, Foosball, and video games and order a burger if they get hungry after a lively game. In balmy weather, patrons can enjoy a beer on the patio.

THE DOG & DUCK PUB
406 West 17th Street
(512) 479-0598
www.doganduckpub.com
This Central Austin bar is as close as Austin gets to an authentic English pub. The food here reflects a mix of English pub grub and popular American dishes, and the bar offers, like any English pub, a wide variety of beers on tap and in bottles.

THE DRAUGHT HORSE PUB AND BREWERY
4112 Medical Parkway
(512) 452-MALT
www.draughthorse.com
From the outside it looks like a reproduction of an English country town pub. Inside, the cozy atmosphere attracts a loyal clientele. In addition to stocking 80 different beer brands, the pub has been experimenting with several homemade brews.

FADÓ IRISH PUB
214 West Fourth Street
(512) 457-0172
www.fadoirishpub.com
Stepping into this Irish pub in the downtown Warehouse District, you almost expect to see John Wayne and Maureen O'Hara at the next table. It's not because the place looks like an old Irish pub, but because it looks more like the Hollywood-set version of an Irish pub. In addition to a menu of Irish-inspired dishes, the bar offers a wide selection of beer and whiskey, and the televisions in the bar tune in to satellite transmissions of rugby games, Gaelic football, hurling, and other interesting sports.

LOVEJOY'S TAP ROOM AND BREWERY
604 Neches Street
(512) 477-1268
The tables here are created from manhole covers, a coffin serves as a coffee table, and the walls are

covered with the work of local artists. The seating ranges from comfy couches to tables and chairs where patrons can enjoy bar food and sample an extensive menu of bottled beers plus several homemade brews. A house specialty is Insomnia Coffee Stout, a strong brew made with coffee.

MAGGIE MAE'S
512 Trinity Street
(512) 478-8541
www.maggiemaesaustin.com
This well-known Sixth Street bar has grown with the years from a narrow, single-room pub noted for its live-music offerings (see The Music Scene chapter) to a major presence in the downtown nightlife scene. The pub has taken over adjacent buildings and has a rooftop patio for Sixth Street viewing.

MOTHER EGAN'S IRISH PUB
715 West Sixth Street
(512) 478-7747
www.motheregansirishpub.com
Imperial pints and frozen margaritas—no place but Texas! Mother Egan's has the feel of an Irish pub, with its wooden floors, cozy nooks, and dark paneled walls, but it also has an outdoor deck and large back room where patrons gather for bluegrass Sunday brunches, Celtic music, pub trivia games, and fish-n-chips nights—buy one, get one free.

NORTH BY NORTHWEST RESTAURANT AND BREWERY
10010 North Capital of Texas Highway
(512) 467-6969
www.nxnwbrew.com
Located just behind the Gateway Shopping Center in northwest Austin, this sleek, sophisticated restaurant and bar features several seasonal brews made on the premises. The glass-and-stone surroundings reflect the quality of the food and the on-premises brews. (See our Restaurants chapter.) North by Northwest also offers beer to go.

Texas beers and barbecue are legend; Texas wines have made their way onto top flight menus; and, not to be outdone, Texas vodka is a favorite. Look for Tito's Handmade Vodka on the bar menu. It is made in Austin in the state's "first legal distillery" and has won industry awards, www.titos-vodka.com.

OLD PECAN STREET ALE HOUSE & SOCCER BAR
310 East Sixth Street
(512) 474-6722
www.alehouseaustin.com
The name says it all here at this cozy Sixth Street alley pub, where the emphasis is on soccer. It serves a variety of beers, mixed drinks, and snacks in an old 19th-century building with limestone walls and well-worn floors, cozy seating, and dimmed lighting. The pub's television sets feature national and international soccer games.

OPAL DIVINE'S FREEHOUSE
700 West Sixth Street
(512) 477-3308

3601 South Congress Avenue
(512) 707-0237

12709 North MoPac
(512) 733-5353
www.opaldivines.com
The original Opal's is housed in an old stone building on Sixth Street, next door to Austin's 24-hour deli, Katz's. This pub is named in honor of the owner's ancestor, who apparently enjoyed the good life as represented by pub food, a wide selection of single malt whiskies, and a large variety of beers. Two additional Opal's have opened, one in South Austin, the other north. All three have both indoor and outdoor seating and offer live music several nights a week.

SCHOLZ GARTEN
1607 San Jacinto Boulevard
(512) 474-1958
www.scholzgarten.net

This old German beer garden is many things to many people. In addition to being a popular restaurant (see our Restaurants chapter), a historical landmark, a favorite postgame gathering spot for University of Texas sports fans, and a political watering hole, the old stage in the shaded garden is also a music venue. A variety of live music is offered here. Check local listings in the *Austin Chronicle* and the *Austin American–Statesman*.

UNCLE BILLY'S BREW & QUE
1530 Barton Springs Road
(512) 476-0100
www.unclebillysaustin.com

Brian Peters is a home brewer turned brewmaster with experience gathered at several Austin micro-breweries. Now he is serving up a wide variety of handcrafted beers—his own and other popular local beers—at this South Central Austin barbecue joint-hangout. The outdoor deck is popular and the menu features beer-appropriate noshes like barbecue sliders and all-you-can-eat 'que on Monday. The takeout menu even offers Peters' handcrafted jugs of brew.

WINE BARS

CORK AND CO.
308 Congress Avenue
(512) 474-2675
www.corkandco.com

A welcome addition to the downtown nightlife scene, this wine bar has an affordable happy hour and offers wine tastings for groups, small and large, plus classes in wine selection. There is also a retail shop on the premises.

CRU
238 West Second Street
(512) 472-9463
www.cruwinebar.com

Several businesses in the Second Street District are Austin branches of Dallas and Houston ventures, as is Cru, a popular wine bar. In addition to flights of wine, the bar and cafe offers "sharing plates" that can be paired with specific flights for optimum taste pleasure.

Sixth Street

Long before Jell-o shots and nachos became a staple of the college diet, Austin's Sixth Street was a social hub of the city. When Austinites refer to Sixth Street, they generally mean the stretch of downtown street that runs west from Interstate 35 to Congress Avenue. On any given weekend there are likely to be 20,000 patrons cruising the 7-block area, where more than 30 bars try to entice them with games, shots, Imperial pints, frozen margaritas, music, and tons of nachos. Many of the bars reinvent themselves with fierce regularity, changing names and decor to fit the fad of the moment.

Some of the venerable Sixth Street institutions remain amid the proliferation of shot bars and sports pubs. Esther's Follies (see Comedy Clubs in this chapter) is home to the city's favorite comedy troupe. Other notable survivors include Joe's Generic Bar at 315 East Sixth Street, a comfy bar noted for its blues music. The street is also popular on holiday nights like Mardi Gras, Halloween and New Year's Eve.

VINO AND VINO
4119 Guadalupe Street
(512) 465-9282
www.vinovinotx.com

This Hyde Park wine bar has an Austin vibe, thanks to its location and the neighborhood clientele. The cafe offers a fresh menu, salads and soups, plus sandwiches and light dishes that might include beef carpaccio, salmon gravlax, vegetable *tians*, and cheese plates. There are also several light and delicious desserts.

COFFEEHOUSES

Austin's coffeehouses reflect their surroundings and the city's artistic, kooky, innovative population. Some are funky neighborhood hangouts, others serve as showplaces for local artists, while still others are favored by political activists.

AUSTIN JAVA COMPANY
1206 Parkway
(512) 476-1829
www.austinjava.com
Austin Java Company has a relaxed feel, with picnic tables on the deck outside for those who enjoy a little sunshine with their coffee. Among the house specialties here are Vietnamese coffee, mocha shakes, and mochachinos, little mocha lattes. The cafe has expanded its menu from snacks and pastries and now serves sandwiches, salads, and pasta dishes. Open daily for breakfast, lunch, and dinner. The coffeehouse also offers a late-night menu until 4:00 a.m. on weekends.

BOULDIN CREEK COFFEE HOUSE & CAFE
1501 South First Street
(512) 416-1601
This south-of-the-river coffeehouse caters to the local neighborhoods that are a mix of old and new Austin. The bright green exterior is in step with this part of the city where old Austin funky meets new Austin gentry. Inside old Austin hippie artists lucky enough to have hung on to their once modest, now high-priced homes rub shoulders with techies and lawyers. The cafe also offers an all-day vegetarian menu.

CAFE MUNDI
1704 East Fifth Street
(512) 236-8034
www.cafemundi.com
The *Austin Chronicle,* which is almost mandatory reading in the city's coffeehouses, has described Cafe Mundi as Parisian-like and an oasis. There is a quirkiness about this quiet eastside coffeehouse that sits amidst a small arts district along the abandoned railroad tracks in the city's eastside barrio, near downtown. The menu features the usual wide variety of coffees, chais and teas, plus breakfast, sandwiches, and salads. Small music groups also perform in the garden; the schedule is posted on the cafe's Web site.

CRESCENT CITY BEIGNETS
1211 West Sixth Street
(512) 472-9622
Tucked back from the busy street, this small restaurant is open from early morning to late evening, serving Cajun specialties in addition to those air-filled beignets coated in powdery sugar that are a hallmark of life in New Orleans. The coffee menu also includes that chicory-coffee blend that is a natural accompaniment.

DOLCE VITA GELATO AND ESPRESSO BAR
4222 Duval Street
(512) 323-2686
www.dolcevitagelato.com
The name means "the sweet life," and there are layers of meaning to that phrase for this Hyde Park–area coffeehouse. The menu is rich with sweets, many with an Italian flavor—gelato, sorbet, granitas, tiramisu, cannoli—and there is also a relaxed, easy-living European atmosphere at this neighborhood cafe. The menu also features Italian sodas, coffees, a full bar, and a variety of grappas. Dolce Vita opens early for breakfast and stays open late for after-theater snacks.

FLIGHT PATH COFFEEHOUSE
5011 Duval Street
(512) 458-4472
Old Austin hands know that this small, neighborhood coffeehouse was once in the flight path for planes landing at what used to be the city's

i Many of Austin's coffeehouses are pet-friendly, particularly those with outdoor decks. For a list of where Fido can curl up with a bowl of latte, check out www.dogfriendly.com. Increasingly, Austin restaurants and bars with outdoor spaces are welcoming well-behaved leashed dogs; call ahead first.

main airport, Robert Mueller Airport. Located in the heart of the Hyde Park neighborhood at 51st Street and Duval, the Flight Path is a popular gathering spot for families, students, and artists, some of whom exhibit their work here.

FLIPNOTICS
1601 Barton Springs Road
(512) 480-8646
www.flipnotics.com
If the oversize cafe au lait doesn't make you flip for Flipnotics, nothing will. It is made from whole milk and condensed milk and served in a cup as big as a soup bowl. Not far from Zilker Park (see our Parks and Recreation and Attractions chapters). Flipnotics offers a light menu of sandwiches, muffins and bagels, wine, beer, and coffee, of course. In the evening, local musicians often perform. It is open until midnight every night except Sunday, when it closes at 11:00 p.m.

GREEN MUSE
519 West Oltorf Street
(512) 912-7789
There is a relaxed, laid-back feel to this South Austin java joint not far from the St. Edward's University campus. The exterior is decorated with murals; inside, the couches, bookcases, and assorted tables give the place a true coffeehouse aura—dare we say groovy? There is a patio out back. Light snacks are on the menu. Given its location near St. Ed's, it is busy in the morning. The coffeehouse is open daily and closes at midnight Sunday through Thursday, and 1:00 a.m. on weekends.

JO'S COFFEE
1300 South Congress Avenue
(512) 441-3627
242 West Second Street
(512) 469-9003
www.joscoffee.com
Jo's is a true neighborhood hangout in SoCo where the locals gather to gossip, read, or hang out. The staff at Jo's is tuned into neighborhood happenings and art events. They even conjure up special happenings like the Average Jo's Fashion Show, held in the neighboring Hotel San José

(see our Hotels chapter) parking lot, featuring retro chic clothes and aimed at raising money for animal rescue groups. Success has led to the opening of a second location in the Second Street District.

LITTLE CITY ESPRESSO BAR AND CAFE
916 Congress Avenue
(512) 476-CITY
www.littlecity.com
Just a few blocks from the capitol, Little City has helped give new meaning to the word *avenue*. Little City was among the first downtown cafes to promote the idea of putting tables and chairs on the wide sidewalks that line the city's main street. The cafe serves coffee, tea, juices, granitas, breakfast items like bagels and muffins, and lunch and snack food, including sandwiches and savory pastries. Little City is open until midnight during the week, until 1:00 a.m. on Friday and Saturday, and until 9:00 p.m. on Sunday.

METRO ESPRESSO BAR
2222 Guadalupe Street
(512) 474-5730
This is the only coffeehouse in Austin that is open all the time, and that means the scene is always changing as the customers come and go. The decor is dark and industrial, with an atmosphere that might have existed in a German cafe between the wars. Upstairs is dedicated to smokers who have a hard time finding a place to puff in Austin, given the city's public smoking laws. The menu includes a variety of coffees, including the popular House Rocket Shake, made with Amy's chocolate ice cream.

MOJO'S DAILY GRIND
2714 Guadalupe Street
(512) 477-6656
A coffee shop with a bohemian bent, Mojo's is popular with UT students and campus habitués. The 19th-century-home-turned-cafe is open 24 hours daily except Sunday. The purple neon lights and the giant coffee mug sign mark the spot. Mojo's prides itself on presenting the work of cutting-edge, and sometimes controversial,

artists working in a variety of mediums including photography, painting, and collage. There are also poetry events held at the cafe; check the listings section of the *Austin Chronicle*. The popular house drink is the Iced Mojo, a cold, creamy brew. Munchie offerings include coffeehouse-style eggs steamed at the espresso machine, bagels, muffins, oatmeal, pastries, and empanadas. Beer is also served at Mojo's.

MOZART'S COFFEE ROASTERS
3825 Lake Austin Boulevard
(512) 477-2900
www.mozartscoffee.com
This West Austin cafe, which boasts a large deck overlooking Lake Austin, is a good spot for a late-afternoon cappuccino or a late-night espresso. On Wednesday and Saturday local artists perform contemporary music under the stars on the deck, which seats 350 people. In addition to an extensive coffee bar menu, the cafe also serves iced, herbal, flavored, and chai (soy-based) teas, granitas, Italian soda, pastries, and snacks. There is a juice bar on the premises as well as a bookstore specializing in arts, travel, and literature. Mozart's also roasts and sells a variety of coffee beans. Mozart's is open until midnight during the week and on Sunday, 1:00 a.m. on Friday and Saturday.

QUACK'S 43RD STREET BAKERY
411 East 43rd Street
(512) 453-3399
Quack's, as the UT students call it, is lively and sometimes noisy at night. Quack's offers work areas, however, for aspiring poets and playwrights to plug in their laptops. The cafe hosts a weekly poetry workshop under the auspices of Austin Poets At Large (APAL). The work of local artists is featured on the walls, and classical music plays in the background. Serving breakfast, lunch, and late-night snacks. Quack's is open until 11:00 p.m. daily.

RUTA MAYA COFFEE COMPANY
3601 South Congress Avenue
(512) 707-9637
www.rutamaya.net
If there was a single coffeehouse that captured

the mood and spirit of Austin, it was Ruta Maya, which occupied an old building in the heart of the warehouse district west of Congress Avenue in downtown Austin. The patrons here were a true Austin mix, and on any given night you could see young professionals, aging hippies, Jack Kerouac wannabes, even a spinning yogi chanting mantras on a rotating platform.

Why do we speak in the past tense? Because Ruta Maya closed down at its old location in early 2002, and Austinites held their breath to see if it would maintain its fabled ambience at a new location near St. Edwards University. Some of the funkiness has gone, but the new industrial-style building offers lots of wallspace for art and space for cultural and political gatherings. In fact, then-Vermont Governor Howard Dean held a fundraiser here in October 2003.

Ruta Maya serves coffees produced in Latin America. In 1990 the company was formed to help Latin American farmers sell their products and make a fair return. Ruta Maya Negra Lager Beer, brewed in El Salvador at La Constancia Brewery, is sold at the coffeehouse. In addition to coffee, the cafe serves soups and snacks. There are regular music events and poetry readings. The walls of the coffeehouse are covered in local artwork and notices on all manner of cultural and political events. Ruta Maya is open until 2:00 a.m. on weekends and 1:00 a.m. during the week and on Sunday.

SARADORA'S COFFEEHOUSE & EMPORIUM
101 East Main Street, Round Rock
(512) 310-1200
Not all the coffeehouse action is in Austin. This Round Rock cafe is housed in an old building in the heart of the town's historic district. Local art-

> **i** Austin touts itself as the Music Capital of the World, so why not join the party? Austin Karaoke, 6808 North Lamar Boulevard, (512) 323-9822, www.austin karaoke.com, rents "designer karaoke" rooms so the whole gang can embarrass themselves in private, BYOB.

ists sell their jewelry and artwork here, and there is live music several nights a week. Saradora's is open until 10:00 p.m. during the week and midnight on Friday and Saturday, and until 6:00 p.m. on Sunday.

SPIDER HOUSE
2908 Fruth Street
(512) 480-9562
www.spiderhousecafe.com
This coffeehouse just north of the University of Texas campus is packed with old stuff—not really antiques and not really junk, just old stuff like Christmas lights and soft drink machines, old radios, and a miscellany of chairs and tables. The large outdoor deck is a stage for local musicians. Late-night noshes include tamales and pasta dishes.

COMEDY CLUBS

Austin is well known as a funny place—especially when the State Legislature is in session. There is not a session that goes by without some Texas legislator making national headlines for offering one wacky proposal or another.

Visitors will find political humor is high on the agenda at local comedy outposts, notably Esther's Follies, a longtime Austin troupe that takes aim at both local and national politicians. There are only a handful of nightclubs dedicated to comedy alone, but a few of the city's live music venues also take a comedy break now and then. That list expands greatly during the annual Big Stinkin' International Improv and Sketch Comedy festival held in April each year (see our Annual Events and Festivals chapter).

CAPITOL CITY COMEDY CLUB
8120 Research Boulevard
(512) 467-2333
www.capcitycomedy.com
This Northwest Austin club has pulled in some of the big names in comedy, including Ellen DeGeneres, Jeff Foxworthy, and Bobcat Goldthwait. While nationally known comics appear on Friday and Saturday nights, up-and-coming

comedians, including local talent, are featured on other nights.

ESTHER'S FOLLIES/ESTHER'S POOL
525 East Sixth Street
(512) 320-0553
www.esthersfollies.com
Like Barton Springs and the old Armadillo World Headquarters, Esther's Follies is part of the fabric of Austin. The comedy troupe performs every Thursday, Friday, and Saturday at Esther's Pool on Sixth Street on a stage where the backdrop is three floor-to-ceiling windows looking out on the street. The audience can watch the antics of the troupe and their interactions with the passersby on Sixth Street.

Esther's is named for Esther Williams, the actress and water ballet artist who made all those swimming movies in the 1950s. The group took that name in the 1970s when they performed skits between music sets at another legendary spot, Liberty Lunch. Founders Michael Shelton and Shannon Sedwick (he is co-owner of Esther's and the announcer, she is a star of the troupe and co-owner) say they chose the name because the troupe would perform in the Texas heat wearing swimsuits and get cooled by the stage sprinklers.

Satire and outrageous, campy comedy are the troupe's mainstays. National and local politicians are spoofed, caricatured, and mimicked. (Before you go you might want to brush up on local and state issues in our Politics and Perspectives chapter.) The show changes routines regularly and puts on special holiday shows, so repeat visitors are never disappointed. There are no reservations taken, and on Friday and Saturday it is wise to arrive early to ensure a seat. Performances are at 8:00 p.m. on Thursday and 8:00 p.m. and 10:00 p.m. Friday and Saturday. Tickets are $18 for students, seniors, and military on weeknights, $20 open seating general admission.

THE HIDEOUT
617 Congress Avenue
(512) HIDEOUT
www.thehideouttheater.com
There are two theater stages where everything

from comedy classes to ghost tours are offered. Improv and parody nights are popular also.

VELVEETA ROOM
521 East Sixth Street
(512) 469-9116
www.thevelveetaroom.com
If Esther's Follies is the jewel in the crown of the Austin comedy scene, then the Velveeta Room is the jester. Housed on Sixth Street, next door to Esther's Pool, local and visiting comic talent try out some of their more outrageous and irreverent routines here. Sketches and improvisations are performed Thursday, Friday, and Saturday nights. There is a $6 admission charge.

DANCE CLUBS AND NIGHTCLUBS

Whether it is the Texas two-step, salsa, merengue, swing, even the Lindy hop, there is a club in Austin where dancers can strut their stuff. Even disco, heaven forbid, is alive and well as the 20-something crowd explores retro fashions. Those looking for a Texas experience should consider visiting one of the city's country dance spots, notably the Broken Spoke, which has been described as the best example of a Texas honky-tonk in Austin. But don't miss out on another important cultural experience: dancing to the Latino beat, ranging from tango to Tejano.

THE 311 CLUB
311 East Sixth Street
(512) 477-1630
An old favorite on Sixth Street featuring blues music. The old-style bar attracts a diverse crowd, and there are open-mic nights when the regulars can sing the blues.

i Want to experience a real Texas country dance hall? Head for The Coupland Dance Hall (512-856-2226, www.coupland dancehall.com) on Highway 95 between Taylor and Elgin, east of Austin. On weekends this old dance hall is "just a two-step back in time," as its slogan says.

ATOMIC CAFE
705 Red River Street
(512) 457-0644
The outside of this downtown nightclub looks as grungy as the inside, but that is part of its charm for the metalhead fans who gather here. The club serves up hard rock nightly, and there are special fetish nights for those who want to show off their chains, piercings, and tattoos.

AZUCAR
Fourth and Colorado Streets
(512) 478-5650
Salsa and merengue continue to be hot trends on the Austin dance scene. This downtown club touts itself as "the only 100 percent salsa and merengue club" in Austin. Salsa is not only an exotic way to get a great physical workout, it can be a good opportunity to spot some of the city's "stars," since many of the Hollywood types enjoy a salsa workout when they are in town, notably film star Sandra Bullock.

BROKEN SPOKE
3201 South Lamar Boulevard
(512) 442-6189
www.brokenspokeaustintx.com
An original honky-tonk that merits the description "legendary" (hence its inclusion in The Music Scene chapter), the Spoke is also a great place to dance a little, drink a little, and eat a lot. There is live music here Tuesday through Saturday, and the cover charges vary. The low ceiling, the tall men in big hats, and the wooden dance floor give this place the feel of an authentic Texas roadhouse. No visit to Austin should end without dropping by the Spoke in South Austin for a longneck.

CLUB CARNAVAL
2237 East Riverside Drive
(512) 444-6396
Southeast of downtown, along East Riverside Drive, there are several authentic Hispanic nightclubs that celebrate Mexican-American and Latin dance traditions. Club Carnaval is noted for its

i The Capital City Murder Mystery Theatre appears at various restaurants around Austin offering a dinner theater experience. The group also performs at private parties. Call (512) 404-9123 or visit www.capcitymystery.com for more information.

norteño dances, which originated in Northern Mexico and flourish in South Texas. Male dancers don Western wear, including large belt buckles, tight pressed jeans, and white cowboy hats, while the women dance in full skirts or jeans and Western shirts. Some of the top names in norteño music play here in a setting that has an Aztec motif. In addition to norteño music, the club also features salsa, Tejano, merengue, and *cumbia* music. Cover charges vary.

COPA BAR AND GRILL
217 Congress Avenue
(512) 479-5002
www.copabarandgrill.com
During the daytime, Copa is a lunchtime spot with a Tex-Mex flavor, but at night it turns into a nightclub swinging to a Latin beat. The Copa also offers salsa lessons several times a week. Patrons tend to be to "dressy" in their attire and there is a cover fee.

DESPERADO'S
9515 North Lamar Boulevard
(512) 834-2640
There are several different kinds of Latino music, but the homegrown kind here in Texas is called Tejano—the state was, after all, named "Tejas" when it was part of Mexico. The music has a fast-paced swing, a sort of cross between country and salsa. The outfit of choice celebrates the "vaquero," the northern Mexican cowboy whose dress influenced cowboys north of the border. Both men and women wear cowboy boots and the men wear cowboy hats, while the women wear either Western-style skirts or jeans. This 11,000-square-foot dance club has three full-service bars.

EL BORINQUEN
2728 South Congress Avenue
(512) 443-4252
This tiny restaurant and bar re-creates the atmosphere of Old San Juan. The food and drinks are Puerto Rican, as are many of the customers, but the dance floor also draws a diverse crowd that enjoys dancing to salsa and merengue sounds on Friday and Saturday nights.

ELEMENT NIGHTCLUB
301 West Fifth Street
(512) 480-9888
This Warehouse District club rocks on after 2:00 a.m., the time when Texas bars close down. Whatever the latest dance craze is you will find it here, and the 1,600-square-foot dance floor is packed into the wee hours. The goal, the owners say, is to create a "hip, big city club," and to that end they have spent $2 million renovating the joint.

FLAMINGO CANTINA
515 East Sixth Street
(512) 494-9336
www.flamingocantina.com
The Flamingo gets consistently good reviews for the bands that it books, and the club also offers rock and reggae that keep the place packed on weekends. The decor and the sounds are designed to evoke the Caribbean with a grass-thatched roof over the stage and pictures of Bob Marley on the walls. There is an upstairs open-air deck where you can dance under the stars.

MENEO
217 Congress Avenue
(512) 479-5002
A combination Mexican restaurant and dance club, this Congress Avenue club features a variety of music including merengue, salsa, and Mexican rock. Customers dress in stylized salsa fashion with women wearing incredibly high heels and sexy skirts. When not dancing, they are drinking the house bombaritas. On the weekends there is also live mariachi music to set the mood. Happy hour features a free food buffet.

MIGUEL'S LA BODEGA
415 Colorado Street
(512) 472-2369
Miguel's is the hot spot in the downtown Warehouse District for the Latino dance scene. Salsa and merengue rule here, and the uninitiated can take midweek lessons on the premises. Live bands on the weekends provide a constant salsa beat, and just to make sure you stay in a south-of-the-border mood, the club serves a Latino menu.

PARADOX
311 East Fifth Street
(512) 469-7615
The *Austin Chronicle* calls this Sixth Street–area club the "Wal-Mart of dance clubs," suggesting it is both popular and cheap. It is always packed on the weekends and is popular with the college crowd. Paradox also stays open after the bars close at 2:00 a.m. The Wal-Mart designation aside, there is a dress code here (primarily on Friday and Saturday). Guys may get turned away at the door if their jeans are too ragged or their T-shirts have gaping holes.

SPEAKEASY
412 Congress Avenue
(512) 476-8017
www.speakeasy.com
Listed in The Music Scene chapter, Speakeasy is also a classy spot for a martini or glass of wine. Housed in one of Congress Avenue's older buildings, recently a used appliance store, the renovation has produced one of the fancier nightspots. A mezzanine overlooks the dance floor, and an old elevator has been restored to give the club that '20s feel. The whole place has a Prohibition theme, hence the emphasis on jazz and gin.

TEJANO RANCH
7601 North Lamar Boulevard
(512)- 834-2640
www.tejanoranchaustin.com
Tejano music is designed for dancing, and some of the biggest acts in the genre appear at this North Austin nightclub, notably on the weekends.

The crowd here is generally older than 30 and familiar with the Tejano scene. The club has a South Texas atmosphere with neon mustangs outside and a large Selena mural inside, plus the chairs are covered in cowhide.

VICCI
404 Colorado Street
(512) 762- 7799
www.vicciaustin.com
Anyone with real memories of the Disco Age is likely to be glad the age has passed, and so has Polly Ester's, the retro dance club that occupied this spot in the Warehouse District. In its place is Vicci, a Las Vegas–style homage to Italian sophistication—even the bouncers wear silk suits here. One of a growing number of clubs in Austin with a dress code: no flip-flops or baseball caps here, and even jeans are discouraged. You will feel more comfortable in a dress, the Web site advises female patrons. There are VIP areas and the luxurious DiLusso Lounge in the basement. Open Thursday, Friday, and Saturday.

GAY NIGHTCLUB SCENE

The gay nightlife scene in Austin seems to divide into two categories—sophisticated downtown clubs where beautiful people gather and country swing clubs. However, there are also a couple of neighborhood bars that offer relaxing atmosphere after work hours.

1920'S CLUB
918 Congress Avenue
(512) 479-7979
This Congress Avenue club, 3 blocks south of the capitol, has a '20s theme. Dubbed a "speakeasy," the club features jazz music and martinis, but there is also a food menu.

'BOUT TIME
9601 North Interstate 35
(512) 832-5339
www.bouttimeaustin.com
Gay patrons, both men and women, are attracted

to this nightclub that aims for a neighborhood tavern theme. Indoors there are pool tables and darts, while outdoors there are sand volleyball courts. The bar also features a big-screen television and video games.

BOYZ CELLAR
213 West Fourth Street
(512) 479-8482
www.boyzcellar.com
This warehouse district club has two bars and a large dance floor. The club also features strippers, movie nights, and special musical events.

CHAIN DRIVE
504 Willow Street
(512) 480-9017
www.chain-drive.com
This Central Austin bar is described as Austin's only "leather bar," but this is soft and cuddly leather. Chain Drive is headquarters for a group calling itself the Heart of Texas Bears, a self-described social group for masculine, bearded, and/or hairy gay men and their admirers. The bar has pool tables and a small dance floor and is open daily from early afternoon until 2:00 a.m.

CHARLIE'S
1301 Lavaca Street
(512) 474-6481
www.charliesaustin.com
A longtime fixture on the gay scene, Charlie's is noted for its clubby atmosphere and party mood on weekends plus drag contests that include an annual Cher look-alike contest. On Sunday night, the downtown club hosts drag shows, while on Tuesday the steak and chicken dinners draw crowds. There is a dance floor, dartboards, pool

i A good source for gossip about the gay nightlife scene in Austin is "The Gay Place" column in the *Austin Chronicle*. The column is a play on the title of the classic Texas novel by Billie Lee Brammer, which was all about old-style Austin politics, not sexuality.

tables, two bars, and television sets for special programming. The outdoor patio is a popular gathering spot when the weather cooperates.

DICK'S DEJA DISCO
113 San Jacinto Boulevard
(512) 457-8010
The gay and lesbian community comes to this downtown club to kick up its collective heels and dance to the top country sounds or the retro sounds of disco music.

OILCAN HARRY'S
211 West Fourth Street
(512) 320-8823
www.oilcanharrys.com
Some have dubbed this Warehouse District bar a neighborhood bar for Austin's gay, beautiful set. Named as one of the top 50 clubs in the world by *Out* magazine, the large bar is a major feature of the club, but the dance floor with its fog machine is the focal point. A patio in the back of the club offers a retreat from the frenzy of the dance floor. Although the majority of the customers are gay, straight patrons also enjoy the atmosphere here—and the dancing. Open 2:00 a.m. to 2:00 p.m. daily.

MOVIES

Check the daily *Austin American–Statesman* and the weekly *Austin Chronicle* for featured movies. The following movie houses feature classic, foreign, and independent films.

ALAMO DRAFT HOUSE
320 East Sixth Street
(512) 476-1320

ALAMO DRAFT HOUSE LAKE CREEK
13729 Research Boulevard
(512) 219-5408

ALAMO DRAFT HOUSE VILLAGE
2700 Anderson Lane
(512) 476-1320

ALAMO DRAFT HOUSE SOUTH
1120 South Lamar Boulevard
(512) 476-1320
www.drafthouse.com

Tired of sitting in movie theaters where the average age of the audience is younger than your family dog? Try the Alamo Draft House, where there is no sticky Coke on the floor and munchie choices go beyond dill pickles and Butterfingers. The original Warehouse District movie theater is now a nightclub, but the old Alamo movie theater was transformed into a concept that has spread throughout the city. Creators decided to feature cult favorites and classics, everything from beach movies to horror flicks served in a nightclub setting where patrons could order beer, wine, and food to accompany the evening's celluloid offerings. The Alamo creators took that concept to three other locations around the city, salvaging old movie houses like the Ritz on Sixth Street. On the weekends there are midnight flicks and sometimes the movie house puts on special presentations, such as a presentation of the movie *Like Water for Chocolate* featuring dishes mentioned in the book. Some of the best independent movies can be found playing in Alamo theaters, also, and if you want a movie at your next party rent the "Alamo Rolling Road Show," a huge 20x40 foot inflatable screen.

DOBIE THEATRE
2021 Guadalupe Street
(512) 472-FILM (3456)
www.landmarktheatres.com

If you're looking for an independent release, foreign film, or art movie, check out the listings for this UT campus-area movie complex. The Dobie is housed in the large and ugly tower at the southern end of The Drag that serves as a residence hall and shopping center for students. Richard Linklater screened *Slacker* here.

PARAMOUNT THEATRE FOR THE PERFORMING ARTS
713 Congress Avenue
(512) 472-5411
www.austintheatrealliance.org

The beautifully restored theater on the city's main avenue hosts a summer film festival featuring the great classics of Hollywood. Also, given Austin's emergence as a movie-making venue, premieres are held at the downtown theater.

THE MUSIC SCENE

If this chapter were set to the tune of Austin music, the savory sounds of country, blues, folk, funk, punk, pop, jazz, bluegrass, Tejano, and rock 'n' roll would waft off these pages and fill the air like a Saturday night on Sixth Street. While we can't reproduce the sounds, we can tell you about some of the artists, the venues, the free concerts, and the record stores that constitute the Live Music Capital of the World. So whether you're a music lover eager to explore the sounds of Austin or you've arrived with a guitar on your back and a pocketful of songs, get ready to enter a truly remarkable realm.

No matter what you may have heard about Austin's live music scene, there really is nothing that prepares newcomers for the jolt of firsthand experience. Music is, indeed, here, there, and everywhere in Austin. On any given Friday night, music lovers can choose from among well over 90 venues offering just about any style of music you can imagine, including those exotic strains created by our true Texas hybrids. No weekend-warrior music mentality exists here, however, as our club scene rocks seven nights a week. From national touring shows and top local acts to the most exciting up-and-coming artists and youngsters (some barely past puberty) taking the stage for the very first time, Austin is tuned in to music.

You'll find live music in record stores and bookstores. There's live music to accompany your Sunday brunch and live music to stir your evening coffee. Austin's premier gourmet grocery offers live music at its two locations on the patio (see our Close-up on Central Market in the Shopping chapter). You can listen to live music in our museums and art galleries, and there's live music in our parks and on our sidewalks. Austin's Sixth Street is an entire district dedicated to live music and dance halls, while our own nationally televised music TV show has celebrated Austin music for nearly a quarter of a century. *Austin City Limits,* which has been called the city's cultural calling card to the world, is Austin's top showcase for musical talent. Every spring, our city also hosts one of the most important live music festivals in the country, South by Southwest (see our Close-up in the Annual Events and Festivals chapter), as well as the ever-popular Austin City Limits Festival in the fall.

Though Austin took the motto "The Live Music Capital of the World" in the early 1990s, it gained prominence long before that as a haven for artists seeking to follow their own music and create their own sounds without much interference from the commercial establishment based in L.A., New York, and Nashville. *Billboard* magazine has called Austin a "mecca for musical mavericks," saying Austin is known as "a creative oasis, a place that puts music first and career far behind." While it's true that many artists are drawn to Austin for its no-strings-attached spirit, so to speak, it is also true that some current and former Austin regulars have found the magic formula that cracks the charts, including Willie Nelson, the late Stevie Ray Vaughan, Pat Green, Shawn Colvin, Jerry Jeff Walker, Christopher Cross, Fastball, and others.

In fact, Austin is one of the few cities in the United States where young musicians can go from learning to play, to having a garage band, to performing in a club, to burning their own CDs, to getting an independent record contract, to earning a major-label deal without ever moving their base of operations.

Austin's music scene appears as dynamic today as ever, as more and more young musicians pour into town seeking the freedom to explore their music and the comfort of Austin's appreciative audiences. The constantly changing array of artists onstage—our classic legends and old mainstays combined with young newcomers and emerging talents—renews Austin's status as a musical mecca each and every night. So whether you prefer a lone singer onstage strumming a folk tune on an acoustic guitar or a 10-piece band rocking off the roof, you'll find that Austin has a sound all its own—the sound of originality.

CATCH 'EM IF YOU CAN

With an entire city of musical artists determined to travel to the beat of their own drummers, it's no wonder Austin offers so many choices for the music lover. A city that re-establishes itself as the world's live music capital seven nights a week makes it hard on those of us trying to assemble a list of all the must-see acts. There are just so many talented musicians worthy of mention. The artists listed here are among Austin's favorites, but don't think for a minute that this list is all-inclusive. A little experimentation and willingness to explore the live music scene will bring its own reward. We've called this section Catch 'em if You Can because Austin's favorite artists are often the most in demand for concerts around the country and around the world. So catch them while they're here. You can't go wrong.

Asleep at the Wheel: Led by founder/ singer/ songwriter/guitarist Ray Benson, Asleep at the Wheel has perhaps done more to preserve and expand the Western Swing sound popularized by the legendary Bob Wills than any other band. From the group's 1973 debut record *Coming Right at Ya* to its recent release, *Asleep at the Wheel* with the Fort Worth Symphony Orchestra, this nine-time Grammy-winning band has continued to impress fans with its fiddle- and steel guitar– driven sound.

ℹ️ *Austin City Limits* is moving to a new, bigger location just north of City Hall, so eventually tickets to the live tapings might not be as hard to come by as they are now. The new digs are set to open in early 2010. When not in use by ACL, the theater will host live acts.

Asylum Street Spankers: *Spanks for the Memories* is our favorite CD title by this seven-piece band that eschews demon electricity in favor of an all-acoustic, string-dominated sound. But with a host of musical voices and a gaggle of instruments among them, who needs a speaker blasting at ya?

Austin Lounge Lizards: With song titles that include "Jesus Loves Me (But He Can't Stand You)," "Put the Oak Ridge Boys in the Slammer," and "Shallow End of the Gene Pool," it's no wonder this group has earned a reputation for its inventive, and quite entertaining, style of satirical bluegrass.

Marcia Ball: *CD Review* called Ball's 1994 release, *Blue House*, "another gusto-filled collection of tunes informed by the grit of Texas honky-tonk, the stomp of Louisiana Delta rhythms, and the soul of New Orleans–style blues." This piano-playing dynamo with a full-bodied, earthy voice continues to enchant audiences across the country.

Lou Ann Barton: It's the voice that gets 'em every time. Austin blues luminary Lou Ann Barton's full-throated voice and scorching onstage performances have been packing clubs in Austin and around the country for years. *Rolling Stone* called her "the most commanding white female belter to erupt out of Texas since Janis Joplin—a singer to whom, in terms of vocal sophistication and emotion, Barton is far, far superior."

Black Joe Lewis: J.J. Lewis, known by his stage name Black Joe, is a rising star on Austin's soul music scene. This young man was inspired by blues greats of the past, but has a sound all his own.

Boombox ATX: With the release of its first CD, *Feel the Boombox,* in 2007, this multi-faceted band finally came together. Although it often is categorized as a hip-hop group (and won a 2007–2008 Austin Music Award in that category), there is something more to these guys. Playing a little bit of jazz and a lot of funk-infused hip-hop, they have been described as "Earth, Wind & Fire meets hip-hop." Most recently they have had a steady Tuesday night gig at Austin Lucky's Lounge, so catch'em if you can.

Junior Brown: There are guitar players—and then there are GUITAR players. Junior Brown couldn't find an instrument that could produce the sounds his mind was hearing—so he invented one. With his deep voice and trademark double-neck "guit-steel," a combination six-string and steel guitar, Brown produces a sound he calls "free-range country," and his fans call just plain out of sight. His music has been labeled country/rock, alternative country, and whatever else label-makers can think of.

Stephen Bruton: Inducted into the Texas Music Hall of Fame in 2003, this guy has done it all since his guitar talents were discovered by Kris Kristofferson in Bruton's hometown of Fort Worth. Kristofferson, who called Bruton "one very devil on the guitar," added the young musician to his band back in 1972 while Bruton was still in his 20s. Since then, Bruton has performed two years as lead guitarist for Bonnie Raitt, written a slew of great songs, and spent much of his professional life as a journeyman guitarist and session player.

Gary Clark Jr.: If blues is your thing, you can't go wrong seeing a show headlining Clark. *Texas Music* magazine has called him "probably the most talented Texas guitarist since a certain SRV." He's a movie actor, too.

W. C. Clark: Few living artists epitomize Austin blues better than W. C. Clark. Born on Austin's east side on November 16, 1939, Clark developed his musical style playing bass and then guitar with the likes of T. B. Bell and Blues Boy Hubbard

at the landmark Victory Grill, Charlie's Playhouse, and other black blues clubs of the era.

Shawn Colvin: With *A Few Small Repairs,* Austin's gem of the New Folk scene solidified her reputation as an important singer/songwriter. Colvin's first platinum album, *Repairs,* produced the single "Sunny Came Home," which won two 1997 Grammys for Record of the Year and Song of the Year and proved to the world what her fans have known all along: This songwriter can play the guitar and owns a set of provocative pipes to boot.

Alvin Crow: At home in Carnegie Hall as much as in honky-tonks and clubs around the country and in Europe, this classically trained musician, who earned a seat with the Oklahoma City Symphony as its youngest violinist, is one of Austin's great fiddlers in the Western Swing tradition of Bob Wills and the Texas Playboys.

Del Castillo: "Our music is kind of like the band, we all come with our own influences," Del Castillo percussionist Mark Holeman once told the *Austin Chro*nicle. "We got a Gipsy Kings/flamenco groove, but then we've got this Steven Tyler–Mick Jagger lead singer out there. It was either going to work or be the biggest train wreck of our lives. Luckily for us, it works." Austin agrees. This six-member Spanish-language band has taken home a slew of Austin Music awards

The Derailers: Combining the country sounds of Buck Owens, Merle Haggard, and others of the Bakersfield Sound era with influences of rock, R&B, and pop, the Derailers are making a major contribution to the music scene in Austin, and now around the country.

The Eggmen: When you just want to hear your favorite radio tunes, you can't go wrong with The Eggmen. The six-member group has been voted Austin's favorite cover band.

Alejandro Escovedo: It's hard to believe that a guy who launched his musical career by playing in his own student film about a rock band that couldn't play could have come so far. His songs, according to his biography, "blend lyrical strings and woodwinds with the gritty sound of crunching, sawed-off guitars and pumping pianos." We couldn't have said it better.

Roky Erickson: When we began this listing back in the 1990s, we never thought we would be including this giant of the 1960s Austin music scene. (See The Music Biz Close-up). Erickson, whose band, 13th Floor Elevators, was one of the seminal groups of that era, suffered mental difficulties and dropped out of sight for decades. But in the late 2000s Erickson staged what the *Statesman* called "one of the most improbable comebacks in music history," winning the *Chronicle*'s 2008 Musician of the Year award. We're not sure how much he will be performing now, but catch him if you can—and find out for yourselves what all the fuss is about.

Fastball: This pop trio had been paying its dues—writing the songs and driving the required hundreds of miles to gigs where a handful of folks, not fans per se, would show up. Then in 1998 Fastball became an overnight sensation with the release of the trio's second album, *All the Pain Money Can Buy,* which *CMJ New Music Monthly* called "measurably more ambitious than the punk-inspired, straightforward pop that had made the trio a local favorite in Austin."

The Flatlanders: The flatlands of West Texas have produced some of our state's most inspired musicians. Buddy Holly, Roy Orbison, and Waylon Jennings all hail from that sparse outpost of pure Texas. In 1972 Jimmie Dale Gilmore and fellow Lubbock singer/songwriters Joe Ely and Butch Hancock formed a little acoustic band called the Flatlanders and recorded *One Road More* in Nashville. When the album fizzled, so did the band. Little did they know the album was to become a collector's item. It was later rereleased under the more appropriate title *More a Legend Than a Band.* All three went on to form successful solo careers and got together once in a while for a show or

two. Fans everywhere got a real treat when the Flatlanders reunited in 2001 for shows across the United States and over into Europe. The three have been performing gigs together ever since. They also make musical magic in records and performances as solo artists—so catch them if you can.

Ruthie Foster: This Texas-born and -raised singer/songwriter has a voice that embodies the Lone Star State in so many ways. A hybrid of blues, gospel, roots, and folk music flows like a backcountry stream whenever she opens her mouth in song.

Kevin Fowler Band: This hot Austin band plays the real stuff: traditional country music that its leader says is for "pickup driving, Wrangler wearing, everyday working-class people like me."

Davíd Garza: "His future's so bright, he's gotta wear shades." That's what the *Austin American–Statesman* said, quoting Austin group Timbuk3 about this pop singer/songwriter following the release of his 1998 major-label debut *This Euphoria.* His music, rooted in quirky yet alluring rock/pop melodies and lyrics, is sort of early Beatles but freshened for the times.

The Geezinslaws: This musical act has become one of Austin's favorite country music attractions. Sammy Allred and Dewayne "Son" Smith, both native Austinites, have been performing together since high school—that would be more than 50 years by our estimate.

Ghostland Observatory: This rockin', experimental duo of front man Aaron Behrens and producer/drummer Thomas Turner has released its third CD, *Robotique Majestique,* and is wowing audiences at home and around the country. Their live performances are inspired.

The Gourds: The music of Austin's rollickin', good-timin' country/rock band is just impossible to describe. No one can ever tell quite where it's going, but everyone knows they're having a grand time anyway. They've been making dang good music around these parts—and around the country—for some time now.

Pat Green: Green's second major-label album, 2003's *Wave on Wave,* which hit No. 1 on Country Music Television's Top 20 Countdown, and an appearance on *Austin City Limits* helped his well-deserved fame spread beyond the Texas border, and now he's packing auditoriums all over the place. His music is personal, and he's found success by doing things his own way.

Patty Griffin: *Billboard* magazine called Griffin's 2002 album, *1,000 Kisses,* "the most magnetic album yet by one of the most compelling recording artists in popular music." Of course, her legions of fans here in Austin and across the country were already well aware of this singer/songwriter's amazing talents. Griffin is a three-time Grammy nominee.

Sara Hickman: A superb live performer, Hickman is an acoustic rock 'n' roller who mixes folk sweetness with open-eyed humor—and not just a touch of mischievousness. This is another Austin artist who breaks the female singer/songwriter mold—due, perhaps, to the fact that she is inspired by all kinds of music.

Tish Hinojosa: Born the last of 13 first-generation Mexican-American children, Leticia "Tish" Hinojosa is a bilingual singer/songwriter with a remarkable ability to weave both languages into her songs. Her rich-textured music and poetic lyrics have earned her a place in Texas music history.

Eric Johnson: Guitar-player extraordinaire and Grammy Award winner Eric Johnson is one of those rare Austin musicians who actually was born here. This tall Texan won his Grammy in 1991 for Best Rock Instrumental Performance for his song "Cliffs of Dover" on the *Ah Via Musicom* album, which proved to the country that lyrics aren't an essential part of rock music. Johnson also sings and writes, but guitar is his forte.

Jimmy LaFave: LaFave's talents as a singer, songwriter, and guitarist have catapulted him to the top ranks of Austin musicians. This poetic lyricist with a wonderfully raspy voice alternates easily between rock numbers and romantic ballads. While he has many CDs, it's still much more fun to see him perform live.

Los Lonely Boys: "Texican rock 'n' roll." That's how this young rock/blues/country/Mexican band describes its unique sound. This hit trio, which composes original songs in both English and Spanish, is made up of the Garza brothers: Henry (guitar), JoJo (bass), and Ringo (drums, of course).

James McMurtry: If that last name sounds familiar to all you fans of the books *Lonesome Dove* and other modern classics by novelist Larry McMurtry, you're on the right track. James is the author's son. This McMurtry, however, has taken a different writing path. As a singer/songwriter known for his intelligent, narrative-oriented rock 'n' roll songs, McMurtry tells stories his own way.

Trish Murphy: A former member, with her brother, of the Trish & Darin group, one of Houston's successful club bands, Murphy went solo in 1995 and has since become one of Austin's most popular singer/songwriters. Look, too, for her band Skyrocket.

Willie Nelson: Willie turned 75 in 2008, but he doesn't appear to be slowing down at all, performing at various venues in Austin throughout the year. Nelson released his four-disc, career-spanning CD, *One Hell of a Ride,* in 2008. His musical style? Do you have to ask?

Okkervil River: *The Chronicle* called Okkervil River's 2007 album *The Stage Names* "a poignant pop masterpiece." This band tours constantly, but stopped home long enough to pick up a 2008 Austin Music Award for Best Indie Band—and perform in the show.

Omar & the Howlers: This dynamite rockin' blues band is one of those quintessential Austin groups that just shouldn't be missed.

Patrice Pike: *Rolling Stone* magazine said, "She's Tina Turner, Bessie Smith, Janis Joplin, and Robert Plant all wrapped up in a tiny but explosive package." The result is a glorious sound all her own. But don't take our word for it. Pike won the overall grand prize in the 2004 USA Songwriting Competition, and was a top-seven finalist in CBS's *Rockstar Supernova*. She tours 24/7, but does make regular appearances at Austin clubs.

Reckless Kelly: "Reckless Kelly . . . could do for alternative-country what Nirvana did for grunge," according to the *Houston Chronicle*. Austin remains impressed with this longstanding quintet, awarding it several Austin Music Awards.

Bob Schneider: The driving force behind several distinctly unique and very popular Austin party bands, Schneider launched a solo career with the self-released CD *Lonelyland* a few years ago—and continues to be a hot live act around the city—and the country. His latest band, Bob Schneider & the Texas Bluegrass Massacre, was voted Best Performing Bluegrass Band at the 2007–2008 Austin Music Awards.

Charlie and Will Sexton: These two brothers, both of whom made major-label record deals when they were just teenagers and then spent more than a decade each developing separate musical identities, are great performers and worth waiting for.

South Austin Jug Band: The South Austin quintet gets its name from the Muppets movie, *Emmett Otter's Jug-Band Christmas*. Now that we've settled that, how about the music? We'll

i An Austin smoking ban prohibits smoking inside restaurants and even bars and clubs. Smokers usually go outside of the venue to light up—or they choose clubs that feature outdoor decks and terraces.

i Want to find out whether one of the Catch 'em bands, or one of your own favorites, is playing in Austin? Use the *Chronicle*'s search engine, www.austin chronicle.com. Type in the band's name and click on the calendar above. For info on local acts, check out the Austin Musicians Database at www.austinchronicle.com/amdb.

just let them describe it: "Call the music . . . whatever you like: bluegrass or newgrass, neo-jug, acoustic country-folk, Texas roots unplugged, swinging Lone Star beatnik country, or anything else that strikes you." However you describe it, the music works.

Darden Smith: UT alumnus Darden Smith is a singer/songwriter who, like Lyle Lovett, had a hard time finding his niche. His sound strongly reflects his Austin folk scene roots—more acoustic rock and ballads—in which the story is the heart of it all.

Spoon: Currently playing at sold-out shows around the country, Spoon took home the most awards at the 2007–2008 Austin Music Awards, including Band of the Year and Album of the Year (*Ga Ga Ga Ga Ga*). Led by songwriter Britt Daniel, this four-man rock band might be hard to find in Austin, but the search is worth it.

The Strange Boys: This quartet is starting to make an impact on the local music scene with its garage rock and pop music. Catch 'em before they really take off.

Jimmie Vaughan: Vaughan was a teenage rock star in Dallas when the Beatles first ruled the world, opened for Jimi Hendrix in Houston, and partied with Janis Joplin just about everywhere else—all before he was 20. Since those days, Vaughan has managed to become a virtual deity—"a living legend with a guitar style so deep that it defies description," according to *Guitar Player* magazine. If you happen to be in town when the blues legend is performing, your trip is made.

(Q) Close-Up

Two Voices: Willie Nelson and Stevie Ray Vaughan

The Red-Headed Stranger has turned gray before our eyes. The Guitar God will remain forever young in our minds. One became guru of Austin's explosive country rock movement. A decade later, the other put Austin blues on the map. Twenty-one years apart in age, Willie Nelson and Stevie Ray Vaughan were both on the run when they discovered Austin in the early 1970s. Their timing couldn't have been better. Austin was perched to take the music world by storm. (See our Close-up on The Music Biz in this chapter.)

Although Patsy Cline had recorded Willie's monumental song "Crazy" in Nashville and took it to No. 1 on the charts in 1961 and Willie himself had made his Grand Ole Opry debut in 1964, Nashville never warmed up to him as a performer. When his Tennessee home burned to the ground in 1970, the 37-year-old musical outlaw decided to return to his native Texas. Here, at least, he wouldn't be tormented for refusing to bend with the winds of Nashville musical fashion—and certainly no one would bother him if he wanted to grow his hair long or tie a red bandana hippie-style around his forehead.

Stevie, a scrawny 17-year-old with a blossoming drug habit when he hit town in 1972, had determined that music would be his ticket out of the stifling prison of high school and the working-class Dallas suburb of Oak Cliff. "For a Dallas kid bound and determined to play guitar for a living, moving to Austin was better than dying and going to heaven," wrote Joe Nick Patoski and Bill Crawford in their book, *Stevie Ray Vaughan: Caught in the Crossfire.*

By August 12, 1972, when Willie first appeared onstage at the Armadillo World Headquarters, it was obvious he had something. In 1973 the Nashville exile recorded his breakthrough album, *Shotgun Willie.* Austin, meanwhile, became the epicenter of a trail-blazing movement in country music as other artists battered by the music establishment found themselves drawn by the city's mounting musical charm. Alternately labeled progressive country, country rock, and redneck rock—because radio stations, the music press, and others didn't quite know what to make of this country music laced with rock and blues—the style created an enormous new class of country-fried hippies. In 1975 Willie recorded the album that would put him over the top: *The Red Headed Stranger.* Featuring the single "Blues Eyes Crying in the Rain," the album established Willie as a country music great. The following year RCA Records packaged previously issued material by Willie, Waylon Jennings, and others on the album *Wanted: The Outlaws.* It became the first country album to sell a million records, sparked a musical revolution, and finally branded Willie as a true outlaw.

Stevie, who saw no use for Willie's outlaws, spent his early years in Austin getting high on the drugs that flowed freely and honing his considerable guitar skills at clubs such as the One Knite and the Soap Creek Saloon. The Soap Creek was "the place where he would develop the sophisticated yet hard-driving style that would become the basis of his legacy," wrote Patoski

Vallejo: Perennial hometown favorite Vallejo is a rock band with a Latin beat.

Kelly Willis: Country crooner and darling of the Austin club circuit, Willis is one of those performers who makes your jaw drop the minute she hits her first note. First, that powerful voice of hers comes charging at you like a bull on wings. Then you realize this young woman is mixing up

some of the best traditional country sounds with a perfect dose of rock 'n' roll.

THE STAGES

Janis Joplin overcame her insecurities and launched her singing career in the early 1960s in an Austin beer joint. George Strait was a relative unknown when he first started singing around town. Stevie Ray Vaughan was just another teen-

and Crawford. In 1975, the year Willie accepted the first of his six Grammy Awards, a blues buff by the name of Clifford Antone opened a club to draw some of the country's blues greats to town. Austin finally had a home for the blues. At Antone's, Stevie would receive the thrill of his young life when his hero, Albert King, invited him onstage to play. "Stevie worked the strings with such brute power and brash confidence, King was taken aback. It was like the young boy had just twisted the cap off the bottle that contained the secrets of all blues and poured every guitar lick known to man right out on stage," Patoski and Crawford wrote. Stevie Ray went on to form Triple Threat Revue and then Double Trouble, the band that would skyrocket him to stardom.

In 1983, the year the National Academy of Popular Music honored its first-ever country artist—Willie Nelson, of course—with a Lifetime Achievement Award, Epic Records released Double Trouble's first album, *Texas Flood*. An international guitar hero was born. Double Trouble's second album, *Couldn't Stand the Weather*, went platinum and was followed by *Soul to Soul*. Double Trouble, fronted by the scrawny young man sporting his trademark flat-brimmed black hat and battered Stratocaster, landed prestigious international touring gigs, an appearance at Carnegie Hall, and legions of worshipers. *In Step*, released in 1988, went platinum and earned the group a Grammy—one of six Stevie would win for his music. In 1990 Stevie Ray and his brother Jimmie finally got together musically for a Grammy-winning album, *Family Style*. It was released two weeks after Stevie Ray's tragic death. In the early morning hours of August 27, 1990, Stevie Ray Vaughan, blues player extraordinaire, was killed in a helicopter crash while returning to Chicago from an Alpine Valley concert in East Troy, Wisconsin. He was 35 years old.

Willie, who was inducted into the County Music Hall of Fame in 1993, has become one of music's most revered performers. Although he tours constantly, he always makes time for his hometown audience—and his Austin concerts invariably wind up as sold-out, standing-room-only events. With only a few chords of "Mamas Don't Let Your Babies Grow Up to Be Cowboys," "Angel Flying too Close to the Ground," "On the Road Again," and countless other classics, his shows turn into a sing-along. After all, every single person in the crowd knows the lyrics by heart.

His face may be chiseled by the years, by the whiskey, and by a life spent on the road, but his music remains as fresh and as gut-wrenchingly powerful as it was when he started out more than five decades ago. He has definitely kept us satisfied.

Stevie Ray, the man who has been called the soul of Austin, lives on through his music and, as such, remains a beloved icon of this city. His phenomenal guitar talents continue to set the standard by which other Austin musicians are judged. A memorial statue of the late blues rocker, erected in 1993, stands by Lady Bird Lake as an eternal reminder of the gentle man and his far-out music. He is always on our minds.

ager with a used guitar and a dream when he found a stage here. Austin's own Willie Nelson is a regular on our club and music hall scene. While not every artist who performs on an Austin stage goes on to fame and fortune, many of the hottest acts on the nation's club scene today got their start on an Austin stage.

From dark, intimate clubs to big concert halls to superb outdoor venues, Austin's club scene swings seven nights a week, bringing a wide array of live music from around Austin and around the country. Few other cities in the nation come close to Austin in the number of live acts performed onstage every night.

If Austin is the Live Music Capital of the World, then downtown is the Live Music Capital of Austin. The lively strip known simply as Sixth Street, on East Sixth between Congress Avenue and Interstate 35 (and now grown to includes side streets as well), touts nearly a score of live music venues, plus restaurants, comedy clubs, T-shirt shops, and tattoo parlors. Because of its national reputation, Sixth Street often gives tourists their first taste of Austin's music scene, but downtown also has the popular Warehouse District and another one developing around Second Street and some good clubs on Congress Avenue. While some of the clubs and restaurants that line East Sixth present hot acts and fascinating up-and-comers, this street also offers plenty of cover bands, DJs, and unproven performers. So experience the awesome Sixth Street scene, but check out downtown's other great clubs and music halls as well as those scattered around Austin.

Of course, what would Austin be without music by the side of the lake? Several spots are known for presenting great live bands—some that cover popular songs and old favorites and others doing original stuff. While the places listed here under The Shores are mainly known as restaurants, we couldn't miss out on telling you about them in this section. Austin music and the lakes are meant to be together like a singer and a guitar.

While there are just too many clubs around Austin to list them all, we've provided you with information about some of Austin's favorites, as well as some of our own. For news about who's playing where, check the listings in the *Austin Chronicle* and *the Austin American–Statesman* (or see our Insiders' Tip earlier in this chapter).

We're not providing specific information on cover charges because these can vary greatly depending on the night of the week, the artist onstage, or, it seems, the alignment of the stars in the heavens. Hours vary, too, so check with the club. Some clubs admit minors; many don't. Again, check with the club. The drinking age in Texas is 21. Most clubs sell tickets at the door only. Some clubs offer tickets for advance purchase. Check out the specific club's Web site to see the policy and order tickets when available.

Around Town

ANTONE'S
213 West Fifth Street
(512) 320-8424
www.antones.net
If there's one existing local club practically the whole world has heard of, it's Antone's, Austin's home of the blues. Since 1975 this club, now in its fourth Austin location, has featured some of Austin's best blues performers as well as top blues artists from around the country. In recent years Antone's lineup has expanded to include rock, pop, and country acts also. This Austin institution swings with live music almost every night of the week, offering a continuous parade of some of the best live music from Austin and around the country. (Read more about Antone's in The Music Biz Close-up in this chapter).

AUSTIN MUSIC HALL
208 Nueces Street
(512) 263-4146,
www.austinmusichall.com
One of Austin's premier venues for national touring shows and local performers, the Austin Music Hall's contribution to the local music scene is enormous. And now, thanks to a major renovation and expansion completed in 2008, including a new, enlarged stage, improved sound system and outdoor covered deck, it is bigger and better than ever. Outstanding performing artists from around the country have performed at this venue, including Bruce Springsteen, the Neville Brothers, Sarah McLachlan, and John Fogerty. This hall, which is indeed a glorified big black box with removable metal chairs for seats, also hosts the annual Austin Music Awards and other South by Southwest events. The Music Hall hosted Zachary Scott Theatre's 2008 production of *Porgy and Bess*, kicking off what promises to be a new dimension of the hall.

THE BACKYARD
13101 West U.S. Highway 71
(512) 263-4146
www.thebackyard.net
www.theglennaustin.net

This delightful open-air venue surrounded by 500-year-old oak trees has become an Austin favorite since it opened in 1993 on a stretch of highway just west of town. Jonny Lang, Bonnie Raitt, Gypsy Kings, the Indigo Girls, Willie Nelson, the Allman Brothers, and many, many more national touring shows favor the Backyard during its March-to-November season. The Backyard amphitheater offers both seated concerts for about 2,400 people and more laid-back affairs in which people bring blankets to sit on. For really popular shows, get your tickets early, as these events sell out fast. At the same address is the smaller outdoor venue The Glenn.

BROKEN SPOKE
3201 South Lamar Boulevard
(512) 442-6189
www.brokenspokeaustintx.com

Willie Nelson calls the Broken Spoke his favorite watering hole. *Texas Highways* magazine has called it the Best Honky-Tonk in Texas, while *Entertainment Weekly* has said it's the best country dance hall in the country. The Broken Spoke has appeared in a host of movies, documentaries, and commercials (including one for Foster's beer that made the Spoke a household name in Australia). Since 1964 the Broken Spoke has been dishing up a steady stream of the best country music Austin has to offer—along with a full menu of down-home Texas cookin'. (Read more about it in The Music Biz Close-Up).

ℹ️ In the old days Austin's downtown east-west streets were named for trees. Sixth Street was called Pecan Street, which is why you still see references to Pecan Street in business names or in our annual Old Pecan Street Festival. The street names were changed to numbers around 1897.

CACTUS CAFE
Texas Union Building
24th and Guadalupe Streets
(512) 475--6515
www.utexas.edu/student/txunion/ae/cactus

This excellent club in the Student Union on the University of Texas campus has been serving up live music for more than 70 years. Opened in 1933 as the Chuck Wagon, the club was among Austin's first hippie hangouts in the 1960s, catering to an emerging group of "folkie" musicians that included a young Janis Joplin. After going through a few names, the club was renamed the Cactus Cafe in 1977 but continues to be one of Austin's prime venues for singer/songwriters presenting acoustic performances. You can also find some bluegrass, swing, jazz, and an occasional rock act here. This venue is a popular daytime hangout for UT students, faculty, and staff. Evening shows draw both students and members of the public.

CAROUSEL LOUNGE
1110 East 52nd Street
(512) 452-6790
www.carousellounge.net

Located just east of I-35, the Carousel Lounge has been serving up drinks and music since 1963. The Carousel features an eclectic range of live music—usually swing, jazz, big band, country, rock, or lounge acts—Tuesday through Sunday nights. The lounge looks much as it did a quarter century ago, with those miniature jukeboxes (not in service) over the tables, an aqua-colored padded bar, and a big jukebox that's loaded with lots of old music. This treasured Austin landmark is now being discovered by a whole new generation of music fans.

CEDAR STREET COURTYARD
208 West Fourth Street
(512) 495-9669
www.cedarstreetaustin.com

Jazz under the trees. Since Cedar Street opened in 1994, this lovely outdoor venue loaded with live oak trees has gained a reputation for featuring excellent local jazz musicians as well as acts from around the country. Tucked between two buildings a few steps down from sidewalk level in the Warehouse District, this intimate setting is the perfect place for live music.

CLUB 115
115 San Jacinto Street
(512) 480-0254
www.club115.com
This upscale club features jazz, hip-hop, and other musical artists. Blue lighting, leather couches, and high cocktail chairs all contribute to the sophisticated atmosphere.

CONTINENTAL CLUB
1315 South Congress Avenue
(512) 441-2444
www.continentalclub.com
Perhaps it's the perennial odor of day-old beer that lends this club its primo atmosphere. More likely, it's the long, long list of top Austin acts that have earned their musical wings at the Continental Club over the years—it celebrated its 50th anniversary in 2007. Whatever the reason, the Continental Club is one of Austin's premier live music venues, with an excellent reputation not only locally but around the country. There's generally always somebody worth seeing within these dark walls.

COOL RIVER CAFE
4001 Parmer Lane
(512) 835-0010
www.coolrivercafe.com
This venue in far north Austin is really three distinct places in one: An elegant, and quiet, restaurant on one side; a sophisticated, and quiet, cognac lounge in the middle; and then a jam-packed and deliciously loud party bar on the other side, featuring live music and lots of dancing Thursday through Saturday. This is one hot spot for both couples and singles, the young and old(er)—anyone who is looking for a good time.

EGO'S
510 South Congress Avenue
(512) 474-7091
This dark, low-ceilinged room on South Congress

Avenue has recently perked up with new cocktail chairs and tables, while the L-shaped corner stage for eclectic musical acts remains intimate and the sound system alert. Strange that one of the city's most likable venues is buried inside a parking garage.

THE ELEPHANT ROOM
315 Congress Avenue
(512) 473-2279
www.natespace.com/elephant
Voted Best Jazz Bar in Austin seven years in a row by the Clarksville Jazz Festival—and in 2007 named by *USA Today* as one of the country's top 10 "places to get jazzed about" —the Elephant Room presents a wide variety of live jazz, including Latin jazz, fusion, traditional, and funk. This cozy basement club presents an excellent assortment of Austin bands as well as bands from around the country. Audiences are treated to the cool sounds of live jazz seven nights a week. (Yes, some of the artists and members of the audience do don sunglasses—it's that cool.)

FRANK ERWIN CENTER
1701 Red River Street
(512) 471-7744,
(512) 477-6060 (Texas box office)
www.uterwincenter.com
Austin's largest venue for national touring musicians is also home to University of Texas basketball as well as Disney on Ice shows, circuses, and scores of other events throughout the year. When it comes to music, however, there just isn't any space in Austin as large or as comfortable for the crowds that have turned out to see world-class musical performers, including, of course, many Austin music legends. The Erwin Center also hosts plenty of classical musical performers. Depending on the stage setup, the Erwin Center can hold anywhere from 4,000 to 18,000 fans. Performances are announced well in advance in the local press.

HANOVERS DRAUGHT HOUSE
108 East Main Street, Pflugerville
(512) 670-9617
www.hanovers.net

i Check out page two of the *Austin American–Statesman* for the "Best Bets" column, which can include recommended music performances for the evening. The *Austin Chronicle* and the *Statesman's* XLent section offer the weekly lineup of live music shows. Pick them up on Thursday.

The suburbs have grown and grown around historic downtown Pflugerville, once a small, quiet Central Texas town (see our Relocation chapter), but not only has new life come to the fields surrounding downtown, but there also has been new life for some of the town's old buildings. Once a saloon, then a hardware store, this 1899 stone building is alive again with the sounds of Texas. The bar features 76 types of beer. In addition to the music stage, there is a back room with pool tables and dart boards, plus a large outdoor beer garden in the back that can seat up to 1,000. For nourishment, there is barbecue, of course.

HILL'S CAFE
4700 South Congress Avenue
(512) 851-9300
www.hillscafe.com
The chicken-fried steak isn't the only thing on the menu at this South Austin landmark. How about a helping of Kevin Fowler, Cory Morrow, or any one of the many other down-home country performers who are giving this place a reputation for presenting great live music?

HOLE IN THE WALL
2538 Guadalupe Street
(512) 477-4747
www.holeinthewallaustin.com
This Austin institution almost didn't make it to its 30th anniversary in 2003. Closed for nearly a year while the building was up for sale, the local Austin Pizza chain revived the space and returned the 200-capacity venue to its original configuration. Bands now play in the front; the back room has pool tables, pinball machines, and a jukebox. Located on The Drag near the University of Texas campus, this really is just a hole in the wall. But over

its three decades in business, this club and eatery has earned a reputation for presenting excellent up-and-coming as well as established bands.

LAMBERTS DOWNTOWN BARBEQUE
401 West Second Street
(512) 494-1500
www.lambertsaustin.com
This spot in downtown's historic Schneider Brothers Building (built in 1873 as one of Austin's first general stores) gained popularity first as a "fancy barbeque" restaurant for both lunch and dinner. Its upstairs stage, however, is now gaining a loyal audience of music lovers, thanks a great deal to the venue's excellent booking choices. Live music, including blues, jazz, Western swing, and other genres, is offered on the weekends.

LA ZONA ROSA
612 West Fourth Street
(512) 463-4146
www.lazonarosa.com
A longtime Austin tradition, formerly a quaint Mexican eatery and music hall, La Zona Rosa now concentrates on outstanding live music. It is high on the list of hot Austin clubs known for providing consistent quality entertainment. La Zona Rosa presents both national touring shows and some of Austin's favorite artists. Its two rooms can be made into one for shows that seat up to 1,200 people.

LUCKY LOUNGE
209 A West Fifth Street
(512) 479-7700
www.theluckylounge.com
Featuring live music six nights a week, this lounge with 60s-inspired decor and soft neon lighting is located in the heart of Austin's Warehouse District. The musical styles—rock, hip-hop, funk, and more—are as eclectic as the patrons who flock to this popular establishment.

MOMO'S
618 West Sixth Street
(512) 479-8848
www.momosclub.com

Close-Up

The Music Biz: Cold Beer and Hot Tunes

Austin luminary Eddie Wilson responds matter-of-factly when asked what launched the spectacular music scene we know today. "Cold beer and cheap pot," he says with a laugh. Wilson, however, humbly neglects to mention his own contributions to Austin's rise as a music mecca. As a founder of the renowned Armadillo World Headquarters in 1970, Wilson helped catapult Austin to the big time.

Of course, the collective talent of the hundreds of artists who have illuminated Austin stages over these many years goes without saying. But Wilson points out, too, that the sizable number of sofas offered to musicians during the '60s and '70s allowed brother and sister performers to find, if not a home, at least a place to bed down.

We're getting way ahead of ourselves, though. Austin's music history goes back much further than the 1960s—all the way back to the dance hall pickers, cowboy crooners, and black blues belters who were making music around Austin long before it had any reputation as a musical mecca. Some performed as far back as the 1800s and would continue to fill our city with their own sound of music despite the various musical invasions that followed.

Some say Austin's modern music scene started with Travis County Beer License No. 01, issued to one Kenneth Threadgill on December 6, 1933. Threadgill, a singer and yodeler who sold gasoline from the front side of his Gulf service station and bootleg whiskey out the back, stood in line all night to be the first to get a beer license after the county voted to go "wet" following Prohibition. Over the years, this little station evolved into a beer joint and haven for music makers. By the early 1960s the ongoing hootenanny at Threadgill's was attracting University of Texas "folkie" musicians, including a freshman named Janis Joplin, who gathered for the regular Wednesday night jam sessions. "The folkie invasion of Threadgill's was a brave move given the general attitude about hippies, beatniks, and long-haired men among the rednecks of the era," Wilson wrote in his book *Threadgill's: The Cookbook*. As things turned out, however, Threadgill's was just the test kitchen for this bizarre social concoction. A decade later, the Armadillo would perfect the recipe when it became a melting pot of blue-haired grannies, bikers, rednecks, and hippies. Threadgill's proved that the music, not the costume, mattered most.

As the '60s stoked up, Joplin joined up with a few budding UT musicians to form the Waller Creek Boys, a folk group that could play just about any kind of music the Threadgill's crowd demanded: blues, country, bluegrass, whatever. Other musicians soon began arriving in Austin and finding their way to Threadgill's. Meanwhile, a few joints near UT, including the Jade Room and the New Orleans Club, were making names for themselves by offering Austin's flower children the kind of live music that appealed to them.

UT's hippies may have invaded Austin, but this was still Texas as sure as shootin', and no amount of folk, blues, or rock 'n' roll could wean this town off good old country and western music. In 1964 a young Austinite fresh from service in the Army established a little roadhouse on the southern outskirts of town. The Broken Spoke, as James White would call his restaurant and club, would become a hub for some of the best country bands in Austin and around the country—and remains so to this day.

By 1965 Joplin had split for San Francisco (being voted the ugliest "male" on campus perhaps hastened the move), and Austin was ripe for a band that could turn on the masses. In the fall of '65 a band called the 13th Floor Elevators burst on the scene at a Jade Room performance. Fronted by a young, good-looking singer/guitarist named Roky Erickson, the Elevators would go on to record two magical albums, break into the top 40, and carve a lasting place for themselves in the collective consciousness of Austin music disciples. (See our Catch 'em If You Can listing).

Despite Austin's own psychedelic sounds, the blossoming of the counterculture revolution, and the drugs that fueled the movement, Austin at that time was still firmly rooted in Bible Belt mores and morality. By the fall of 1967 "there wasn't a hint of the now-bustling music biz in our town," Spencer Perskin, a member of another notable Austin band of the time, Shiva's Headband, wrote in the *Austin Chronicle* in 1993. "To perform only original material was considered almost outrageous by our musician friends, and there was zero tolerance for us at the few bars around town [serving beer only at the time]. Only the opening of the Vulcan Gas Company gave us the foothold we would need."

The Vulcan Gas Company, Austin's first musical haunt for hippies, opened in 1967 at 400 Congress Avenue, just 10 blocks from the state capitol. The 13th Floor Elevators, Shiva's Headband, and another esteemed Austin band called the Conqueroo all found a home at the Vulcan, while "groundbreaking acts such as the Velvet Underground, Moby Grape, and the Fugs would have bypassed the entire state of Texas if not for the Vulcan," wrote Joe Nick Patoski and Bill Crawford in their book, *Stevie Ray Vaughan: Caught in the Crossfire*. The experiment lasted only three years. The Vulcan closed in 1970. As the new decade dawned, however, Austin was set to explode onto the national music stage.

On August 1, 1970, Armadillo World Headquarters opened as a counterculture concert hall. "We wanted to create an entertainment facility that was different from anything Austin had ever seen," Wilson told the *Insiders' Guide*. Indeed. Despite early wobblings, the Armadillo succeeded in drawing throngs of fans desperate to hear top touring bands and even more of the original music that was by then the "in" thing. As the music grew better and better and the number of fans multiplied, talented musicians from around the country started appearing at the Armadillo. Other entrepreneurs riding the coattails of the Armadillo's success began opening clubs all over town.

"Through the interest of a curious national press and word-of-mouth communication by touring musicians, Austin gained almost overnight a reputation as one of the most exciting centers of music activity in the country," Austinite Jan Reid wrote in his book, *The Improbable Rise of Redneck Rock*.

Still, the list of ingredients that went into Austin's magical musical brew was far from complete. Willie Nelson's return to his native Texas led the way for a rising tide of young musicians whose music was labeled progressive country, country rock, and redneck rock. A young country rock group led by Marcia Ball called Freda and the Firedogs catered to this new breed of music listeners. San Antonio native Doug Sahm, who'd found musical success on the West Coast, came home to Texas while Jerry Jeff Walker also settled in. Michael Murphey released his album *Cosmic Cowboy Souvenirs* in 1973, which unwittingly gave a name to the musical rebels. With the arrival of these and other "cosmic cowboys," Austin burst on the national scene as the hub of the redneck rock movement.

Suddenly, hippies and rednecks found themselves bonded by a common sound, rock- and blues-infused country and western music. Local radio station KOKE-FM began exalting the new sound, calling it "progressive country." The pickup truck became the preferred mode of transportation, while no self-respecting, long-haired, cowboy-hatted "goat roper" would be caught dead drinking anything but a longneck beer.

"This was a direct reversal of the previous decade's attitudes, when the city's young pacesetters, rebelliously rejecting haircuts while embracing rock, folk, and blues, would have preferred to drink muddy water and sleep in a hollow log rather than betray affinity with their hillbilly cousins," Clifford Endres wrote in his book, *Austin City Limits*.

Before long, however, Willie was on to his next incarnation as a musical outlaw and Austin moved on to new sounds.

continued

The time had come for Austin's music scene to go national. With Willie Nelson as a featured act, Austin's own country music program, *Austin City Limits,* hit the airwaves in the spring of 1975. The program, still airing on Public Broadcasting Stations around the country, features the best-known acts in music today. In the past three decades, *ACL* has taken its place among the city's music legends.

The cosmic cowboys may have dominated the music scene for a good spell during the 1970s, but theirs wasn't the only sound in town. Down at the Broken Spoke, fans of traditional country music found a refuge away from the city's invading hippies. (Austin lore has it that young men with hair longer than their dates' were refused service at the Spoke during these years.)

On other stages, a band that included a young guitarist by the name of Eric Johnson (see the Catch 'em If You Can section in this chapter) blasted out a radically different tune. The Electromagnets, as the quartet called itself, "generated fan reaction proportional to the volume of its music, gathering an intense, almost worshipful, fan base that seemed to expand with each live date," *Austin American–Statesman* music critic Michael Point wrote in a 1998 article celebrating the re-issue of the Electromagnets self-titled album.

A group of West Texas singer/songwriters also migrated to Austin during the 1970s. Joe Ely, Butch Hancock, and Jimmie Dale Gilmore (see them collectively as the Flatlanders in the Catch 'em listings) found Austin audiences receptive to the original music they wanted to make—and stayed to make a contribution. So did a teenage Dallas transplant named Jimmie Vaughan. Vaughan's group, Storm, would be just the beginning of the blues tradition Vaughan would help to inspire in his new hometown. Austin's musical tree, it appeared, was destined to produce many branches.

Yet another Austinite geared up in the '70s to take his place in music history. Clifford Antone, a Port Arthur, Texas, native of Lebanese descent, came to Austin at age 19 to run the family gourmet grocery business. In 1973 the tiny back room of Antone's Imports became the unofficial launching pad for a group of blues artists that included Jimmie Vaughan's little brother, Stevie Ray. Antone opened his first club on Sixth Street on July 15, 1975, featuring such blues greats as Muddy Waters, Albert King, and Sunnyland Slim—in just its first year. Antone's is credited with helping to develop a blues tradition in Austin where none existed before, at least not in the predominantly white area west of Interstate-35.

By the time Armadillo World Headquarters closed in 1980, Austin's status as a "mecca for musical mavericks" had solidified. And there was still more to come.

A star among Austin's rebels during this time was a lanky Texan by the name of Townes Van Zandt. Born in 1944 to a prominent Fort Worth oil family, Van Zandt had rejected the easy life to become a singer/songwriter. The writer of such country hits as "Pancho and Lefty," recorded by Willie Nelson and Merle Haggard, and Emmylou Harris's "If I Needed You," Van Zandt's work would influence a generation of Texas songwriters. Despite his near-constant struggles with alcohol, his recording career spanned more than a quarter of a century. During his many years living and performing in Austin, Van Zandt became one of our city's most revered musicians—and a magnet for other musical storytellers. In fact, it's been said that he helped establish the "couch circuit" for drifting musicians. "I really, honestly believe Townes was one of the main reasons Austin received a reputation for quality," Jimmie Dale Gilmore told the *Austin American–Statesman* after Van Zandt's death, at age 52, in 1997. Van Zandt had died of a heart attack while recovering from hip surgery in Tennessee. His music lives on, however, and there have been many posthumous releases of his work.

The Sixth Street music scene, which had taken root in the 1970s, fired up in the 1980s and has since become a dominant district for live music and dancing. Well-established Sixth Street hangouts like Maggie Mae's saw the once-tranquil strip turn into a frenzy of clubs turning out live music seven nights a week, and now the greater downtown area packs in more outstanding live music than anyone could ever experience in a short visit here. Many of Austin's

continued

most notable live clubs, including Antone's, La Zona Rosa, and the Continental Club, can all be found in greater downtown. Wilson himself went on to revive the old Threadgill's saloon, turning it into one of Austin's most illustrious restaurants (featuring live music, of course). Threadgill's now touts two Austin locations, including one near the spot of the former Armadillo and appropriately named Threadgill's World Headquarters (see our Restaurants chapter).

Austin's star on the world stage continues to rise as more and more young artists flock to The Live Music Capital of the World yearning to make a name for themselves. In what's been called "the second coming of the outlaw attitude," this century has witnessed a stunning national revival in Texas's unique brand of country music. Hot, hot, hot among the cities showcasing the talents of hometown "Texas Music" artists is Austin. Pat Green, Kevin Fowler, and other young artists are just the latest links in Austin's talent-heavy outlaw chain. Of course the Austin beat goes on in so many other musical realms as well. As Wilson told us, "There are many more quality musicians and 10 times more music in Austin today than there was during the days of the Armadillo."

Indeed.

One of the best things about this downtown club, besides the live music of course, is the rooftop patio, which offers a view over the city and a look at the inside stage and dance floor. The club has had several incarnations and now features all sorts of music, including singer/songwriters.

SAXON PUB
1320 South Lamar Boulevard
(512) 448-2552
www.thesaxonpub.com
Saxon Pub started out as a folk music club when it opened in South Central Austin in 1990, but Saxon is now gaining a reputation as a great blues club. Country and rock bands also have found a home. To the delight of music fans, some of the country's most popular musicians also have been known to drop in for a jam session or two, including Bonnie Raitt and Kris Kristofferson.

SPEAKEASY
412 Congress Avenue
(512) 476-8017
www.speakeasyaustin.com
This upscale club in the Warehouse District downtown features live music on most nights. This is the place to play billiards and hear bands play some great standards from the '30s and '40s as well as some original music. The Speakeasy offers plenty of blues, jazz, salsa, lounge music,

swing, and some country tunes. The rooftop terrace (for those willing to make the trek up the 59 stairs) offers a fantastic view of downtown.

Sixth Street

The Sixth Street Entertainment has grown over the years to include parts of Fifth and Seventh Streets, as well as a few blocks of Red River Street on the east end of Sixth. This listing includes our favorite clubs in the expanded district.

BEERLAND
711½ Red River Street
(512) 479-7625
www.beerlandtexas.com
The Austin American–Statesman calls this punkish club with a gay vibe "the heart and soul of Red River Street," although well-established Emo's down the block might dispute that. The decor is Old World cabaret.

THE CHUGGIN' MONKEY
219 East Sixth Street
(512) 476-5015
www.thechugginmonkey.com
With a name like Chuggin' Monkey, this club was destined for Sixth Street. The stage is tiny but it is right up front on Sixth. The Monkey packs in the crowds.

ELYSIUM

705 Red River Street

(512) 478-2979

www.elysiumonline.net

Specializing in synthpop, gothic, industrial, rock, EBM (electronic body music), as well as alternative rock and electronica genres, Elysium is one popular night spot for those who eschew the ordinary. The club presents live music on Thursday and Friday; DJs the other nights.

EMO'S

603 Red River Street

(512) 477-3667

www.emosaustin.com

This Austin club just off Sixth Street is drawing oodles of fans for its eclectic mix of underground music. With two stages, one inside and one outside, there's always an act worth seeing. If it's punk/indie/electronica/garage/emo stuff you like, Emo's is your place.

FLAMINGO CANTINA

515 East Sixth Street

(512) 494-9336

www.flamingocantina.com

Calling itself "Austin's Good Vibes Club," this place is where Austin goes to hear the city's best reggae music. Carpeted bleachers line two walls, offering great views of the band onstage. Of course there's a dance floor, for when swaying in your seat just isn't enough, and an upstairs open-air deck for dancing under the stars.

MAGGIE MAE'S

323 East Sixth Street

(512) 478-8541

www.maggiemaesaustin.com

With three different stages offering simultaneous music on weekends, an airy rooftop bar upstairs, and private courtyard downstairs, Maggie Mae's has no trouble drawing a crowd. Named for a famous London lady of the evening, Maggie Mae's offers live music most nights. One band is featured during the week, but on Friday and Saturday this two-story club rocks with different types of music in three different rooms, including

i Austin's venerable Paramount Theatre and Bass Concert Hall have in the recent past begun booking pop music performers—to great success. Check out their Web sites at austintheatre.org and utpac.org for a list of upcoming shows.

at least two live bands. The building, originally a general store built in 1874, predates Sixth Street's historic Driskill Hotel by a dozen years. Maggie Mae's, one of this strip's longest running and most successful clubs, is also acclaimed for its extensive beer selection and the beer tastings it holds.

MOHAWK

912 Red River Street

www.mohawkaustin.com

This popular spot on the outer limits of the Sixth Street Entertainment District says it draws its inspiration "not from the hairdo," but from the Native American culture of the Northeast. An eclectic mix of music—hip-hop, jazz, indie, rock, and so on—is offered on both the indoor and outdoor stages Thursday through Sunday. By the way, the club says if you happen to have a mohawk (the hairdo) "bring it on over."

THE PARISH

214 East Sixth Street

(512) 478-6372

www.theparishroom.com

This has been a hot Sixth Street nightclub for quite some time, and deservedly so. *Austin American–Statesman* music critic Michael Corcoran has called it "one of the last places to hear live original music on Sixth Street" and "Austin's most handsome room." All sorts of bands play in this acoustically excellent space.

RED EYED FLY

715 Red River Street

(512) 474-1084

www.redeyedfly.com

The emphasis seems to be on rock and funk here, but really it's an electrically eclectic mix of great sounds, with some heavy metal and a bit of country rock tossed in the mix. There's definitely some musical experimentation going on here.

RED 7
611 East Seventh Street
(512) 476-8100

If you like punk music—and who doesn't? —you'll love Red 7.

STUBB'S
801 Red River Street
(512) 480-8341
www.stubbsaustin.com
www.frontgatetickets.com

It's hard to say which is more enticing at this Austin hangout, the excellent barbecue or the live music acts that perform on both the indoor and outdoor stages. The building itself is a historical gem. Built in the 1850s, the building has been remodeled into a 6,000-square-foot two-level restaurant with mahogany and cherry bars that date from the 1870s. Outdoors, two decks and bars overlook the stage. Today Stubb's showcases both national touring acts and some of Austin's finest musicians. The Gospel Brunch every Sunday at Stubb's is not to be missed.

THE 311 CLUB
311 East Sixth Street
(512) 477-1630

R&B star Joe Valentine is not just one of the 311 Club's owners, he's also the featured attraction here several nights a week. When Joe Valentine and the Imperials aren't onstage, other blues and R&B bands from around Austin and around the country perform.

THE VIBE
508 East Sixth Street
(512) 474-0632
www.liveatthevibe.com

It didn't take long for word to get out about this club, which features a variety of live music. The crowd is multigenerational, multicultural—and everybody is here to have a good time.

The Shores

Music snobs may reckon that venues known primarily as lakeside eateries are unworthy of mention in the same listing with such Austin classics as Antone's, the Broken Spoke, and others. You might not always hear original music at these restaurants, but sometimes you will. Besides, even the cover bands we've heard at several of these places beat the music many visitors will find at home. And you get to enjoy being out on the lakes at the same time. Water and music—now that's an unbeatable Austin combination. This is just one more dimension of the Live Music Capital of the World. To find more about most of these eateries, see our Restaurants chapter.

IGUANA GRILL
2900 Ranch Road 620
(512) 266-8439
www.iguanagrillaustin.com

The excellent view of Lake Travis and the great Mexican restaurant draw crowds of Austinites and out-of-towners, but the Iguana also offers live music mainly on Friday and Saturday starting around 6:30 p.m., but also on random other nights. Check the Web site for the music calendar.

THE PIER
1701 River Hills Drive
(512) 327-4562
www.pierlakeaustin.com

A huge stage shaded by 60-foot elms, a large concrete slab of a dance floor, and plenty of picnic tables for dining and drinking make this one great place to hear all varieties of music, including cover bands and Austin acts playing original music. You can even drive your boat right up to the dock on Lake Austin and listen from there or join the crowds that gather for the show. Live music is presented Friday and Saturday nights and Sunday evenings.

SKI SHORES WATERFRONT CAFE
3101 Pearce Street
(512) 346-5915
www.skishores.com

Getting raves from Austin crowds since 1954, this is another supercasual place where you can just boat right up to the dock and hop in for a burger, a beer, or an evening of live music. Located on Lake Austin, Ski Shores is one of our favorite outdoor eateries. The stage, presenting Austin singer/songwriters during the summer, is so close to the water that the wake from the boats going by could almost serve as the rhythm section.

STARLIGHT TERRACE AT THE OASIS
6550 Comanche Trail
(512) 266-2441
www.oasis-austin.com
Situated high above Lake Travis, the Oasis is famous for its fabulous view of the sunset. But the multilayered outdoor decks are also perfect for dining—and for listening to live music. The bands play all kinds of music, including Top 40, jazz, salsa, and much more. Austin bands, performing both original hits and popular contemporary music, make this place an inviting stop for those who want to experience the outdoor music scene in Austin.

Free Concerts
AUSTIN'S FOURTH OF JULY PICNIC
Auditorium Shores, Riverside Drive and South First Street
(512) 476-6064
www.austinsymphony.org
Austin's biggest free concert is the performance by the Austin Symphony Orchestra at the annual July Fourth Concert and Fireworks Show on the shores of Lady Bird Lake. See our Annual Events and Festivals chapter for more on this giant concert/picnic/party.

FALL CONCERT SERIES
Frost Bank Plaza
816 Congress Avenue
(512) 442-2263
Members of the Austin Federation of Musicians, in conjunction with the Downtown Austin Alliance, offer free outdoor concerts on Friday from noon to 1:00 p.m. at this downtown outdoor

i Passport to Texas" featuring Joel Block is a 90-second radio series about the Texas outdoors. The program, airing weekdays, features interviews with experts on everything from birding and biking to wildlife management and habitat restoration. The radio series is heard on approximately 100 Texas radio stations and over the Internet. For a schedule of programs, visit www.passporttotexas.com.

venue. The series runs from mid-September to early November. Bring your lunch along and enjoy a taste of Austin.

WATERLOO PARK CONCERT SERIES
Waterloo Park, 403 East 15th Street
(512) 442-2263
Formerly held at Auditorium Shores on Lady Bird Lake, this popular series of summer concerts has featured some of Austin's top performers over the years. These concerts, a typical Austin mix of music styles, are fun for the whole family and offer an excellent opportunity to get acquainted with the Austin music scene. Shows are held each Wednesday night from 7:00 to 9:00 p.m. from the end of April through June. This is another project by the Austin Federation of Musicians.

ZILKER HILLSIDE THEATER CONCERTS
2206 William Barton Drive
(512) 477-5335
www.ci.austin.tx.us/zilker/hillside.htm
The fabulous natural amphitheater near Barton Springs Pool in Zilker Park presents an array of free concerts during its season, which runs from late March to mid-October. Performances are given by the Austin Symphony, the Austin Civic Orchestra, the Austin Civic Wind Ensemble, and many other groups. Special events include the Mother's Day, Pops, and Earth Day Concerts.

MUSIC STORES

Record stores, yet another dimension to the city's music scene, feature a wide variety of music from jazz to Tejano, hip-hop to blues, classical to funk, and of course, Austin's own local artists. Furthermore, some of these stores go out of their way to promote Austin's music scene by sponsoring live in-store performances, setting aside special sections featuring CDs by local musicians, and offering advice and tips on the Live Music Capital of the World. Stop in any of the shops we've listed here for a taste of Austin. The large chain bookstores all over town, including Borders and Barnes & Noble, also sell records.

ANTONE'S RECORD SHOP
2928 Guadalupe Street
(512) 322-0660
www.antonesrecordshop.com
Reflecting the music played at the venerable Austin club of the same name (see the listing in this chapter), Antone's focuses on blues music. There is also a large selection of Texas and Cajun music, country sounds, soul, vintage rock 'n' roll, rockabilly, and jazz at this Central Austin store. Customers can buy, sell, and trade here. This is also the place to buy advance tickets to shows at Antone's club (see The Stages section of this chapter).

CHEAPO DISCS
914 North Lamar Boulevard
(512) 477-4499
www.cheapotexas.com
Housed in the old Whole Foods store, just north of the West Sixth shopping district, not far from downtown in Central Austin, Cheapo features used CDs, one of the largest selections in Austin. The shop buys used CDs. Technically, Cheapo is part of a small Minnesota-based chain, but it retains the atmosphere of an independent outfit.

END OF AN EAR
2209 South First Street
(512) 462-6008
www.endofanear.com
This fairly recent arrival on the Austin record store scene wasted no time in capturing a loyal clientele base with its eclectic mix of sounds, not to mention its huge collection of used LPs. Music lovers can find everything from indie and French pop, to jazz, techno, soul, funk, punk, reggae, and much more. It also hosts free in-store music events. This is a good-size shop as independent record stores go, making it an inviting place to browse.

MUSICMANIA
3909-D North I-35
(512) 451-3361
East of the interstate in the Fiesta grocery store center, this East Austin record store has a reputation for one of the best R&B and rap music collections in the country. In addition to CDs, the store has a large collection of vinyl records, posters, magazines, and music-related merchandise.

SOUND ON SOUND
106 East North Loop
(512) 371-9980
www.soundonsoundrecords.com
"If it doesn't suck we sell it. And if it does, we sell it for a dollar!" That's the promise made by this locally owned shop "run by music-obsessed and friendly record dorks." Indeed, we find the selection of both new and used CDs, as well as used LPs, quite impressive for a small shop, and we like the LP listening stations. This is a great place to shop for those who want to expand their musical tastes beyond the top 40, as the music junkies who run the place are quite helpful in offering advice.

TURNTABLE RECORDS
507 West Mary Street
(512) 462-2568
Just west of South Congress Avenue's funky shopping district, this small store sells breakbeat, retro, disco, Top 40, and other sounds, including both domestic and imported albums and singles.

WATERLOO RECORDS
600–A North Lamar Boulevard
(512) 474-2500
www.waterloorecords.com
Consistently voted the Best Record Store in town in the annual *Austin Chronicle* Readers'

Poll, Waterloo is at the heart of the West Sixth Street shopping district. The shop has a fabulous selection of records and CDs—both new and used—reflecting a wide variety of styles and sounds, and there are plenty of listening stations to sample the music. In-house performances and CD-release concerts are held regularly to highlight the work of popular artists, both up-and-coming and well known. Waterloo arranges its records alphabetically instead of by music type, which makes this store extremely user-friendly. Waterloo also stocks lots of other music-related items. Trying to decide what band to hear when you're in town—and you can't find any on our "Catch 'em If You Can" list? Stop in at Waterloo and ask the advice of owner John Kunz or any other member of the knowledgeable sales staff. Waterloo is also one place to purchase tickets for shows around town and for wristbands or individual tickets for SXSW events and the Austin City Limits Music Festival (see our Annual Events and Festivals chapter). It's no wonder this store has been going strong since 1982.

SHOPPING

You can never be too adventurous to enjoy shopping in Austin. Sure there are big malls with big parking lots to match, but while they provide Austin shoppers with the opportunity to buy appliances at national discount chain prices, local merchants present a dazzling array of arts, crafts, collectibles, folk art, funk, vintage redux, and just plain fun items.

We give you the big, the bold, and the beautiful. First is a look at the city's shopping districts, then a brief overview of the area's major malls and outlet stores. This is followed by listings, by category and area, of shops in the Austin area. It is impossible to list every noteworthy and intriguing shop in the city, especially as the city grows and the shopping districts multiply, but this list aims to give the reader the flavor of the shopping scene in Austin, plus tips on finding shops that are unique to the city.

Several categories of shops are not included here—bookstores appear in our chapter on The Literary Scene, art galleries are showcased in The Arts chapter, and music stores are featured in The Music Scene. In addition, sporting goods that cater to a specific sport are found in our Parks and Recreation chapter.

In recent years there has been a blossoming of retail in Austin. On the one hand, national giants such as Whole Foods Market and Dell Computer have emerged from the Austin earth; on the other hand, the personal has flourished. Older boulevards and city streets in Austin have seen small, unique shops sprout like cabbages as young at heart Austin goes in search of expression and joy.

Given Austin's lively night scene, many bookstores and specialty food shops keep late hours. The burgeoning shopping scene along South Congress Avenue is one example of a late-night shopping district—some of the stores stay open until midnight, particularly on weekends. On the first Thursday of each month, the South Congress shopping district has a shopping, eating, and drinking celebration called "First Thursday" (www.firstthursday.info), and that unique monthly event is profiled in our Arts chapter. During the Christmas holiday season, many stores and malls also extend their hours.

SHOPPING DISTRICTS

One of the liveliest shopping districts is on South Congress Avenue, in the neighborhood called "SoCo," south of Lady Bird Lake in South Central Austin. Congress Avenue is wide and magnificent here, but for many years the shops and businesses along the street decayed and stagnated. Now there is new life on the avenue, and resale shops featuring vintage clothing, toy emporiums, retro furnishing stores, and folk art shops flourish (if they can afford the escalating rents, a controversial subject these days)—some staying open in the night hours to give the street an after-dark vitality.

West of the South Congress shopping district is South Lamar Boulevard, where some of the city's really funky stores can be found. Vintage clothing stores, "junque" shops, antiques stores, and several thrift stores are located on this road to downtown Austin. Running parallel and in between South Lamar and Congress is South First Street, which is also home to offbeat stores and eateries.

The nexus of West Sixth and North Lamar Boulevard is one of the hippest shopping districts in Austin. At its heart is the Whole Foods Landmark Market, the natural foods grocery store that is a leitmotiv for the Austin economy. Founded more than 20 years ago as a natural foods store by a couple of hippies with a vision, it now serves as the anchor of the country's largest natural foods grocery store empire. Next door is Austin's quintessential bookstore, Book People, a place where incense fills the air and the titles outnumber any chain store in town. In 2003 Whole Foods broke ground on a site immediately to the south of the current store. The new 80,000-square-foot store is a flagship for the chain (see our Close-ups in this chapter and the Restaurants chapter).

The area east of the Sixth Street-Lamar nexus, leading to the so-called Warehouse District, is also seeing a boom in bars, restaurants, shops and galleries catering to the fast-rising number of downtown residents. Just south of the Warehouse District is downtown's most upscale shopping, the Second Street District (www.2ndstreetdistrict .com) anchored around City Hall and the neighboring lofts. The shops here are trendy, upscale (that word that is creeping into the Austin lexicon) and many of them aimed at dressing those downtown loft-dwellers and decorating their habitats.

Another shopping district in the making is the area along Burnet Road leading from North Austin down into Central Austin. This is a mix of antiques shops, ethnic bakeries and grocery stores, and crafts stores catering to potters and glassmakers.

One of the city's shopping corridors lies east of MoPac along 35th Street, flowing into 38th Street and then north on Lamar Boulevard to Central Park, home of the city's second-biggest tourist draw, Central Market (see our Close-up in this chapter), a grocery store that belies its pedestrian name. There are no big signs here, but Austin residents know this is where they can find some of the best shops in Austin in small shopping centers like 26 Doors and Jefferson Square along 35th Street.

To the northwest along U.S. Highway 183 is the Arboretum, the Rodeo Drive of Austin. This is where some of the top merchandising names in the country have a foothold. Saks has a store in the Great Hills Trail area near the open air Arboretum shopping center.

To the north of the city, just east of MoPac Boulevard and north of U.S. Highway 183 is The Domain (www.thedomainaustin.com), a definitely upscale shopping experience built to resemble a European town center. Here you will find Tiffany's, Neiman Marcus, Burberry, Coach, and several top-notch resturants, cafes, and even a tea room. A large Whole Foods is planned for the development, also.

To the east, at 10901 North Lamar Boulevard, is another exciting addition to the Austin shopping scene, Austin's new Chinatown, www .chinatownaustin.com. The Chinatown Center, anchored by the MT Supermarket (see our Food shopping listings) is home to several restaurants and cafes featuring Chinese, Indian, Japanese, Korean and Vietnamese food, plus home decor and herb shops.

Back in the central city is The Drag, the section of Guadalupe Street that runs alongside the University of Texas campus. Here there is an odd mix of hip fashion stores and Vietnamese egg roll stands, old hippie vendors and souvenir shops selling all things Longhorn. Just north of The Drag is The Triangle, another town center concept that is home to small shops and cafes.

The Austin ethos dictates that nobody shops simply to shop; Austinites shop to find, to discover, to enjoy. If these listings are packed with stores selling folk art, food, and plants, it is an indication that Austin residents are sensual folk who love to dip into the unknown, find the new, and enjoy the past.

MALLS

We have it on good authority that when the Queen of England came to Austin, her staff and ladies-in-waiting ventured to a local shopping mall to sample the wares. There are some local merchants in the area's malls, but like much of America, the shopping mall is the home of chain stores, big-name department stores, and fashionable merchants of the moment.

The malls are open seven days a week, usually from 9:00 a.m. to 9:00 or 10:00 p.m. Monday through Saturday and from noon to 6:00 p.m.

on Sunday, although hours are extended greatly during the Christmas shopping season and for special promotional sales.

The major shopping malls include The Arboretum (10000 Research Boulevard) in northwest Austin, an open-air mall that is home to many upscale national stores. Barton Creek Square, a large indoor mall, sits atop a hill in West Austin at 2901 Loop 360 (Capital of Texas Highway) and is home to several department stores, including Foley's, Nordstrom's, Sears, Dillard's, and JCPenney. Lakeline Mall (11200 Lakeline Mall) serves the fast-growing northwest greater Austin area. It also is home to such major department stores as Foley's, Sears, Dillard's, and JCPenney. Highland Mall (6001 Airport Boulevard) was Austin's first mall in what was then far North Austin and is now considered the edge of Central Austin, near the intersection of Interstate 35 and U.S. Highway 290. It has several major department stores on the premises.

New malls include the aforementioned Domain at 11506 Century Oaks Boulevard and the Hill Country Galleria, home to many well-known national merchandising names, located in the Village of Bee Cave at the intersection of U.S. Highway 71 and RM 620 in what was once rolling, empty hill country pasture west of the city—proof that much of Austin's growth has been in the coveted land near the lakes.

Shoppers who love to hunt for bargains at outlet stores have a major source of pleasure in San Marcos, about 45 minutes south of Austin. Both sides of I-35 are lined with outlet stores located in two malls, Prime Outlet Mall and Tanger Outlet Center, both located at exit 200 on the interstate.

ANTIQUES/COLLECTIBLES/ FOLK ART

Central

BOB LARSON'S OLD TIMER CLOCK SHOP
1803 West 35th Street
(512) 451-5016
www.bobsclocks.com

The Old Timer Shop has been a treasured resource for years for Austin residents. The shop not only sells beautiful old clocks and watches but also offers a fine repair service.

DREYFUS ANTIQUES BROCANTE
1901 North Lamar Boulevard
(512) 473-2443
www.dreyfusantiques.com

The large wrought-iron replica of the Eiffel Tower is a surefire tip to what shoppers will find inside—a selection of 18th- and 19th-century French antiques, including armoires, tapestries, tables, architectural pieces, and chairs.

EL INTERIOR
1009 West Lynn Street
(512) 474-8680
www.elinterior.com

This Clarksville store is one of the best and oldest folk art stores in Austin. The owners really know where to find the best pottery, jewelry, and textiles south of the border. The selection of Oaxacan ceramics is notable, and the store also stocks Guatemalan fabric by the yard. The store features the work of notable Mexican and Southwestern folk artists and often brings them to the store for special appearances.

KERBEY LANE DOLL SHOPPE
3706 Kerbey Lane
(512) 452-7086
www.kerbeylanedollshop.com

This store sells both antique dolls aimed at the collectors' market and exquisite, new dolls for

There are three large antiques marketplaces in the Austin area that house dozens of small dealers under one roof. Two are in north Austin, Austin Antique Mall, 8822 McCann Drive, (512) 459-5900, and Antique Marketplace, 5350 Burnet Road, (512) 452-1000. A third, large marketplace is in Round Rock, just north of Austin, The Antique Mall of Texas, 1601 South I-35, (512) 218-4290.

that special niece or granddaughter. The owners also offer on-site doll repair.

LA COSECHA
3703 Kerbey Lane
(512) 445-0347

A popular store in the Kerbey Lane shopping scene, part of the 35th through 38th Street corridor, this store features Latin American folk art and clothing, hats, and jewelry, plus custom-designed fashions and accessories by local Austin artists.

LOTUS ASIAN ART AND ANTIQUES GALLERY
1211 West Sixth Street, Ste 100
(512) 474-1700
www.lotusasianart.com

Don't just think Chinese here, in addition to a large collection from Asia, the gallery also has African antiques, ancient pottery and even some Viking pieces.

WHIT HANKS ANTIQUES AND DECORATIVE ARTS
1009 West Sixth Street
(512) 478- 2101
www.whithanksantiques.com

Several top flight antiques and arts dealers can be found under one roof at Whit Hanks, an antiques showcase on West Sixth Street at the heart of one of Austin's best shopping districts. The Web site has a detailed list of the stores under one roof here and links to individual dealers, some of whom show extensive catalogs online. From the large, Tuscan-style pottery urns on its lawn to the myriad collectibles inside, this is one of the most pleasant and amenable antiques venues in Austin. The building, located next door to Treaty Oak (see our Attractions chapter), is a popular spot for a weekend outing. Several Austin artisans display their original iron, ceramic, and woodworking pieces here also.

ZANZIBAR
West Sixth Street and Lamar Boulevard
(512) 472-9234
www.zanzibarhome.com

The West Sixth area has evolved into one of the hippest shopping districts in Austin. Named for the great African port, this store evokes the spirit of an old bazaar with a melange of Chinese furniture, kilim rugs, Arabic-style lamps, tribal baskets, ethnic jewelry, and primitive cooking utensils, pots, and tools. The entrance to the store is on Lamar Boulevard across from Whole Foods. In addition to wonderful old finds, the store sells small treasures, home furnishings, and children's items. A great place to shop for Christmas gifts for someone who has everything.

South Central

THE ARMADILLO
1712 South Congress Avenue
(512) 443-7552

Hand-carved furniture takes center stage here, but the store also sells antique furniture pieces, jewelry, pottery, and ceramics that capture the spirit of Texas and the Southwest.

MAYA
1508 South Congress Avenue
(512) 912-1475
www.mayastar.com

This family-owned store has been a fixture of the South Congress shopping district for many years. Nowadays you'll find an eclectic and colorful mix of jewelry and furniture (sofas, chairs, ottomans) and kitchenware, cards, lamps, purses, pillows, mirrors, and unusual gifts. Some of the items in the store are Parisian imports—kitchen gadgets, kitchen brooms, and serving spoons.

MI CASA
1700A South Congress Avenue
(512) 707-9797
www.micasagallery.com

i Keeping up with the dizzying pace of Austin's design and fashion scene is made easier by reading "Design Notebook" and "The Goods," two blogs on the *American Statesman's* Web site, www.statesman.com.

The entrance to this rabbit's warren of treasures is actually on West Milton, just half a block off Congress Avenue. Room after tiny room features rustic ranch and primitive furniture, while the walls hang with Southwestern and Mexican folk art. The store also sells textiles and cotton clothing from Mexico and Guatemala.

TEN THOUSAND VILLAGES
1317 South Congress Avenue
(512) 440-0440
www.tenthousandvillages.org
This store is part of a growing number of "fair trade" stores across the country and Canada that sell crafts, jewelry, and home furnishings from countries around the world. The goal is to offer support for Third World countries and communities.

TESOROS TRADING CO.
1500 Congress Avenue
(512) 479-8377
www.tesoros.com
Nudged off Congress Avenue north of the river by a hotel development, Tesoros has relocated in SoCo. Tesoros is one of our favorite Austin stores. It features a wide selection of Mexican and Latin American folk art, jewelry, Day of the Dead tableaux, amulets, loteria art, old Mexican postcards, Moroccan mirrors, jewelry from all over the world, purses made in Vietnam from old Pepsi cans, Mexican grocery store calendars, retablos, Peruvian good luck pigs, etc., etc. The store's Christmas ornaments, particularly those from Latin America, are popular Austin collectibles. Look out for the occasional warehouse sale advertised in the local press. This SoCo store is one of those must-see stops for any visitor.

THORNTON ROAD STUDIO COMPLEX
2311 Thornton Road
(512) 443-1611
www.thorntonroadstudios.com
A gathering of 10 artists maintains studios in a small complex located on Thornton Road behind the Office Depot store at the corner of South

Lamar Boulevard and Oltorf Street. Painters, sculptors, jewelry-makers, ironworkers, and mosaic artists have their studios here. The group holds a special sale in late November as the Christmas shopping season kicks in.

THE TURQUOISE DOOR
1208 South Congress Avenue
(512) 480-0618
Mexican folk art, notably works from famous ceramic artists like Josefina Aguilar, plus wonderful Southwestern jewelry make this store a popular spot for folk art collectors.

UNCOMMON OBJECTS
1512 South Congress Avenue
(512) 442-4000
www.uncommonobjects.com
There seems to be a competition in the South Congress shopping district to see which store can qualify for the Best Stuff award. Here, Mexican doors, architectural elements, lamps, and clothing all compete for attention, making the store a surefire contender for top spot.

WEST MARY ANTIQUES
910 West Mary Street
(512) 916-9561
While some of the stores in the South Congress shopping district lean more toward the funky than the classic, this small store is the exception. The antiques here are the real deal.

Northwest
MARCO POLO'S ATTIC
9828 Great Hills Trail, Suite 330
(512) 342-0111
www.marcopolosattic.com
Walking around owner Renata Marsilli's "attic" is like going on a trek through the world's exotic places. There are many large pieces suitable for the garden or for grabbing attention in any room—antiques from Tibet and Thailand, Indian textiles and Italian marble. Some really unique stage setters here.

North

AUSTIN HOME COLLECTION
5101 Burnet Road
(512) 377-5000
www.austinhomecollection.com

In addition to the English antiques offered here, there are some high-quality furniture consignment pieces for sale.

COURTYARD SHOPS
5453 Burnet Road
(512) 477-1616

Several antiques dealers and crafters are creating a small shopping and craft center on Burnet Road, all part of the spontaneous revival of this street as a place to roam for special items and bargains. The center of the shopping area is a small courtyard decorated by garden artist Bud Twilley. He uses old garden stoneware from Europe and Mexico to create fountains, topiaries, and garden art.

DRAGON'S LAIR COMICS & FANTASY
4910 Burnet Road
(512) 454-2399
www.dlair.net

Comic books, games, fantasy fiction, and videos, particularly those featuring the work of John Wu and Jackie Chan, are sold here. Japanese comic books are particularly popular. The Austin Board Game Group meets here every month, as the store hosts games on-site.

GYPSIES ANTIQUES
5202 Burnet Road
(512) 451-6200
www.gypsiesantiques.com

The store owner gathers European and American antiques, often mixing them with whimsical finds and affordable gift items like British bread boards and old china. Gypsies also participates in the spring Round Top antiques show (see our Annual Events and Festivals chapter).

TURQUOISE TRADING POST
6103 Burnet Road
(512) 323-5011
(888) 887-7864
www.turquoisetradingpost.com

In addition to offering a wide selection of contemporary and traditional Native American jewelry, the store also has a collection of Zuni fetishes and Navajo kachinas, plus pottery and sculpture from the Southwest.

ARTS AND CRAFTS

Central

ARTISTS' MARKET
715 West Sixth Street
(512) 535-5761
www.theartistsmarket.com

This juried art show, usually held on Sundays next door to Mother Egan's pub, features the work of local artists and craftsmen, paintings, sculpture, jewelry and glasswork.

CLARKSVILLE POTTERY & GALLERIES
Central Park, 4001 North Lamar
Boulevard, Suite 200
(512) 454-9079

9722 Great Hills Terrace, Suite 380
(512) 794-8580
www.clarksvillepottery.com

This pottery shop found life in the old Central Austin neighborhood of Clarksville (hence the name); however, this shop and gallery now has two locations, one in Central Park on North Lamar Boulevard and the other in the Arboretum area. Both stores feature pottery by local artists, including decorative pieces and very practical, sturdy everyday ware; also stone fountains, lamps, beautiful wooden boxes, and hummingbird feeders. The Central Park store also showcases unusual and unique jewelry pieces, including a collection of wedding rings.

KERBEY LANE DOLLHOUSES AND MINIATURES

3503 Kerbey Lane

(512) 454-4287

www.kerbeylanedollhouses.com

Granddads looking for wallpaper, roof shingles, or carpet for that dollhouse project can find it here. The store also features a large collection of dollhouse furniture along with tiny household accessories.

THE NEEDLEWORKS

26 Doors, 1206 West 38th Street

(512) 451-6931

www.theneedleworks.com

A mecca for needlework enthusiasts, this store in the 26 Doors shopping center features all manner of needlework supplies and kits, including traditional yarns, specialty fibers, accessories, books, instruction, and finishing.

RENAISSANCE MARKET

West 23rd and Guadalupe Streets

Some folks joke that Austin is an elephant's graveyard for old hippies, and Renaissance Market may be evidence of that. This small plaza on The Drag is home to a variety of crafters and artists who specialize in Woodstock-era items—tie-dyed shirts and skirts, silver jewelry, suncatchers, leather pouches and purses, etc. The outdoor market also attracts jugglers and mimes. A mural, dubbed "Austintatious," shows the city's life in the hippie heyday. Despite its laissez-faire atmosphere, the market is tightly regulated, and the operation is under the auspices of a special city oversight committee that makes sure only authentic hippie stuff is sold here. No place but Austin!

i Christmas shopping takes on special meaning in Austin because of two popular annual events: the Austin Junior League Christmas Affair in late November and the Armadillo Christmas Bazaar in December. Check our Annual Events and Festivals chapter for details.

SILK ROAD

3910 North Lamar Boulevard

(512) 302-0844

www.srfabrics.com

A plain-looking, small building across from Central Market houses this store that sells natural fabrics from around the world, including cottons, silks, linens, batiks, and velvets. The store has an unusual collection of bone, glass, jet, pewter, and wood buttons.

South Central

FANNY'S OUTLET FABRIC STORE

1150 South Lamar Boulevard

(512) 442-8255

The antithesis of an outlet, this small, friendly south Central Austin neighborhood shop features an assortment of fabrics and samples, plus decorating staples such as wide linen and Egyptian cotton. It is also a good spot to pick up information on the Austin fashion scene and the various events and classes held in the area.

HILL COUNTRY WEAVERS

1701 South Congress Avenue

(512) 707-7396

www.hillcountryweavers.com

For over two decades this store has been a vital resource for the "fiber community" that includes weavers, knitters and basketmakers. Supplies, classes and news about shows and events.

Southwest

COWGIRLS AND LACE

1111 US 290 West, Dripping Springs

(512) 858-4186

(800) 982-7424

www.cowgirlsandlace.com

A 15-minute drive (that's in non-rush hour traffic) from the Austin city limits along US 290 West in Southwest Austin, this outlet store sells designer fabrics at wholesale prices. In addition to more than 1,000 bolts of designer fabrics at discount prices, Cowgirls and Lace also stocks 100-inch-wide designer sheeting fabric.

North

FEATS OF CLAY

4630 Burnet Road

(512) 453-2111

www.featsofclay.com

Local potters buy supplies at this Central Austin store, plus the store offers kiln firing for home-made pieces. The store also features stoneware, earthenware, and porcelain by local potters. Pieces include dinnerware, batter bowls, large tureens, teapots, and bird feeders.

RENAISSANCE GLASS COMPANY

5200 Burnet Road

(512) 451-3971

www.rencoglass.com

Specializing in stained glass, this arts and crafts store also sells supplies for stained-glass artists. It is a good place to find tools for cutting glass and metal foil tapes for picture frames.

East

FIRE ISLAND HOT GLASS STUDIO, INC.

3401 East Fourth Street

(512) 389-1100

www.fireislandglass.com

Owners and artists Matthew LaBarbera and Teresa Uelschey create fine art pieces, custom designs, and small items for sale at their East Austin studio. The smaller items include perfume bottles and paperweights. The artists also offer demonstrations on Saturday morning September through January and March through May.

MITCHIE'S FINE BLACK ART GALLERY AND BOOKSTORE

6406 North I-35

Lincoln Village Shopping Center

(512) 323-6901

www.mitchie.com

Mitchie's celebrates African-American, African, and Caribbean culture, selling arts, crafts, and books that illustrate these regions and the work of the people who live there. The store has a large print collection celebrating the lives of sports figures, cultural and religious heroes, historical figures from the American Civil Rights movement, and celebrations of African and African-American life and art.

CLOTHING/FASHION

Central

BLACKMAIL

1202 South Congress Avenue

(512) 326-7670

www.blackmailboutique.com

One of several quirky fashion spots in SoCo, it's all about black here (although an occasional dash of red or spot of brown creeps in) and both the clothes and the home furnishings urge shoppers to "think noir!"

BY GEORGE

524 North Lamar Boulevard, Suite 103

(512) 472-5951

1400 South Congress Avenue

(512) 441-8600

www.bygeorgeaustin.com

The two By George shops are a favorite among young, hip, and well-heeled dressers. The look is simple and very modern; the price tag is not so simple. Designers featured include Stella McCartney, Vera Wang, Lanvin, Marc Jacobs, plus some lesser known names.

CAPRA & CAVELLI

3500 Jefferson Street, Suite 110

(512) 450-1919

www.capracavelli.com

This men's boutique features classic looks and designs, casual wear or button-down office outfits. The aim is to provide personal service to customers who want to look their best and be comfortable in the Austin climate.

CREATURES

1206 South Congress Avenue

(512) 707-2500

Sweatshop-free fashions by Misile and kooky shoes by the likes of French designer Colico give the wares here a decidedly young, hip feel. The boutique also has clothes for men and babies, really cute shoes for toddlers.

EMERALDS
624 Lamar Boulevard
(512) 476-4496

Emeralds is a favorite shopping spot for hip young women looking for simple, well-designed fashions. The store also has a shoe collection and a variety of modern accessories, plus decorative items for the home.

FETISH
1112 North Lamar Boulevard
(512) 457-1007

Sexy, smart, sleek shoes by designers like Isaac Mizrahi and Cynthia Rowley are sold here. The shop also stocks fashions to match, with designs by Diane von Furstenberg and Laundry, among others.

INSTEP
3105 Guadalupe Street
(512) 476-5110
www.instepaustin.com

This shoe store next door to Wheatsville Co-op features Birkenstock shoes and sandals. If your trusty Birkenstocks ever need fixing, this is the place; a repair shop is on site. The store also sells a line of leather-free "vegan" shoes.

JULIAN GOLD
1214 West Sixth Street
(512) 473-2493
www.juliangold.com

Catering to well-dressed, well-heeled (both in the bucks and the shoes departments) Texas women, Julian Gold has four stores in the state, where shoes, clothes, and accessories by designers like Escada, Bill Blass, and Valentino can be found, plus popular collections created by Ellen Tracy, Missoni, Ferragamo, Anne Klein, and Isaac are featured in the shoes department, and there are bridal, fur, evening wear, and cosmetic departments also.

SCARBROUGHS
Central Park, 4001 North Lamar Boulevard
(512) 452-4220
www.scarbroughs.com

For more than 100 years, this family-owned business has operated in Austin. The original downtown location opened in 1894. Now the family runs this upscale clothing store with a wide variety of evening, day, and resort wear in the Central Park Shopping Center.

T. KENNEDY
1011 West Lynn Street
(512) 478-0545

The emphasis is on natural women's clothing here—easy, natural design and natural fabrics including linen, cotton, and flax. Batik clothing is a specialty, and the store also features jewelry and accessories.

THE TEXAS CLOTHIER
2905 San Gabriel Street
(512) 478-4956
www.texasclothier.com

Owners Dain and LaDonna Higdon have survived the economic roller coaster in 20 years of business in Austin. After working for years in retail, Dain Higdon started his own store in 1976, and ever since Austin's busy, top businessmen and attorneys have turned to him for fashion advice. Higdon's clients insist on quality and are willing to pay for it.

TROPICAL TANTRUM
Central Park, 4001 North Lamar Boulevard, Suite 520
(512) 302-9888

Headed for an island getaway or just a backyard luau? Then check out the clothes at this small Central Park shop. The comfortable wear for both men and women includes hand-painted clothing and batiks for tropical nights and days on the Seychelles or Sixth Street.

South Central

THERAPY
1113 South Congress Avenue,
SoCo Center
(512) 326-2331
www.therapyclothing.com
SoCo is alive with shops, including several vintage clothing stores (see listings later in this chapter). While some of the fabrics used for Therapy's featured designs might be vintage, the creations are contemporary works by talented Austin designers. Owner Jyl Kutsche looks to local talent for clothing and accessories, notably handbags, and also imports smart, urban designs from New York and elsewhere. The store's Web site maintains a dialogue with customers and offers news on the latest fashions featured at the store.

Southwest

LAST CALL
Brodie Oaks Shopping Center,
4115 South Loop 360
(Capital of Texas Highway)
(512) 447-0701
This is Neiman Marcus without the posh surroundings and posh prices. The famous department store has its outlet store at this location in a small mall in Southwest Austin. The store features men's, women's, and children's fashions, shoes, some small decorative furniture items, and a few household items including sheets, pillows, and knickknacks. Items are discounted up to 70 percent.

SUE PATRICK
5222 Burnet Road, Suite 150
(512) 452-7701
www.suepatrick.com
Dressing comfortably and smartly in Austin's climate can be a challenge given the hot summer weather and sudden temperature changes in the winter. Sue Patrick offers a wide variety of casual and dressier fashions well suited to the Austin lifestyle. Some of the casual but comfortable fashions often have a hint of Texas in their cut or design.

CLOTHING/KIDS

Central

BRIGHT BEGINNINGS
1006 West 38th Street
(512) 454-KIDS

701 South Capital of Texas Highway
(Loop 360)
(512) 328-8989
www.bestdressedkids.com
Owner Sally Whitehouse keeps the Austin lifestyle in mind when stocking her store. Just like their elders, Austin kids like to play, and that means casual clothes, preferably in natural fabrics. Even the dress-up clothes here emphasize easy wearing and easy caring.

PICKET FENCES AND DOWN CHERRY LANE
1003 West 34th Street
(512) 458-2565
More than a kids clothing store, Picket Fences features (hence the name) picket-fence kids beds, plus nursery necessities, baby books, baby bags, decorative accents for the nursery or playroom, fabrics by the yard, window treatments, comfy nursery chairs for Mom or Dad, and maternity clothes. Custom orders are welcomed.

WILD CHILD AND WILD CHILD TOO!
1600 West 38th Street
(512) 451-0455, (512) 453-4335
Wild Child features "fashion-forward" clothing and shoes for infants and kids through size 6X. Wild Child Too! has the same hip clothing for preteen and junior kids. The store also stocks "preppy" clothes for preteens. including madras shirts, twill pants, and simple T-shirts.

North

DRAGONSNAPS
2438 West Anderson Lane
(512) 445-4497
Owned by the same folks who own Terra Toys (see our Toys section in this chapter), Dragonsnaps seeks to bring the Terra Toys free spirit to

kid's clothing. The clothes are easy to wear, fun, and eye-catching.

West

LAMBS-E-DIVEY
3663 Bee Caves Road
(512) 306-0566

This West Austin store features both casual wear for kids and outfits for those special occasions, such as Easter, Christmas, and family weddings.

CLOTHING/WESTERN

There is an old saying in Texas: "That boy is all hat," meaning, of course, there's too much image and not much substance. If you are going to don Western wear, you have to have the panache and some bucks. Good boots, a well-made hat, and a sturdy leather belt with a finely made belt buckle do not come cheap.

Not everyone in Texas dresses Western-style; in fact, "cowboys" come in various styles across the state. In Houston and Dallas you are more likely to see a businessman in a Brooks Brothers suit with a finely made pair of cowboy boots. In Amarillo or Midland, you might see a lawyer, cattleman, or oilman dressed for a business meeting in a Western-cut suit, a bolo tie, and boots. In the state's smaller towns and on farms and ranches, you are sure to see well-worn boots and traditional cowboy hats, while in El Paso and the Rio Grande Valley, the influence of Mexico's vaqueros (literally cowboys) can be seen in the design of belt buckles and boots.

In Austin, Western attire is not seen as much as in other parts of the state, although at some Western and Mexican dance clubs (see our Nightlife chapter) you will see both men and women dressed in fine Western wear. While you won't see a lot of Stetsons in Austin (outside the dance halls), you will see boots, particularly well-worn, much loved old boots, usually worn with jeans or a long skirt. Boots with no hat is okay, but a hat and no boots is a social faux pas. Nothing says Yankee like a guy in a cowboy hat and a pair of loafers.

There are several boot outlet stores in Austin, but the well-heeled will turn to one of the city's master boot makers or specialty shops for a custom-made pair—well-heeled because a good pair of boots can run to several hundred dollars. If you can't afford a pair, settle for a kerchief or two. A faded cotton kerchief, dipped in cold water and tied around your neck on a hot day, is an authentic cowboy tradition.

One word about two stores not listed in this section. Cabela's, a national chain catering to all things outdoors in terms of hunting and fishing, plus Callahan's, a local Austin "feed store" and more, both sell Western wear. We chose to list them in our Food section since they are both wonderful resources for foodies, selling cookware, preserving tools, and all manner of gadgets, but they are also a great resource for Western wear.

TEXAS HATTERS
911 Commerce Street
Lockhart
(512) 398-4287, (800) 421-HATS
www.texashatters.com

What does Prince Charles have in common with Willie Nelson? They both own hats created by one of the most famous Western wear artists in the United States, the late Manny Gammage. For decades, country western music stars, politicians, presidents, and future kings have worn what are generically called "cowboy hats." The walls of Gammage's workshop and store in the small community of Buda, just south of Austin off I-35, were covered with photos of famous folks. Gammage, like his father before him, blocked his hats by hand rather than by machine. Gammage passed away in 1995, but his family has carried on the tradition out of their Lockhart store.

Central

CAPITOL SADDLERY
1614 Lavaca Street
(512) 478-9309
www.capitolsaddlery.com

Singer Jerry Jeff Walker made this leather shop famous when he sang about the talents of late master boot maker Charlie Dunn. The store has an old-fashioned air, with boots, saddles, tack, and assorted leather wear stacked everywhere. Look for the large boot-shaped sign hanging outside the old building, just a few blocks west of the Capitol.

South Central

ALLEN BOOTS
1522 South Congress Avenue
(512) 447-1413
www.allenboots.com
This Western wear store has been on South Congress for years and now finds itself in the midst of a South Austin shopping revival. This is a great place to find Western wear and boots at reasonable prices. Enjoy the ambience. This is a Western wear shop without the glitz and urban cowboy atmosphere found in some other large Texas cities.

COMPUTERS

Austin has more computer stores than Los Angeles has car dealers. Perhaps not factually true, but metaphorically speaking it captures the tech mood in Austin. In addition to several major chain operations, there is an ever-growing subculture of small stores and resale outlets in Austin. Judging from online ads, it might appear that there's more money in motherboards than mother's old Buick. However, putting a system together from bits of this and that is easily done in Austin, provided you know your bytes from bits. Keep track of the ads, know who is a fixture on the landscape as opposed to a fly-by-night operation, and ask questions. Here is one unique Austin store for geeks:

GOODWILL COMPUTER WORKS
1015 Norwood Park Boulevard
(512) 637-7501
www.austincomputerworks.org
Whether you're looking for a cheap PC or an old classic Mac, this may be the place. Given Austin's intense high-tech industry growth and level of computer ownership, the town's closets are filled with old models. So Goodwill decided to provide a home for the abandoned. Old computers are donated to the shop, fixed up, and sold at bargain-basement prices. It's a great place to find a computer for a schoolchild or grandma without spending a fortune. There is an informal "museum" on-site, also.

FLEA MARKETS

Central

AUSTIN CITY-WIDE GARAGE SALES
Palmer Events Center
900 Barton Springs Road
(512) 441-2828
www.cwgs.com
The Palmer Events Center on Lady Bird Lake is host to a large sale, usually held once a month, featuring more than 180 vendors selling a variety of flea market merchandise. Dates vary, so check the Web site for each monthly sale.

Northeast

AUSTIN COUNTRY FLEA MARKET
9500 US 290 East
(512) 928-2795
www.austincountry.citymax.com
This is the real thing: an old-fashioned, take-your-chances flea market. A jumble of clothing, rugs, pottery, tools, records, furniture, CDs and videos, and sporting goods—all under one roof so that you can wander around, rain or shine. Beware, some of the "brand-name" items may not be the real thing. The market's Mexican herb stalls and Latino music stands give the market a south-of-the-border flavor. You also can have your palm or tarot cards read, or enjoy a snow cone and a barbecue sandwich. The market is approximately 5 miles east of I-35 and is open only on weekends.

Southwest

MARKET DAY
Lions Field, Wimberley
(512) 847-2201
www.visitwimberley.com/marketdays
On the first Saturday of the month, April through December, flea market mavens flock to Wimber-

ley, southwest of Austin, to comb the multitude of stalls at the famed Wimberley Market Day. Vendors number in the hundreds, and the wise get there early—to get first choice get there by 7:30 a.m. The Lions Club sells sausage wraps for breakfast and barbecue later in the day, plus a couple of local churches operate cake and cookie stands.

FARMERS' MARKETS

A good resource for keeping track of local farmers' market activities and the status of locally produced vegetables and fruits is the Web site www.localharvest.org which not only lists markets, but also farms where visitors and customers are welcome. The Texas Department of Agriculture's Web site www.picktexas.org is also another invaluable resource, especially if the family plans a peach-pickin' weekend.

Central

AUSTIN FARMERS' MARKET
422 Guadalupe Street
(512) 236-0074
www.austinfarmersmarket.org
The downtown market is the latest addition to the farmers' market scene in Austin, turning Republic Square, 2 blocks west of Congress Avenue, into a busy mix of food stalls and craftspeople every Saturday morning from 8:00 a.m. to noon. The market's Web site lists many of the vendors and links to their Web sites, offering information on Texas goat cheese, Oaxacan tamales, herbs, locally smoked salmon, mesquite spoons, and longhorn beef. The Web site also lists Capital Metro bus information. Midweek, the market holds a sale at The Triangle, the town center-like development at 46th Street between Lamar Boulevard and Guadalupe Street.

WHOLE FOODS FARMERS' MARKET
601 North Lamar Boulevard
(512) 476-1206
www.wholefoods.com
The downtown Whole Foods Market flagship store holds a weekly afternoon farmers' market in

i It is really a love story, a tale of how Sara Bolton with her family and friends created an award-winning goat cheese dairy and farm in the hills just west of Austin. Sara passed away at 52, surrounded by her loved ones, but her family continues to produce incredibly delicious cheese at Pure Luck Farm and visitors can arrange for tours. There are also open house days and special classes. Check the farm Web site www.pure lucktexas.com.

front of the store. The market is usually held on Wednesday afternoon from spring through fall, but check with the store for times.

South

SOUTH AUSTIN FARMERS' MARKET
2910 South Congress Avenue
(512) 285-4758
www.austinfarm.org
Local farmers set up shop in the parking lot of the El Gallo restaurant on Saturday morning from spring to fall.

Southwest

SUNSET VALLEY FARMERS' MARKET
3200 Jones Road
(512) 280-1976
www.sunsetvalleyfarmersmarket.com
The Westlake Farmers' Market grew to such a size that it has moved to this larger site at the Toney Burger stadium parking lot in southwest Austin. Some of the best-known names in Austin foodie circles have a presence here, including Sweetish Hill Bakery (see our Restaurants chapter), and food purveyors from the Hill Country like Chatauqua River Salmon can be found here Saturday morning.

Northwest

WHOLE FOODS FARMERS' MARKET
Gateway Shopping Center,
9607 Research Boulevard
(512) 345-5003
www.wholefoods.com

Whole Foods at Gateway holds a seasonal farmers' market spring through fall, usually on Monday afternoon. Call the store for times.

East

BOGGY CREEK FARM
3414 Lyons Road
(512) 926-4650
www.boggycreekfarm.com

It is almost unbelievable that just 2½ miles east of downtown Austin in an old East Austin neighborhood is a five-acre organic farm that offers its products for sale every Wednesday and Saturday morning throughout the year. Boggy Creek Farm is noted for its fruit and vegetable crops, particularly its tomatoes. Owners Larry Butler and Carol Ann Sayle send out a weekly e-mail to customers, announcing what is in season. But there's more; the e-mail also includes wonderfully written glimpses into farm life that offer busy urbanites a moment's pause for reflection.

FOOD/GOURMET/ KITCHENWARE

Austin is a city that considers food a significant part of life, not in a highfalutin way, although the city's restaurants boast a fair number of top-notch chefs, but in a way that celebrates the mix of food and friends, new tastes and familiar comforts. It is no surprise that when out-of-town visitors arrive, many Austinites take them on a discovery tour of the city's food stores (see Close-up in this chapter).

Central

ACE MART RESTAURANT SUPPLY CO.
2415 South Congress Avenue
(512) 482-8700

9411 North Lamar Boulevard
(512) 832-9933
www.acemart.com

A little-known secret in cooking circles is that many restaurant supply companies are open to the public. Ace sells both to the trade and to the individual customer. Thrifty cooks and host-esses will check out the price of plates, glasses, silverware, and party ware here. There are two locations, a new one in central Austin since its Fifth Street location was sold to a loft developer, and a second in north Austin.

ANDERSON COFFEE COMPANY
Jefferson Square
(512) 453-1533
www.andersonscoffee.com

Jefferson Square, just off West 35th Street near Kerbey Lane, is a collection of small, older homes turned into cozy shops, a fitting setting for Anderson Coffee Company, founded in 1972 and which sells coffees, teas, mugs, and teapots, plus culinary spices—comfort stuff. Singer-songwriter Lyle Lovett is said to be a fan of Anderson's coffee.

BREED & COMPANY
718 West 29th Street
(512) 474-6679

3663 Bee Caves Road
(512) 328-3960
www.breedandco.com

This is the kind of store that actually can bring couples closer together, even heal marriages. One partner can stroll the nuts and bolts section, while the other daydreams about the days when the entire collection of cooking equipment will find its way to his or her kitchen. The store stocks hard-to-find and everyday hardware and paint supplies, cleaning solutions, china and crystal, a perfumery, a specialty food section, garden supplies, picture frames, decorative accessories, throw rugs, coffee beans, bird feeders, knives, cutting boards, and all manner of cookware.

i Shopping for a special birthday cake, desserts for a dinner party, or fresh breads for a picnic on Lady Bird Lake? Check out our Restaurants listings for three popular Austin bakeries—Sweetish Hill Bakery on West Sixth Street, Texas French Bread with several locations around the city, and Upper Crust Bakery on Burnet Road.

Breed also offers bridal and gift registries and cooking classes and events.

CENTRAL MARKET
**Central Park, 40th Street and
Lamar Boulevard
(512) 216-1000**

**Westgate, Ben White and South
Lamar Boulevards
(512) 899-4300
www.centralmarket.com**
Both Central Market supermarkets are must-see stops for foodies. See our Close-up in this chapter.

CIPOLLINA
**1213 West Lynn Street
(512) 477-1237
www.cipollina-austin.com**
The name is Italian for a special, small sweet onion, often grilled or roasted in a sweet balsamic vinegar, and it is a fitting symbol for this popular take-out deli in the Clarksville neighborhood created by the owners of one of Austin's favorite restaurants, Jeffrey's (see our Restaurants chapter). A great place to stop for picnic fare or a take-home dinner feast.

PASTA & CO.
**3502 Kerbey Lane
(512) 453-0633
www.austinpasta.com**
Pasta to go is the theme here. The company makes numerous kinds of pasta and sauces, including jalapeño fettucine, wild-mushroom ravioli, and ancho-pecan pesto. For those who can't bring themselves to boil a pot of water, the store also features ready-cooked pasta dishes that simply need reheating. For Valentine's Day, the store makes special heart-shaped varieties.

PORTABLA
**1200 West Sixth Street
(512) 481-TOGO (8646)
www.portabla.com**
Casual eating is a hallmark of the Austin scene, and this take-out deli (affiliated with nearby Sweetish Hill Bakery; see below) offers a variety of dishes, many with a Mediterranean flavor. Portabla also caters small and large parties. During football season, there is a tailgate menu offered to feed the fans in style. Closed Sunday.

SPEC'S LIQUORS
**5775 Airport Boulevard
(512) 366-8300**

**4960 West US Highway 290
(512) 366-8260**

**10515 North MoPac Boulevard
Arborwalk shopping center
(512) 342-6893
www.speconline.com**
This Houston-based liquor store, wine shop and deli was a welcome addition to the Austin foodie scene for bargain hunters. There are three locations, one central, one southwest and a third northwest. Pay with cash or a debit card and get an extra discount.

SWEETISH HILL BAKERY
**1120 West Sixth Street
(512) 472-1347**

**98 San Jacinto Boulevard
(512) 472-1347
www.sweetishhill.com**
One of Austin's most noted bakeries, Sweetish Hill is famed for its breads, cookies (the lemon bars are addictive), and European-style pastries. This is a great place to order a special birthday cake and many Austinites insist on a chocolate or *mocha buche de noel* (a French cake shaped and decorated like a log, complete with meringue mushrooms) at Christmas time. The bakery is also a popular breakfast and lunch spot (see our Restaurants chapter).

WHEATSVILLE FOOD CO-OP
**3101 Guadalupe Street
(512) 478-2667
www.wheatsville.com**
Wheatsville is an old-fashioned cooperative grocery store where the customers own the store.

Close-Up

Austin's Feeding Frenzy

One surefire way to judge how people regard their hometown is to ask them where they take out-of-town visitors for an Insider's view of their city. Austin residents are lucky. The list of favorite spots is long and varied, but three spots appear on most short lists—Barton Springs Pool, the State Capitol, and the grocery store. The grocery store? Yep, but not just any grocery store and not just one. Austin is the birthplace of two marvelous grocery stores, Central Market and Whole Foods. One is the creation of an old Texas family-owned grocery store chain, H-E-B; the other grew out of the imaginations of several hippies, for want of a better word, who took the old concept of a health food store to places they could only dream of 25 years ago. We have described both stores below and, in fairness, listed them alphabetically, but any serious food enthusiast should visit both and take a large shopping bag.

Central Market now ranks among the city's most visited landmarks, and it has become a living symbol of the city's lifestyle. Since it opened in January 1994, this central city grocery store has been a popular spot to give visitors a real peek at the Austin approach to living. On any given weekend, when the store is at its busiest, it is possible to see Austinites from all parts of the city, of all ages and backgrounds, speaking a variety of languages. They will be meandering through the store's aisles, tasting this, sampling that, and finding all manner of ingredients, some familiar, others exotic. Many are eagerly showing out-of-town guests or relatives the bounty at hand. So popular was the original Central Market, a second has opened in Southwest Austin—Central Market Westgate.

On the eve of holidays such as July Fourth, Thanksgiving, and Christmas, finding a parking place at either of the shopping centers can be an exercise in patience. What draws the crowds to these central Austin grocery stores? It is a combination of ambience, incredible variety, and the notion that cuisine is an integral part of the Austin lifestyle, particularly on weekends when Austinites light their barbecues, fire up their smokers, pack their picnic baskets, and fill up their ice chests.

The Central Market concept is the creation of the H-E-B grocery store chain, a family-owned South Texas chain now headquartered in restored buildings in the historic King William District in San Antonio. H-E-B has been an innovator, both in its concept developments and its growth; in fact, the company has opened grocery stores in northern Mexico and is enjoying success in that country. The original Central Market in Austin is the model for others around the state, where residents quickly demanded their own Central Markets. However, each one is a little different in design and content. Central Market is designed to stimulate the imagination, educate the shopper, and broaden his or her horizons. In doing so, the store captured the hearts (and pocketbooks) of Austin foodies—although it should be noted that while luxury items do abound here, prices for everyday items are competitive with neighborhood grocery stores.

The operative word here is *market*—Central Market is designed to evoke the spirit of an Old World marketplace. Visitors enter a vegetable and fruit market first, then proceed to a fish and meat market, a wine shop, a specialty food area, a bakery, a deli, and a cheese shop, finally reaching the front of the store, where a flower shop stands. The original Central Market building itself is a blend of local materials and design elements taken from 19th-century Texas buildings with a hint of Italian inspiration. The limestone walls and tin roof reflect buildings from the Texas frontier, while the terra-cotta columns evoke Tuscan architecture. A large tile mural by Austin artist Malou Flato at the front of the store depicts Barton Springs pool. The second location also borrows Austin icons, and there is a replica of the city's moonlight towers (see our Attractions chapter) out front, plus more tile murals of wildflowers by Flato.

Among Central Market's most crowded spots on the weekend are the butcher shop and fishmonger. The meat market features aged premium choice beef, lamb, veal, naturally raised pork, and poultry raised on organic grains, as well as 48 varieties of custom-made sausage. Special cuts of meat can be ordered, and many Austinites put in their orders for holiday turkeys or rib roasts. The 75-foot-long seafood counter at the original store offers up to 100 varieties of both saltwaterand freshwater fish, shellfish, and sushi, plus up to six varieties of fresh salmon in season.

The store's wine and beer shop offers 2,700 domestic and imported wines and more than 330 varieties of beer produced by American microbreweries and foreign brewers. Many of the wine selections are available for less than $10, and the store's wine shop has been voted Austin's best by the *Austin Chronicle* several years in a row. The specialty foods section of the store features more than 175 olive oils, 165 varieties of vinegar, 60 varieties of barbecue sauce—and the list goes on. Freezers hold Indian and Chinese foods and sorbets made from exotic fruits; the dairy case is filled with butter from Europe and milk in glass bottles from Texas cows. The coffee and tea shop has coffee beans from Africa, Brazil, Mexico, and Hawaii; teas from the Himalayas; biscotti from Italy. Then there is the bakery, where French baguettes are baked daily (along with a large variety of other breads, including a personal favorite, southern Burgundy walnut bread), and fresh tortillas roll off the conveyer belt of the tortilla machine. The deli has prosciuttos from Italy, smoked salmon from Scotland, pâtés, and organic cold cuts. Then there is the pasta shop, where shoppers can match handmade pasta with fresh sauces or pestos, and the cheese shop with cheeses from the best producers in the United States and Europe. Across the way is the salsa, pickle, olive, and antipasto bar. One final stop—the flower shop at the front of the market. Here shoppers can find a wide variety of ready-made bouquets, including Hill Country wildflower bouquets in season, special holiday arrangements, and dried-flower creations. You can also get custom-designed bouquets for any occasion.

On the second floor of the original store is the Central Market Cooking School, where internationally known chefs as well as top Austin chefs have taught. Both stores also feature a Central Market Cafe (see our Restaurants and Kidstuff chapters), a popular family gathering spot where patrons can eat inside or listen to a variety of local musicians while eating on the deck. The original location at 4001 North Lamar Boulevard is open from 9:00 a.m. to 9:00 p.m. daily, and the cafe is open from 7:00 a.m. to 10:00 p.m. daily. Call (512) 206-1000 for general information, (512) 206-1013 for the meat market, (512) 206-1012 for the seafood market, and (512) 458-3068 for the cooking school. The Westgate location at 4477 South Lamar Boulevard is open from 9:00 a.m. to 9:00 p.m. daily, and the cafe from 7:00 a.m. to 10:00 p.m. daily. Call (512) 899-4300 for all departments. During the holidays, notably Thanksgiving and Christmas, both stores extend their hours in the evening. For more information check out www.central market.com.

The first **Whole Foods Market** was in a tiny store not much bigger than a 7-11—the premises are now occupied by Cheapo Discs at 914 North Lamar Boulevard. But just 2 blocks to the south is the world headquarters of Whole Foods, where the corporate offices make the old store look like a crowded VW bus. Whole Foods was founded in 1980 when three local health food store owners came together. Back then the store had 19 employees, now it has 32,000 and operates 180 stores in three countries, including Canada and the United Kingdom. Its stock is listed on NASDAQ, and like the Austinites who bought stock in Dell years ago, it has made some people very, very happy. But commercial success aside, the company strives to keep the old ethic going that it developed in its first days, according to CEO John Mackey. In the beginning, Whole Foods developed a team member approach where employees shared profits and had input into company policy, and that is still the approach, making a Whole Foods job a prize for some. (The store's Team Members tend to be a unique group as any stroll through the store will reveal, and some are musicians, writers, poets, etc., who like to express their individuality both on and off the job.) The company's philosophy is laid out on the Whole Foods Web site where you can find a sort of company constitution, dubbed a "Declaration of Interdependence."

continued

One thing Whole Foods is communicating these days is that Austin is its birthplace, and to that end Austinites deserve the best. In March 2005 the company opened its newest and largest store, the Landmark Store in Austin, located next to its six-story corporate headquarters. At 80,000 feet the new store is the largest in the chain, which now boasts stores in the most chic parts of New York, London, and San Francisco. The entrance to the store is through Market Hall, a semi-outdoor area meant to evoke a farmers' market. Shoppers can either park in a small lot in front of the store or underground where their purchases can be delivered curbside.

True to its roots, much of the produce is organic, and the store also has a large health care and supplements section, plus organic products of all kinds including clothing, paper goods, soaps, and cleaners. But it is also a veritable gold mine of foods from various cultures—aisles are dedicated geographically in some cases—and for a multitude of taste buds. The meat and seafood departments are large and offer not just various cuts but also smoked meats, aged beef, shucked oysters, and ready-to-go cooked foods of all varieties. There is a barbecued meat counter, smoked fish counter, and a large variety of fresh sausages.

From the moment the shopper enters the store and sees Lamar Street Greens, a fresh food cafe, he or she is surrounded by not just a multitude of grocery choices but also in-house mini-restaurants, small food counters where a customer can get a full meal or a snack. Pasta, salads, a cheese and wine bar, ethnic foods, a pizza oven, a smoked nut bar, noodles and sushi, satays and soups, coffee and raw foods, you name it, Whole Foods likely has it and you can eat it here, on the rooftop garden, or take it home. There is also a large wine and beer section, a bakery, and a chocolate bar with freshly made truffles, a deli, a cheese shop, an olive bar, and a Candy Island where fresh fruit is dipped in chocolate. Did we mention the smoothie bar, the dessert shop, the mashed potatoes, the grilled veggies? Did we miss anything? Yes.

Just in case you can't find what you want, there is a concierge desk at the front of the store where you pick up an iPod and take a tour. The store's concierge also will shop for you if you don't have time and even offers a pantry-stocking and makeover service, plus wine cellar management. For concierge services call (512) 542-2243. For those of us who remember the old Whole Foods with its cramped aisles and tiny parking lot, the new Landmark Store sums up the journey Austin has been on for the last 25 years, literally from soup to nuts. The Whole Foods Landmark Store is open from 8:00 a.m. to 10:00 p.m. daily and is located at 525 North Lamar Boulevard, (512) 476-1206, www.wholefoods.com. A second, smaller store is located in northwest Austin in the Gateway Plaza, 9607 Research Boulevard, (512) 345-5003.

Members pay a nominal annual fee or purchase a share, but anyone can shop here. The co-op specializes in natural foods, and there is a vegetarian deli.

WIGGY'S
1130 West Sixth Street
(512) 474-WINE (9463)

1104 North Lamar Boulevard
(512) 479-6045

If you are picking up a picnic at nearby Portabla, Cipollina, or Sweetish Hill, these two small central Austin stores are a good place to find a wine to complement your menu. The staff is knowledgeable and the shops offer a wide range of wines, some bargains, others more expensive. The stores also have a large selection of cigars and spirits.

South Central

CISSI'S MARKET
1400 South Congress Avenue
(512) 225-0521
www.cissismarket.com

It's all about the essentials here—essential deli meats, pastries, breads, wines, coffees. Food for the soul to eat on the premises, take home for a easy supper, or pack for a picnic in Zilker Park.

FARM TO MARKET GROCERY

1718 South Congress Avenue
(512) 462-7220
www.fm1718.com

A loaf of bread, a jug of wine, and a can of tomatoes. This SoCo neighborhood grocery store (look for the big radish sign) provides essentials and staples for home cooks in the nearby neighborhoods. The owners emphasize local and organic produce and products.

LA MEXICANA BAKERY

1816 South First Street
(512) 447-1280

Mexican pastries are intended to be mood-lifters, a little sweet bite to accompany midmorning coffee, or a late-night snack with a cup of hot Mexican chocolate. Many contain no salt or preservatives, so they are best eaten the day they are made. La Mexicana offers a variety of cookies and cakes, empanadas stuffed with pumpkin, gingerbread pigs, and sugarcoated conchas (shell-shaped cakes). Be sure to ask the names of the varieties—often they are a wonderful play on the shape, ingredients, or taste of the item. The bakery also sells Mexican sodas.

PHOENICIA BAKERY & DELI

2912 South Lamar Boulevard
(512) 447-4444

4701 Burnet Road
(512) 323-6770
www.phoenicabakery.com

Phoenicia is a deli specializing in imported foods from those countries and regions that ring the Mediterranean. In addition to olives, olive oils, peppers, spices, sauces, pasta, and grains, the store also sells cold cuts, plus cheeses from the region, pickles, stuffed grape leaves, freshly made tahini, and hummus. There is a frozen food section where bakers can find phyllo dough. The deli also makes sandwiches and has a small bakery selling pita bread and baklava, plus other regional delights. In addition to the original location in South Central Austin, a second, larger new store has opened in uptown Austin on Burnet Road.

Northwest

FARADAYS

1501 RR 620 North
Lakeway
(512) 266-5660
www.faradayskitchenstore.com

Cooks don't have to drive into Austin to shop for the best culinary tools or even take cooking classes. Faraday's offers the best in the hills near the lakes west of Austin.

North

ASAHI IMPORTS

100 West North Loop Boulevard
(512) 453-1850

It is easy to miss this store with its unassuming storefront in a strip shopping center, but its selection of everyday Japanese ceramics, sake sets, rice bowls, teapots, plus origami kits and Japanese food items (tea, rice candy, plum wine) is well worth seeking out, both for price and quality.

GRAPE VINE MARKET

7938 Great Northern Boulevard
(512) 323-2900
www.grapevinemarket.com

This 18,000-square-foot gourmet food and wine shop also offers classes and tastings and has a rare-wine room where exceptional wines can be bought for special occasions. The store also designs gift baskets, sells gourmet foods and special take-out dishes, offers a bridal registry, and has a large selection of cigars and spirits. The store is located just east of MoPac off Anderson Lane. Closed Sunday.

HONG KONG SUPERMARKET

8557 Research Boulevard
(512) 339-2068
www.hongkong-supermarket.com

A stroll around this North Austin supermarket is like a culinary tour of Asia. Formerly a neighborhood grocery store, the owners took over the facility and filled it with Asian foodstuffs, fresh, frozen, and canned, to meet the needs of Austin's growing Asian population. The meat and fresh fish section features cuts and types of fish and fowl popular among cooks. There is a cooked meat section with barbecued ducks and meats, plus several aisles featuring kitchen and household goods. It is a good place to buy noodles, tea, and rice in bulk.

LAMME'S CANDIES
5330 Airport Boulevard
(512) 310-2223, (800) 252-1885
www.lammes.com

The Lamme family has been making candies in Austin since 1885. Famed for Texas Chewie Pecan Pralines, Lamme's also heralds the early summer with its chocolate-dipped strawberries. The company's headquarters is on Airport Boulevard, but there are other locations around the area: Lamar Village at 38th Street in Central Austin, downtown at Sixth and Congress, Northcross Mall in North Austin, Barton Creek Mall in West Austin, Highland Mall in North Austin, Lakeline Mall in Northwest Austin, R.R. 620 and I-35 in Round Rock, and at San Marcos Factory Outlet stores.

LA VICTORIA BAKERY
5425 Burnet Road
(512) 458-1898

Owner Anita Becerra creates Mexican specialties at this small bakery on Burnet Road. One seasonal item worth seeking out is her pan de muerto or Day of the Dead bread, which celebrates the annual Mexican holiday on All Souls Day. (See our Annual Events chapter for more on All Souls Day.)

MANDOLA'S ITALIAN MARKET
4700 West Guadalupe Street
(512) 419-9700
www.mandolasmarket.com

The creation of Texas chef Damian Mandola, this store and cafe features all the essential Italian ingredients and goodies. Fresh bread, meats and cheeses, pastas both dried and homemade, olive oils, vinegars and antipasto essentials. For desserts, there is a gelati bar and bakery with biscotti and ladyfingers for tiramisu.

MGM INDIAN FOODS
7427 Burnet Road
(512) 459-5353
www.mgmindianfoods.com

This is the city's oldest Indian grocery, stocking herbs, vegetables, dried fruits and nuts, and other vital ingredients for Indian cuisine. Recently the owner, who hails from the state of Kerala in India, has added foods from Ghana and Nigeria to meet customer demands.

MT SUPERMARKET
10901 North Lamar Boulevard
(512) 454-4804
www.mtsupermarket.com

This 55,000 square foot supermarket serves Austin's growing Asian population and aficionados of Asian cuisine. The supermarket is the anchor to Austin's Chinatown market (www.chinatown austin.com), and has vast aisles of fresh vegetables, fish tanks, and staples to stock Chinese, Thai, Japanese, Indian, Filipino, Korean, and Vietnamese kitchens. Chinatown is the location for traditional Asian festivals like Chinese New Year and the shopping center joined in the Chuy's Christmas children parade (see our Annual Events and Festivals chapter) with a popular Hello Kitty float.

SAIGON ORIENTAL MARKET
8610 North Lamar Boulevard
(512) 837-6641

This grocery stocks a full line of Vietnamese ingredients and also sells cooking utensils, incense, and traditional festival decorations.

SUR LA TABLE
11410 Century Oaks Terrace
(512) 833-6905
www.surlatable.com

This Austin branch of the foodie favorite national chain offers chef's tools; the best cooking pots, pans, and devices; plus wonderful linens and crockery. Spend a few dollars or go whole hog on tools to enhance your kitchen skills. Sur La Table is located on the ritzy main street of The Domain shopping center.

East

CALLAHAN'S GENERAL STORE
501 U.S. Highway 183
(512) 385-3452
www.callahansgeneralstore.com
The closest thing to an old-fashioned general store in Austin, Callahan's sells sausage-stuffing machines, canning equipment, cast iron cookware, and all manner of supplies for cooks. In addition, they have Western wear, boots, saddles, and supplies for the farm and ranch.

EL MILAGRO
910 East Sixth Street
(512) 477-6476
www.el-milagro.com
El Milagro—the Miracle—is an authentic tortilla factory that sells both wholesale to Austin grocery stores and restaurants and retail to the walk-in customers. Buying from the source can be fun, and it gives you an opportunity to see the inner workings of an authentic culinary tradition both south of the border and in Texas. Ambitious cooks who plan to follow a Texas tradition and make Christmas tamales can buy freshly ground masa (cornmeal) from the factory. Some Austin foodies swear the "Blancas" white corn tortillas are the best in town. Check out the Web site for its great music and recipes.

FIESTA MART
3909 North I-35
(512) 406-3900

5510 South I-35
(512) 373-7800
www.fiestamart.com
A branch of the Houston supermarket chain, Fiesta takes a multicultural approach to the grocery store business. Everything from banana leaves for tamales to British custard mixes can be found on the shelves here. If your Puerto Rican pen pal or your great-aunt from Australia is coming to town, check the shelves here for those grocery essentials.

South

CABELA'S
15570 I-35
Buda
(512) 925-1100
www.cabelas.com
Maybe the only store that some shopping-averse men will go to with enthusiasm. This national chain sells all things for the outdoor life, hunting, fishing, camping, etc., but we like it for its wide range of foodie supplies. Cast iron cookware, home preserving and sausage-making equipment. Big fryers for that southern fried turkey, chili pots big enough to feed the team, plus picnic and barbecue supplies.

West

GREAT HARVEST BAKERY
3201 Bee Caves Road
(512) 329-9216

4815 West Braker Lane
(512) 345-0588
www.greatharvest.com
Noted for their crusty, rustic, flavorful European-style breads, Great Harvest has two locations and also sells its breads to local restaurants and grocery stores.

TRIANON COFFEE ROASTERS
3201 Bee Caves Road
(512) 328-4033
www.trianon.com
This French-style coffee boutique sells freshly roasted beans, pastries, chocolate, and candies.

Round Rock

LONE STAR BAKERY
106 West Liberty
(512) 255-3629
www.roundrockdonuts.com
Lone Star claims to make the best doughnuts in Texas, and there is no harm in testing their claim, even coming back for seconds or thirds to make sure the boast is true.

SARADORA'S COFFEEHOUSE & EMPORIUM
101 East Main Street
(512) 310-1200
In addition to a coffee bar, this store in the historic town center sells roasted beans, fresh breads, and pastries to go, plus homemade fudge and Austin's own Amy's ice cream.

GARDENING

Central

GARDENS
18118 West 35th Street
(512) 451-5490
www.gardens-austin.com
The small garden in front of this Central Austin garden shop is living proof that wonderful gardens can be created not only in small spaces but also in the Austin climate, where summer heat and drought can be a challenge. The creators have been featured in *Martha Stewart Living* and top design magazines. Don't be fooled by the outward appearance of this shop in the 35th Street shopping corridor; it may look small, but inside there is a mother lode of resources for serious gardeners—imported pottery from Italy, Japanese garden elements, English garden tools, books, seeds, and an outdoor nursery of herbs and plants, many of them unusual and eye-catching. This is a must-stop for any ardent gardener. The small store also sells exquisite home furnishings with a natural, handmade appeal that reflects the store's aesthetic.

South Central

FLORIBUNDA
2401–B South Lamar Boulevard
(512) 441-6145
www.floribundawork.com
Tucked behind a bead shop and a vintage clothing store, Floribunda is like a small magic garden. Austin-friendly plants, vibrant pots, seeds, tools, and garden ornaments are arranged artfully in this hidden garden. Ivan Spaller, a young Austin garden artist who once worked at the Bush Kennebunkport, Maine, home, has designed several garden follies, including a literal lawn chair—an oversize lawn-covered sofa that sits in one corner of the garden—and a four-poster lawn "bed."

THE GREAT OUTDOORS
3730 South Congress Avenue
(512) 448-2992
www.gonursery.com
Huge live oaks cover this South Austin nursery across from the St. Edward's University campus, making it a pleasant place to meander while choosing plants and daydreaming about garden projects. The garden center offers advice on growing in the challenging Austin climate and has special tips on bamboo, fruit trees, banana palms, and other tropicals that can tolerate both hot summers and sudden cold snaps. Another attraction is the on-site outdoor cafe, the Mad Bird Juice Garden, where smoothies, coffee, muffins, cookies, and sandwiches are served amid the horticultural surroundings.

South

IT'S ABOUT THYME
11726 Manchaca Road
(512) 280-1192
www.itsaboutthyme.com
Newcomers to Austin who enjoy gardening may be frustrated if they try to grow plants that flourish in cooler, northern climes, but they won't be disappointed if they stick to native plants and those herbs that do well in Mediterranean countries—rosemary, oregano, basil, and thyme. This South Austin herb nursery, 2 miles south of Slaughter Lane, has a wide selection of herbs and related items. The shop also sells antique roses, which do quite well in the Austin climate, and xeriscape and pond plants.

Southwest

THE NATURAL GARDENER
8648 Old Bee Caves Road
(512) 288-6113
www.naturalgardeneraustin.com
Owner John Dromgole is a well-known radio personality who preaches the benefits of organic

gardening every Saturday morning on KLBJ–AM The nursery, tucked away on a country road in Southwest Austin, is always busy on the weekends as Austin gardeners flock here for plants, flowers, vegetables, seeds, and a wonderful variety of tools and garden ornaments. There is an antique rose collection, plus xeriscape plants for low water–maintenance gardens. The nursery also sells a line of soils and fertilizers, including Dillo Dirt, a soil enhancer made from recycled Austin sewage wastes. Shoppers can bag their soils or have large amounts delivered.

West

BARTON SPRINGS NURSERY
3601 Bee Caves Road
(512) 328-6655
www.bartonspringsnursery.com
This West Lake Hills nursery features an extensive collection of native plants. Newcomers soon learn that native is often the best way to go in the Austin climate, and many varieties and species can be found here. The owners and staff have a warehouse of knowledge to help gardeners overcome the challenges of Hill Country gardening. The center also has a collection of wildflower seeds and garden ornaments.

POTS AND PLANTS
5902 Bee Caves Road
(512) 327-4564
www.plasticpinkflamingos.com
"That crazy flamingo place" is how you will hear radio ads refer to this West Austin garden center. Austin gardeners know spring is on the way when

i It is a dream shopping trip for anyone fascinated by architectural salvage, plus the drive is a pretty one on a spring day. Discovery Architectural Antiques, 409 Saint Francis Street, in Gonzales, a small town 60 miles southeast of Austin, boasts a vast array of doors, old ceiling tiles, sinks, bathtubs, and hardware—all salvaged from old homes. (830) 672-2428, www.discoverys .net.

a few pink flamingos show up on the front lawn of Pots and Plants at the intersection of Bee Caves Road and Loop 360. Later, the rest of the pink plastic flock arrives and Austin gardeners know the planting season goes into full swing. The garden center has a wide selection of native plants, plus deer-resistant varieties and the Web site has a Web cam with live shots of the flamingos.

East

BIG RED SUN
1102 East Cesar Chavez Street
(512) 480-0688
www.bigredsun.com
This garden design and landscaping business also houses a wonderful garden shop with strikingly modern planters, imported ceramic pots, and "retro-botanicals" that match the Austin climate and hip personality. A small store on-site, Little Green Moon, sells unusual clothing for children, reflecting the fact that this is a family business, and there is a housewares section also.

PITCHFORKS AND TABLESPOONS
2113 Manor Road
(512) 476-5858
www.eastsidecafe.com
They grow their own vegetables and herbs at the Eastside Cafe (see our Restaurants chapter), so it was only logical that a small food and garden shop open on-site at this—the name says it all—eastside cafe. In addition to gourmet and homestyle pantry items, patrons can find balm to soothe those garden-stressed hands, birdhouses and butterfly kits, herbs, and natural fertilizers.

GIFTS

Central

ATOMIC CITY
1700 San Antonio Street
(512) 477-0293
Toys are us—for grown-ups that is. Atomic City is the place to find Godzillas that spit fire, fighting nuns, and other Japanese toys to keep on the desk for those moments when the brain

bombs. The store also has a large collection of tin toys, lava lamps, Hawaiian shirts, even boots and shoes to add just the right sartorial touch to a toy player's tropical outfit.

CAPITOL COMPLEX VISITORS CENTER
112 East 11th Street, Capitol Annex
(512) 305-8400
www.texascapitolgiftshop.com
The capitol police report the occasional ardent tourist attempting to remove part of the capitol's wrought-iron fence, a doorknob, or door hinge as a memento. But law-abiding visitors head to the capitol's gift shop where gifts reflecting these architectural elements can be bought without risking arrest. Replicas of the capitol's door hinges serve as bookends; other architectural elements are reproduced in paperweights. The store has a first-class collection of posters, flags, and books about Texas flora, fauna, travel, and history. The small shop also sells Texas foods and T-shirts.

COWGIRLS AND FLOWERS
508 Walsh Street
(512) 478-4626
www.cowgirlsandflowers.com
One of the most popular flower shops in the central city, Cowgirls is noted for its jewelry and craft items. If you are looking for a very artsy flower presentation, plus a special gift, check out this Central Austin store.

THE MENAGERIE
1601 West 38th Street, Suite 7
(512) 453-4644
www.themenagerie.com
Bucatelli, Christofle, Saint Louis, and Wedgwood are just some of the top names in crystal, china, and silver that can be found at this small, elegant Jefferson Square shop. The bridal registry is a favorite among some of Austin's old families. The shop also sells jewelry and collectibles.

MORNING STAR TRADING COMPANY
1919 South First Street
(512) 476-1726
The major trade here is in oils and essences aimed at making folks feel better. The store sells massage, relaxation, and bath oils, plus other body-care products.

OAT WILLIE'S
617 West 29th Street
(512) 482-0630
www.oatwillies.com
Remember the term "head shop"? A visit to Oat Willie's is a jaunt down memory lane for anyone who grew up in the '60s. Whenever you see an "Onward through the Fog" bumper sticker, you are a looking at an Austin hallmark—this was Oat Willie's slogan. Oat Willie once ran for president, and his T-shirts are now collectors' items. T-shirts are still sold at Oat Willie's, along with comic books, videos, toys, and clothing.

THE OLD BAKERY AND EMPORIUM
1006 Congress Avenue
(512) 477-5961
Austin's senior citizens sell their crafts in this old store just a block south of the capitol (see our Attractions chapter). Located in a beautiful, restored 1876 building, the Old Bakery also has a sandwich shop and visitor information desk.

PAPER PLACE
4001 North Lamar Boulevard, Suite 540
(512) 451-6531
www.paperplaceaustin.com
The stock here goes beyond invitations, celebratory cards for all occasions, and stationery to include a large stock of handmade papers that can be used in a variety of crafts.

POSITIVE IMAGES
1118 West Sixth Street
(512) 472-1831
Part of the so-called West End shopping district, this store has a delightful mix of handcrafted jewelry, wooden boxes, and glass art. The store also sells fantastical furniture—carved, painted, and decorated with inspirational and witty sayings—woodland animals, pastoral scenes, and fairy-tale fantasies.

THINGS CELTIC
1806 West 35th Street
(512) 472-2358
www.thingsceltic.com
The name says it all here. The shop features arts, crafts, and food items from the Celtic world—Scotland, Ireland, Wales, Cornwall—and Celtic artists in the United States. Celtic lace, Bewley china, Waterford crystal, and Irish tea are sold in this small shop in the 35th Street shopping area. The shop also sells kilts, socks, walking sticks, and Celtic jewelry. The shop's operators have information on the Austin Celtic Association, which holds an annual festival in October (see our Annual Events and Festivals chapter). The Web site offers online shopping and a link to the association.

UNIVERSITY CO-OP
2244 Guadalupe Street
(512) 476-7211
www.coop-bookstore.com
If God isn't a Longhorn, why did he paint the sunset burnt orange and then fill this store on The Drag with all that burnt-orange stuff? That philosophical question needs no answer in Austin. UT fans can find just about anything in their team colors here.

South Central

THE HERB BAR
200 West Mary Street
(512) 444-6251
www.theherbbar.com
Herbs, both culinary and medicinal, can be found here, plus tinctures and body oils designed to soothe what ails you. The small SoCo shop also offers massage and alternative medicine information.

HOME FURNISHINGS

Central

BELLA
1221 West Sixth Street
(512) 474-1157
www.bellahomeaustin.com
Italian design holds sway here. The owner visits the design capital Milan every year and brings back an array of modern home furnishings for her West Sixth Street shop.

FEATHER YOUR NEST
3500 Jefferson Street
(512) 206-3555
www.featheryournestaustin.com
Luxurious European linens, table linens, lamps and home furnishings are sold at the charming Jefferson Square shop in the 35th Street shopping district.

FINCH
417 West Second Street
(512) 236-1414
www.shopfinch.com
Frankly, some of the newcomers to the shopping scene lack an "Austin feel," but not Finch in the hip Second Street District. Owner Kristi Pruett favors pieces that reveal the hand of the maker and have a modern, but charming look and feel.

HOMEGIRLS FURNISHINGS
4634 Burnet Road
(512) 420-2647
www.homegirlsaustin.com
Ever wondered what you could do with that chest of drawers you spotted at Goodwill? Mother and daughter Kathryn and Sarah Blanchard have a Goodwill-hunting eye we all could envy. Their uptown shop features vintage and retro furnishings, some restored, others revived, all with an Austin vibe.

JAYA
902 North Lamar Boulevard
(512) 457-1255
www.jayafurniture.com
David and Jacque Hooks travel to China, India, and Southeast Asia to bring back exotic furniture and home furnishings for their central Austin store. They also take special orders that craftsmen in faraway places construct to meet your needs. Many of them are built from old woods to modern specifications.

SPAZIO
1214 West Sixth Street
(512) 474-5768
www.spaziointeriors.com
Some of the top names in the world of contemporary design are featured here, including Frank Gehry, Eames, Isamu Noguchi, Minotti, etc. The store's gallery also is national curator for the works of Charles Umlauf, the late Austin sculptor whose home and garden serves as a showcase for his work (see our Arts chapter).

TIPLER'S LAMP SHOP
1204 West Fifth Street
(512) 472-5007
www.tiplerslampshop.com
Tipler's has a selection of hanging lamps from the 1900s to 1940s, plus a large variety of antique and custom-made lamps. The store also has an extensive selection of lampshades and provides repair and restoration services.

WILDFLOWER
908 North Lamar Boulevard
(512) 320-0449
www.wildflowerorganics.com
Natural is the keyword at this home furnishings boutique in the North Lamar–West Sixth shopping district. Natural bedding, shabby slipcovers, organic cotton mattresses, and furniture from reclaimed wood are among the items for sale in this boutique. The store also sells natural clothing for the whole family, including babies.

South Central

AVIARY
2110 South Lamar Boulevard
(512) 916-4445
www.aviarydecor.com
Proof that South Lamar Boulevard is a shopping destination that reflects Austin creativity, Aviary is a mix of travel finds from Canada, Sweden, Argentina—not your usual finds in Austin where Latin America, Italy, and France often dominate—plus local home furnishing creations by local designers.

OFF THE WALL
1704 South Congress Avenue
(512) 445-4701
www.offthewallaustin.com
A mix of antiques, retro furniture, vintage china and glassware, even old cowboy boots in the store's "Odd Stuff" corner that might include souvenir glasses, vintage cameras, old cigarette lighters, etc., are for sale in this SoCo store.

YOUR LIVING ROOM
220 South Congress Avenue
(512) 320-9909
www.yourlivingroom.com
The Colorado River divides downtown Austin from what is now being dubbed SoCo, the hip neighborhood that lines South Congress Avenue as it rises to the south. One glimpse in the storefront window offers an idea of what SoCo is all about—hip, modern furniture with a splash of retro and a sense of humor.

West

FURNITURE BROKERS OF WESTLAKE
4201 Westbank Drive
(512) 329-8421
The showroom for this upscale furniture consignment store is in a small shopping center across from Westlake High School. Given its West Austin location, much of the furniture here comes from some of Austin's more affluent residents. The store also sells collectibles and artwork.

North

ASIAN LIVING
2135 West Anderson Lane
(512) 323-5495
www.asianlivingimports.com
Restored and new pieces from Tibet, Mongolia and China at this import store where the prices are reasonable. Inventory includes screens, chests, chairs, lamps, and decorative panels.

CIERRA
5502 Burnet Road
(512) 454-8603
www.cierrainteriors.com
Cierra presents primitive folk art and furnishings from the Southwest and Mexico, including rustic tables, wrought-iron lamps and candleholders, cabinets, and chairs evocative of Old Mexico.

IKEA
1 IKEA Way, I-35 Exit 256
Round Rock
(512) 828-4532
www.ikea.com
The Round Rock branch of this worldwide home furnishings giant is always busy on the weekends as Central Texans scoop up those IKEA bargains, contemporary design to bring comfort and a modern feel to a home office, kitchen or any room in the house or garden. And then there is the cafe with those famous Swedish meatballs.

Southeast
FOUR HANDS HOME
2090 Woodward Street
(512) 371-7575
www.fourhands.com
Imported furniture from the Far East and India, much of it with an ethnic, but modern feel. Massive wooden tables, Oriental cabinets, leather chairs with a contemporary, boxy look, are among the many pieces sold out of the warehouse just southeast of the intersection of I-35 and Ben White Boulevard. Look for the yearly sales for bargains.

JEWELRY

Central

GALLERIE ESTATE JEWELERS
3500 Jefferson Street, Suite 105
(512) 451-3889
www.galleriejewelers.com
Antique and estate sale jewelry is sold at this Jefferson Square–area jeweler. The store also accepts consignments.

RUSSELL KORMAN
3806 North Lamar Boulevard
(512) 451-9292
www.russellkormanjewelry.com
This is another Austin success story. Back in the '70s, Korman worked on The Drag near the university selling beads; now he is selling custom-made pieces made from precious metals and jewels.

North
NOMADIC NOTIONS
2438 West Anderson Lane
(512) 454-0001
www.nomadicnotions.com
Nomadic Notions sells beads from more than 35 countries, some 5,000 varieties ranging in price from pennies to around $50 apiece. The store also sells jewelers' supplies and offers instruction to those eager to make their own distinctive jewelry.

PHOTOGRAPHY

Central

PRECISION CAMERA AND VIDEO
3810 North Lamar Street
(512) 467-7676
www.precision-camera.com
A favorite among Austin's professional and amateur photographers, Precision has grown from a small shop near the university to this large store just north of 35th Street. Services include film processing, camera rental, and repair. Check out the store's used-camera department.

South Central
HOLLAND PHOTO
1700 South Lamar Boulevard
(512) 442-4274
www.hollandphoto.com
This is a full-service photographic lab used by many of Austin's professional photographers. It offers a variety of services to both professionals and amateurs alike, including two-hour E-6 processing, computer imaging, custom enlargements, and film and photo supplies.

RESALE SHOPS/CHARITY

Recycling is a subject close to Austin's heart, so it is no wonder that resale shops abound. Many are dedicated to raising money for charity; others seek to extend the life of bell-bottoms well beyond their expected life span. Goodwill (www. austingoodwill.org), the Salvation Army (www. satruck.com), the MaryLee Foundation, the Junior League, St. Vincent de Paul (www.svdpusa.org), and other worthy institutions all operate thrift stores in Austin. Donations are encouraged, and listings for the stores can be found in the Yellow Pages. Here we have listed those charity stores with a specific mission or those with a unique presence in Austin.

Central

BUFFALO EXCHANGE
2904 Guadalupe Street
(512) 480-9922
www.buffaloexchange.com
Founded in Phoenix, Buffalo Exchange shops are sprouting across the country. The innovative concept is to recycle and re-use clothes by encouraging customers to bring in their cast-offs and swap them or get cash in return. The shops even accept old fur coats and recycles them into beds for injured wildlife.

JUNIOR LEAGUE OF AUSTIN RESALE SHOP
6555 Burnet Road
(512) 459-4592
www.jlaustin.org
One of several fund-raising efforts by the Junior League (the popular Christmas Affair show is another; see our Annual Events chapter). The store is a good place to find children's clothing.

NEXT TO NEW
5308 Burnet Road
(512) 459-1288
The Next to New shop is a nonprofit organization sponsored by St. David's Episcopal Church. Staffed by community volunteers, the store's profits go to community outreach programs and to the restoration of historic church buildings.

TOP DRAWER THRIFT
4902 Burnet Road
(512) 454-5161
www.topdrawerthrift.com
This store supports people living with HIV/AIDS. Proceeds from the sale of donated merchandise benefit Project Transitions, which provides a homelike environment to meet the physical, emotional, and spiritual needs of persons experiencing the dying process.

Northwest

GOODWILL OUTLET
12317 Technology Boulevard
(512) 249-5231

916 Springdale Road
(512) 928-8832
www.austingoodwill.org
Known in Austin's sewing and fashion circles as the "Blue Hanger" stores—their original name—these two Goodwill stores generate millions for the group each year in Austin. All clothing is $1.25, no matter how fancy or plain. Rummaging through the piles are bargain hunters, moms with a tight budget and funky fashion mavens on the prowl for retro looks. The second store is in East Austin.

East

HABITAT FOR HUMANITY RE-STORE
310 Comal Street
(512) 478-2165

7434 North Lamar Boulevard
(512) 225-9264
www.re-store.com
The large Comal Street warehouse features donated household fittings such as faucets, mini-blinds, bathroom cabinets, stove tops, even the kitchen sink, plus doors, windows, and construction lumber. Many of the items are used and have been donated by homeowners and builders upgrading or replacing older items, but some are new. All proceeds benefit Habitat for Humanity, the organization that builds homes in low-income neighborhoods. A second Habitat store is located in North Austin on Lamar Boulevard.

RESALE/VINTAGE CLOTHING AND STUFF

Vintage clothing stores abound in Austin, so much so that the Austin Convention and Visitors Bureau provides a "treasure map" of vintage stores around town and the *Austin Chronicle* Web site offers the definitive vintage and kitsch list. There are four general areas where the stores can be found: the South Congress Avenue shopping district (see the chapter introduction), on South Lamar Boulevard between Barton Springs Road and Oltorf Street, along The Drag, Guadalupe Street near the university campus, and around North Loop Street and 51st Street in North Austin.

Central

BANANA BAY TRADING COMPANY
2908 San Gabriel Street
(512) 479-8608
www.camonow.com

Banana Bay is Austin's version of an Army-Navy store. Located on a triangle of land east of Lamar and just north of 29th Street, Banana Bay features a variety of military clothing, ammo boxes, tents, and survival kits.

HOG WILD
100A East North Loop Boulevard
(512) 467-6515

Is this a toy store or a clothing emporium? It's both, thanks to joint owners with different interests. On the clothing side, customers find Hawaiian shirts, velvet bell-bottoms, miniskirts, and leisure suits, all divided by decade. On the toy/collectible side there are *Star Wars* toys, Barbies, even *Welcome Back Kotter* games.

South Central

BIG BERTHA'S BARGAIN BASEMENT
1050 South Lamar Boulevard
(512) 444-5908

It is not in a basement, but it is in an old shopping center that seems to capture the essence of South Austin (see our Relocation chapter). The word *funky* is overused in Austin, but this is one case where it fits. The funky shopping center is home to several resale shops, a classic gym, a Salvation Army store, a music store, and this clothing resale store that owner Henry Tarin calls "extreme vintage." The store has a wild assortment of clothes that attracts retro fans and the theatrical community in Austin.

BITCH'IN THREADS
1030–D South Lamar Boulevard
(512) 441-9955

Grace Faulkner is a diminutive woman with a small treasure trove of a shop, located near her good friend Henry Tarin's Big Bertha's (see above). A native of Australia, she relies on an old school chum to ship her pre-World War II kimono (she will politely tell you that the plural of kimono is kimono, not kimonos) from Japan. Collectors come from throughout the country to see what she is offering. In addition to kimono, Grace also sells "top-quality" vintage fashion, suits, cocktail dresses, evening gowns, shoes, and purses, classy enough to clad Audrey Hepburn on a world cruise.

BOHEMIA RETRO-RESALE
1606 South Congress Avenue
(512) 326-1238

Good junk from every era is the boast here. The ever-changing stock includes clothes, furniture, and housewares. Like other South Congress stores, Bohemia keeps late hours to encourage after-dinner browsing.

FLASHBACK
2047 South Lamar Boulevard
(512) 445-6906

The shops along the 1000 and 2000 blocks of South Lamar Boulevard are tucked between businesses, bus stops, car washes, and apartment homes, and, if anything, they are even funkier than those found on the burgeoning South Congress Avenue shopping strip. This vintage clothing store is one of the longtime fixtures in this area and boasts a large selection of shoes.

FLIPNOTICS
1603 Barton Springs Road
(512) 322-9011
www.flipnotics.com
If the retro clothes here smell a little more like coffee than the usual thrift shop aroma, it is because there is a coffee shop with the same name on the premises. Among the finds here are surfer shirts, 50s-style rock 'n' roll wear, and fanciful little cocktail dresses.

LET'S DISH
1102 South Lamar Boulevard
(512) 444-9801
The vintage clothing at Let's Dish ranges from the turn of the 20th century through the ever-popular '70s disco style. The store also has an extensive vintage jewelry collection and sells pottery, dishware, and maps dating from the 1920s to the 1950s.

LUCY IN DISGUISE WITH DIAMONDS AND ELECTRIC LADYLAND
1506 South Congress Avenue
(512) 444-2002
www.lucyindisguise.com
That's the real name of the store, perhaps the most famous shop in SoCo, certainly one of the most photographed storefronts. The emphasis here is theatrical, with both gorilla suits and French maid's uniforms in stock. Disco wear also is big, and the store boasts that Bob Dylan shopped here.

North
IT'S NEW TO ME
7719 Burnet Road
(512) 451-0388
A variety of furniture is displayed in the store's 8,000-square-foot showroom, including some good-quality pieces from furniture producers such as Henredon. This is a consignment shop where Austin residents sell their quality furniture.

TOYS

Central
HOG WILD
100 East North Loop Boulevard
(512) 467-9453
These toys are for grown-ups who long for their childhood years—retro toys at a retro clothing store (see above under Resale/Vintage Clothing).

KIDS-N-CATS
5808–A Burnet Road
(512) 458-6369
All things feline here—toys, jewelry, china cats, pens shaped like kitties, posters, cards, and kitty knickknacks. Despite its name, the store also has other sections devoted to dinosaurs, horses, and spacemen—in other words, all things kids hold dear. The shop is also a good resource for party favors.

MOMOKO'S
705 West 24th Street
(512) 223-9801
www.momokos-gifts.com
This small store and bubble tea shop sells all things by Sanrio. If you don't know Sanrio, then likely you don't know any preteen girls who love the star of the Sanrio line, Hello Kitty. There is also a sushi restaurant and bubble tea bar in the store.

ROOTIN' RIDGE
26 Doors, 1206 West 38th Street
(512) 453-2604
www.rootinridge.com
Georgean and Paul Kyle have been making toys since 1975, and their store in 26 Doors features their own creations, plus handcrafted quality wooden toys, puzzles, and musical instruments.

TOY JOY
2900 Guadalupe Street
(512) 320-0090
www.toyjoy.com
"You are never too old to play" might be the motto of this store, which boasts of selling toys

for kids and grown-ups. Japanese toys are a specialty, plus there is a large selection of lava lamps, stickers, novelty items, and puppets.

North

TERRA TOYS
2438 West Anderson Lane
(512) 445-4489
www.terratoys.com
This is a favorite place for shopping for stocking stuffers and unusual children's toys for Christmas. Terra Toys left its longtime Congress Avenue location as rental rates climbed when SoCo became a hip address, but fortunately, this wonderful toy shop has found a new home in north Austin.

WORLD WIND KITE SHOP
7208 McNeil Drive
(512) 250-9454
www.worldwindkites.com
The store's slogan is "A Hobby to Some. A Way of Life to Us!" Listing it under "toys" may be misleading, since this shop sells not only indestructible kid kites but also high-grade kites for competition. The store also offers repair services and kite-flying lessons.

East

PIÑATA PARTY PALACE
1704 East Cesar Chavez Boulevard
(512)-236-0975
Custom-made piñatas for parties, particularly kid's birthday parties, can be ordered here. Piñatas are papier-mâché forms, covered with colorful tissue paper and stuffed with candies and little toys. The piñata is strung up over a tree limb and the birthday boy or girl is blindfolded and given a baseball bat to take whacks at the piñata until it breaks open—then there is a mad scramble for the candy and toys. The store also sells ready-to-go piñatas.

South Central

ANNA'S TOY DEPOT
2620 South Lamar Boulevard, Suite B
(512) 447-8697
www.annastoydepot.com

None of the frenzy of a modern toy shop here. Anna's sells traditional toys, some of them gently used. It also caters to special-needs children and youngsters who can benefit from play-therapy toys.

TRAVEL/ADVENTURE/ OUTDOORS

For sporting goods stores focused on a particular sport (e.g., soccer or cycling), see our Parks and Recreation chapter and also see listings for Cabela's and Callahans in our Food shopping section.

Central

ARMADILLO SPORT
1806 Barton Springs Road
(512) 478-4128
An Austin surf shop? Housed in a former diner-style restaurant along the Barton Springs restaurant row (see our Restaurants chapter), Armadillo also sells sports equipment that you can use in nearby Zilker Park, including in-line skates, wakeboards, swimsuits, and lacrosse equipment.

McBRIDE'S GUNS
30th Street and North Lamar Boulevard
(512) 472-3532
www.mcbridesguns.com
Popular among hunters, anglers, and collectors, McBride's is noted for its extensive collection of antique guns. The store also sells archery equipment and provides gunsmithing services. The store also has a complete line of fishing tackle and lures.

ROOSTER ANDREWS
3901 Guadalupe Street
(512) 454-9631

8650 Spicewood Springs Road
(512) 258-3488
www.roosterandrews.com
He stood 5 feet tall, but Rooster Andrews was a giant in University of Texas folklore. His real name was William Andrews, but the diminutive man was called "Rooster" since his World War II

days as a manager for the UT Longhorns football team. Andrews owned two sporting goods stores in Austin and was a major organizer and booster of UT sports. His stores sell sports equipment and shoes, offer sports services such as racket restringing and custom T-shirt printing, and stock all the burnt orange Longhorn sportswear any UT fan could want.

WHOLE EARTH PROVISION CO.
2410 San Antonio Street
(512) 478-1577

1014 North Lamar Boulevard
(512) 476-1414

Westgate Shopping Center,
4477 South Lamar Boulevard
(512) 899-0992
www.wholeearthprovision.com

Before Austinites head for the hills, they head for Whole Earth. Not only does the store sell the top labels in camping, hiking, diving, biking, and kayaking gear, it also has wonderful rainwear and sweaters, plus imported clothes from Latin America. The shoe shop has everyday, sturdy wear and great hiking boots. Whole Earth also sells tents, backpacks, climbing gear, toys, guidebooks, knives, flashlights, freeze-dried foods, desktop Zen gardens, and telescopes. If you are not sure you want to buy a tent, you can rent one here. There are three stores, one central, the second uptown, and the third in Southwest Austin.

West

SPORTSMAN'S FINEST
12434 Bee Cave Road
(512) 263-1888
www.sportsmansfinest.com

This West Austin store sells new and used firearms, hunting and fishing gear, travel equipment, and offers information on guide services and classes.

North

GOLFSMITH
11000 North I-35
(512) 821-4050
www.golfsmith.com

This North Austin outlet is a mecca for golf enthusiasts. The facility boasts that it has the largest golf inventory in the world, where shoppers can buy Golfsmith and Harvey Penick golf clubs. The store has a snack bar, computerized swing analyzer, and educational and practice facilities. In addition, visitors can take a factory tour. There is a second, smaller store at the Arboretum.

ATTRACTIONS

First, a word of appreciation to our sponsor: Nature. It is, after all, our greatest attraction. The bluebonnets in springtime; the sparkle of sunlight on the lakes; the limestone cliffs and green rolling hills; the crisp, rushing creeks; the fresh air; the fauna; the fault and the foliage. Austin's natural beauty and bounty attracted our first visitors, drew our first settlers, and continue to entice our newest arrivals. Nature was Austin's greatest artist, perhaps an inspiration to the others who came to create some of the phenomena that give Austin its individuality. So while you're busy enjoying the production that is Austin, take a moment to acknowledge the set design.

While some of the sites below come to us courtesy of Nature, we've devoted much of this chapter to giving you a tour of the landscape of invention, the visual sensations contributed by the ingenuity of Austin's own people over the past 150 years or so. Here you'll find attractions to tickle your fancy, tease your brain, touch your heart, and, perhaps, stir your own imagination. Among these curiosities, historic treasures, and modern marvels you'll discover a provocative portion of Austin's story.

The Austin Museum Partnership was formed in 1998 by 31 Austin-area museums. The consortium promotes collaborations for the mutual benefit of the public and the museums. The membership includes art and science museums, historic sites, nature habitats and preserves, the University of Texas library and art repositories, a children's museum, and a Presidential library and museum. In the fall the partnership hosts a citywide museum day that attracts thousands of visitors to the various facilities. The partnership's Web site, www.austinmuseums.org, is a treasure trove of information about area attractions.

We've pointed out some of our most interesting pieces of public art. Here, you'll receive an introduction to a few of the sculptures, statues, paintings, murals, and fountains that are on view for all to appreciate. These artistic creations enhance Austin's natural beauty and provide a window into the city itself.

Of course, Austin wouldn't be Austin without the many spots dedicated to celebrating our unique natural habitat. So for many more outdoor attractions, don't miss our chapter on Parks and Recreation, where we've introduced you to Lake Travis, Lady Bird Lake (formerly Town Lake), and many, many other alfresco wonderlands. If you still yearn for more things to see and do, check out our chapters on The Arts, Kidstuff, The Music Scene, Nightlife, and Spectator Sports. Come to think of it, much of this book is dedicated to Austin attractions, in one form or another. *NOTE:* Because of the high concentration of Attractions in Central Austin, we've divided this section into three smaller parts to make it easier for you: Downtown, The University of Texas, and Central.

DOWNTOWN

ART AT THE AUSTIN CONVENTION CENTER

500 East Cesar Chavez Street

(512) 404-4000

www.austinconventioncenter.com

Even if you're not in town for a convention, stop in here to see artwork by six Austin-area artists. One of those artists, Damian Priour, raised some eyebrows with his sculpture *The Waller Creek Shelves*, made of limestone, glass, metal, and found objects. Priour used material collected at Waller Creek by homeless people. (Some of Austin's transients were displaced when the Convention Center was built in 1992.) Priour nevertheless proceeded with his plan, and the results are fascinating. A wall-mounted installation of 400 powder-coated geometrically shaped metal components titled *Index for Contemplation* is the work of artist Margo Sawyer. The paintings of Rolando Braseño comprise a series of 12 triptychs, the result of the artist's investigation into the relationship between the natural and cultural worlds in a work titled *Macro-Micro Culture*. John A. Yancey with Steve Jones created *Riffs and Rhythms*, a broken-tile wall mosaic, and Jill Bedgood has contributed 20 oil paintings, called *Texas Botanicals*. These six artists have made a significant contribution to the center's appeal and to Austin's Art in Public Places program. The doors are open during the fairly constant stream of events at the center. However, visitors should check first to make sure the building is open. For a listing of events at the Convention Center and Palmer Events Center, check the Web site at www.austinconventioncenter.com.

THE AUSTIN HISTORY CENTER

810 Guadalupe Street

(512) 974-7480

www.cityofaustin.org/library/ahc

While Austin was among the last major Texas cities to build a public library, the city made up for its delay by constructing a facility that was both inspiring and advanced in its design. This Moderne-influenced, Classical Revival–style building opened in 1933 to replace the city's temporary public library, a wooden structure built in 1926. A showcase for some of Austin's finest crafters in its day, the building features loggia frescoes, a carved mantel, and ornamental ironwork balconies. The ironwork was done by a noted family of ironworkers, the Weigls, whose workshop is now a barbecue restaurant, Iron Works Barbecue (see our Restaurants chapter). The History Center building, which served as the city's library for nearly 50 years, now houses the leading local history collections in the state. Here, visitors will find more than one million items documenting the history of Austin from before it was founded to the present day. The center has received national recognition for its collection of more than 600,000 photographic images, which document the people, events, architecture, and social customs of this region. The center also has more than 1,000 maps of Austin and Travis County from the mid-1800s to the present as well as 25,500 drawings and documents from local architectural projects. The History Center serves as the official repository for the records of the City of Austin as well as those of Travis County. This is also the place to come to find issues of local newspapers dating back more than a century. The center also features regular temporary exhibits of interest to the Austin community. The History Center, part of the Austin Public Library system, is next door to Austin's main public library at the corner of Ninth and Guadalupe Streets in downtown Austin. It is open from 10:00 a.m. to 9:00 p.m. Monday through Wednesday, from 10:00 a.m. to 6:00 p.m. Saturday, and from noon to 6:00 p.m. on Sunday. The library also has a Web site featuring on-line exhibits: www.cityofaustin.org/library/ahc/austin_treasures.htm.

THE BATS

Congress Avenue Bridge at Lady Bird Lake

Get your cooler and a comfy blanket and head

---

i Austin's Convention Center features a 43,300-square-foot Grand Ballroom with enough space to entertain 3,240 people, making it the biggest ballroom in Texas. And that ain't just Austin brag.

out to Lady Bird Lake for a truly unique Austin experience. The largest urban bat colony in North America—as many as 1.5 million Mexican free-tails—resides in the crevices beneath the Congress Avenue Bridge for nearly eight months of the year. When they take off from under the bridge for their evening flight for food, the spectacle is astounding. On their nightly forage the bats devour up to 30,000 pounds of insects. August is the best month for viewing the bats because they often come out before sunset. But they can be seen at other times during their stay here, from about mid-March to early November. You can see the bats from either side of Lady Bird Lake under the bridge or from the top of the bridge. Check out our chapter on Hotels and Motels for the hotels in the area that also provide great bat views. Information kiosks are at the Austin *American–Statesman*'s information center on the south shore and on the north bank below the Four Seasons Hotel. The *Statesman* also operates a bat phone (512) 416-5700; category 3636) with estimated time for the nightly flight. Austin was scandalized when the huge colony first took up residence here in the early 1980s, even going so far as to petition to have the colony eradicated. But when citizens learned that the bats consume so many insects—thus cutting down the need for chemical insecticides—and that the bats pose no danger to the community, Austin changed its mind in a big way. Today our bat colony is a welcome addition to Austin. Our hockey team is called the Ice Bats (see our Spectator Sports chapter). Of course, no one should ever try to handle a bat.

For more information on these nocturnal creatures, read the information provided at the kiosks.

THE BOB BULLOCK TEXAS STATE HISTORY MUSEUM
1800 North Congress Avenue
(512) 936-8746
www.thestoryoftexas.com
This museum was Bob Bullock's dream. Who was he? Perhaps the quintessential Texas politician

of the last half of the 20th century. Bullock rose to become the state's lieutenant governor and was known for his tough politics and his unmitigated love of all things Texas. President George W. Bush, a Republican, has credited Bullock, a Democrat, with being a major influence on his political life, and the two men grew to be very close. They sometimes disagreed, but they also were committed friends; in fact, Bush was with Bullock during his final hours. When "Governor Bullock"—all lieutenant governors in Texas are called "Governor"—set a goal, nothing could stop him. He decided the great state of Texas needed a museum, just as he decided the Texas State Cemetery where he now rests needed a much needed restoration (see later in this chapter). The building echoes the colors, textures, and style of the nearby Texas Capitol, and its huge star out front says "This is Texas!" There are three floors inside, the first named "Encounters on the Land," where the ancient cultures and pre-Republic days are celebrated. The second floor is dubbed "Building the Lone Star Identity" and takes visitors through the volatile days of the Republic of Texas, followed by admission to the Union and the tragedy of the Civil War. "Creating Opportunity" is the theme on the third floor, where all the energy that has made modern Texas is chronicled.

In addition to permanent exhibits, the museum has rotating exhibits on each floor, borrowing art and artifacts from around the state. There is an IMAX theater, plus the Texas Spirit Theater that echoes the traditional Texas town opera house and where an electronic Sam Houston introduces the audience to a colorful history of Texas. There is even a cafe with an outdoor dining deck in the museum and a museum store. No visitor to Austin should miss a tour of this wonderful addition to the historic center of the city. The museum is open from 9:00 a.m. to 6:00 p.m. Monday through Saturday and from noon to 6:00 p.m. on Sunday. Parking is available nearby or for a fee in the underground parking lot. Ticket prices are affordable. There are additional admission prices for the IMAX Theatre and Texas Spirit Theater.

CAPITOL COMPLEX VISITORS CENTER
112 East 11th Street
(512) 305-8400
www.texascapitolvisitorscenter.com

The Capitol Complex Visitors Center definitely must be added to any list of places to visit while in Austin, for both what it was and what it is today. Built in 1856 and 1857, this is the oldest remaining state office building in Texas and, both for its architectural and historic values, one of the most significant properties owned by the state. Designed by German-born architect Christopher Conrad Stremme for use as the Texas General Land Office, the building is an excellent example of Medieval-inspired architecture and is listed on the National Register of Historic Places. Professor Stremme's design is a unique blending of the German Rundbogenstil (round-arch style) and the Anglo-American Norman style. Today, the two-story "castle" hosts a variety of exhibits relating to the State Capitol and to the history of the Old Land Office itself.

We recommend stopping here before taking a tour of the Capitol. For one thing, the 20-minute film *Lone Star Legacy: A History of the Capitol,* narrated by Walter Cronkite, will serve as a great initiation to the capitol tour itself. There's also a wonderful exhibit on the massive restoration and extension of the State Capitol and grounds completed in 1997. And don't miss the space next to the "small, dark spiral stairway" dedicated to William Sydney Porter, better known as O. Henry. (See our listing for the O. Henry Museum in this chapter.) The famous short-story writer worked as a draftsman in the Land Office from 1887 to 1891, and two of his stories are set in the Land Office, "Georgia's Ruling" and "Bexar Scrip No. 2692," in which he refers to the spiral stairway.

Upstairs in the wing dedicated to the history of the Land Office, visitors will find two surveyor's transits—those scopes we see surveyors using on the side of the road. Peek through a transit to get a perfect close-up view of the Goddess of Liberty who stands so regally on top of the Capitol Rotunda. (Remember, her features are exaggerated to be seen from afar.) The gift shop here is great and so are the people who work as informa-

tion assistants just inside the front entrance. The Capitol Complex Visitor Center is open 9:00 a.m. to 5:00 p.m. Monday through Saturday and noon to 5:00 p.m. on Sunday.

DEWITT C. GREER BUILDING
125 East 11th Street

What with the splendor of the State Capitol, this building just across the street is easy to miss. But take a moment to enjoy its wonderful Art Deco architecture. Built in 1933, the building features three bronze panels over the main entrance depicting changes in Austin's modes of transportation. The first shows a Native American on horseback, the second is a covered wagon, and the third an automobile. There are also two stylized eagles over the entrance and a number of other details from the era that are worth a look. The building houses the administrative offices of the Texas Transportation Commission and was named for Greer, a state highway engineer and commissioner from 1969 to 1981.

THE DRISKILL HOTEL
122 East Sixth Street
(512) 474-5911
www.driskillhotel.com

Built in 1886 for cattle baron Jesse Driskill, the Driskill Hotel was restored in 1998 to its original splendor. This Richardsonian Romanesque–style hotel is uniquely Austin and should not be missed. (See our chapter on Hotels and Motels for more details.)

GOVERNOR'S MANSION
1010 Colorado Street
(512) 463-5518
www.governor.state.tx.us/mansion

Fire caused by a suspected arsonist greatly damaged a good portion of the Governor's Mansion in the early morning hours of June 8, 2008. The mansion, which was in the midst of a major renovation project, was unoccupied at the time of the blaze and no injuries were reported. The mansion will remain closed to the public for the foreseeable future. Check the Web site for information about when it might reopen for tours.

You've most likely heard of the legendary Texas Rangers. But have you heard of the Downtown Rangers? These friendly folks roam the greater downtown area, offering help, advice, and making sure all is well. These rangers are not police and do not carry weapons, but they use two-way radios that allow them to contact authorities if anyone needs help.

MILLET OPERA HOUSE
110 East Ninth Street

Now the private Austin Club, tourists can enjoy this edifice from the outside only. But it's definitely worth a walk by when you're visiting downtown. Built in 1878, the opera house became a cultural center for the city. Its auditorium boasted 800 movable seats. The building, made of Texas limestone, was listed on the National Register of Historic Places in 1978.

MOONLIGHT TOWERS
Corner of Ninth and Guadalupe Streets

At this location, which features a historical marker, visitors will find just one of the 17 Moonlight Towers that remain in Austin from 1895, when the towers provided the city's first public electric lights. Austin is the only city in the world to preserve its earliest electric street lamps. And they still work. At 165 feet, they're the city's tallest street lights and a truly unique attraction. The City of Austin contracted the Fort Wayne Electric Company to install 31 towers with carbon arc lamps, believing they would be easier to maintain than many small street lamps throughout the city. Some residents of Hyde Park, however, weren't so sure. They feared that the lights, sometimes called Austin moonlight, would trick the vegetables in their gardens into growing day and night. The 17 towers that remain, now with mercury vapor lights, can be found around downtown, in Hyde Park, and in Clarksville. The Moonlight Tower in Zilker Park, moved to the park from Congress Avenue in the 1960s, is used every Christmas to support the 3,500 multicolored lights on the Zilker Park Christmas Tree (see our chapters on Kidstuff and Annual Events).

O. HENRY MUSEUM
409 East Fifth Street
(512) 472-1903
www.ci.austin.tx.us/parks/ohenry.htm

William Sydney Porter, who earned international fame as a short-story writer under his pen name, O. Henry, lived in this simple Queen Anne–style cottage for 3 of his nearly 11 years in Austin. Simply Will Porter when he arrived as a bachelor in 1884, Porter would see some of his greatest personal triumphs and his most devastating public humiliation during his era in Austin. It was here where Porter married, had his daughter, sold his first short story to a national publication—and was convicted of embezzlement and sentenced to prison. (A mock court trial conducted at the UT School of Law in 1998, the 100th anniversary of the original trial, exonerated him.) Porter, who lived the dapper bachelor life, singing at parties and serenading girls, worked a variety of odd jobs before he married Austinite Athol Estes when he was 24.

His most stable career before writing took over his life was at the Texas General Land Office, where he worked drawing maps for four years. The Land Office was later to appear in two of O. Henry's short stories. (See our listing on the Capitol Complex Visitor Center.)

When his politically appointed job ended, Porter was finally able to find another job handling accounts at the First National Bank of Austin. During this time, Porter also launched his weekly newspaper, *The Rolling Stone,* which revealed the beginnings of a great talent but lasted only one year. Porter was fired from the bank when the bank discovered shortages in his accounts. He was indicted several months later, fled to Honduras, and later returned—due largely to the failing health of his wife in Austin—to face the music. He was sentenced to five years in federal prison in Columbus, Ohio, and never returned to Texas. Porter spent the last eight years of his life drinking, gambling, living the extravagant life, and publishing 381 short stories. He died at age 47 in New York of cirrhosis of the liver, an enlarged heart, and complications of diabetes.

The cottage is much as it was during Porter's three years in it, from 1893 to 1895. Once slated for demolition, the home was moved twice in the 1930s from its original location at 308 East Fourth Street. Here visitors will find many furnishings and personal possessions belonging to Porter, his wife, and daughter, Margaret. Here also are first editions of O. Henry books, magazines featuring his stories, copies of *The Rolling Stone* newspaper, and family photographs. The museum conducts the O. Henry Writing Clubs for Austin schoolchildren and hosts several annual programs, including the O. Henry Pun-Off World Championship, a lively and popular event held every May since 1977.

The museum is open from noon to 5:00 p.m. Wednesday through Sunday. Admission and parking are free. Guests are asked to wear flat, soft-soled shoes to prevent damage to the original Bastrop pine floors.

THE OLD BAKERY AND EMPORIUM
1006 Congress Avenue
(512) 477-5961
www.ci.austin.tx.us/parks/bakery1.htm
When Swedish immigrant Charles Lundberg opened his bakery in 1876, Austinites gathered to buy such delicacies as ladyfingers, sponge cake, and glazed kisses. Used as a bakery until 1936, the building then housed a number of different businesses, including a nightclub. By 1963 the Old Bakery, vacant and deteriorating, was scheduled for demolition. That's when the Austin Heritage Society and the Junior League stepped in to save it, through hard work and donations. Today the Old Bakery is registered as a national landmark. Owned and operated by the Austin Parks and Recreation Department, the bakery features a sandwich shop where you can still buy cookies but no ladyfingers or sponge cake. Most interesting, however, is the gift shop. Here visitors will find scores of handicrafts made by Austin's most experienced artists, those aged 50 and older. Custom orders are accepted, too. The Old Bakery also has a hospitality desk that provides information and brochures about Austin attractions. Just a half block down Congress from the State Capitol, the Old Bakery is a great place to stop on your tour of Austin. It's open Monday through Friday

9:00 a.m. to 4:00 p.m., though it opens on Saturdays in December before Christmas. It generally is closed on weekends and holidays.

PARAMOUNT THEATRE
713 Congress Avenue
(512) 472-2901
www.austintheatre.org
An Austin jewel, the Paramount Theatre opened in 1915 under the name Majestic Theatre. Now, beautifully restored to the last detail, the neo-classic structure is one of the nation's classic theaters. Today it hosts Broadway shows, local productions, musical events, and classic movies. Katharine Hepburn performed here, as did Sara Bernhardt, Helen Hayes, and Cab Calloway. The Paramount series for kids is a summer extravaganza. Unfortunately, the Paramount does not offer tours, so the only way to see the theater from the inside now is to buy a ticket to an event, although virtual tours are offered on the Web site. (See our chapter on The Arts.)

SCHOLZ GARTEN
1607 San Jacinto Boulevard
(512) 474-1958
www.scholzgarten.net
Built in 1866 by German immigrant August Scholz, the Scholz Garten has been serving up beer and German food ever since. This building is listed as a National Historic Site and as a Texas Landmark. General Armstrong Custer, who was stationed 2 blocks away during Reconstruction, reportedly ate here, and the University of Texas football team celebrated its first undefeated season here in 1893. Photographs from days of old adorn the walls. For more information see our chapters on Restaurants and Politics and Perspectives.

SIXTH STREET ENTERTAINMENT DISTRICT
Downtown between Congress Avenue and Interstate 35
If you haven't spent an evening in the Sixth Street area, you haven't really experienced Austin. These few blocks, filled with live music venues, DJ clubs, shops, and restaurants, continue to make up the entertainment district for Austin in many

people's minds, even though downtown now offers several other hip areas. Within walking distance of many hotels, Sixth Street is one of Austin's top tourist draws. Nowadays, the Sixth Street District also encompasses parts of Fifth and Seventh Streets on either side of Sixth, as well as Red River Street on the eastern side. This district really comes alive after five. (See our Music Scene chapter for a listing of some of the clubs, and see the Close-up about Sixth Street in the Nightlife chapter.)

SYMPHONY SQUARE
1101 Red River Street
(512) 476-6064
www.austinsymphony.com/about/square
Four historic limestone buildings and a wonderful 350-seat outdoor amphitheater still used for live performances make up this complex, which serves as the offices of the Austin Symphony Orchestra and the Women's Symphony League and houses Serrano's Cafe, a popular Mexican restaurant (see our Restaurants chapter). Located on the banks of historic Waller Creek since the 1970s, Symphony Square represents the efforts of a group of leading citizens, the City of Austin, the Urban Renewal League, and the Symphony itself to save and restore these 19th-century buildings. The provocative triangular shaped building at the corner of 11th and Red River Streets is believed to be one of just three stone triangular buildings remaining in Texas today. Built in 1871 by Jeremiah Hamilton, one of nine African-American legislators who served in the Texas Legislature, the building today bears his name and is used as the symphony's main office. Symphony Square also contains the Michael Doyle House, considered one of the few remaining examples of a simple, one-story stone cottage in Austin. The Hardeman House, also of native limestone, was moved from its original location to the square and is home to Serrano's Cafe, which features a lovely outdoor patio overlooking the amphitheater. Serrano's caters private parties in the fourth building in this complex, the New Orleans Club Mercantile, a beautifully restored 19th-century building. On Wednesday mornings in June and July, the Aus-

Capital Metro's "Tour the Town" bus operates on weekends and runs between many of Austin's cultural, historic, and outdoor attractions. Bus route 470 starts at the LBJ Library and passes the State History Museum, the Austin Art Museum, Barton Springs Pool, and many more sites. It's an inexpensive, easy way to get around town. Check it out at www.capmetro.org/riding/tourthetown.asp.

tin Symphony Orchestra hosts Children's Day activities in the square. For information on that and for other children's activities sponsored by the symphony, see our chapter on Kidstuff. Also see our chapter on The Arts for more about the Symphony and its seasonal performances at the Bass Concert Hall.

TEXAS STATE CAPITOL
1100 Congress Avenue
(512) 463-0063
www.tspb.state.tx.us
"Here glitters a structure that shall stand as a sentinel of eternity to gaze upon the ages." Now, more than a century since those words were spoken, visitors from all over the world come to gaze upon this magnificent monument to Texas. Temple Houston, the youngest son of Texas hero Sam Houston, dedicated Texas's new State Capitol, our "sentinel of eternity," on May 16, 1888. This Renaissance Revival–style structure made of Texas pink granite and native limestone, now stands as gracious and grand as Texas itself on the hilltop overlooking Austin's historic Congress Avenue. Perched atop the soaring Rotunda—which at 311 feet is taller than our nation's Capitol—is the 15½-foot statue called the *Goddess of Liberty*, a 1986 aluminum replica of the original zinc goddess. Marble statues of Stephen F. Austin and Sam Houston carved by German-born sculptor Elisabet Ney grace the south foyer as does a portrait of Davy Crockett, martyr of the Alamo, holding his famous coonskin cap. The painting of the *Surrender of Santa Anna*, which depicts a watershed event in Texas history, is among the meaningful works of art that can be found throughout the building.

More than a monument, more than a museum, the State Capitol is the seat of Texas government. In this building, among the pioneers of Texas's past, work the leaders of Texas's future. Among many other state government headquarters, the offices of the governor and secretary of state are here, along with the magnificent Senate and House chambers, occupied during the legislative sessions held every two years.

No trip to the capitol is complete unless you've stood on the Rotunda floor and looked up at the Texas star and the 2-foot letters spelling out T-E-X-A-S on the ceiling. From below, they look about 3 inches tall. After you've gazed up, be sure to look down. Here are the seals of the six nations whose flags have flown over Texas: France, Spain, Mexico, the United States, the Confederate States of America, and, of course, the Republic of Texas. On the Rotunda's circular walls you will find the portraits of every president and governor of Texas beginning with the current chief executive. That means that each time a new governor is elected, every portrait in the Rotunda must be moved back one space.

Visitors can choose to walk through the capitol themselves or take a free regularly scheduled guided tour. We suggest the tour. Not only are the guides interesting and informative, they also will point out details you might miss and can also take you into areas otherwise locked, such as the Senate and House chambers. And these are definitely worth a look. When the Legislature is in session—every other year on odd years—visitors can watch our lawmakers in action from the third-floor public gallery, open on a first-come, first-served basis. Guided tours are also available of the capitol grounds. The massive grounds, with their many statues, sculptures, and beautiful old trees, are a sight unto themselves. When you're visiting the capitol, take a moment to enjoy this Austin treasure also. And don't forget to visit the Capitol Complex Visitor Center nearby. (See our previous listing in this chapter.)

A 1983 fire in the capitol set off such an alarm over the future integrity of the overcrowded, deteriorating building that plans were made to renovate and enlarge the capitol complex, which sits on 26 acres. By 1997 the massive restoration project, construction of an impressive underground extension, and restitution of the vast capitol grounds were complete. The project restored our legacy for future generations and the building that Temple Houston had said "fires the heart" was radiant once again.

The capitol is open 7:00 a.m. to 10:00 p.m. weekdays, 9:00 a.m. to 8:00 p.m. on weekends and holidays. Tours are offered on weekdays from 8:30 a.m. to 4:30 p.m., Saturday 9:30 a.m. to 3:30 p.m., and Sunday noon to 3:30 p.m.

THE UNIVERSITY OF TEXAS

The University of Texas at Austin (www.utexas.edu), founded in 1883 on 40 acres, has grown to 357 acres, and that's just the main campus. Its historical significance, size, and allure as one of Texas's most beloved universities make UT a major tourist attraction. The university is roughly bounded by 26th Street on the north, Martin Luther King Boulevard on the south, Interstate 35 on the east, and Guadalupe Street on the west.

Getting information about UT and its many small and large treasures is much easier these days, thanks largely to user-friendly improvements to the university's Web site. For a campus overview, go to the main site at www.utexas.edu. For more specific information about tours, go to www.utexas.edu/tours. We highly recommend spending some time navigating the tours section of this site before you arrive on campus, as it will provide you with some good basic information about what to see. Plus, it offers some interesting virtual tours, including "The University of Texas Virtual Campus," which provides photographs and details about the 40 acres. Here's where you go to find out about student-led campus walking tours, the after-dark tour called the Moonlight Prowl, and tours of the UT Tower Observation Deck. Also, after a long wait, UT finally added an excellent self-guided tour to its Web site, so download a copy of that before heading to campus. There's a recorded message about tours at (512) 475-6636 or (877) 475-6633 and a small Visitor Information Center in the Texas Union just off Guadalupe Street. Frankly, though, the Web stuff is much better.

Those interested in visiting the UT campus should be aware that streets inside the campus are closed to normal traffic (cars must bear an authorized sticker to enter) during school hours. It's okay to enter after 4:00 p.m. daily. The university recommends that visitors use one of the seven public parking garages scattered around campus, although these, too, can fill up. For information and maps about UT parking, go to www.utexas.edu/parking/parking/visitor. If you happen to find a parking space near UT on The Drag, don't buy a lottery ticket for a while, as you've just used up your luck for the foreseeable future.

Information on the university's most noteworthy attractions follows.

BATTLE OAKS
Near 24th Street and Whitis Avenue

In an interesting twist of words, the historic Battle Oaks, three live oak trees at the northwest corner of the campus, are named in honor of the man who saved them, not the battle he waged to do so or the other trees in the grove that were destroyed earlier to build a fortress to protect the capital. The trees are named for Dr. W. J. Battle. His efforts to save the trees, slated for the ax to make room for a new biology building, have now taken on mythic grandeur. Some stories have him perching with a shotgun on one of the largest branches; others say he was on the ground with the shotgun to keep the tree choppers away. Neither version is probably true, but the story is fun anyway.

Of course, way before Battle, and perhaps one of the reasons he saved the trees—the site for the biology building was later moved—was a UT legend about this grouping of trees. According to the story, the largest of the three trees, which existed when Austin was home to Native Americans, learned to speak the native tongue. This tree brought eternal happiness to a young man when it whispered the name of the woman who loved him. When the new settlers came, the trees learned the ways of these

people and provided shelter for them beneath their branches. When the only son of an old man was killed in battle, the oaks brought comfort. And when Northern troops were descending on Austin during the Civil War, all the trees in this grove, but the three remaining, gave their lives for the fortress.

JACK S. BLANTON MUSEUM OF ART
Martin Luther King Jr. Boulevard and Congress Avenue
(512) 471-7324
www.blantonmuseum.org

The Blanton Museum opened in early 2006, featuring 18,000 feet of exhibition space to show off the University of Texas's enormous art collection. For more about the museum, see our chapter on The Arts.

THE DRAG
Guadalupe Street
from Martin Luther King Boulevard to 26th Street

The University of Texas meets Austin on this lively strip filled with restaurants, coffeehouses, bookstores, shops, and the outdoor Renaissance Market (see our Shopping chapter), where you can buy tie-dyed clothes and jewelry made by Austin artisans. This is a great place to select UT T-shirts and other memorabilia or just take a break from sightseeing on the UT campus. There are a couple of inviting coffeehouses along this strip, providing a perfect place for a rest—and a snack. Check out the University Co-op for books and gifts. Nomadic Notions is a top-notch shop for finding unique beads, jewelry-making items,

> **i** Ahhhhh, Austin in springtime. The weather is perfect, and the fields and roadsides are filled with miles of bluebonnets. It's an annual tradition to find a field of bluebonnets and take your loved ones' pictures against this stunning backdrop. The Lady Bird Johnson Wildflower Center has tons of bluebonnets, but there are plenty all around the city.

and gifts. The Dobie Mall is here, too, along with the Dobie Theater, which runs popular movies as well as some great offbeat films (see our Nightlife chapter). The Drag, once made up of mostly locally owned shops, is starting to see more and more national chains move in. You'll find a Gap clothing store, Barnes & Noble Booksellers, Sunglass Hut, and Einstein Brothers Bagels.

THE LYNDON BAINES JOHNSON LIBRARY AND MUSEUM
2313 Red River Street
(512) 721-0200
www.lbjlib.utexas.edu/

While Americans have not gone in for a lot of fanfare about our former presidents, other than the Washington memorials, we do make an exception when it comes to our presidential libraries. And one of the greatest expressions of this American political tradition is the library and museum dedicated to President Lyndon Baines Johnson. Nowhere on earth can visitors see, hear, and learn as much about this compelling figure in American history and about the official politics of the turbulent 1960s as in the LBJ Library. This facility is the largest and most-visited presidential library in the country. But one doesn't just visit the LBJ Library; one experiences it. The Vietnam War, the Civil Rights Movement, the War on Poverty, and the Great Society all are represented, as well as some aspects of the '60s cultural scene. Here visitors will learn about Johnson's long and colorful political career, view mementos of the lives of President Johnson and First Lady, Lady Bird Johnson, and visit the replica of the Oval Office as it was during Johnson's time (note especially the number of television sets and the news wires here. Johnson was a real newshound).

There also are two short video presentations of LBJ himself. A five-minute tape shows how he worked, and a seven-minute presentation gives great insight into the humor and personality of this charismatic Texan who was the nation's 36th president. For even better perspective, start your tour by watching the twenty-minute movie that traces Johnson's life from his childhood on the banks of the Pedernales River west of Austin

(see our Day Trips chapter) to the nation's highest office. The library houses 40 million pages of historical documents. The permanent exhibits are exceptional, and so are the temporary exhibits, a number of which the museum hosts each year. The museum and gift shop are open from 9:00 a.m. to 5:00 p.m. every day of the year except Christmas. And, because Johnson did not want people to have to pay to see his museum, it's the only presidential library that does not charge an entrance fee. Parking is free, too, in the lot on Red River Street.

LITTLEFIELD BUILDING
At the northwest corner of
24th Street and Whitis Avenue

Built in 1894, this ornate red stone-and-brick Victorian mansion belonged to Major George W. Littlefield, an important UT benefactor and member of the Board of Regents. Standing on the edge of the original 40 acres, the mansion was bequeathed to the university in 1939. It was first used as practice rooms for UT music students and in World War II as headquarters for Naval Reserve Officers Training Corps, who set up a firing range in the attic. The first floor, restored to its original splendor, is open for visitors Monday through Friday from 8:00 a.m. to 5:00 p.m. Visitors are asked to enter the mansion through the east door.

LITTLEFIELD MEMORIAL FOUNTAIN
21st Street and Whitis Avenue

Visit this fabulous fountain to enjoy its beauty and to mingle with the college students who come here to sit, have lunch, and socialize. Dedicated on March 26, 1933, the fountain has become a prominent landmark on the UT campus. Designed by Italian-born sculptor Pompeo Coppini, the fountain is meant to symbolize the revival of American patriotism during World War I, a spirit that Coppini felt had been lost during the Civil War. The large fountain consists of three-tiered pools with water jets spraying the larger-than-life bronze goddess standing on the prow of the battleship Columbia as it rushes to aid democracy abroad. The goddess Columbia holds in one hand the torch of freedom and in the other the palm of peace. The bronze figures of three horses rearing out of the water represent the surging ocean. On the left side of the grouping stands a young lad representing the army. Over the years this fountain has attracted all kinds of mischief. Soap bubbles and detergent have turned the normally still waters into a foaming spectacle, while an interesting array of reptiles, including alligators, have turned up in the fountain. The memorial, which includes the nearby statues of Texas and national notables, is dedicated both to "the men and women of the Confederacy who fought with valor and suffered with fortitude that states' rights be maintained . . ." and to the "sons and daughters of the University of Texas" who died in World War I. The fountain is about half a block east of Guadalupe Street at 21st Street.

THE MUSTANGS SCULPTURE
San Jacinto Street
at the base of the Texas Memorial Museum
Dedicated to the "spirited horses that carried the men who made Texas," this gorgeous statue of seven plunging mustangs is a landmark at the University of Texas. Unveiled in 1948, the statue is the work of Phimister Proctor, a famous sculptor of Western subjects. Proctor reportedly spent almost a year observing and measuring the anatomical details of a herd of painstakingly chosen puros españoles, Spanish mustangs. (FYI: It was the Spanish who introduced these powerful and wonderful horses to Texas.) The results are marvelous. Proctor created a band of horses that, since 1948, appears as if it could come to life at any moment.

HARRY RANSOM CENTER
Near Guadalupe and 21st Streets
(512) 471-8944
www.hrc.utexas.edu
Among the Ransom Center's exceptional properties are a rare Gutenberg Bible and the world's first photograph. The center is much more inviting to the general public since a major renovation was completed in 2003. See The Arts chapter for more about the center's world-class collections.

SANTA RITA OIL RIG
At the corner of Trinity Street and
Martin Luther King Boulevard
History buffs will want to search out this rig while touring the University of Texas campus. This little piece of machinery stands as a powerful symbol of the riches UT gained from the legendary Santa Rita oil well in West Texas. On the morning of May 28, 1923, oil gushed forth from the well in Big Lake Oil Field on UT lands. For 19 years this oil rig worked to draw the black gold to the surface and help catapult the struggling university to fame as a first-class institution. (UT became one of Austin's economic pillars along the way.) For just short of 67 years, the Santa Rita oil well pumped money into the UT system.

TEXAS MEMORIAL MUSEUM
2400 Trinity Street
(512) 471-1604
www.utexas.edu/tmm
Opened in 1939 as a permanent memorial of the Texas Centennial celebrations, the Texas Memorial Museum is a showcase for the natural and social sciences. Here, among the bones, rocks, fossils, and dinosaur tracks, visitors will discover the distant—and not so distant—past. This museum is a must for anyone interested in the fields of geology, paleontology, zoology, botany, ecology, anthropology, or natural history. Life-size dioramas of Texas wildlife, habitat groups of native Texas birds, and displays of Texas's poisonous and harmless reptiles are just some of the treasures awaiting visitors in this museum.

Among the museum's many special attractions is the original 16-foot statue of the Goddess of Liberty that stood atop the State Capitol for nearly 100 years until she was replaced with a replica in 1986. The star she holds in her hand, however, is not the original. That can be viewed in the Capitol Complex Visitor Center. There's also the Onion Creek mosasaur, which serves as the centerpiece of the Hall of Geological History. The museum has an outstanding collection of fossil vertebrates. Here ancient amphibians and reptiles mingle with some of the giant Ice Age mammals, including saber-toothed cats and

🔍 Close-Up

Lady Bird Johnson: A National Treasure

One of the first display cases that visitors encounter at the Lyndon Baines Johnson Library and Museum contains mementos of the whirlwind courtship between the future president of the United States and the woman who would be his bride, Lady Bird Taylor. Among the documents is a handwritten letter from the 21-year-old recent University of Texas graduate to her suitor.

"Lyndon, please tell me as soon as you can what the deal is," the letter reads. "I am afraid it's politics—Oh, I know I haven't any business—not any 'proprietary interest'—but I would hate for you to go into politics . . ."

The year was 1934. Mrs. Johnson spent more than six decades in the public eye. During those years she evolved from the shy, nervous girl who deliberately dropped her grade point average in high school to avoid making the speech required of the class valedictorian to become one of the great First Ladies in American history. Although Mrs. Johnson died in 2007, she will forever remain an American treasure, a Texas icon, and Austin's most beloved citizen. Each spring, Central Texas residents need only look to the roadside to see Lady Bird Johnson's reflection: There wildflowers abound, planted by both Mother Nature and the state highway department as a tribute to her advocacy.

On November 22, 1963, an assassin's bullet thrust Mrs. Johnson into the role of First Lady of the United States. Asked later what image she hoped to project to the nation, Mrs. Johnson replied, "My image will emerge in actions, not words."

Indeed. A genteel Southern woman whom fate would place at the very center of the turbulent 1960s, Mrs. Johnson's vigorous campaign in the Bible Belt helped the JFK-LBJ ticket take Texas and win the 1960 national election. In 1964, when it was her husband's turn to seek the presidency in his own right, Mrs. Johnson embarked on a massive whistle-stop tour through eight Southern states, often facing hostile crowds because of Johnson's support for civil rights. As First Lady she traveled to some of America's poorest regions to address the crisis of poverty in the country.

She also became the first First Lady to actively campaign to get a bill made into law. In 1965, despite strong opposition, her noble vision for America paid off with the passage of the Highway Beautification Act, which sought to eliminate billboards and other eyesores from America's highways.

In 1977 President Gerald Ford gave her the nation's highest civilian honor, the Presidential Medal of Freedom. President Ronald Reagan added the Congressional Gold Medal in 1988. "She claimed her own place in the hearts and history of the American people. In councils of power or in homes of the poor, she made government human with her unique compassion and her grace, warmth, and wisdom. Her leadership transformed the American landscape and preserved its natural beauty as a national treasure," reads her Medal of Freedom certificate, on display along with the medal at the LBJ Library.

mastodons. There are also fascinating examples of dinosaur troikas. Tracks found in a 105-million-year-old limestone bed near Glen Rose, Texas, record forever the passage of several kinds of dinosaurs.

The Texas Memorial Museum, dedicated to the study and interpretation of the natural and social sciences, also contains internation-ally known research collections and laboratories. Although the museum focuses on Texas, there's also much to be seen about the Southwest and Latin America. The building itself is a work of art and a true attraction. The museum is open from 9:00 a.m. to 5:00 p.m. Monday through Friday, 10:00 a.m. to 5:00 p.m. Saturday, and 1:00 to 5:00 p.m. on Sunday. There's no entrance fee, but con-

As a child growing up in the small East Texas town of Karnack, the girl born Claudia Alta Taylor on December 22, 1912, came to cherish the native flowers that flourished around her home. The daughter of Thomas Jefferson "T. J." Taylor, the wealthy owner of the town's general store, and Minnie Pattillo Taylor, Claudia was just 5 years old when her mother died after falling down a flight of stairs. The role of mothering was left to her maiden Aunt Effie Pattillo, a well-educated, cultured woman who came from Alabama to help raise Claudia and her two older brothers. It was a nursemaid who gave Claudia the name that would remain with her for life, saying she was just "as purty as a lady bird."

Lady Bird was 17 years old when she entered the University of Texas at Austin in 1930. Four years later she graduated with honors with degrees in journalism and history as well as with a teaching certificate. In Austin she met Lyndon Baines Johnson, the up-and-coming assistant to a Washington congressman. Within one day of their meeting, Johnson proposed and within two months they were married in San Antonio. He had literally swept her off her feet.

After World War II broke out and LBJ joined the service, Lady Bird ran his congressional office for the half a year Johnson was away. In 1943 the Johnsons, with Lady Bird at the helm, bought a small Austin radio station, KTBC. Mrs. Johnson, who did everything from paint the station walls to sign the checks, proved she was an astute businesswoman. On Thanksgiving Day 1952, KTBC became Central Texas's first television station and the cornerstone of the family's multimillion-dollar fortune.

Following President Johnson's death, Mrs. Johnson divided her time between Austin and the family ranch in Stonewall, which the Johnsons donated to the American people as a national historic site. Through all these years she remained at the forefront of the American environmental movement, not as a figurehead but actively involved in the effort to preserve and protect the nation's natural beauty. In Austin she chaired the Town Lake Beautification Project, a community effort that resulted in the creation of the city's magnificent Lady Bird Lake Hike and Bike Trail (see our Parks and Recreation chapter). The city wanted to name Town Lake for Lady Bird, but she demurred. Following her death on July 11, 2007, however, Town Lake was officially renamed Lady Bird Lake in her honor. In 1982, on her 70th birthday, Mrs. Johnson founded Austin's National Wildflower Research Center. On a glorious spring day in 1998, the acclaimed center (see the listing in this chapter) was officially renamed the Lady Bird Johnson Wildflower Center in honor of this remarkable woman, whom First Lady Laura Bush called "the conductor of the symphony of wildflowers that bloom across Texas."

Mrs. Johnson, wearing a sunflower-bright yellow suit and her trademark radiant smile, received a warm standing ovation as she stood to unveil the new name on the center's logo. "I had great fun campaigning with Lyndon and falling in love with the natural beauty and diversity of this country," she told the audience, speaking in the soft East Texas drawl that charmed even her staunchest opponents throughout her lifetime.

tributions are encouraged. Supporters may wish to consider joining the museum's membership organization.

THE UT TOWER
(512) 475-6633, (877) 475-6633
www.utexas.edu/tower
Just look up when you're on the UT campus and you'll find this 307-foot landmark, the most recognizable symbol of the university, which stands at the very heart of the original 40-acre campus. The Tower of the Main Building was completed in 1937 on the site of the university's first academic building, Old Main. The 27-story tower features a clock whose four faces are 14 feet, 8 inches, in diameter and the Knicker Carillon with its 56

bells that chime on the quarter hour and hour and are played at other times by the university's carillonneur.

The tower once shared the Austin skies with only one other soaring rival, the State Capitol. Its construction drew the ire of some Austin citizens back then, most notably Austin's master storyteller and UT professor J. Frank Dobie, who suggested the tower be laid on its side. Why, he complained aloud, with all the space in Texas, did a building here have to look like one in New York.

The soaring observation deck, however, afforded an excellent view of the city and quickly became a popular tourist attraction. But a tragic mass murder committed from the tower (see our History chapter) as well as a rash of suicides caused university officials to close the tower to the public in 1975. After being closed for nearly 25 years, the tower underwent a renovation and is once again open to the public for guided tours on weekends and on selected evenings during the summer only. Tickets for the nearly hourlong tour, including about 35 minutes on the observation deck, cost $5. Advance reservations are strongly recommended, as the tours fill up early. Call the numbers listed above to reserve. Tickets cannot be reserved on the Web site, but the site contains other important information about the ticketing process.

The Spanish Renaissance–style structure, designed by Paul Cret of Philadelphia and built of Bedford Indiana limestone, is lighted to commemorate achievements in athletics and academics. There are so many different lighting schemes, each with its own significance, that the university once issued a guide to Tower lighting.

Umlauf Sculptures

Around campus visitors will find 10 sculptures, most of them outdoors, created by Austin artist Charles Umlauf. (See our write-up on the Umlauf Sculpture Garden & Museum in this chapter.) Outside the Jack S. Blanton Museum of Art at the corner of San Jacinto and 23rd Streets is the bronze *Seated Bather II*. Outside the Alumni Center at 2110 San Jacinto is *Mother and Child*. In Centennial Park at Red River Street near 15th Street, across from the Frank Erwin Center, is *Three Muses*. And in front of the Business-Economics Building at West 24th Street is *The Family*, a 15-foot-tall bronze done in 1962. At the Harry Ransom Center near Guadalupe and 21st Streets, visitors will find two busts. There's a bronze portrait bust of Dr. Ransom in the entrance lobby and a portrait bust of Dr. Merton M. Minter. At the Peter Flawn Academic Center, on the main mall in front of the building, is Umlauf's 1962 bronze sculpture, *Torchbearers*, which is 12 feet high. The Law School Building at 727 East Dean Keeton Street features a portrait bust of General Ernest O. Thompson, done in 1953. The University Catholic Center, located at 2010 University, has Umlauf's *Pieta* done in bronze inside the Newman Chapel.

CENTRAL

THE NEILL-COCHRAN HOUSE MUSEUM
2310 San Gabriel Street
(512) 478-2335
www.neill-cochranmuseum.org

Austin's master builder Abner Cook designed and built this stately home in 1855 following a design plan that is similar to the Cook-built Governor's Mansion (which suffered extensive damage in a June 2008 fire). Now operated as a museum by the Colonial Dames of America in the State of Texas, the home is a glorious example of Greek Revival architecture. Classic furnishings from the late 18th and early 19th centuries can be viewed throughout this beautifully kept home. The National Trust for Historic Preservation has called this house a "jewel and perfect example of the Texas version of the Greek Revival in the South." The home, originally built for Washington L. Hill, was purchased in 1876 by Colonel Andrew Neill. Judge T. B. Cochran bought the house in 1895 and made additions. The museum is open from 2:00 to 5:00 p.m. Tuesday through Saturday. General admission is $5.

ELISABET NEY MUSEUM
304 East 44th Street
(512) 458-2255
www.ci.austin.tx.us/elisabetney
This museum, once the Hyde Park home and studio of celebrated artist Elisabet Ney, features an array of about 50 portrait busts and full-figure statues of European notables, Texas heroes, and other figures. An entire section of the museum is dedicated to the life of this amazing sculptor who helped to establish Austin's artistic traditions. This is one museum that should not be missed on any tour of the arts in Austin. For more information about the museum and the home Ney built in the late 1800s, called Formosa, see our chapter on The Arts. The museum is open Wednesday through Saturday from 10:00 a.m. to 5:00 p.m. and Sunday from noon to 5:00 p.m. Admission is free.

TREATY OAK
Baylor Street, between West Fifth and West Sixth Streets
The poignant tale of Austin's beautiful and historic Treaty Oak will tug at your heart strings. Estimated to be between 500 and 600 years old, the Treaty Oak once stood more than three stories high and its branches covered more than half an acre. In the Hall of Fame of Forestry, the tree was described as "the most perfect specimen of a tree in North America." Legend has it that the Father of Texas, Stephen F. Austin, and leaders of local Indian tribes signed a treaty under the mighty oak, supposedly dividing the city between them. Although there is no historic evidence that this meeting ever took place, the legend persevered and people came from all over the country just to look at this incredible specimen.

Poisoned in 1989 by a man who was later caught and sentenced to nine years in prison, the majestic Treaty Oak is now about a third its original size but still definitely worth a visit. Austin's heroic effort to save the Treaty Oak is another chapter in the tree's rich history. Specialists were brought in, sunscreens were erected, and people from all over the country prayed and sent letters along with more than $100,000 in donations to

i Xeriscaping is environmentally friendly landscaping that requires about 40 percent less water than traditional landscaping and often less chemical fertilizers and pesticides. In pro-environmental Austin a xeriscaped lawn is a wise choice—and can be beautiful and colorful to boot.

help save the tree. Since then, acorns and cuttings from the tree have been planted in Austin and the Treaty Oak was cloned so that identical copies of it are growing in Texas and other parts of the country. It's a story of survival. It's a story of Austin.

AROUND AUSTIN

South Central

AUSTIN NATURE AND SCIENCE CENTER
301 Nature Center Drive
(512) 327-8181
www.cityofaustin.org/ansc
A perfect place to enjoy Austin's great outdoors, the Austin Nature and Science Center in the Zilker Park Nature Preserve features 2 miles of trails with cliffs and a scenic outlook (see our Parks and Recreation chapter). But the facilities here go far beyond trails. Here, in the Visitor Pavilion, guests will learn about the two ecosystems—Hill Country and Caves, and Grasslands—that meet right smack in the middle of Austin. Displays also provide information on two minor ecosystems found throughout Central Texas: Ponds and Creeks, and Woodlands. Wildlife exhibits and a birds of prey exhibit are just a couple of the attractions found at this wonderful spot. (See our Kidstuff chapter for more information on the Austin Nature and Science Center.) The center is open from 9:00 a.m. to 5:00 p.m. Monday through Saturday and from noon to 5:00 p.m. on Sunday throughout the year. Admission is free.

PHILOSOPHERS' ROCK SCULPTURE
Entrance to Barton Springs Pool
This exquisite bronze sculpture by artist Glenna Goodacre depicts three of Austin's illustrious

figures engaged in animated conversation—just as they were accustomed to doing in life. Life-size images of historian Walter Prescott Webb, naturalist Roy Bedichek, and J. Frank Dobie, humorist and folklorist, are presented in this large work, installed November 21, 1994. Webb stands fully clothed next to the rock (he never swam), while Dobie and Bedichek are seated, wearing swimming trunks. As you view this lively sculpture, it's difficult not to wonder what these three great "philosophers" are discussing.

UMLAUF SCULPTURE GARDEN & MUSEUM
605 Robert E. Lee Road
(512) 445-5582
www.umlaufsculpture.org
The outdoor setting of this wonderful sculpture garden combines Austin's love for the outdoors and for the arts. Acclaimed artist Charles Umlauf, whose works are on display in museums and public collections across the country, lived in Austin from 1941 until his death and was a University of Texas professor until 1981. The garden is the perfect outdoor setting for 62 of Umlauf's bronze and cast-stone pieces. (For more on this inspiring Austin museum, see our chapter on The Arts.) The museum is open Wednesday through Friday from 10:00 a.m. to 4:30 p.m. and on Saturday and Sunday from 1:00 to 4:30 p.m. Nominal admission charge.

STEVIE RAY VAUGHAN MEMORIAL
Auditorium Shores,
South side of Lady Bird Lake
near Riverside Drive and First Street
This larger-than-life bronze statue of the late blues/rock legend stands near the site where Vaughan played his last Austin concert on Auditorium Shores. The sculpture by artist Ralph Helmick depicts Vaughan in a relaxed pose wearing his trademark black hat and holding his guitar like a walking stick in his left hand. A long bronze shadow trails behind. When it was dedicated on November 21, 1993, Vaughan fans gathered in tribute to the Austin-based music man who died in a helicopter crash in 1990. The piece continues to draw admirers of both the artist it depicts and the artist who

created it. (For more on Stevie Ray Vaughan, see the Close-up in our chapter on The Music Scene.)

ZILKER BOTANICAL GARDEN
2220 Barton Springs Road
(512) 477-8672
www.zilkergarden.org
The eight theme gardens in this beautiful spot are just some of the attractions at this lovely botanical garden, managed jointly by the Austin Area Garden Council and the City of Austin Parks and Recreation Department. Here visitors stroll among the 31 acres of displays and gardens to learn about different species of plants, get ideas for their own gardens, or just appreciate the beauty of nature. The Rose Garden features more than 800 bushes. The Butterfly Garden and trail has been filled with flowers and plants that attract many species of Texas butterflies. The Green Garden is a showcase of water-tolerant plants and the principles of xeriscaping. The Prehistoric Garden re-creates a dinosaur habitat, in tribute to the dinosaur tracks and bones discovered here in 1992. The habitat includes a waterfall, pond, bog, and stream. In the Oriental Garden visitors will discover a series of waterfalls, lotus ponds, and an authentic teahouse. There is also a Cactus Garden and an Herb and Fragrance Garden. The Garden Council also sponsors a number of educational and cultural programs on-site as well as several popular annual events, including the Zilker Garden Festival in the spring. This is the place to come for anyone interested in gardening, as the Garden Center has information on all its member Austin garden clubs.

Here, too, visitors will find Pioneer Village, which includes two original log structures from the 1800s, a blacksmith shop, and an organic garden. The Swedish Log Cabin, built about 1838 on the "Govalle" Ranch—meaning "good grazing land" in Swedish—and moved to the botanical garden in 1966, is fully furnished with such 19th-century necessities as a spinning wheel, loom, and baby cradle. The small cabin was built by S. M. Swenson, a settler who encouraged migration of other Swedes to Texas and opened the cabin as a social center for the Swedish community.

(Most of the activities must have taken place outdoors, however, as not too many people could have moved about here comfortably.) Right next to the cabin is the Esperanza School Building. Built in 1866, the log building was one of the earliest one-room rural school houses in Travis County. The interior of this school also is furnished as schoolchildren would have occupied it in the 19th century. The Botanical Garden is open from 7:00 a.m. to about 7:00 p.m. daily except on Thanksgiving, Christmas, and New Year's Day. Admission is free. There is a parking charge on weekends from March through November.

North

THE REPUBLIC OF TEXAS MUSEUM
510 East Anderson Lane
(512) 339-1997
www.drt-inc.org/museum.htm
This fascinating space, which is meticulously run and cared for by the Daughters of the Republic of Texas, is packed with Texas history. Here visitors will learn about the men and women who fought for Texas independence and led the Republic of Texas from 1836 to 1846. The museum features award-winning permanent exhibits and a variety of touring shows. One outstanding section is called Great Grandma's Backyard, where visitors get to see and touch the household implements used by families in the mid-19th century. The museum also features an excellent collection of guns from that period, portraits and statues of Texas leaders, and much, much more. (See also our chapter on Kidstuff.)

South

ST. EDWARD'S UNIVERSITY
3001 South Congress Avenue
(512) 448-8400
www.stedwards.edu
Don't miss the beautiful Gothic Revival–style Main Building and the other great attributes of this 180-acre campus. The Main Building is one of Austin's most stunning landmarks—a grand structure in the Southwest when it was built in 1889 and just as grand today. (For more informa-

tion on this historic university, see our Higher Education chapter.)

SOUTH AUSTIN MUSEUM OF POPULAR CULTURE
1516 South Lamar Boulevard
(512) 440-8319
www.samopc.org
A true Austin original, this funky little space it worth a stop for any visitor who wants to view some of the music posters and other graphic art that were created during the 1960s psychedelic era, the 1970s cosmic cowboy era, and into the 1980s. For more information, see the listing in The Arts chapter.

Southwest

AUSTIN ZOO
10807 Rawhide Trail
(512) 288-1490, (800) 291-1490
www.austinzoo.org
Located on the edge of Hill Country about 20 minutes from downtown Austin, the Austin Zoo is a great escape from the hustle and bustle of the city. Here visitors get a close-up view of domestic and exotic animals as well as a relaxing, enjoyable experience in a natural setting. (For more on Austin's zoo, see our Kidstuff chapter.)

BARSANA DHAM
400 Barsana Road
(512) 288-7180
www.barsanadham.org
About 20 minutes from downtown Austin, this Hindu temple and ashram is a stunning sight to behold in the Texas Hill Country. Located on 200 acres, the 35,000-square-foot architecturally magnificent compound is one of the largest Hindu temples in the United States. The most impressive feature is the dome, which towers high above the temple, but that is only one of the attractions here. The main hall and prayer hall, as well as the compound's fountains, pools, and shrines also are impressive. The temple, which represents the holy district of Braj, India, is surrounded by fields of wildflowers, a stream

and ponds in a park-like setting that includes picnic benches and other outdoor seating. Best of all, this temple is extremely visitor friendly. General visiting hours are 8:30 to 10:00 a.m. and 3:00 to 5:00 p.m. daily, but visitors also are invited to attend prayer services. The temple also hosts festivals throughout the year, as well as an open house and fair in the spring, which features carnival games, booths, entertainment, Indian food and sometimes even elephant and camel rides! Check the Web site for a virtual tour and the calendar of events.

LADY BIRD JOHNSON WILDFLOWER CENTER
4801 La Crosse Avenue
(512) 292-4100
www.wildflower.org
Established in 1982 as the National Wildlife Research Center, this delightful center was renamed in March of 1998 in honor of its founder, Austin's own Lady Bird Johnson. (See our profile of the former First Lady of the United States in this chapter.) This 42-acre Hill Country gem overflows with a brilliant variety of native plants and flowers and has become one of Austin's most visited spots. Here visitors will see and learn about our own state flower, the bluebonnet, as well as the glorious Indian paintbrush, which is as splendid as its name, and more than 500 other species of native plants. The center's 23 lovely perennial and seasonal gardens display in living color the bounty of Texas's botanical beauties. Much more than a showcase for the magnificent plant life of Texas, however, the center is an ecological sanctuary dedicated to the preservation and reestablishment of native plants—wildflowers, grasses, shrubs, and trees. It's the only national nonprofit organization fulfilling that mission and has become the leading national authority on native American plant life. Researchers, staff, and volunteers are committed to reversing the threat of extinction to about 3,000 endangered native plant species in North America, nearly 25 percent of the continent's natural plant life. This loss contributes to ecological havoc that goes way beyond vanished beauty. Accolades for

the center's original conservation and ecological techniques have come from such prestigious organizations as the Smithsonian Institution and the National Wildlife Federation.

The center, which opened its impressive facilities in 1995, features stone buildings designed in German Mission and ranch-style architecture to reflect the region's cultural diversity. There's also a wonderful observation tower offering an excellent view of the surrounding Hill Country, and a central courtyard and stone fountain, a nature trail, ponds, and picnic spots. The Wildflower Cafe is a great spot to have a sandwich or refreshment. The gift shop has a good selection of arts, crafts, posters, and books.

The center also features North America's largest rooftop rainwater collection system, which provides water for all the gardens. The place to begin the tour of this unique center, however, is at the Visitor Gallery. Here visitors are introduced to the Wildflower Center and can view interesting displays on the region's plant life. Young children especially will delight in hearing Ralph, the talking lawn mower, just one of the many features designed to appeal to children. Those interested in finding out more about specific plants can browse the research library. Education remains the center's primary goal. To that end, the center sponsors a number of conferences, lectures, and workshops on a variety of topics, many in the center's 232-seat auditorium. It also operates a clearinghouse so that people from across the country can obtain information about plants native to their region. *The Wildflower Handbook,* a source book on wildflowers and native plant landscaping, with nursery and information directories for all 50 states, is published by the Wildflower Center.

The grounds are open Tuesday through Saturday from 9:00 a.m. to 5:30 p.m, and Sunday noon to 5:30 p.m, though check the Web site for extended hours in the spring. The Visitors Gallery is open Tuesday through Saturday from 9:00 a.m. to 4:00 p.m., and from noon to 4:00 p.m. on Sunday. Admission is $7, with reduced rates for children and seniors. Regular visitors and supporters of the environment may wish to become members—or volunteers.

Northwest

CYPRESS VALLEY CANOPY TOURS
1223 Paleface Ranch Road
Spicewood
(512) 264-8880
www.cypressvalleycanopytours.com
When we visited Costa Rica a few years ago, one of our most thrilling adventures was taking the zip-line canopy tour, soaring hundreds of feet above the forest floor over the treetops suspended only by wires and harnesses. You can imagine our pleasant surprise, then, when we learned that the patriarch of a former Austin family had done the same—and decided to open up a canopy tour in the cypress-covered area near his family's new home about 35 miles northwest of downtown Austin in Spicewood. Three different tours are offered: The Canopy Tour (1½ hours), the more advanced Canopy Challenge (2 hours) and the Sunrise Birding Tour (2 to3 hours). Check the Web site for details, as there are minimum and maximum weight requirements as well as other restrictions. There is also an option of staying overnight—and zipping to your room!

East

FRENCH LEGATION MUSEUM
802 San Marcos Street
(512) 472-8180
www.frenchlegationmuseum.org
After King Louis Philippe of France officially recognized the fledgling Republic of Texas in 1839, he named Alphonse Dubois de Saligny as charge d'affaires and sent him to Austin. De Saligny, a flamboyant character, bought 22 acres of land on a beautiful Austin hilltop and began construction on his luxurious residence and carriage house, which are considered modest by today's standards. De Saligny, who insisted he be called Count, was anything but noble and more like a no-account scoundrel, leaving a trail of debts and angry citizens during his short stay here. While he awaited completion of his residence, de Saligny lived in downtown Austin, where he launched the infamous Pig War. Complaining that his neighbor's pigs were destroying his garden, de Saligny ordered his servant to shoot any pig that even looked as though it was going after the garden. The neighbor, Richard Bullock, retaliated by whacking the servant and threatening to come after de Saligny himself. That was about all de Saligny could take of Texas, and vice versa. He headed back to Louisiana and never occupied the home. The home was purchased by Dr. Joseph Robertson in 1848, and it remained in the family's hands for a century. In 1948 the state of Texas bought the property and placed it in custody of the Daughters of the Republic of Texas. They restored the home and opened it to the public in 1956. Today visitors will find many of the Robertson family furnishings as well as other period pieces. Guided tours include a visit to the original house and the reconstructed French Creole kitchen, which is fully equipped and contains many unique items. The replica of the carriage house contains an 1828 carriage, other exhibits, and a gift shop. Tours are conducted Tuesday through Sunday 1:00 to 4:00 p.m. The French Legation is also a popular spot for weddings. Nominal admission fee.

The French equivalent of our Independence Day, Bastille Day, July 14, is celebrated here with French song, food, and dance, and the legation also hosts a popular Christmas event when Pere Noel arrives to celebrate the season with a Gallic flair (see the listing in our Annual Events chapter).

GEORGE WASHINGTON CARVER MUSEUM AND CULTURAL CENTER
1165 Angelina Street
(512) 974-4926
www.ci.austin.tx.us/carver
Following a major renovation and expansion, this museum and cultural center—which is distinguished for being the first African-American neighborhood museum in the state of Texas—reopened in 2005. The new 36,000-square-foot facility includes four galleries, a 134-seat theater, a dance studio, conference room, classroom, darkroom, and archival space. The museum's core exhibit is on Juneteenth, the oldest nationally celebrated commemoration of the ending of slavery in the United States. There also is a

permanent exhibit on Austin African-American families, an Artists Gallery, and a children's exhibit on African-American scientists and inventors, including George Washington Carver, of course. It's open 9:30 a.m. to 6:00 p.m. Monday and Friday, 9:30 a.m. to 8:00 p.m. Tuesday, Wednesday, and Thursday, and 1:00 to 5:00 p.m. Saturday.

HUSTON-TILLOTSON UNIVERSITY
900 Chicon Street
(512) 505-3025
www.htc.edu

While the campus has modernized over the past 125 years, two of Huston-Tillotson's historic buildings remain as splendid examples of turn-of-the-20th-century architecture. The Evans Industrial Building, built in 1911–12, was completely renovated in 1984 and designated as a Texas Historical Site. The Old Administration Building, constructed in 1913–14, is one of the few remaining examples of the Modified Prairie Style popularized by Frank Lloyd Wright. This building was entered in the National Register of Historic Places in 1993 and is slowly being restored. (For more on this historic African-American university, see our chapter on Higher Education.)

OAKWOOD CEMETERY
16th and Navasota Streets

Austin's oldest cemetery is a scene of tranquility and beauty. Created in 1839, the cemetery is the final resting place for many Austin pioneers, prominent Austin families, and community leaders from the past and present. Athol Estes Porter, wife of short-story writer O. Henry, is interred here, as are former Texas Governor James Hogg and his daughter Ima. Mary Baylor, a driving force in the preservation of the Clarksville neighborhood, was buried here in 1997. The cemetery is chock-full of towering trees that provide wonderful shade in summer. The cemetery was added to the National Register of Historic Places in 1988.

PARQUE ZARAGOZA
Recreation Center Murals
2608 Gonzales Street
(512) 472-7142

Austin artist Fidencio Duran has captured the essence of the center's Hispanic neighborhood in a series of three immense—and immensely moving—narrative paintings that relate the story of the Hispanic experience in Austin to sweeping historical events in Mexico. *Cinco de Mayo* and *Diez y Seis* are the two 25-foot-tall murals in vivid color and detail that line the sides of the main entrance hall. Both begin with two infamous dates in Mexican history. *Cinco de Mayo,* or May fifth, depicts the Mexican battle at Puebla that resulted in the defeat of French invaders in 1862; *Diez y Seis* marks the event on September 16, 1810, when Father Miguel Hidalgo y Costilla uttered the famous Grito de Dolores, or cry, for independence from Spanish rule. These two epic paintings include homages to the 1929 Diez y Seis de Septiembre celebration in Austin, the neighborhood's first independence day festival. Residents will discover several East Austin landmarks within these works. Another stunning Duran mural, *Comite Patriota,* is in the conference room. This series of murals highlights Austin's Hispanic culture and should not be missed. The center is open from 10:00 a.m. to 10:00 p.m. Monday through Thursday, 10:00 a.m. to 8:00 p.m. Friday, and 10:00 a.m. to 5:00 p.m. Saturday.

TEXAS STATE CEMETERY
901 Navasota Street
(512) 463-0605
www.cemetery.state.tx.us/

A must-see for anyone who wants to comprehend the scope of Texas history, the 18-acre Texas State Cemetery manages to be both tranquil and exhilarating at the same time. Visitors who walk among the tombs of many of Texas's most noted heroes and legends can't help envisioning the drama of the lives and times of these leaders. Ste-

> **i** When planning outdoor activities, remember that Austin does have four seasons: November, December, January, and Summer. Or, as some like to say, Almost Summer, Summer, Like Summer, and Christmas.

phen F. Austin, the Father of Texas, is buried here under a bronze statue that shows him standing with his right hand raised and holding a manuscript in his left hand inscribed with the words TEXAS 1836. Confederate General Albert Sidney Johnson lies under the recumbent statue of him carved by Elisabet Ney, the German-born sculptor who made Austin her home. Among the other Texas leaders interred here is Barbara Jordan. A beloved scholar, teacher, and politician, Jordan was the first African American from Texas elected to the U.S. House of Representatives. Three-term Texas Governor John B. Connally is buried here along with the bullet fragments left in his body from when he was wounded during the Kennedy assassination. Lt. Governor Bob Bullock, the force behind the Texas State History Museum (see earlier in this chapter), is also interred here. And there are many more, including 10 other Texas governors, many famous writers and historians, and about 2,200 white marble headstones for veterans of the Confederate Army. Among the graves is that of General Edward Burleson, a vice president of the Republic of Texas and the first person to be buried in the cemetery after its creation in 1851.

A $4.7 million renovation and restoration project at the cemetery included construction of the visitor center made of Texas limestone and inspired by the long barracks of the Alamo. The visitor center serves as the main entrance to the cemetery and houses a permanent exhibit on Texas cemeteries. The landscaped grounds, stone recycling pond, and the lovely Plaza de los Recuerdos (Plaza of Memories) all contribute to the sense of serenity created at this very Texas location, often called the Arlington National Cemetery of Texas. The cemetery is open from 8:00 a.m. to 5:00 p.m. every day. The visitor center is closed Sunday, however. Guests can call ahead to arrange for guided tours, or they can do a self-guided tour with the help of information packets available at the visitor center.

West

AUSTIN MUSEUM OF ART AT LAGUNA GLORIA
3809 West 35th Street
(512) 458-8191
www.amoa.org
One of two facilities of the Austin Museum of Art, Laguna Gloria is important as much for its facilities as for the artworks it exhibits. Constructed in 1915–16 as a private residence, the Mediterranean-style villa covers more than 6,000 square feet. The outdoor amphitheater hosts a variety of performance artists throughout the year. It's also a great place just to sit by the lake and have a picnic. The sculpture garden is wonderful. (For more information on Laguna Gloria, see our chapter on The Arts.)

MOUNT BONNELL
At the top of Mount Bonnell Road
off West 35th Street
This scenic spot overlooking Lake Austin has been attracting nature lovers—and romantic ones—for more than 150 years. At 785 feet above sea level, Mount Bonnell is one of the highest points in the Austin area and offers a view to end all views. Choose your partner wisely to make that first climb up the steps. According to local lore, two people who make their first climb together will fall in love. Some say Mount Bonnell was named after George W. Bonnell, a newspaperman and mercenary. Others claim it was named for Golden Nell and her "beau"—beaunell—who leapt off the summit to their deaths in order to avoid capture by Native Americans. Visitors can also reach Mount Bonnell off Farm-to-Market Road 2222 (Bull Creek). (For more information on Mount Bonnell, see our chapter on Parks and Recreation.)

Northeast

JOURDAN-BACHMAN PIONEER FARMS
11418 Sprinkle Cut-Off Road
(512) 837-1215
www.pioneerfarms.org
This living history museum, originally part of a

2,000-acre cotton farm, treats visitors to a journey back in time to witness the lifestyle of Central Texas's early settlers. From the dwellings to the farm implements and household items to the guides' dress, everything out here is historically correct. There are plenty of hands-on activities for the whole family. See our chapter on Kidstuff for more about this enlightening slice of early Texas life.

Lake Travis

THE OASIS
6550 Comanche Trail
(512) 266-2442
www.oasis-austin.com

Consistently named one of the Top 10 Austin Area Attractions by the Austin Convention and Visitors Bureau, the Oasis offers one of the most stunning views in this entire area. From a vantage point of 450 feet above Lake Travis, the multitudes of outdoor decks and the indoor dining rooms look out across the lake and the Texas Hill Country. Struck by lightning on June 1, 2005, much of the Oasis was destroyed by the resulting fire. Within weeks the Starlight Terrace was reopened and other decks were being reconstructed. This is one of the best places to drink a margarita or two while watching a fabulous Austin sunset. The Oasis hosts live bands Thursday through Sunday nights. This establishment is also a full-service restaurant leaning heavily on Tex-Mex cuisine.

NATIONAL REGISTER DISTRICTS

While Austin has numerous residences and commercial buildings listed on the National Register of Historic Places, many of which we've mentioned in this chapter, the city also boasts a number of entire districts listed on this important National Register for historic preservation. Those who don't want to miss one stop on their tour of historic Austin should consider taking a walking tour of some of these uniquely Austin locations. See our listing under Austin Tours in this chapter if you're interested in a guided walking tour of some of the following neighborhoods, or pick

up copies of the free "Historic Walking Tours" series at the Austin Visitor Center at 209 East Sixth Street (512-478-0098 or 800-866-GOAUSTIN). The National Park Service also has information on its Web site, www.cr.nps.gov/nr. They have brochures for Hyde Park, the Bremond District, and Congress Avenue and East Sixth Street. These brochures describe each building in more detail and give some interesting tidbits about the buildings' former owners. There's also a brochure available on Camp Mabry.

Barton Springs Archaeological and Historic District

This district within Zilker Park in South Central Austin includes our favorite swimming spot and a most endangered treasure, Barton Springs Swimming Pool. Named to the National Register in 1985, this place is Austin through and through and should not be missed on any tour of Austin, prehistoric, historic, or otherwise. Barton Springs, comprising four principal springs, is the fifth-largest group of springs in the state of Texas. One of the many reasons this site is listed on the National Register of Historic Places is that human habitation has been traced back to approximately 6000 B.C. Archaeologists have found chipped-stone arrowheads, bone fragments, and prehistoric ceramics while digging in this area.

The springs are named for one of Austin's earliest modern settlers, William Barton, who moved to the springs in 1837 and built a home. While nothing remains of his homestead, there is evidence (a cistern) of the home built on the property in 1867 by the Rabb family, who came to Texas as part of Stephen F. Austin's first colony of Anglo settlers (see our History chapter). More modern structures that contributed to the springs' selection for the National Register include the concrete Zilker Amphitheater, built around one of the springs by Austin civic leader and philanthropist Andrew Jackson Zilker in the first decade of the 20th century. And then there's the famous Bath House. Built in 1946, this cool structure has been a source of pride for Austin for more than half a century. During a period when

Texas architecture was largely ignored by the national press, the Bath House was the subject of a long article in *Architectural Digest* magazine. The article praised architect Dan Driscoll's ingenuity in designing an imaginative structure that was entirely appropriate for its site. The Bath House, still in use today next to the pool, is practically unchanged from the day it was built. (For more information on this 1,000-foot-long spring-fed pool, see our chapter on Parks and Recreation.) The pool itself is located at 2201 Barton Springs Road, but the register district is bounded on the north by Barton Springs Road, on the east by Robert E. Lee Road, and on the west by Barton Creek and is situated on both banks of the creek.

Bremond National Register District

For a glimpse into the lifestyles of the rich and prominent from a century ago, include the Bremond Block on your tour of downtown Austin. Here are some of the most elegant and elaborate 19th-century homes still found in the city. Italianate, Greek Revival, Colonial Revival, Queen Anne, and Second Empire are just some of the architectural styles borrowed for this collection of fourteen homes built between 1854 and 1910. Many of these fabulous homes are historic landmarks.

Three of the homes—the Walter Bremond House, the Pierre Bremond House, and the stunning John Bremond Jr. House—were built by Austin builder George Fiegel, who is notable for having planned, constructed, or remodeled many of the buildings on historic Congress Avenue.

The histories of those who built and occupied these dwellings are as interesting as the structures themselves. Eugene Bremond and his siblings grew up just a couple of blocks away as the children of wealthy merchant John Bremond Sr. As it happened, the Bremond homestead was catty-cornered from the homestead of another Austin merchant, John Robinson Sr. The warm friendship between the patriarchs of these two families must have cast a spell over both houses, because Eugene and two of his sisters married Robinsons. Eugene, who parlayed his father's wealth into a fortune first as a lender—it's said

he charged 18 percent interest on loans made to early settlers—and then as a banker, bought the north half of the block in 1866 that was to bear his family's name. Over the years, as the families' children grew and married, the block became the Bremond family compound, just as Eugene had envisioned. Not all the homes in this district were owned by the Bremond line, however. Other wealthy Austinites also lived in this compound, including the Harvey North family, the Henry Hirshfelds, and William Phillips, one of Austin's first doctors. The district is between Seventh and Eighth Streets and Guadalupe and San Antonio Streets.

Camp Mabry National Register District

Established in 1892 as a permanent training ground for the Texas Volunteer Guard, Camp Mabry is the third-oldest active military post in Texas. Today the West Austin camp is headquarters to the Texas Army National Guard, Texas Air National Guard, the Texas State Guard, and the Reserves. Among the many historic buildings on these huge grounds is the Texas Military Forces Museum, built in 1918 as the mess hall for the School of Automobile Mechanics. The mess hall accommodated 4,000 men and had the largest kitchen of its kind in Texas, covering 45,000 square feet. Today the museum stands alone in presenting the history of the Texas military from the Texas Revolution to the present. Another special attraction on the grounds is the pond and picnic area that has been attracting Austinites for more than 100 years. Here visitors will find a rustic limestone dam, built in 1892 to create a bathing pool for the Texas Volunteer Guard.

i *The Unforeseen* is a new documentary film about the forces of real estate developers on Austin's beloved Barton Springs. The award-winning film is moving, magical—and not just a little sad—but it is a wonderful way to discover the strong feelings many Austinites have about Barton Springs. Rent it if you can.

The Volunteer Guard, by the way, became the National Guard in 1903. The remaining buildings and grounds have been open to the public for self-guided walking tours, and there's a great cinder track and workout trail that Austinites have used for exercise. There are some vintage aircraft on display near the track. Security concerns in the fall of 2001 caused some areas of the camp to be closed, and future public access may continue to be limited.

Take special note of the many facilities here that were built by the Works Progress Administration (WPA), the federal program that put people to work during the Depression and wound up providing some of the country's best infrastructure. WPA projects at Camp Mabry include the stone wall and guard post that visitors pass upon entering the camp, the stone arch bridges near the picnic area, and a number of workshops and warehouses. The WPA also replaced the dam's original brick with limestone in 1938. Some of these WPA projects were built in the so-called CCC-rustic style, named after the Civilian Conservation Corps. One of the unique structures at Camp Mabry is the multicolored totem pole, presented to the camp in 1949 by the Royal Canadian Air Force in honor of the Texans who joined the RCAF to fight in World War II. The totem pole represents the Thunderbird family and the figures, from top to bottom, are the son, who makes thunder and wind; the daughter, keeper of hail storms; the mother, maker of lightning, thunder, and rain; and Chief Thunderbird, who attempts to subdue a dragon and make huge storms at the same time. The dragon is at the bottom of the totem pole. Camp Mabry was named in honor of Adjutant General Woodford Mabry of the Texas Volunteer Guard, among the first to see the need for a permanent training ground for the Texas military.

The museum is open Wednesday through Sunday from 10:00 a.m. to 4:00 p.m. The grounds are open from 6:00 a.m. to 10:00 p.m. The camp, listed on the National Register in 1996, is at 2200 West 35th Street. For more information call the camp at (512) 465–5001.

Clarksville National Register District

Clarksville is one of four Austin communities founded by African Americans in the years following the end of slavery, on June 19, 1865. Named for Charles Clark, the name taken by freed slave Charles Griffin, the neighborhood started when Clark purchased two acres of wilderness land on what was then just west of the Austin city limits. In 1977 Clarksville became the first African-American neighborhood in Texas to be listed on the National Register of Historic Places. Many of the homes in this neighborhood were built between the 1870s and the 1930s (see our Relocation chapter). Today visitors can find the 1930s basilica-style building that houses the Sweet Home Missionary Baptist Church at 1725 West 11th Street (see our Worship chapter). The church was founded in the 1880s by the freed men and women who built new lives in this district. The neighborhood is in Central Austin and is bounded by MoPac on the west, 10th Street on the south, Waterston Avenue on the north, and West Lynn Street on the east. And don't miss Mary Baylor Clarksville Park at 1811 West 11th Street. This park was named in 1997 in honor of Mary Baylor, who passed away earlier that year. This dynamic community leader, the great-granddaughter of original Clarksville residents, spent a lifetime fighting to preserve Clarksville's unique character. The annual Clarksville Jazz Festival is held in June just outside this neighborhood in nearby Pease Park and other area venues. Look for more information in our Relocation chapter.

Congress Avenue National Register District

With our grand Texas State Capitol as its crowning glory, Congress Avenue is a showcase for some of the city's finest late-19th-century commercial architecture. As you walk this 10-block district from the capitol south to Cesar Chavez Street, keep in mind that this street was once Austin's main thoroughfare and the nerve center for the capital of a fledgling frontier state. We've introduced you to several of this district's most important structures under the individual listings above, including the State Capitol, the Old Bakery, and the Paramount Theatre. We'll point out a few others here. The first is not a structure at all, but a small, unassuming park located at 11th Street and Congress Avenue. This easy-to-miss parklet actually has significant historical value. There was once a building here, built in 1881, that served as our State Capitol while the grander one you see just across the street was under construction. The University of Texas also held its first classes here in the fall of 1884. But as with an amazing number of Austin's old buildings, this one burned down in 1899. You can still see its foundation and cistern.

Also of note on this street is the Johns-Hamilton Building at 716 Congress Avenue. Built in 1870 with an elegant Gothic Revival storefront, the facade has been reconstructed. Just a few doors down are the Walter Tips and Edward Tips Buildings at 708–712 Congress Avenue. These two German-born brothers emigrated to the United States about 1850. Older brother Edward opened his hardware business at 708 Congress Avenue in 1865 and gave his brother a job as clerk. Not to be outdone, Walter built a much more elaborate structure for his business next door, which dealt in heavy machinery. The Walter Tips Building is a three-story structure that features Corinthian architecture on the first floor and Venetian Gothic architecture on the top two floors. Interior columns and girders in this building are made of recast exploded Confederate shells.

At the corner of Sixth Street and Congress Avenue is the Littlefield Building, which we mentioned in our chronicle of the Sixth Street Historic District. Down the block, at 512–520 Congress, is the Littlefield's rival, the Scarbrough Building, which housed the preeminent department store in Texas until the early 1980s. Built in 1909 in the Chicago style, the building's exterior was changed to an Art Deco style in 1931. Next to Scarbrough's, at number 504, is the Robinson-Rosner Building. Built in the mid-1850s, this is the oldest known building on Congress Avenue. We must also point out one of Abner Cook's buildings on this avenue. Cook was Austin's master builder during this era and is responsible for some of the city's most historic landmarks,

including the old Governor's Mansion (which suffered extensive damage in a June 2008 fire) and the Neill-Cochran House (see the listings in this chapter). He also built the Sampson-Henricks Building at 620 Congress Avenue in 1859. This, too, is one of Congress's oldest buildings and is distinguished for its Italianate style and excellent craftsmanship.

Hyde Park National Register District

Hyde Park represents the vision of Monroe Martin Shipe, an entrepreneur who came to Austin from Abilene, Kansas, in 1889. As president of the Missouri, Kansas, and Texas Land and Town Company, Shipe had resources as big as his dream. He bought the tract of land that was then in far North Austin, named it Hyde Park, for the distinguished London address, and spent the rest of his life living in and promoting his beloved neighborhood. Elisabet Ney, the sculptor famous for carving the marble statues of heroic Texans found in Austin, was among the first to build her home and studio in this 207-acre suburb, now listed as a National Register District. (See more about Elisabet Ney in this chapter.)

The site of the State Fair of Texas from 1875 to 1884, the area back in Shipe's day still had a prominent horse racing track, and those who raced horses there would walk their horses up and down one of the main streets, which became known as the Speedway because of it. Speedway is still one of the major avenues in this Central Austin area.

One of Shipe's first actions to promote development of this suburb was to connect it to the city via his own electric streetcar system. Then he turned the southwest section into a resort that included a dance pavilion and tree-lined walking paths. The middle-class homes, built mostly of wood between 1892 and 1925, reflect a variety of architectural styles and tastes (see our Relocation chapter). The first of Austin's historic Moonlight Towers was built in this neighborhood, and it still works. You'll find it at 41st Street and Speedway (see the previous listing in this chapter). A lovely park and playground, now called Shipe Park, was added in 1928 and remains a popular spot for neighborhood families today. The homes are privately owned and not available for tours. Do take a moment to stop in at the Avenue B. Grocery at 4403 Avenue B. This small neighborhood store will take you back in time. This district is in Central Austin between 39th and 44th Streets and Avenue B to Avenue H.

Moore's Crossing
National Register District

This community just south of the new Austin-Bergstrom International Airport in Southeast Austin was added to the National Register of Historic Places in 1996. The community dates to before the turn of the century and reached its peak of prosperity between 1880 and 1920. More than a dozen structures and sites contribute to this historic place, including homes, a henhouse, a barn, an abandoned metal-truss bridge, and, most significantly, a small country store, known as the Berry & Moore Bros. Store, which dates back to between 1900 and 1914. The store is particularly impressive and important to our historic preservation because these examples of country stores, which were the economic nucleus of rural communities, are becoming harder and harder to find. Moore's Crossing is in the area roughly bounded by Farm-to-Market Road 973, Old Burleson Road, and Onion Creek.

Rainey Street
National Register District

Located downtown near the Austin Convention Center between Driskill and River Streets, the Rainey Street district includes 21 Victorian cottages as well as 1930s bungalows and other historic structures. This was a working-class neighborhood during the late 19th and early 20th centuries. None of the structures is open to the public.

Shadow Lawn
National Register District

This district includes a couple of blocks of residences within the Hyde Park neighborhood in Central Austin. The Depression-era homes are mostly one-story brick structures, many with Tudor Revival–style touches. The Shadow Lawn district is on Avenue G and Avenue H and includes part of the 3800 block of Duval Street.

Sixth Street National Register District

By night, this strip defends its reputation as Austin's most-visited strip when tourists and residents out for a good time pack its lively, music-filled clubs and restaurants. (Don't miss our chapter on The Music Scene for the story of Sixth Street after dark.) By day, Sixth Street takes a breather. That's the time to stroll along the uncluttered sidewalks and take in the sites of one of Austin's most historic streets. This section is about East Sixth Street by day, when the sun illuminates the past. Known as Pecan Street in Austin's early days, this district is filled with more than two dozen fascinating examples of Victorian commercial architecture. Many of the buildings here were constructed during the building boom of the 1870s. Others followed in the 1880s and 1890s. Of course, these structures don't disappear at night. They're just a little harder to appreciate. The district encompasses a 9-block street from Lavaca Street on the west to I-35 on the east.

Start your tour at the corner of Sixth and Brazos Streets at the famous Driskill Hotel, built in 1886. (See our chapter on Hotels and Motels for more on this landmark.) As you walk east on the north side of Sixth Street, you'll discover many more examples of Victorian architecture. Among the noteworthy structures on Old Pecan Street is the Hannig Building. Built in 1875 at 206 East Sixth Street, this Renaissance Revival–style structure is considered one of Austin's finest late-19th-century, Victorian commercial buildings. The Padgitt-Warmoth Building, built in 1885, is next at number 208. Once a saddlery and leather business, this is one of Old Pecan Street's most interesting buildings, with its fleur-de-lis cutouts and a Star of David cap.

In the next block is the Platt-Simpson Building at 310 East Sixth Street. This structure, built in 1871, was a livery stable and later a hardware store. St. Charles House, at number 316, was built in 1871 and once was a hotel and restaurant. Among the historic structures in the 400 block is the beautifully restored Dos Banderas at 410 East Sixth Street. Once a saloon and bawdy house, the building was closed in 1961 for housing "nefarious activities." Next door is the Quast Building, built in 1881 as a residence and later operated as a grocery store. This is one of the oldest stone buildings on the strip. The Risher-Nicholas Building at 422–424 East Sixth Street is another of the building-boom structures. Built in 1873, it became a drugstore in the early 1900s. Owner J. J. Jennings, a black physician, was once lauded for his work at building up "a trade that would do justice to any drugstore owned by any other race." The *Austin Watchman*, an early African-American newspaper, was published here in the early 1900s.

On the south side of Sixth Street, at 421 East Sixth Street, is the two-story stone and masonry Paggi Carriage Shop, constructed around 1875. Owner Michael Paggi is said to have been the first to bring an ice-making machine from France to Texas. Also on this block, visitors will find two 1875 structures, the J. L. Buass Building at number 407 and the Driskill-Day-Ford Building at number 403. The Cotton Exchange Building next door at 401 East Sixth also was built about this time. Across the street, at 325 East Sixth Street, is the Smith-Hage Building. Built in 1873, this building is a good example of commercial Victorian architecture during this time period, with its three arched windows on the second floor and topped by an elaborate metal cornice. One of Austin's few remaining cast-iron–front buildings can be found at 209 East Sixth Street. This is the Morely-Grove Drug Store, originally built as a two-story structure in 1874. The third floor and a Queen Anne bay window were added about 20 years later. At the corner of Sixth and Congress is the Littlefield Building. Completed in 1912 and built for Major George Washington Littlefield (whose opulent home and the fountain named for him are on the UT campus), this elegant

When you're looking for downtown attractions or lodging, remember that an address that includes the word south means south of Lady Bird Lake. Also know that Lady Bird Lake is that river-looking body of water downtown. It's a lake only because the river is dammed.

structure once was the tallest building between New Orleans and San Francisco. The building originally had eight floors, but Littlefield added another floor when the rival Scarbrough Building matched the Littlefield's height.

Swedish Hill National Register District

This district is close to the Oakwood Cemetery just east of I-35 in East Austin. Visitors who walk along East 14th Street, East 15th Street, Olander Street, and Waller Street will discover 10 architecturally significant residences built from about 1880 to 1938, none open to the public. The neighborhood, now only partially intact, got its name from the area's Swedish immigrants.

Willow-Spence Streets National Register District

This district is in East Austin. Willow Street is a block south of First Street, just east of I-35. Spence Street is another block south of Willow. Along these two streets, visitors will find 38 historically noteworthy buildings constructed from about 1900 to the 1930s. None is open to the public.

Zilker Park National Register District

This great Austin Park, which includes many historic structures and buildings, including a limestone Boy Scout hut, built in 1934, and a Girl Scout lodge built the same year, was added to the National Register of Historic Places in 1997. (For more on Austin's favorite community park, see our chapter on Parks and Recreation.)

TOURING GREATER AUSTIN . . .

. . . On Foot and On Wheel

AUSTIN ASTRONOMICAL SOCIETY TOURS

Wild Basin Wilderness Preserve
805 North Loop 360 (Capital of Texas Highway)
(512) 327-7622
www.austinastro.org/wbtours.html

A bit off the beaten path but well worth the time are the monthly Stargazing and Moonlighting tours offered at Wild Basin Wilderness Preserve by members of the Austin Astronomical Society and Wild Basin volunteers. Although the tours can be canceled if the sky is overcast, these events are extremely popular and do fill up, so reservations are highly recommended. The operators suggest that visitors bring a flashlight, binoculars, drinking water, and a cushion or small folding chair. The preserve entrance is about 1 mile north of Bee Caves Road on the east side of Loop 360.

AUSTIN CONVENTION AND VISITORS BUREAU

(512) 478-0098, (800) 866-GOAUSTIN
www.austintexas.org

The visitor bureau offers free guided walking tours from March through November of the capitol grounds, historic Congress Avenue and Sixth Street, and the Bremond District. Tours of the capitol grounds are conducted on Saturday at 2:00 p.m. and Sunday at 9:00 a.m., while the walking tour of Congress Avenue begins at 9:00 a.m. sharp Thursday through Saturday and at 2:00 p.m. on Sunday. The Bremond Historical District tour begins on Saturday and Sunday at 2:00 p.m. These tours leave from the south steps of the capitol building. While the visitor bureau does not run the tours of the State Capitol, it does provide information about the tours.

i Visit the Austin Visitor Center at 209 East Sixth Street to pick up brochures and find out about current events. Tickets to theater events can also be purchased at the center.

AUSTIN OVERTURES

(512) 659-9478
www.austinovertures.com

From the vantage point of a comfortable bright-fuchsia van, Austin Overtures offers 90-minute narrated tours of Austin that include 30 of Austin's major historical and cultural attractions on a 30-mile tour route. Experienced tour operators Dow and Mary Davidson launched this company in 2003, offering interesting, fun-and-fact-filled introductions to many of the places and people that make Austin what it is, such as *Austin City Limits,* the LBJ Library, Barton Springs, and the Congress Avenue bat colony. The tours are narrated by Dow, a Texas history buff whose great-great-grandfather founded the Texas town of Leakey. There are three daily scheduled departures from the Austin Convention and Visitors Bureau, at 9:30 a.m., 11:30 a.m., and 1:30 p.m. Special group tours can also be arranged.

HAUNTED TEXAS TOURS

(512) 443-3688
www.hauntedtexas.com

Boo! For those looking for the decidedly unusual, the well-established Haunted Texas Tours and Austin Ghost Tours offer a variety of adventures unlike any other tour company. Jeanine Plumer serves as both historian and storyteller as she takes visitors through Austin's haunted haunts. The Ghosts of the Capitol District Tour conjures up the spirit world in a 90-minute walking tour that includes stops at the capitol and the Driskill Hotel. The Servant Girl Annihilator Tour traces the steps of the girl who terrorized our city in the 1880s. There is also the Haunted Sixth Street Tour and the Ghosts of the Warehouse District Tour. All tours are conducted in the evening.

TEXPERT TOURS

(512) 383-8989
www.texperttours.com

Known locally as "the Texas Back Roads Scholar," Howie Richey offers entertaining, insightful tours of Austin and the Texas Hill Country based on his excellent knowledge of and love for this region. His enlightening tours of downtown Austin provide much more than a look at buildings and scenery. He's got the scoop on the history, geography, and quirky qualities of our fair city and exudes a hearty respect for the region's natural wonders. You'll think you've got your very own university professor in the vehicle with you. Howie is a longtime Austinite and University of Texas grad (twice!), who also hosts shows on Austin public radio. While the Heart of Austin tour is probably his most popular, he also offers the delightful Keep Austin Weird tour, that includes some of the city's more offbeat sights, as well as a Hill Country tour. Howie also can tailor an outing to satisfy any group's interests. His Austin tours are three hours long; the Hill Country trips run about four hours. He offers departures at 9:00 a.m., 1:00 p.m., and 7:00 p.m. most days. It's important to reserve in advance, as he customizes the trip for each group and provides refreshments, maps, souvenirs, and printed schedules. Reservations can now be made on his Web site.

. . . On Hoof

AUSTIN CARRIAGE SERVICE
Tours starting and ending at several downtown locations
(512) 243-0044
www.austincarriage.com
With Austin's weather so beautiful most of the year, one great way to see the sites of historic downtown and enjoy the outdoors in style is to hop on a Vis-A-Vis. That's French for face to face. Indeed. These white horse-drawn carriages operated by the Austin Carriage Service have seating for up to six people, facing one another, and each features a top that can be raised in case of light rain or harsh sunlight. The carriages, reproductions of a servant-driven carriage from the 18th century, are drawn by draft horses that stand about 6 feet tall and weigh 1,800 to 2,200 pounds. Austin Carriage Service offers a variety of regular tours that take in the sights on Congress Avenue, Sixth Street, the State Capitol, Lady Bird Lake, and more. Tours depart from several

downtown restaurants and hotels, including The Driskill, the Four Seasons, the Hyatt Regency, Embassy Suites, and DoubleTree Guest Suites. The service offers day, evening, and late-night rides. Call for their schedule. In most cases, there's no need to make a reservation. Just walk up and enjoy the ride. A carriage can also be dispatched to a specific location by making arrangements in advance. Drivers are friendly and also serve as guides on your historic tour. Fees vary according to the length of the tour, which ranges from about 20 minutes to 80 minutes.

DIE GELBE ROSE CARRIAGE
(512) 477-8824
www.diegelberosecarriage.net
From its base of operations near the Radisson Hotel & Suites at East Cesar Chavez Street and Congress Avenue, this carriage company offers horse-drawn carriage tours around downtown's most comely sights. Starting around sunset daily, you can hail a carriage to the State Capitol or design your own tour. Call ahead if you prefer to have a carriage waiting at a certain time to whisk you away. Magnificent Clydesdales are the most common horses used for this task.

. . . On Rail

AUSTIN STEAM TRAIN
(512) 477-8468
www.austinsteamtrain.org
All aboard! Like the carriage rides above and the boat rides that follow, the mode of transportation for these tours is a big part of the fun. Take one—or all—of a number of rides on this popular train that runs on weekends year-round. Choices, depending on the season, include a daylong trip through the Texas Hill Country, a half-day Hill Country tour, a two-hour ride through East Austin, and specialty evening excursions, such as the Storybook Special for families with young children and the Murder Mystery Special and the New Year's Eve Special, both adult oriented. The Hill Country trains, which depart from Cedar Park in north Austin, run on the same tracks built in 1881 for the Austin & Northwestern Railroad. The

pink granite used to build our State Capitol was hauled over these tracks in the 1880s.

The main locomotive for these trips is a steam engine, Southern Pacific #786, built in 1916. However, the vintage locomotive was still undergoing a massive overhaul in 2006, and diesel-powered engines were temporarily called into action. Check out the Web site for a schedule, rate information, and news on when the steam train will be back in service. The trains are operated by the Austin Steam Train Association, a community-based nonprofit organization whose volunteers go out of their way to make these trips fun for all.

. . . On Water
AUSTIN DUCK ADVENTURES
(512) 4-SPLASH (477-5274)
www.austinducks.com

What's that strange yellow truck with the big tires rolling down Congress Avenue? It is one of the Austin Duck Adventure trucks, a combo vehicle that can ride on roads and splash into Lady Bird Lake for a cruise along the river. Tickets can be purchased at the Austin Convention and Visitors Bureau, 209 East Sixth Street.

CAPITAL CRUISES
At the Hyatt Regency Hotel,
208 Barton Springs Road
(512) 480-9264
www.capitalcruises.com

For private or public cruises of Lady Bird Lake, Capital Cruises offers a variety of tour options. Public tours, held March through October, include weekend dinner cruises and sightseeing tours as well as the popular nightly bat-watching excur-

sions. Capital Cruises also offers private cruises by reservation year-round. These include private and group dinner cruises, party boat cruises, and company outings. This company also has canoes, kayaks, pedal boats, and pontoons for rent. Tickets are required.

LAKE AUSTIN RIVERBOATS
On Lake Austin
(512) 345-5220
www.austinriverboats.com

These two stern-wheeler riverboats are for chartered cruises of Lake Austin, complete with food and beverage service if you like. *Commodore's Pup* is for groups of 50 to 100 people, while the riverboat *Commodore* is designed for 100 to 300 people. Entertainment can also be arranged for that special party. Call them for rates.

LONE STAR RIVERBOAT
On the south shore of Lady Bird Lake
between the Congress Avenue Bridge and
South First Street Bridge
(512) 327-1388
www.lonestarriverboat.com

A double-decked paddle-wheel riverboat takes visitors on a one-hour cruise of scenic Lady Bird Lake from March through October. *Lone Star* offers a variety of cruise times, including a sunset tour and a close-up view of the evening flight of the bats from the Congress Avenue Bridge (see the previous listing in this chapter). There's also a moonlight cruise on Friday night during summer. Group and private charters are also available. The schedule changes according to the time of year. Call for current tours. No reservations are required. Fees vary according to the type of cruise.

KIDSTUFF

"**O**ne morning hundreds of years ago, an acorn fell and grew in the earth. And that was me." So begins *The Tree That Would Not Die,* a wonderful, beautifully illustrated children's book by Ellen Levine and Ted Rand about Austin's legendary Treaty Oak. It may seem odd to begin a section on children's activities by mentioning a book, or our remarkable tree for that matter. However, this short, poignant book, available in most area bookstores, offers an excellent introduction to Austin for both children and adults. Folklore, history, and a somber slice of contemporary life intermingle to deliver a unique perspective on this fascinating city. And don't forget to take your little acorns to visit the real Treaty Oak in Central Austin (see our Attractions chapter). Did we say little acorns? It seems to us that Austin views its children—both residents and visitors—as if they were wee acorns: little pods of potential that, if nurtured, will grow upright, strong, and resilient. So whether yours is a little sprout, a precocious sapling, or a young tree whose branches are reaching for the sky, Austin offers plenty of sunshine, water, and fertilizer for all.

From the Austin Children's Museum to children's theater, the Austin Zoo, indoor skating rinks, and great outdoor activities, Austinites have put a great deal of energy into providing recreational, educational, cultural, and simply fun activities for youth of all ages. The Central Texas area provides even more diversion, including that guaranteed kid-pleaser, the giant amusement park. All the Kidstuff activities and attractions we've included in this chapter can be found within 90 minutes of Austin, but most are right here at home. A word on ticket prices: Generally speaking, public institutions, museums, science centers, etc., charge nominal, family-friendly admission prices. Some of the privately run attractions in central Texas, particularly those focused on the area's natural wonders, charge a little more. Admission for a family of four to these attractions can cost around $50. Commercial attractions, including the major theme parks, are more expensive, and tickets for a family of four can cost more than $140 for a daily admission, unless you look for Internet or promotional discounts in advance.

OVERVIEW

If you want your sprouts to enjoy their trip to Austin, be sure to visit some of the places listed here. We've provided six categories designed to direct you to Central Texas's most appealing attractions for "growing" children.

Fertilize Well: While this list includes those attractions designed to stimulate the mind, there's plenty of fun to be found, too.

Just Add Water: What would Central Texas be without diversions designed to get you nice and wet?

Supply Sunshine: These are a few of Austin's outdoor delights that appeal to children.

Let 'em Grow Crazy: For when the kids just need to let loose and have fun.

A Garden of Delights: Check this out for relaxing and entertaining spots that are sure to please.

Don't Eat the Daisies: Sure, Austin has all the fast-food chains that appeal to children, but here are a few local favorites, both homegrown and outside imports. See our Restaurants chapter for even more places to feed yourself and the kids.

Don't miss our chapter on Parks and Recreation for information on many more activities that are practically guaranteed to delight kids of all ages. Our chapters on Attractions, Spectator Sports, and The Arts offer events and attractions for the young and young at heart. The Literary Scene chapter provides information about our libraries and bookstores, which all have storytimes or other activities designed especially for kids.

FERTILIZE WELL

AQUARENA CENTER
921 Aquarena Springs Drive, San Marcos
(512) 245-7575, (800) 999-9767
www.aquarena.txstate.edu
Take a ride on a glass-bottom boat on Spring Lake to view the pristine waters and aquatic life of Aquarena Springs, one of Central Texas's natural wonders. The freshwater springs that created the San Marcos River were formed millions of years ago by a fracture in the earth's crust, known today as the Balcones Fault. The river is home to more than 100 varieties of aquatic life, including several endangered species found nowhere else on earth. Well-informed tour guides take you on a relaxing adventure as you witness, through the bottom of the boat, the springs bubbling up from the Edwards Aquifer. There are also the underwater remains of an archaeology dig that unearthed 12,000 years of history, including mastodon bones, Spanish gold coins, and arrowheads left by the hunter-gatherers who once lived here. This is a perfect place to spend a couple of hours.

This former theme park was acquired in 1994 by Texas State University, which changed the focus here from amusement to preservation and education. Aquarena Center features a lovely park next to the lake, a historic village, a gift shop, and snack bar as well as a fascinating endangered species exhibit where visitors learn about the Texas blind salamander, the San Marcos salamander, and other aquatic life. Admission to the park and exhibits is free, but a fee is charged for a variety of boat tours, including ones focusing on ecology, endangered species, archaeology, and history. The center has offered special kids programs in summer, but check to see if they're still running. Aquarena Center is generally open seven days a week from 9:30 a.m. to 7:00 p.m., but do confirm closing times if you're planning to arrive late. To get to the springs, take Interstate 35 south from Austin, exit 206 to Aquarena Springs Drive, and go about 1.5 miles west.

AUSTIN CHILDREN'S MUSEUM
Dell Discovery Center
201 Colorado Street
(512) 472-2499
www.austinkids.org
Fun AND educational. What better combination is there to please children and parents alike? The Austin Children's Museum at Dell Discovery Center is a 7,000-square-foot playscape filled with galleries and hands-on activities designed to entertain and educate even the youngest visitors. This two-story facility (three if you count the small third-level Time Tower that includes exhibits of Austin history and features a tube slide to the first floor) is just packed with permanent and temporary exhibits—all aimed at encouraging youngsters to explore and use their imaginations.

In early 2010 the museum plans to move to a new space just north of City Hall downtown, so check the Web site for updates on the move—and the new digs. The museum is open Tuesday through Saturday 10:00 a.m. to 5:00 p.m. and Sunday noon to 5:00 p.m. Admission is by donation on Wednesday from 5:00 to 8:00 p.m. and free Sunday from 4:00 to 5:00 p.m. The museum also offers a wide range of summer camps and special activities for children throughout the year.

i *Austin Family* magazine, www.austin family.com, sponsors a Camp Fair each January. This is a great place for long-time residents and newcomers alike to check out the many kids' camps available in Austin.

AUSTIN MUSEUM OF ART AT LAGUNA GLORIA
3809 West 35th Street
(512) 458-8191
www.amoa.org
Housed in a historic villa, this great West Austin museum also hosts the city's art school for children and adults alike. While small children may feel too restricted in the exhibition space, the museum sits on a 12-acre site, complete with sculpture garden, that gives kids plenty of room to move around while still enjoying works of art. The school is in a separate building on-site. The museum also hosts several family-friendly outdoor festivals each year. Regular operating hours are 11:00 a.m. to 4:00 p.m. daily for the Villa, and 9:00 a.m. to 5:00 p.m. Monday through Saturday and 11:00 a.m. to 5:00 p.m. Sunday for the grounds. Public tours are held at 1:00 p.m. on weekends. (See The Arts chapter for more details about the villa and the art school.)

AUSTIN NATURE AND SCIENCE CENTER
301 Nature Center Drive
(512) 327-8181
www.cityofaustin.org/ansc
Children will get a kick out of using the Eco Detective kit to discover signs of Austin wildlife on the Eco Detective Trail, learn about plants and animals in the Discovery Lab, and work in a paleontological dig in the Dino Pit at this great center in the Zilker Park Nature Preserve. Injured owls, hawks, and vultures are featured in the Birds of Prey exhibit, while the Small Wonders exhibit displays 20 of Austin's small animals. The Nature and Science Center is a perfect introduction to Austin's unique ecosystems and to the wonders of Austin nature. (For more on the center see our chapter on Attractions.) The center is open 9:00 a.m. to 5:00 p.m. Monday through Saturday and Sunday noon to 5:00 p.m. Admission is free.

THE BOB BULLOCK TEXAS STATE HISTORY MUSEUM
1800 North Congress Avenue
(512) 936-8746, (866) 369-7108
www.thestoryoftexas.com
This new downtown museum just north of the capitol is a must visit for visitors of all ages, but kids will love the colorful exhibits, many of them interactive, which present the story of Texas from before we were even called Texas. Because this is a non-collecting museum, some exhibits come and go—so visit often! The museum also houses Austin's only IMAX theater and the Spirit Theater. (For a complete description of the museum, see our Attractions chapter.)

GEORGE WASHINGTON CARVER MUSEUM AND CULTURAL CENTER
1165 Angelina Street
(512) 974-4926
www.ci.austin.tx.us/carver
Distinguished for being the first African-American neighborhood museum in the state of Texas, the George Washington Carver Museum and Cultural Center is a 36,000-square-foot facility that includes four galleries, a 134-seat theater, a dance studio, conference room, classroom, darkroom, and archival space. The museum's core exhibit is on Juneteenth, the oldest nationally celebrated commemoration of the ending of slavery in the United States. There also is a permanent exhibit on Austin African-American families, an Artists Gallery, and a children's exhibit on African-American scientists and inventors, including George Washington Carver, of course.

INNER SPACE CAVERN
I-35, exit 259, Georgetown
(512) 931-CAVE
www.innerspace.com
People tend to think that attractions located right beside the interstate are just tourist traps designed to get your money. This one, however, is one of the best and most accessible attractions around for both children and their families. Estimated to be 100 million years old, Inner Space Cavern was discovered in 1963 by workers testing core samples for construction of the interstate. It seems everywhere they drilled they found air pockets. Now opened for all to appreciate, this living cavern—meaning it continues to grow and develop—features an excellent array

of formations beyond the typical stalactites and stalagmites. Guides on the Adventure Tour will lead you on a 75-minute walk and point out such fascinating shapes as the Flowing Stone of Time, the Lake of the Moon, and more, including the bones of prehistoric animals who died in here. Other tours also are offered. At a temperature of 72 to 74 degrees, this is the perfect spot to escape both the sizzling summer heat and the winter chill. Outside, the family can pan for gems and minerals. The cavern has a large gift shop and snack bar. The cavern, located just 24 miles north of downtown Austin, is open 9:00 a.m. to 6:00 p.m. daily during the summer, with shorter hours during the off-season. Tours depart regularly throughout the day with the last one beginning at 5:50 p.m.

JOURDAN-BACHMAN PIONEER FARMS
11418 Sprinkle Cut-Off Road
(512) 837-1215
www.pioneerfarms.org
Children will enjoy stepping back in time to witness the lives of Central Texas settlers at this living history museum, which is open to the public on Sunday from 1:00 to 5:00 p.m. and Friday from 10:00 a.m. to 2:00 p.m. The farm, originally part of a 2,000-acre cotton farm, presents the story of rural life in the late 19th century. Visitors can stroll around the three historic farmsteads and view demonstrations of blacksmithing, woodworking, spinning, and weaving. They also can see firsthand the historically correct crops, food, clothing, farm implements, and dwellings on this large property. On other days, farm personnel offer guided tours for schoolchildren and other groups. Admission is $8 for adults and $6 for children.

MEXICAN AMERICAN CULTURAL CENTER
600 River Street
(512) 478-6222
macc@ci.austin.tx.us
Opened in late 2007, the Mexican American Cultural Center (MACC) is a wonderful addition to the Austin kids' scene. This Hispanic-focused facility (see The Arts chapter) offers countless activities for children, from classes in dance, sewing, filmmaking, writing and, of course, art, to children's theater and music productions. Any time is a good time to visit, but the last Sunday of each month has a special focus on kids' activities.

NATURAL BRIDGE CAVERNS
26495 Natural Bridge Cavern Road
(210) 651-6101
www.naturalbridgecaverns.com
Located just north of San Antonio and southwest of New Braunfels off I-35 exit 175, Natural Bridge Caverns boasts more than 10,000 formations, including such wonders as Sherwood Forest, the Castle of the White Giant, and the King's Throne. These living caverns, discovered in 1960, present many spectacular sights, including one underground room that's as big as a football field. The cool caverns (average temperature is 72 degrees) are nestled amid Texas Hill Country terrain and provide plenty of shaded space outside for picnicking or relaxing. There's also a gift shop. The 75-minute tours depart about every 30 minutes beginning at 9:00 a.m. daily and ending at 6:00 p.m., except Thanksgiving, Christmas, and New Year's Day. Closing time varies depending on the season. Several different tours are offered at various prices.

THE REPUBLIC OF TEXAS MUSEUM
510 East Anderson Lane
(512) 339-1997
www.drt-inc.org/museum.htm
Do you know where and when the Texas Declaration of Independence was signed? How about the year Santa Anna was elected president of Mexico or the reason washing clothes was dangerous for women in the 1800s? The answer to these questions, and many more, can be found in the Republic of Texas Museum, a compact but fun and educational space for the whole family. Children and adults are given a separate list of scavenger hunt questions, the answers to which can be found by touring the exhibits. The littlest ones get to answer questions such as where is the chair with the two ears located or find the

three chickens in the museum and what are their names? This museum, run by the Daughters of the Republic of Texas, is dedicated to the era of the Texas Republic (1836–1846). Young children especially like Great Grandma's Backyard, a collection of hands-on household items and implements used by families in the mid-19th century. There's something of interest for people of all ages here. The museum is open 10:00 a.m. to 4:00 p.m. Monday through Friday. General admission is $2, $1 for kids.

SPLASH! INTO THE EDWARDS AQUIFER
2201 Barton Springs Road
(512) 478-3170
www.ci.austin.tx.us/splash
This hands-on educational center at Barton Springs Pool is a 1,400-square-foot interactive exhibit on the Barton Springs Edwards Aquifer. Splash! features a continuously running four-minute video, *Carved in Stone*, which shows how the springs were formed. An interactive three-dimensional relief map that uses animated lights to show the movement of the water lets children push the buttons to make the water flow. There's also a fascinating aquascape model of the aquifer. Aquariums here house specimens of the aquifer's aquatic life. This is a great place to learn about the Barton Springs salamander, an endangered species found only in Austin. Splash! is part of the Beverly Sheffield Education Center run by the Austin Parks and Recreation Department. The various exhibits are designed for use by children in fourth grade and up. Splash! is free to the public, although there may be a charge for guided tours. Call for hours of operation. (For more about Barton Springs, see our Close-up in the Parks and Recreation chapter.)

STAR GAZING
T. S. Painter Hall Observatory,
near 24th Street and Speedway
(512) 232-4265
No. We're not talking about the kind of stargazing that involves Austin's film industry. This is the old-fashioned, out-of-this-world kind. The University of Texas astronomy department offers free stargazing experiences on the UT campus every Sat-

urday night for the general public (from 10:00 to 11:00 p.m. for UT students and faculty on Friday), weather permitting, during the school year. Families with children seem especially attracted to this kind of educational fun. Astronomy students lead visitors on a tour of the stars, using a cool 10-inch-diameter telescope built in 1932. The fun starts around 8:30 p.m., but call ahead to confirm. No reservations are required. Parking is easy at this time of night, except when big UT events, like a Longhorns football game, are scheduled. For further information on other celestial events and stargazing activities, call the UT Sky Watchers Report at (512) 471-5007.

TEXAS STATE CAPITOL
1100 Congress Avenue
(512) 463-0063
www.tspb.state.tx.us/SPB/capitol/texcap.htm
There's just no better way to introduce your youngsters to the legends and lore of Texas history than taking them on a tour of the Texas State Capitol. We've found the guides to be especially kind and patient with children, making sure to answer all their questions. (For more on this monument to Texas, including hours of operation, see our Attractions chapter.)

UMLAUF SCULPTURE GARDEN & MUSEUM
605 Robert E. Lee Road
(512) 445-5582
www.umlaufsculpture.org
Ask for the treasure hunt map when you visit the Umlauf Sculpture Garden, and your child will be delighted to chase around looking for some of Charles Umlauf's magnificent sculptures. (The diversion will allow you more time to enjoy the sculptures, too.) Because most of the statues are outdoors, this is a great place to introduce children to a museum. They don't have to keep quiet, and they don't have to keep their hands to themselves. (Yes, they can touch the outdoor sculptures!) They'll love you for it. (To find out more about this outdoor garden and indoor museum, including the hours of operation, see our Attractions chapter.)

WONDER WORLD PARK
1000 Prospect Street, San Marcos
(512) 392-3760
www.wonderworldpark.com
Unlike other caves in Texas that were formed by rushing water, this fascinating underground fissure was formed by a massive earthquake millions of years ago. You can actually see where the earth split, leaving jigsaw puzzle–like sections of rock that would fit right into each other if pushed back together. And because it's not growing, kids get to put their hands anywhere they like. Wonder World, said to be the only earthquake-formed cave in the country open for tours, drops more than 160 feet beneath the earth's surface but is accessible for children of all ages. Kid-friendly guides take visitors on a 45-minute tour of this Texas marvel, pointing out all the prehistoric treasures and naturally glowing rocks. Wonder World also has a 190-foot aboveground observation tower, a deer-petting zoo, and an antigravity house. Theme park prices and coupons are available on the Web site. Kids younger than age 5 are admitted free. Admission for just the cave is $11 for adults and $9 for children. The cave is by far the best feature here. Wonder World is open 8:00 a.m. to 8:00 p.m. Memorial Day to Labor Day; shorter hours the rest of the year.

JUST ADD WATER

BARTON SPRINGS
Zilker Park, 2201 Barton Springs Road
(512) 476-9044
www.ci.austin.tx.us/parks/bartonsprings.htm
There's nothing like a cool—and we mean cool—dip in Austin's treasured spring-fed swimming pool to chill out the kids on a hot summer day and make them feel like real Austin Insiders. The water in the pool remains a constant 68 degrees throughout the year. (For more on this historic spot and for Austin's other great swimming spots, see our Parks and Recreation chapter.)

DEEP EDDY POOL'S SUMMER MOVIES
401 Deep Eddy Avenue
(512) 472-8546
www.ci.austin.tx.us/parks

Take a float along with you when you go to Deep Eddy's Summer Movies—and watch the flick from the pool. That will keep you cool.

Leave it to Austinites to figure out a way to combine water fun and flicks. West Austin's Deep Eddy Pool, one of our favorite swimming spots, presents family movies right next to the pool on Saturday night throughout the summer, starting in late June. The schedule has included such winners as *Antz, 101 Dalmatians, George of the Jungle, Dr. Doolittle,* and *Creature from the Black Lagoon,* presented in 3D. Come around 8:00 p.m., and bring a picnic basket or buy pizza at the pool. The films begin at about 9:00 p.m. or so, just around sunset. A nominal admission fee is charged.

SCHLITTERBAHN WATERPARK RESORT
305 West Austin Street,
New Braunfels
(830) 625-2351
www.schlitterbahn.com
Never mind that this waterpark is about 50 miles south of Austin in New Braunfels. Schlitterbahn is one place many Austin families visit at least once, if not several times, during summer. Located on the banks of the spring-fed Comal River, Schlitterbahn is 65 acres of high-tech water rides, slides, pools, inner tube floats, and kiddie parks. The park has plenty of hair-raising rides sure to please the stoutest thrill-seeker in your group. Schlitterbahn also claims the world's first uphill water coaster. Picnic baskets (no glass or alcohol, please) are welcome here, and there are plenty of shaded areas and tables. The park is open late April to late September, but on weekends only during the school year. The fun starts at 10:00 a.m. daily and goes until closing time, which varies from 6:00 to 8:00 p.m. One-day admission is $38 for ages 11 and up and $30 for ages 3 to 11. Two-day passes, tickets for the Comal River Rapids only, and season tickets also are available. Parking is free. Schlitterbahn also runs two riverside resort hotels (at the same phone number).

SEA WORLD ADVENTURE PARK
10500 Sea World Drive, San Antonio
(800) 700-7786
www.seaworld.com

Promise your youngsters a trip to Sea World and you're sure to get at least a day or two of good behavior in exchange. While there are plenty of thrilling water rides, wet playscapes, cool amusement park adventures, and shows, kids can actually learn something here, too. But keep that part under your hat. This giant park features the only major display of hammerhead sharks in North America, dozens of penguins, sea lions, whales, and, of course, the great Shamu. Sea World says it's the world's largest sea life adventure park. While not all the rides are designed to get you wet, there are plenty to keep you cool on a hot summer day. Be sure to pack the swimsuits. Sea World is open March through October, mostly on weekends until school gets out. But all summer long this exciting place is open 10:00 a.m. to 10:00 p.m. Admission is in the $43 to $51 range, but print your tickets online and save 10 percent. Two-day passes and season tickets also are available. This is definitely worth a trip to San Antonio.

TUBING
City Park, near University and
Bobcat Drives, San Marcos
(512) 396-LION
www.tubesanmarcos.com

To many Texans, the Hill Country is synonymous with river tubing, in which you ride down the river on big inner tubes. This inexpensive, low-tech pastime is loads of fun, especially on hot summer days. While some tubing areas can be dominated by older kids and young adults, the Lions Club operates a family-oriented tubing, swimming, and snorkeling spot on the San Marcos River in nearby San Marcos. They provide

i If you go to Schlitterbahn, most locals know to stake a claim on a picnic table early in the day. Put your coolers and towels there and make it your base of operations. Don't leave valuables, of course.

rides back to the park once you've gone downriver. You can even rent an extra tube, tie it to your own, and cart a cooler downstream if you like. This is refreshing and exhilarating fun, and all proceeds go to charity. All-day rental prices are very reasonable. It's open daily late May to early September from 10:00 a.m. to 7:00 p.m. The Lions Club also rents life vests for the little ones and lockers. Take I-35 south to exit 206 and follow Aquarena Springs Drive. Turn left onto Charles Austin Drive, then turn right behind Strahan Basketball Stadium and follow the signs.

VOLENTE BEACH WATER PARK
16107 F.M. 2769, Leander
(512) 258-5109
www.volentebeach.com

For those hot, hot, hot summer days in Austin, this compact water park on Lake Travis offers some cool options. It features four great water slides of varying thrill levels, as well as a pool for swimming or volleyball and other fun water activities. Sprouts can play in the shallow pool and climb on the pirate ship in the middle. The sandy beach on the lake is large, even if the swimming area is not. There are WaveRunners and other boats for rent. Volente Beach is Austin's only water park and is quite small in comparison to a sprawling Fiesta Texas or Splash Town water park, but that doesn't prevent it from being a popular spot for kids of all ages. The Sundowner Grill serves entrees, desserts, and beverages, and visitors may also bring ice chests with food and soft drinks. (No glass, of course.) The water park is open weekends in April, May, and September and daily June through August.

SUPPLY SUNSHINE

AUSTIN'S PARK 'N PIZZA EXPERIENCE
16231 North I-35
(512) 670-9600
www.austinspark.com

Open 365 days a year, this 22-acre park offers fun activities for all the kids—and for the kid in all of us. The hardest part of the day is trying to choose from among the park's many attractions, which include miniature golf, bumper boats, laser tag, go-karts, batting cages, a driving range, an indoor climbing wall, a huge arcade, and a thrill ride: the Ejection Seat, which shoots passengers 150 feet into the air. Of course all this exercise is going to work up some huge appetites. For that, there's the reasonably priced all-you-can-eat pizza, pasta, salad, and dessert buffet. The nice thing about this park is that attractions are individually priced, so you don't have to spend the whole day to get your money's worth. Family packages are also available. The park, 15 miles north of downtown Austin at exit 248, is open Sunday through Thursday from 9:00 a.m. to 10:00 p.m., Friday and Saturday from 9:00 a.m. to 11:00 p.m., but call or check the Web site as hours can vary by season.

AUSTIN ZOO
10807 Rawhide Trail
(512) 288-1490, (800) 291-1490
www.austinzoo.org

This Hill Country escape about 20 minutes southwest of downtown Austin is a perfect place to bring young children for a close-up look at the animals, a picnic, a pony ride, or a train ride. Compared to the sprawling superzoos many cities boast, Austin's zoo is small, rustic, and very laid-back. That makes it easy on young ones and their parents—you don't need to rush madly around the park to see everything. In fact, it was voted "Best Nature Day Trip" in the 2007 *Austin Chronicle* readers' poll. Here visitors will find Bengal tigers, wallabies, capybaras, African lions, antelope, pot-bellied pigs, and many more animals. There's a petting corral where you can purchase food to feed the animals. The zoo features a wonderful tortoise barn in which children can get a close-up view of several species. The Austin Zoo is open 10:00 a.m. to 6:00 p.m. daily. It's closed on Thanksgiving and Christmas. Admission is $7 for adults ($4 for 55 and older), $4 for children ages 2 to 12, and free for children younger than 2. This is a non-profit organization and prefers payment in cash. Checks are not accepted.

BUTLER PARK PITCH & PUTT GOLF COURSE
201 Lee Barton Drive
(512) 477-4430

Tiger Woods would have loved this place when he was just a toddler trying to master the game of golf. This specially designed, nine-hole Par 3 course in South Central Austin features holes about a third as long as standard ones—61 to 118 yards long—and also rents short clubs for the kids. Of course, adults who want a quick game of golf enjoy this wonderful course, too, which includes all the fun and frustrations of a regular course, including water hazards and the rough. Run by the Austin Parks and Recreation Department, this golf course is sure to please. It's open year-round. Greens fees are family-friendly. Club rental is extra.

CHILDREN'S DAY ART PARK
Symphony Square, 1101 Red River Street
(512) 476-6064
www.austinsymphony.org

Children are encouraged to bang the drums, blow the horns, and fiddle the strings at the instrument "petting zoo," just one exciting feature of the Austin Symphony Orchestra's summer art park for children. These delightful outdoor events, held every Wednesday morning in June and July at historic Symphony Square, feature performances by symphony ensembles and by a variety of children's performers, including salsa bands, folk singers, and ballet folklorico. Symphony musicians are on hand each week to demonstrate the use of various instruments and to provide guidance. When the musical performance ends, children follow the Pied Piper down Waller Creek for more hands-on activities and face painting under a big tent. The Austin Symphony, Austin's oldest performing group, has sponsored these art parks for kids for more than 25 years. They're designed

i Kids can test their gaming skills at the giant chess set (knee-high to adults) in Woolridge Park downtown almost every Saturday year-round from about 12:30 p.m. to 3:30 p.m.

for kids ages 3 to 8, but everyone is invited. Very small admission fee. Check out the art park from 9:30 to 11:30 a.m. (See our chapter on The Arts for more symphony events for the whole family.)

PETER PAN MINI-GOLF
1207 Barton Springs Road
(512) 472-1033
If you've got a hankering to play miniature golf until midnight—at least on Saturday—this is the place for you. Peter Pan offers two 18-hole miniature golf courses and a whole lot of fun for the little ones. What is it about this game that attracts so many kids and adults? It must be the challenge of trying to get that little ball up the hill around the obstacle and into the hole without screaming! Peter Pan is open year-round. Admission is $5 for adults and $3 for children 5 and younger. You can arrive 20 minutes before opening to get signed up.

SLAUGHTER CREEK METROPOLITAN PARK
4103 Slaughter Lane
Do you have an in-line skating fanatic in the family? This is the outdoor place for those who just couldn't leave home without the skates. The park features a 3-mile veloway (it's nice and smooth) and is popular with skaters and bikers. The park also offers a playground, nature trail, sports courts, and picnic facilities, too. This Southwest Austin park is next to the Lady Bird Johnson Wildflower Center. (See our Parks and Recreation Chapter for more about indoor roller rinks.)

WILD BASIN WILDERNESS PRESERVE
805 North Loop 360
(Capital of Texas Highway)
(512) 327-7622
www.wildbasin.org
Open from sunup to sundown, this is a perfect place to educate the kids, and yourself, about Austin's beautiful Hill Country terrain. This 227-acre preserve in West Austin is also great for nature walks as it features a trail system that runs throughout the area. The preserve gives school tours during the week, so tour guides know just

how to talk to youngsters and are prepared for the guided tours for visitors on weekends. Or you can take a self-guided tour and explore this park yourself. For the budding astronomer in the family, the Austin Astronomical Society holds a family-oriented stargazing party here each month as well as many other kid-friendly events. Nominal admission fee. Call (512) 416-5700, ext. 3560, for details. (See our Parks and Recreation chapter for information about other parks and preserves in the area.)

ZILKER PARK
2100 Barton Springs Road
(512) 472-4914
If, as they say, Barton Springs is the crown jewel of Austin, then Zilker Park is the crown. This 400-acre park is the city's largest park and definitely one of its most popular. There's a great playscape for kids, miniature train rides, jogging trails, and plenty of space to just run, play soccer, throw a Frisbee, or toss a ball. Tuck your swimsuits in the trunk when you head for the park, as Barton Springs Pool is right here and you might be tempted. (See our Parks and Recreation chapter for more details.)

LET 'EM GROW CRAZY

BLAZER TAG ADVENTURE CENTER
1701 West Ben White Boulevard
(512) 462-0202
www.blazerlazer.com
Billing itself as the "largest laser tag arena in Texas," this giant complex is blaster Nirvana. Whether your kids need to release some pent-up energy after a week of school or a weekend of sightseeing, Blazer Tag is the place to go. The three-story, 10,000-square-foot arena offers players of all ages plenty of space to track down and then blast away at their opponents. Games are 20 minutes long and start every 20 minutes. The center also has a video arcade, snack bar, and Austin's only revolving rock-climbing wall. It's also a popular spot for parties of all kinds. Blazer Tag is closed Tuesday and Wednesday for private functions.

CHAPARRAL ICE CENTER
14200 North I-35
(512) 252-8500

2525 Anderson Lane
(512) 451-5102
www.chaparralice.com

Kids can come daily for skating on their own or sign up for Learn-to-Skate classes at the I-35 facility and the recently renovated rink on Anderson Lane in Northcross Mall. These well-run, well-maintained skating rinks offer a wonderful variety of year-round activities for children and adults, so be bold and lace up some skates for yourself. The I-35 location is also the "Bat Cave," home to the Austin Ice Bats hockey team. (See our Spectator Sports chapter). There also are classes in ice dance and hockey as well as hockey leagues for children and adults. Chaparral does birthday parties and has a full summer of camps for children. Call for the current schedule. Admission and skate rental fees are family friendly.

CHUCK E CHEESE
8038 Burnet Road
(512) 451-0296

502 West Ben White Boulevard
(512) 441-9681

401 West Louis Henna Boulevard
(512) 385-2575

Ahhhh, the coveted token! There just never seem to be enough of those discs of gold to satisfy even the youngest of competitors. To match wits with a machine and win those esteemed tickets is, at that very moment, the most awesome adventure on the planet. All of Austin's Chuck E Cheese locations are filled with interactive arcade games, playscapes, and air hockey tables that are sure to please. The good news for parents is that the food is pretty darn good too. There is pizza and hot dogs, snacks and soft drinks, and even a salad bar. At the end of the day, your youngsters get to go home with the prizes they've won in exchange for the tickets. Chuck E Cheese does birthday parties, too. The stores are open Sunday

through Thursday from 10:00 a.m. to 10:00 p.m., Friday and Saturday 10:00 a.m. to 11:00 p.m.

CYPRESS VALLEY CANOPY TOURS
1223 Paleface Ranch Road
Spicewood
(512) 264-8880
www.cypressvalleycanopytours.com

There is a minimum weight requirement of 70 pounds for the thrilling zip-line rides at Cypress Valley Canopy Tours, but your older kids—especially your teenagers—will have a blast soaring through the cypress trees and over the creek at this spot not far from Austin (See the Attractions chapter). Make your reservations in advance if you will have only limited time in Austin. And check out the "one child flies for free" offer on the Web site.

MAIN EVENT
13301 N. U.S. Highway 183
(512) 401-0000
www.maineventusa.net

With 75,000 square feet of entertainment space, there is something here for kids of all ages. With bowling (including exciting Laser Jam events), laser tag, rock climbing, cool arcade and interactive games, and even an 18-hole glow-in-the-dark miniature golf course, the kids will want to spend hours here. But that's not a bad thing because Main Event caters to adults, too. The Shots Bar offers an assortment of alcoholic and non-alcoholic drinks, as well as billiards and darts. When it's time for a food break, the whole family can enjoy burgers, pizzas, nachos, wings, subs and more at the Main Street Cafe. Main Event is open daily from 11:00 a.m. (10:00 a.m. on Saturdays) and closes as late as 2:00 a.m. on some nights, although minors under age 18 can only stay until 10:00 p.m. The games are priced individually.

SIX FLAGS FIESTA TEXAS
17000 Interstate 10 West, San Antonio
(210) 697-5050, (800) 473-4378
www.sixflags.com

You'll need to drive down to San Antonio for this

one, but our resident kid advisor for this chapter insists you'll gain major points with your children by letting them know that, yes, Central Texas offers a fantastic amusement park. Fiesta Texas is a blast—and not just for the kiddies. Thrilling rides, the only floorless coaster in the Southwest, and a huge wooden coaster called the Rattler will have your heart in your throat in no time. There also are plenty of exciting rides sure to get you wet—and cool! This giant park offers rides for people of all ages, a special children's area, plenty of shops and restaurants, great shows, and, to top it off, a wonderful waterpark—don't forget to bring your swimsuits. This immaculate facility is so fun and so huge that many people purchase two-day or season passes. Fiesta Texas is open 10:00 a.m. to 10:00 p.m. daily throughout the summer and on weekends, with shorter hours in spring and fall. Call for a schedule. The park is closed November to March. Daily admission is around $47 for teenagers and adults and around $32 for children, but print tickets online and get a nice discount. Seniors are eligible for discounted adult tickets.

YMCA
1100 West Cesar Chavez Street
(512) 322-9622 (main office)
Locations throughout the area
www.ymca.com
With five Austin locations and more in Pflugerville and Round Rock, there's sure to be a YMCA somewhere near you. They all offer plenty of sporting facilities and equipment, classes, and just plain fun. The good news for Austin members is that your membership card at one "Y" allows you access to all Austin locations. There is an initiation fee, and membership is offered by the month.

A GARDEN OF DELIGHTS

CAFE MONET
4477 South Lamar Boulevard, Suite 560
(512) 892-3200
www.cafemonet.org
This paint-your-own pottery studio is tucked away in a small storefront in the Westgate Central Market Center in Southwest Austin. Patrons simply pick out the ceramic piece they want to decorate, choose their colors, paint, and leave the pottery to be fired, picking it up three days later. The cafe offers children's parties for a minimum of eight kids at family-friendly prices. The studio also can be rented for private parties for the young and creative at heart of all ages. On Friday the studio offers special prices for an all-evening session. You can bring along your own snacks and beverages.

CERAMICS BAYOU
3620 Bee Cave Road
(512) 328-1168
www.ceramicsbayou.com
This paint-it-yourself ceramics studio offers a wide range of items—everything from simple tiles and coffee mugs to plates, platters, and animals. Children will delight in using their creative powers to design and paint their own piece. At Ceramics Bayou you pay for the piece plus $6 per studio hour per person. Finished pieces are fired in the kiln and ready for pickup in a few days. Hint: These make excellent gifts for parents, friends, or Grandma or Grandpa on their birthday. Speaking of birthdays, Ceramics Bayou hosts those too, as well as private parties. The studio is open Monday, Tuesday, Wednesday, and Saturday from 10:00 a.m. to 6:00 p.m., Thursday and Friday from 10:00 a.m. to 9:00 p.m., and Sunday noon to 6:00 p.m.

PARAMOUNT THEATRE KIDS' CLASSICS
713 Congress Avenue
(512) 472-5470
www.austintheatre.org
Austin's historic Paramount Theatre (see our chapter on The Arts) presents many productions aimed specifically at children. The Paramount brings in some of the country's top children's

i The upscale Arboretum Shopping Center at 10000 Research Boulevard in Northwest Austin has a lovely park that features five life-size granite cows that kids like to climb on. An Amy's ice cream shop and picnic tables are right there.

ℹ The luxury Omni Austin Hotel at Southpark (see our Hotels chapter) offers a spacious Kid's Sensory Suite, which not only is decorated in kid-appealing colors, it is stocked with bean bag chairs, toys, games, and an art table. The youngsters even get goodie bags upon check-in. Parents get an adjoining room and a list of emergency phone numbers.

performers and theater companies for an exciting season of plays, musicals, and performing arts. The season has included such productions as *Jack and the Giant Beanstalk, Swiss Family Robinson*, Scholastic's *Magic School Bus* on tour, and more. This is fun for the whole family, and a great way to introduce youngsters to live theater. Many people subscribe to the full season.

THE BATS
Congress Avenue Bridge at Lady Bird Lake
Children ogle in wonder when North America's largest urban bat colony sets off en masse on the evening flight for food during spring and summer. This is a spectacle the whole family can enjoy. (For more on these Mexican free-tails, see our Attractions chapter.)

ZILKER PARK TRAIL OF LIGHTS AND CHRISTMAS TREE
Zilker Park, 2100 Barton Springs Road
(512) 472-4914
It only lasts a few weeks once a year, but this is one of THE places to take your kids if you're here around the Christmas holiday. The "tree" is formed using Zilker Park's 165-foot-tall Moonlight Tower as the trunk and strings of multicolored lights—3,500 of them—to form the tree's cone shape. Children love to stand inside the tree and twirl around until the lights blur. Austin's annual Yule Fest celebration, which features the Trail of Lights, is another tradition that children love. (See our December Annual Events for more on this and on the Lighting of the Zilker Park Christmas Tree.) Admission to the park is free.

DON'T EAT THE DAISIES
BIG TOP CANDY SHOP
1706 South Congress
(512) 462-2220
If you prefer to visit the museums or the malls, but can't convince the kids, try bribing them with the promise of a trip to the Austin-original Big Top Candy Shop in the trendy SoCo neighborhood south of Lady Bird Lake. This big store with a circus theme is chock full of sugar in all its best forms, both in pre-wrapped form and in bulk. Of course, one giant bin is dedicated to circus peanuts. On First Thursdays, the monthly street party on South Congress, the store features entertainers such as clowns and musicians. There's an old fashioned soda fountain here, too. (A few doors down, and operated by the same owner, is the toy store Monkey See, Monkey Do).

CENTRAL MARKET CAFE
4001 North Lamar Boulevard
(512) 206-1020

4477 South Lamar Boulevard
(512) 899-4300
www.centralmarket.com
The great outdoor patio filled with picnic tables and a playscape that's close enough to keep your eye on the kids are among the attractions for families at North Lamar Central Market Cafe. This casual restaurant, an extension of Austin's gourmet grocery store, has an extensive menu for people of all ages: burgers, pasta, salads, pizzas, gourmet fare, and much more, including great desserts. The second location on South Lamar has a patio, but not the wide green space of the original. You place your order at the counter and retrieve your meal when your beeper lights up. Both Central Market locations also have indoor dining for when it's just too hot outside to breathe. There's live music on the patio at both locations several evenings a week. It's a great way to introduce children to the Austin music scene and get them fed, too. (For more about Central Market see our Close-up in the Shopping chapter.)

DAVE & BUSTER'S

9333 Research Boulevard

(512) 346-8015

www.daveandbusters.com

Guests ages 18 and under must be accompanied by an adult at this establishment, even in the gaming area, but that doesn't prevent it from being one extremely popular spot with Austin kids. Why? Eat well, play games, win prizes! One side of the huge facility is filled with all sorts of arcade and interactive games, including table shuffleboard and pocket billiards. Yes, adults must come along here, too. The dining room, which is separated from the gaming room, is much more upscale than the typical fun center, one of the reasons this Dallas-based chain is growing. It offers plenty of kid-pleasing menu items, including burgers, pizza, and pasta. For heartier appetites there are steaks, chicken, and ribs. D&B's is open daily from 11:30 a.m. Closing time varies.

GÜERO'S TACO BAR

1412 South Congress Avenue

(512) 447-7688

www.guerostacobar.com

This Austin institution on funky South Congress Avenue is a popular family eatery. While Chelsea wasn't with former President Clinton when he ate here several years ago, we're sure she would have been satisfied with the Mexican fare. The kid's menu includes quesadillas, breakfast tacos, chicken breast tacos, and enchiladas. All entrees come with rice and beans. The salsa bar is serve-it-yourself, so the food isn't too spicy for the kids. You won't have to chide the kids for squirming here. It's just comfy Austin.

HUT'S HAMBURGERS

807 West Sixth Street

(512) 472-0693

www.hutsfrankandangies.com

Are the kids screaming for burgers? Why take them to one of those ubiquitous fast-food chains? You won't know whether you're in Austin, Boston, or Kalamazoo. Hut's, a '50s-style diner decorated with college sports memorabilia, is an Austin legend. Better yet, your kids will love the food. The menu includes 20 types of burgers—or mix and match to build your own—plus chicken-fried steak, fried chicken, meat loaf, and, of course, french fries and thickly sliced onion rings. True to diner law (it must be written somewhere), Hut's also offers a daily blue plate special. If you want to experience a real Austin burger joint, visit Hut's on West Sixth Street. And if the kids are leaning more toward pizza and pasta instead of burgers, we can suggest the Hut's-affiliated Frank and Angie's Pizzeria, which is just behind Hut's at 508 West Avenue.

KERBEY LANE CAFE

3704 Kerbey Lane

(512) 451-1436

2606 Guadalupe

(512) 477-5717

12602 Research Boulevard

(512) 258-7757

2700 South Lamar Boulevard

(512) 445-4451

www.kerbeylanecafe.com

Children just seem to love the huge plate-dwarfing pancakes served round the clock at this popular Austin eatery. But there are many more delicacies sure to please. The children's menu includes enchiladas, tacos, hamburgers, peanut butter and jelly sandwiches, ham and cheese, and other guaranteed kid pleasers. Prices are very reasonable, and with four Austin locations Kerbey Lane is easy to find. All four are open 24 hours a day.

MAGNOLIA CAFE

2304 Lake Austin Boulevard

(512) 478-8645

1920 South Congress Avenue

(512) 445-0000

www.cafemagnolia.com

Homegrown and down home, Magnolia Cafe serves an excellent assortment of meals for children, including some nutritious items, like steamed broccoli with cheese or a grilled chicken dinner. There are plenty of other kid pleasers as well, including a chicken black bean taco, kid burger with home fries, fish taco, kid French toast, and a kid breakfast that includes an egg, pancake, and sausage or bacon and is served all day. There's nothing fancy about Magnolia Cafe but the food. Adults will be happy, too, and there's a good selection of vegetarian dishes. Both Magnolia Cafes are open 24 hours a day.

PHIL'S ICEHOUSE
5620 Burnet Road
512-524-1212
www.philsicehouse.com
An outdoor playscape complete with bridges and slides, a shuffleboard game, and plenty of outdoor seating create the perfect kid-friendly atmosphere at this newer Austin burger joint, brought to you by the folks at Amy's ice cream. Burgers—big beefy ones, mini ones, chicken ones, veggie ones—and fries (a mix of regular and sweet potato) are the stars at Phil's, but there are also footlongs, corn dogs, frito pies, fish sandwiches and more. And if our recommendation isn't enough, Austinites voted Phil's the best place to bring the kids in the *Chronicle*'s readers' poll. To finish off the meal, take the family next door for some Amy's ice cream. Phil's even hosts occasional live music and outdoor movies, so check Phil's Web site for upcoming events.

SHADY GROVE
1624 Barton Springs Road
(512) 474-9991
www.theshadygrove.com
This super-casual eatery with both indoor and outdoor dining spaces is sure to please the kids. The menu offers everything kids love, including hot dogs, burgers, tacos, and nachos, as well as plenty of nourishment for adults. (See our Restaurants chapter). The "Unplugged at the Grove" music series features Austin musicians performing live every Thursday evening in the spring and fall.

ANNUAL EVENTS AND FESTIVALS

Weekends are the raison d'être for life in Austin. Weekday workdays are the equivalent of bench time, as far as many Austinites are concerned. The generally benign climate affords residents and visitors the opportunity to live life outdoors, and perhaps that is why so many weekend activities are linked to appreciation of sun, sky, and landscape. It is significant to note that springtime is the most active of all seasons when it comes to outdoor fiestas and festivals. This, after all, is when the Hill Country blossoms, the sun shines, and the sky is generally blue. (It is also the time when hotels are full and few rental cars are available.)

It is impossible to list all the annual events and festivals that take place in Austin and the surrounding Central Texas area. We have chosen our favorites and those that are both widely popular and long-standing. One characteristic of this list is the number of annual events that celebrate local culture, ethnic traditions, and historic events. Texans, nonnatives and newcomers will note, are eager to explore their past and have a strong sense of their state's history and culture. Other events are just sheer expressions of what could be called Texas joy, an embracing of local life and folkways. Whether it is a Woodstock-style romp or an old-fashioned church picnic, the operative word is *celebration*. So go forth and celebrate!

One note before you do: Admission prices, times, and even dates may vary from those listed. Many events are sponsored by nonprofit groups that face the vagaries of economic needs and demands, so it is a good idea to check the local media and make a call for additional information before you go.

JANUARY

FRONTERAFEST
Hyde Park Theatre, 511 West 43rd Street
(512) 479-PLAY
www.hydeparktheatre.com
The annual performance festival runs for five weeks beginning in late January and includes more than 50 productions put on under the auspices of Frontera @ Hyde Park Theatre, the theater company in one of the most popular neighborhoods in Central Austin (see Hyde Park in our Relocation and The Arts chapters). Ticket prices vary and usually begin at around $3. Discount passes are available.

FEBRUARY

BLACK HISTORY MONTH
(800) 926-2282 or (866) GO-AUSTIN
www.austintexas.org

Throughout February there are numerous celebrations and events relating to African-American history. In the very early days of the city, almost a quarter of the city's residents were African Americans, some 155 out of 856 people living in the city. The Austin Convention & Visitors Bureau (telephone and Web site listed above) produces the *Austin African-American Visitors Guide*, listing historic sites, cultural facilities, clubs, churches, and a guide to Austin's historic African-American neighborhoods. The guide can be picked up at the visitor center at 301 Congress Avenue. Another great resource for events and celebrations in the African-American community is the Carver Branch Library, 1161 Angelina Street, (512) 974-1010, www.austinlibrary.com.

i Need a breath of fresh air on New Year's Day? Take a blanket to the hills or shores around Lake Travis (see our Parks and Recreation chapter) and watch the Austin Yacht Club's Annual Redeye Regatta, www.austinyachtclub.com.

CARNAVAL BRASILEIRO
Palmer Events Center, 900 Barton Springs Road
(512) 452-6832
www.carnavalaustin.com

For more than 20 years, Austin has danced to the Brazilian beat of samba in a pre-Lenten festival of conga lines, costumes, and cacophony. A couple of thousand or more revelers gather, usually the Saturday before Lent, which can fall in February or March, to emulate Rio's famous Carnival. The costumes are hilarious and sometimes minimalist, which makes this a decidedly grown-up affair. The live music features top names in samba. Tickets are on sale at various popular record and bookstores in Austin.

MARCH

SPAMARAMA
Waterloo Park
Red River and 15th Streets
(512) 467-7848
www.spamarama.com

Spam sushi? Spam kebobs? Perhaps Spam Jell-O? This annual event, dubbed the "Pandemonious Party of Potted Pork," is a tribute to that World War II staple, Spam. Cooks, some of them serious professional chefs, compete for prizes, but for those who would rather play with their food there is a Spam Toss, a Spam Relay featuring a Spam baton, and, of course, a Spam Jam, which features some of Austin's live bands and popular musicians. Usually held in late March, sometimes early April, the location has changed over the years, so check the entertainment listings in the local paper. Admission charge.

SPRING FESTIVAL AND TEXAS CRAFT EXHIBITION
Winedale, near Round Top
(979) 249-2085
www.roundtop.org

This tiny village near Round Top, some 90 miles east of Austin, has served as the center for study of Texas culture under the auspices of the University of Texas. The collection of historic buildings is now a center for cultural events and antiques shops and home to artists and crafters. (See our Day Trips chapter for more information on this historic area.) The third weekend in March, Winedale holds its annual Spring Festival and Texas Crafts Exhibition. This area is an easy drive from Austin but worth an overnight stay at one of the country bed-and-breakfasts in the area.

STAR OF TEXAS FAIR & RODEO
Travis County Exposition
and Heritage Center, 7311 Decker Lane
(512) 919-3005
www.staroftexas.org

For two weeks in mid-March, country music fans flock to the livestock and rodeo show at the Expo Center in far East Austin, where top-name stars perform. The live music begins after the rodeo performances each night. In addition to the music, there are livestock shows, a carnival, barbecue and food booths, and children's activities. Rodeo tickets are in addition to grounds admission fees. There is extensive coverage of the event in the local media. *NOTE:* The show usually overlaps with the SXSW Festival (see our Close-up in this chapter), and hotel rooms and rental cars are at a premium in March. (See our Spectator Sports chapter for more information.)

ZILKER GARDEN FESTIVAL
Austin Garden Center
Zilker Botanical Gardens
(512) 477-8672
www.zilkergarden.com

To paraphrase the pitch for the popular local public television show *Central Texas Gardener*, what flourishes in gardens elsewhere can end up in the compost heap in Austin given the local climate—sometimes too much rain, too much drought, sudden frost, summer heat, year-round shade, year round sun, and occasional high wind. That is not to say gardening cannot be rewarding in Austin; it simply means newcomers have to learn the rules. Garden enthusiasts can find many of the answers at this annual event, plus plants for sale, advice, brochures, books, gardening tools, and equipment. There is a small admission fee.

ZILKER KITE FESTIVAL
Zilker Park, 2100 Barton Springs Road
(512) 647-7888
www.zilkerkitefestival.com
March winds help more than 200 handmade kites take flight in one of the city's most popular free outdoor events. Usually held on the second Sunday of the month in the city's large downtown park. Anyone can come fly a kite, but there is also an organized competition. Categories include the smallest kite, the strongest-pulling kite, the highest kite, and the most creative kite, but everyone's favorite is the largest kite. The event begins at 11:00 a.m. and is free. Parking at Zilker Park events can be a headache. In addition to parking in the park, additional space is available under the MoPac overpass to the west.

i It seems not a month goes by that the historic Hill Country town of Fredericksburg does not have a spring festival. In July there is the Night in Old Fredericksburg festival that celebrates the town's German roots and Hispanic culture, the Food and Wine Festival and the Mesquite Art Festival in October, and the Candlelight Homes Tour at Christmas. Check the calendar at the Chamber of Commerce Web site, www.fredericksburg-texas.com and our Day Trips chapter.

APRIL
THE ANNUAL AUSTIN RUGBY TOURNAMENT
Zilker Park, 2100 Barton Springs Road
www.austinrugby.com
Since 1968 this rugby tournament has attracted enthusiasts from across the region. Organizers tout it as the oldest and largest rugby tournament in the Southwest. There are several divisions of play in the two-day tournament and, true to rugby tradition, a post-tournament party on Sixth Street. The tournament's Web site lists telephone numbers for team contacts. (See the Rugby section in our Parks and Recreation chapter for more information on the local rugby scene.)

ANNUAL BLUEBONNET FESTIVAL
Historic Square, Burnet
(512) 756-4297
www.burnetchamber.org
This is one of several Hill Country events celebrating the wildflower season. Burnet is northwest of Austin on U.S. Highway 281. In addition to an arts and crafts show, children's activities, a parade, and 5K and 10K runs, the festival also features a golf tournament, a classic car show, and special appearances by an association of vintage airplane owners. The festival is held in conjunction with the Highland Lakes Bluebonnet Trail, a scenic route through the Hill Country where many of the best stands of wildflowers can be viewed. Maps and stories about the best bluebonnet spots are frequently printed in the Austin newspaper.

ART CITY AUSTIN
City Hall and the Second Street District
downtown area
(512) 610-4211
www.artsallianceaustin.org
This juried art show features the works of more than 200 nationally recognized artists. To make the event festive there is music and children's activities. The festival is sponsored by the Austin Arts Alliance , and both the exhibitions and the creations of craftsmen that are offered for sale are top quality. Admission fee.

i The Austin Convention and Visitors Bureau maintains an extensive Web site calendar for all kinds of events in the city: www.austintexas.org.

AUSTIN INTERNATIONAL POETRY FESTIVAL
Various venues
P.O. Box 41224
Austin, TX 78704
www.aipf.org

Usually held in mid-April, this citywide festival celebrates poetry in a variety of forms. Readings are held in bookstores, coffee shops, and pubs as well as public places and feature published poets and inspired amateurs. The festival also includes several workshops and films.

THE BOB MARLEY FESTIVAL
Auditorium Shores
Riverside Drive and South First Street
(512) 684-2525
www.austinmarleyfest.com

This laid-back music concert celebrates the life of reggae singer Bob Marley. There's no admission charge, but attendees are asked to bring a donation for the food bank. The event has collected more than 100,000 pounds of food for the needy. The all-day festival features both local and national reggae favorites.

THE CAPITOL 10,000
Downtown, shores of Lady Bird Lake
(512) 445– 3598
www.austin360.com

This 10K race is listed among the top 100 road races in the country by *Runner's World* magazine. First held in 1978, it has become a very popular event and attracts approximately 15,000 competitors and hundreds of spectators. The course changes every year but always ends on the shores of Lady Bird Lake. Entry fees vary.

EEYORE'S BIRTHDAY PARTY
Pease Park, Parkway Street off West 12th Street
(512) 448-5160
www.eeyores.sexton.com

You don't have to be a full-time flower child to enjoy Eeyore's Birthday; however, it helps if you have a touch of Woodstock in your heart. (That makes it easier to understand the Summer of Love drumbeat.) Both old and young free spirits meet on the final Saturday of the month at Pease Park in Central Austin to listen to music, dress up (costumes with a pun are favored), paint their faces, dance, watch the jugglers—all for free from midmorning to sunset. Despite the Winnie the Pooh connection, some aspects of Eeyore's Birthday Party might not be suitable for children, but there are areas set aside for face painting and other kid-friendly activities.

OLD SETTLER'S MUSIC FESTIVAL
Salt Lick Pavilion
Camp Ben McCullough Road, Driftwood
(512) 346-0999
www.oldsettlersmusicfest.org

This folk music festival originated in Old Settler's Park in Round Rock, north of Austin, hence its name. But as it grew, the celebrants sought a larger site and moved south to Driftwood, a tiny community about 12 miles south of U.S. Highway 290 on FM 1826, southwest of Austin. The two-day celebration of acoustic, bluegrass, jazz, and folk music is usually held on the first weekend of the month, drawing crowds that make a weekend of the event by camping out on-site. A two-day ticket costs about $50, but call ahead. One-day tickets are also available.

SAFARI
Austin Nature Center, West Zilker Park
(512) 327-8181
www.ci.austin.tx.us/ansc

This annual family festival on the last weekend of the month is a celebration of nature and a great event for a family outing. There are wildlife and environmental exhibits, games, entertainment, food, hands-on crafts activities, and rides. It is learning disguised as fun and a great way for children to become familiar with both their natural surroundings and the resources the nature center offers year-round (see our Kidstuff chapter). Admission fee.

TAYLOR JAYCEES NATIONAL RATTLESNAKE SACKING CHAMPIONSHIP
Murphy Park, Lake Drive, Taylor
(512) 352-6364
www.taylorjaycees.org
Not for the faint of heart, this annual event takes place in the small community of Taylor, northeast of Austin. Amateur teams compete for the prize; even young snake handlers test their skills. Visitors can also answer that age-old question—does fried rattlesnake meat taste like chicken? Admission fee.

THE TEXAS HILL COUNTRY WINE & FOOD FESTIVAL
Various locations
(512) 249-6300
www.texaswineandfood.org
Texas chefs, vintners, cheesemakers, herb growers, and gourmets gather in Austin on the first weekend in April to celebrate Texas wine and foods. The first festival was held in 1985 and was the brainchild of several nationally and internationally recognized chefs, including Dean Fearing, executive chef of Dallas's Mansion on Turtle Creek, and Robert Del Grande, executive chef of Houston's Cafe Annie. Events take place at restaurants, posh and funky, throughout the city and locations outside the city. Experts in cuisine, wine, cigars, and famous chefs and culinary authors from across the country conduct seminars and tastings, create special menus, and host field trips. Admission to events varies from triple digits for a ticket for a celebration dinner to an affordable amount for a Taste of Texas sampler, featuring Texas foods, wine, and beer at a country barbecue. Chocolate cigars might be the dessert at a dinner, while bock beer–battered quail is likely to be on the menu at the outdoor tasting. For a brochure and information, write to the festival at 1006 MoPac Circle, Suite 102, Austin, TX 78746.

THE TEXAS RELAYS
The University of Texas Memorial Stadium, San Jacinto Street at Manor Road
(512) 471-3333, (800) 982-BEVO
www.texassports.com
The relays have been run at UT for more than 70 years and feature top high school and collegiate track and field competitors from across the nation. Usually scheduled for the first weekend in April, sessions begin on Friday morning and end Saturday afternoon. The preliminaries are held on Wednesday and Thursday and are free. Tickets available for one day or the entire event. An all-session ticket costs $10. Call the toll-free number for additional information and advanced ticket purchase.

THE UNIVERSITY OF TEXAS PRESS BOOK SALE
2100 Comal Street
(512) 471-7233
www.utexas.edu/utpress/about/booksale/html
Usually held in late April or early May, this annual sale is a great place to find book bargains, especially books on subjects like Texana, Latin-American studies, archaeology, Texas and Western history, plus titles that represent doctoral dissertations on subjects of all sorts. The sale is advertised in the local media. Early birds get the best selection.

WILDFLOWERS DAYS FESTIVAL
Lady Bird Johnson National Wildflower Research Center, 4801 La Crosse Avenue
(512) 292-4100
www.wildflower.org
The research center celebrates the Hill Country spring wildflower season with a daylong festival featuring native plant experts and authors, an arts and crafts exhibit, and live music. Admission is $3.50 for adults, $2.00 for students and seniors, and $1.00 for children 5 and younger.

YESTERFEST AND THE SALINAS ART FESTIVAL
Bastrop City Park and Main Street
Bastrop
(512) 626-5308
www.bastroptexas.com
Bastrop, the historic small community just east of Austin on Highway 71, is a town that has worked

🔍 Close-Up

South by Southwest

Since 1986 when the first SXSW Music and Media Conference (South by Southwest, for the uninitiated) was held, it has grown to significant proportions. There is so much energy, growth, and creativity associated with this annual festival that it literally takes over the city, as nightclubs, theaters, conference halls, restaurants, and hotels get in on the action. The economic impact on Austin is estimated in the millions, and the number of musicians and entertainment professionals is counted in the thousands. In addition to the SXSW Music festival, there is now a SXSW Film Festival and Conference and a SXSW Interactive Festival. The essence of the festival is to produce a creative critical mass that spills out and energizes all who come into contact with it. Hence, the city of Austin is awash in musicians, filmmakers, and high-tech multimedia types for the last two weeks of March. (A word of warning to anyone planning to come to Austin during the festival—make your hotel, air, and car rental reservations well in advance.)

In the beginning, the conference was seen as a vehicle to focus attention on the Texas music scene, the so-called Third Coast. The festival is still kicked off at the Austin Music Hall with the Austin Music Awards, a decidedly funky version of the Grammys in which winners are chosen by the public at large—and top names in Austin music perform. The local alternative newspaper, the *Austin Chronicle,* organized the first festival (and remains a primary host), but the conference quickly grew and has expanded at record rates every year. The number of bands participating is approaching the 1,000 mark, performing at more than 50 venues in Austin. The acts include national and international headliners. So extensive is the performance list that SXSW press releases tend to look like the contract you sign to buy a refrigerator at Sears: yards and yards of tiny print.

Everyone is on alert during the festival to seek out the next wave. The panelists at the conference count among their numbers major record producers and influential music and film professionals who have come to view SXSW, according to festival sponsors, as "one of the most influential musical events in the world." While conference participants sign up for the whole shebang of seminars and panel discussions ("Parenting in the Music Business" and "So IS Paul Dead?"), music enthusiasts opt to pay for a wristband that allows them to roam the nightclub scene and hear as many of the bands as possible. Conference fees cost several hundred dollars, but wristbands have been described as affordable. However, grumbling has been heard in recent years as wristband prices approached $100. Availability and cost of wristbands have caused rumors of rebellion in the Austin ranks, but that has not detracted from the success of SXSW.

The creators of SXSW also launched a SXSW Film Festival, which has been described as "early Sundance," since entrants must be chosen by a panel in order to show their films. The four-day festival includes panels, workshops, meetings, mentor sessions, demo reel sessions, and the presentation of more than 150 films at various locations in Austin. Major agents, directors, and up-and-coming film producers attend. Another spin-off festival held in conjunction with the film and music conferences is the SXSW Interactive Festival, dedicated to discussions and explorations of new media technology. Again, there are panel discussions, star speakers, and a trade show featuring local and national high-tech companies. The entertainment events include such things as cyberoperas and intercontinental Internet concerts. The best way to absorb all the SXSW possibilities is to visit www.sxsw.com or get on the mailing list. Write to SXSW, P.O. Box 4999, Austin, TX 78765, call (512) 467-7979, or fax (512) 451-0754.

hard at maintaining its ties to the past. Several historic buildings line Main Street, where the art festival takes place on the third Saturday of the month. Out at the city park, the locals celebrate their pioneer past with historical exhibits, reenactments, craft demonstrations, music, and food. It all winds up in a Main Street dance at night and a campfire stew dinner. Admission charge to the park. Parking is available at the Bastrop High School, and shuttles run to the park. Yesterfest begins at 10:00 a.m. and closes at 5:00 p.m.

MAY

AUSTIN WINE FESTIVAL
The Domain
11410 Century OaksTerrace
(576) 649-9578
www.austinwinefestival.com
The new Domain shopping center where upscale shops line a European-style town center hosts this annual festival celebrating just Texas wines. There is music, food and kids' activities. Admission fee benefits the Austin Farmer's Market.

AUSTIN WOMAN'S FILM, MUSIC AND LITERARY FESTIVAL
Ruta Maya Coffeehouse
3601 South Congress Avenue
(512) 707-9637
www.blowinupaspot.com
This arts festival encourages submissions from women not just in the Austin artistic community, but beyond.

CATHOLIC CHURCH SPRING PICNIC
American Legion Park, Shiner
(512) 594-4180
www.shinertx.com
Shiner is a small Central Texas town southeast of Austin well known as the home of Shiner beer. The town retains much of its German-American flavor, and one of the best ways to experience that is to visit the annual Catholic church picnic. The event, which dates back to 1897 and is one of the biggest church picnics in the area, is free and features a country store, food, games like

horseshoes, and dancing all day to polka bands. The fun continues into the evening with more dancing and a church dinner, featuring Shiner Picnic Stew, sausage, fried chicken, and all the fixin's. The event is held the Sunday before Memorial Day.

CHISHOLM TRAIL ROUNDUP
City Park, Lockhart
(512) 398-2818
www.lockhart-tx.org
Back in 1840, Lockhart residents fought their way into the history books by defeating the Comanches at the Battle of Plum Creek. Later this small town southeast of Austin became a staging center for cattle being driven north on the Chisholm Trail to Abilene, Kansas. Lockhart had a reputation as a wild town, famous for its shoot-outs and feuds. The town history is celebrated with a reenactment of the battle, city tours, and a chili cook-off. The weekend-long festival in late May also includes dances, arts and crafts shows, and live music. Admission for events varies.

CINCO DE MAYO
Fiesta Gardens
2101 Bergman Street
On May 5, 1862, Mexican General Ignacio Zaragoza (who was born in Texas) defeated the army of French Emperor Louis Napoleon at Puebla, east of Mexico City. That blow against European imperialism is now a special holiday celebrated in song and dance both in Mexico and Texas. In addition to celebrations at Fiesta Gardens in East Austin, folkloric dancers and mariachi bands often perform at the State Capitol in the rotunda. Most Cinco de Mayo events are free, but some of the evening celebrations at Fiesta Gardens may charge an entrance fee. Another place where celebrations of Mexican-American life are held is the new Mexican American Cultural Center, 600 River Street, (512) 478-6222, www.ci.austin.tx.us/macc.

FUSE BOX FESTIVAL
Downtown Austin
(512) 927-1118
www.refractionsarts.org

A 10 day contemporary arts festival celebrating theater, film, dance, music and art on Austin's downtown streets and in buildings, even bridges—the emphasis here is on modern.

HISTORIC HOMES TOUR
Various locations in Austin
(512) 474-5198
www.heritagesocietyaustin.org
On Mother's Day weekend, the Heritage Society of Austin offers history buffs an opportunity to tour some of the city's most historic homes. Each year, the tour has a different theme. The society has played an important role in saving Austin buildings. One of its first projects was to rescue the Driskill Hotel on Sixth Street back in the 1970s. Tickets are available in advance or at the homes on the tour.

KERRVILLE FOLK FESTIVAL
Quiet Valley Ranch, Kerrville
(210) 257-3600,
(800) 435-8429, tickets only
www.kerrville-music.com
This legendary 10-day folk festival is held on a beautiful Hill Country ranch, southwest of Austin near Kerrville. There is a wide variety of bands—reggae, folk, country, etc. The festival usually begins the Thursday before Memorial Day. Quiet Valley Ranch has scenic campgrounds for those who want to stay for several days. Admission fees and campsite prices vary. Call for information. The fans, particularly those who camp out for the festival, are known as "Kerrverts." Tom Pittman, a member of the Austin Lounge Lizards, told an *Austin American–Statesman* writer: "The typical Kerrvert is a builder, a cellular phone salesman or something like that . . . they just want to get away from ringing telephones for two weeks." Some camp out primitive style; others pack up the fancy RV and head to the hills. The festival is also noted for its campfire gatherings and nightly revelry.

THE O. HENRY WORLD CHAMPIONSHIP PUN-OFF
O. Henry Museum
409 East Fifth Street in Brush Park
(512) 472-1903
www.ci.austin.tx.us/parks/ohenry.htm
If you are a pun-lover, and apparently there are hundreds of them in Austin, this is the event for you. Each year, on the first Sunday in May, up to 2,000 people gather at the O. Henry Museum (see our Attractions chapter) to watch and participate in the pun-off. The famous short-story writer William Sydney Porter, who wrote under the nom de plume of O. Henry, was a master punster. The event is free. To join the pun-off, simply show up.

THE SUMMER CONCERT SERIES
Waterloo Park
Red River and 15th Streets
downtown Austin
(512)440-1414
Organized by the Austin Federation of Musicians, this series of free outdoor summer concerts is held every Wednesday in May at 7:00 p.m. on Auditorium Shores, the south shore of Lady Bird Lake, just west of South Congress Avenue. Concerts also are held on Sunday afternoon at the Zilker Hillside Theater at 3:00 p.m. The concert series features a variety of bands and music, including rhythm and blues, Tejano, samba, and jazz. Bring a blanket or a lawn chair. Some refreshments are sold at concession stands, but many music lovers bring along a picnic.

JUNE

AUSTIN SYMPHONY ORCHESTRA CHILDREN'S DAYS
1101 Red River Street
(512) 476-6052
www.austinsymphony.org
Each Wednesday in June and July the symphony entertains and educates children in the little stone amphitheater at Symphony Square. There's music, dance, stories, and a little education thrown in for good measure.

BLANCO LAVENDER FESTIVAL
Courthouse Square, Blanco
(830) 833-5101
www.blancolavenderfestival.com
The Hill Country is now home to a burgeoning new crop—lavender and this festival celebrates its role in the culinary and home-keeping arts. Tours of local lavender farms are offered and stalls on the courthouse square demonstrate lavender arts and sells crafts and food. There's music, also.

CLARKSVILLE-WEST END JAZZ & ARTS FESTIVAL
Various locations
(512)477-9438
This concert salutes jazz greats with a series of club dates around Austin and a free concert in Pease Park, near the old Central Austin where the festival originated. The event is held on the second weekend in June.

FESTIVAL INSTITUTE AT FESTIVAL HILL
Round Top
(409) 249-3129
www.festivalhill.org
In the early 1970s, classical pianist James Dick founded the festival at Round Top, the small German settlement east of Austin in Fayette County. Round Top has come to represent the best of the Texas cultural scene, combining great music, historical settings, and a bucolic atmosphere. There are concerts once a month throughout the year at the institute site, but a special midyear series dubbed Summerfest takes place on each weekend in June and the first two weekends of July. Concerts range from the strictly classical to the popular. For a concert schedule write to Festival Institute, P.O. Box 89, Round Top, TX 78954.

JUNETEENTH
Various locations
Juneteenth is an original Texas celebration and marks the day that Texas slaves learned of the Emancipation Proclamation. On June 19, 1865, Union commander Major General Gordon Granger took Galveston and announced to Texas slaves that they had been freed two years earlier. The day is now marked by festivals of music, barbecues, parades, celebrations of African-American culture, and gospel sings. Check the *Austin American–Statesman* and community newspapers for details of this yearly event. Juneteenth is now a state holiday.

ORIGINAL ROUND TOP ANTIQUES FAIR
Round Top
(512) 237-4747
www.roundtopexasantiques.com
Round Top is a wonderful, culture-rich community located in Fayette County, about 65 miles east of Austin. Two of the most renowned antiques fairs in the United States, one in the spring, the other in October, are held here. *Country Home* magazine has named this fair "one of the ten best antique fairs in the country," and dealers come from all over the United States and even the world to sell, shop, and mingle. Founded by the legendary dealer Emma Lee Turney, the show at the Big Red Barn on State Highway 237 is now held by Susan Franks and features furniture and home furnishings from all regions of the country, plus British and European works. (For more information on Round Top, see our Day Trips chapter.) In addition to the two big fairs, there are other antiques sales events and crafts shows, as well as theater presentations and music concerts throughout the year, so check out the small town's Web site: www.roundtop.org.

JULY

AUSTIN CHAMBER MUSIC FESTIVAL
Various locations
(512) 454-0026
www.austinchambermusic.org
Imagine a chamber ensemble performing in the Victorian ballroom of the Driskill Hotel, or a music workshop for kids at the Austin Children's Museum. This three-week festival celebrating chamber music utilizes a variety of locations around the city, including churches, public spaces indoors and out, and evocative settings like the Driskill's ballroom.

AUSTIN SYMPHONY ORCHESTRA JULY FOURTH CONCERT AND FIREWORKS

Auditorium Shores
Riverside Drive and South First Street
(512) 476-6064
www.austinsymphony.org

As Austin grows, the size of the crowd gathering on the shores of Lady Bird Lake to watch the July Fourth concert gets larger and larger. The orchestra sets up on the southern shore of Lady Bird Lake on Auditorium Shores. The grand finale is, of course, Tchaikovsky's "1812 Overture," complete with cannon and fireworks. The music begins at 8:30 p.m., but many families come down earlier and enjoy a family picnic. Parking is a major headache, and after the concert the city's major thoroughfares out of the downtown area are jammed, making the trip home a slow one. The concert is free.

BARTON SPRINGS DIVING CHAMPIONSHIPS

Barton Springs Pool
2201 Barton Springs Road
(512) 476-9044
www.ci.austin.tx.us/parks/bartonsprings

Elvis is alive and diving at Barton Springs. At least he was in 1997, when he won the "Most Original" prize in this annual contest. The contest includes best splash, best dive, and most-original dive categories. Participants range in age, and their entry fees help fund environmental exhibits. Local musical groups also perform before and after the diving competition, which takes place on the third Sunday of the month. Flyers advertising the event and containing registration forms are widely distributed at Austin's pools, local grocery stores, and other outlets. Spectators pay an admission charge. Participants pay a registration fee. You can save a few dollars by preregistering.

BASTILLE DAY

The French Legation,
802 San Marcos Street
(512) 472-8180
www.frenchlegationmuseum.org

The legation was the home and office of Comte Alphonse Dubois de Saligny, charge d'affaires to the Republic of Texas. Francophiles and homesick French citizens gather on the Sunday closest to July 14 to celebrate the French equivalent of our July Fourth. The food is French, of course, and very good since it is concocted by local chefs. The music also is French, and the dancers, jugglers, and mimes celebrate traditional French culture. Admission fee.

SHAKESPEARE AT WINEDALE

Winedale Historic Center, near
Round Top
(979) 278-3530
www.shakespeare-winedale.org

Each summer, University of Texas English literature students gather at historic Winedale (see our Day Trips chapter) to study and perform Shakespeare's plays. The students perform three plays in the theater barn in the historic settlement, beginning the last week of July and continuing through mid-August. Performances are Thursday and Friday at 7:30 p.m. and Saturday at 2:00 and 7:30 p.m. Admission fee. Winedale is about a 90-minute drive east of Austin.

WILLIE NELSON'S JULY FOURTH PICNIC

Willie Nelson is renowned for his concerts, and no one gets shortchanged when he takes to the stage. Over the years, the picnic has changed locations, so it is wise to keep an eye on local music coverage in the media for prices, admission, and ticket numbers. It is an event that is popular, and concertgoers from all over Texas come to hear Willie sing, so book tickets in advance.

ZILKER SUMMER MUSICAL

Zilker Hillside Theater, Zilker Park
(512) 479-9491
www.zilker.org

Each summer, for more than 40 years, talented Austin musicians and actors have put on a popular Broadway musical in the open-air hillside "arena" adjacent to Barton Springs in the city's major downtown park. The musical is free and performances are at 8:30 p.m. Thursday through Sunday from mid-July through August.

AUGUST

AUSTIN CHRONICLE HOT SAUCE FESTIVAL
Waterloo Park, 403 East 15th Street
(512) 454-5766
www.auschron.com
This combination cook-off and foodie fest brings together amateurs, chefs, and commercial salsa makers who try to woo the taste buds of Austin's hot sauce aficionados. There is a competition, lots of samples, plus music—so what better way to cool off on a hot summer than with some hot sauce.

AUSTIN LATINO COMEDY FIESTA
713 Congress Avenue
(512) 472-5470
www.teatrohumanidad.com
The historic Paramount Theatre is home to this annual comedy festival that celebrates Austin's Latino culture. Stand-up comics and sketch artists perform at the weekend festival.

BAT FEST
Ann Richards Congress Avenue Bridge
(512) 441-9015
www.roadwayevents.com
Underneath the bridge lives the two-million-strong colony of Mexican free-tail bats (see our Attractions chapter) and mid-summer is a great time to watch the swarm fly out at dusk to feast on bugs all around Central Texas. This family-friendly festival features all things "batty," including a "bat wing" eating contest (think chicken) and all manner of bat costumes and bat hats. Admission fee.

i Looking for that Abraham Lincoln letter stuck under the slats of a rocking chair, or a discarded Navajo blanket? Roaming the "junque" and antiques markets is a favorite weekend pastime for many of us. We've listed just a few of the country flea markets here that hold regular sales. Look at our Shopping chapter for more, plus a section on holiday shopping.

FALL CREEK GRAPE STOMP
Fall Creek Vineyards, Llano County
(915) 379-5361
www.fcv.com
This Hill Country vineyard has established a national reputation for the quality of its wines. Located on the shores of Lake Buchanan, about 70 miles northwest of Austin, Fall Creek is a popular place to visit while touring the Hill Country. The peace and quiet of the winery is broken by the cheers and hollers of barefooted kids and grown-ups stomping the grapes. The winery opens its doors from 11:00 a.m. to 5:00 p.m. so that visitors can roll up their jeans, strip off their socks, and jump into vats of red grapes. The experience is free.

GILLESPIE COUNTY FAIR
Fairgrounds, Highway 16, Fredericksburg
(830) 997-6523
www.gillespiefair.com
This is the oldest county fair in the state and is well worth a visit for a glimpse of a time when the county fair was an important date on the local calendar. The fair includes a traditional livestock show, handicrafts and home-baked goods, horse races, a carnival, and dances in the evening. The fair usually takes place at the end of August over four days and nights. Fairground admission is $5, free for children. Additional admission charges may be in place for other events.

ZILKER PARK JAZZ FESTIVAL
Zilker Park Amphitheatre, Zilker Park
(512) 440-1414
www.ci.austin.tx.us/zilker
There is no better way to spend a warm summer night than listening to the cool sounds of jazz float across Zilker Park, the city's favorite gathering spot throughout the seasons. (See our Parks and Recreation chapter.) Bring a blanket and something cold to drink, and enjoy the free summer festival.

SEPTEMBER

ANNUAL SHAKESPEARE FESTIVAL
Zilker Park, 2201 Barton Springs Road
(512) 454-BARD (2273)
www.austinshakespeare.org
The Sheffield Zilker Hillside Theater is the outdoor site of this late September, early October dramatic festival. Usually, one of the Bard of Avon's comedies is presented along with a drama on alternate nights. Bring along a blanket, a picnic, and perhaps a sweater if cooler weather has arrived.

AUSTIN CITY LIMITS FESTIVAL
Zilker Park
2100 Barton Springs Road
www.aclfest.com
The same folks who brought America the legendary *Austin City Limits* television show on PBS sponsor this three-day festival of music, food, arts, and crafts in the city's most famous park (see our Parks and Recreation chapter). There are multiple stages across 15 acres of parkland, plus an "Austin Food Court" and an art show. Capital Metro provides transportation to the site. The festival runs a very detailed Web site, where lists of bands, schedules, and information can be found and tickets may be purchased. Daily or three-day tickets are offered.

AUSTIN GAY AND LESBIAN INTERNATIONAL FILM FESTIVAL
Various venues
(512) 302-9889
www.agliff.org
In keeping with Austin's building reputation as a film center, this two-week festival brings a variety of films to Austin theaters around the city.

DIEZ Y SEIS DE SEPTIEMBRE
Various locations
This is a major fiesta both north and south of the border, celebrating Mexico's demand for independence from Spain. Like the U.S. July Fourth celebration, serious history and fun are combined on Diez y Seis. Mariachi bands perform, folkloric dancers celebrate their heritage, and everyone eats really well. Austin's celebrations center on Fiesta Gardens, on the shores of Lady Bird Lake in East Austin. Nearby Elgin also holds its Chili Pepper Fest, with celebrations of the Mexican fiesta. There are ceremonies in Austin on the actual day of the holiday, but the fiesta is usually carried over to the weekend closest to the 16th, with events on several consecutive days. Check the local newspaper for details.

OATMEAL FESTIVAL
Bertram
(512) 335-2197
www.bertramtx.com
This tongue-in-cheek Labor Day weekend festival has helped to revive a small community northwest of Round Rock on F.M. 243. The festivities include an oatmeal cook-off and eat-off, an oatmeal sculpture contest, and the Miss Bag of Oats (you have to be 55-plus) pageant. For the kids, there is a grasshopper parade where children can parade their pet insects. Most events are free.

TEDDY BEAR PICNIC
Central Park
40th Street and Lamar Boulevard
Toddlers and baby boomers alike can be seen clutching their teddies as they make their way to the annual Teddy Bear Picnic sponsored by the Austin Junior Forum. They are all hoping their bear will win one of the contests at the event—best dressed, silliest, most lovingly worn—which is held on the second weekend of the month. The picnic is a fund-raiser for the Forum, which buys teddy bears for children who are in crisis.

TEXAS WILDLIFE EXPOSITION
4200 Smith School Road
(512) 389-4472
www.tpwd.state.tx.us/expo/
This large, free two-day fair in late September, early October is a favorite among outdoors enthusiasts. Exhibits focus on fishing and hunting skills, equipment, and skill improvement. There are field dog trials, target shooting and archery

contests, plus a variety of activities for children. The exposition is held in the Southeast Austin headquarters of the Texas Parks and Wildlife Department. (See our Parks and Recreation chapter for more information on hunting and fishing.)

OCTOBER

AUSTIN FILM SCREENWRITERS CONFERENCE AND AUSTIN FILM FESTIVAL
Various locations in the city
(512) 478-4795
www.austinfilmfestival.com

This fall festival, usually held at the beginning of the month, is fast becoming recognized as a significant film and cultural event. The conference offers screenwriters the opportunity to listen to panel discussions by top screenwriters, directors, and studio executives. Participants have included director Oliver Stone, actor Dennis Hopper, Mike Judge (creator of *King of the Hill* television show), screenwriters Eric Roth (*Forrest Gump*), Randall Wallace (*Braveheart*), Al Reinart (*Apollo 13*), and Buck Henry (*The Graduate*), and many more. The accompanying film festival features either movies scheduled for release or movies that are making the festival circuit. The two festivals vary in admission prices. Tickets to individual films are available on show day. Passes to panel discussions and films also can be purchased for around $200, and full registration is approximately double that. The festival also includes a juried competition for screenwriters, and some of the winners have seen their work make it to the big silver screen as a result of the exposure here.

i October is Texas Archaeology Month, celebrated statewide with hands-on exhibits, demonstrations, workshops, and opportunities to explore the rich Texas past. The Texas Historical Commission posts an events calendar on its Web site, www.thc.state.tx.us, or archaeology buffs can call (512) 463-6096 for more information.

EMMA LEE TURNEY'S ROUND TOP FOLK ART FAIR
Round Top
(281) 493-5501
www.roundtopfolkartfair.com

Twice a year the cognoscenti of the antiques world flock to this small Texas town (see the fair listing in April for details). The fall event celebrates American folk art and is under the direction of the legendary antiques dealer Emma Lee Turney.

FRONTIER DAYS
Old Settlers Park, Round Rock
(512) 255-5805
www.roundrocktexas.gov

The only shoot-outs these days in Round Rock involve high school basketball tournaments. The only masks being worn are those donned by high-tech workers. But Round Rock, now a booming suburban community, was a typical frontier town back in 1878 when the streets were the setting for one of the most famous of Texas shoot-outs between the law and outlaw Sam Bass. "Texas's Beloved Bandit," as Bass was dubbed, rode into town intent on robbing the bank, but he ended the day buried in the local cemetery. Bass likely was dubbed "Beloved" because, in the grand Texas tradition of Bonnie and Clyde, bank robbers are somehow elevated to folk hero status. On the second weekend of the month the community celebrates Frontier Days, complete with a reenactment of the shoot-out, which is the headline event of the two-day festival. There is also a frog-jumping contest and hands-on demonstrations of butter-churning, whittling, soap making, and other pioneer skills. Admission fee.

HALLOWEEN ON SIXTH STREET
Sixth Street, between Congress Avenue and I-35

Wholesale Halloween madness is one way to describe this event. As many as 60,000 costumed revelers have gathered on the street for the celebration. Several blocks are roped off to vehicular traffic. The noise level is high, and some party-goers do become a little rowdy. This is strictly a grown-up celebration and not recommended for children.

HOGEYE FESTIVAL
Elgin
(512) 285-5721
www.elgintx.com/hogeye
Famed for its sausage, Elgin is a small town 19 miles east of Austin on U.S. Highway 290 East. This typical Texas small-town festival features cow patty bingo, a sausage cook-off (of course), a hog-calling contest, music, arts and crafts, and a street dance.

LIVE STRONG CHALLENGE
Various sites in the city
(888) 4-CHALLENGE
www.livestrongchallenge.org
One of Austin's most beloved residents is legendary bicyclist Lance Armstrong. According to the Lance Armstrong Foundation, Lance's cycling buddies first organized a Ride for the Roses race to show support for Lance's battle with cancer in 1997. The original race paralleled the training ride Lance and the group made through the hills west of Austin. Today the event has become the Live Strong Challenge and takes place in four cities. It has multiple features and spans a weekend. Some 7,000 participants enter bicycling events, plus there is a gala, silent auction, a 5K fun run, a health and sports expo, a Kids CARE ride at Auditorium Shores, and music venues featuring local and national bands.

OKTOBERFEST
Market Square, Fredericksburg
(830) 997-4810
www.oktoberfestinfbg.com
Fredericksburg has a strong German heritage; in fact, some of the older residents still speak in a form of German heard in 19th-century Europe. The traditional community festival features beer-hall singing, waltz contests, and lots of sausage. Admission fee; free for those 6 and younger.

NOVEMBER

AUSTIN CELTIC FESTIVAL
Fiesta Shores on Lady Bird Lake
www.austincelts.org/festival
Touted as the largest gathering of the clans in Central Austin this three-day festival features Celtic music and dance, plus food. Admission fee.

AUSTIN JUNIOR LEAGUE CHRISTMAS AFFAIR
Palmer Events Center
900 Barton Springs Road
(512) 467-8982
www.jlaustin.org
A sure sign that Christmas is just around the corner is the transformation of Palmer Events Center into a shopping wonderland. More than 200 specialty merchants offer a variety of Christmas gift ideas, some easily affordable, others high-priced. Not everyone shops at the affair, although the league raises hundreds of thousands of dollars for its community projects at the event; some just stroll, sip some Christmas spiced wine, and window-shop or gather decorating ideas for their own holiday celebrations. The affair is held the third weekend in November. Daily admission fee.

CHUY'S CHILDREN GIVING TO CHILDREN PARADE
Congress Avenue
(888) 439-2489
www.chuysparade.com
This is a great way to teach children to give thanks on Thanksgiving weekend. Balloons, some up to 80 feet high, depicting popular children's characters lead the parade, followed by marching bands, floats, dancers, clowns, and trucks filled with toys donated by children along the route. The donations go to the Austin Police Department's Operation Blue Santa, which gives toys to needy kids at Christmas. The parade is sponsored by Chuy's, the popular local restaurant (see our Restaurants chapter).

DIA DE LOS MUERTOS
Mexic-Arte Museum
Fifth Street and Congress Avenue
(512) 480-9373
www.mexic-artemuseum.org
It means "Day of the Dead," and this quintessentially Mexican fiesta is celebrated on All Souls Day, November 1. In Mexico, families take food to the local cemetery on that day for a two-day celebration in honor of their ancestors. Families set up altars at the gravesite, offering food and drink. Day of the Dead folk art is highly collectible, and much of it is humorous, mocking human foibles. Mexic-Arte Museum (see The Arts chapter) sponsors several Day of the Dead events, including the construction of a variety of *ofrendas* by local artists at its downtown museum site. Admission fee. There is also a parade down East Sixth Street onto Congress Avenue in celebration of Mexican and Chicano culture. Spectators are urged to wear typical Day of the Dead costumes, angels or skeletons, and watch low riders, dancers, and musicians parade on the avenue. Check the local paper for additional Dia de los Muertos events.

INTERNATIONAL CHILDREN'S FESTIVAL
Austin Children's Museum
201 Colorado Street
(512) 472-2499
www.austinkids.org
The children's museum hosts this celebration of Austin's growing diversity. Arts and crafts by Austin children representing over 30 cultures from around the world are on display during this one-day art festival.

POWWOW AND AMERICAN INDIAN HERITAGE FESTIVAL
Toney Burger Center
3200 Jones Road
(512) 414-0159
www.austinpowwow.org
In 1991 the Austin Independent School District and local Native Americans joined to offer this free one-day, insightful festival to Austin residents. The goal was to share Native American culture with neighbors in Central Texas. Attendance has grown to more than 20,000 for the powwow, which usually is held on the first Saturday of November. The highlight of this free event is a dance competition, which features hundreds of dancers from dozens of tribes. Toney Burger Center is in Southwest Austin near the intersection of US 290 West and Loop 360 (Capital of Texas Highway).

TEXAS BOOK FESTIVAL
Texas Capitol and various locations
(512) 477-4055
www.texasbookfestival.org
This very successful celebration of Texas literature (thanks in great part to First Lady Laura Bush) includes book signings, seminars, discussions, and celebrations of literary history. (See The Literary Scene chapter for more on this event.)

WURSTFEST
Wurstfest Grounds, Land Park,
New Braunfels
(830) 625-9167, (800) 221-4369
www.wurstfest.com
Wurstfest is the city's version of Oktoberfest and attracts tens of thousands of visitors, who eat sausage, drink beer, sing songs, and spend money. Admission fee. Children 12 and younger are free.

DECEMBER

ARMADILLO CHRISTMAS BAZAAR
Austin Convention Center,
Second and Trinity Streets
(512) 447-1605
www.armadillobazaar.com
This annual arts and crafts fair was originally held at the legendary Armadillo World Headquarters (see The Music Scene chapter) but now is housed in the Austin Convention Center. The 'Dillo is long gone, but the spirit of the bazaar lives on as a showplace for local artists and craftspeople, some of them creating fanciful jewelry and whimsical toys. Local musicians also perform nightly at the two-week event, which begins in mid-December and ends Christmas Eve. It is open from 11:00

a.m. to 11:00 p.m. daily. Admission fee. Children younger than 12 are admitted free.

CHRISTMAS AT THE FRENCH LEGATION
French Legation, 802 San Marcos Street
(512) 472-8180
www.frenchlegationmuseum.org
The Daughters of the Texas Republic offer a glimpse of Christmas past as it might have been celebrated in the mid-19th century. The legation (see our Attractions chapter) was built for Comte Alphonse Dubois de Saligny, France's charge d'affaires to the Republic of Texas. In addition to Christmas displays, choirs perform Christmas carols and holiday refreshments are offered. Pére Noel, the French Santa Claus, is on hand. The celebration takes place on the first Sunday of the month from 1:00 to 5:00 p.m. Admission fee.

CHRISTMAS MUSIC AND THEATER
Various locations
With its rich and talented arts community, Austin offers a large variety of Christmas musical events. There are the long-standing traditions of the holiday, like the annual performances by the Austin Civic Ballet of *The Nutcracker* at Bass Concert Hall, (512) 469-SHOW. Handel's "Messiah" is performed by several musical entities, plus there is the annual "Sing It Yourself Messiah" at St. Matthews Episcopal Church, where the audience can join in with the Austin Civic Chorus. Call (512) 454-TIXS for information and tickets. Local theater and comedy troupes offer a variety of performances. Check the listings in the *Austin American–Statesman*.

CHRISTMAS OPEN HOUSE
Winedale Historic Center, near
Round Top
(409) 278-3530
www.roundtop.org
Christmas at Winedale is celebrated each year in a different historic home in this wonderful old settlement in Fayette County, east of Austin (see our Day Trips chapter). Usually held the Sunday before Christmas, the celebration features seasonal music and food. The many antiques shops

offer one-of-a-kind Christmas gifts. Call for hours. There is a small admission charge.

FAMILY CHRISTMAS NIGHT
Downtown Round Rock
(512) 255-5805
On the first Saturday of the month, the City of Round Rock closes the downtown streets for a family celebration. At the heart of the event is the town's historic town square where Santa appears to assure Round Rock kids that he knows who has been naughty and who has been nice. The festivities begin at 7:00 p.m., and admission is free.

FELIZ NAVIDAD!
Various locations
There are a variety of Christmas events with a Mexican flavor held in Austin during the holidays. Plays depicting the Nativity, folk music concerts, and folk art are popular at this time of year. *La Pastorela*, the traditional Latino Nativity play, is performed by several groups. But one of the most interesting and authentic traditions takes place in mid-December as members of Our Lady of Guadalupe Church, 1209 East Ninth Street, enact La Posada. This is a tradition both in Mexico and Texas as the faithful reenact Joseph and Mary's search for a place to stay in Bethlehem. The faithful follow members, who are dressed as the Holy Family, as they go from door to door, asking for shelter. When the parade reaches the church there is a mass followed by Christmas treats, tamales, and Mexican hot chocolate. Check the arts and events listings in the *Austin American–Statesman* and local community newspapers.

FIRST NIGHT
Downtown Austin
(512) 391-1551
www.firstnightaustin.org
This family-friendly celebration is a farewell to the old year and a great way for the whole family to ring in the new. A "celebration of the arts," it is centered around City Hall on the northern banks of Lady Bird Lake (formerly Town Lake) and is a gift by various major corporate donors to the city. There is poetry, dance, mummers and

musicians, artwork and clowns, some exhibitions have a Cirque de Soleil feel and even the buildings become canvases for artists. There is an early evening welcoming for the New Year, plus the traditional midnight fireworks and its free!

KWANZAA
Various locations
The Swahili word means "fruits of the harvest," and Kwanzaa, created in 1966, has proved fruitful as millions of African Americans embrace the celebration's principles. From December 26 to January 1, the seven days of Kwanzaa are dedicated to seven principles. In recent years African-American leaders in Austin have taken Kwanzaa from a family event to a community celebration. During the festival there are a variety of public events. Check the *Austin American–Statesman* and local community newspapers for details.

THE LIGHTING OF THE ZILKER PARK CHRISTMAS TREE
Zilker Park, 2100 Barton Springs Road
This annual event and Austin ritual on the first Sunday of the month is a true sign that Christmas is nigh. One the city's moonlight towers (see our Attractions chapter) was moved to the park and serves as the main "trunk" of the tree. Thousands of colored Christmas lights are strung from the top of the 165-foot tower to resemble a Christmas tree shape. Tradition calls for children to stand inside the pyramid and whirl around, making the lights blur. Young children are whisked around in their parents' arms. It is one of those simple holiday traditions that children never forget. Admission to the park is free.

LIGHTS OF THE BLACKLANDS
Small towns east of Austin
(512) 285-5721
www.elgintx.com
The holidays can be stressful, but one of the most relaxing ways to enjoy the season is to take a leisurely evening drive through some of the area's small towns and view the Christmas decorations. The towns east of Austin in what are called the Blacklands, a reference to the rich blackland prairie soil, suggest a tour beginning in Elgin on US 290 and then on through Coupland, Thrall, Bartlett, and LaGrange. The route is featured on the Elgin City Web site.

NEW YEAR'S CELEBRATION ON SIXTH STREET
Sixth Street, between Congress Avenue and I-35
(512) 441-9015
New Year's Eve in Austin's club scene is wild. Many clubs and downtown restaurants have special performances or menus in celebration. Check the local entertainment press for the particulars. Local television and radio stations camp out on Sixth Street rooftops to watch Austin's version of the "big ball" fall. The big ball falls at midnight, but that doesn't end the craziness as the party goes on in clubs and on the street itself until the wee hours.

PIONEER FARM CHRISTMAS CANDLELIGHT TOUR
Jourdan-Bachman Pioneer Farm
11418 Sprinkle Cut-Off Road
(512) 837-1215
www.pioneerfarm.org
Traditional Christmas activities reflecting the pioneer lifestyle are celebrated each weekend leading up to Christmas, many of them conducted by candlelight just as they would have been done in frontier days. Admission is $6. (See our Kidstuff chapter for information on the farm.)

TEXAS HILL COUNTRY REGIONAL CHRISTMAS LIGHTING TRAIL
Various locations
(860) 997-8515
www.fredericksburgtexas.com
Some of the most picturesque Christmas light shows can be seen in the small towns around the Austin area. Most of the lights are put up in early December and taken down after New Year's Day. Below are a few locations well worth visiting. The phone numbers are for the local chambers of commerce and visitor bureaus. Check the chambers Web sites, also.

Bastrop, to the east, decorates its historic downtown and Old Iron Bridge, (512) 321-2419. **Blanco,** southwest of Austin, decorates the old courthouse with thousands of lights, (210) 438-2914. **Johnson City,** west of Austin, is ablaze as the local residents cover homes, businesses, and the Blanco County Courthouse with lights, (830) 868-7684. **Llano,** northwest of Austin, decorates the historic town square and the old courthouse with 10 miles of lights, (915) 556-5172. **Marble Falls,** northwest of Austin, boasts it uses one million lights to decorate its Walkway of Lights, (800) 759-8178. In **Austin** the local television meteorologists often highlight spectacular Austin neighborhood decorations. One of the best is 37th Street, east of Guadalupe Street in Central Austin. Walking through this neighborhood is recommended, rather than driving. In **Round Rock** the downtown historic district is decorated for the holidays, and in **Cedar Park** the Hill Country Flyer (see our Attractions chapter) departs from the train station in midafternoon for Burnet, then returns in the evening so that passengers can view the Hill Country homes decorated with lights. Call (512) 477-8468 for information.

YULE FEST
Zilker Park, 2100 Barton Springs Road
(512) 478-6875
www.ci.austin.tx.us/tol
For the last two weeks of December, the southern banks of Lady Bird Lake in Zilker Park are the site of Yule Fest and the Trail of Lights. This nighttime Christmas pageant features lighted set pieces decorated according to various Christmas themes. It is a popular family event that has seen lines grow longer and longer, prompting the city in 1998 to eliminate the special nights set aside for drive-through spectators and confine the trail to pedestrian traffic, bicycles, and special trams for the disabled. Capital Metro provides shuttle service to the park.

There is one Austin neighborhood that takes Christmas decorating very seriously. On 37th Street east of Guadalupe Street in Central Austin's Hyde Park neighborhood, neighbors try to outmatch each other in Christmas light exhibitions. Walk or drive the street, but be sure to make a donation to the electricity fund.

THE ARTS

What do 20-something slackers, a zany town named Tuna, a statewide high school competition, a giant university, and a celebrated European sculptor have in common? They all have added a few broad brush strokes to the colorful canvas of Austin arts. Austin attracts artists. While that phenomenon dates back to the 1800s, Austin's status as a hub for artists has developed largely since the 1970s, when enough musicians, actors, writers, and painters had gathered to form an arts scene. Over the past few decades, more and more talented artists have found inspiration in Austin's artistic communities, and many of those have helped Austin earn a reputation for both appreciating and producing high-quality art. Read about the dynamic people and places in this chapter as well as in The Music Scene, Nightlife, and Attractions to discover many of the reasons Austin always gets such high praise in the national media. In this chapter we'll tell you about the visual artists and theater troupes, the dancers and filmmakers, the classical performers, and the choirs that make Austin sing.

OVERVIEW

Elisabet Ney, who had sculpted some of the great figures of Europe, was nearly 60 when she moved to Austin in the late 1800s. Back then, Austin had more gambling dens and brothels than galleries and theaters. Ney's celebrity status attracted influential men and women, many who believed, as did she, that art, music, and dance rank up there near water and air to sustain life. As Ney's hands transformed crude blocks of marble into glorious statues of Texas heroes, her spirit and her passion shaped a culture that prized the arts. Along the way, she became a pioneer of artistic development in the state of Texas. Her ability to inspire others during a time when the arts weren't exactly on the top of the Texas agenda led to the creation of the Texas Fine Arts Association (now called Arthouse) and later the Texas Commission on the Arts and the University of Texas art department.

The University of Texas gets major billing among the stars of Austin's cultural scene. The university's highly respected film and fine arts schools have turned out some of the best-prepared graduates in the country. It's impossible to estimate the number of UT alumni, and profes-

sors, who are making significant contributions in Austin and around the country in the fields of dance, film, visual art, theater, literature, and music. UT's Performing Arts Center is a world-class venue for world-class performers. The University Interscholastic League (UIL), a program started in 1910 to encourage educational development in Texas high schools through competition, began as a sports program. Since the 1920s the UIL has included an annual theater competition in which high school students from across the state vie for top honors. This Texas theater tradition, which produced Broadway's Tommy Tune and others, gets students hooked on theater at an early age.

Speaking of addictions, Austin—and most of the country, it seems—has developed a taste for Tuna. The crazy-quilt of characters that inhabit the fictional Tuna (Texas's third-smallest town) come to comic life onstage through actors Joe Sears and Jaston Williams, the Austinites who cowrote (with Ed Howard) *Greater Tuna* and its spin-offs. *Greater Tuna*, an Off-Broadway hit in the early 1980s, was followed by *A Tuna Christmas* and *Red, White and Tuna*. Quick-change artists Sears and Williams perform the parts of more than two dozen characters—male and female—in their fictional town of Smut Snatchers and hanging judges. Tuna fanatics know Aunt Pearl Burras and her sister Bertha Bumiller, Didi Snavely, Petey Fisk, and Vera Carp as well as they know their own families. *Greater Tuna,* presented in touring versions around the country, in an HBO production, in command performances at the White House, and in theaters all over the United States, has placed Austin on the national theatrical map.

What Tuna is to theater, *Slacker* is to film. This 1991 low-budget film by Austinite Richard Linklater made a bundle when it was released nationally and proved to the country that Austin has what it takes to make movies. A year later, Austin's Robert Rodriguez hit it big with *El Mariachi.* Since those films debuted, Austin filmmaking has jelled into an industry. Austin's large and small theater companies, visual artists, cutting-edge dancers, and performance artists are doing their parts to shake up the arts world, not just locally. Austin's rapid artistic development has not come without speed bumps. Today there isn't always enough space for many of Austin's performing and visual artists. While small warehouse-type theaters/galleries were popping up all over, Austin still cried out for larger state-of-the art venues. In response, a dedicated team of arts patrons mounted a $77 million private fundraising campaign to convert Palmer Auditorium on the south shore of Lady Bird Lake (formerly Town Lake) into a world-class facility. Renamed the Joe R. Long and Teresa Lozano Long Center for the Performing Arts—The Long Center for short—it opened in the spring of 2008. Austin will always need more performance space, but with the opening of The Long Center and other facilities around town, things are looking up. This chapter presents the Austin art scene on center stage—and the curtain is rising.

PERFORMING ARTS

Theater

When William Shakespeare wrote that "all the world's a stage," he might have been looking into the future at Austin. With more than 250 different shows a year produced by both national touring companies and the dozens of local troupes that perform at varying intervals, it often seems as though the whole city has been bitten by the bug. Check our local theater listings if you're in doubt. Many times, theater patrons have the luxury of choosing from as many as two dozen productions—at once.

Austin does theater in a variety of ways: big Broadway shows like 2007's *Lion King* at the University of Texas Performing Arts Center; sold-out performances by the wacky Tuna guys at the Paramount; the ambitiousness of a locally done *Angels in America* at Zachary Scott Theatre; lots of experimental shows staged in small converted warehouses; delightful productions geared toward kids; bilingual comedies and dramas; and performances celebrating the Bard himself on an outdoor stage.

Austin also is becoming increasingly known as an incubator of playwrights, many of them qualifying as finalists for the Actors Theatre of Louisville's Heideman Award, a prize given for the best play submitted to ATL's National Ten-Minute Play Contest. In fact, an Austinite has won the prize in the past. Each of these writers came out of the dynamic local organization, Austin Script Works (www.scriptworks.org), which offers services to playwrights at every stage of project development.

While theater can pop up in just about any nook and cranny around the city, we've identified Austin's main performance stages and theater troupes here. The stages are divided into three categories: The Main Stages are the city's larger, cushier, most formal theaters; The Outdoor Stage presents Austin's natural amphitheater; and The Warehouse Stages highlight vintage buildings and warehouses that are increasingly being converted into small theaters by or for Austin's up-and-coming theater troupes. Additionally, we have a category called The Gypsies, which includes our favorite young theater troupes that perform anywhere they can find a space. Keep in mind that theater is very fluid here in Austin, so those troupes we've associated with a particular stage may perform in other locations as well.

This list will direct you to some of the best and most interesting theater Austin offers. For even more theater, check out the lineup at Austin's colleges and universities. The Austin Circle of Theaters (see Arts Organizations in this chapter) calculates there are about 80 theater companies in our city. Some present works occasionally, while others, as you'll see here, are busy all the time.

We may all be actors on the stage of life, as Shakespeare suggested, but those who choose the theater as their life make it so much more interesting for the rest of us—as we like it.

The Main Stages

THE LONG CENTER
701 West Riverside Drive
(512) 474-LONG
www.thelongcenter.org
www.thelongcenter.frontgatesolutions.com
(for tickets)
A 15-year-effort to bring another world-class performing arts center to Austin paid off in the spring of 2008 with the grand opening of The Joe R. Long and Teresa Lozano Long Center for the Performing Arts, known as The Long Center. Located on beautiful Auditorium Shores on Lady Bird Lake, the center is the new performance venue for Ballet Austin, the Austin Lyric Opera, and the Austin Symphony. Additionally, it presents an eclectic mix of both local and nationally known artistic performers—everything from Broadway-style shows to musical acts to children's theater and much more.

The center features the 2,400-seat state-of-the-art Dell Hall, whose acoustics can be arranged to maximize the effect of each performance. It also has the smaller black-box-style Rollins Studio Theatre, also acoustically excellent, which can be arranged to seat anywhere from 80 people in a cabaret-style configuration, to 232 people in a theater-in-the-round design.

While Dell Hall is a sight to behold, one of the main attractions at The Long Center is the spectacular view of the shores, the lake, and the downtown Austin skyline. Lobbies on either side of Dell Hall, one glass-enclosed and one open-air,

were designed to maximize the view. The center not only sits on the site of a long-time Austin icon, the former Palmer Auditorium, its construction actually incorporates about 65 percent of the old Palmer, including its columns, its distinctive ring shapes and, most notably, the green, brown and beige metal tiles that adorned Palmer's roof. (Some of the hail-dented tiles are used as decorative accents inside the new building).

The center is operated by a non-profit arts organization, which raised $77 million from more than 4,000 Austin donors to finally get this new Austin icon up and running.

ONE WORLD THEATRE
7701 Bee Caves Road
(512) 330-9500,
(512) 32-WORLD (96753) for tickets
www.oneworldtheater.org
It was originally intended to be a large, even huge, home in West Austin, but it took a man who was dubbed "a California dreamer" by the *Austin American–Statesman* to turn it into a wonderful performing arts center. Hartt Stearns has created what theater critic Michael Barnes has dubbed "a wonder." Stearns, who studied samba under Brazilian master Mayuto Corea, runs the theater for a nonprofit group, Barton Creek Arts Center Limited. In addition to his commitment to bringing world-class artists to Austin, he also helped found a mission to help schoolchildren enjoy cultural offerings from around the world. The One World program is one of the most popular in Austin schools.

One World Theatre is a modern, Italianate structure that is an eye-grabber along Bee Caves Road. From its verandas visitors can look out over the Hill Country and the burgeoning high-priced neighborhoods in the area. Inside, the 300-seat auditorium wraps around the stage, offering the audience close-up, intimate views of the performers. The eclectic offerings in past seasons have included Russian ballet stars, Tibetan monks, world-famous classical guitarists, the top names in chamber music, popular contemporary music stars, rock groups, and jazz legends.

PARAMOUNT THEATRE FOR THE PERFORMING ARTS
713 Congress Avenue
(512) 472-5470, (866) 4GET-TIX
www.austintheatre.org

On a stage once graced by the Ziegfeld Follies, Helen Hayes, George M. Cohan, John Philip Sousa, the Marx Brothers, and more of history's great performers, the Paramount Theatre presents top artists from Austin and around the country. Built in 1915 as the Majestic Theatre, a vaudeville house that presented variety acts, this elegantly restored venue was designed by one of the most respected theater architects in the United States, John Eberson of Chicago. This is one of the few theaters left in the country that showed the movie *Casablanca* when it was originally released more than half a century ago.

Now listed on the National Register of Historic Places, the Paramount itself is one of the city's main attractions. And the attractions onstage are just as important. This major performing arts venue, which seats nearly 1,300, is active almost 300 nights of the year, bringing live theater, dance, music, and comedy to audiences of all ages. This is where Austin's own blockbuster comedy *Greater Tuna* (www.greatertuna.com) got its start and where the two Tuna sequels packed the house. *The Foreigner*, another highlight of the Paramount's past, starred Tuna creators Jaston Williams and Joe Sears and was co-produced by Austinite Charles Duggan, who also produces Broadway shows in New York. The Paramount is also the theater of choice for the up-and-coming TexArts company (www.texarts.org), the latest Austin effort to bring locally produced Broadway-caliber musical theater to the city. Co-founded by Todd Dellinger, a former Broadway dancer, and Robin Lewis, former director of the Martha Graham Dance Center, the company got its feet wet with productions of *The Music Man*, *Big River* and *Carousel*. After much hard work and positive audience response, TexArts was included in the Paramount's 2008 season, presenting its version of *Damn Yankees*.

i R–E or E–R? Austin can't seem to collectively decide whether to call its performing arts companies and venues "theaters," the American spelling, or "theatres," the British version. Some venues use both. If you're trying to find one of these spots on the Internet, check which comes first: the "E" or the "R." There's also "teatro," the Spanish way.

For those who can't get enough of big musical productions, this is one company to watch. In 2000 the Paramount joined with its neighbor, the State Theater, to create the Austin Theatre Alliance, which offers season packages that include productions at both. Tickets may be purchased in person at the Paramount box office or over the phone with a credit card.

RIVERBEND CENTRE
4214 North Loop 360
(Capital of Texas Highway)
(512) 327-9416,
(512) 469-SHOW (Star Tickets)
www.riverbendcentre.com

Musical and theatrical stars performing in a house of prayer? Well, yes. This elegant 2,300-seat venue in one of Austin's most picturesque settings opened for public events in 2002 and has drawn acts like bluegrass singer Alison Krauss, pop star Kenny Loggins, and the Austin Symphony Orchestra. Built in 1998 as the Riverbend (Baptist) Church's "Home for Hope," the hall is one of Austin's largest performing arts venues, although it has a limited schedule. Check the Web site for listings.

i Clara Driscoll, whose historic Italianate villa is now home to the Austin Museum of Art at Laguna Gloria, is renowned for saving the Alamo from destruction in 1903. She simply bought the former mission for $75,000.

THE STATE THEATRE
719 Congress Avenue
(512) 472-5143, (866) 4GET-TIX
www.austintheatre.org

This performing arts center presents shows of all kinds throughout the year but is home to the State Theatre Company, an outstanding professional company operating in Austin since 1982. The company presents an eclectic array of productions during its five-play main-stage season that runs from September through June. Productions include musicals, comedies, dramas, and at least one world premiere each season. The theater's commitment to developing and producing new and award-winning works has led to the staging of outstanding productions. The State, located next door to Austin's classic Paramount Theatre, joined the Paramount in 2000 to create the Austin Theatre Alliance, so now it's possible to get a season package that includes productions at both. The renovated State Theatre, which includes two theaters of 400 and 100 seats each, rehearsal halls, scene and costume shops, and offices, made its debut in 1999. The expanded facility allowed the company to double the size of its School of Acting, which provides professional training to children, teens, and adults.

UNIVERSITY OF TEXAS
PERFORMING ARTS CENTER
23rd Street and East Campus Drive
(512) 471-1444,
(512) 477-6060 (Texas Box Office)
www.utpac.org

We've said it before, and we'll say it again. Having one of the country's largest universities in our own backyard has its advantages. The UT Performing Arts Center (PAC) is one of the biggies. This huge network of theaters, studios, rehearsal halls, and classrooms spreads to several campus locations. At the heart of the PAC system is the complex at 23rd and East Campus Drive.

This immense structure, which houses two theaters as well as rehearsal halls, offices, and massive support facilities, is one of the finest performing arts centers in the United States. Bass Concert Hall, UT's flagship theater, is a 3,000-seat auditorium with an atrium lobby and an orchestra pit that can accommodate even the largest musical group. Some of the finest touring artists and companies in the country also perform at Bass Concert Hall. Big Broadway touring shows in the recent past have included *Mamma Mia* and *Chicago*. Bass, which closed at the end of the 2007 season for an 18-month $14.7 million renovation, reopened in January 2009 with state-of-the-art acoustics, an expanded atrium area, improved lighting, and restaurant space for patron dining. Also in this complex is the McCollough Theatre, which seats 400 people and is used by both professional and student performers.

Many people, including local residents, tend to think of the Performing Arts Center as the Bass complex alone. In fact, there's much more. The Performing Arts Center also includes Bates Recital Hall in the Music Building adjacent to Bass. The recital hall is a 700-seat theater designed for acoustic excellence and equipped with a three-story pipe organ. This theater hosts musical performances by some of the best virtuoso performers of the day, as well as leading names in jazz, chamber and organ music, and more.

Other theaters around campus that contribute to the Performing Arts Center are the B. Iden Payne Theatre, a 500-seat facility used for both professional events and student theatrical productions, and Hogg Auditorium, a recently reintroduced theater that's almost as large as the Paramount and is also used for both professional and student events. A few smaller theaters and a dance studio complete the Performing Arts Center.

While the PAC is perhaps most known to the public at large for the world-class events it presents, we can't fail to mention the quality and range of many student productions offered at some of these theaters throughout the school year. UT students of theater, dance, film, and music present shows that are definitely worthwhile for any fan of the performing arts. Texas Box Office, with locations in H.E.B. grocery stores all over the area, is an easy way to buy tickets to PAC events. Tickets are also on sale directly at the PAC box office and other locations in town.

ZACHARY SCOTT THEATRE CENTER
1510 Toomey Road
(512) 476-0541
www.zachscott.com

One of Austin's most exciting and innovative professional theater companies, Zachary Scott has been wowing Austin audiences for years with its broad spectrum of plays and musicals, including many performed for the first time by a regional theater in the United States. Additionally, Zach (as it's known locally) has given Austin audiences wildly popular revues such as *Beehive* as well as *Shear Madness,* the longest-running play in Austin history.

Zach, Central Texas's oldest resident theater, began in 1933 when it was incorporated as the Austin Civic Theatre. The theater took a major leap forward in 1972 with construction of its first 240-seat theater at the current location. The theater was renamed that year in honor of Zachary Scott, an Austin-raised actor who went on to a successful Hollywood film career. A second 130-seat theater and costume shop, classroom, rehearsal studio, and administrative offices were added later, during the time Zach was moving from community theater to become one of Austin's premier professional theaters. Several of Zach's shows have been so popular that the company has needed to rent Austin's larger Paramount Theatre to accommodate all audiences. A new 500-seat auditorium at South Lamar Boulevard and Riverside Drive is in the planning stage.

Zach presents 8 to 10 productions during its yearlong season that runs from September through August on both stages, the main Kleberg Stage and the Whisenhunt Arena Stage. The Zachary Scott Theatre Center also operates a hugely popular Performing Arts School that draws thousands of children, teens, and adults each year. Zach's Project InterAct, a professional company of adult actors, performs children's shows for school students throughout the Southwest, including some outstanding original productions. Theater buffs should include a visit to Zach Scott on any tour of Austin.

The Outdoor Stage

ZILKER HILLSIDE THEATER
2206 William Barton Drive
(512) 477-5335
www.ci.austin.tx.us/zilker/hillside.htm

Casual outdoor free arts! What better tribute to Austin than this great venue on a natural grassy amphitheater that hosts some of our city's most anticipated free shows. Start with the annual Zilker Summer Musical, an Austin tradition for nearly 50 years. This big, splashy show draws more than 2,000 people a night to Zilker Park for some of the best outdoor performances Austin offers. Another outstanding Austin event, Shakespeare Under the Stars, held each fall for more than 20 years, draws upward of 15,000 to the Hillside for a four-week engagement of an excitingly staged and costumed Shakespeare play. Past performances have included *Macbeth* and *Twelfth Night*, produced in association with the National Shakespeare Company. Officially named the Beverly S. Sheffield Zilker Hillside Theater, this spot also is home to the annual Trail of Lights Festival in December, the event that kicks off Zilker Park's wonderful Trail of Lights. You don't have to wait for an annual event to experience this great Austin theater, however. Bring a blanket and a picnic basket and enjoy the outdoors while watching any number of dance, musical, or theatrical events held in this comfy spot near Barton Springs Pool that has room for more than 2,500 spectators. All events are free, but there is a small charge for parking.

The Warehouse Stages

ARTS ON REAL
2826 Real Street
(512) 472-2787
www.artsonreal.com

"Yelavich . . . is almost single-handedly responsible for the most exciting, most incredible, most downright stupendous theatre miracle that's hit Austin in many a year." That's what the *Austin Chronicle* had to say in 2003 about the grand opening of Blake Yelavich's East Austin space,

Arts on Real. This former meat plant and ice factory has been converted into a 120-seat theater, complete with a bar and gallery and including rehearsal space and a scene shop. This is now home to Yelavich's Naughty Austin Productions, which, as its name implies, has produced risqué shows as well as gay-themed plays. In fact, it was Naughty Austin's hit production of *Making Porn* in 2002 that helped finance this new facility. Naughty Austin, which has since branched out into more traditional theater, first gained prominence around here by producing musical parodies of local theater productions, a la Forbidden Broadway. In keeping with the edgy nature of the venue, it recently added Colosseum Wrestling— that's erotic entertainment in the form of mock "sexy" wrestling matches—to its calendar. Yelavich, a director, producer, writer, and actor, is now executive director of the nonprofit Arts Entertainment Group Inc. that operates the space. Rental dates are immediately snatched up by other groups around the city, so check the Web site for a listing of upcoming shows.

AUSTIN PLAYHOUSE
3601 South Congress Avenue, Building C
(512) 476-0084
www.austinplayhouse.com
Home to the Austin Playhouse theater troupe and site of most of Austin Shakespeare Festival's productions, this facility is located in the sensitively redeveloped Penn Field complex off South Congress Avenue. Built in 1914 at a flight training center for the Army Air Corps, the building reopened as a 150-seat theater in 2002. It also has a bar, coffee shop, and gallery. Austin Playhouse, which says it "is dedicated to providing opportunities for Austin artists and audiences to celebrate the human experience," is a professional company that presents four shows during its September-to-June season. The lineup has included original plays, including *Travesties* by Austin playwright Tom Stoppard, as well as such perennial favorites as *Kiss Me Kate* and *Private Lives*. Also presenting shows at this venue is Onstage Theatre Company (512-445-9866, www .onstagetheatreco.org), founded as a showcase

for vintage comedies and dramas. Its goal is to present quality presentations of classic theater to audiences in landmark theaters and opera houses throughout Texas. Its list of past productions includes *Educating Rita, Barefoot in the Park, The Gin Game,* and *The Mousetrap.*

BLUE THEATER
916 Springdale Road
(512) 927-1118
www.refractionarts.org
A former truck shop built in the 1950s, this facility is operated by Austin troupe Refraction Arts Project. It features a 100-seat theater and a smaller proscenium space that seats about 40 people. Located in a warehouse complex in East Austin, it opened as an arts venue in 2000 to offer theatrical productions, visual art, dance, music, and film. When Refraction Arts isn't performing, other events are taking place here, so check the calendar often.

DOUGHERTY ARTS CENTER
1110 Barton Springs Road
(512) 397-1471,
(512) 454-TIXS (box office)
www.ci.austin.tx.us/dougherty/
theaterhome.htm
Built in the 1940s as a Naval and Marine Reserve Center, this wonderful facility was taken over by the Austin Parks and Recreation Department in 1978 and turned into one of the busiest arts venues in town. The Dougherty Arts Center (DAC) has it all: a comfortable 150-seat theater that's always hosting one show or another, an 1,800-square-foot art gallery, classrooms, and plenty of studio-lab spaces. It's impossible to list all the arts-related activities that go on at this center.

Teatro Humanidad has performed here, as has Austin's Ballet East Dance Theater. Teatro DAC also has hosted some shows for the Big Stinkin' International Improv and Sketch Festival, an annual event that draws comics from around the world to Austin. The Julia C. Butridge Gallery at DAC hosts art shows of all kinds by Austin-area artists and arts organizations. Exhibitions have been organized by Women Printmakers of Austin, the Texas Music Museum, Austin Community College, and La Peña, a nonprofit organization dedicated to promoting Latino art and artists. La Peña's annual Serie Print Project, presented here in the spring, is a great way to see up-and-coming artists.

Austin's only city-run arts complex, DAC provides arts enrichment to citizens of all ages and economic levels. Admission prices to DAC performing arts events are often very reasonable, while gallery admission is always free. Many of Austin's other excellent arts programs are operated out of the Dougherty Arts Center, including Art in Public Places, which commissions artworks for placement in city facilities for all to see and enjoy. (Be sure to see our chapter on Attractions for information on some of Austin's easily accessible artworks.) DAC runs a wide variety of programs for adults and students, including the nationally recognized Totally Cool, Totally Art program, in which professional artists work with teenagers at local recreation centers. DAC sponsors art classes in many genres and runs a wonderful summer camp program.

ESTHER'S FOLLIES
525 East Sixth Street
(512) 320-0553
www.esthersfollies.com
We tell you more about this laugh-a-minute riot of a comedy troupe in our chapter on Nightlife. They call themselves Texas's premier musical comedy revue, and we can't argue with that. We've taken more than one out-of-town guest to see Esther's Follies' great show, which combines some classic routines with constantly updated political satire. The follies can be found in a converted 1800s-era building on Austin's historic and hip East Sixth Street.

THE HIDEOUT
617 Congress Avenue
(512) 443-3688
www.thehideout.org
Near downtown's Paramount and State theaters, this inviting coffeehouse/bar also includes

performance space for 150 souls on two stages and offers comedy, theater, music, and local film screenings. Improvisational comedy is especially big at this venue, with events by the Austin Improv Collective and others taking place regularly. The Hideout even offers improv classes and improv jams for those brave enough to test their comedic wits in front of others. Opened as The Hideout in 1999, it's in an 1846 building (see our Nightlife chapter).

HYDE PARK THEATRE
511 West 43rd Street
(512) 479-7530,
(512) 479-7529 (box office)
www.hydeparktheatre.com
Since its founding in 1992, Hyde Park Theatre has grown into one of Austin's most well-respected and popular small troupes, presenting bold alternative works by both Austin artists and others from around the country, including several world premiere events each season. Hyde Park also runs the largest and most intriguing performance festival in the Southwest: Fronterafest. This annual five-week fringe festival, held in January and February, provides a venue for hundreds of high-caliber local, regional, and national artists who present nearly 100 separate acts (see our Annual Events and Festivals chapter). Fronterafest is produced in collaboration with Austin Script Works, a group dedicated to supporting emerging playwrights and developing new dramatic works. In addition to producing its own shows, Hyde Park Theatre also serves as performance home to other Austin gypsy troupes and fringe artists.

THE OFF CENTER
2211–A Hidalgo Street
(512) 474-7866
www.rudemechs.com
This 93-seat theater in a converted feed store presents shows by one of our city's most "Austin-tacious" theater troupes: Rude Mechanicals. Founded in 1995, Rude Mechs (512-476-7833) has become one of Austin's most renowned and original companies and is known for its enormously creative—and brave—theatrical vision.

The company received national attention and acclaim for its stage adaptation of *Lipstick Traces*, which played in New York in 2001 and other American cities in 2002. A longtime favorite among Austin theater buffs, Rude Mechanicals was featured in the *New York Times* as one of three companies in the country "making theatre that matters." It also manages The Off Center.

SALVAGE VANGUARD THEATER
2803 Manor Road
(512) 474-7886
www.salvagevanguard.org

Salvage Vanguard is an exciting experimental company that has earned a reputation for presenting hot new writers to Austin in shows that, in recent seasons, were paired with a local band—so music fans no longer have to miss out on an interesting theater experience. Catering to Austin's hip crowd, Salvage Vanguard is known for performances that rock the ceiling. The nonprofit company presents several mainstage shows, some of them world premieres, between March and December. Over the winter holidays SVT also presents its annual five-minute new-play festival and sing-along. It's a blast. The company operates out of its new 9,600-square-foot, 100-seat facility in East Austin.

SANTA CRUZ CENTER FOR CULTURE
1805 East Seventh Street
(512) 524-4278

This established cultural center is home to Austin's well-respected Aztlan Dance Company (see the Dance and Music listing in this chapter) as well as the ProArts Collective and Proyecto Teatro. The theater, which opened in 1988 in a converted WWI-era warehouse, seats 120 people and has become a center for both well-established and up-and-coming Latino arts projects on the East Side.

THE VORTEX
2307 Manor Road
(512) 478-5282,
(512) 454-TIXS box office
www.vortexrep.org

Home to Austin's Vortex Repertory Company since 1994, the Vortex has become the place to go to see original cutting-edge performances that have included *Wisdom of the Crone*, conceived and directed by producing artistic director and Vortex founder Bonnie Cullum. Among the leaders of Austin's alternative theater scene, Vortex has produced scores of successful works since it was founded in 1988. World premieres, new plays, Texas premieres, and vibrant works by Shakespeare have all been presented on the Vortex stage. Vortex Productions is also very well known for its other incarnation, Ethos, an electronic music and multimedia performance troupe. Among the troupe's original works are the award-winning cybernetic opera *The X & Y Trilogy* and *Elytra*, the story of four female insect-angels who awaken in Heaven and find it in need of repair. Audiences love the extraordinary spectacle of these shows. This East Austin theater, a once-abandoned warehouse that has been converted to an intimate 90-seat venue with comfortable theater seats, is used by other individual performers and theatrical companies for shows of all kinds. Vortex presents several major productions a year as well as a number of smaller performances that showcase this company's talents. Vortex also has earned a reputation in Austin for presenting shows by nationally known performance artists. Whether it's a simple one-person show with only a chair onstage or a full-scale production with elaborate scenery, lighting, and sound, the Vortex has done it all. The theater also sponsors Summer Youth Theater, which brings teenagers from around Austin to the theater to create, produce, and perform a theatrical show. Other Austin theater companies also perform here.

The Gypsies

AUSTIN SHAKESPEARE FESTIVAL
P.O. Box 683, Austin 78767
(512) 454-2273
www.austinshakespeare.org

Mention Austin Shakespeare Festival around these parts and folks will immediately think of the wonderful free outdoor Shakespeare Under the Stars plays produced annually for the past two decades at the Zilker Hillside Theatre. These days, however, the name implies much, much more. Austin Shakespeare Festival now offers a year-round season of plays, both indoors and out. Additionally, while the primary focus is on Shakespeare, the company's productions are not limited to works by the Bard. Guy Roberts has led this professional company in delightful new directions since his first season as artistic director in 2002–03. The results are impressive. Roberts, an actor, director, and educator who has served in many capacities on the Austin theater scene over the years, now brings entertaining, stimulating, and, most important, extremely accessible Shakespeare to our city. ASF most often performs at Zilker and at Austin Playhouse.

CITY THEATRE
3823 Airport Boulevard, Suite D
(512) 524-2870
www.citytheatreaustin.org
Although City Theatre Company is one of the newcomers on the Austin stage, it wasted no time in catching the public's—and the critic's—eye. It already has won rave reviews and several local theater awards with its productions of *Parallel Lives* and *The Boys Next Door*. Operating out of this venue in East Austin, City Theatre is also one of the most ambitious companies around, opening a new production within days of closing another. It presents classics such as *Death of a Salesman* and *The Taming of the Shrew,* as well as dramas from the likes of Neil Labute and Tom Stoppard. Its season also includes summer productions aimed at kids.

COLD TOWNE THEATER
4803 Airport Boulevard, Suite B
(512) 524-2807
www.coldtownetheater.com
Tragedy in the form of 2005's Hurricane Katrina brought members of this exciting comedy improv troupe from New Orleans to Austin. Since the group's founding, Cold Towne has won a bundle of impressive awards, including

the B. Iden Payne Award for Outstanding Improv Ensemble, *Chronicle* Readers' Poll awards for Best Comedy Troupe, Frontera Fest—Best of Week and the O. Henry Pun-Off World Championship. All forms of comedy are performed at the theater, including improv, sketch, and stand-up. Check the Web site for the current schedule of events. The Cold Towne Conservatory also offers sketch-writing classes.

DIFFERENT STAGES
(512) 454-TIXS
www.main.org/diffstages
Started in 1980, Different Stages is a nonprofit community theater company that produces works by playwrights who are defining forces in theater: Moliére, Shakespeare, Shaw, and O'Neill, to name a few. The company also has been the first to introduce Austin to new playwrights and has produced original works by Austin playwrights Ann Ciccolella and Tom White. Under the artistic directorship of Norman Blumensaadt, the company has presented dozens of plays, including romantic, neoclassic, realistic, and surrealistic. In 2007 the company's production of Edward Albee's *The Goat* won Austin's prestigious B. Iden Payne awards for best production of a drama, best actor and best actress. Different Stages presents a full season of performances from the beginning of November to July, both here and at other Austin locations. Of late, the troupe has performed most often at the Austin Playhouse or the Vortex.

SECOND YOUTH
P.O. Box 26186, Austin TX 78755
(512) 386-8292
www.secondyouth.com
Billed as "theatre for the young at heart," Second Youth presents a wonderful array of family-friendly productions, most often at the Dougherty Arts Center but also on other stages around town and beyond. In 2007 Second Youth won the B. Iden Payne Award for Outstanding Production of a Play for Youth with its version of *The Page and the Caterpillar*. Other productions have included *The Lion, the Witch, and the Wardrobe* and *Alice*

in Wonderland. The Second Youth Educational Outreach Program sends professional actors into schools and community centers to entertain and interact with students.

DANCE AND MUSIC

More and more Austin audiences are getting the "pointe" about Austin's rich dance scene, which includes a number of established companies and even more individual dancers and choreographers who bring their unique styles to stages all over the city. In addition to the dance companies we've listed here, be sure to look for special performances by troupes formed for a specific production. Austin dancers offer a wonderful cross section of styles, including classical ballet, tap, modern, postmodern, and folklorico. The leader among Austin dancer/choreographers is Deborah Hay, nationally recognized as one of the pioneers of postmodern New Dance. If you love dance, be sure to look for occasional performances by the Deborah Hay Dance Company (www.deborah hay.com). Andrea Ariel and Toni Bravo are other Austin dancers of note. Austin's main dance organization, Dance Umbrella, also sponsors dance and performance-art shows throughout the year by Austin talent as well as nationally and internationally known performers (see the Arts Organizations listing in this chapter).

Whether you like a toe-tapping good time, the skirt-swirling grandeur of a Mexican folk dance, the awesome power and grace of a dancer on pointe, or the stylized foot- and bodywork of modern dance, you'll be inspired by Austin's dance performances.

While Texas's mecca for classical music artists is about 70 miles east of Austin in Round Top (see our Day Trips chapter), you'll be pleased to know that you don't have to travel to hear exciting ensembles. In fact, in 2003 Austin's classical music scene took a giant leap forward when the University of Texas snagged highly coveted string ensemble the Miró Quartet (www.miroquartet .com) as its resident quartet. This internationally renowned foursome performs for the public

at large. Additionally, Austin claims about two dozen classical music groups, about half choral, half instrumental. The two mentioned here are among Austin's leaders, but look, too, for outstanding performances by the Austin Choral Union, the Austin Vocal Arts Ensemble, River City Pops, the Austin Lyric Opera Chorus, and the Texas Chamber Consort. Those interested in performing will discover that these and many other musical groups, including barbershop and gospel choruses, accept new members by audition. Austin also claims several groups for children.

The classical guitar scene is also alive and well in Austin and has attracted enough outstanding guitarists to maintain the Austin Classical Guitar Society. The only nationally syndicated classical guitar program is produced right here in Austin and airs out of radio station KMFA. The crème de la crème of Austin's classical guitarists is world-class player and recording artist Adam Holzman (www.adamholzman.com). This virtuoso, who plays recital halls throughout the world, including Carnegie Hall, has won many prestigious international guitar competitions and has created UT's classical guitar program. In a music city dominated by singer/songwriters and rock 'n' rollers blasting chords through amplifiers, Holzman is the artist the *Austin American–Statesman* has called "the best guitar player in Austin you've never heard of."

Dance

AZTLAN DANCE COMPANY
Santa Cruz Center
1805 East Seventh Street
(512) 524-4278
www.aztlandance.com
Both the critics and the public are raving about this dance company, which combines original contemporary choreography with traditional Latino folk steps, often set to the music of popular Latino recording artists. Founded in 1974, this company for many years performed mainly the classic regional folk dances of Mexico. In the past few years, however, choreographer and general director Roen Salinas has introduced a modern

🔍 Close-Up

First Thursday: SoCo's Monthly Celebration

Live music, beer gardens, casual dining, shopping—and free hugs! Those are just a few of the attractions at the increasingly popular First Thursday event in the trendy SoCo district of South Congress Avenue from about the 1200 block to the 1800 block. On the evenings of the first Thursday of each month, district merchants keep their doors open until 10:00 p.m. (or later), many of them hosting special events or activities, while outdoor marketeers offer their wide assortment of handicrafts and other goods in several spots along the strip.

The focus here is on dining, shopping and services—and why not? Few other strips offer the eclectic assortment of choices available on South Congress. Visitors can find new, designer clothes as well as vintage apparel, costume rentals, hair salons, toys and candies, antiques, art galleries, fine jewelry, home furnishings, international imports and much more. There is even Allens Boots, a whole store dedicated to cowboy boots and Western wear, as well as an Amy's Ice Cream shop, and Austin's famous Continental Club live music venue (which really gets going after the festivities).

This is not a rollicking street party like that which occurs regularly on Sixth Street because alcoholic drinks are served only in the restaurants and beer gardens, but it is a lively event nonetheless, with plenty of live music under the stars. And this was a first for us: There is even live music regularly at Pink Hair Salon! It's no wonder the event is popular with the old and young alike, including singles, families, groups of friends and couples. There even are more than a dozen college-age kids offering free hugs—and each one is most warmly received. While you are here, take a moment to check out the roof at Lucy in Disguise with Diamonds (in the 1500 block) to enjoy a piece of Austin's landmark art, a giant zebra dressed as Carmen Miranda—complete with the fruit-filled headpiece!

This also is a perfect place to find Austin originals, from the "Keep Austin Weird" T-shirts and mugs, (as well as the alternative "Keep Austin Batty," a tribute to our local bat population) to handcrafted jewelry, candles and soaps, as well as photographs of Austin scenes. One of our favorite booths is one that offers handbags made of vintage LP covers and snack bowls made of old records—very creative! SoCo also offers an assortment of restaurants, including the extremely popular Güero's Taco Bar and El Sol y La Luna restaurant (see our Restaurants chapter). Beyond those two, there is Doc's MotorWorks Bar & Grill, which features a large outdoor patio, as well as hamburger and pizza joints, an outdoor coffee shop, Japanese fast food, and more.

Parking is available right on South Congress, but those spots fill up quickly. The best bet is to park in the free lot at One Texas Center (505 Barton Springs Road) and then grab the free orange 'Dillo trolley car that runs all evening. For information on the event, and the SoCo merchants, see the Web site at www.firstthursday.info.

format that reflects the danza folklorico heritage but addresses the Hispanic culture of today's Texas. Instead of the flamboyant costumes typical of some regional dances of Mexico, for example, Aztlan dancers have worn blue jeans and T-shirts while dancing to the music of Los Lobos.

Aztlan still does Mexican folk dances, and does them extremely well, but this new choreography adds an exciting artistic dimension to the troupe. The company is based at East Austin's Santa Cruz Center but also performs at the Paramount and the Bass Concert Hall. Aztlan also has performed at venues all over the country and in Hong Kong and Great Britain. Academia Aztlan, which aims to promote a greater understanding of the Hispanic cultural arts, offers dance classes, workshops, lectures, art exhibits, and more at the Santa Cruz Center and elsewhere in Austin.

BALLET AUSTIN
501 West Third Street
(512) 476-9151,
(512) 476-2163 (Box Office)
www.balletaustin.com

Austin's premier classical ballet troupe has soared to new heights since 2000, when Stephen Mills stepped up as artistic director. Mills, who has been with the organization since 1987 as dancer, choreographer, and associate artistic director, received rave reviews and attention from across the country for his world-premiere production of *Hamlet* during his first year as director. In 2002 the company performed sold-out shows of *A Midsummer Night's Dream* at the Kennedy Center in Washington, D.C. Mills's national and international accomplishments as both a dancer and a choreographer are astounding. Under his leadership Ballet Austin is becoming one of the nation's finest developing ballet organizations.

Ballet Austin presents five seasonal ballets, including the much anticipated annual performances of *The Nutcracker* in December. Other Austin favorites have included performances of *Firebird, Ulysses,* and *Cinderella.* This accomplished company traces its roots to 1956, when it was chartered as the Austin Ballet Society. Over the years, the ballet evolved from a civic, all-volunteer organization to become a professional organization.

One major aspect of this company is the Ballet Austin Academy, also established in 1956, which offers classical ballet training as well as jazz, modern dance, and fitness classes to dancers from age 3 to adult. Ballet Austin II, an apprentice program, provides professional development for the 10-member second company. Ballet Austin's performances are held at The Long Center on West Riverside Drive. The company also offers full-length and mixed-repertoire performances throughout Texas. This community-based company goes all out to educate school students and adults alike. The season runs from October to May.

BALLET EAST
At Dougherty Arts Center
(512) 385-2838,
(512) 454-TIXS (8497) (for tickets)
www.balleteast.org

Founded by Rodolfo Mendez in 1982, Ballet East is a well known community dance troupe made up of professional and emerging dancers and choreographers from many ethnic backgrounds. The company in residence in East Austin has a solid reputation for developing young dancers and for showcasing the talents of some of Austin's finest dancers and choreographers, including Toni Bravo, Andrea Ariel, and Melissa Villarreal. The company also works with guest choreographers from nationally known companies, including the Alvin Ailey American Dance School in New York and the Joyce Trisler Danscompany. Ballet East, which most often offers mixed repertoire programs, performs several times a year at various locations in Austin, most often at the Dougherty Arts Center.

BLUE LAPIS LIGHT
6701 Thomas Springs Road, Suite A
(512) 288-1929
www.bluelapislight.org

Choreographer and performer Sally Jacques is the creative mastermind behind some of the most spellbinding and offbeat dance/performance art productions around these parts. She creates so-called site-specific aerial dance performances, meaning that one production is developed for, say, a temporary construction scaffolding while another is developed for an airport hangar, and another for Barton Creek, and so on. A native of England, Jacques has received many Austin awards as well as important grants in recognition of her work, including those from the National Endowment for the Arts, Art Matters of New York City, and the Texas Commission on the Arts. "As an artist I am always searching for ways to inspire and reveal a universal understanding of what it is to be alive in these times," she says on her Web site.

KATHY DUNN HAMRICK DANCE COMPANY

P.O. Box 160432, Austin 78716
(512) 891-7703
www.kdhdance.com

This modern dance company has dazzled Austin audiences and critics since its first performance in 1999. *So Close*, performed with dancers moving behind, in front of, and through the audience, was named one of the Top Ten Dance Events of the year by the *Austin Chronicle*. It was no surprise, then, that by its second season the company had moved performances from a small studio to the larger State Theater to keep up with growing attendance. The company and its founder/artistic director/dancer/choreographer Kathy Dunn Hamrick have won plenty more awards since then—and with good reason. Dunn Hamrick, a UT graduate, creates imaginative dances often accompanied by live musical ensembles.

ROY LOZANO'S BALLET FOLKLORICO DE TEXAS

1928–C Gaston Place Drive
(512) 928-1111
www.rlbft.org

Be sure to check the dance listings for performances by Austin's own Ballet Folklorico de Texas, a company started in 1983 by the late Roy Lozano, a University of Texas alumnus who studied with the world-renowned Amalia Hernandez Ballet Folklorico de Mexico. Now under the artistic directorship of Jesus Chacon, this energetic company presents traditional Mexican folk dances from 19 regions of the country, each with its own dance style and stunning costumes. Ballet Folklorico is a professional troupe that performs all over Texas and has also been asked to perform in Mexico. This company knows Mexican folk dance. The authentic, brightly colored costumes Ballet Folklorico is known for only add to the appeal of this fine dance troupe. Ballet Folklorico also operates a youth dance company and a dance school to train young dance talent in the many styles of traditional Mexican dance. Don't miss the company's annual show, *Fiesta*, at the Paramount in May.

TAPESTRY DANCE COMPANY

507–B Pressler Street
(512) 474-9846
www.tapestry.org

Founded in 1989 by rhythm tap dancer Acia Gray and ballet/jazz artist Deirdre Strand, Tapestry is an acclaimed multiform dance company that has delighted audiences all over Austin and in other parts of the country during the company's national performance tours. This professional, nonprofit company presents seasonal multiform concerts from October to June at the Paramount and has thrilled Austin audiences by hosting a number of international dance and musical artists. Tapestry's annual Soul to Sole Tap Festival brings the world's finest rhythm tap artists to Austin for tap jams, concerts, film screenings, and more. The company also operates a pre-professional program and a downtown dance academy that offers classes for children and adults in rhythm tap, jazz, and ballet. Tapestry is also known for hosting numerous ethnic and cultural events, including Irish step dancing, clogging, and tango.

Music

AUSTIN CIVIC CHORUS

(512) 719-3300
www.chorusaustin.org

Founded in 1965 with just 32 singers, Austin Civic Chorus today has 100 voices ranging from high school students to senior citizens. This excellent chorus performs two or three major choral/orchestral masterpieces a year for huge audiences from all over Central Texas and is often a featured chorus with the Austin Symphony Orchestra. Past performances of Austin Civic Chorus have included *Songs of the American People*, a concert of spirituals and other American music that featured a guest gospel choir and the singing voice of Austin's accomplished Judy Arnold. The Civic Chorus also has performed "The Passion According to St. John" by Bach and works from many other masters.

Other highlights of the year include the annual Sing-It-Yourself Messiah in December, a holiday tradition for hundreds of Austin families. Austin Civic Chorus also produces and performs the annual *Summer Musical for Children*, a fully costumed and choreographed show presented free in eight performances attended by more than 2,000 people. The group works in cooperation with the Austin Vocal Arts Ensemble to present a choral education program in all of Austin Independent School District's middle schools. The Austin Civic Chorus performs mainly in churches around Austin, most often Northwest Hills United Methodist Church.

AUSTIN LYRIC OPERA
901 Barton Springs Road
(512) 472-5927, (512) 472-5992 (tickets)
www.austinlyricopera.org
Since its founding in 1986, Austin Lyric Opera has grown dramatically to a seasonal attendance of nearly 35,000 persons and has expanded its season to include 12 performances of three operas, most of them sold-out events. That's an outstanding attendance record for a city the size of Austin, and much of the credit goes to Joseph McClain, the opera's cofounder and general manager until 2003.

The company, led by internationally renowned conductor Richard Buckley, is known for presenting both the most popular of the operatic repertoire as well as works that explore the boundaries of opera, including *The Ballad of Baby Doe*, the company's first American work. Central Texas's only professional opera company brings major international and American artists to Austin each season, and the results have included many world-class performances. *The Barber of Seville, Andrea Chenier,* and *La Bohème* are just a few of the performances that have highlighted past seasons. In 2008 the company teamed up with the gang at Esther's Follies for a comedic, all-Austin version of Johann Strauss's *Die Fledermaus.*

The season features an opera every other month from November through March and has included a free outdoor performance at the Zilker Hillside Theater each October. All main-stage performances are held at The Long Center on West Riverside Drive. Opera attendance is on the rise nationwide, and one of the reasons is the use of supertitles, the simultaneous translation into English of the opera on a small screen above the stage. Patrons of Austin Lyric Opera and of operas throughout the country no longer have to speak a foreign language to understand the story. Austin Lyric Opera has its own 65-member orchestra and a 60-member semiprofessional chorus.

Austin Lyric Opera has opened a modern facility, the Armstrong Community Music School at Barton Springs Road, which houses a recital hall, a multimedia lab, classrooms, and teaching studios.

AUSTIN SYMPHONY ORCHESTRA
1101 Red River Street
(512) 476-6064, (888) 4-MAESTRO
www.austinsymphony.org
Austin's oldest performing arts group, the Austin Symphony Orchestra was founded in 1911. In 1998 American Peter Bay arrived in Austin as the symphony's conductor and music director, following a two-year search for the perfect conductor to lead the orchestra to new artistic challenges and to expand its audience even further in Austin. Bay, especially known for his skill at conducting large contemporary scores and complex pieces, has introduced more works of American composers and thematic programs, including music from film scores, to the orchestra's extensive repertoire of classical music. In 2003 the symphony performed with famous singing group the 5th Dimension. The orchestra also presented concerts commemorating President John F. Kennedy on the 40th anniversary of his assassination. The performance of "JFK: The Voice of Peace" (a work by local composer Dan Welcher) was narrated by ABC News's Hugh Downs and accompanied by the symphony.

The Austin Symphony Orchestra, which performs its September-through-May concert series at The Long Center, also presents festive Holiday and Promenade Pops Concerts, in which the audience brings their own picnic dinners and sits at tables for an evening of lighthearted music. The orchestra offers an assortment of nationally recognized youth programs, including the Young

People's Concerts in the spring, which bring more than 28,000 elementary students to Bass Concert Hall for live performances, and the Halloween Children's Concert at the Paramount Theatre.

The symphony also conducts free family concerts throughout the year and is especially known for its popular July Fourth concert and fireworks show on the shores of Lady Bird Lake, which draws more than 60,000 people a year. (See our Attractions chapter to learn more about Symphony Square, the complex of historical buildings that houses symphony offices and features an outdoor amphitheater and restaurant.)

CONSPIRARE
(512) 476-5775
www.conspirare.org

Since its founding in 1991, Conspirare has developed into a world-class ensemble known for its entertaining, innovative, and varied vocal music concerts. This professional chorus and orchestra specializes in music for the human voice. Conspirare has never been known to limit itself to just one genre. Choral, classical, jazz, ethnic, experimental, Broadway, old masterworks, and contemporary compositions are all presented by this company of 30 singers from Austin and across the United States. Founded as New Texas Festival by renowned conductor Craig Hella Johnson, Conspirare started out as an annual weeklong series of vocal music performances. Now the choir performs additional concerts throughout the year, including the annual "Christmas at the Carillon" show performed in a historic chapel in West Austin.

THE VISUAL ARTS

We can think of few better ways to spend an afternoon or a whole day than by visiting some of Austin's exceptional art museums and galleries. Access to the master artists of the past and present, including celebrated Austin and Texas artists, couldn't be easier. Austin offers two significant museums dedicated to the works of eminent sculptors Elisabet Ney and Charles Umlauf, who both lived and worked in Austin until their deaths.

The gallery scene offers an excellent opportunity to view works by both established and emerging artists. There's always a chance you'll come face to face with the artists themselves, either working or simply enjoying the company of people like yourself who've come for the experience. You may return home with an art treasure that will delight you for years to come, or perhaps turn out to be a shrewd investment. At the very least, we guarantee you'll be enlightened. Austin seems dominated by so many "alternative" galleries that the term has lost its meaning to a certain extent. Alternative to what? we might ask. Prepare yourself for the unusual.

Austin still has not achieved the status of Dallas and Houston as a major hub for art buyers, but what it lacks in patrons is more than made up by a dynamic artistic community. Austin has several artists whose work is recognized, and coveted, far beyond our state's borders. What better way to become acquainted with these talented visionaries, as well as our city's many emerging artists, than by seeing exhibits of their work on their home turf. You'll be astounded by the range of styles and the diverse media on display by the painters, sculptors, photographers, and fine crafters working in Austin today.

Austin also is distinguished for producing fine arts prints. Master printmaker Sam Coronado, Flatbed Press, and Slugfest are leading the way in that arena. Austin's galleries are not limited to our own artists, however. Among the galleries we've listed below you'll find work by some of the most interesting and well-known artists in the country today.

Don't let the idea of visiting a museum or gallery intimidate you, even if you're not an art expert. Austin's showrooms are staffed by knowledgeable, accessible experts, sometimes artists themselves, who are more than willing to offer on-the-spot advice, tips, and information about the artists and their works. Those of you who want to extend your study of the visual arts even further may want to check out some of the true art colonies that circle Austin in small towns like Salado, Wimberly, and Fredericksburg. For more i In recent years a huge community of artists has sprung up just east of Interstate 35 from the Cesar Chavez Street area up to around 38½ Street. The best way to see the more than 100 artist studios in this area is to take part in the annual East Austin Studio Tour (E.A.S.T.) event, www .eastaustinstudiotour.com.

information on local museums and galleries, visit the Austin Museum Partnership's Web site at www.austinmuseums.org.

Art Museums

AUSTIN MUSEUM OF ART—DOWNTOWN
823 Congress Avenue
(512) 495-9224
www.amoa.org

After the Austin Museum of Art (AMOA) outgrew its location at Laguna Gloria, the institution opened this additional 12,000-square-foot space in November 1996. The downtown space focuses on presenting temporary exhibits of significant 20th-century American visual art. Works by artists from the United States, Mexico, and the Caribbean are presented, including a strong showing of artists from Austin and around Texas.

The museum hosts 10 to 12 exhibitions annually, including those organized in-house and by other museums around the country. Since even before the museum expanded to this space, however, efforts had been made to build a larger permanent facility in downtown. After many failed attempts, the museum has announced it will break ground in 2009 on a new 40,000-square-foot facility just south of Republic Square Park downtown.

Meanwhile, the current location is open Tuesday through Saturday from 10:00 a.m. to 6:00 p.m. (until 8:00 p.m. on Thursday) and Sunday from noon to 5:00 p.m. Nominal admission fee. Reduced parking rates are available at the 823 Parking Garage on Ninth Street, or you can try to find a spot at the meters on the street.

AUSTIN MUSEUM OF ART AT LAGUNA GLORIA
3809 West 35th Street
(512) 458-8191
www.amoa.org

One of Austin's most cherished treasures, Laguna Gloria is a restored Italian-style villa, which is registered as a National Historic site. Built in 1916 and designed with meticulous care by its original owner, Clara Driscoll, the five-story, 15-room villa sits on 12 acres beside Lake Austin. The gardens surrounding the estate, including a sculpture garden, also have been restored to reflect Driscoll's vision. The grand lady herself ensured that her home would one day become a museum, deeding it in 1943 to the Texas Fine Arts Association (known today as Arthouse). The museum presents small-scale, long-term exhibitions and special events and is home to the museum's educational programs. This West Austin site was the only city art museum until the larger downtown facility opened in 1996. Members receive free admission to the museum, invitations to special events, subscriptions to museum publications, and more. The museum is open Tuesday through Saturday from 10:00 a.m. to 5:00 p.m., Thursday from 10:00 a.m. to 8:00 p.m., and Sunday noon to 5:00 p.m. The Art School at Laguna Gloria, in a separate facility on the grounds, offers both children's classes and instruction for adults in painting, sculpture, graphic arts, and more. The school can be reached at (512) 323-6380.

JACK S. BLANTON MUSEUM OF ART
Martin Luther King Jr. Boulevard and Congress Avenue
(512) 471-7324
www.blantonmuseum.org

i Want to take in the stunning view from the new Long Center, but can't afford the price of admission to the major events in Dell Hall? Buy a ticket instead to the usually less expensive events in the center's Rollins Theatre and then wander on over to the Dell Hall's scenic-view lobbies.

The University of Texas's new Jack S. Blanton Museum of Art, a 180,000-square-foot complex featuring two art buildings as well as a sculpture garden and pergola-covered walkways, is a key component of Austin's cultural scene. The complex includes The Mari and James A. Michener Gallery Building that houses the permanent collection and temporary exhibitions. The Blanton Museum's outstanding permanent collections are the most expansive in Central Texas, especially in the areas of American and contemporary art, Latin American art, and prints and drawings from all periods. Especially noteworthy is the museum's celebrated Suida-Manning Collection of Renaissance and Baroque paintings, drawings, and sculptures, as well as the Michener Collection of 20th-century American paintings (see our Close-up of Michener in The Literary Scene chapter). In all, the collection includes more than 17,000 works of art spanning the history of Western civilization from antiquity to the present.

The Blanton, named for former chairman of the UT Board of Regents and arts advocate Jack Blanton, offers a constantly changing array of temporary exhibits of works by internationally known artists, major Texas artists, and University of Texas fine arts graduate students. The museum, a strong research-oriented teaching institution, also hosts an ongoing series of public lectures by museum curators, artists, and art historians from UT and around the country.

MEXICAN AMERICAN CULTURAL CENTER
600 River Street
(512) 478-6222
macc@ci.austin.tx.us

One of the newest additions to the Austin arts scene, the Mexican American Cultural Center opened in September 2007—though in many ways it was hundreds of years in the making. Known as the MACC, the center celebrates Hispanic art, history, and culture through exhibitions, film, dance, music, educational programs and more. It features a large, airy art gallery that presents the works of well-known and up-and-coming Latino artists. It also has an auditorium for performances, film presentations, and lectures. The MACC sits literally a stone's throw from Lady Bird Lake on a sprawling lawn (some of it earmarked for future MACC expansions) that makes a perfect spot for outdoor performances and activities—as well as picnicking on a warm Austin afternoon. The center is family friendly and offers classes of all kinds for kids and adults. On the last Sunday of each month, the MACC hosts the artists' market *Hecho a Mano*, featuring artists' booths, live entertainment and food. Admission to the center is free, though there could be a charge for special programs.

MEXIC-ARTE MUSEUM
419 Congress Avenue
(512) 480-9373
www.mexic-artemuseum.org

Since its founding in 1984, Mexic-Arte Museum has been dedicated to presenting and promoting art created by both local and internationally known Mexican and Latino artists. The museum presents works from Mexic-Arte's permanent collection as well as from touring shows and exhibits organized by the museum staff .

Among the more memorable shows in recent years, and there have been many, is *From Revolution to Renaissance: Mexican Art from the Aaron Collection,*which included works by Rufino Tamayo, David Siqueiros, Dr. Atl, and others. The annual Young Latino Artists Exhibition showcases the work of artists under age 35. Mexic-Arte works with the Mexican Consulate in Austin to bring exhibitions and programs from throughout Mexico.

This museum was founded by Sylvia Orozco, Pio Pulido, and Sam Coronado, three Austin artists who painted a mural at the former Arts Warehouse in Austin in exchange for exhibit space back in 1983. In its current location since 1988, the museum also presents musical, theatrical, and performing arts events. The museum also houses an impressive gift shop that offers works by local artists. It's open 10:00 a.m. to 6:00 p.m. Monday through Thursday and 10:00 a.m. to 5:00 p.m. Friday and Saturday. Admission is free on Sunday.

ELISABET NEY MUSEUM
304 East 44th Street
(512) 458-2255
www.ci.austin.tx.us/elisabetney

Celebrated sculptor Elisabet Ney put her artistic career back on track when she moved to Austin's Hyde Park in the late 1800s and built Formosa, now an extraordinary museum dedicated to the life and works of this sophisticated woman. Here visitors will discover a provocative array of about 50 portrait busts and full-figure statues of Texas heroes and of the European notables Ney sculpted as a young artist in Europe. Also here are the glorious sculptures of Lady Macbeth, Prometheus Bound, and Sursum (a Latin word meaning "to uplift your heart"), a delightful sculpture of two young nude boys.

The building itself, which Ney designed as her home and studio, also glorifies Ney's artistic sensibilities. Built in two phases and named Formosa, meaning "beautiful" in Portuguese, the studio lives up to its name. The first studio section, reminiscent of a Greek temple, was built in 1892, when Ney was 59 years old. Living quarters, which included a Gothic tower study for her husband, philosopher/scientist Edmund Montgomery, were added 10 years later. Today Formosa is listed on the National Register of Historic Places as well as both the Austin and Texas Registers. The museum includes a wonderful section on the life of Ney herself. Here visitors will find many of the artist's tools as well as a hat, watch, teacup, glasses, and many other items used by the artist. Excellent written accounts of her life are on display here also. Visitors will learn that this great talent came to Texas from Europe with the idea of forsaking her career for, as she put it, the "more important art of molding flesh and blood"—in other words, to raise her two boys. Tragically, one son died at age 2. Twenty years later Ney accepted a commission to sculpt the figures of Sam Houston and Stephen F. Austin that stand in the Texas State Capitol today. Her career had resumed.

The museum stands as a monument to Ney's influence on the arts in Texas. Her ability to inspire others during a time when Texas slighted the arts led to the creation of the Texas Fine Arts Association (known today as Arthouse) and later the Texas Commission on the Arts and the University of Texas art department. The Elisabet Ney Museum, one of the oldest museums in Texas, was founded after her death in 1907 by those Ney inspired during her lifetime. Ney's work can also be seen at the Texas State Cemetery, at UT, at the Smithsonian Institution in Washington, D.C., and in other museums in the United States and Europe. The museum is open Wednesday through Saturday 10:00 a.m. to 5:00 p.m. and Sunday from noon to 5:00 p.m. Admission is free, as is parking on the residential streets around the building.

HARRY RANSOM CENTER
Near Guadalupe and 21st Streets
(512) 471-8944
www.hrc.utexas.edu

Officially named the Harry Ransom Humanities Research Center, the emphasis here has always been on providing researchers with access to the once-stodgy building's world-class collections of art, literary manuscripts, photography, music, and more. However, a 20-month, $14.5 million renovation completed in 2003 lets the light shine in on this Austin gem. The new glass walls and open spaces invite visitors to come in and stay awhile, while the arrangement of the collections makes it much easier for the general public to enjoy. There certainly are plenty of reasons to spend some time here. Among the center's exceptional properties is a 1455 Gutenberg Bible, one of just five existing complete copies of the first book printed with movable type, as well as the world's first photograph, taken by Frenchman Joseph Nicephore Niepce in 1826. There are important paintings by Mexican artists Diego Rivera, Frida Kahlo, and Rufino Tamayo, as well as artworks done by some literary greats, including D. H. Lawrence and Tennessee Williams. Literary manuscripts include works by Ernest Hemingway, William Faulkner, and Samuel Beckett.

In all, the Ransom Center houses 30 million literary manuscripts, 1 million rare books, 5 million photographs, and more than 100,000 works of art. Obviously it's impossible to display all these treasures at once, so the Center presents numerous exhibitions and events showcasing its collections. The galleries are open from 10:00 a.m. to 5:00 p.m. Tuesday, Wednesday, and Friday; from 10:00 a.m. to 7:00 p.m. Thursday; and from noon to 5:00 p.m. on weekends. Admission is free.

SOUTH AUSTIN MUSEUM OF POPULAR CULTURE
1516 South Lamar Boulevard
(512) 440-8319
www.samopc.org
The more Austin gentrifies and sprawls—not only literally, but figuratively as well—away from its core, the more need there is for a museum like this. A visit to this funky South Austin hole in the wall is a trip down musical memory lane for some and a portal into the past for those who missed the 1960s, '70s, and even into the '80s when Austin was making its biggest impact on U.S. popular culture. On these walls, visitors will find posters advertising music shows around town, underground cartoons, as well as other music-related graphics and ephemera of the era. And they will also learn about the personalities that put Austin graphic art on the map during those years, including Jack "Jaxon" Jackson, Jim Franklin, Ken Featherston, Frank Kozik, and others. One of the feature attractions here is a giant mural, *Peyote Dreams*, done by Featherston in 1974. This museum was opened in 2004, so it really is just getting going in establishing its collection, which is to include more paintings, album covers, T-shirts of the era, musical recordings, photographs and other important music memorabilia from the psychedelic period, through the cosmic cowboy years and beyond (see The Music Biz Close-up in The Music Scene chapter).

UMLAUF SCULPTURE GARDEN & MUSEUM
605 Robert E. Lee Road
(512) 445-5582
www.umlaufsculpture.org
Directors of the Umlauf Sculpture Garden & Museum like to say this garden epitomizes Austin:

It's outdoors, casual, and lovely. And they have a great point. Here, in a totally Austin xeriscape garden and pond next to Zilker Park, visitors are treated to the fabulous sculptures of acclaimed artist Charles Umlauf, who came to Austin in 1941 and remained for the rest of his life.

The garden, terrace, and surrounding land provide a perfect outdoor setting for 62 of Umlauf's bronze and cast-stone sculptures. The pieces, which range from the realistic to the abstract, represent a wide range of subject matter, including children, family groupings, mythological and religious figures, refugees, small animals, and sensuous nudes. There are many other smaller sculptures made of exotic woods, marbles, and terra-cotta inside the glass-enclosed museum.

Umlauf, who taught in the University of Texas art department for 40 years and retired in 1981 as professor emeritus, won nearly every professional award offered, including a Guggenheim Fellowship and a Ford Foundation Grant. His works can be seen in museums and public collections across the country, including the Smithsonian Institution in Washington, D.C., and the Metropolitan Museum of Art in New York. Umlauf's pieces can also be found on the UT campus and at a dozen sites around town, including the grounds of the Austin Museum of Art at Laguna Gloria and the Texas State Cemetery (see our listings in this chapter).

In 1985 Umlauf and his wife, Angeline, donated their longtime home and studio and more than 200 pieces of his work to the City of Austin. The museum, built with private funds, opened in 1991. This is a wonderful place to visit and is also popular for weddings and other outdoor events. The museum is wheelchair accessible and offers special programs for the visually and hearing impaired. It also hosts workshops for both children and adults and is a great place to bring children (see our Kidstuff chapter). The museum is open Wednesday through Friday from 10:00 a.m. to 4:30 p.m. and 1:00 to 4:30 p.m. on Saturday and Sunday. Nominal admission fee.

ℹ️ The Arthouse Texas Prize, the nation's biggest regional award for early career visual artists, comes with a whopping $30,000 no-strings-attached gift. The biannual prize recognizes innovation, talent, and a marked contribution to the Texas art scene.

Galleries

ART ON 5TH
1501 West Fifth Street
(512) 481-1111
www.arton5th.com

One of Austin's largest and most diverse art galleries, Art on 5th features work by famous artists such as Miró, Picasso, and Dr. Seuss as well as exceptional undiscovered artists from around the world working in many genres. This well-designed, visitor-friendly gallery is owned by Joe Sigel, who owned galleries in Santa Fe and California for many years. It's open Monday through Saturday 10:00 a.m. to 6:00 p.m. and Sunday noon to 6:00 p.m.

AUSTIN GALLERIES
1219 West Sixth Street
(512) 495-9363
www.austingalleries.com

After a tour of Austin and the surrounding Hill Country, you might be tempted to search out paintings that capture the stunning beauty of our hills. Among the more than 2,000 original works of art offered at Austin Galleries is a huge selection of Texas landscape paintings, as well as Impressionist, abstract, and classical paintings and original prints signed by Andy Warhol, Picasso, Jasper Johns, and others. And that's just the beginning.

AUSTIN SPIRIT GALLERY
1206 South Congress Avenue
(512) 444-8500
www.austinspiritgallery.com

Featuring the work of acclaimed Austin artist Fidencio Duran and other local artists, this invit-ing space on funky South Congress is perking up some ears. Duran, whose work includes the giant murals that greet passengers checking in at the airport and several other important murals around town, is an important local artist whose work is well worth seeing. The gallery also hosts temporary exhibits of other artists' work.

CLARKSVILLE POTTERY & GALLERIES
4001 North Lamar Boulevard
(512) 454-9079

9828 Great Hills Trail, Suite 110
(512) 794-8580
www.clarksvillepottery.com

Clarksville Pottery & Galleries has grown from a small, one-man pottery shop and studio back in the '70s into a major retailer of fine arts and crafts with two prominent Austin locations. The stores offer handmade pottery by local and nationally known potters as well as an impressive selection of jewelry, glass, wall art, fine woodcrafts, fountains, and more. The stores do a brisk business because in addition to offering some of the finest crafts available in Austin today, the local owners stock a good supply of items that are affordable. Started by former art professor Arnie Popinsky and his wife, Syd, in the Clarksville neighborhood of Austin, the business has been chosen by *Niche* magazine as a "Top 100 Retailer of American Crafts." Insiders love to take out-of-town guests to Clarksville.

F8 FINE ART GALLERY
1137 West Sixth Street
(512) 480-0242
www.f8fineart.com

ℹ️ Many people have asked us whether Austin has a museum dedicated to the musicians who put Texas on the map. The answer is yes—and no. The collection is mounting but no permanent exhibition space has yet been found. To follow the progress, or donate a building, visit www.texasmusicmuseum.org.

Photography buffs will recognize this gallery's name as a camera aperture, putting the, umm, focus, shall we say, on fine art photography. F8, however, offers a wide range of works, including oils and mixed media, from the nearly three dozen artists it represents. The Web site features a profile of each artist and his or her works. Once a month, the gallery offers a new exhibition featuring two photographers as part of West End Gallery Night. This inviting space is worth a visit.

FLATBED PRESS AND GALLERY
2830 East Martin Luther
King Jr. Boulevard
(512) 477-9328
www.flatbedpress.com
Flatbed Press's master printmakers work with some of the finest artists of the day to create limited editions of original etchings, lithographs, and woodcuts. This press has a national reputation for producing state-of-the-art work. Additionally, the gallery exhibits and sells original paintings as well as works on paper by leading contemporary artists, including Austin's Michael Ray Charles and Melissa Miller. Flatbed also offers about a dozen classes in printmaking and other techniques for novice to experienced artists.

IMAGES OF AUSTIN AND THE SOUTHWEST
4612 Burnet Road
(512) 451-1229
www.imagesofaustin.com
Austin artist Mary Doerr runs this gallery in a small house in Central Austin that showcases Doerr's attractive illustrations and watercolors, often depicting Austin, as well as the work of a number of other selected artists. The gallery features Southwestern sculptures and wall hangings as well as pottery, gourds, jewelry, limited-edition prints, and paintings.

THE JONES CENTER FOR CONTEMPORARY ART
700 Congress Avenue
(512) 453-5312
www.arthousetexas.org

Arthouse operates this downtown gallery as part of its efforts to nurture artists, promote contemporary Austin and Texas artists, and improve public awareness and appreciation of the state's visual artists. Formerly called the Texas Fine Arts Association, Arthouse was established in 1911. It is the oldest statewide visual arts organization in Texas and the only one devoted solely to contemporary art. Arthouse hosts a variety of exhibitions throughout the year, as well as special programs devoted to contemporary art. It is open daily except Monday, but operating hours vary.

SLUGFEST PRINTMAKING WORKSHOP & GALLERY
1906 Miriam Avenue
(512) 477-7204
www.slugfestprints.com
Slugfest is a stellar printmaking operation that produces limited-edition original prints for both novice and established artists. Opened in 1996 by Margaret Simpson and Tom Druecker, both MFAs in printmaking and teachers at Austin universities, this press has an excellent reputation for producing museum-quality prints. The gallery hosts an excellent variety of shows. Slugfest also offers introductory workshops in lithography, relief printing, monotype, collograph, book arts, and letterpress.

EL TALLER GALLERY
2438 West Anderson Lane, Suite C-3
(512) 302-0100
www.eltallergallery.com
Established in 1980 and owned by Olga O. Piña, El Taller Gallery has for many years been Austin's leading gallery for Southwestern art. El Taller carries work by Michael Atkinson, Amado Peña, R. C. Gorman, Poteet Victory, Darryl Willison, and others. In recent years the gallery has expanded to include traditional landscapes, florals, and engravings by several Austin artists, including Rick Hodgins, Betty Rhodes, Earlayne Chance, and Sue Kemp.

WILD ABOUT MUSIC
115 East Sixth Street
(512) 708-1700
www.wildaboutmusic.com

What better combination for Austin than an art gallery and gift shop that celebrates music? Everything in the locally owned shop has a music or performing arts motif, including accessories, clothing, jewelry, glass, and stationery. Wild About Music (WAM) features exceptional work by more than 100 artists, including some nationally known Central Texas artists as well as others from around the country. Acclaimed Austin musician Joe Ely is the most prominent of WAM's artists who also are bona fide musicians, but there are other musicians/visual artists as well as dozens of visual artists who are inspired by music. This gallery also hosts a variety of special events, including art demonstrations, touring art shows, and live music performances.

WOMEN & THEIR WORK
1710 Lavaca Street
(512) 477-1064
www.womenandtheirwork.org

This statewide nonprofit organization dedicated to promoting women in the arts celebrated its 30th anniversary in 2008. Make no mistake—this is much more than just an art gallery. Women & Their Work is the only organization of its kind in Texas that embraces all the arts. The organization promotes women artists in visual art, dance, music, theater, literature, and film, and it is one of Austin's premier resources for the arts. There's

Half-price tickets to select Austin performances are available at www.texasperforms.com and at the AUSTIX booth at the Austin Visitor Center, 209 East Sixth Street. Full-price tickets also are available Tuesday through Saturday. The Austin Circle of Theaters also hosts one of our favorite Web sites for upcoming events in the performance and visual arts: www.nowplayingaustin.com.

also a nice gift shop here that, like the gallery, is open Monday through Saturday. Gallery exhibitions featuring painting, sculpture, photography, fine crafts, and works on paper change regularly. Women & Their Work presents more than 50 diverse events each year, including juried and invitational exhibitions of Texas artists as well as solo and group exhibitions. The organization also produces dance, musical, and theatrical performances featuring local, regional, and national performing artists, often collaborative ventures with other groups. We especially like this organization's motto: "Women & Their Work is dedicated to the belief that women artists should be seen and heard. And paid."

YARD DOG FOLK ART
1510 South Congress Avenue
(512) 912-1613
www.yarddog.com

Fascinating is the word that comes to mind to describe the work of the folk artists, many of them nationally known, represented here. Art dealer Randy Franklin opened this gallery in South Central Austin in 1995 and handles work by artists from the American South. Be sure to ask him about the various artists represented here; they have interesting stories. The outsider art of well-known Austin artist Ike Morgan, a mental patient who has lived many years in the Austin State Hospital, is for sale here as is the work of Sybil Gibson, the Rev. J. L. Hunter, and many more. This area of South Congress Avenue is a fun place to visit even if you're not a folk art buff. The strip is lined with other funky shops and restaurants that will satisfy any craving for the unusual.

ARTS ORGANIZATIONS

ART IN PUBLIC PLACES
1110 Barton Springs Road, Suite 201
(512) 397-1455
www.ci.austin.tx.us/aipp

Established in 1985, the City of Austin's Art in Public Places (AIPP) program was Texas's first municipal effort to purchase and place works of art in public areas. Since then, AIPP has installed artworks at the Austin-Bergstrom International Airport, the Austin Convention Center, libraries, parks, recreation centers, and many more spots for everyone to enjoy. The program has involved talented artists of local and national renown, while the collection represents the broad range of media, styles, and cultural sensibilities. The organization's Web site has recently added an excellent map to the art installations around the city.

AUSTIN CIRCLE OF THEATERS
701 Tillery Street, Suite 9
(512) 247-2531
www.acotonline.org
Long before they sell a single ticket, take their first bows, or earn a rave review, many of Austin's theater companies first pass through the door at Austin Circle of Theaters (ACoT). This outstanding nonprofit organization works to nurture and promote the city's performing arts community and attract new audiences to the arts. ACoT's annual B. Iden Payne Awards are the most prestigious performing arts awards in the city. For the public at large, ACoT sponsors the excellent AUSTIX box office, which offers easy access to full- and half-price tickets for the city's performing arts events. It offers the ease of finding great local performances simply by flipping to the large ACoT advertisement on newspaper arts pages. For its more than 70 theater, music, and dance member groups, ACoT provides opportunities to help them develop survival strategies, and it helps start-ups by serving as an umbrella organization. ACoT is a strong voice of arts' advocacy in the community. In other words, this is one toasty art incubator for Austin. Anyone can reap the many benefits of becoming an ACoT member. Check the Web site for details.

AUSTIN VISUAL ARTS ASSOCIATION
(512) 457-0075
www.avaaonline.org
For more than 30 years the Austin Visual Arts Association has worked to promote knowledge and appreciation of the visual arts in the city. Its members include working artists as well as arts' patrons, museum professionals, and gallery owners. AAVA not only provides its members with a networking structure and opportunities to exhibit, it also hosts seminars and other events for the city's visual artists.

DANCE UMBRELLA
3710 Cedar Street, Suite 286
(512) 450-0456
www.danceumbrella.com
Whether it's bringing local and internationally renowned dance companies to the Austin stage or helping a young dance company find its legs, Dance Umbrella has been supporting the movement arts in our city since it was founded in 1977. This nonprofit organization with about 100 artistic members also aims to promote dance and dance companies throughout the region with its many programs and services. After all, the organization is based on the philosophy "that the arts help describe, define, and deepen our experience of living." Membership is open to one and all and provides discounts on performances.

TEXAS FOLKLIFE RESOURCES
1317 South Congress Avenue
(512) 441-9255
www.texasfolklife.org
Modern-day Texas culture is a rich blend of ethnic and regional traditions dating back hundreds of years. There's no better way to discover how well those traditions have survived than by attending events sponsored by Texas Folklife Resources (TFR). This dynamic nonprofit organization brings the best of those living, breathing cultures to the forefront of public awareness today through a comprehensive calendar of events in Austin and around the state.

TFR works with folk artists all over Texas to document living traditions and present them to the public in many forms, including exhibitions, concerts, radio programs, and demonstrations. Among TFR's many successful projects is Texas

Folk Masters, which puts outstanding traditional Texas musicians onstage at the Paramount Theatre. The organization also offers photography exhibitions that showcase traditional Texas blues clubs and its honky-tonk culture. And there's more: gospel music, powwow craft traditions, works in wood by folk artists, and songs and ballads of the Texas-Mexico border.

TFR also operates the Apprenticeships in the Folk Arts program, which encourages master folk artists to pass their traditions on to qualified apprentices in their community. Check the Web site often to keep fully informed of TFR's extensive list of events. Better yet, join TFR and help present, preserve, and promote the folk arts and folklife of the Lone Star State.

THE LITERARY SCENE

"The tempo of the earth-dwellers to whom I have been listening for many years is the tempo of growing grass, of a solitary buzzard sailing over a valley, of the wind from the south in April, of the lengthening of a tree's shadow on a summer afternoon, of the rise and fall of flames in a fireplace on a winter night. . . ." With those words, J. Frank Dobie, Texas's first nationally known writer, introduced his book *Tales of Old-Time Texas,* published in 1928 and still available, along with many of his other two dozen collections, at bookstores today. In this chapter we'll delve into Austin's rich literary history and describe its current status as a writers' mecca. But for those of you in a rush to explore the Austin of letters, we'll get right to the point: If you like books, you'll love Austin.

J. Frank Dobie is one of the reasons. Dobie, a University of Texas professor from 1914 to 1947, with occasional absences, was born in the Texas brush country and lived in and around Austin for most of his adult life—that is, when he was not off wandering around Mexico and the American Southwest in search of someone with a tale to tell.

"Frank Dobie became a hunter of legends and a gatherer of folk tales and the result was one of the most important bodies of literature produced by a Southwesterner," wrote Neil B. Carmony, who edited a collection of Dobie's stories for the book *Afield with J. Frank Dobie,* published in 1992, 28 years after the writer's death.

Names of other luminaries grace Austin's past, including historian Walter Prescott Webb and naturalist Roy Bedichek, who together with Dobie formed a triumvirate of intellectuals that electrified the city's literary ambience. William Sydney Porter, who later was to gain international notoriety as the short-story writer O. Henry, published his first short fiction here in his literary magazine the *Rolling Stone.* A Porter story that appeared in the October 27, 1894, issue of the *Rolling Stone* gave Austin one of its most endearing nicknames: City of the Violet Crown. (See our chapter on Attractions for more about O. Henry.) Austinite and LBJ aide Billy Brammer is still known around these parts for his 1962 political novel, *The Gay Place.*

John Henry Faulk, for whom our central library is named, was a multitalented writer, actor, New York radio show host, and defender of the First Amendment. As vice president of the American Federation of Television and Radio Artists, Faulk insisted the union take a stand against McCarthy-era blacklistings of entertainers—and was himself blacklisted. Faulk fought back and as a result won the largest libel judgment awarded up to that time. He was one of Dobie's students.

Internationally celebrated short-story writer Katherine Anne Porter (1890–1980) grew up 20 miles down the road from Austin in the small town of Kyle. Her relationship with Texas, however, was a stormy one. It infuriated her, for example, that the Texas Institute of Letters chose to honor Dobie instead of her when it gave its 1939 award for the best book by a Texas writer. (Folklorist Sylvia Ann Grider has written that "Porter's emotional attachment to her home state fell victim to the cowboy mentality that has traditionally proclaimed Texas a fine place for men and horses, but hell on women and oxen.") Of course her fame eclipsed Dobie's, which probably brought her no small amount of satisfaction. While Porter lived most of her adult life outside Texas, she nevertheless wrote some of her finest fiction about her home state and chose to be buried in Texas.

Pioneering Texas journalist Bess Whitehead Scott, who broke gender barriers in 1915 as the first woman news reporter in Houston, was a beloved member of the Austin writers community until her death in 1997 at age 107. Noted folklorist and poet J. Mason Brewer, the first African American to become a member of the Texas Institute of Letters and the first African-American vice president of the American Folklore Society, found inspiration among members of his own family in their East Austin home. Dobie called Brewer's work "genuine and delightful." Pulitzer Prize–winning author James Michener is another illustrious writer who found inspiration in Austin—and inspired others. (Find out more about Michener's contributions to Austin's literary scene in our Close-up in this chapter.)

Austin also was home to liberal syndicated columnist and best-selling author Molly Ivins, who forever will be known for her sharp tongue, her ability to skewer politicians, and her colorful commentary on what she called the "reactionary, cantankerous and hilarious" state of Texas. She also was the person who gave President George W. Bush the nicknames "Dubya" and "Shrub." Sadly, Ivins died in January 2007 at the age of 62.

Some of these trailblazers not only established Austin's literary traditions but also helped this city earn a reputation as a haven for writers and free thinkers, a distinction that has endured. Austin's literary scene, in fact, is more vibrant today than ever before. Perhaps even Dobie would be amazed at the sheer number of Austin writers and at the contributions many of them have made to the nation's literary wealth. To read Austin writers is to take a joyride on the roller coaster of literary expression: novels, mysteries, science fiction, cyberpunk, suspense, history, poetry, travel, books for children and young adults, essays, memoirs, how-to books, cookbooks, political satires, biographies, screenplays, short stories. The list goes on. Our city claims best-selling and award-winning writers in a number of genres—including 2007 Pulitzer Prize winner Lawrence Wright (*The Looming Tower: Al-Qaeda and the Road to 9/11*)—as well as a host of successful poets, playwrights, and screenwriters.

> **i** Readers unite in Austin as part of the Mayor's Book Club, an initiative that includes selection of the book to be read, book discussions at area libraries, and a party with the chosen author at City Hall. For information, see what the mayor has to say at www.ci.austin.tx.us/library/mbc08_intro.htm.

It's impossible to pinpoint just one catalyst for Austin's literary explosion. We'd have to include Austin's own magnetism. Once experienced, Austin is hard to abandon. The superlative efforts of the Writers' League of Texas to promote and encourage the city's writers have had impressive results. The league, with more than 1,500 members, is one of the largest writers' organizations in the country.

Two Austin publications, *Texas Monthly* magazine and the *Texas Observer,* have long and rich traditions of attracting excellent writers to Austin, many of whom have gone on to achieve literary fame. The vibrant music scene and flourishing film industry, illuminated by excellent local songwriters and screenwriters, add further dimension to Austin's literary landscape. (See our chapter on The Music Scene and our Close-up on the film industry in The Arts chapter.) Of course, the presence of outstanding intellectuals at the University of Texas, St. Edward's University, and our other colleges and universities has added untold riches to Austin's writing legacy. Adding further dimension to the scene are the university presses and many small- and medium-size publishing houses that are willing to gamble that an author's work will be of interest to others.

The last decade of the 20th century roused an unprecedented flurry of interest in Austin's literary arts. Major bookstore chains Barnes & Noble and Borders Books, which opened here in the mid-1990s, joined Austin's esteemed superstore, BookPeople, so that now book lovers don't have far to go to find a giant bookstore. These stores host an astounding assortment of readings by national and local authors, as well as book signings and other literary events that bring the

🔍 Close-Up

James Michener: A Memorable Character

Pulitzer Prize–winning author James Michener, whose 1991 memoir is titled *The World Is My Home,* chose Austin as his home for many of the last, always prolific, years of his life. Over the course of the Michener Age here, Austin was to become a richer city, not merely because of the millions in art and monetary endowments he gave to the University of Texas but also because of Michener's generosity of spirit.

Here was a man whose own life was one of America's great rags-to-riches tales; a man whose appetite for adventure and unquenchable thirst for knowledge were matched only by a gift— he called it a passion—for telling a story; a man who spent his life, and most of his fortune, giving back to the people and communities that had embraced him.

Michener was no stranger to the Capital City when he arrived in 1982 to begin work on his sweeping saga of the Lone Star State. He had known the Austin of the 1940s, when he came as an editor following publication of his first book, and he'd known the Austin of the 1960s, when he returned to donate his huge 20th-century American Art collection to the University of Texas. By the time the 1980s rolled around, Michener had been decorated with America's highest civilian honor, the Presidential Medal of Freedom. His reputation as America's Storyteller was as solid as his hefty novels—and so was his fame as one of the country's most generous writers. At the time of his death, it was estimated that Michener had given $117 million to museums, libraries, individuals, and universities around the country. The largest beneficiary of Michener's generosity was the University of Texas at Austin, which received $44.2 million from the late-in-life Austinite.

Michener's first novel, *Tales of the South Pacific,* published in 1947 when the author was 40 years old, had earned him a Pulitzer Prize. The bestsellers that followed, including *The Fires of Spring, The Bridges at Toko-ri, Sayonara, Caravans, The Source, Iberia, Centennial, The Drifters,* and *The Covenant,* earned him millions of loyal readers who found his fictionalized version of history more exciting, more moving, and even more educational than anything they'd read in nonfiction. It warranted not even a pause when critics called his work too preachy, his characters too one-dimensional, or his dialogue too contrived. Readers made Michener famous as they

written word to life. Several of Austin's small- and medium-size bookstores have long traditions of providing venues for local and national writers of poetry and prose, as do a number of other venues around town, including the Harry Ransom Center at the University of Texas and St. Edward's University in South Austin. The James Michener Center for Writers, appropriately housed in J. Frank Dobie's former home on Waller Creek, sponsors a wonderful series of readings by national and international writers.

Texas Writers Month, first organized in 1994, has become an outstanding statewide celebration of Texas's literary artists. The annual May festival, held in Austin and other major cities around the state, includes book panels, readings, chil-

dren's events, literacy benefits, signings, musical events, and film. Texas Writers Month, originally conceived to convince booksellers to give local authors more prominence in their stores, has become a premier celebration of Texas writers.

The Texas Book Festival, started in 1996, is another major Austin event for writers and readers alike. Laura Bush was a driving force behind the festival when she was first lady of Texas. The November festival, which raises money for Texas public libraries, features readings and panel discussions by more than 100 authors who have been published the previous year. Texans, Texas natives, and those who've written about the Lone Star State are invited to participate. A giant book fair, musical events, children's activities, and more stampeded to the bookstores to get their hands on his latest epic. Perhaps it was his ability to create characters with whom readers could identify that won him such a loyal following.

"I have endeavored to center my writing upon ordinary but memorable characters whose lives shed a kind of radiance, whose behavior, good or bad, illuminated what I was striving to impart, and whose noble, craven, godlike or hellish deportment stood surrogate for the behavior of human beings the reader has known," he wrote in his memoir.

Bill Clements, then governor of Texas, invited Michener to Austin in 1981 to work on a book about Texas for the sesquicentennial. Published in 1985, when Michener was 78, the 1,096-page epic turned out to be his longest work. Like *Hawaii, Space,* and *Chesapeake* before it, and *Poland, Alaska, and Mexico* that followed, *Texas* required no dramatic title. The image the title conjured in people's imaginations, and the bold name of the author below it, was enough to turn *Texas* into a million-copy blockbuster.

Michener and his wife, Mari, found a home in Austin during the years the author spent researching and writing his Texas saga. According to the Austin *American–Statesman,* Michener once told a friend as they walked down the West Austin street where he lived, "You know, I think I'm happier living on this street than any street I've lived on in my life." That statement said a great deal about the man who considered the world his home. His memoir features a cover photograph of the author sitting atop Austin's breathtaking Mount Bonnell (see our Attractions chapter).

In his half century of work, Michener wrote nearly fifty books of nonfiction and fiction, many of them as thick as bricks. Along the way, Michener found time to establish the Texas Center for Writers—renamed the James Michener Center for Writers following his death in 1997—to enlighten writers for generations to come.

In a 1988 interview on *Good Morning America,* Michener talked about his craft. "I think I have a passion for telling a story and then working on it until I think it's coherent," he said. "I'm proud of my profession. I'm a writer. I never say I'm an author, that's somebody else. I'm a real good writer."

He was also a real good human being.

highlight this celebration of the state's literary heritage. The Austin International Poetry Festival, held in April since 1993, draws poets and poetry fans from around the globe to Austin.

BUY THE BOOK

As if in a scene by Kafka, you innocently walk through a door and suddenly you're transformed—into a worm, no less. As you look around you realize the room is crawling with all kinds of worms: big ones, baby ones, curly-haired ones, bearded ones, coffee-drinking worms, worms wearing ties, worms taking notes. It's a community, a coterie, a coven of worms. Ahhhh.

You're right at home. Whether it's 10:00 in the morning or 10:00 at night, Austin's bookstores are teeming with those literate critters known as bookworms. Austin consistently ranks among the top 10 cities in per capita sales of books, according to nationwide studies done by the book industry. From small specialty stores to giant superstores, Austin's booksellers cater to the complex tastes of our readers. Readings and book signings by nationally known and local authors, comfy couches, and cafes are just a few of the features some bookstores offer to lure readers—and to add life to Austin's literary scene. For those of you who can't wait to savor the Austin bookstore experience, read below for a listing of some of our outstanding shops.

Throughout Greater Austin

BARNES & NOBLE BOOKSELLERS
Six stores in Austin and Round Rock
(512) 328-3155
www.bn.com

This large New York–based chain arrived in Austin in 1994 and has grown to include six superstores around the greater metropolitan area. Barnes & Noble wasted no time in becoming part of, and promoting, Austin's literary, musical, and artistic communities. Each store hosts a number of monthly book discussion groups on a variety of areas of interest, including fiction, nonfiction, science fiction, and Texana. The stores are a popular place to attend regular book readings and book signings by local, national, and international writers and screenwriters. The stores also are extremely active in promoting and hosting events for the annual Texas Writer's Month celebration in May. There's so much going on at Barnes & Noble that each store publishes a monthly calendar of events. Several stores feature a large music section with headphones for sampling a variety of artists. The children's sections are wonderful, and so are the numerous story times the stores host each week. Barnes & Noble also works in conjunction with local and national organizations that promote literacy and is involved with the Austin Independent School District's Adopt-a-School program. The inviting aroma of coffee permeates these stores, thanks to the great cafe and pastry shop inside each one. In addition to the Barnes & Noble stores, this chain also owns Austin's Bookstop and the B. Dalton's bookstores. The Web site gives the addresses of all B&N stores in the area.

BORDERS BOOKS, MUSIC AND CAFE
Four stores in the Austin area
(512) 339-1352
www.bordersstores.com

These superstores, despite not being "home-grown," have earned an excellent reputation for their support of the Austin literary and music communities. Readers, writers, music lovers, and musicians all have found a place in each of Borders' four Austin area locations. Like the other major bookstores, Borders hosts book discussion groups, book readings, and signings by local and national authors, book discussion panels, and other events of interest to the literary community. Borders also is active in sponsoring events for the annual Texas Writers Month celebration in May. The children's departments are always buzzing with activity, and the stores host regular story times for children each week. In addition, Borders have well-stocked music departments, including special sections for Austin and Texas artists. The inviting coffee shops serve a wide range of gourmet coffees as well as pastries and sandwiches. Don't miss the monthly calendar of events to stay abreast of the latest happenings at Borders. The Web site store locator gives the addresses of all Borders stores in the area.

HALF PRICE BOOKS
Five stores in Austin and Round Rock
(512) 454-3664
www.halfpricebooks.com

With four Austin locations and another in Round Rock, Half Price Books offers Central Texans easy access to its wide selection of used and new books, including rare and out-of-print titles and Texana and Americana titles not easily found elsewhere. We especially like the well-stocked used magazine section, where patrons often can find recent issues of their favorite magazines without having to pay full price for them. For the environmentally minded—and this is Austin, so there are many of us—this is a great place to recycle used magazines and books. The Dallas-based chain opened its first Austin store in 1975 and gradually built up to its current number. Half Price Books has a good selection of children's books as well as music in all formats, magazines, and videos. New books sell for half the current retail price or less. The store buys used books, magazines, videos, and music.

Central

AUSTIN BOOKS

5002 North Lamar Boulevard

(512) 454-4197

www.austinbooks.com

This locally owned store, serving Austin since 1977, has gone through several incarnations over the years and now specializes in comic books, Japanese manga, anime action figures, Japanese graphic novels, and trade paperbacks. The store stocks about 500 new titles of comic books as well as thousands more classics and collectibles. For collectors and diehard comic book fans, the store offers an e-mail service listing new titles for the week, as well as a simple response asking employees to set aside certain titles for pickup later.

BEVO'S BOOKSTORE

1202 West Avenue

(512) 477-2992

www.bevos.com

Located near Austin Community College's Rio Grande campus, Bevo's sells ACC textbooks, school supplies, study aides, gift items, and souvenirs. This store and its branch in North Austin at 11900 Metric Boulevard near the ACC Northridge campus stock thousands of titles of textbooks and also offer collegiate clothing. Originally located on The Drag across from the University of Texas, this locally owned business was once a shop for UT supplies, hence the name Bevo's.

BOOKPEOPLE

603 North Lamar Boulevard

(512) 472-5050

www.bookpeople.com

This Austin institution was the city's first book superstore and continues to be one of Austin's major literary venues. With more than 200,000 titles, BookPeople is one of the largest bookstores in Texas. It definitely is one of Austin's favorite spots to shop for books and to hear authors read from their works. Founded in 1970 by two University of Texas students, the store later became Grok, an alternative bookstore. BookPeople, still locally

i One of our favorite Austin picture books in recent years is *Wildly Austin: Austin's Landmark Art,* by Vikki Loving. It features more than 30 photographs and stories of many of the zaniest landmark sculptures around town. It's a fun tour guide and it makes a great gift or memento.

owned and operated, has grown to encompass a huge selection of books in all genres and is especially known for an excellent selection of books on alternative healing, computers, and cooking. The store features a wonderful children's section and great newsstand as well as books on tape, gift items, and computer software for children and adults. BookPeople's contributions to the Austin literary scene through the years have been enormous. This store goes out of its way to sell books written by local authors, even going so far as to buy books that are self-published. The store features a section of books about Texas and another dedicated to Texas authors. Book-People sponsors regular book discussion groups and hosts three weekly story times for children, including one for preschoolers. Check out the store's monthly calendar for upcoming events.

BOOKSTOP

4001 North Lamar Boulevard

(512) 452-9541

www.barnesandnoble.com

Started by Austin entrepreneur Gary Hoover, this discount bookstore chain scored an immediate hit with the Austin book-buying public, which delighted in the store's huge selection—and special prices. Owned since 1989 by Barnes & Noble Booksellers, Bookstop continues its discount tradition. Hoover's idea was for regular customers to buy a membership card, which then afforded them discounts on *New York Times* best-sellers, magazines, and other purchases. The idea has been adopted by major booksellers like Barnes & Noble. Other Bookstop stores have assumed the B&N name, but this popular store retains the Austin homegrown name.

BOOK WOMAN
5501 North Lamar Boulevard, Suite A–105
(512) 472-2785
www.ebookwoman.com
This Austin original, the only feminist bookstore in Texas, celebrated its 33rd anniversary in 2008. Book Woman specializes in new books by and about girls and women, but that tells only part of the story. Since 1975 this shop has been a showcase for women writers and musicians. Book Woman, owned by Austinite Susan Post, sponsors a monthly book club for women and hosts readings and book signings by local and national writers. The regular music series held on the third Friday of each month features women singers and songwriters. In addition to its great fiction section, the shop stocks an impressive collection of books on such subjects as self-help, women's health and psychology, girls and teens, memoirs, biographies, spirituality, and feminism. It has a wonderful section dedicated to Latina and Chicana books and another section of lesbian fiction and nonfiction works. There's also a small used-book section. Book Woman also has a great selection of T-shirts that laud women artists and feminist politics. The community bulletin board, which displays information on events and services of interest to women, is a popular feature of this store. Book Woman is part of the feminist bookstores network and can do special orders from that catalog.

FUNNY PAPERS
2021 Guadalupe Street
(512) 478-9718
www.funnypapers.com
This is one of Austin's one-stop shops for fans of comic books, role-playing games, collectible card games, collectible figurines, and more. Funny Papers sells comic book–related collectibles and many types of players' handbooks that go along with role-playing games. This unique store, which opened in Dobie Mall near the UT campus in 1990, receives about 100 new comic book titles each week and also stocks a wide selection of back issues and trade paperbacks. Funny Papers

i For offbeat encounters with Austin's literary scene, don't miss the annual O. Henry Pun-Off in May at the O. Henry Museum (see our chapter on Annual Events), or check newspaper listings for local Poetry Slam events.

has an assortment of collectible card games as well as Magic cards and all the supplies needed for card collectors. Regular comic book subscribers receive a discount.

HART OF AUSTIN ANTIQUARIAN BOOKS
1009 West Sixth Street
(512) 477-7755
Locally owned and operated since 1992, this large antiquarian bookstore is tucked away inside the delightful Whit Hanks Antiques complex. Owner Pat Hart offers several thousand used and rare books in all genres. The store also buys book and offers appraisals.

UNIVERSITY CO-OP BOOKSTORE
2246 Guadalupe Street
(512) 476-7211, (800) 255-1896
www.universitycoop.com
Founded in 1896, the University Co-op is owned by the students, faculty, and staff of the University of Texas at Austin. The bookstore offers UT and Austin Community College textbooks as well as books for UT Extension classes, correspondence courses, and informal classes. This is also a great place to shop for UT apparel, gifts, and souvenirs as well as greeting cards, art, and school supplies. The store has been on The Drag right across the street from the UT campus since 1919. The Co-op East Bookstore at 2902 Medical Arts Street also has some souvenirs but mainly carries textbooks for the UT Law School, the nursing program, and other graduate programs. The co-op has expanded recently to include two other locations on Guadalupe Street: the Annex and the Co-op for Women. There also are locations at 605 West 13th Street and 2237 East Riverside Drive.

South Central

RESISTENCIA BOOK STORE
1801–A South First Street
(512) 416-8885
www.resistenciabooks.com

Founded by the late Austin poet Raul Salinas, Resistencia adds an important dimension to the Austin literary scene. This specialty store, established in Austin in the early 1980s and located in South Central Austin since 1992, is well known for promoting the literary arts through its sponsorship of regular poetry readings, book signings, and book readings by local and national authors. The store specializes in Native American, Chicano, Latino, African-American, and feminist literature, poetry, and history. Resistencia also features CDs and tapes by local and international musicians in its specialty areas. The store offers literary magazines, T-shirts, and posters and features a community bulletin board announcing literary events. On the first and third Friday of each month, Resistencia hosts "Cafe Libero," a poetry reading and open-mic event for poets to try out their stuff. This is one store that Austin relies on for more than books.

WHOLE LIFE BOOKS
1006 South Lamar Boulevard
(512) 443-6794
www.wholelifebooks.org

This nonprofit bookstore, music store, and gift shop specializes in books on alternative health, metaphysics, spirituality, meditation, health, and New Age topics. Whole Life Books, which opened in 1983, is the only store of its kind in Austin that does not exist for commercial purposes. Austinite Ted Lanier, former UT graduate student in psychology and the former owner of a "hippie bicycle shop," started the operation as a reading room so that people could investigate for themselves the possible approaches to discovering nonmaterial spiritual reality. His patrons, however, wanted to buy the books they discovered in the reading room—and a business was born. The store now stocks about 50,000 titles as well as a wide assortment of CDs. Candles, wind chimes, incense, and jewelry can also be found at Whole Life Books. One nice thing about this store is it hours. It's open Monday through Saturday from 11:00 a.m. to 10:00 p.m., and Sunday noon to 7:00 p.m.

North

B. DALTON BOOKSELLER
Highland Mall, 6001 Airport Boulevard
(512) 452-5739

This national chain of mall bookstores now owned by Barnes & Noble has been serving Austin for nearly three decades. The store stocks a full range of hardbacks, paperbacks, children's books, and books on CD as well as national and local magazines. The store also sponsors occasional book signings and book readings.

SUE'S BOOK EXCHANGE
1205 Round Rock Avenue, Round Rock
(512) 244-9193

This Round Rock store features new and used books of all kinds. And Sue's accepts trade-ins for discounts on books—a very popular aspect of this bookstore. About half the Austin store is dedicated to romance books and includes both best-sellers and series romances. Romance fans will also find the trade magazine *Romantic Times*. The store also stocks a number of fiction and nonfiction books of all types. Sue's offers up to a 20 percent discount on new books and sells used paperbacks for half the cover price. With the trade-in of a comparable book, clients can buy used paperbacks for a quarter of the cover price.

BORROW THE BOOK

As centers of learning and for community outreach, Austin's public libraries are among our greatest public assets. Despite the bookstore boom of the 1990s, which brought hundreds of thousands of books to our community, more and more citizens are turning to the public libraries for their reading material. Of course there's no place like the library for doing research, getting on the Internet free of charge, or checking out that vintage recording. Those attractions, and the surge in Austin's population in recent years, have put a

i The Austin Public Library operates a Youth Services Hotline at (512) 974-7302 that provides information about kid-oriented activities at city libraries, including author visits, story times, musical events, and more. Also learn about the library's Wired for Youth programs, which give young people access to computer technology, at www.wiredforyouth.com.

strain on our already limited library resources.

Authorities say the materials collection at the current Central Library is about a third the size it should be to meet Austin's needs. Despite limited resources, however, the library system has won a number of awards for its efforts to make reading and research materials available to everyone, to increase literacy in the city of Austin, and to provide after-school tutoring. Our library was named Library of the Year in 1993 by *Library Journal* and Gale Research for its innovative and creative approach to programming in the face of funding shortages. Although Austin has outgrown its existing Central Library, voters approved a major bond issue in late 2006, and the projected opening date for a brand new downtown facility is 2012.

The Austin public library system is made up of 22 facilities that include the John Henry Faulk Central Library, the Austin History Center, and 20 branch libraries located all over the city.. Austin's strong neighborhood associations have convinced the City of Austin to construct more and more branch libraries, and these same groups have successfully thwarted attempts to close smaller branches. If anything, Austin's branch libraries are getting bigger and better, what with major renovation, expansion, or rebuilding projects taking place throughout the system for many years now. Austin's branch library system provides easy access to books and to the Internet for citizens all over the city. Some branches are within a mile or two of each other. The hub of the interconnected system continues to be the Central Library, however, which is more than 10 times the size of some of our branches. While branch libraries do not always have the book you want,

the library system allows for books to be sent from the Central Library or another branch, usually within a couple of days. The Central Library is open seven days a week, as are three main libraries around the city: Carver, Little Walnut Creek, and Manchaca Road. The other branches are open daily except Sunday.

Central

AUSTIN HISTORY CENTER
810 Guadalupe Street
(512) 974-7480
This building, which served as Austin's city library for nearly half a century, is now home to one of the leading local history collections in the state. The History Center houses more than one million items documenting the history of Austin to the present day. It's closed Thursday and Friday. (See our Attractions chapter for more about this wonderful facility.)

JOHN HENRY FAULK CENTRAL LIBRARY
800 Guadalupe Street
(512) 974-7400
Named for revered Austinite John Henry Faulk, Austin's Central Library has more than 360,000 books, manuscripts, periodicals, artistic prints, and recordings. It also features 26 computers that connect to the Internet as well as wireless Internet connections for those who wish to connect to the Web using their own computers. The library is open Monday through Thursday from 10:00 a.m. to 9:00 p.m., Friday and Saturday from 10:00 a.m. to 6:00 p.m., and Sunday noon to 6:00 p.m.

There is also one branch library in Central Austin:

YARBOROUGH BRANCH
2200 Hancock Drive
(512) 454-7208

South Central

TWIN OAKS BRANCH
2301 South Congress Avenue, #7
(512) 442-4664

This facility is being rebuilt and is scheduled to open in August 2009.

North

LITTLE WALNUT CREEK BRANCH
835 West Rundberg Lane
(512) 836-8975

NORTH VILLAGE BRANCH
2139 West Anderson Lane
(512) 458-2239
This facility is being rebuilt and is scheduled to open in late January 2009.

South

MANCHACA ROAD BRANCH
5500 Manchaca Road
(512) 447-6651

PLEASANT HILL BRANCH
211 East William Cannon Drive
(512) 974-3940

East

CARVER BRANCH
1161 Angelina Street
(512) 974-1010

CEPEDA BRANCH
651 North Pleasant Valley Road
(512) 974-7372

OAK SPRINGS BRANCH
3101 Oak Springs Drive
(512) 926-4453

TERRAZAS BRANCH
1105 East Cesar Chavez Street
(512) 974-3625-

West

HOWSON BRANCH
2500 Exposition Boulevard
(512) 472-3584

Northwest

MILWOOD BRANCH
12500 Amherst Drive
(512) 339-2355

OLD QUARRY BRANCH
7051 Village Center Drive
(512) 345-4435

SPICEWOOD SPRINGS BRANCH
8637 Spicewood Springs Road
(512) 258-9070

Northeast

SAINT JOHN BRANCH
7500 Blessing Avenue
(512) 974-7570

UNIVERSITY HILLS BRANCH
4721 Loyola Lane
(512) 929-0551

WINDSOR PARK BRANCH
5833 Westminster Drive
(512) 928-0333

Southeast

RUIZ BRANCH
1600 Grove Boulevard
(512) 974-7500

SOUTHEAST AUSTIN COMMUNITY BRANCH
5803 Nuckols Crossing Road
(512) 462-1452

Southwest

HAMPTON BRANCH AT OAK HILL
5125 Convict Hill Road
(512) 892-6680

University of Texas Libraries

It pays to have one of the largest universities in the country right in your own backyard, especially when that university has a great library system—the fifth-largest academic library in North America to be exact. The UT library system comprises 17 facilities, including 14 general libraries—all but the Marine Science Library located in Austin and most open to the public. Visitors who wish to use these UT libraries may acquire a Courtesy Borrower Card, available for a $100 annual fee, or apply for a free TexShare card from the Austin Public Library. Information is available at the Courtesy Borrower Desk at the main UT library, the Perry-Castañeda Library (512-495-4305). Brochures describing the libraries, their locations, and hours of operation, which vary, can also be obtained at the Borrower Desk. For general information call (512) 495-4350. On-site use of the other three system libraries—the Center for American History, the Harry Ransom Humanities Research Center, and the Tarlton Law Library—is free.

We've provided information about the main libraries here. For information about all UT libraries and their locations, visit the library system's Web site at www.lib.utexas.edu. Vehicular access to the main campus is restricted during normal school hours, so if you'd like to visit one of the UT libraries, it's best to park in one of the lots or parking garages located off campus nearby.

PERRY-CASTAÑEDA LIBRARY
21st and Speedway Streets
(512) 495-4250
www.lib.utexas.edu/pcl/
The main library of the UT system contains about three million volumes in all subject fields. The PCL, as it is known, emphasizes the humanities, the social sciences, business, and education. Subject strengths are American and British history,

> **i** If you have a TexShare card from the public library in Austin, you can borrow materials from the University of Texas, Austin Community College, and public libraries outside the city without having to pay a membership fee. Ask at your local library for details.

the South, 20th-century American literature, and modern German literature. The PCL also houses the Map Collection, the East Asian Program, South Asian Program, and the Middle Eastern Program. U.S. government and United Nations documents can also be found here, along with other collections. Most of the books available for loan are found on levels 3 to 6.

THE NETTIE LEE BENSON LATIN AMERICAN COLLECTION
Sid Richardson Hall, Manor Road
Between Red River Street and East Campus Drive
(512) 495-4520
www.lib.utexas.edu/benson/
Adjacent to the LBJ Library on campus, the Nettie Lee Benson Latin American Collection is an internationally renowned collection of books and many more materials on subjects relating to Latin America and writings by Latin Americans. The collection includes the Mexican American Library Program, which collects materials relating to all aspects of Spanish-speaking people in the United States, especially Mexican Americans.

FINE ARTS LIBRARY
Doty Fine Arts Building, Third Floor
Near 23rd and Trinity Streets
(512) 495-4481
www.lib.utexas.edu/fal/
The library includes materials on art, the performing arts, and music, including plenty about Austin's modern music scene. The art collection emphasizes 19th- and 20th-century art of the Americas but includes materials on all art movements and schools, the philosophy of art, art education, and aesthetics. The music collection provides support for teaching and research in applied music, music education, musicology, and more. The performing arts collection is designed to support studies in drama history, performance, play production, playwriting, drama education, and dance. The library also houses the Historic Music Recordings Collection, with facilities to play selections.

Community Libraries

CEDAR PARK PUBLIC LIBRARY

550 Discovery Boulevard, Cedar Park

(512) 401-5600-

www.cedarparktx.us/cp/li.aspx

Opened in 1981, the Cedar Park Public Library now holds more than 70,000 book titles as well as videos, books on tape, music CDs, and more than 100 magazine and newspaper titles. The library also has Internet-connected computers for public use. The library is free for Cedar Park residents. Others may obtain a card for $20 for six months or $35 per year. The library is open Monday through Thursday from 9:00 a.m. to 9:00 p.m., Friday and Saturday from 9:00 a.m. to 5:00 p.m., and Sunday 1:00 to 6:00 p.m.

LAKE TRAVIS COMMUNITY LIBRARY

2300 Loman's Spur, Suite 100

(512) 263-2885

www.laketravislibrary.org

This library serves Lake Travis community residents as well as all those summer visitors who flock to the lake. In addition to the fiction and nonfiction sections, the library features a good-size children's section, large print books, newspapers and magazines, audio and video cassettes, as well as Internet computers for public use. This library also features an ongoing bag-of-books sale to raise funds. Volunteers who staff this library in summer say this program is especially popular with out-of-town visitors. The library is open Monday and Tuesday from 10:00 a.m. to 7:00 p.m., Wednesday through Friday from 10:00 a.m. to 6:00 p.m., Saturday from 10:00 a.m. to 4:00 p.m., and Sunday from 1:00 p.m. to 4:00 p.m.

PFLUGERVILLE COMMUNITY LIBRARY

102 Tenth Street, Pflugerville

(512) 251-9185

www.cityofpflugerville.com/library

Once housed in an old home in what was euphemistically called "downtown" Pflugerville, the library, like other city services, found itself overwhelmed by the growth of the once-quiet little town northwest of Austin. A bond program raised the funds for the new facility, which is located between the local high school and a middle school. There are now 38,500 volumes on the shelves, eight computers plus three "kid-friendly" computer stations, a reference library, and a children's library, appropriate for a community where many of the residents are young families. There is no fee to belong to the library. Open Monday through Thursday 10:00 a.m. to 9:00 p.m., Friday 10:00 a.m. to 6:00 p.m., Saturday from 10:00 a.m. to 4:00 p.m., and Sunday from 1:00 p.m. to 6:00 p.m.

ROBERT G. AND HELEN GRIFFITH ROUND ROCK PUBLIC LIBRARY

216 East Main Street, Round Rock

(512) 218-7000

www.roundrocktexas.gov/library

The city's library, located in the heart of Round Rock's historic district, has expanded from 11,000 square feet to 43,000 square feet and has been renamed in honor of library patrons Robert G. and Helen Griffith. The library now boasts 153,000 items, including books, videos, CDs, and books on CD. There are 23 computer stations, including seven filtered computers for young patrons to use to access the Internet. There is no fee for residents of Round Rock; patrons from outside the city limits pay $25 per year for an individual library card, $40 for a family. The library is open Monday through Thursday 9:00 a.m. to 9:00 p.m., Friday and Saturday 9:00 a.m. to 6:00 p.m., and Sunday 1:00 to 6:00 p.m.

WRITERS' ORGANIZATIONS

Writers, like other addicts, need support and there's no better comfort to be found than at the meetings of the groups listed here. We have yet to hear of one that has cured writing fever, however.

TEXAS INSTITUTE OF LETTERS

www.texasinstituteofletters.org

This honorary organization, established in 1936, recognizes practicing writers who have demonstrated substantial literary achievement, as well as others who have had a positive influence on the literary arts. Members, who are invited to join, must have a substantial connection to Texas. Most important for nonmembers, the TIL, as it is known, determines the winners of about $20,000 in annual writing prizes that are backed by foundations or individuals. The prizes include the prestigious $6,000 Jesse Jones Award for the best fiction book and the $5,000 Carr P. Collins Award for the best nonfiction book. Other awards are given for poetry, journalism, short stories, children's books, and book design. Additionally, the TIL and the University of Texas determine two annual winners of the Paisano Fellowship, which gives writers a six-month residence at J. Frank Dobie's Paisano ranch and a large stipend. The goals of the TIL are to stimulate interest in Texas letters, recognize distinctive achievement in the field, and promote fellowship among those interested in the literary and cultural development of the state.

WRITERS' LEAGUE OF TEXAS
611 South Congress Avenue, Suite 130
(512) 499-8914
www.writersleague.org
Established in 1981, the Writers' League of Texas has grown from a group of writers gathered in an Austin backyard to include more than 1,500 members, more than half living outside Central Texas. Formerly called the Austin Writers' League,

the name was changed to reflect the membership base as well as the many programs the league offers to writers throughout the state. This fine organization, the largest in Texas, is highly involved in developing the Austin literary scene and providing support for its members. League members host many informal classes, workshops, and retreats for writers of many genres. The league also honors members with a number of annual awards and cash prizes. The Violet Crown Awards are given in three categories: fiction, nonfiction, and literary nonfiction. The Teddy Book Award goes to a writer of children's books. There's also a Manuscript Contest, Memoir Contest, and Storytelling Contest that recognize high writing achievement in those areas. Additionally, the league awards thousands of dollars each year in writing fellowships.

The nonprofit organization maintains a library and resource center that contains more than 1,500 volumes and includes books written by members that can be checked out. The league's monthly newsletter, *Scribe*, provides a wealth of information for writers and book lovers. General meetings, open to the public, are held the third Thursday of each month and feature a speaker or panel of experts on topics of interest to writers. The league also has information about local writers' groups for specific genres. Regular membership is $50 a year.

PARKS AND RECREATION

N o one who has stood on the edge of a Hill Country pasture in springtime could deny the beauty of Central Texas, but even long after the riot of colorful wildflowers is gone there is much to admire in the landscape of the Hill Country. Familiarity breeds admiration and learning about the particulars makes both residents and visitors appreciate the whole. Central Texas is not only home to some of the world's intriguing and delicate fauna and flora but is also a land where residents enjoy a generally benign climate. This is a place where Christmas Day may be celebrated with a walk in the sun along Lady Bird Lake or a swim in Barton Springs Pool. Life, for much of the year, is lived outdoors in Austin. Though Austin's nightlife and music scenes are touted, it is also the city's fondness for outdoor activities and an abundance of parks, greenbelts, and preserves that give Austin a reputation as a livable city. Pockets of greenery are fiercely defended against the pressures of urban sprawl. The Highland Lakes, which bring nature into the heart of the city via Lady Bird Lake, serve as a natural lifeline between the Hill Country and the city dweller. The city also rises to the modern challenge to provide its citizens with something to do on the weekends other than mow the lawn. There are 5K runs, 10K runs, marathons, bicycle races, kite-flying contests, and rugby games. There are rocks to be climbed and Frisbees to be thrown. This chapter offers a look at area parks and gives an overview of the many recreational activities popular in Central Texas. It is divided into three general sections: Parks, Recreation, and Watersports.

PARKS

State Parks

There are at least two dozen state parks within an easy two-hour drive of Austin under the management of the Texas Parks & Wildlife Department (800-792-1112, www.tpwd.state.tx.us). This is a first-class Web site with downloadable maps and PDF files that detail the state's parks, wildlife management areas (WMAs), and areas of interest, including biking, camping, driving tours, equestrian activities, fishing, hunting, and wildlife viewing. Visitors can make reservations online or by e-mail, plus fax and telephone numbers for campsites and cabins are listed.

Among the 41 historical sites are several national landmarks, including the Admiral Nimitz Museum and Historical Center in Fredericksburg and Lyndon Johnson State Park in Stonewall, both to the west of Austin and easily accessible (see our Day Trips chapter).

Other state parks in Central Texas offer visitors an opportunity to experience Texas natural history. Most offer camping, water sports, nature trails for hiking, walking, or mountain biking, plus picnic facilities and perhaps equestrian trails.

Admission to most state parks is between $1 and $5 per person. There is a 12-month pass, the Texas State Parks Pass, which sells for $60 for each family vehicle and allows unlimited visits to state parks and historic sites. Pass holders also qualify for a 50 percent camper's discount (some restrictions apply on popular holidays), a 10 percent discount at state park stores and a reduced subscription rate to *Texas Parks and Wildlife* magazine. The state also offers the Texas Parklands Passport, also called the Bluebonnet Pass, which offers discounted admission to parks and historic sites for seniors, veterans and disabled visitors.

Most state parks have camping facilities. Advance reservations are advised. Most parks are open for day visitors from 8:00 a.m. to 10:00 p.m., but call ahead for hours of operation, particularly

i The best time to call the state parks reservation number (512-389-8900) is midweek (Wednesday and Thursday), when call volumes are lighter. Monday and Tuesday and the week before major holidays are the busiest times. Before you go, visit the park you have chosen online at www .twpd.state.tx.us to download a detailed map in PDF format.

on holidays. Parks that have certain natural attractions, greenbelts, nature trails, or swimming holes may have special hours and blackout dates.

BASTROP STATE PARK
Highway 21,
1.5 miles east of Bastrop
(512) 321-2101
This 3,503-acre park 32 miles east of Austin is popular, perhaps because its landscape is so different from the surrounding countryside. The park is home to the "Lost Pines," a forest of pine trees (Texans call them "piney woods") that would seem to be more at home in East Texas. During the Depression, the Civilian Conservation Corps built several log cabins at the park, which are now popular for family getaways. There are 12 cabins accommodating from two to eight persons. Reservations and a deposit are required. All cabins have bathrooms, kitchen facilities, air-conditioning, and wood-burning fireplaces. Prices range from $65 to $110. For reservations call (512) 389-8900. No pets are allowed except for those aiding the physically challenged. The park also has camping facilities, a swimming pool open in the summertime, fishing on a 10-acre lake, hiking, golfing on a nine-hole course, and hiking trails. Park rangers offer guided nature tours, popular from January to March during the breeding season of the endangered Houston toad. Scenic Park Road 1 connects with Buescher State Park, 15 miles east.

BUESCHER STATE PARK
F.M. 153 off Highway 71, Smithville
(512) 237-2241
This 1,016-acre park, pronounced "Bisher" State Park, is a favorite spot for area fishermen. A 30-acre lake is stocked with trout, bass, and other fish. There are campsites, screened shelters, and picnic areas. Unlike nearby Bastrop State Park, oak trees and Blackland prairie dominate the landscape here. Popular activities at the park include biking, hiking, swimming, and boating.

COLORADO BEND STATE PARK
F.M. 580, west of Lampasas near Bend
(915) 628-3240
This 5,328-acre park offers primitive camping, hiking, fishing, swimming, mountain biking, birding, cave tours, and nature walks to the beautiful 60-foot-high Gorman Falls, particularly popular with bird-watchers.

ENCHANTED ROCK STATE NATURAL AREA
Rural R 965, north of Fredericksburg
(830) 685-3636
The major feature of this 1,643-acre park is Enchanted Rock, a 640-acre granite outcropping, a vast stone dome that rises above the Hill Country landscape, similar to its geological cousins Uluru (Ayers Rock) in Australia and Stone Mountain in Georgia. Hikers who are in good form can hike to the top (it's easier than Uluru) to enjoy an unparalleled view of Texas. See the Fredericksburg section of our Day Trips chapter to learn more about the Native American origins of the "enchanted" part of the name. It is the "rock" part of the name that beckons the more down-to-earth types who are interested in rock climbing. In addition, there is camping, both tent and primitive; hiking; nature trails; and picnicking. Given its spectacular views and easy access from major population centers, the park reaches its visitor and parking limits early on weekends. Get an early start.

INKS LAKE STATE PARK
Highway 29 on Park Road 4, near Burnet
(512) 793-2223
This 1,201-acre Highland Lakes park 9 miles west of Burnet offers camping, mini-cabin facilities, recreational vehicle hookups, backpacking, hiking, golfing, boating, canoeing (canoes and paddleboats

for rent), water-skiing, scuba diving, and fishing. It is a favorite for boaters and anglers. The park offers nature trail walks and canoe tours in spring and fall. There is a sunset bat watch, and a grocery store is on-site. A nine-hole golf course is operated by Highland Lakes Golf Club (512-793-2859), and the daily fee is $10 or less, depending on the day and time.

McKINNEY FALLS STATE PARK
5808 McKinney Falls Parkway, Austin
(512) 243-1643
Located just 13 miles southeast of downtown Austin off U.S. Highway 183, this 744-acre park encompasses the lands around the confluence of Williamson and Onion Creeks. The park is named for Texas pioneer Thomas McKinney, whose ruined home still stands near the confluence of the creeks. He was one of Stephen F. Austin's original 300 colonists. The pool under the falls is a popular swimming spot, but it is limited to those days when park rangers deem it safe. On some days the bacteria count may be high due to pollution from upstream, nonpoint sources, so call ahead if you want to swim. The park also has hiking, biking, fishing, picnicking, several screened shelters with bunk beds (no mattresses), and camping facilities. There are nature study areas, a dirt-bike trail, and group picnic facilities.

PEDERNALES FALLS STATE PARK
F.M. 3232, near Johnson City
(830) 868-7304
The spectacular falls are the highlight of this 5,211-acre park, formerly part of the Circle Bar Ranch. The falls are even more spectacular after a sudden spring rain, when the Pedernales River exhibits all the dangerous beauty of a Hill Country river in flash flood. With its vast tumble of boul-

ders and Hill Country plants and trees, the falls are beautiful, even on dry summer days. The park has fishing and nature study facilities, picnic sites, a hike and bike trail, swimming in the lower 3 miles of the river, and an equestrian trail.

The Lake Parks
The image of Texas as a land of deserts and vast, treeless wilderness owes a lot more to Hollywood than reality, but in Central Texas, where lakes abound, most of them are not nature's work but owe their existence to people with gigantic imaginations who roamed the Texas political landscape in the first half of the 20th century.

Between 1843 and 1938 several devastating floods washed through the Hill Country along the path of the Colorado River. The horror of flooding was contrasted with the blight of drought. Texas leaders looked to the hills and dreamed of damming the river to stem the floods, defeat droughts, and harness the river's power to electrify the wilderness. With the help of engineers and laborers, they succeeded, and now the Highland Lakes climb 646 feet, stretch more than 150 miles long, and encompass 56,000 acres of water and 700 miles of shoreline, making up the greatest concentration of fresh water in Texas.

In 1934 the Texas Legislature created the Lower Colorado River Authority (LCRA), a state agency that administers the chain of artificial lakes and dams created to harness the Colorado River. Today it is one of the most influential state agencies in terms of environmental policy.

Hydroelectricity may be a very small part of the function of the Highland Lakes these days, but the lakes are still a vital force in the battle against floods and are a critical water supply for some communities in the area. They also provide water for rice farms downstream, a major Texas agricultural crop, and are a huge draw to tourists.

There are three major links in the lake chain in the area around and in Austin. The most urban link in the chain is Lady Bird Lake, 5 miles long from Tom Miller Dam in West Austin, near Redbud Trail, to Longhorn Dam in East Austin near Pleasant Valley Road.

i The Texas state parks system celebrated 75 years of stewardship in 1998. One handy guide to the state system is a map of Texas showing all the state park sites. Call (800) 786-8644. The cost is $3.11 to cover postage and handling.

Lake Austin is 20 miles long, stretching from Mansfield Dam on Lake Travis to Tom Miller Dam. Lake Austin is the oldest of the Highland Lakes.

Lake Travis is 64 miles long and was formed by the construction of the 266-foot-high, 7,089-foot-long Mansfield Dam, which was built in 1941 and named for Texas Congressman J. J. Mansfield. Not only is the lake an increasingly popular recreational spot but its shores also are prized real estate.

With the booming growth, the Highland Lakes are just one focus of the debate among environmentalists and the development community. On the recreation front, there are increasing concerns about crowding on the lakes as personal watercraft, yachts, swimmers, scuba divers, water-skiers, windsurfers, and cigarette boats vie for space. Personal watercraft have been banned from the lakes during the three major summer holiday weekends: Memorial Day, Fourth of July, and Labor Day. Following verbal clashes and some accidents between motorized crafts and sailing vessels, there has been some discussion by the LCRA of "zoning" the lakes for various activities.

To the west of Lake Travis is Lake Buchanan, pronounced Buck-ANN-un by the locals (see our Texas Pronunciation guide in the Overview chapter). Created by the Buchanan Dam, the 31-mile-long lake is the highest in the chain and covers the largest surface area, although Lake Travis contains more water. The LCRA has set aside 16,000 acres for parks and reserves along the Colorado River—developed parks, environmental learning centers, recreational areas, and river access sites. The LCRA's Web site is a valuable resource and offers detailed guides and downloadable maps, which can be very handy when trying to locate remote areas and boating docks. These parks typically feature little artificial landscaping—hills have not been leveled, and large green spaces are usually Hill Country meadows rather than planted lawns. Picnic and campsites are shaded by oak trees and trails are lined with juniper trees.

For more information about all the Highland Lakes, see our Day Trips chapter.

THE LOWER COLORADO RIVER AUTHORITY (LCRA)
(512) 473-3200,
(800) 776-5272, ext. 3366
www.lcra.org
In addition to a wealth of information on water safety and quality, weather forecasts, and utility, energy, and conservation issues, the agency also offers newcomers and visitors a park visitor's package.

LCRA Primitive Areas

The river authority operates a primitive recreation system along the lake system. These campsites are in natural areas where the typical rugged Hill Country landscape has been minimally disrupted. Most of the sites are in out-of-the-way places, and visitors will need detailed directions or a good area map to find them. Call (512) 473-3200, ext. 4083 for directions and information. Some charge a nominal use fee, around $5.00.

GLOSTER BEND PRIMITIVE AREA
Lake Travis, off F.M. 1431
Approximately 6 miles west of Lago Vista, this lakeside site has camping and picnic facilities. Day use only is recommended, but the boat ramp is available 24 hours a day.

GRELLE PRIMITIVE AREA
Lake Travis,
off Highway 71 near Spicewood
Grelle is a 400-acre park with woods, trails, camping, and access to the lake. The hiking trails are challenging. Next door is the popular Krause Springs swimming hole (see the Swimming section of this chapter). Overnight camping is allowed.

MULESHOE BEND PRIMITIVE AREA
Lake Travis,
off Highway 71 past Bee Cave
A 900-acre facility with trails, lake access, camping, and picnicking near the Ridge Harbor subdivision on Burnet County Road 414. This wilderness area is very popular with mountain bikers.

THE NARROWS PRIMITIVE AREA
Lake Travis,
off Highway 71 near Spicewood
This rugged site has a boat ramp, picnic areas, and primitive campsites. This is one of the smallest parks in the system, encompassing only 250 acres. It is used primarily as a boat ramp facility (the only public ramp on the upper south side of the lake), since there are neither potable water nor restrooms on-site.

SHAFFER BEND PRIMITIVE AREA
Lake Travis, off F.M. 1431
A 535-acre park with camping, picnicking, and lake access about 17 miles west of Lago Vista. The terrain is rough and suitable to trucks and four-wheel-drive vehicles.

TURKEY BEND (EAST) PRIMITIVE AREA
Lake Travis, off F.M. 1431
A 400-acre park with great views of the lake and surrounding countryside. The park has camping and picnic facilities and lake access. The park is about 10 miles west of Lago Vista.

Travis County Parks

Travis County, home to the capital city, operates 20 parks under its Travis Natural Resources department (TNR), many of them on the banks of Lake Travis and Lake Austin, and other small, urban parks in suburban areas beyond municipal limits. Generally the Lake Austin parks charge no fees, but those on Lake Travis may have vehicle charges and individual entrance fees. You can reach Travis County Parks Visitor Information and Reservations at (512) 473-9437, www.co.travis .tx.us/tnr/parks.

ARKANSAS BEND
Sylvester Ford Road, off R.M. 1431
This 195-acre LCRA park on the shores of Lake Travis is not as primitive as some other LCRA parks and is operated by the county. The Hill Country landscape is a backdrop to picnic areas equipped with barbecue pits. The park has hiking trails, swimming facilities, a boat ramp, and campsites.

BEN FISHER
F.M. 973 off U.S. Highway 290 East
This park is in eastern Travis County and has picnic and barbecue facilities, hiking trails, and sports courts. The landscape east of Austin is called Blackland Prairie, and much of it is fertile farmland. Parks in this area have undulating hills, meadows covered with wildflowers both spring and fall, and large pecan trees. Pecan harvesting is a favorite fall pastime.

BOB WENTZ PARK AT WINDY POINT
On Lake Travis,
access from Comanche Trail
This 21-acre LCRA lakeside park has barbecue pits, picnic sites, hiking trails, playgrounds, a swimming area, showers, and a boat ramp for sailboats. It is popular among windsurfers and scuba divers.

CYPRESS CREEK
On Lake Travis,
Anderson Mill Road at R.M. 2769
The landscape in this LCRA park on Lake Travis retains its wild character, but there have been some additions, including barbecue pits and picnic areas. The park offers access to the lake for swimming and primitive camping.

DINK PEARSON PARK
On Lake Travis near Lago Vista
Dink Pearson is a lakeside park with picnic and barbecue facilities, access to the lake for swimmers, and a boat ramp.

FRITZ HUGHES
Lake Austin, near Mansfield Dam
This is a good spot for family picnics but is not suitable for swimming. The park has picnic and barbecue facilities plus a playscape.

HIPPIE HOLLOW
Lake Travis,
near Comanche Trail off R.M. 620
This is an Austin landmark. (Its formal name is MacGregor Park, but nobody calls it that.) This clothing-optional LCRA park is open to individu-

als age 18 and older and is particularly popular among gay sun seekers. You can swim in the lake, sunbathe on the park's beach and rocks, or hike on the trails (shoes recommended). Admission fees. Day use only.

LITTLE WEBBERVILLE
On the Colorado River near F.M. 969
This Colorado River park 20 miles east of Austin, near the community of Webberville, has both picnic and barbecue areas. The park also has play-scapes and a boat ramp. It is a popular entry point on the river for kayakers and canoeists.

MANSFIELD DAM
Rural Route 620
On Lake Travis, just west of Mansfield Dam, this county park offers picnic and barbecue facilities, swimming, a boat ramp, and overnight camping facilities. It is a short walk to the dam, which offers a close-up view of engineering feats in Central Texas. The dam is also a favorite place for hawks and other birds of prey to ride the thermal wind currents.

PACE BEND
2701 F.M. 2322,
4.6 miles off Highway 71
(512) 264-1482
This 1,000-acre-plus park (sometimes called Paleface Park) has equestrian facilities, trails, campsites, picnic and barbecue facilities, plus swimming in the lake.

RICHARD MOYA
Burleson Road, 2.6 miles from the intersection of US 183 and Burleson Road in eastern Travis County
This park is a favorite spot for family picnics, particularly on Mexican-American holidays and birthdays, when the smell of fajitas cooking and the sound of piñatas being whacked fill the air. Portions of the original downtown Congress Avenue Bridge, c. 1884, now span Onion Creek in the park. This day-use park is only twenty minutes from downtown and is a popular location for baseball and softball tournaments.

SANDY CREEK
On Lake Travis off Lime Creek Road
Another rugged hillside park on Lake Travis, this park has hiking trails, offers access to the lake for swimmers and boaters, and has primitive camping facilities.

SELMA HUGHES PARK
Lake Austin off Quinlan Park Road
This is the site of a popular boat ramp on busy Lake Austin. There are picnic facilities with barbecue pits.

TOM HUGHES PARK
Lake Travis on Tom Hughes Park Road, off Rural Route 620
Swimming is the popular attraction in this small county park, which is open in daylight hours only.

WEBBERVILLE
F.M. 969
This large and popular county park is 3 miles east of Webberville in eastern Travis County on the banks of the Colorado River at the Travis/Bastrop County line. There are picnic and barbecue facilities, hiking trails, playscapes, a boat ramp, ballfields, sports courts, and equestrian facilities. The large picnic pavilions can be reserved for gatherings by calling the Travis County parks reservations number at (512) 473-9437.

WINDMILL RUN
US 290 West and Highway 71
Windmill Run is a neighborhood park near the Windmill Run subdivision in Oak Hill, with picnic and barbecue facilities, hiking trails, and ballfields.

Austin City Parks

The city boasts nearly 208 city parks, 25 hike and bike trails and greenbelts, plus 11 nature preserves (see our Nature Preserves section in this chapter), all encompassing more than 16,076 acres of urban retreats.

Given the large number of city parks, we have picked out several of particularly interesting character and detailed them below. The city offers detailed information about all city parks in several brochures, available on request from the Parks and Recreation Department (PARD) and on the city's Web site, both listed below. The parks are listed alphabetically, ending with Zilker Park, the city's major park in the heart of the city and home to Barton Springs Pool, an icon that is perhaps the ultimate natural symbol of Austin life (see our Close-up in this chapter).

Austin has more than 20 miles of surfaced scenic paths in the city's natural greenbelts, plus untold miles of wooded tracks. Bicycles are permitted, but motorized vehicles are not. Pets on leashes are allowed. The city's parks department has been building separate trails for hikers, joggers, walkers, and bikers, but there are several popular trails, notably around Lady Bird Lake, where the groups must coexist. Rock climbers on the Barton Creek greenbelt also have been at odds with mountain bikers. Peaceful coexistence is encouraged.

The curfew on all trails is 10:00 p.m. They reopen at 5:00 a.m. To access a greenbelt, head for the address listed with each park. Parking is limited at some greenbelt locations, and space is at a premium on weekends, particularly when the weather sends much of Austin outdoors.

AUSTIN PARKS AND RECREATION DEPARTMENT (PARD)
200 South Lamar Boulevard
(512) 974-6700
www.ci.austin.tx.us/parks
Residents and visitors alike should stop by the main office of PARD and pick up a wealth of material on Austin recreational activities and facilities. The city's Web site also has extensive information and downloadable maps.

BARTON CREEK GREENBELT
3755-B Loop 360 (Capital of Texas Highway)
This is one of the city's most popular, and most crowded, greenbelts. The trail follows Barton Creek through the canyon that cuts across Southwest Austin. Barton Creek has six official access points, called trailheads, and one very popular

unofficial entry. The designated trailheads are at Zilker Park, west of Barton Springs Pool; the intersection of Spyglass Drive and Barton Skyway; 2010 Homedale Drive, behind Barton Hills Elementary School; the Gus Fruh Access at 2642 Barton Hills Drive; the Brodie Oaks office complex, off Loop 360 west of Lamar Boulevard; and the intersection of Camp Craft Road and Scottish Woods Trail. The Gus Fruh and Brodie Oaks access points are wheelchair accessible. The unofficial access point is easily spotted on a balmy weekend afternoon. The shoulder of the access road leading from Loop 360 (Capital of Texas Highway) onto MoPac south is lined with cars. Just a few yards away, a wide stretch of the creek creates a swimming hole that attracts large crowds on warm days.

BOGGY CREEK GREENBELT
1114 Nile Street
This East Austin trail runs 3 miles from Rosewood Park to Zaragosa Park. Trails in the eastern half of the city, roughly defined as east of Interstate 35, have different flora from those in the western half. The eastern half of the city is built over Blackland Prairie—rich, black soil, compared with the rocky, limestone landscape in the west. The creeks and greenbelts in the east are often shaded by pecan trees and have woodland plants along their banks.

BULL CREEK PARK AND GREENBELT
7806 North Capital of Texas Highway
This is a popular spot, particularly in spring when the rains fill the creek, attracting swimmers and waders. In summer the creek is usually very low or dry. There are picnic facilities and hike and bike trails. The 120-acre greenbelt attracts hikers and mountain bikers. The park is off Loop 360 (Capital of Texas Highway) and south of Spicewood Springs Road.

EMMA LONG METROPOLITAN PARK (CITY PARK)
1600 City Park Road
(512) 346-1831
This large 1,147-acre park with 3 miles of Lake

Austin shoreline has boat ramps and picnic sites. It is the oldest city park and is more traditional, showing the human hand in its landscaping and facilities.

JOHNSON CREEK GREENBELT
2100 Enfield Road

A mile-long urban trail runs from Lady Bird Lake to Enfield Road, paralleling MoPac. Trail users can access the greenbelt from the Austin High School parking lot.

LADY BIRD LAKE METROPOLITAN PARK

Along the Colorado River from Tom Miller Dam in West Austin to the US 183 bridge in East Austin, this park graces the Colorado River as it winds through the heart of downtown Austin. No other Austin city park, with the exception of nearby Zilker Park, so captures the Austin spirit. From dawn to beyond dusk, the Hike and Bike Trail is filled with joggers, walkers, bicyclists, nature lovers, and dog walkers enjoying the riverside pathways. Spring is an especially beautiful time for a stroll along Lady Bird Lake (formerly Town Lake) as flowering cherry trees, some of them gifts from Japan, bloom alongside native redbud trees. The parks department also periodically offers the public the opportunity to plant a tree in the park and dedicate it to a loved one.

The southern shore of Lady Bird Lake, just west of South First Street, is known as Auditorium Shores and is the site for outdoor concerts, including the annual July Fourth Pops Concert (see our Annual Events and Festivals chapter) and various festivals.

In quieter moments, wildlife, particularly turtles, ducks, and swans, can be seen swimming and feeding along the banks of Lady Bird Lake. Only nonmotorized craft are allowed on this stretch of the lake, such as canoes, kayaks, and paddleboats, which can be rented in nearby Zilker Park (see our Boating section in this chapter). The Austin Rowing Club has its clubhouse on the north shore near the Four Seasons Hotel, and lone rowers can be seen sculling in the early morning through the light fog rising from the lake. No swimming is allowed in the lake.

On the northern bank of Lady Bird Lake and east of I-35 is Fiesta Gardens, a popular community concert and celebration spot. Two notable Mexican-American holidays are celebrated here, Cinco de Mayo and Diez y Seis de Septiembre (see our Annual Events and Festivals chapter).

LAKE WALTER E. LONG METROPOLITAN PARK
6614 Blue Bluff Road
(512) 926-5230

In Northeast Travis County, this 1,300-acre lake is well known for its fishing and water activities. There are campsites, hike and bike trails, plus park roads that are popular with bicyclists and runners.

MARY MOORE SEARIGHT METROPOLITAN PARK
907 Slaughter Lane

The 344 acres contain an 18-hole disc (Frisbee) golf course, a 2-mile hike and bike trail, a 2½-mile equestrian trail, and a fishing pier over Slaughter Creek. There are basketball, tennis, and volleyball courts, plus baseball and soccer facilities, barbecue pits, and a picnic gazebo for large parties.

MOUNT BONNELL PARK
3800 Mount Bonnell Road, off Scenic Road

For 140 years tourists have been coming to Mount Bonnell and climbing the 99 steps (785 feet) to the peak for a great view of the city. No mountain, but a sturdy climb. Several local legends purport to account for the mount's name. One claims it is named in honor of George W. Bonnell, a New Yorker who came to Texas to fight in the War of Independence against Mexico. He fought the Native Americans and was a sometime newspaper editor. He met his death on December 26, 1842, when he was captured and shot by Mexican troops. Others say the name is a corruption of the names Beau and Nell, two lovers who were married on the peak minutes before a Native American attack. After their first kiss, they leapt to their death. Other legends are variations on this theme, involving Native American princesses and beautiful Spanish senoritas, all forced to take a dive. On a serious note, visitors should be careful at the peak, since an unfortunate few have slipped and fallen down the hillside. Mount Bonnell is the stuff of romance and a popular spot for young couples who want to watch the stars come out over Austin—a particularly romantic spot for University of Texas students, who can get a clear view of the UT Tower, aglow in orange light when the university's athletic teams win. It is also a great spot for a picnic with a view. The park opens at 5:00 a.m. for sunrise viewing and closes at 10:00 p.m.

PEASE PARK
1100 Kingsbury Street

Along Shoal Creek between 12th and 24th Streets, this Central Austin park is popular among lunchtime picnickers and joggers. The land was donated by former Governor Elisha M. Pease, hence the name. During the Civil War General George Armstrong Custer camped on this site and buried 35 of his men here. There are legends of buried treasure here involving a lost cache of money supposedly stolen by a paymaster in the Mexican Army. Digging, of course, is forbidden. These days it is known for happier occasions, including Eeyore's Birthday, an annual free-spirit celebration—sort of a mini Woodstock-meets-Mardi Gras event—that includes both the whimsical and the outrageous (see our Annual Events and Festivals chapter).

SHOAL CREEK HIKE AND BIKE TRAIL
Lamar Boulevard, from 38th Street to Lady Bird Lake

i Woolridge Square is a little gem of a park in downtown Austin—squeezed between the Travis County Courthouse and the Austin History Center, 9th and 10th Streets on Guadalupe. The park's Victorian bandstand sits in the center of a natural amphitheater and has been the site of weddings, political rallies, small concerts, and one murder (according to legend).

This wide, 3-mile-long greenbelt along the urban pathway of Shoal Creek, roughly paralleling Lamar Boulevard, winds through the heart of Central Austin and can be accessed at many points along the way. Like other urban Austin creekbeds, Shoal Creek has an early-warning system in place to alert residents and emergency workers of flash floods. These high-tech devices can be seen near bridges and low crossings on city creeks. They look like large traffic signal boxes and are equipped with solar panels and antennas.

SLAUGHTER CREEK METROPOLITAN PARK
507 West Slaughter Lane

Adjacent to the Lady Bird Johnson Wildflower Center in Southwest Austin, this park is at its best in spring, when the Hill Country wildflowers bloom. The prime attraction is the 3-mile velo-way, which attracts bicyclists and in-line skaters. The park also has a nature trail, picnic facilities, playground, soccer fields, volleyball, and basketball courts.

WALLER CREEK GREENBELT
703 East 15th Street

Stretching from 15th Street to Lady Bird Lake, the Waller Street greenbelt is a mixture of urban greenbelt and urban blight. The northern stretch is quite pleasant. City voters recently approved a bond election to improve the southern end of the trail.

WATERLOO PARK
403 East 15th Street

This central city park lies just east of the capitol and is a quiet retreat in the heart of the city. It is also a popular spot for several gatherings during the year (see our Annual Events chapter).

ZILKER BOTANICAL GARDENS
2200 Barton Springs Road
(512) 477-8672

Just north of Zilker Park (see the subsequent listing) and part of the Zilker experience, the gardens are also home to the Austin Garden Center. There are several gardens within the grounds, including a rose garden (a popular site for weddings), a cactus and succulent garden, fragrance and butterfly gardens, and woodland trails. There is also a xeriscape garden, where native plants are shown off to great advantage. Admission to the garden center is free except for certain weekends (see our Annual Events and Festivals chapter) when garden shows are held on the grounds.

The most beautiful part of the garden center is the Taniguchi Oriental Garden, created by the late Isamu Taniguchi, a native of Osaka, Japan. Taniguchi moved to the United States as a young man, worked as a farmer in California and the Rio Grande Valley, and then retired to Austin in the 1960s. Taniguchi, whose son was a noted Austin architect, spent 18 months creating the garden along the hillside site. He worked for free with his own plans and no oversight or interference from city planners. His creation is a symbol of peace, just as Taniguchi wished. He died in 1992 at age 94. The best time to visit the garden is on a quiet weekday, since it is a popular attraction on weekends.

ZILKER PARK
2100 Barton Springs Road
(512) 472-4914

This 400-acre downtown park became a city park in 1917 when Colonel A. J. Zilker donated the land to the city. The most famous and revered attraction in the park is Barton Springs Pool (see our Close-up in this chapter), but it is also a place of pilgrimage for other reasons. At Christmas one of the city's so-called moonlight towers (see our Attractions chapter) serves as the trunk of the Zilker Park Christmas Tree (see our Annual Events and Festivals chapter), visible from miles around. The "tree" is created by Christmas lights strung in maypole fashion from the tower to the ground. Tradition calls for children to stand inside the tree and spin around until the lights are blurred and the kids are dizzy. Small children are spun around in a grown-up's arms, making both kid and grown-up enjoy the dizzy spell.

Zilker is home to a miniature train, playscape, picnic grounds, a "folf" course, rugby and soccer fields, and a canoe and kayak concession (see our

Boating section in this chapter). A grass-covered hillside serves as a natural amphitheater for summer musicals (see our Annual Events and Festivals and The Arts chapters for more information). The park is open daily from 6:00 a.m. to 10:00 p.m. and is free. There is a small parking fee on weekends when the park is very busy.

Round Rock

The city's parks department operates about 30 parks in the city limits, most of them small neighborhood parks that serve as play areas for neighborhood children and places to relax, perhaps jog, play tennis, or shoot a few baskets for teens and adults. Parks with hike and bike trails, swimming pools, or tennis courts are listed in the Recreation and Watersports sections of this chapter under those specific categories. The city's three major parks are described below.

ROUND ROCK PARKS AND RECREATION DEPARTMENT (PARD)
301 Bagdad Street, Suite. 250
(512) 218-5540
www.roundrocktexas.gov

The city's PARD publishes a program brochure and guides to the city's parks that are available on request. In addition to athletic programs, PARD offers country and ballroom dance classes, Jazzercise, programs for toddlers and seniors, preschool and youth programs, plus Cool Kids Camp, an afternoon recreation program for elementary kids.

LAKE CREEK PARK
800 Deerfoot Drive

Home to the municipal swimming pool, this 23-acre park also has a playscape area and a pavilion, which can be used for community events.

OLD SETTLERS PARK
3300 East Palm Valley Boulevard

This large, 570-acre park has soccer and softball fields, hike and bike trails, playscapes, a folf course, and picnic areas. It is also the site of Old Settler Week (see our Annual Events and Festivals ℹ️ Wildlife, notably birds and deer, are abundant around Austin, but so are insects and snakes, so pack insect bite treatment and wear sturdy boots when hiking on nature trails. Snakes play a vital role in the ecosystem and are usually shy creatures that avoid human contact. Most snakebites can be treated successfully if aid is sought quickly. If you plan to be outdoors frequently in Austin, familiarize yourself with the snakes found in the Texas countryside.

chapter), when Williamson County celebrates its pioneer roots with music, food, and carnivals, plus a reenactment of the shootout between outlaw Sam Bass and the law.

ROUND ROCK MEMORIAL PARK
600 Lee Street
The city's other major park is home to the Legion Field softball complex. In addition to the softball fields, the park features a hike and bike trail, playscape, and picnic areas.

Pflugerville
PFLUGERVILLE PARKS AND RECREATION DEPARTMENT (PARD)
400 Immanuel Road
(512) 251-5082
www.cityofpflugerville.com
The city of Pflugerville boasts that the city's parks are a "hometown kind of place, where you and your friends and coworkers can celebrate without a lot of big-city fuss and bother." The city's PARD has developed a master plan aimed at helping the city make the transition from a tiny, rural town to a growing suburban community. The city's parks are connected by an integrated trail system, connecting many of the neighborhoods in the city. PARD also provides swimming, gymnastics, aerobics, soccer, volleyball, and basketball programs. There is the Summer Pfun Camp and PARD-organized events such as 5K Pfun Run and Walk, Pfall Pfest, and the Pumpkin Pflyer bicycle tour.

GILLELAND CREEK PARK
700 Railroad Avenue
The anchor for the city's integrated trail system, Gilleland also boasts a community swimming pool, picnic areas, and volleyball courts.

PFLUGER PARK
515 City Park Road
This large city park is home to soccer and softball fields, sand volleyball facilities, and basketball courts. The park's picnic area has barbecue pits and a playscape, and there are several nature trails running through the park.

Cedar Park
CEDAR PARK PARKS AND RECREATION (PARD)
715 Discovery Boulevard, Ste. 111
(512)- 401-5500
www.ci.cedar-park.tx.us
As Cedar Park grows, the number of city parks increases as the city attempts to keep up with the area's booming population. There are 11 neighborhood parks, most of them with picnic facilities and playscapes. Many also have tennis and basketball courts, and some have sand volleyball facilities. The city's parks and recreation department offers information on all city parks and recreation programs. A proposed parks master plan is posted on the city's Web site.

ELIZABETH M. MILBURN COMMUNITY PARK
1901 Sun Chase Boulevard
This is the crown jewel of the Cedar Park park system. At the heart of the park facility is an eight-lane, 25-meter lap pool, with an adjoining recreational pool with a water playscape and a 117-foot water slide. The new park has several soccer fields, plus a large pavilion with picnic tables for reunions and special events. There are also three large gazebos in the park. Scattered throughout the park are picnic tables and barbecue grills, plus tennis courts, a basketball court, a sand volleyball area, playscapes, and a hiking path circling the park.

Austin's Beloved Waterin' Hole

Barton Springs Pool has been called the soul of Austin, and that is really not an exaggeration. This treasured, spring-fed pool stands both as a symbol of Austin's lifestyle, a measure of its commitment to the environment, a political rallying point, and even a place of spiritual and psychological renewal. This 1,000-by-125-foot unchlorinated swimming pool, fed by natural spring waters, stands at the heart of Zilker Park and serves as a touchstone for all that was and is Austin.

The pool is fed by spring waters that bubble up at the rate of 35 million gallons a day through the 354-square-mile Edwards Aquifer, an underground limestone formation that stretches from downtown Austin west through the Hill Country. Rains that fall on the hills west of the city filter down through the limestone and emerge at temperatures between 67 and 70 degrees Fahrenheit.

For hundreds of years, before European explorers ventured onto Texas soil, Native Americans gathered around the springs, according to archaeologists. Later, Spanish explorers paused to rest here. In the 19th century among the settlers who came to Austin was William "Uncle Billy" Barton. He set up a homestead near the springs in 1837 and eventually gave his name to both the springs and the creek. City records show that on December 16, 1839, Barton agreed to "give possession of the stream of water from my big spring" for a sawmill. For the next 70 years, the land passed through several owners, eventually being sold to Colonel A. J. Zilker in 1907.

During those years, more and more Austinites began to use the pool. At first just male residents swam there, but in 1880 a ladies swimming club was formed. While some ethnic minorities swam there in the latter years of the 19th century, by the 1950s the overwhelming majority of African Americans and Mexican Americans did not swim at the pool. That changed with the Civil Rights Movement, and now the city pool is a gathering place for all Austinites and visitors.

In 1917 Zilker deeded the springs and the surrounding 35 acres to the city, and Zilker and his gift are now memorialized in the name of the city park where Barton Springs Pool stands. An additional 330 acres were added to the park in 1932 when Zilker gave the land to Austin schools, which then, as part of the agreement, sold the acreage to the city for $200,000. The bathhouse that now stands at the entrance to the pool was built in 1947. For a time there was talk of making the springs a city municipal water source, but contamination from fecal coliform was found in some samples and that idea was discouraged. Contamination is still occasionally found in samples, particularly after heavy rains.

The concrete sides of the pool, which mark the current length and breadth, were built in 1929. The pool was by then an Austin fixture. Former Texas Congressman Bob Eckhardt, a well-known environmentalist, swam there as a five-year-old boy in 1918. His father, a doctor, would come home from the office and pack the family off for an afternoon swim.

Eckhardt's support for Barton Springs had special meaning in 1998; that was the year he and many others engaged in the Great Salamander Debate.

Since the late '60s, Austin environmentalists, let's dub them the "Greens," have faced off against the "Developers" (see our History and Politics and Perspectives chapters). Barton Springs became a symbol of that fight when the Save Our Springs Alliance (SOS) was formed in the 1980s to do battle against development over the Edwards Aquifer, the watershed that feeds the springs. Armed with federal conservation legislation, laws such as the Endangered Species Act (ESA), the Greens lobbied federal regulators and took cases to federal court to fight development.

The Greens saw an opportunity to add another arrow to their quiver in the fight when it was discovered in the early 1990s that the tiny salamander that had been swimming underfoot for years was in fact a rare species found only in the waters of the spring and pool. The inch-long salamander has a pale yellow-cream body, flat snout, long limbs, four toes on its front legs, five on the back, and a short, finned tail marked with a narrow orange-yellow stripe and is unique to the springs. In the early '90s the Greens pressed for the salamander to be listed as an endangered species.

In 1994 the Clinton Administration announced that the salamander would be listed. Then Interior Secretary Bruce Babbitt changed his mind about listing it. Federal and state officials announced a water conservation agreement instead that was touted as a way to protect the aquifer, the springs, and the pool waters. The Greens were very critical of the compromise and went to federal court to force the listing of the salamander. U.S. District Judge Lucius Bunton of Midland, Texas, agreed with them and ordered the administration to review its decision. In spring 1997 the Barton Springs salamander was placed on the ESA list.

In January 1998 an attorney who had, in the past, represented landowners and developers, filed suit on behalf of two scientists against the city, charging that the City of Austin was violating the ESA by killing salamanders during routine pool cleanings, when the water level was lowered and the pool bottom scrubbed. The Greens said the lawsuit was aimed at shutting down the pool and claimed that mean-spirited developers were behind the action, but the attorney and his clients insisted they only wanted the city to follow the federal laws and protect the salamander. The local media was filled with supporters and detractors, and some observers said the Greens had been hoisted on their own petard.

The Greens cried foul and questioned the motives of the plaintiffs. After a great deal of legal maneuvering, U.S. District Judge Sam Sparks of Austin refused to stop the pool cleanings, issuing his ruling in a poem:

> Barton Springs is a true Austin shrine,
>
> A hundred years of swimming sublime.
>
> Now the plaintiffs say swimmers must go
>
> 'Cause of "stress" to critters,
>
> 50 or so.
>
> They want no cleaning 'cause of these bottom feeders,
>
> Saying it's the law from our
>
> Congressional leaders.
>
> But really nothing has changed in all these years
>
> Despite federal laws and these plaintiff's fears
>
> Both salamander and swimmer enjoy the springs that are cool.
>
> And cleaning is necessary for both species in the pool.
>
> The City is doing its best with full federal support,
>
> So no temporary injunction shall issue from this Court.
>
> Therefore, today, Austin's citizens get away with a rhyme;
>
> But, the truth is they might not be so lucky the next time.
>
> The Endangered Species Act in its extreme makes no sense.
>
> Only Congress can change it to make this problem past tense.

continued

The city set about developing new cleaning methods with the blessings of the federal regula-tors. During all this legal wrangling, Barton Springs Pool had been shut down for extended periods for time-consuming cleanings that involved sending biologists to search the pool bot-tom and scoop up any stranded salamanders and return them to the spring while city workers carefully scrubbed the pool bottom. By late summer 1998, the city was holding hearings hoping to devise an acceptable cleaning program, plus make some modifications to the pool so that salamanders and swimmers could peacefully coexist.

The salamanders have now become a popular feature on T-shirts and in paintings that decorate the pool bathhouse. They also have joined the pantheon of Austin-area endangered species, which includes golden-cheeked warblers and black-capped vireos, both songbirds.

Few swimmers claim to have actually seen a Barton Springs salamander, but for those who regard Barton Springs Pool as more than a place to swim, the knowledge that the little crea-tures also enjoy the waters just adds to the beauty and wonder of the place.

For information about pool hours and admission, see our listing under Swimming in this chapter.

NATURE PRESERVES

Within the Austin city limits are several nature preserves that offer visitors a glimpse of the wild beauty of both the Hill Country and the prairie to the east of Austin. In addition to city preserves, Travis County and the LCRA are also guardians to several nature areas.

Austin Nature Preserves

The city operates 11 nature preserves and a nature center. There are strict rules of behavior within the preserves, designed to protect the ecosystems. Access to some of the preserves is by prearrangement only, and group tours are available. For information call (512) 327-7723. The preserves' pages on the city's PARD Web site offer downloadable maps and brochures.

Motorized vehicles, bicycles, pets, firearms, and hunting are prohibited in the nature pre-serves. Visitors are required to keep noise levels low and stay on trails and may not remove plants or animals from the area.

AUSTIN NATURE AND SCIENCE CENTER
303 Nature Center Drive
(512) 327-8181
The center's central exhibit is "The Nature of Aus-tin," illustrating four habitats found in the area—ponds, grasslands, woodlands, and a Hill Country cave. The live exhibits feature Texas wildlife—animals that have been rescued and because of permanent injury or extensive human contact cannot be returned to their habitat. The center also has a discovery lab and is surrounded by 80 acres of nature preserve with 2 miles of trails. The "dino pit" exhibit features fossils and bones found at a Congress Avenue building site.

BARROW PRESERVE
7715 Long Point Drive
This 10-acre preserve is on the upper reaches of Bull Creek in Northwest Austin. It has spring-fed canyons and hiking trails.

BLUNN CREEK PRESERVE
1200 St. Edwards Drive
This preserve near the St. Edward's University campus in South Austin boasts two lookout points that offer great views of the city, one of which is atop a 100-million-year-old coral reef. This area of Central Texas once was an inland sea. Within its confines can be seen the remains of volcanic ash deposits spewed out by a dozen active volcanoes that rumbled in this area some 80 million years ago.

COLORADO RIVER PRESERVE
US 183 at the Montopolis Bridge
5827 Levander Loop
On the banks of the Colorado River, west of the Montopolis Bridge in East Austin, this 43-acre preserve offers views of river life, including turtles, herons, and cranes along the sandy banks of the river.

INDIANGRASS WILDLIFE SANCTUARY
Walter E. Long Metropolitan Park
6614 Blue Bluff Road,
off US 290 East
The sanctuary is in a 200-acre section of Walter E. Long Park in Northeast Austin and is designed to protect Blackland Prairie habitat, notably a variety of prairie grasses. The wetlands along Lake Long are home to an abundance of wildlife. Access is limited to guided tours only.

KARST PRESERVE
3900 Deer Lane
This interesting preserve is off Brodie Lane in Southwest Austin and adjacent to the Maple Run subdivision. Karst is the name scientists have given to the type of honeycombed limestone formations found in several areas of the world, including the Texas Hill Country. This eight-acre site, and this part of Austin, is riddled with sinkholes, caves, and honeycombed limestone.

MAYFIELD PRESERVE
3505 West 35th Street
This is a small city enclave that reflects 19th-century Austin. The 22-acre preserve in Central Austin embraces five lily ponds, palm trees,

i Austin Metropolitan Trails Council is a coalition of public, private, and non-profit organizations, neighborhood associations, and individuals working to "promote a comprehensive system of greenways and trails in the greater Austin area." You can contact the council through the Austin Parks and Recreation Department at (512) 499-6700.

woodlands, and several old cottages, including one from the late 19th century. A cross between a preserve and a park, this quiet spot is very popular with children, who can approach the peacocks (watch out, they have tempers!) and tame deer for close-up viewing. The preserve is next door to Austin Museum of Art Laguna Gloria (see The Arts chapter) in West Austin.

ONION CREEK PRESERVE
7001 Onion Creek Road
This secluded preserve is north of Highway 71 along Onion Creek and is open to guided tours by reservation only.

VIREO PRESERVE
1107 North Capital of Texas Highway
East of the 100 and 200 blocks of Loop 360 North (Capital of Texas Highway), this rugged section of Hill Country is home to the rare black-capped vireo, one of several bird species threatened by development in Central Texas. The preserve is open for guided tours only.

ZILKER NATURE PRESERVE
This is a 60-acre preserve at the western end of the park (see the listing under Austin Parks in this chapter), which includes 2 miles of trails along cliff edges on the banks of Barton Creek.

Balcones Canyonlands
The Austin growth boom has led to a great loss of natural habitat, particularly west of Austin in the rugged Hill Country, a land whose outward appearance belies its sensitivity. Following a grand political tug-of-war between pro-development forces and environmentalists (see our Politics and Perspectives chapter), city leaders, environmentalists, developers, and concerned landowners sat down and forged an agreement for a unique preservation effort, dubbed the Balcones Canyonlands Conservation Plan (BCCP).

What has emerged is one of the most significant preservation efforts in Texas. The BCCP embraces more than 30,000 acres west of Austin, and more acreage is being sought to add to this

i Inside the City of Austin, dogs must be leashed, but even Fido can enjoy the city's famous free-spirit lifestyle in certain designated parks (www.ci.austin .tx.us/parks/dogparks). One of the most popular spots is in Zilker Park in an area bounded by Stratford Drive, Barton Springs Road, and Lou Neff Drive. For a complete list of places to let Fido feel the wind in his hair, free and unfettered, call the parks department at (512) 974-6700, or check the city's dog parks Web site www.ci.austin .tx.us/parks/dogparks.htm.

vast area just west of the city. Part of the BCCP is the Balcones Canyonlands National Wildlife Refuge, an area run by the U.S. Fish and Wildlife Service. The City of Austin, Travis County, the LCRA, and several private landowners also are part of the BCCP effort. The Austin BCCP office is located in Marble Falls, northwest of Austin, but this Austin area telephone number provides information on hours and programs, (512) 339-9432. All the agencies involved have information about the BCCP and maps to access points on their respective Web sites, but one way to get a wealth of information and find links to all the agencies and environmental groups involved in the effort is to visit www.friendsofbalcones.org.

BALCONES CANYONLANDS NATIONAL WILDLIFE REFUGE

The public areas of the refuge are located near the community of Lago Vista, northwest of Austin. The refuge gets its name from the Spanish explorers who, when they saw the terraced hills west of what is now Austin, dubbed the land "Balcones." From afar, the land looks dry and scrubby, but numerous creeks run through, over, and under the terrain, and wildflowers, grasses, trees, and plants abound. This is home to the endangered golden-cheeked warbler and black-capped vireo, two little birds whose songs can still be heard thanks to efforts like the BCCP.

The refuge has two public areas: Warbler

Vista Trail, just outside Lago Vista on F.M. 1431, and Doeskin Ranch, located on F.M. 1174. Warbler Vista has two trails through the limestone terraces—Cactus Rocks Trail is a 0.6-mile one-way trail and is an easy to moderate hike. This trail winds through golden-cheeked warbler habitat of juniper and hardwood trees. The warblers arrive from Mexico and Latin America in mid-March and leave in July. Pick up a guide pamphlet at the parking lot kiosk. Keep in mind this is a delicate ecosystem dedicated to the birds, so no pets or rowdy activity. The Vista Knoll Trail is 1.2 miles round-trip and is a moderate hike. This trail offers great views of Lake Travis and Lago Vista. The Shin Oak Observation Deck is set in the middle of black-capped vireo habitat. The deck is closed for a short period in spring just as the vireos arrive to minimize the disturbance to the birds. Check the refuge Web site for the specific dates the deck is closed each year. Once the birds settle into nesting activities, the observation deck is reopened to visitors. The refuge is open from sunrise to sunset, but some areas may be closed for public hunts or bird nesting activities.

The Texas Ornithological Society and the Travis Audubon Society conduct field trips to the refuge, and several annual events throughout the year offer information and tours. One of the most popular events is the Annual Texas Songbird Festival hosted by the Lago Vista community in late April or early May. Master naturalists lead area birding expeditions, some to the refuge and others to backyard habitats. There are workshops and seminars on bird photography, butterfly gardening, landscaping fort wildlife, etc. Local craftspeople also show their wares. Contact the Lago Vista Chamber of Commerce at (512) 267-7952, (888) 328-5246, or visit songbirdfestival .homestead.com/.

LCRA Preserves

The Lower Colorado River Authority (LCRA) operates two preserves near Austin—McKinney Roughs and Westcave Preserve, listed below—and Canyon of the Eagles, detailed in our Day Trips chapter.

McKINNEY ROUGHS PRESERVE
North Bastrop, Highway 71
(512) 303-5073,
(800) 776-5272; ext. 8021
www.lcra.org

Located a little more than 13 miles east of the Austin-Bergstrom International Airport on Highway 71, this 1,100-acre preserve includes rolling canyons, wildflower meadows, and meandering river bends illustrating four unique ecosystems. The preserve is open to canoeists, hikers, horseback riders, birders, and picnickers who simply want to enjoy the pastoral scenes. The Mark Rose Environmental Learning Center hosts educational programs and activities for students, teachers, and the general public. The center has a 128-room dormitory and is home to the Academy in the Roughs, an overnight environmental learning program for children. There is small entrance fee, reduced for seniors and children; horseback riders pay a larger fee and provide their own horses.

WESTCAVE PRESERVE
Hamilton Pool Road, R.M. 3238
(830) 825-3442
www.westcave.org

Not far from Hamilton Pool Preserve (see below) is an almost mystical place, a natural collapsed grotto that was formed 150,000 years ago, effectively creating a giant terrarium covered by towering cypress trees. The sheltered environment creates a unique ecosystem where orchids and other semitropical plants flourish. Temperature differences between the grotto floor and the surrounding countryside above can be as much as 25 degrees—a wonderful place for a summer escape. Westcave's 30 acres also are home to several endangered species, including the golden-cheeked warbler. The preserve is operated by the LCRA and the private Westcave Preservation Corporation and is open only on weekends or for special visits. Access is limited to guided tours at 10:00 a.m., noon, and 2:00 and 4:00 p.m. Tours also are limited to 30 persons at a time. In March 2003 a study center designed by well-known Texas architect Robert Jackson opened on the site, and this sensitively designed building now operates as a study and education center. There is a nominal entrance fee.

Travis County Preserves
HAMILTON POOL PRESERVE
Hamilton Pool Road, R.M. 3238
(512) 264-2740
www.co.travis.tx.us/tnr/parks

Hamilton Pool Preserve is part of the Balcones Canyonlands (see the listing above). At the heart of the preserve is the pool, a natural pool fed by a waterfall along Hamilton Creek, a branch of the Pedernales River. The waters spill out over limestone outcroppings and create a 50-foot waterfall into the box canyon. The flora of the canyon and the surrounding grasslands vary in color and texture with the seasons. In addition to endangered and rare birds, there are several rare plant species in the preserve. Because of the sensitive, fragile nature of the land, visitors are limited to 75 a day; and because of the beautiful swimming, the parking lot fills up fast. Call ahead, or perhaps plan a weekday visit. Visitors may picnic, hike, or engage in group nature walks and study groups. There is no overnight camping, and pets are not allowed. Guided tours are available every Sunday at 10:00 a.m. or by appointment. Sturdy shoes and lots of drinking water are recommended. During dry weather the waterfall may slow to a trickle, but the pool remains filled; however, the pool is closed to swimming when the bacteria count climbs. In heavy rains the park may be closed because of typical Hill Country flooding. The preserve has no concessions. Admission fee.

WILD BASIN WILDERNESS PRESERVE
805 North Capital of Texas Highway
(Capital of Texas Highway)
(512) 327-7622
www.wildbasin.org

The traffic whizzes by on Loop 360, but just a few steps off the roadway is a 227-acre wilderness literally within minutes of downtown Austin. Travis County operates this preserve, but it exists because of the efforts in the 1970s of seven extraordinary women who were dubbed the "Now or Never" group. Their goal was to establish the natural area as an outdoor lab for children's science education and teacher training, and the seven women took the task on as a Bicentennial Project. For more on how they won the day, visit www.wildbasin.org, the home page of the volunteers who still help maintain and fund the project. There are 2.5 miles of hiking trails that pass through woodland, grassland, and streamside habitats that are home to threatened and endangered species and hundreds of native plants, animals, and birds. Wild Basin's nature education programs are funded by special events, memberships, corporate donations, and grants. The entrance to Wild Basin is on the east side of Loop 360 at 805 North Capital of Texas Highway, 1.5 miles north of Bee Caves Road, or 3.25 miles south of the Loop 360 bridge over Lake Austin. The preserve is open from sunrise to sunset, and while there are no entrance fees, donations are accepted. There is a small gift shop at the site.

RECREATION OPPORTUNITIES

Looking to play rugby? Climb a rock wall? Join a soccer club? Find the best place to go in-line skating, or view the sunrise from a hot-air balloon? This Recreation section offers a play-by-play breakdown on sports activities in Austin. First, some general information:

AUSTIN PARKS AND RECREATION DEPARTMENT (PARD)
200 South Lamar Boulevard
(512) 974-6700
www.ci.austin.tx.us/parks
The City of Austin Parks and Recreation Department (PARD) operates 17 recreation centers throughout the city, which offer a wide variety of activities, day camps, youth programs, lessons in sports activities, and league supervision. PARD is a good place to begin when researching availability of facilities, lessons, and league activity.

CEDAR PARK PARKS AND RECREATION (PARD)
715 Discovery Boulevard, Suite. 111
(512)-401-5500
www.ci.cedar-park.tx.us
Cedar Park's parks and recreation department is developing a variety of programs to meet the town's growing population, including league sports, swimming, aerobics, and water safety classes.

PFLUGERVILLE PARKS AND RECREATION DEPARTMENT (PARD)
400 Immanuel Road
(512) 251-5082
www.cityofpflugerville.com
Pflugerville PARD offers swimming, gymnastics, aerobics, soccer, volleyball, and basketball programs. Since Pfun is part of the Pflugerville lifestyle, the PARD also organizes a Summer Pfun Camp and events such as 5K Pfun Run and Walk, Pfall Pfest, and the Pumpkin Pflyer bicycle tour.

ROUND ROCK PARKS AND RECREATION DEPARTMENT (PARD)
301 West Bagdad Street
(512) 218-5540
www.roundrocktexas.gov
The Round Rock PARD organizes several adult sports leagues, including flag football, basketball, and softball and offers a wide variety of adult programs—country dance, ballroom dance, and Jazzercise classes—for all age groups. Youth programs include gymnastics, karate, dance, and tennis classes. The Cool Kids Camp is an afternoon recreation program designed for elementary-age children. Program schedules and information are available on request.

UNIVERSITY OF TEXAS RECREATIONAL SPORTS OUTDOOR PROGRAM
(512) 471-3116
www.utrecsports.org
The university offers noncredit courses in outdoor sports, including canoeing, rock climbing,

windsurfing, cycling, hiking, fitness and personal training, massage, and health education. Classes are open to UT staff, students, faculty, and members of the community. They are very popular, so sign up early.

YMCA

There are six YMCA branches in the greater Austin area. A branch in Round Rock area and another in Cedar Park are both under the auspices of the Williamson County YMCA. As the area grows, additional facilities are planned.

METRO YMCA OFFICE
(512) 322-9622
www.austinymca.org
This office offers information on programs and facilities at all Y branches in the area. The Web site has detailed descriptions of each branch, plus downloadable maps and information on child care, summer camps, and special events.

EAST COMMUNITIES BRANCH
5315 Ed Bluestein Boulevard
(512) 933-9622

NORTH PARK FAMILY BRANCH
9616 North Lamar Boulevard, Suite 130
(512) 973-9622

NORTHWEST FAMILY BRANCH
5807 McNeil Drive
(512) 335-9622

PFLUGERVILLE CENTER
15803 Windermere Drive
(512) 928-9622

SOUTHWEST FAMILY BRANCH
6219 Oakclaire Drive
(512) 891-9622

TOWNLAKE BRANCH (DOWNTOWN)
100 West Cesar Chavez Boulevard
(512) 542-9622

YMCA OF GREATER WILLIAMSON COUNTY
812 North Mays Street
Round Rock
(512) 246-9622

200 Buttercup Creek Boulevard
Cedar Park
(512) 250-9622

204 East Little Elm Trail
Cedar Park
(512) 250-9622
www.ymcagwc.org
The Y is always a good place to seek out other athletes with similar interests. The downtown location is just north of the Lady Bird Lake Hike and Bike Trail, which makes it a popular fitness club for downtown workers. The Southwest location is in "downtown" Oak Hill in a former privately owned fitness club that was acquired by the Y. The clubs are popular and have up-to-date fitness equipment, whirlpools, saunas, swimming pools, steam rooms, gyms, indoor running tracks, etc. The Oak Hill branch has a rock-climbing wall and racquetball courts. The newest addition to the YMCA's facilities in Austin is in East Austin, an area that has lacked top flight recreational facilities. The new Y is built on 125 acres donated by IBM along Walnut Creek. Other corporate citizens came together to build a first-class facility with a fitness center, swimming pool with water slides, lap pool, and even a computer lab.

Bicycling

Bicycling has taken off in the Hill Country, where both road-racing and mountain-biking enthusiasts face some rugged challenges. One of Austin's most famous residents is international racing champion Lance Armstrong. (See the Close-up profile of Armstrong in our Spectator Sports chapter.)

The 3-mile Veloway in Slaughter Creek Metropolitan Park (see the Austin Parks section of this chapter) is a popular spot for cyclists. Other popular trails include Loop 360 west of the city and the Lady Bird Lake Hike and Bike Trail. Local mountain bikers also enjoy riding the trail in the Barton Creek Greenbelt. Check the Parks section of this chapter for other area venues for road and off-road cycling.

The Bull Creek Greenbelt in Northwest Austin (see our Parks listings above for more details on all these sites) has a hilly bike path in unspoiled, natural surroundings. The Shoal Creek Hike and Bike Trail wends through the center of the city in a more urban parklike setting, while the 2-mile trail in Southwest Austin at the Mary Moore Seabright Metropolitan Park flows through the rolling, wooded hills, typical of the natural landscape in this area.

Local cycle shops sell maps of the area showing popular trails. Among the most popular are Colorado Bend State Park (again, see our Parks listings above) and McKinney Falls State Park. The latter has a 3.5-mile trail characterized by woodlands and gently rolling hills. Since McKinney is just 13 miles southeast of Austin, this is easily accessible to local riders.

One popular road route among cyclists is Park Road 1C between Buescher and Bastrop State Parks, about a 40-minute drive east of Austin. This is a very challenging ride, as the 13 miles of paved road climbs through steep hills.

The emergence of cycling as a popular sport has brought road-racing events to Austin. Bicyclists are respected in Austin—the city even has a bicycle coordinator on its planning staff (see our Getting Here, Getting Around chapter).

AUSTIN CYCLING ASSOCIATION
(512) 282-7413
www.austincycling.org
The group publishes a monthly newsletter that previews upcoming events, describes the best places to test your skills, and keeps track of the bicycle scene, including recreational and transportation issues.

> **i** The LCRA's excellent Web site (www .lcra.org) offers several "adventures" pages, which give tips to mountain bikers and equestrians, among others. The site also has links to parks and preserves that are wheelchair friendly.

> **i** The 3-mile veloway in the Slaughter Creek Metropolitan Park was designed for cyclists, but in-line skaters also find this winding paved trail through the park a wonderful place to roll. No joggers are allowed on the veloway. The park is located at 4103 Slaughter Lane in Southwest Austin and is open seven days a week from sunrise to sunset.

AUSTIN FLYERS
www.austinflyers.com
This club touts itself as "everybody's cycling club," and its Web site offers extensive listings about area activities for cycling enthusiasts.

AUSTIN RIDGE RIDERS
www.austinridgeriders.com
Dedicated to the Austin mountain-biking community, the Ridge Riders organize fun rides and races and offer information on popular trails in Central Texas.

BICYCLE SPORT SHOP
5175 South Lamar Boulevard
(512) 477-3472

10947 Research Boulevard
(512) 345-7460
www.bicyclesportshop.com
Just west of Lamar Boulevard and Riverside Drive, this local shop offers sales, rentals, and information on the local scene. A second location is on Research Boulevard (US 183) in Northwest Austin.

MELLOW JOHNNY'S
400 Nueces Street
(512) 473-0222
www.mellowjohnnys.com
When famed cyclist and Austin resident Lance Armstrong announced his plans for Mellow Johnny's he told the *Austin American–Statesman* he was planning "the coolest bike shop in the world" and this downtown paean to all-things cycle-ly is just that. It is an homage, albeit a very practical one, to cycling. The shop sells the best bikes in

the world and not just the famed Trek brand Lance rode to glory, but all manner of machines suited to play and transportation. The shop also has a coffee bar where customers can view bike mechanics at work. There are showers and lockers for commuting cyclists—Lance is a big advocate of biking to work—and there are training facilities in the large store, which occupies an old warehouse space in downtown Austin. Biking memorabilia, including some of Lance's Tour de France mementos, decorate the walls—in a word, a mellow place indeed.

UNIVERSITY CYCLERY
2901 North Lamar Boulevard
(512) 474-6696
www.universitycycle.com
This University of Texas area store offers rentals, sales, repairs, and information on the Austin cycling scene.

Bird-watching

Texas is the center lane of the migratory pathway of many North American birds, making the state a popular spot for bird-watching. Local environmentalists are working hard to raise the consciousness of newcomers about endangered species in the area, and several nature preserves are dedicated to protecting these species. For more information see the Preserves section of this chapter.

TRAVIS COUNTY AUDUBON SOCIETY
3710 Cedar Street
(512)- 300-BIRD (2473)
www.travisaudubon.org
There are more than 2,500 members of this local chapter of the society, which meets every month and usually holds at least one field trip a month. From backyard birding to treks into the Hill Country in search of elusive and endangered species such as the golden-cheeked warbler, the society offers practical advice to both members and nonmembers who are eager to protect and conserve the ecosystems so vital to bird life in Central Texas. Every December the group holds a Christmas bird count, its contribution to the national count.

VANISHING TEXAS RIVER CRUISE
Lake Buchanan
(512) 756-6986, (800) 474-8374
www.vtrc.com
In addition to offering wildflower cruises in spring, this company also offers winter river cruises up the Colorado River Canyon to view the largest colony of American bald eagles in the state.

Bowling

Austin has hosted professional bowling tournaments, and most lanes offer facilities for disabled bowlers plus party planning for large groups. The latest craze to hit local lanes is Electric Bowling, known in other parts of the country as Extreme Bowling or Glow-in-the-Dark Bowling. By pumping up the music and bringing down the lights, the bowling facility owners hope to attract a younger crowd and boost interest in the sport.

Two area associations are a good place to obtain information about local bowling activity and league play: the Austin Bowling Association located at 8820 Business Park Drive (512-670-9315, www.austin.bowling.org), and the Austin Women's Bowling Association, located at 5700 Grover Avenue (512-453-8714).

HIGHLAND LANES
8909 Burnet Road
(512) 458-1215
www.highlandlanes.com
This North Austin bowling facility is home to Electric Bowling three times a week, on Friday and Saturday from 11:00 p.m. to 1:00 a.m. and Tuesday evening from 8:00 to 10:00 p.m. Highland Lanes also offers bumper bowling for kids, eliminating gutter balls and ensuring that kids hit at least some of the pins. There are leagues on-site for teens, women, men, and seniors. The lanes are open from 9:30 a.m. to midnight Sunday through Thursday and 9:30 a.m. to 1:00 a.m. Friday and Saturday.

SHOWPLACE LANES
9504 North I-35
(512) 977-0394
A large 52-lane facility in North Austin, Showplace is open 24 hours a day. There is a sports bar on-site, plus two video game rooms and a nursery. A dart league also holds its events here.

WESTGATE LANES
2701 William Cannon Drive
(512) 441-2695
www.westgatelanes.net
Home to several popular summer youth leagues, Westgate has 40 lanes and is located in South Austin. The bowling alley is open daily from 10:00 a.m. to midnight Sunday through Thursday and 10:00 a.m. to 2:00 a.m. on Friday and Saturday.

Camping

Camping is not just a recreational activity in Central Texas, it is a way of life for some residents who have chosen to make their homes in the area's private facilities. Perhaps the most famous "campsite" for motor homes is the Shady Grove RV Park smack in the middle of town in an old pecan grove and a few blocks from Zilker Park. Campsites catering to short-term visitors can be found along the Interstate 35 corridor and on the shores of the Highland Lakes.

The Parks section lists area parks with camping facilities, and we have included some of the most popular here in this section, along with privately operated facilities. The Lower Colorado River Authority operates several parks with primitive camping areas (see the LCRA Primitive Areas section). Two guides that are very useful for campers visiting Central Texas are *The Texas State Travel Guide*, published by the Texas Department of Transportation (800-452-9292), and the *Lower Colorado River Authority (LCRA) Visitors Package* (800-776-5272, ext. 4083, or 512-473-4083).

In addition to the Web sites for the state, county, city, and LCRA (see above), other good resources include:

AUSTIN CONVENTION & VISITORS BUREAU
301 Congress Avenue, Ste. 200
(512) 474-5171, (800) 926-2282
www.austintexas.org

TEXAS ASSOCIATION OF CAMPGROUND OWNERS
6900 Oak Leaf Drive, Orange
(512) 459-8226, (409) 886-4082
www.tacomembers.com

TEXAS PARKS & WILDLIFE DEPARTMENT
4200 Smith School Road
(512) 389-4800, (800) 792-1112
www.twpd.state.tx.us

TEXAS TRAVEL INFORMATION CENTER
Old General Land Office Building
Capitol Grounds
112 East 11th Street
(512) 463-8586, (800) 452-9292
www.traveltex.com

AUSTIN LONE STAR RV RESORT
7009 South I-35
(512) 444-6322
www.austinlonestar.com
There are 159 RV sites, eight cabins, and camping facilities at this South Austin campground. Campsites rent and cabins are available for under $50 a night. Access to the site is controlled, and there are facilities for handicapped visitors. The main lodge has a fireplace, a full kitchen, color

ℹ️ Many Texas landowners, farmers, and ranchers have turned to ecotourism to help them survive difficult financial times in rural America. Others simply want to share the wonders of Texas with visitors. The state agency charged with boosting Texas tourism, the Texas Department of Economic Development (TDED), has developed a Web site where visitors can find ecotourist opportunities, including birding, trail riding, wilderness camping, and fishing—check out traveltex.com.

television, jukebox, and swimming pool. There is a small grocery store and laundry facilities on-site. Telephone hookups, compatible with modems, and television hookups also are available.

AUSTIN RV PARK NORTH
4001 Prairie Lane
(512) 244-0610

The 25 spaces at this North Austin park, near the intersection of I-35 and F.M. 1325, may be rented on a daily basis for around $20 a night, a little more than $100 a week, and around $400 a month. The sites all have electricity, water, and sewage hookups.

ARMADILLO RV
4913 Hudson Bend Road
(512) 266-9012

This Lake Travis–area RV park has 38 large shaded lots, all with a view of Lake Travis, that rent for around $20 a day, or approximately $250 to $275 a month. Cable television and telephone hook-ups are extra. There is an on-site laundry facility, a grocery store nearby, and three marinas within a half mile of the facility. Children and pets are welcome.

BUESCHER STATE PARK
F.M. 153, off Highway 71, Smithville
(512) 237-2241

A popular spot for angler, Buescher (pronounced "Bisher") State Park has 34 campsites (20 for tents or pop-ups and 14 for RVs) and four screened shelters. Showers and restrooms are available for campers. Admission to the park is $3 and free for those 13 and younger. Tent campsites are $12 a night; RV sites with water and electricity are $15 a night.

EMMA LONG METROPOLITAN PARK (CITY PARK)
1600 City Park Road
(512) 346-1831

This large 1,147-acre Austin park with 3 miles of Lake Austin shoreline is a popular weekend camping spot (see the Austin City Parks section of this chapter). There are 20 sites with water

and electricity, plus 50 tent sites. Campers may stay for up to two weeks. The entry fee to the park is $3 during the week and $5 on weekends. Tent sites are $6 per night and $10 for sites with utilities. The campsites are on an alluvial plain, adjacent to Lake Austin with the hilly park in the background. This is a very popular site, so reservations should be made early.

ENCHANTED ROCK STATE NATURAL AREA
R.R. 965, north of Fredericksburg
(915) 247-3903

This popular and legendary state park, detailed above under State Parks, is 18 miles north of Fredericksburg (see our Day Trips chapter). Only walk-in campers and backpackers may pitch their tents in this carefully protected natural area. There are no facilities for RVs or pop-up campers. Campers must call the state's camping reservations number at (512) 389-8900. Walk-in campers pay the park admission fee of $6 for those 13 and older, plus $15 a day camping fee with a maximum of eight people at a walk-in site. Backpackers pay the entrance fee, plus $10 daily camping rate with a maximum of four people at each campsite.

HUDSON BEND RV PARK
5003 Hudson Bend Road
(512) 266-8300
www.hbrv.com

Sites are available at this Lake Travis–area facility by the day ($25), week ($85), or month ($280), and all are served with water, electricity, and free cable television. There are 29 pads at this shady site and also six storage sheds available for rent to extended-stay campers.

MCKINNEY FALLS STATE PARK
5808 McKinney Falls Parkway
(512) 243-1643

Its location, just 13 miles southeast of downtown Austin off US 183, ensures that this 640-acre state park is usually filled with campers on holidays and weekends. (See our State Parks section for a full description of the park.) There are 81 sites in the park for tents, pop-ups, or RVs, and these cost

$12 a night, including water and electricity. There are eight walk-in primitive sites for hikers, costing $12 a night. The park entrance fee is $4 per person, free for those 13 and younger. McKinney also rents three screened shelters for $30 a night. The two-room shelters are furnished with eight bunk beds, a cold-water sink, picnic table, and barbecue grill.

PACE BEND PARK
2701 F.M. 2322,
4.5 miles off Highway 71
(512) 264-1482
This 1,000-plus-acre Travis County park (sometimes called Paleface Park) is likely to be packed with campers on weekends and during summer holidays. The park, described in our Travis County Parks section above, has more than 400 sites for tents, pop-ups, and RVs. There are also primitive tent sites. Admission to the park is $8 per vehicle, $15 for overnight stays. Sites with water and electricity cost $20 a night. The park has a strict quiet time in effect from 10:00 p.m. to 7:00 a.m., and dogs can be allowed to run free if their owners are in control of them. Reservations are critical at this park, since it fills up very quickly on major holiday weekends.

RECREATION PLANTATION
County Road 198, Dripping Springs
(512) 894-0567
www.recreationplantation.com
If you're looking to camp with a crowd, then consider renting this self-described "event facility." For $750 a weekend, the minimum rate, you can rent this 40-acre campsite with its own creek frontage and swimming hole. The facility also has a two-bedroom cabin on the property and a stage. There are tent sites and RV hookups, also, making this a great place for family reunions and corporate getaways.

City Leagues
One of the best resources for information on local team sports is the city's parks and recreation department or PARD offices. See the full listing

i League officers change with the seasons, and with the advent of the Internet many city sports leagues are relying on their Web site to reach out to fellow sport fans—abandoning the answering machine in favor of e-mail. Consequently, some listings in this chapter show only a Web site. If you have no access to the Internet, call the city PARD office at (512) 974-6700; they will put you in contact with the appropriate league official.

of PARD offices in the previous Recreation introduction.

Another good resource for information on team sports is the YMCA. The Y has six locations in Austin, offering basketball, volleyball, soccer, basketball, and T-ball. Listings for the facilities are also listed in the previous section.

The area has an abundance of baseball leagues for all ages. Check with the area PARD for Little League, Optimist, and Kiwanis league teams. The Austin PARD supervises several basketball leagues, and the Y offers league and pickup games.

Central Texas is home to soccer moms and dads by the thousands, but the sport also attracts Gen-Xers and even older "footballers" from the expatriate crowd in Austin. There are numerous soccer leagues; the vast majority fall under the auspices of two organizations.

The Capital Area Youth Soccer Association at 1029 Reinli Street, Suite 6 (512-302-4580, www.caysa.org), has more than 15,000 members. It is an umbrella group that oversees youth league and tournament play in the Central Texas area. The association also offers coaching and referee training sessions and hosts two annual invitational tournaments.

The Austin Municipal Soccer Association (512-288-5133, www.amsapremier.com) is also an umbrella association that organizes men's, women's, and coed league and tournament play in Austin. The Web site offers soccer news from around the world.

One of the best ways to keep track of league

play at all levels is to visit one of the Austin area soccer stores. Soccer World has four locations: 5446 US 290 West (Southwest area), (512) 899-1135; 221 South Lamar Boulevard (Central), (512) 320-8447; 13376 Research Boulevard (Northwest), (512) 257-8560; and Soccer World Indoor Center, 1404 Royston Lane, (512) 990-3100.

Another center of soccer activity in the Round Rock–Pflugerville area is the Longhorn Soccer Club, run by Laszlo Marton, a former Hungarian and Austrian professional soccer player. The club offers top-quality coaching and training for soccer players of all ages and summer camps. Contact the camp at 1235 Blackthorn Drive, Round Rock (512-990-1234, www.longhorn soccerclub.org).

Softball is an extremely popular sport year-round in Austin. The Austin PARD serves as the major clearinghouse for schedules, league, and fee information. Call the PARD Athletics Office at (512) 480-3015. Many of the teams play at the Pleasant Valley Sports Complex, 1225 South Pleasant Valley Road, (512) 445-7595. For softball league information in Round Rock, call (512) 218-5540.

Disc Golf (Folf)

Pitching a Frisbee at a target is a popular sport in Austin, and many of the area's neighborhood parks feature either 9- or 18-hole folf courses. The discs can be found at local sporting goods stores. On the Web, www.discrevolution.com rates courses around the United States—Austin's rank from three to four stars, with five being tops.

AUSTIN RECREATION CENTER
1301 Shoal Creek Boulevard
(512) 476-5662
www.ci.austin.tx.us
The Austin Recreation Center offers classes to would-be folf masters.

BARTHOLOMEW PARK
5201 Berkman Drive
(512) 974-6700
This 18-hole course is in Northeast Austin.

MARY MOORE SEARIGHT PARK
907 Slaughter Lane
This 18-hole course is part of a fairly new park in Austin's growing southern suburbs.

OLD SETTLERS PARK
3300 Palm Valley Road, Round Rock
This course is in Round Rock's major city park and claims to be the longest folf course in America (see our Parks section above).

PEASE PARK
1100 Kingsbury Street
This course is very popular among University of Texas students who live in the neighborhood.

SLAUGHTER CREEK METROPOLITAN PARK
5507 Slaughter Lane
This pleasant, relatively new Southwest Austin park boasts a new nine-hole folf course and gets four stars from discrevolution.com.

WELLS BRANCH GREENBELT
Wells Branch Parkway at Wells Port Drive
(512) 251-9814
A new nine-hole course in the Wells Branch subdivision of North Austin, this facility is open to Wells Branch residents only.

ZILKER PARK
2100 Barton Springs Road
You"ll find this nine-hole course at the western edge of the city's premier park. It's a popular weekend course, also ranked at four stars.

Fishing

Texans have a reputation for telling tall tales, but when it comes to fishing they have lots to boast about. The state has more than 5,175 square miles of inland fresh water, including lakes, rivers, and creeks, plus 624 miles of shoreline. There is a wide variety of fish available for the taking, provided the fish are biting. Native fish include black bass, crappie, bluegill, and catfish. Freshwater fishing areas also have been stocked with nonnative species, including Florida bass, walleye, and rainbow trout, and saltwater species, including redfish and striped bass. The Texas Parks & Wildlife Department reports that several Texas lakes are producing striped bass weighing over 30 pounds—some Texas tale!

Texas residents can buy an annual combination fishing-hunting license for $25. Fishing licenses vary in cost and can be purchased on an annual or two-week basis by residents. Nonresident anglers over the age of 17 must purchase a license, and these can cost $30 for an annual license or $20 for a five-day license. There are additional charges for stamps for certain fish.

Licenses are sold at sporting goods and tackle stores, some county courthouses, Parks & Wildlife offices, and by some local game wardens. The Texas Parks & Wildlife Department also produces several excellent guides to Texas fishing. The department's magazine (see our Media chapter) is also an excellent resource.

TEXAS PARKS & WILDLIFE DEPARTMENT
4200 Smith School Road
(512) 389-4800, (800) 792-1112
www.tpwd.state.tx.us
The Highland Lakes are popular among anglers (see our Parks listings in this chapter for access and location). Lake Austin record catches include a 43-pound striped bass. Bass fishing is popular in the quieter areas of Lake Austin and Lake Buchanan. Fishing is permitted on Lady Bird Lake in Central Austin, and after years of concern about urban runoff, the city has lifted its warning about consuming your catch. In fact, the river has been stocked with trout.

BASTROP STATE PARK, BASTROP
Highway 21, 1.5 miles east of Bastrop
(512) 321-2101
Lake Bastrop boasts a lighted pier. The record catch here is a 43.5-pound catfish. See our State Parks section of this chapter for a description of facilities here.

BUESCHER STATE PARK, SMITHVILLE
F.M. 153, off Highway 71
(512) 237-2241
This state park is considered an angler's paradise

by some. The park's 30-acre lake is stocked with catfish, bass, crappie, perch, and rainbow trout.

Fishing Gear

GIT BIT
(512) 280-2861
www.gitbitfishing.com
This fishing guide service, run by Mike Hastings, a national tournament fisherman and commentator, offers half-day and full-day bass fishing trips on Lake Travis, a noted hot spot for summertime bass fishing.

SPORTSMAN'S FINEST
12434 Bee Cave Road
(512) 263-1888
www.sportsmansfinest.com
This West Lake Hills angling and outdoor sports supply and travel company provides guides and other services to hunters and fishermen.

Fitness Centers

Fitness centers, gyms, aerobics classes, tai chi sessions, health clubs—Austin has them all. Some offer activities priced per session, while others offer membership. There is a wide range of services and amenities, from the basic nuts-and-bolts weight rooms to highly personalized training programs. Several national chains are present in Austin, and the number of fitness centers has grown with the city. Here, we list some of the non-chain centers that have an Austin "vibe." A great source of information on local gyms and other fitness resources is *Austin Fit* magazine (www.austinfitmagazine.com).

CRENSHAW ATHLETIC CLUB
5000 Fairview Drive
(512) 453-5551
www.crenshaws.com
This is an old Austin favorite, home for more than 50 years to generations of Austin's families. Located in Central Austin, Crenshaw is noted for its family facilities and popular children's gym. The club has an indoor pool and track, plus weight rooms and cardio training equipment.

GREGORY GYMNASIUM
2101 Speedway on the UT campus
(512) 471-6370
www.utrecsports.org
Under the auspices of its RecSports program (see the Recreation Opportunities listing earlier in this chapter), students, ex-students, faculty, staff, and community members can enjoy the extensive facilities at the UT gym. The facilities are vast and include basketball and volleyball courts, indoor jogging, squash courts, weight rooms, climbing walls, even a big-screen TV and a coffee shop.

THE HILLS FITNESS CENTER
4615 Bee Caves Road
(512) 327-4881
www.thehillsfitness.com
Located on a beautiful 12-acre wooded campus, the center features both indoor and outdoor pools; racquetball, squash, and basketball courts; and a child-care center and cafe, among other amenities.

HYDE PARK GYM
4125 Guadalupe Street
(512) 459-9174
www.hydeparkgym.com
"No chrome. No contracts." is the advertising motto of this university-area gym in one of Austin's favorite and most colorful neighborhoods, Hyde Park. The owners describe the place as down-to-earth, and it is, with cement floors, free weights, and no fancy contracts to sign. Personal trainers are available.

PREMIERE LADY AND SPA
7028 Wood Hollow Drive
(512) 418-9399

6800 Westgate Boulevard 78745
(512) 707-7700
A very popular fitness center in Northwest Austin, this facility caters to women only. In addition to fitness equipment, the center also has a pool, whirlpools, and steam and sauna rooms. There are aerobics and fitness classes, plus clients can avail themselves of personal care services, such as a hair and nail treatment, facials, massage therapy, and tanning. The club has in-house child care available.

ST. DAVID'S HEALTH AND FITNESS CENTER
900 East 30th Street
(512) 544-4263
www.sdhcp.com
Month-to-month memberships are available at this Central Austin health club, which is affiliated with the St. David's Medical Center. The club has rowing machines, step machines, Cybex weight machines, ski machines, treadmills, and stationary bikes. Aerobics classes and individual exercise programs are offered.

YMCA
See a list of YMCA branches under Recreation Opportunities, earlier in this chapter.

Flying
See our Getting Here, Getting Around chapter for information on flying lessons and sightseeing tours.

Hiking
Austin's greenbelts, hike and bike trails in Cedar Park, Pflugerville, and Round Rock (see our Parks section above), and hundreds of miles of trails in nearby state parks offer a great variety of terrain, levels of difficulty, and scenic views for hiking enthusiasts.

Some of the easiest trails to access are within the Austin Greenbelt network. For more information and brochures showing trails and access points, call Austin PARD at (512) 499-6700. One good way to get started is to join the Sierra Club for its city hikes (www.sierra club.org/austin). The Lone Star Chapter is headquartered at 54 Chicon Street in Austin, (512) 477-1729.

Popular scenic hikes include the trails at McKinney Falls State Park in Southeast Austin and Wolf Mountain Trail in Pedernales Park and Hamilton Pool Park, both west of Austin (see our Parks section in this chapter). A good resource for hikers is the Hill Country Information Service

(512-478-1337, www.txinfo.com), which offers U.S. Geological Survey maps and other illustrated guides to Hill Country. Other good resources are outfitters listed in our Shopping chapter.

The Colorado River Walkers of Austin (512-495-6294, www.onr.com/user/dbarber/crw) organizes scenic hikes. Another Hill Country group that carries on a German tradition of hiking is Volkssporting in Fredericksburg. Call (800) 830-WALK for information on Texas and national activities. If you need to learn more about backpacking and hiking, consider taking a course at the University of Texas Recreational Sports Division, (512) 471-1093.

Horseback Riding

True to its Texas character, there are several major rodeo and equestrian events in Austin each year. (See our Annual Events and Festivals chapter for details.) Several area ranches offer horseback riding—be sure the owner/operator has a Texas Department of Health certificate posted.

BEAR CREEK STABLES
13017 Bob Johnson Road
(512) 282-0250
This 25-acre private trail riding facility is located in the area Austin residents call Manchaca, a small South Austin community that has been swallowed up by the growing metropolis. The horses are well behaved and the scenery bucolic, making it a great place for a family outing. Children under 7 years of age may not ride.

i Looking for the ultimate city slicker experience? How about a few days at a Central Texas dude ranch? The Hill Country town of Bandera, about 120 miles southwest of Austin, is home to several well-known dude ranches that offer horseback adventures, evenings on the front porch, and chuck wagon food; some find it quite high class. Check out www.duderanches.com/Texas.

CAMERON EQUESTRIAN CENTER
13404 Cameron Road
(512) 272-4301
This Northeast Austin stable and training center offers English- and Western-style lessons and riding opportunities.

WHITE FENCES EQUESTRIAN CENTER
10908 Jones Road
Manor
(512) 282-6248
www.whitefencesaustin.com
The trail rides here meander through the rolling hills east of the city, where riders are likely to see a variety of Texas fauna and flora in quiet, serene surroundings. Family rides are available, and the little guys can rent ponies for the trek. The large facility also has a sale barn, picnic sites, and White Fences offers several types and levels of lessons

Hot-Air Ballooning

The skies over Austin are filled with balloons each September during the annual Lone Star Weekend Aloft. Before floating away, check the pilot's FAA certification. Most flights begin in the early morning, and prices per person can range from $150 to $350.

CENTRAL TEXAS BALLOONING ASSOCIATION
(512) 479-9421
www.main.org/ctba
This group maintains a list of members who hold commercial hot-air balloon certificates.

Hunting

Deer hunting is a popular pastime in the Texas Hill Country, where more white-tailed deer live than in any other part of the country. So dense is the population that suburban Austin residents often find their gardens have become a favorite noshing place for small herds of deer. Driving in the Hill Country at night also can be a challenge, since the abundant deer love to graze on the roadside grasses—usually the grass on the other side of the road.

The Hill Country also is home to several exotic game ranches where, for a hefty fee, hunters can track and hunt wild Corsican rams, African aoudad sheep, Indian blackbuck antelope, and axis and sika deer. (Axis deer is a popular item on some area restaurant menus, notably Hudson's-on-the-Bend, one of Austin's leading restaurants. Read about it in our Restaurants chapter.)

Much of the hunting in Texas takes place on private lands where landowners rent out leases or allow hunters to come onto their land for a fee during peak season. The Texas Parks & Wildlife Department 4200 Smith School Road, Austin, (512) 389-4800 or (800) 792-1112, offers several free comprehensive guides to Texas hunting, including *The Guide to Texas Hunting*. The Web site (www.tpwd .state.tx.us/hunt) is a vast source of information on where hunters may apply online for permits.

Ice Sports

Ice sports are becoming more and more popular in Austin, perhaps because of the influx of new residents from colder climates. Youth ice hockey leagues are growing fast.

CHAPARRAL ICE CENTER
14200 North I-35
(512) 252-8500

Northcross Mall location
2525 West Anderson Lane
www.iskateaustin.com
Public skating, classes, hockey leagues, birthday parties, and broom ball are all offered at these facilities in North Austin. They also offer a pro shop and locker facilities. Round Rock PARD offers ice-skating classes at the I-35 location. Skating admission is $5, and skates rent for $3 a pair. The Lone Star Curling Club meets at the new Northcross rink every Sunday morning. Call for hours and admission charges.

Rock Climbing

This is a fast-growing recreational activity in Austin. Central Texas Mountaineers Association (www .texasclimber.com) keeps track of area activities.

A favorite outing for local rock climbers is to Enchanted Rock Park near Fredericksburg, about 90 miles west of Austin (see above under State Parks).

ASPIRE ADVENTURES
11008 Jollyville Road, Suite. 219
(512) 343-1071
www.climbtexas.com
Hutto, just a stone's throw from Austin, is now regarded as part of the greater Austin metro area. Aspire is a guide service for rock climbers and also offers classes at facilities around Austin. The company's Web site lists numerous links to rock-climbing clubs and facilities around the state and beyond.

AUSTIN ROCK GYM
4401 Friedrich Lane, Suite 300
8300 North Lamar Boulevard
(512) 416-9299
www.austinrockgym.com
This Austin gym with two locations, one south, the other north, has a 30-foot rock wall and offers classes for both kids and adults. There is a pro shop, plus patrons can rent equipment. Austin Rock also offers guide services for climbs around Central Texas.

UNIVERSITY OF TEXAS RECREATIONAL SPORTS
(512) 471-3116
www.utrecsports.org
Information about the classes is detailed in the Recreation section of this chapter. Rock climbing classes are included in the curriculum.

YMCA SOUTHWEST
6219 Oakclaire Drive,
off US 290 West
(512) 891-9622
www.ymca.org
The Southwest branch of the Y has a rock-climbing wall and offers classes. Membership is required to enjoy the Y's facilities; however, guests may pay for one annual visit if they are accompanied by a member.

Roller-skating

These roller-skating facilities are generally open in the evenings until 11:00 p.m. Some offer afternoon sessions, particularly on weekends; however, be forewarned the rinks do close for private parties, so it is wise to call ahead. Admission prices are generally $4 and under; in-line skates cost a couple of dollars more. They also offer a variety of party packages ranging in price from around $5 to $9 per person, depending on whether party favors and snacks are included.

PLAYLAND SKATING CENTER
8822 McCann Drive
(512) 452-1901
www.playlandskatingcenter.com
The Northeast Austin center offers rollerskating, in-line skating, and special adults nights.

ROUND ROCK ROLLER RINK
15501 North FM 620
(512) 218-0103
This center touts its family activities, including skating for families and Christian music on Monday.

SKATEWORLD
9514 Anderson Mill Road
(512) 258-8886
www.skateworldaustin.com
Skating lessons and hockey leagues are featured at this Northwest Austin skating rink.

Rugby

Rugby can be an exciting game to watch, even if you don't understand the rules—or apparent lack of them. Spectators should remember rugby is a tough sport that often encompasses certain off-pitch lifestyle habits; i.e., revelry. There are three rugby clubs in Austin; several of their players hail from foreign countries where rugby is popular. Both teams have won titles, gone on tour, and hosted visits from foreign teams.

THE AUSTIN HUNS
(512) 459-HUNS
www.hunsrugby.org
The Austin Huns RFC Pitch is in Zilker Park, and games are usually played on Saturday afternoon. After the game the Huns head for Nasty's, "Homeland of the Huns," a neighborhood bar at 606 Maiden Lane in Central Austin. The Austin Huns Rugby Football Club was founded in 1972 when the second side of the Austin Rugby Football Club broke away to form their own team.

THE AUSTIN RUGBY FOOTBALL CLUB
P.O. Box 12932, Austin 78711
(512) 419-4784 hot line
(512) 926-9017 clubhouse
www.austinrugby.com
The Austin Rugby Football Club was founded in the spring of 1967 and was the first club in the Southwestern United States. In 1978 the club became the first rugby club in the United States to purchase its own grounds, and in 1985 the team built a clubhouse—it is one of only two rugby clubs in the United States with its own clubhouse and grounds. Call the clubhouse for directions to the club in East Austin, which can be difficult to find without detailed directions.

AUSTIN VALKYRIES
www.austinvalkyries.com
The Austin Valkyries Women's Rugby Football organization is eager for new members. Ranked No. 2 in the Western United States, the Valkyries train Tuesday and Thursday at Burr Field, a facility the club owns in Northeast Austin. The site is hard to find, and the dirt road into the pitch is muddy in rainy weather. The Valkyries suggest using a four-wheel-drive vehicle on wet days. Check the Web site for directions.

Running/Walking

There are 5K, 10K, and marathon events throughout the year in Austin. RunTex, which sells running equipment is a good source of calendar events (www.runtex.com). There are several in Austin and more planned: 422 West Riverside Drive, (512) 472-3254; 9901 North Capital of Texas Highway, (512) 343-1164; -and 2201 Lake Austin Boulevard, (512) 477-9464. The Austin Runner's Club serves as a clearinghouse of information; visit www.austinrunners.org. See the Austin Parks listings in this chapter for hike and bike trails in the city.

Tennis

In addition to private facilities at some of the area's top resorts (see our Resorts Close-up in the Hotels and Motels chapter) and country clubs, there are 28 first-come, first-served municipal tennis court facilities, some with two courts, others four, located in all sectors of Austin. Tennis players also have access to several school courts during the summer months. For a complete list contact PARD at (512) 974-9350 (www.ci.austin .tx.us). Courts are concrete, asphalt, or laykold and are available free of charge. A wonderful resource for tennis players of all ages is www.austin-tennis-resource.com. This Web site has maps of tennis court locations, retail support for tennis players in the city, special events and tournaments, league stats, even some national and international tennis news.

Reservations are necessary and fees are charged to play on the courts at the city's four municipal tennis center facilities, which are larger and have lighting. All courts are laykold and lighted. Fees are $3.00 for adults and $2.50 for children in prime time, which is Monday through Thursday after 6:00 p.m. and Saturday and Sunday before 6:00 p.m. Fees are lower at other times.

The Capital Area Tennis Association at 3625 Manchaca Road, (512) 443-8384, www.austinten nis.org, is an excellent resource for tennis players. Organized in 1974 and dedicated to promoting amateur tennis competition, the association keeps its members informed of tennis activities in the greater Austin area; conducts educational tennis clinics and seminars; organizes competitive events to fund youth programs and new

i There is a popular new sport on the Austin scene—cricket! Given the influx of immigrants from countries formerly colonized by the Brits, many of whom work in the high-tech industry, the sport has taken hold in Texas. There are four clubs in the area—the Round Rock Cricket Club, the Hill Country Cricket Association, the Austin Cricket Club, and the University Cricket Club. The cricket enthusiasts also are teaching area kids the sport. Schedules, contacts, league results, and special events are listed at www.centraltxcricket.org.

court construction; and offers consulting services to public officials about the development of tennis facilities. Membership fees are less than $15 a year for adults.

AUSTIN HIGH
1715 Cesar Chavez Street
(512) 414-2505s
This tennis facility is in Central Austin, just east of MoPac at Austin High School. There are eight courts available after school is out during the school year and daily during the summer months.

CASWELL
24th Street and Lamar Boulevard
(512) 478-6268
www.lovetennis4caswell.com
This Central Austin tennis center has nine courts and is open from 8:00 a.m. to 10:00 p.m. Monday through Thursday, Friday 8:00 a.m. to 9:00 p.m., and Saturday and Sunday from 8:00 a.m. to 6:00 p.m. A summer tennis league is headquartered here, and lessons are offered.

PHARR
4201 Brookview Road
(512) 477-7773
This tennis center in North Austin has eight full courts and is open daily from 8:30 a.m. to 10:30 p.m. Monday through Thursday and until 7:00 p.m. Friday, Saturday, and Sunday.

SOUTH AUSTIN
1000 Cumberland Road
(512) 442-1466
The city's South Austin facility has 10 courts and is open Monday through Friday from 9:00 a.m. to 10:00 p.m. and Saturday and Sunday from 9:00 a.m. to 6:00 p.m. In the summer, beginning in June, the center opens 30 minutes earlier.

WELLS BRANCH COMMUNITY CENTER
2106 Klattenhoff Drive
(512) 251-9814
The two lighted courts here are open to Wells Branch residents in this North Austin neighborhood.

Round Rock
Several of the city's parks have free courts, including Frontier Park, 1006 Oakridge Drive; Greenslopes Park, 1600 Gattis School Road; McNeil Park, 3701 North I-35; Round Rock West Park, 500 Round Rock West; Stark Park, 1409 Provident Lane; and Stella Park, 803 Nancy Drive. Call Round Rock PARD at (512) 218-5540 for information.

Cedar Park
The city's newest park, Elizabeth M. Milburn Community Park, 1901 Sun Chase Boulevard, has tennis facilities. Call the Cedar Park PARD at (512) 401-5500 for information.

Volleyball
Sand Volleyball
There are several sand volleyball courts in the city's parks, plus a few commercial locations where volleyball enthusiasts gather. Check out www.austinvolleyball.com.

AUSSIE'S BAR AND GRILL
306 Barton Springs Road
(512) 480-0952
(512) 474-2255 (volleyball hot line)
www.aussiesbar.com
This is a haven for local sand court players. The restaurant operates league play throughout the summer.

AUSTIN PARK FACILITIES
Austin PARD
(512) 974-6700
There are four public sand volleyball courts with nets in Zilker Park in a green space area north of Barton Springs Road. The three courts at Pease Park lack nets, but you can rent them from PARD.

CARLOS 'N CHARLIE'S
5981 Hiline Road
(512) 266-1683
www.cncaustin.com
Cousin to those wacky Mexican restaurants south of the border, made popular by spring breakers in Cancun, this Emerald Point restaurant has a well-regarded sand volleyball complex. The restaurant rents out the volleyball court and party room for $200 a day for private parties.

VOLENTE BEACH
16107 Wharf Cove
(512) 258-5109
www.volentebeach.com
Volente Beach is a private lakeside park that offers volleyball, windsurfing, swimming, and other beach/lake activities. It opens at 11:00 a.m. daily, closing at 10:00 p.m. during the week and 11:00 p.m. on weekends. There are three lighted sand volleyball courts on site. Admission is $4.

Indoor Volleyball
The Austin PARD operates two indoor volleyball leagues: one located at the Austin Recreation Center, 1301 Shoal Creek Boulevard, (512) 476-5662, and one located at the Northwest Recreation Center, 2913 Northland Drive, (512) 458-4107. League play is year-round and includes men's, women's, and coed teams.

WATER SPORTS
Newcomers to the Texas Hill Country often are taken aback by the abundance of lakes, rivers, and creeks in the area. There are several invaluable resources for the water sports enthusiast:

THE AUSTIN PARKS AND RECREATION DEPARTMENT (PARD)
(512) 974-6700
www.ci.austin.tx.us.parks

PARD offers classes in canoeing, kayaking, and sailing. The department also operates Emma Long Metropolitan Park (see our Austin City Parks section above), the closest boat ramp to downtown Austin and the only city-run ramp on Lake Austin—Walsh Landing, 1 block north of the western end of Enfield Drive.

THE LOWER COLORADO RIVER AUTHORITY (LCRA)
(512) 473-3200
www.lcra.org

Much of the Highland Lakes area falls under the auspices of the LCRA. In addition to operating parks along the lakes, the LCRA also offers boating safety classes. There are several public boat ramps in the LCRA parks and primitive areas (see our Lake Parks section in this chapter).

TEXAS PARKS & WILDLIFE DEPARTMENT
4200 Smith School Road
(512) 389-8900
www.tpwd.state.tx.us

This state agency is not only charged with maintaining the state's parks but also enforcing water safety laws (see our Boating Safety information in this chapter). Copies of the rules and guidelines on water safety can be obtained from the agency, in addition to information about state facilities, including boat ramps, on Texas lakes and rivers.

TRAVIS COUNTY PARKS
(512) 473-9437
www.co.travis.tx.us/tnr/parks

In addition to state parks and wildlife and LCRA wardens, the Travis County Sheriff's Office also has deputies aboard patrol boats on some areas of the lakes. Many of the county parks (see our Travis County Parks section above) include boat ramps.

Boating
Safety

Alarmed by the rising numbers of accidents on Texas waterways, the state legislature passed tougher boating laws in 1997. The highlights include:

* Teenagers 13 to 15 must take a boating education course before they can legally operate a boat of 15 HP or more without adult supervision. Since 2001 all 13- to 17-year-olds must complete water safety courses before they can operate a boat or watercraft without adult supervision.
* Children younger than 13 must be accompanied by an adult when operating boats of 10 HP or more or a sailboat longer than 14 feet.
* Jet Skis and other personal watercraft cannot be operated except at slow speed within 50 feet of other personal watercraft, stationary objects, the shoreline, or other boats.
* Driving a boat or personal watercraft while intoxicated is against the law.

Boat Rentals and Marinas

Literally dozens of companies rent boats, sailboats, canoes, pontoon boats, and even large party boats in the Austin area. Most also rent personal watercraft. Several of the larger marinas and rental companies are listed below. It is wise to check the Yellow Pages, then call around to check prices and availability. For busy holiday weekends, rentals should be made far in advance. Most require a deposit in the form of a credit card, and renters will be held liable for any damage to the craft.

Marinas offer both storage slips for sail and power boats, plus full service for gasoline and marine supplies. Many also rent boats, houseboats, and personal watercraft.

AQUAVENTURES
(512) 327-2200
www.austinaquaventures.com

This Austin boat rental company delivers ski boats, personal watercraft, and pontoons to marinas on Lake Travis and the Highland Lakes.

AUSTIN AQUA FUN
2507 Westlake Drive
(512) 459-4FUN

This company rents boats on both Lake Austin and Lake Travis. Their stable includes pontoons, personal watercraft, and ski boats. The company also offers ski instruction. Pickups are arranged at various locations on the lakes.

BEACH FRONT BOAT RENTALS
Volente Beach, 16120 Wharf Cove
(512) 258-8400
www.beachfrontboats.com

The marina at this private lakeside park at the northern end of Lake Travis off R.M. 2769 rents personal watercraft and ski boats.

EMERALD POINT MARINA
5973 Hiline Road
(512) 266- 5910
www.emeraldpointmarina.com

The marina is next door to the popular Carlos 'N Charlie's Bar & Grill on Lake Travis. In addition to being a full-service marina with store and gas station, the facility rents houseboats, ski boats, and personal watercraft.

JUST FOR FUN WATERCRAFT RENTAL
5973 Hiline Road
(512) 266-9710
www.jff.net

Hurst Harbor Marina
16405Clara Van Street
www.hhmarina.biz

This boat rental on Lake Travis Emerald Point Marina and Hurst Harbor offers a variety of craft, including pontoon boats and party craft for groups up to 150 people.

LAKEWAY MARINA
103A Lakeway Drive
(512) 261-7511
www.lakewaymarina.com

One of the larger marinas on the lake, this business offers boat rentals, lessons, fishing guides, and sunset cruises.

Canoeing and Kayaking

AUSTIN CANOE & KAYAK
9705 Burnet Road
(512) 719-4386
www.austinkayak.com

This North Austin store boasts the largest selection of kayaks and canoes for sale in Central Texas. In addition to sales of several major brands, the shop also offers rentals.

AUSTIN PADDLING CLUB
www.austinpaddling.org

The club is dedicated to promoting canoeing, kayaking, and rafting and meets monthly at the LCRA Hancock Building, 3701 Lake Austin Boulevard.

CAPITAL CRUISES
Hyatt Regency
(512) 480-9264
www.capitalcruises.com

Looking for a unique way to view the evening bat flight at the Congress Avenue Bridge? Consider renting a canoe, kayak, or electric pedal boat from this boat company based on Lady Bird Lake (formerly Town Lake).

ZILKER PARK CANOE RENTALS
2000 Barton Springs Road
(512) 478-3852
www.fastair.com/zilker

Since no motorized craft is allowed on Lady Bird Lake, one of the best ways to enjoy it is in a canoe or kayak, which can be rented at this concession in Zilker Park from 11:00 a.m. to dusk daily, March through Labor Day.

Cruises

AUSTIN PARTY CRUISES
2215 Westlake Drive
(512) 328-9887 (Lake Austin)
(512) 266-3788 (Lake Travis)
www.austinpartycruises.com

Party boats can be rented for sunset cruises, birthday parties, scenic cruises of both lakes, and corporate events. The company also offers catering services.

CAPITAL CRUISES
Hyatt Regency
(512) 480-9264
www.capitalcruises.com

In addition to renting electric boats and canoes (see previous listing), Capital also offers dinner cruises on Lady Bird Lake, bat-watching parties, and sightseeing trips up and down the downtown lake.

RIVERBOATS
6917 Greenshores Drive
(512) 345-5220
www.austinriverboats.com

The company's two riverboats, *Commodore Riverboat* and *Commodore's Pup*, can accommodate 50 to 500 people as they cruise Lake Austin. The boats can be rented for parties, receptions, and corporate outings. Full food and beverage service is available on both boats.

VANISHING TEXAS RIVER CRUISE
Lake Buchanan
(512) 756-6986
www.vtrc.com

In addition to eagle-watching cruises (see Birdwatching in this chapter), Vanishing River offers fall foliage cruises, summer sunset dinner cruises, trips to admire the wildflowers in spring, and even tours of Fall Creek Vineyards (see the Close-up on Texas foods in our Restaurants chapter).

Rowing

AUSTIN ROWING CLUB
223–B East Cesar Chavez Boulevard
(512) 472-0726
www.austinrowing.org

The advent of rowing on Lady Bird Lake has given Austinites the opportunity to view one of the most picturesque of early-morning city sights: a lone rower skimming the waters of Lady Bird Lake in the morning mist. The rowing club is on the northern bank of Lady Bird Lake, near the Four

> **i** There are several sports programs for disabled children in Austin. The Austin Parks and Recreation Department offers therapeutic recreation programs, and the YMCA has several programs for special-needs children and adults.

Seasons Hotel. The club serves as headquarters for collegiate team events on Lady Bird Lake and serves noncollegiate members of the rowing club. Classes are offered for beginners.

Sailing

THE AUSTIN YACHT CLUB
5906 Beacon Drive
(512) 266-1336
www.austinyachtclub.com

The club sponsors races every Sunday out on Lake Travis and hosts several regattas and races throughout the year. The club is a good source of information on local sailing opportunities and practices, resources, and classes (see our chapters on Spectator Sports and Kidstuff).

COMMANDER'S POINT YACHT BASIN
4600 Commander's Point Drive
(512) 266-2333

One of the few marinas on the lake that rents sailboats and offers training for beginners, Commander's Point is home to a large sailing fleet. The marina also rents captained boats for visitors who want to enjoy a sail on Lake Travis but do not know the ropes.

SAIL AWEIGH
(512) 250-8141
www.ccsi.com/~sailaweigh

Sailing lessons with a U.S. Coast Guard–licensed master are offered by this Austin business. The company also offers chartered, captained cruises on Lake Travis.

TEXAS SAILING ACADEMY
103 Lakeway Drive, Lake Travis
(512) 261-6193
www.texassailing.com

The academy has been offering sailing lessons on the lake since 1965. Day and weekly charters, captained cruises, and sailboat rentals are also available.

Scuba Diving

OAK HILL SCUBA INC.
6156 Highway 290 West
(512) 892-4900
www.oakhillscuba.com
This longtime scuba store offers several levels of instruction, also information on safety practices, and coordinates scuba trips both affordable and exotic.

TOM'S DIVE & SKI
5909 Burnet Road
(512) 451-3425
www.tomsscuba.com
Offering classes at all levels from beginners to advanced, plus specialties such as underwater archaeology, this North Austin diving facility has a 3,000-square-foot, 10-foot-deep pool. The school organizes local fun dives, outings to the Gulf of Mexico, and international dive trips to such places as Cozumel in the Yucatan.

Swimming

The Central Texas climate can make swimming a joy or, on a hot day, a necessity. Even on the coldest days of the year, enthusiasts will head for the constant 68 degrees of Barton Springs Pool (see our Close-up in this chapter), which, unlike many municipal and neighborhood pools, is open year-round. Of course, the area's lakes and creeks are open throughout the year, but there are dangers there. Diving into creek or riverbeds can be dangerous, as water depths can vary with the seasons, and rocky bottoms pose hidden dangers. The lakes are really water-filled valleys; rocks, buried tree limbs, and duckweed can pose dangers. No swimming is allowed in Lady Bird Lake, and it is unlikely you would want to swim there anyway given urban runoff problems. Instead, head for one of the many neighborhood pools, natural-fed pools, or favorite water holes in the area.

Swimming Lessons

AMERICAN RED CROSS
(512) 928-4271
www.centex.redcross.org
The Red Cross serves as a referral service to swimming lessons offered by various entities in the Austin area.

CAPITAL AREA REHABILITATION CENTER
919 West 28½ Street
(512) 478-2581
The center offers classes for adults, children, and handicapped students. There are also sessions for persons suffering from chronic disorders such as arthritis.

CRENSHAW ATHLETIC CLUB
5000 Fairview Drive
(512) 453-5551
www.crenshaws.com
Fitness and water aerobic classes for swimmers with chronic disabilities, or those embarking on a health regimen, are offered at this Central Austin fitness center.

YMCA
All Y facilities listed in our Fitness section earlier in this chapter have indoor pools and a full schedule of swimming classes for all ages and ability levels.

Austin City Pools

There are two categories of city-run outdoor pools in Austin: municipal pools and neighborhood pools. Municipal pools are large, deep pools and charge small fees for daily use. Multivisit passes are available from the PARD. All municipal pools have wading areas, lap lanes, diving boards, concessions, and sunbathing areas. There are picnic sites adjacent to the pools. Generally neighborhood pools are free, open during summer months, and no deeper than 5 feet. All pools have lifeguards, and all may be rented before and after regular operating hours.

There are 27 neighborhood pools throughout the city. Call the Aquatics office below for a list and a map. The neighborhood pools usually open in May and operate on a weekend-only schedule until Memorial Day, when they go into daily operation. In mid-August they resume weekend-only operation and then close before Labor Day. Admission and hours of operation vary at each location.

AUSTIN AQUATICS OFFICE
400 Deep Eddy Avenue
(512) 974-9333
www.ci.austin.tx.us/parks/aquatics
This city PARD hot line lists class schedules, fee information, and status of city pools.

BARTHOLOMEW POOL
1800 East 51st Street
(512) 928-0014
This municipal pool serves Northeast Austin. Specific times are set aside for recreational swims, lap swimming, and lessons.

BARTON SPRINGS
Zilker Park, 2201 Barton Springs Road
(512) 476-9044
Revered as an icon, the "soul of Austin," this hallowed swimming pool is featured in our Close-up in this chapter. The pool is open daily, and even during the coldest days of winter you'll see swimmers enjoying the 68-degree water. It is open in spring and fall, from mid-March to Memorial Day, Labor Day to October 31, from 5:00 a.m. to 10:00 p.m. There are no lifeguards on duty from 5:00 to 9:00 a.m. and from 8:00 to 10:00 p.m. The pool closes on Monday and Thursday at 7:30 p.m. From Memorial Day to Labor Day, the pool is open from 5:00 a.m. to 10:00 p.m. There are no lifeguards from 5:00 to 9:00 a.m. and from 9:00 to 10:00 p.m. The pool closes at 7:30 p.m. Monday and Thursday. From October 31 to mid-March, hours are 5:00 a.m. to 10:00 p.m., and there are

no lifeguards on duty from 5:00 to 9:00 a.m. and dusk to 10:00 p.m.

There are no entrance fees during the winter season. Admission during the rest of the year is $3 for adults; $2 for juniors (12 to 17); and $1 for seniors and children 11 and younger. Call to make sure the pool is open—cleanings and occasional heavy rains do close the pool. There is a gift shop and information booth at the bathhouse, plus a snack bar.

DEEP EDDY
401 Deep Eddy Avenue
(512) 472-8546
This West Austin pool is fed by an artesian well, and its fresh water is a major attraction, especially for families who let the little ones wade in the large, shallow end of the pool. Eilers Park at the intersection of MoPac and Lake Austin Boulevard is home to the pool. The early morning hours are set aside for lap swimmers.

GARRISON
6001 Manchaca Road
(512) 442-4048
Serving South Austin, Garrison opens in early May and closes in mid-August. Lap swimmers have the pool to themselves during early morning and late evening on weekdays. Recreational swimming and swim lessons also have designated hours on weekdays and weekends.

MABEL DAVIS
3427 Parker Lane
(512) 441-5247
This Southeast Austin pool opens in mid-May and closes in August. Lap swimmers have the pool to themselves on weekdays from 9:00 to 10:00 a.m. Swim lessons are also offered here during the week.

NORTHWEST AUSTIN POOL
7000 Ardath Street
(512) 453-0194
This Northwest Austin municipal pool opens a little earlier (late April) and closes a little later

(mid-September) than some of the other city pools. Lap swimmers enjoy early-morning and late-evening weekday hours here.

WELLS BRANCH POOL
2106 Klattenhoff Drive
(512) 251-9932
This facility, in the Wells Branch Municipal District in far North Austin, is dedicated for the use of Wells Branch residents.

Round Rock City Pools

There are two municipal pools in Round Rock. Call the city's Parks Department at (512) 218-5540 for operating hours and information about swimming lessons and summer fun activities at the pools.

LAKE CREEK SWIMMING POOL
Lake Creek Park, 800 Deerfoot Drive
(512) 218-7030
The pool opens in mid-May on weekends only and then shifts to a daily schedule on Memorial Day for the summer, shutting down in mid-August.

MICKI KREBSBACH MEMORIAL POOL
301 Deepwood Drive
(512) 218-7090
This city pool opens in early May and operates on a weekends-only schedule until Memorial Day. The pool is open daily through the summer, then shifts to a weekend schedule from mid-August to the end of September. Daily admission to both city pools is $1.25 for those 18 and older and 75 cents for children 17 and younger. Swim passes are available for multiple visits.

Pflugerville City Pool

GILLELAND CREEK PARK POOL
700 Railroad Avenue
(512) 990-4392
The community pool is located in the city's major park that serves as the focal point of a citywide trail system. Picnic sites are adjacent to the pool, which is open daily throughout the summer. The city's PARD offers swimming and aquatics lessons here.

Cedar Park Pools

BUTTERCUP CREEK POOL
407 Twin Oak Trail
(512) 250-9578
The pool opens in early May and operates much of the month on a weekend-only schedule, then switches to a daily schedule following Memorial Day, closing down in mid-August. The pool has a lap swimming area and 1-meter and 3-meter diving boards. The city's PARD offers swimming lessons, water aerobics, and family nights at the pool.

ELIZABETH M. MILBURN AQUATIC FACILITY
1901 Sun Chase Boulevard
(512) 331-9317
This swimming complex includes an eight-lane, 25-meter lap pool and an adjoining recreational pool with a water playscape and a 117-foot water slide. The pool's bathhouse has showers, a concession area, an arcade, and an aquatics office. The lap pool is heated and remains open year-round.

Swimming Holes

There are three natural swimming holes within a 90-minute drive of Austin. Not all are open year-round, and some may be closed when high water proves dangerous or park operators limit human traffic to protect delicate ecosystems. It cannot be overemphasized that swimmers must exercise caution when swimming in natural locations. Underwater hazards can prove deadly, and not a summer goes by without area residents mourning the loss of someone killed from diving into a natural hole.

BLUE HOLE
333 Blue Hole Lane, County Road 173,
Wimberley
(512) 847-0025
Blue Hole has passed from private ownership to the City of Wimberley. *Texas Monthly* magazine named this swimming hole (featured in several movies) as one of the top 10 in Texas. It is along

Cypress Creek, near Wimberley. There is a small admission fee and season passes are available for $10.

HAMILTON POOL
Hamilton Pool Road,
F.M. 3238, off Highway 71
(512) 264-2740
www.co.travis.tx.us/tnr/parks/hamilton
The pool and the grotto that serve as the crown jewel of this 232-acre park (see our Travis County Parks section above) were formed when the dome of an underground river collapsed thousands of years ago. The grotto is now a unique ecosystem. The emphasis is on the environment here, so access to the pool for swimmers is limited. Calling ahead is vital. Once the 100-car parking lot is full, the park closes. Admission is $8 per car, $3 for pedestrians and bicycles.

KRAUSE SPRINGS
Spur 191, off Highway 71
(830) 693-4181
Devotees of swimming holes tout this natural pool as a great place to take the family, since the waters are clear and shallow. The pool, which is listed on the National Register of Historic Places, is about 7 miles west of the point where the Pedernales River meets Highway 71. Turn north on Spur 191 and follow the signs. The pool is on privately owned land that is shaded by large cypress trees. There are picnic and camping facilities at the pool. Daily admission is $4 for adults and $3 for children ages 4 to 11. There are additional fees for overnight stays. No pets allowed.

Windsurfing
Windsurfing is a popular pastime on the Highland Lakes. There are two areas of Lake Travis where windsurfers tend to gather—Mansfield Dam and Windy Point, both near Travis County Parks. Mansfield Dam Park is on R.M. 620 and Windy Point is off Bob Wentz Park (see our Travis County Park section).

AUSTIN WINDSURFER CLUB
www.geocities.com/austinwindsurf/
The club has adopted Bob Wentz Park as its club project, working to keep the park clean and litter free. In addition to serving as a clearinghouse for windsurfers, the club also meets socially every month, usually at a Lake Travis–area restaurant.

VOLENTE BEACH
16107 Wharf Cove
(512) 258-5109
www.volentebeach.com
This private lakeside park at the northern end of Lake Travis off R.M. 2769 rents windsurfers. Admission is free for children two years of age and under; $14.99 for individuals under 42 inches in height; and $19.99 for anyone measuring over 42 inches.

Waterskiing
There are two area ski clubs that offer information on classes, tournaments, and tips about good ski locations.

AUSTIN SKI CLUB
(512) 327-1115
The club sponsors two major tournaments each year—the Texas State Championships in mid-July and the Austin Ski Club Novice Slalom in late August.

CAPITAL AREA WATER SKI CLUB
P.O. Box 180875, Austin 78718
www.waterskiaustin.com
The club offers several tournaments throughout the year and touts itself as a "competitive ski club" where members can test their skills against members with similar skill levels. Coaching and clinics are also part of the club's activities.

GOLF

Austin is the home of the famous *Little Red Book*. "Aha!" some might say—at last, proof that Austin politics is decidedly more left-footed than the rest of Texas. Although we are not talking about Chairman Mao's little book here, but Harvey's. Harvey Penick was the revered golfing pro and teacher who is credited by some of the best players, both amateur and pro, with helping them better their game and reach inner golfing peace. Penick, who lived from 1904 to 1995, is more than an Austin legend. Long known in U.S. golfing circles, Penick became a worldwide legend in the final three years of his life when his small, succinct, plain-talking books of golf wisdom became international best sellers. In 1992 Austin writer and screenwriter Bud Shrake teamed up with Penick to write the *Little Red Book*. When it became a runaway hit, they followed with a second little book, *And If You Play, You're My Friend,* followed by a third, *For All Who Love the Game*. They were working on a fourth when the much-loved Penick died.

Two weeks before he died in an Austin hospital, Penick was visited by one of his longtime students, pro golfer Ben Crenshaw, who was having trouble with his putting game. Penick gave him the advice he needed. Also, just days before he died, Penick saw another of his star pupils score a major breakthrough. Davis Love Jr. won the Freeport McMoran Classic in New Orleans and made the cut for the Masters. Penick died before the Masters ended, but Crenshaw and Love battled it out that year—Crenshaw winning, Love coming in second. Crenshaw said he felt Penick was the 15th club in his bag. Penick's "simple philosophies about golf and life" had helped him win.

Harvey Penick's life spanned almost a century of golf in Austin. He began as a caddy in 1913 and after high school took a job as the pro at the Austin Country Club (ACC). He taught Crenshaw and Tom Kite at the old ACC, now the Riverside Golf Club (see our listing in this chapter), and passed on his quiet knowledge of the game to several generations of golfers. A bronze statue of Penick, shown passing on tips to Tom Kite, stands near the ninth green of the ACC course in the hills of West Austin.

Penick, a religious man, mixed his love of golf with a wonder and praise of nature—easy to do on some of Austin's attractive golf courses. In addition to having some of the most beautiful and challenging golf courses in the country, Austin is also an egalitarian place. The city maintains several excellent municipal courses that can be played at very reasonable rates.

OVERVIEW

This chapter is divided into four parts—Austin Municipal Courses, Daily-Fee Courses, Private Courses, and Driving Ranges. For greens fees and cart rental prices, use the price code chart.

And for the ultimate pampered golf experience, we've listed several golf resorts.

Price Code

(for greens fees or cart rental)

$	under $25
$$	$26 to $50
$$$	$51 to $100
$$$$	$101 and up

AUSTIN MUNICIPAL COURSES

There are five municipal golf courses in the Austin area. Each course offers public league and tournament play, and lessons are available at each course. The city also hosts the Austin Junior Golf Academy for children ages 8 to 18. Call either the Austin Parks and Recreation Department's golf office at (512) 480-3020 (www.ci.austin.tx.us/parks/golf) or the office at each course listed below.

Annual cards allow you to play weekdays at any municipal course and seven days a week at the Hancock course. You also pay a small surcharge of around $2.00 per round for seniors and juniors and a little more per round for adults. (Fees, of course, may change as government budgets are scrutinized every year.) Seniors and juniors also get a considerable discount on daily greens fees, which top out at around $25.00 on prime weekend play days.

Approximate prices for the annual cards are:

- Individual: $750
- Senior: $380
- College Golf Team Member: $280
- Junior: $240
- Summer Junior: $70

JIMMY CLAY GOLF CLUB $
5400 Jimmy Clay Drive
(512) 444-0999
There are two courses at this municipal golf club located in Southeast Austin. The 6,749-yard Roy Kizer Course is 18 holes, par 71, and has a driving range. The course is described as a "thinking man's golf course" because of its carefully laid out design. It is named after a legendary figure in Austin golf who was the course superintendent at the Lions course (below) from 1937 until 1973. The 57 acres of lakes and marshes surrounding the course add to its natural beauty. Tee times for weekdays are taken three days in advance; Friday, Saturday, and Sunday tee times are taken on Tuesday beginning at 7:00 a.m. Greens fees depend on the day of the week and time of day. The 6,857-yard Jimmy Clay course has 18 holes,

par 72. Tee times for weekdays are taken one day in advance; weekend tee times are taken Friday beginning at 7:00 a.m.

HANCOCK GOLF COURSE $
811 East 41st Street
(512) 453-0276
Built in 1899, this is the oldest golf course in the state of Texas. Located in Central Austin, not far from the popular old Hyde Park neighborhood (see our Relocation chapter), this is a pretty course with rolling hills and a small creek that meanders through its heart. The nine-hole course is 2,633 yards, par 35. Reservations are not required, but groups of four or more can make a reservation one day in advance. Sunday group reservations must be made Friday. Seniors and juniors pay reduced fees, and there are lower fees for evening and sunset play.

LIONS MUNICIPAL GOLF COURSE $
2910 Enfield Road
(512) 477-6963
In West Austin, south of Enfield and west of MoPac, this is the oldest municipal course in Austin, but nevertheless very popular. Ben Hogan, Byron Nelson, Tom Kite, and Ben Crenshaw have played here. This is a 6,001-yard course, par 71. There is an irons-only driving range, also. Tee times for weekdays are taken one day in advance; weekend tee times are taken Friday beginning at 7:00 a.m.

MORRIS-WILLIAMS GOLF COURSE $
4300 Manor Road
(512) 926-1298
This 18-hole municipal course is in East Austin, southeast of the old Robert Mueller Municipal Airport. When the airport site is developed, this golf course is likely to be a prime selling point

for the residences that will be part of the new neighborhood. The 6,636-yard, par 72, course is built on an undulating landscape and has a driving range. Tee times for weekdays are taken one day in advance, weekend tee times are taken Friday beginning at 7:00 a.m. Greens fees depend on the age of the golfer, the time of day, and day of the week.

Round Rock

FOREST CREEK GOLF CLUB $$–$$$
99 Twin Ridge Parkway
(512) 388-2874
www.forestcreek.com

This municipal golf course has gained a great reputation not only for its challenging design but also for the quality of the pros who have worked at the club. J. L. Lewis, who went on to the PGA, was the club's first pro. The club is open daily. The par 72 course has 18 holes in 7,154 yards.

The club has a golf shop, driving range, putting green, dining facilities, and even a stocked fishing lake.

DAILY-FEE COURSES

BLUEBONNET HILL GOLF COURSE $–$$
9100 Decker Lane
(512) 272-4228

Located in northeast Travis County near Manor, this public course was built to attract beginning golfers and has become very popular. It is popularly known as "the home of the four-hour round." It takes its name from the rolling Hill Country landscape, particularly beautiful in spring when the bluebonnets bloom. Bluebonnet is rated one of the top 25 public courses in Texas according to the *Dallas Morning News*.

The 6,503-yard course is 18 holes, par 72. Facilities include a driving range, snack bar, putting green, and chipping green.

BUTLER PARK PITCH AND PUTT
GOLF COURSE $
1201 West Riverside Drive
(512) 477-9025

For almost 50 years Winston Kinser operated this tiny private, very inexpensive course on city-owned land just south of Lady Bird Lake in the heart of Austin. Kinser died in 2000, but his dream lives on. The par 27, 805-yard course is tucked away just east of Lamar Boulevard and south of Riverside Drive. Each of the nine holes is par 3, and the longest hole is No. 8, 118 yards. This is a great place to find out if golf is for you. You can rent clubs (you won't need a cart). The course opens at 8:30 a.m. and closes at dusk.

GREY ROCK GOLF CLUB $$$
7401 Highway 45
(512) 288-4297
www.thegolfclubatcirclec.com

This club was designed to give patrons of a daily-fee course a country-club feel. Near the southern end of MoPac in Southwest Austin in the Circle C subdivision, the course apparently succeeded. It was named one of the best new clubs in Texas in 1992 and has remained popular. The course was designed by Jay Morrish to attract new golfers and is regarded as a fun place to play. Circle C is next door to the Lady Bird Johnson National Wildflower Research Center, and the same rugged beauty preserved at the center is apparent around the golf course.

The 18-hole course is 6,859 yards, par 72. Players can avail themselves of the driving range, putting green, dining room, meeting rooms, and the 24-hour/10-day advance tee hot line. There is also shuttle service from area hotels.

RIVERSIDE GOLF COURSE $$
1020 Grove Boulevard
(512) 386-7077

This course is a part of golf history. Now a public course in Southeast Austin, this was the home of the Austin Country Club and the place where Harvey Penick taught golf luminaries like Ben Crenshaw and Tom Kite. Penick was the club pro when Austin Community College moved here in 1950. The course is lined with old oak and pecan trees that once stood witness as some of Austin's wealthiest citizens and future national golf champions played. Now it is owned by Austin Community College and open at very low fees to all comers. The 6,500-yard course is 18 holes, par 71. There is a snack bar and picnic area on site, plus a putting green, golf shop, and chipping green.

Pflugerville

BLACKHAWK GOLF CLUB $$
2714 Kelly Lane
(512) 251-9000
www.blackhawkgolf.com

Build it, and they will come! This is true of the Blackhawk Golf Club, which was built in the early '90s by John and Martha Leach in what was then the small country town of Pflugerville, northeast of Austin. These days the club is surrounded by the suburban boomtown of Pflugerville. John Leach turned to his sister-in-law for the design of the course—she is Hollis Stacy, three-time U.S. Women's Open Champion, who decided to enter the male-dominated profession of golf course architecture. Working with local architect Charles Howard, they turned a dairy farm into a highly praised public golf course with abundant water and trees. The 6,636-yard course is 18 holes, par 72. Facilities include a driving range, golf shop, and snack bar. Greens fees include a cart. There are reduced fees for twilight play and for seniors during the week.

PRIVATE COURSES

AUSTIN COUNTRY CLUB $$$
4408 Long Champ Drive
(512) 328-0090
www.austincountryclub.com

This is the spiritual home of Harvey Penick, who was the club's first pro. A bronze statue of the revered teacher stands near the ninth green. He is shown giving tips to former student Tom Kite, the international golf champion who holds the course record, 64. This is the third home for the club, which was chartered in 1898, one of the two oldest in the state. The current course in West Austin was designed by Pete Dye, one of the world's top golf course designers. Experts rate this course as one of the toughest in the Central Texas area. The 6,822-yard course is on the shores of Lake Austin—18 holes, par 72.

BALCONES COUNTRY CLUB $$
Balcones Course
8600 Balcones Club Drive
(512) 258-1621

Spicewood Course
11210 Spicewood Club Drive
(512) 258-6672
www.balconescountryclub.com

There are two courses at this Northwest Austin club south of U.S. Highway 183, near Spicewood. Each course has its own club and pros, plus members enjoy an additional central clubhouse. The club is one of the largest in the Austin area and has given special emphasis to its junior program. The rolling hills of the Balcones course are favored by walkers. The 6,649-yard course is 18 holes, par 70. The 6,706-yard Spicewood course is 18 holes, par 72. Spicewood has greater elevation changes, plus more water elements. Twilight rates, after 4:00 p.m., are half price.

GREAT HILLS GOLF CLUB $$
5914 Lost Horizon Drive
(512) 345-7342
www.greathillscc.com

This club is known for its wonderful, authentic Hill Country landscape with rolling hills, cliffs, and canyons. It is in West Austin but priced in a much more affordable range than its nearby neighbors—Barton Creek Resort and Austin Country Club. Great Hills is regarded as a great bargain and a challenging course. The 6,599-yard course is 18 holes, par 72. The clubhouse has both casual and formal dining rooms, a swimming pool, and tennis courts.

HILLS OF LAKEWAY GOLF COURSE $$$
26 Club Estates Parkway
(512) 261-7200
www.thehillscc.com

This Hill Country course west of R.M. 620 near Lake Travis has been ranked among the top five in Texas. It was designed by Jack Nicklaus, one of his first courses in Texas. The course follows a creek and offers wonderful vistas of the surrounding rugged hills. This 6,954-yard, 18-hole, par 72 course has a marina, tennis courts, swimming pool, driving range, and putting green on-site. The club also has three additional courses, plus club facilities.

LOST CREEK COUNTRY CLUB $$$
2612 Lost Creek Boulevard
(512) 892- 1205
www.lostcreekclub.com

Located just west of Loop 360 (Capital of Texas Highway) in an area of rugged canyonland, this club is not far from Austin's most noted golf resort, Barton Creek. The land around the Lost Creek fairways and greens is rugged, and the precipitous drops along the edges of the course make control even more important than usual. The natural rise and fall of the land, plus the hazards, make the course challenging. This 18-hole course is 6,522 yards, par 72. The clubhouse offers both golf and tennis pro shops, a swimming pool, and formal and casual dining areas. There is a driving range, practice bunker, and putting green on site. Closed on Monday.

ONION CREEK COUNTRY CLUB $$$
2510 Onion Creek Parkway
(512) 282-2162
www.onioncreekclub.com

This course was designed by Masters Champion Jimmy Demaret in collaboration with George Fazio. It has been described as a classic golf course, and for many years it was the home of the original Legends of Golf tournament on the Senior PGA Tour. The Legends was played here for 12 years, and it proved to be a major building block for the seniors' tour. Located in far South Austin, the course is the anchor for a country club–style residential development. The clubhouse has all the amenities. The 18-hole course is 6,367 yards, par 70.

RIVER PLACE GOLF CLUB $$
4207 River Place Boulevard
(512) 346- 1114
www.riverplaceclub.com

On the shores of Lake Austin, west of the city, this course has been a symbol of the economic

i Avid golfers sometimes build a vacation trip around a visit to Austin's Golfsmith megastore, located in North Austin at 11000 North Interstate 35, (512) 837-1245, toll-free (800) 815-3873 (www .golfsmith.com). The complex is home to the Harvey Penick Golfing Academy, created with the blessing of the legendary Austin teacher whose legacy is noted in the introduction to this chapter.

roller-coaster ride of the past 20 years. Originally planned to be part of an upscale Hill Country development on the shores of Lake Austin, it was caught up in the development versus antigrowth wars, then the real estate downturn of the 1980s. Finally, in 1991 it was placed on the auction block by the Resolution Trust Corporation. Now, after a redesign by professional golfer Tom Kite, the course is described as attractive and sometimes challenging. The 18-hole course is 6,611 yards, par 71. Facilities include a driving range, snack bar, and putting green. Greens fees include carts. Twilight fees go into effect after 2:00 p.m.

GOLF RESORTS

The three resorts listed here are detailed in the Close-up in our Hotels and Motels chapter.

BARTON CREEK CONFERENCE RESORT
AND COUNTRY CLUB $$$$
8212 Barton Club Drive
(512) 329-4000, (866) 572-7369
www.bartoncreek.com

This resort with its four highly praised golf courses and beautiful 4,000-acre site is built on one of the most sought after and fought over pieces of land in Austin. Located just a dozen miles from downtown, the resort was created along the banks of Barton Creek, which winds through the hills before feeding the underground spring that, in turn, feeds Barton Springs. Some of Austin's most vocal environmentalists protested its construction, but others have praised the development for its ecological sensitivity—the golf courses are maintained without many of the traditional fertilizers typically used on golf courses, and efforts have been made to embrace the local flora in the resort design. The greens and fairways are planted with drought-resistant grasses to cut down on water usage.

The club has four courses, described below, all designed by leading names in golf course architecture. Given the resort's popularity as both a country club and conference center, not all four courses are available every day to resort play, with the exception of the Lakeside course. Golf packages are available.

While golf is a great reason to visit the Barton Creek club, the resort also offers other recreational facilities, including skeet shooting, tennis, and "supersports" for groups—volleyball, tug-of-war, and obstacle courses. Jogging, swimming, boating, fishing, horseback riding, sightseeing, even factory outlet mall tours are available. The resort has several dining facilities, including one of the few restaurants in Austin where a jacket is required. On-site there is a fitness center and a spa where you can have everything from facials to salt rubs, marine fango massages to aromatic loofah scrubs. There are 147 guest rooms at the resort with views of the golf course and the surrounding Hill Country. An additional 158 rooms were added to the resort in 2000.

The Crenshaw & Coore Course: This was designed by Austinite Ben Crenshaw and his partner, Bill Coore. True to Crenshaw's philosophy, the course is traditional and follows the terrain with broad, rolling fairways. This 18-hole course is 6,678 yards, par 71.

The Fazio Foothills Course: This is dubbed the resort's signature course, and its dramatic design shows the distinctive signature of Tom Fazio. There are cliff-lined fairways, waterfalls, and even caves. *Golf Digest* has rated this Fazio course one of the Best Resort Courses in America, second in Texas and 60th in the ranking of the 100 greatest golf courses in America. The course also has won the USGA's National Environmental Steward Award.

The Fazio Canyons Course: A second Fazio course has been added to the resort, and this one features more of the stunning Hill Country features Fazio incorporated into the first course, including hilltop views, meandering creeks, and small canyons where the native flora has been maintained.

The Arnold Palmer–Lakeside Course: Arnold Palmer designed this course, which opened in 1986 as the Hidden Hills Country Club. Barton Creek now owns and operates the course about 25 miles from the resort on the shores of Lake Travis. The course has been named among the most beautiful in Texas by the *Dallas Morning News*. Golfers enjoy great views from the clubhouse overlooking the lake. The 6,956-yard course is 18 holes, par 72.

LAKEWAY INN $$$$
101 Lakeway Drive
(512) 261-6600, (800) LAKEWAY
www.lakewayinn.com

This resort hotel on Lake Travis, west of the city, offers golfers and tennis players opportunities to pursue their sports while enjoying the other recreational activities available at the Highland Lakes. The hotel underwent a major restoration in 2000 and reopened with refurbished rooms, facilities, and restaurants. There are four golf courses made available to Lakeway Inn guests, including the nearby Nicklaus-designed Flintrock Falls course at The Hills of Lakeway, and tennis players can enjoy the World of Tennis with its 26 indoor and outdoor courts. There is also a fitness center, outdoor jogging trails, two swimming pools, spa, and a marina.

Live Oak Golf Course was created in 1964 by designer Leon Howard. Development restrictions were not in place back then, and Howard was given permission to dredge soil from the lake bottom to spread on the course. Twelve years later, Howard built the Yaupon Course at the resort. Both offer dramatic views of the lake—two holes on Live Oak are adjacent to the marina.

Live Oak is 18 holes, 6,643 yards, par 72. Yaupon is 18 holes, 6,565 yards, par 72. The resort offers a variety of packages, and greens fees are included in the price of packages.

WOLFDANCER GOLF CLUB $$$-$$$$
The Hyatt Regency at Lost Pines
575 Hyatt Lost Pines Road
Bastrop
(512) 308-WOLF
www.visitlostpines.com
The club at this plush new resort just west of Austin in historic Bastrop is named in honor of the Tonkawa Indians who once roamed the woods here, named the "Lost Pines" since they are far from the typical piney woods of East Texas. The course is set down amid wild grasses, and the natural fauna and flora of the area have been preserved. The 18-hole, 72 par course designed by Arthur Hill has been ranked as one the top fifty courses in Texas by the *Dallas Morning News*. The club also includes a short game area, two putting greens, a 13-acre driving range, and a clubhouse.

DRIVING RANGES

GOLFSMITH PRACTICE FACILITY
11000 North I-35
(512) 837-1810
Located next door to the Golfsmith Factory Outlet, the driving range has 70 lighted tees. Golfsmith offers custom golf clubs, clinics, practice greens, computerized swing analysis, factory tours, snack bar, and Harvey Penick irons and woods.

MISTER TEE
13910 North R.M. 620
(512) 335-4444
There are 25 lighted tees at this Northwest Austin driving range.

OAK HILL GOLF RANGE
5243 U.S. Highway 290 West
(512) 892-5634
This Southwest Austin driving range has 65 lighted tees.

SPECTATOR SPORTS

Let's face it. When it comes to professional sports, Austin isn't exactly in the big leagues. While the thousands of Austinites who enjoy major league sports find themselves sitting in left field, so to speak, there is still much to celebrate when it comes to sports in Austin. What our city lacks in major league sports is more than made up by Austin's passion for University of Texas sports teams. While UT didn't coin the phrase "Winning isn't everything, it's the only thing," it has lived by that sentiment for more than a century of athletic achievement and has produced national championship teams in a wide range of sports time and time again. UT's nationally recognized Hook 'em Horns hand signal wasn't voted the best in the country by *Sports Illustrated* magazine in 1997 for nothing.

Austin also is home to the Ice Bats, a minor-league professional ice hockey team that draws die-hard fans from all over the region; an arena football team, the Austin Wranglers; and an NBA development team, the Austin Toros. Our neighbors in Round Rock claim a very popular minor league baseball team, the Round Rock Express.

Sports spectators will discover that Austin boasts an important annual rodeo, a horse track, hugely popular marathons, and several spectacular boat races each year. Bicyclists and cycling fans will be pleased to note that not only is Austin home to seven-time Tour de France winner Lance Armstrong but our city also hosts his foundation's annual Ride for the Roses. (See the Close-up of our hometown hero in this chapter.)

Another plus for sports fans is Austin's unique location between San Antonio, Dallas, and Houston, all within a three-hour drive of our city—and an even shorter flight. San Antonio is 80 miles south on Interstate 35. This quirk of logistical fate affords Austinites incredible choices among major league sports teams in both men's and women's basketball, baseball, soccer, ice hockey, and, of course, football—the national pastime of Texas. In fact, one of the best spectator sports to be seen in this part of the world is the weekly high school football game, usually held on Thursday or Friday during the season, particularly those in some of the small towns where the game is the social event of the week. Check the sports pages of the *Austin American–Statesman* for schedules, and take in a game on a cool fall evening.

Whether your competitive spirit is most roused by a whistle, a buzzer, a starter's pistol, or those simple words, "batter up," you're sure to find a Texas sport to call your own.

MINOR LEAGUE SPORTS

Baseball

ROUND ROCK EXPRESS
Dell Diamond, 3.5 miles east of I-35 on Highway 79, Round Rock
(512) 255-2255
www.roundrockexpress.com
It took several major league players to bring minor league baseball to Round Rock, but when former Texas Ranger Hall of Famer Nolan Ryan and heavyweight techie Michael Dell are on the team, success is assured. Naming the team was easy, given Ryan's nickname as "The Ryan Express" for his awesome fastball during his playing days. The Round Rock Express rolled into the Dell Diamond in 1999. The team was so successful, both in performance and in fan attendance, that owners felt confident enough to move on up from Double-A ball, announcing the purchase

i Sign up with Texas Box Office to receive notice—and advance purchase opportunities—of sporting events, concerts, family shows, and other events at the Frank Erwin Center and elsewhere around town. The Web site is www.texasboxoffice.com/register.

of the Triple-A Edmonton Trappers of Canada, who began play as the Express in 2005.

In preparation for the new team, more luxury suites were added to the 10,000-seat Dell Diamond, named to honor the Round Rock computer giant's efforts to bring minor league ball to Central Texas. The stadium is designed with families and comfort in mind, and even the cheapest seats have chairbacks and cupholders. There's also a swimming pool complex and a children's fun center, which includes a climbing wall. General admission prices are family friendly, but make your reservations well ahead of time. Tickets are available through the Web site or at the Dell Diamond Ticket Office. The season runs from April to September.

Basketball

AUSTIN TOROS
Austin Convention Center
500 East Cesar Chavez Street
(512) 236-8333
www.austintoros.com
Minor-league basketball jumped into Austin in the fall of 2005 with the Austin Toros, one of four teams, all in the Southwest, added to the young NBA Development League. Head coach Quin Snyder is a former coach of the University of Missouri men's basketball team. The Toros play about 23 home games during their November-through-April season. The venue only holds 3,200 people, meaning fans are close to the action.

Ice Hockey

AUSTIN ICE BATS
Chaparral Ice Center
14200 I-35 North
(512) 927-PUCK,
(512) 469-SHOW (Texas Box Office)
www.icebats.com

The perfect place in Austin for those with a "bat attitude" is the Chaparral Ice Center on Ice Bats game night. The center is known fondly as the "Bat Cave." The team, formed in 1996 and currently a member of the Western Professional Hockey League, consistently draws thousands of "rabid" fans to its fast-paced and exciting home games. The season begins in October.

MAJOR LEAGUES AROUND TEXAS

NFL Football

DALLAS COWBOYS
Dallas Cowboys New Stadium
925 North Collins Street
Arlington
(972) 785-5000
www.dallascowboys.com
The Dallas Cowboys have competed in the Super Bowl a record eight times and have taken home the trophy in five of those games to tie with San Francisco as the winningest team in Super Bowl history. The Cowboys are building a brand new state-of-the-art stadium in Arlington, to be opened by the first kickoff in the fall of 2009. The "New Stadium" is the working name for the project.

HOUSTON TEXANS
Reliant Stadium, 2 Reliant Park, Houston
(866) GO-TEXANS
www.houstontexans.com
In 2002 the Houston Texans became the first NFL team in 41 years to win its expansion debut when the team stunned intrastate rival the Dallas Cowboys 19–10 in the Texans' brand-new stadium. Major league football, which had disappeared from Houston with the departure of the Oilers, was back. Reliant Stadium, a 69,500-seat state-of-the-art facility, is the world's first retractable-roof football stadium, which makes sense in a city whose perennial weather forecast is partly cloudy with a chance of rain.

NBA Basketball

DALLAS MAVERICKS
American Airlines Center
2500 Victory Avenue, Dallas
(877) 316-3553
www.nba.com/mavericks

Dallas was home to the Chaparrals of the American Basketball Association from 1967 to 1973 but lost its professional basketball team when the Chaparrals moved to San Antonio as the Spurs in 1973. Seven years later pro basketball returned to Big D at the 18,042-seat Reunion Arena when the Dallas Mavericks became an expansion team of the NBA. Three years later the Mavs recorded their first winning season.

HOUSTON ROCKETS
Toyota Center, 1510 Polk Street, Houston
(866) 446-8849
www.nba.com/rockets

Two-time National Basketball Association champions, the Houston Rockets joined the NBA in 1967 as the San Diego Rockets. The team moved to Houston four seasons later and rewarded supporters with NBA titles in 1994 and 1995. After 28 years in the same complex, the Rockets moved downtown to the Toyota Center for the 2003–2004 season, where they have played ever since.

SAN ANTONIO SPURS
1 AT&T Center Parkway
San Antonio
(210) 444-5050,
(210) 224-9600 (Ticketmaster)
www.nba.com/spurs

Austin's closest major league sports venue is about 80 miles down I-35 in San Antonio. The four-time NBA champions San Antonio Spurs is a popular team for basketball fans throughout Central Texas, and the Spurs make a special effort to promote the team in Austin by making appearances at schools and in shopping malls. The regular season runs October through April.

WNBA Basketball

HOUSTON COMETS
Reliant Arena, One Reliant Park
Houston
(713) 627-9622
www.wnba.com/comets

The Houston Comets dominated the Women's National Basketball Association for the first four years of its existence, winning the championship in 1997, 1998, 1999, and 2000. The WNBA has grown dramatically since its eight-member inaugural season and now totals 14 teams across the country. Although their "brothers" in the NBA continue to play at Houston's Toyota Center, the Comets moved to the more-compact Reliant Center beginning with the 2008 season. The season runs from May to September.

Major League Baseball

HOUSTON ASTROS
Minute Maid Park
501 Crawford Street, Houston
(877) 9-ASTROS
www.houston.astros.mlb.com

Established in 1962 as the Houston Colt .45s, the team became the Astros in 1965 and moved into the then-new Houston Astrodome. The Astros have won several Central Division pennants, including in 1997 and 1998, but haven't yet made it to the World Series. In 2000 the team moved to a new state-of-the-art facility in downtown Houston. The park, which is located near the George Brown Convention Center and next door to Union Station, is a tribute to old ballparks revered by lovers of the game. One unique feature is the retractable roof that can move into place within 12 minutes if inclement weather threatens.

TEXAS RANGERS
The Ballpark at Arlington
1000 Ballpark Way, Arlington
(817) 273-5100
www.texas.rangers.mlb.com

Formerly the Washington Senators, the team came to Dallas in 1972 as the Texas Rangers. The Rangers have had a large and loyal following over the years and in 1996, 1998, and 1999 treated fans to an American League West division championship. Playing since 1994 in a $191 million state-of-the-art complex, the Rangers claim one of the top stadiums in the country. Even if you're not a baseball fan, the Ballpark is a sight to behold. In addition to the 49,166 seats and boxes, the Ballpark features the Legends of the Game Baseball Museum, which contains some 1,000 baseball artifacts from the 1800s to the present, including some items on loan from the National Baseball Hall of Fame. The complex also features a children's learning center with a 12-acre lake, interactive exhibits, and a youth ballpark. The Ballpark was built under the direction of George W. Bush when he served as the Rangers managing partner. An ardent baseball fan, Bush has been heard to say that baseball should be played on grass, with wooden bats, and outdoors—the Ballpark is living proof of his belief.

National Hockey League

DALLAS STARS

American Airlines Center
2500 Victory Drive, Dallas
(214) 387-5600,
(214) 467-8277 (Tickets)
www.stars.nhl.com

Despite the Sunbelt climate, ice hockey has a long history and loyal following in Big D. The city's first professional ice hockey team played in Fair Park Ice Arena in 1941. In 1993 the major league Dallas Stars walked onto the ice. In 2001 the team began the season in the then-new American Airlines Center. The arena was erected on a cleared industrial site in the northwest section of downtown and can be seen by motorists traveling through downtown on I-35 East. (Take the Continental Drive exit to get a closer view of the arena.) The $325 million arena "sits on a buried superhighway of fiber-optic cable," enabling the fans to enjoy high-tech replay boards, state-of-the-art public address systems, even Internet access in the suites and conference rooms. The popularity of NHL hockey in Dallas is evident to anyone who visits the arena. Season tickets for the NHL Dallas Stars

i For a rock-n-rolling good time, check out the Texas Rollergirls, www.tx rollergirls.com, a high-spirited, heart-pumping roller derby born in Austin. Catch games played by the league's four teams— Hell Marys, Hotrod Honeys, Honky Tonk Heartbreakers, and Hustlers—at Playland Skate Center, 8822 McCann Drive.

have been sold out since 1998, and a single-night ticket, if you can find one, is costly.

Arena Football

THE AUSTIN WRANGLERS
Frank Erwin Center, 1701 Red River Street
(512) 491-6600, (512) 339-3939 (tickets)
www.austinwranglers.com

A professional football team finally took the "field" in Austin in 2004 after the Arena Football League (AFL) awarded a franchise to the Austin Wranglers. Arena football, one of today's fastest-growing professional sports, is a fast-paced game in which big nets guard the end zone instead of goal posts and foam boards surround the field of play. The Wranglers now draw thousands of die-hard fans to their games, which are played indoors at the 16,000-seat Erwin Center from February through July.

UNIVERSITY OF TEXAS SPORTS

LONGHORNS BASEBALL
Disch-Falk Field,
I-35 and Martin Luther King Drive
(512) 471-3333, (800) 982-BEVO
www.texassports.com
www.texasboxoffice.com

UT baseball fans from across Austin share the blissful moment of striding past the turnstile, ticket in hand, through the stadium tunnel, and

i If your child is hooked on sports, check out the Web sites of the professional teams in our area. Some of them offer kids' birthday parties on the court or field!

into the arena that is widely recognized as the best collegiate baseball facility in the country. This team, founded in 1895, has won an impressive six national championships, the latest in 2005. Disch-Falk Field, built in 1975 at a cost of $2.5 million and named for two former Longhorn coaches, holds 5,000 baseball fans in the main chairback area and can be expanded to hold more. As many as 8,000 fans have packed this facility for important, hotly contested collegiate games. However, this is one UT sporting event for which tickets can most often be purchased at the gate.

LONGHORNS FOOTBALL

Darrell K Royal–Memorial Stadium,
23rd Street and Campus Drive
(512) 477-6060 (Texas box office)
www.texassports.com
www.texasboxoffice.com

No sporting event in Austin comes close to Texas football for the sheer number of burnt orange–clad fans that turn out to support this team. Longhorns fans—students, Texas Exes, and just plain football buffs—unite as one big family in Darrell K Royal–Memorial Stadium when the Longhorns play at home. In fact, Texas football is so popular here that many times over the years more than 84,000 fans have stood to watch hotly contested games, jamming the stadium to way over capacity.

To attend a UT football game is to become part of a Texas tradition that dates back more than a century. Established in 1893, the Longhorns have left an impressive mark on national collegiate football. Over the years, Longhorn loyalists have been rewarded with a number of national and conference titles and more than three dozen NCAA postseason bowl games. In 2005, the Longhorns won their fourth National Championship, defeating USC 41–38 in a thrilling Rose Bowl game. In addition to witnessing these victories, fans have been treated to performances by Heisman Trophy–winner and future NFL Hall-of-Famer Earl Campbell, as well as by dozens

of All Americans, future NFL players, and other trophy winners. In 1998 senior halfback Ricky Williams broke conference and national collegiate records, culminating his UT career with a Heisman Trophy. The list of accolades for this team goes on and on. Mack Brown, former head coach of the North Carolina Tar Heels, became Texas's 28th head football coach in 1998.

Known simply as Memorial Stadium since it was inaugurated in 1924, UT added legendary head football coach Darrell K Royal's name to the stadium in 1996. The five or six seasonal home games are usually played on Saturday afternoon during the fall football season, which runs from September through November. It's best to get your tickets early, as these games can sell out. The Longhorns play an average 30 home games a year during the January through May season.

LONGHORNS SOFTBALL

McCombs Field
Martin Luther King Drive and
Comal Street
(512) 471-3333, (800) 982-BEVO
www.texasboxoffice.com

McCombs Field is a $4.5 million softball complex that's arguably one of the best in the country. Of course the team that plays on it is also top notch. A varsity team since the late 1990s, the Longhorns have won three Big 12 Conference Tournament titles and two Big 12 regular-season titles and have appeared several times in the College World Series, most recently in 2006. The team has included noted pitchers Christa Williams, a 1996 and 2000 Olympic gold medalist on the U.S. Women's Softball Team, and Cat Osterman, who won an Olympic gold medal in 2004 as a member of the U.S. team.

The Longhorns play about 15 home games, mostly double-headers, during the regular season, which runs February through April. These games can and do sell out, so get your tickets early. The team also has an exhibition-game schedule in the fall.

LONGHORNS BASKETBALL

Frank Erwin Center
1701 Red River Street
(512) 471-3333,
(512) 477-6060 (Texas box office)
www.texassports.com
www.texasboxoffice.com

Few teams on the UT campus have captured the attention and admiration of Austin sports fans like our women's basketball team. Over the past 20 years, the team has attracted the most fans in women's basketball history with a total attendance of well over 1.5 million. Success on the court is the reason. During the 14-year history of the Southwest Conference, the Longhorns took 10 regular-season titles and won nine tournaments. In 1986 the Longhorns became the first women's basketball team in the history of the National Collegiate Athletic Association to record a perfect season with a 34–0 record. The Longhorns, who moved to the Big 12 conference at the start of the 1996–97 season, draw an average of more than 5,000 fans to the Frank Erwin Center for the approximately 16 home games played during the regular season, which runs November through February.

RUNNIN' HORNS

Frank Erwin Center
1701 Red River Street
(512) 471-3333,
(512) 477-6060 (Texas box office)
www.texassports.com

i While UT football is often just as exciting as any professional game, remember that this is a college game. No smoking is allowed and no alcoholic beverages are sold or allowed in the stadium. The Texas Ex-Student's Association, fondly known as the Texas Exes, hosts a lively outdoor pregame celebration just across the street from the stadium on San Jacinto Street. They sell food, beer, and soft drinks—and will tell you how to join the organization. The event is open to the public.

i The University of Texas Longhorn Band, "the Showband of the Southwest," performs at UT football games and also makes appearances at important events around the country. The band owns the largest bass drum in the world, nicknamed "Big Bertha."

With crowds averaging 13,000 fans for each home game, UT's Runnin' Horns men's basketball team is one of the biggest draws in town—and in college basketball anywhere. Founded in 1906, the Horns were members of the Southwest Conference (SWC) from 1915 to 1996. During that time the Horns racked up an impressive 22 SWC titles (12 outright) and a 648–449 total record. In 1997 the Horns along with Southwest Conference members Baylor, Texas A&M, and Texas Tech merged with Big Eight teams to form the Big 12. The Runnin' Horns hold court for regular season games at the Erwin Center November through February.

THE BEST OF THE REST

Car Racing

THUNDER HILL RACEWAY

24801 I-35, Kyle
(512) 262-1352
www.thunderhillraceway.com

Located just off I-35 exit 210, about 25 miles south of Austin, Thunder Hill Raceway presents exciting racing events every Saturday evening from March through September. This is not a sport to watch, it's a sport to experience as the cars speed around a 3⁄8-mile oval asphalt track, sometimes faster than 120 miles per hour. Thunder Hill, Central Texas's newest and most modern track, opened in 1998 and features a 3,600-seat open-air stadium. The raceway presents hobby stock cars, superstocks, and limited late models regularly and each week also adds a special feature race, such as Texas pro sedans, super late models, and American race trucks. Thunder Hill also sponsors RV shows, car shows, and fairs as well as an ongoing live music concert series. Gates open at 5:30 p.m. Racing starts at 7:00 p.m. Tickets are on sale at the door. Admission is $10.00 for adults, $7.50 for children ages 6 through 12. Children younger than 6 are admitted free.

Running

AUSTIN CONVENTION AND VISITORS BUREAU
201 East Second Street
(512) 478-0098
www.austintexas.org

Two Austin footraces draw lots of spectators each year. The Motorola Marathon (www.motorolamarathon.com), usually held the second Sunday of February, draws more than 10,000 participants. Runners start in far Northwest Austin and wind up, hopefully, 26 kilometers later on the shores of Lady Bird Lake downtown. The prize money purse totals $100,000, with $10,000 awarded to both the overall male and overall female winners. In April Austin hosts the Statesman Capitol 10,000, among the top 100 road races in the country. This 10K event draws about 15,000 competitors as well as crowds of spectators. (See our Parks and Recreation chapter for more information on running events and venues.)

Rodeo

STAR OF TEXAS FAIR & RODEO
7311 Decker Lane
(512) 467-9811,
(512) 477-6060 (Texas box office)
www.rodeoaustin.com
www.texasboxoffice.com

Yee haw!! There's nothing like a great rodeo to let you know you've arrived in Texas. Austin's big event is the annual Star of Texas Fair & Rodeo, a two-week affair that begins around early March. This huge competition, on the official Professional Rodeo Cowboys Association (PRCA) circuit, draws thousands and thousands of people from all over the state for fun-filled days and nights of bull riding, calf roping, team roping, steer wrestling, barrel racing, saddle bronc riding, bareback riding,

and much, much more. Rodeo events aren't the only highlight of this celebration. This is also the Travis County Fair and offers fun for people of all ages, including carnival rides and booths galore . To top it all off, the rodeo features a major concert performance each evening. Brooks & Dunn, Merle Haggard, Gretchen Wilson, Willie Nelson and many more outstanding musical performers have appeared at this wildly popular event.

Sailboat Racing

AUSTIN YACHT CLUB
5906 Beacon Drive
(512) 266-1336
www.austinyachtclub.org

Austin wouldn't be Austin if it didn't have a spectator sport that took advantage of our great waterways. The Austin Yacht Club sponsors a number of major annual sailboat regattas as well as a number of other races throughout the year. Sailors may call the Yacht Club for information on how to participate in these events, while those with sailing experience may post information about themselves on the club's bulletin board if they would like to crew these boats. The Austin Yacht Club, founded in 1952, aims to promote the sport of sailboat racing. The club sponsors a summer sailing class for adults and camps for children.

Horse Racing

MANOR DOWNS
US 290 East and Manor Downs Road, Manor
(512) 272-5581
www.manordowns.com

Established in 1974 as a quarterhorse racetrack for racing enthusiasts, Manor Downs became a pari-mutuel betting track in 1990 after Texas legalized that form of gambling. The Downs, offering Thoroughbred racing, too, features live horse racing on weekends starting about 1:30 p.m. during the spring season (from about February to around the end of May). Manor Downs also offers simulcast racing from tracks around the country on screens at other times during the

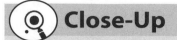

Close-Up

Lance Armstrong—Austin's Hometown Hero

"He's from Austin, you know."

Who among Lance Armstrong's hometown fans—and there are so many of us—has never heard those words drop impulsively from our lips? It's not just that Lance is a champion cyclist who won the Tour de France a stunning seven consecutive times. And it's not only because he first had to triumph over an advanced case of cancer, or because he formed a cancer foundation to help others even before he knew whether he'd survive the disease himself, although those are part of it, too. We're mostly proud of our hometown hero because he's lived his life—on and off the bike—with such style, such dignity, such humanity, such heart. So when we casually mention that Lance Armstrong is one of us, or when we call the world's most famous bicycle race the Tour de Lance, we pay tribute to the neighbor we've come to admire these past years. He has reminded us just how high the human spirit can soar.

Each October, cyclists, cancer survivors, and supporters from around the world converge on our city to participate in the Lance Armstrong Foundation (LAF)'s Ride for the Roses Weekend (see the Annual Events and Festivals chapter). Founded in 1997, the LAF has raised more than $26 million to fund cancer survivorship programs and research. Not bad for an organization that Lance has said "started on a paper napkin in a Mexican restaurant in Austin, Texas." The foundation, however, is just one of the many ways Lance has reached out to others. In 1995, before he became a household name, he created the Junior Olympic Race Series to promote cycling among America's youth. He has co-written two best-selling memoirs that address in candid detail his struggle to survive cancer and get back to the business of living. And when he's not out there training for or winning races, Lance travels the globe on behalf of his foundation and others to raise cancer awareness and help strengthen the resolve of those stricken with the disease.

Born September 18, 1971, in the Dallas suburb of Plano, Lance gained fame in 1991 by winning the U.S. Amateur Cyclng Championship. In 1993, after picking himself up from a humbling last-place finish in his professional debut, Lance secured his spot in U.S. cycling history with his victory in the million-dollar Triple Crown. By 1996 he was the number one–ranked cyclist in the world. Later that year he was diagnosed with testicular cancer, which had spread to his lungs and brain. Given less than a 50/50 chance of survival, Lance underwent two operations and a debilitating treatment program. While still battling the disease, he created the LAF. By 1998 he was cancer free—and ready to ride into history.

His stunning comeback victory in the 1999 Tour de France is now legendary, and the six Tour wins that followed are nothing short of miraculous. In 2002 *Sports Illustrated* named Lance its Sportsman of the Year, calling him "more than a bicyclist now, more than an athlete. He's become a kind of hope machine."

Wherever he goes from here, one thing is certain: Coasting is not in Lance Armstrong's nature.

---

spring meet and throughout the year. While not the fanciest racetrack in Central Texas, Manor Downs is the closest Austinites can get to live horse racing. It's also a wonderful gathering place for the state's horsemen and women who come in from all over to take part in this age-old Texas tradition.

i Bevo, the live Longhorn steer that serves as the UT mascot, made his first appearance at a UT football game on Thanksgiving Day 1916.

RETAMA PARK

1 Retama Parkway, Selma
(210) 651-7000
www.retamapark.com

This ultramodern horse racing park features

Thoroughbred and quarterhorse racing May through June and Thoroughbred racing late July to mid-October. Retama also offers simulcast racing year-round from top tracks across the country, including the Kentucky Derby, Preakness, Belmont, and the Breeders Cup. Retama has a spectacular indoor grandstand and clubhouse as well as a sports bar and terrace dining. Live racing May to June begins at 6:30 p.m. Thursday through Saturday and 5:00 p.m. on Sunday. Races for the Thoroughbred meet begin at 6:30 p.m. Wednesday through Saturday. Selma is about 65 miles south of Austin on I-35. Take the 174-A exit and follow the signs. Retama is just west of the interstate.

DAY TRIPS AND WEEKEND GETAWAYS

Covering 267,339 square miles and boasting hundreds of miles of seashore, soaring mountains, plunging valleys, vast plains and prairies, pine forests, deserts, islands, lakes of all sizes and shapes, giant metropolises, small towns, and wide-open spaces galore, Texas is much more than a state—"It's a Whole Other Country," as our boosters like to say. At the very heart of it all, in spirit if not precise geographic center, is Austin. It's no wonder, then, that when Central Texans plan a vacation we often look no farther than our own great big bountiful backyard. In fact, for the day trips and weekend getaways we cover in this chapter, we can't even include all the fascinating sights Texas has to offer. Some are just too far away to make even a weekend trip feasible. You'll soon find, however, that there are plenty of places to escape to right here in Central Texas.

OVERVIEW

One journey takes you to Johnson City, boyhood home of our country's 36th president. We'll also introduce you to LBJ's beloved ranch, the "Texas White House" during the Johnson Administration, and the place where the elder statesman came home to retire following a lifetime of public service. Both of these areas make up the LBJ National Historic Park.

Not to overlook Texas's other U.S. presidents, we'll present Bryan/College Station, home of the George Bush Presidential Library and Museum, site of sprawling Texas A&M University, and domicile of UT's archrivals, the A&M Aggies. Of course #41, as the Bush family calls former President George H. W. Bush, has a library, while #43, President George W. Bush, just has a ranch for now. Located in Crawford, a tiny unincorporated community southwest of Waco, Prairie Church Ranch is well hidden from public view, but visitors to town can drop by the local coffee shop and pick up a Crawford souvenir. It is an easy side trip on the way to or from Dallas.

We'll tell you about Gruene, a former ghost town that emerged from ruin to become a thriving community, especially on weekends when the chicken-fried steak disappears faster than the time it takes to pronounce the city's name

correctly. This is one place Austinites visit regularly to shop for antiques or to crowd into the historic Gruene Hall for an evening of first-class live music.

We had to include Round Top and Winedale, two communities east of Austin renowned as meccas of classical music and theater. One of the state's oldest communities, Round Top is home to the International Festival Institute, founded by a concert pianist. Winedale hosts the annual Shakespeare at Winedale festival. Austinites flock to these cities throughout the year to partake of their great annual events and to step back in time.

The little town of Salado, just a stone's throw from Austin, could have been a contender. An up-and-coming town in the 1880s, Salado was bypassed when the railroad finally came to Central Texas. While railroad towns thrived, Salado slipped into obscurity. Discovered by artists in the second half of the 20th century, Salado is now back on track, so to speak, and a popular day trip or weekend getaway from Austin.

Of course, we couldn't forget Fredericksburg, one of Austin's favorite weekend getaways and a prime example of Hill Country living. This quaint town, founded by German immigrants in 1846, boasts a Main Street that has earned a spot on the National Register of Historic Places. Main Street shops offering antiques, apparel, and arts and crafts do a bustling business on weekends as visitors pour in from all over the region. This is one great place to spot a movie star or two, or perhaps just enjoy an authentic German meal.

Considering the important German influences on the culture and development of Central Texas over the past 150 years, it wouldn't do to mention just one German-infused town. New Braunfels, too, retains much of its German flavor, literally. From the great German restaurants to the annual Wurstfest sausage festival, New Braunfels is a delight for the taste buds. We'll give you two other reasons this town attracts Central Texans year-round.

Appropriately, the Highland Lakes come last. After you've spent even a little time trying to see all the sights Central Texas has to offer, you may need to just get away from it all and relax for a while on a boat or on a beach. Any one of the four lakes we describe in this section will do the trick.

Before you head out, check our Annual Events and Festivals chapter for events in these day trip destinations. Also have a look at our Texas Pronunciation Guide in the Area Overview chapter so that you'll sound like an Insider when you get there.

Whether you decide to head north, south, east, or west to major cities, small towns, or a place of quiet solitude, you're sure to find a spot that is Texas through and through.

UP NORTH

Salado

The Village of Salado, 55 miles north of Austin on Interstate 35, is just that—a village, and a charming one, that owes its existence now to the fact that history passed it by. Founded in 1859 at a low-water crossing of Salado Creek, it looked like Salado was destined to become a growing community, especially with the founding of Salado College in 1859. By 1884 the community was on its way to being a town with 7 churches, 14 stores, 2 hotels, 2 blacksmiths, and 3 cotton gins. But when the railroads were built to the north

> **i** If you're planning to explore several state parks, be sure to purchase a one-year Texas State Parks Pass for $60, which provides unlimited entry to all 120 state parks and historic sites, as well as a host of other benefits. The pass can be purchased at all Texas state parks and historic sites, (512) 389-8900. It is not yet available for purchase online.

and east, Salado slipped back to being a village.

Salado's population dwindled from 900 in 1882 to 400 by 1914 and only slightly more than 200 in 1950, according to the community's publications. But then artists and artisans began to settle in the area, buying up the old buildings and opening art galleries and antiques shops. Now the village has more than 130 businesses and attracts weekend visitors who come here to relax, browse the stores, and soak up the area's history. A great resource is the Salado Web site (www.salado.com), which offers information on lodging, shops, dining, events, and recreation in this historical community.

One of the best ways to learn about the area is to request a copy of the Driving Tour Tape prepared by the Bell County Historical Commission. Visitors can write to the Bell County Historical Commission, Bell County Courthouse, Belton, TX 76513, or ask at one of Salado's landmarks, like the Stagecoach Inn, 1 Main Street, on the east side of I-35, (254) 947-5111, www.inn-at-salado.com.

The modern 82-room Stagecoach Inn stands adjacent to what remains of the Shady Villa Hotel, where Sam Houston was said to have slept in 1850. Other famous guests include General George Armstrong Custer and cattlemen Charles Goodnight and Shanghai Pierce, who stopped at this historic spot along the Chisholm Trail.

What remains of the old hotel is part of the inn's restaurant, which also includes an open-air atrium built around a 500-year-old burr oak. Newer dining rooms adjoining the original two-story clapboard building serve guests at lunch and dinner, but in keeping with tradition the waitresses always recite the menu by heart—

prime rib, plate-size steaks, fried chicken, baked ham and lamb, plus desserts such as homemade pie and cobbler.

Salado abounds with historical connections. In the 1830s Sterling C. Robertson, himself of Scottish heritage, established a colony here; many of the settlers were Scots. In November Salado hosts the Annual Gathering of the Clans on the Village Green near the Stagecoach Inn. Hundreds of Texans and Americans of Scottish descent descend on Salado for the weekend festival. Call (254) 947-5232 for information.

Visitors also flock to Salado for the annual Christmas Stroll & Holiday Home Tour, held on weekends in December. Salado is a favorite choice of Central Texans for Christmas shopping and celebrating the season, so the village's hotels and guest houses are booked in advance. There is also a large July Fourth picnic, a summer art fair in August, and a December village artists' sale. Call the Salado Chamber of Commerce, (254) 947-5040, for information on these events or check the calendar at www.salado.com. At the Table Rock Amphitheater, (254) 947-9205, an outdoor dinner theater in the community, the Tablerock Theatre group puts on annual performances of a historical pageant, Salado Legends, during the summer and dramatizations of Dickens's *A Christmas Carol* in December.

More than 130 buildings in Salado are listed on the National Register of Historic Places, and several of them serve as guest houses and bed-and-breakfast inns. Some are small cottages with cozy fireplaces, while others are large Victorian homes. Some are located in rural settings, others are just a few steps from the shopping district and most are listed on the chamber's Web site, www.salado.com. Duffers may want to ask about the Mill Creek Country Club & Guest Houses (254) 947-5141, www.millcreekgolfresort.com, which has a Robert Trent Jones II 18-hole golf course as well as swimming and tennis facilities. The old homes also offer romantic and charming backdrops for dining in Salado. Several serve lunch and afternoon tea, including Browning's Courtyard Cafe on Salado Square, (254) 947-8666; Cathy's Boardwalk Cafe, (254) 947-8162; and

the Pink Rose Tea Room on Main Street, (254) 947-9110. Gourmet dinners are served on weekends at the Inn on the Creek, (254) 947-5554, a Victorian bed-and-breakfast on Center Circle. Reservations are required. Pietro's Italian Restaurant & Pizzeria, 302 North Main Street, (254) 947-0559, offers a change of pace for lunch and dinner. The Range at the Barton House, Main Street (254) 947-3828, offers American cuisine with French and Mediterranean touches for lunch and dinner Wednesday through Sunday. No Texas village would be complete without Mexican food, which can be enjoyed at the Salado Mansion, Main Street, (254) 947-5157. Mexican food served in an 1857 mansion—no place but Salado.

Sustenance is necessary in Salado since the village has so many shops it is impossible to list them all here. There are herbalists, antiques dealers, custom furniture stores—Barnhill-Britt sells handcrafted furniture constructed of antique longleaf pine taken from 19th-century Texas buildings; Benton's has custom-order iron beds—Amish quilts, children's fashions, Oriental rugs, Christmas ornaments, folk art, bride's gifts, rare books, top women's fashion, native plants, tribal art, gourmet foods, jewelry, and rabbits everywhere (Wigglesworth Place, Rock Creek at Main, a Salado Christmas favorite), paintings and sculpture, and on and on.

Salado is an unincorporated village, but the chamber of commerce estimates the population of permanent residents is about 1,500—which means there is a shop for about every 10 residents in the area. Most of the shops are open daily, although some do close on Sunday. Most are in the immediate area of Main Street.

DOWN SOUTH

New Braunfels

Only an hour's drive from Austin, New Braunfels attracts visitors for two primary reasons—antiques shopping and water sports. The latter draws thousands of visitors, especially in summer, to a variety of artificial and natural waterways to tube, raft, swim, paddle, and plop in the cool, wet stuff.

The two sides of New Braunfels have led to a growth boom, and Comal County has been cited as the fastest growing county in Texas in recent years. Many of the visitors come to enjoy swimming in Landa Park, (830) 608-2165, the downtown home of the state's largest spring-fed pool and also home to a stretch of the Comal River. Another popular destination is Schlitter-bahn, the state's biggest water park, which is detailed in our Kidstuff chapter. Given all the activities available in the area, crowds flock to New Braunfels on weekends in the peak summer season, but thanks to its old German roots the town has maintained its charm. The town is named after Prince Carl of Solms-Braunfels, a member of the Mainzer Adelsverein, or League of Nobles, who encouraged German emigration in the 1840s as an escape from economic hard times in Germany.

The young Republic of Texas offered land grants to the nobles as an inducement for European settlers. Prince Carl brought over a large contingent in 1844, many of whom died on the coast of Texas due to an epidemic. The survivors settled in New Braunfels in 1844, and by 1855 the town was the fourth largest in Texas. Meanwhile, Prince Carl had gone home since his fiancée refused to come to Texas.

There are several invocations of the Prince's name in and around the town, including Prince Solms Park, where tubers pay a small admission fee to tube in the Comal River, and the Prince Solms Inn, 295 East San Antonio Street, (830) 625-9169, www.princesolmsinn.com, an upscale bed-and-breakfast in a restored Victorian home. Advance reservations are a must at this popular guest house. Another hotel with great character is the Faust Hotel, 240 South Seguin Street, (830) 625-7791, www.fausthotel.com, just 1 block south of the town plaza. The Faust, now a National Landmark Hotel, was built in 1928 and has been restored to reflect that period. The rooms here all have character and are decorated individually.

New Braunfels is of great interest to architecture buffs, particularly for the tiny Sunday houses built by German farmers in the 19th century as weekend town cottages. Many have been restored, but others stand waiting for the deep pockets and eager hands of would-be restorers. Many of the town's antiques shops are housed in old German homes. The New Braunfels Chamber of Commerce, 390 South Seguin Street, (830) 625-2385, www.nbcham.org, offers an "antique crawl" map.

The chamber also provides a historic walking tour map to guide visitors through the vibrant downtown area, where there are more than 30 historic buildings. The heart of the community is the plaza, where the traffic is slowed by a roundabout, and the restored buildings reflect the prosperity enjoyed by the town's forefathers.

Early life in New Braunfels is depicted at the Sophienburg Museum, 401 West Coll Street, (830) 629-1572. Named for Prince Carl's fiancée, who declined to head for the frontier, the museum is built on a small hill where the prince had planned to build his honeymoon castle. The building housed his administrative offices and now has several exhibits showing life on the Texas frontier. The museum is open daily from 10:00 a.m. to 5:00 p.m. except Sunday, when it is open from 1:00 to 5:00 p.m. There is a small admission fee.

Another New Braunfels museum is one of those little gems often tucked away in small towns that receive little attention in these days of theme parks. The Museum of Texas Handmade Furniture, 1370 Church Hill Drive, (830) 629-6504, features more than 75 examples of handcrafted furniture made by German cabinetmakers working in the mid-19th century on the Texas frontier. Housed in the Breustadt House, c. 1858, and listed in the National Register of Historic Places, the museum is open to the public daily during the summer and on weekends the rest of the year.

Nearby, at 1300 Church Hill Drive, the city's Conservation Society has relocated a number of historic buildings in Conservation Plaza. They include several homes, a one-room schoolhouse, a music studio, a barn, and a general store. Some have been completely restored; others are awaiting restoration. The society holds a folklife festival here in early May, (830) 625-8766, and the buildings are open at irregular hours during the rest of the year (www.nbconservation.org).

Another good way to capture the spirit of 19th-century New Braunfels is to eat at one of the town's German-style restaurants. Krause's Cafe, 148 Castell Street, (830) 625-7581, has been serving German dishes, barbecue, and just plain, old-fashioned American cooking since 1938. This is where the courthouse crowd and the business leaders come for breakfast and lunch. The cafe also serves dinner, including chili (William Gebhardt perfected his chili powder formula in downtown New Braunfels a century ago), steaks, and burgers. Leave room for pie—Krause's has a wide selection. The cafe is open for breakfast, lunch, and dinner daily; closed Sunday and for three weeks in September. No credit cards are taken here.

True to its German roots, New Braunfels is noted for its sausage. The New Braunfels Smokehouse, (830) 625-2416, www.nbsmokehouse.com (they ship!), at the intersection of I-35 and Highway 46, began life as a smokehouse for local farmers and ranchers more than 50 years ago. Now it is a restaurant featuring several varieties of sausage and barbecue, plus smoked hams and turkeys. The restaurant is open for breakfast, lunch, and dinner daily, and there is a gift shop and mail-order business on the premises.

Sausage is celebrated with relish (and onions) at Wurstfest, the annual 10-day festival that attracts tens of thousands of visitors to New Braunfels every November. The festival centers on sausage-eating, beer drinking, and polka dancing (see our Annual Events and Festivals chapter).

Gruene

It is pronounced "Green," and for the savvy developers who revived this ghost town north of New Braunfels, the name proved propitious. These days, old Gruene (www.gruene.net, www.touringtexas.com/gruene/) is anything but a ghost town, particularly on weekends when visitors stroll the narrow streets looking for antiques bargains, visiting craft shops and studios, kicking up a storm at the local dance hall, or digging into a chicken-fried steak. Ernest Gruene originally settled in New Braunfels and then moved his family to this area, about 5 miles north of New Braunfels, in 1872. His son, Henry D. Gruene, became very influential, and so the town was named after him.

After Henry died in 1920, Gruene suffered two fatal blows—the boll weevil killed the cotton crop and the Depression hit. The city turned into a ghost town, and the old buildings lay empty for years. When investors discovered the community, it looked as if time had stopped back in the '30s. Now this community on F.M. 306 just north of New Braunfels and about an hour's drive south of Austin on I-35 is listed on the National Register of Historic Places. There is only one intersection in Gruene, and most businesses lie either on Gruene Road or Hunter Road, making a tour of the town easy on the legs.

You will want to save some energy if you plan to spend the evening at Texas's oldest dance hall, Gruene Hall, (830) 606-1281 (www.gruenehall.com), where some of the top names in country music have played, including Garth Brooks. The first dance was in 1878, and now the bar-cum-dance hall opens daily around midday so visitors can enjoy a longneck or two. The old hall has remained stuck in the years between the two world wars. The posters on the walls are advertisements from the era; there is no air-conditioning—the windows and doors are opened wide to catch the breeze—and there are burlap bags hanging from the ceiling. Cover charges for evening performances vary.

During the week, Gruene is quiet unless a popular band is playing, but on the weekends the little town fills up. Tubers are attracted to the Guadalupe River in summertime (Gruene is on the north bank of the river), while antiques hunters and shoppers come to the village to stroll the stores and galleries.

There is an abundance of bed-and-breakfast accommodations in town and the upscale Gruene Mansion Inn, located at 1275 Gruene Road, (830) 629-2641 (www.gruenemansioninn.com), where guests stay in restored 1870 cottages with views of the Guadalupe River. The hotel also operates the Restaurant at Gruene Mansion Inn, (830) 620-0760, which serves lunch and dinner daily inside or out on the deck overlooking the river.

The menu features a variety of cuisines, including Cajun, German, and continental. The Gruene Homestead Inn sits on eight acres of farmland, and several of the old farm buildings have been renovated and converted to unique bedrooms. Cottages and old homes from the area also have been relocated on the farm and restored. The rooms at the inn are all individually decorated and have sitting areas or porches for relaxing after a day of activities on the river or among the shops nearby. The inn is located at 832 Gruene Road, (800) 238-5534 or (830) 606-0216, www.greunehomesteadinn.com.

Also overlooking the river is the Grist Mill Restaurant, (830) 625-0684, 1287 Gruene Road, housed not in a gristmill but in a converted 100-year-old cotton gin. Lunch and dinner are served daily, and the menu features typical all-American fare—burgers, sandwiches, salads, steaks—plus some Tex-Mex and barbecue dishes.

Most of the businesses in Gruene offer free brochures illustrating walking tours of the community. One popular stop on the tour is the Guadalupe Valley Winery, also housed in an old cotton gin, at 1720 Hunter Road, (830) 629-2351.

Hunter Road has several antiques stores and the old Gruene General Store, built in 1878, that now sells Texana, including cookbooks, cookies, and kitchen equipment, and offers sodas from the old-style soda fountain. Several artisans, including potters and ironworkers, have studios along Hunter Road, and the Greune Antique Mall is home to several dealers. Gruene is popular year-round, but visitors mark their calendars for the monthly Market Days (www.gruenemarketdays.com), held the third weekend of the month from February through November, when more than 100 arts and crafts vendors gather in Gruene. For more information on Gruene, call the Gruene Information Center at (830) 629-5077.

OUT EAST

Round Top and Winedale

These two tiny communities in Fayette County, about 90 miles east of Austin, have become

Traveling around Texas by car will eventually lead you to a two-lane state highway. When these highways have wide shoulders, it's customary for slower vehicles to drive on the shoulder briefly to allow faster cars to pass. Frankly, we don't know if that's legal, but it's the Texas way.

world-renowned for their cultural events, their celebrations of music and theater that take place in several beautifully restored 19th-century Texas buildings set in landscaped grounds, and two nationally renowned antiques fairs. But even when there are no events scheduled at Round Top or Winedale, a day trip to the area can be an opportunity for city dwellers to catch a glimpse of small-town Texas.

Round Top is one of the state's oldest communities—the first Fourth of July in Texas was celebrated here in 1828, long before Texas was a republic or a state in the Union. In the mid-19th century, several German and Swedish families settled here, but the community never grew beyond a mere handful of homes. Then in the 1960s, artists and wealthy Texans began to be attracted to the area's natural beauty, buying up the old homes and restoring them.

In 1971 concert pianist James Dick chose Round Top as the home for his music institute, designed to offer students an opportunity to study with leading musicians. Dick established the International Festival Institute in historic Round Top. During its first five years, the Festival Institute leased facilities, but a master plan for development of a 200-acre campus was adopted. The first major facility, the Mary Moody Northern Pavilion, was acquired in 1973. It was the largest transportable stage in the world and was used for open-air concerts until 1983. Later it was housed in the 1,200-seat Festival Concert Hall, on which construction began in 1980, until the permanent stage was completed in the Concert Hall in 1993. An abandoned school building and six acres of land east of Round Top were acquired in 1973 for the campus, now named Festival Hill. The grounds are open to the public, and they make a great setting for a spring picnic.

Several historic buildings were moved to the festival site. The first historic structure moved to Festival Hill came from nearby LaGrange and was named the William Lockhart Clayton House in honor of the man who created the Marshall Plan. Built in 1885, it was renovated in 1976 for faculty offices, teaching facilities, and indoor concerts. The Menke House, built in 1902, was moved to Festival Hill from Hempstead and renovated as a faculty residence and conference center in 1979. Its Gothic Revival ceilings, woodwork, and staircases make it a showcase of Texas carpentry.

The historic sanctuary of the former Travis Street United Methodist Church of LaGrange, built in 1883, was moved to Festival Hill in 1994 for restoration as a center for chamber music, organ recitals, lectures, and seminars. It was renamed the Edythe Bates Old Chapel to honor one of the great Texan patronesses of the fine arts and houses an 1835 Henry Erben pipe organ. The Festival Institute Museum and Library exhibits art collections in the Festival Concert Hall and the historic house restorations.

There are now 17 musical programs during June and July each year. The August-to-April Concerts Series, the Early Music Festival, and other programs bring the total number of year-round concerts to more than 50. These include orchestral, chamber music, choral, vocal, brass, woodwinds, and solo performances. The repertoire extends from ancient to contemporary music.

The campus is also used for conferences, meetings, and retreats by businesses and professional organizations. A series of distinguished museum lectures is presented at Festival Hill each year. The campus, famed for its gardens, rare trees, herb collections, cascades, fountains, and unusual landscaping is a destination for visitors from all over the world; the grounds are open daily.

Tickets may be purchased at the Concert Hall beginning one hour prior to each concert, and season tickets are available. For information on the musical season or individual concerts, call (979) 249-3129, www.festivalhill.org.

Nearby Winedale has been a center for ethnic studies since Ima Hogg, daughter of a former Texas governor, donated the grounds and several historic buildings to the University of Texas in 1967. Winedale is also home to the Shakespeare at Winedale festival where UT students perform several of Shakespeare's plays in an 1894 barn-turned-theater at various times during the year (www.shakespeare-winedale.org).

Like Round Top, the grounds are open to the public, and there is a small admission charge. Winedale is open May through October on Saturday from 10:00 a.m. to 6:00 p.m., Sunday from noon to 6:00 p.m., and November through April from 9:00 a.m. to 5:00 p.m. on Saturday and noon to 5:00 p.m. on Sunday. Tours of the on-site historic buildings can be arranged, (979) 278-3530, and there is a marked nature trail. There are several annual events that bring visitors to Winedale, including a Christmas Open House featuring seasonal music and food, a spring festival and Texas Craft Exhibition, and a German Oktoberfest.

There are numerous bed-and-breakfast and guest house accommodations in the Round Top/Winedale area, and many are listed on the round-top.org Web site. Some Austin residents prefer to stay overnight in the area after a concert or play, turning a night outing into a weekend getaway. Accommodations range in price. If you plan an overnight stay, book well in advance during those times when concerts and theater presentations are scheduled.

Several restaurants in the area feature country cooking, including Klump's restaurant, (979) 249-5696, in Round Top. It's open Wednesday through Saturday for breakfast, lunch, and dinner and Sunday and Tuesday for breakfast and lunch. Closed Monday.

The area also has become popular among antiques collectors. In addition to shops in the communities of Round Top, Winedale, Shelby, Warrenton, and Carmine, antiques dealers come from across the country for the first weekend in April and October to the Antiques Fair (see our Annual Events and Festivals chapter).

To reach Round Top or Winedale, take U.S. Highway 290 east toward Houston from Austin.

Just beyond Giddings look for Highway 237; head south and follow the signs to Round Top. Winedale is just east of Round Top on F.M. 2714. Many of the merchants in the area have tourist maps showing the locations of the various small communities and lists of accommodations and area attractions, and there is a visitor center on the square in Round Top. Another good place to gather information about local happenings is the Round Top Mercantile Company, on Highway 237, (979) 249-3117, www.roundtopmercantile .com, which is open seven days a week. Look for the store's Texaco pumps on the west side of the highway as you drive into Round Top.

Bryan/College Station

Given the intense sports rivalry between the University of Texas and Texas A&M University, it's practically treason for an Austinite to tout the merits of College Station—home of the Aggies of A&M. This college town and neighboring Bryan (you can't tell where one begins and the other leaves off) offer all kinds of treats for the day-tripper or weekend visitor. College Station, 101 miles northeast of Austin, is an easy, stress-free drive along a route now designated as the "Presidential Corridor."

The corridor—US 290 East and Highway 21—connects Texas's two presidential libraries, the Lyndon Baines Johnson Library in Austin and College Station's George Bush Presidential Library and Museum, (979) 260-9552, www.bushlibrary. tamu.edu, which opened at Texas A&M University in November 1997. It's worth the trip alone to visit this massive facility dedicated to the life and times of the 41st president of the United States. With more than 25,000 square feet of exhibition space, the museum chronicles Bush's life from his youth in Greenwich, Connecticut, to his service as a pilot in the U.S. Navy and through his bold move to the Texas oil fields in the mid-1940s.

In vivid detail, visitors learn about Bush's career as a congressman, ambassador to the United Nations, director of the C.I.A., then vice president and president of the United States. Here visitors will find the largest and most com-plete exhibit in the country dedicated to the 1991 Gulf War. There's also a huge slab of the Berlin Wall, graffiti and all. One section of the museum is dedicated to former First Lady Barbara Bush's efforts on behalf of literacy, volunteerism, and AIDS prevention. Of course the library is also a research institution and includes 38 million pages of President Bush's official and personal papers. The library, located on the A&M West Campus, is open Monday through Saturday 9:30 a.m. to 5:00 p.m. and Sunday noon to 5:00 p.m. There is a small admission fee, but children age 5 and younger are admitted free. (Construction on the George W. Bush presidential library will begin in 2009. It is to be located on the Southern Method-ist University campus in Dallas).

Just a short distance from the Bush library is the main campus of Texas A&M University, Tex-as's oldest public college. A&M, the state's land grant college, was founded in 1876 as an all-male military college. On August 23, 1963, the name of the Agricultural and Mechanical College was changed to Texas A&M University. Today A&M is among the 10 largest universities in the United States, with more than 46,000 students, and ranks among the top three institutions nationally in undergraduate enrollment in agriculture, busi-ness administration, and architecture.

A&M's nationally known Corps of Cadets program—now open to men and women—has produced more military officers than any other institution in the country except for the service academies. Start your tour of this sprawl-ing campus with a visit to the Appelt Aggieland Visitor Center in Rudder Tower on the main campus, (979) 845-5851, www.tamu.edu. Some points of interest include the Academic Building, built in 1912 on the site of Old Main, the first building on campus; the Albritton Bell Tower, a 138-foot tower that contains a 49-bell carillon; the Memorial Student Center, opened in 1950 and dedicated to former students who died in World War II; the Student Recreation Center, the largest student rec center of its kind in the coun-try, completed in 1995; the Cadet Quad, home to those world-famous cadets; and Kyle Field, the

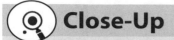

Close-Up

Hitting the Trails to Hill Country Wines

It likely comes as no surprise to wine aficionados that Texas makes some excellent wines, many of them medal winners in national and international competitions. Those who are new to, or visiting, Central Texas, however, might be surprised to learn that the wine-making tradition in this region is alive and well—and growing. Today, the Texas Hill Country alone boasts almost two dozen wineries that vary in size, ambience, wine-making style, and, of course, "flavor." Austin, which sits at the eastern edge of Hill Country, is the gateway to all, as well as to other award-winning wineries within driving distance to the east and south of us.

As the popularity of Texas' homegrown wines has increased, so have the number of wine-related events.

Foremost on the list of Austin-area happenings is the Hill Country Wine & Food Festival, a four-day event held annually in April, www.texaswineandfood.org. It is hard to pinpoint the highlight of this classy festival, which takes place at venues in Austin and the Hill Country, as every aspect of it is a true experience. The Village at the Shores, an outdoor food, wine, and live music extravaganza, and the Stars Across Texas Grand Tasting, a gala affair, are two of the most popular features, as are the cooking classes and the luncheons at Hill Country wineries.

Sixteen of our neighboring wineries have joined forces to create the Hill Country Wine Trail, www.texaswinetrail.com, to introduce newcomers to the wineries and to present the newest vintage. The calendar begins in February, with the Wine Lover's Trail held around Valentine's Day. The focus of this event is on the new vintage, but guests can enjoy "sweetheart" dinners, chocolates, and, of course, wine—in case the "bouquet" you want to present to your sweetheart is not the kind presented in a vase. The Wine & Wildflower Trail in April is timed to coincide with the annual spring blossoming of the Hill Country's bluebonnets. August brings the Harvest Wine Trail, October features the Texas Wine Month Passport Trail, while the Holiday Wine Trail is held in December. Another set of trails is outlined on the Texas Wine Trails Web site, www.texaswinetrails.com, which includes two trails in our region. Some wineries are found on more than one trail, but if you want to get a fuller spectrum, check out all three.

It is not possible to visit all the wineries in the region in a day. Then again, why would anyone want to rush while visiting the quaint towns in the Hill Country? We suggest you select one area of the wine map on each trip and visit the wineries in that vicinity. First-timers might want to start in Fredericksburg, as it is the hub for several excellent wineries. And don't forget to take along a picnic basket. The Hill Country offers some excellent picnic spots, some at the wineries themselves.

To celebrate Texas Wine Month in October, don't miss the Fredericksburg Food & Wine Fest and the Gruene Music and Wine Fest, both within an easy drive of Austin. There's no need to wait for a special event to visit the wineries, however, as wine tastings and tours are held throughout the year. You might even come across a good old-fashioned grape stomp!

impressive 70,210-seat football stadium—home to UT's archrival.

Check, too, for a listing of events at A&M's Reed Arena, (979) 862-7333, reed.tamu.edu. Opened in 1998, the arena features sporting events, concerts, ice shows, circuses, and much more. Also in College Station is Wolf Pen Creek Amphitheater, (979) 764-3408. This lovely out-

door arena hosts a wide range of music and entertainment, including some of Austin's finest musical performers.

Bryan is home to the Brazos Valley Museum of Natural History, (979) 776-2195, www.anthropology.tamu.edu/brazosvalleymuseum. The museum features a collection of fossils found in the Brazos Valley as well as a constantly changing array of temporary exhibits. Youngsters will find plenty to do in the nature lab and discovery room. The museum is open Monday through Saturday 10:00 a.m. to 5:00 p.m., and Sunday 1:00 to 5:00 p.m. And be sure to take your children to the new Children's Museum of the Brazos Valley, (979) 779-5437, www.mymuseum.com. The museum features a wonderfully whimsical upside down entrance, and all kinds of hands-on learning activities and displays, including the inspiration gallery in which children can perform a puppet show, disassemble a VCR, or paint a Volkswagen Beetle. The museum is open Monday through Saturday 10:00 a.m. to 5:00 p.m. and Sunday 1:00 to 5:00 p.m.

One of our favorite spots in Bryan is the Messina Hof Winery at 4545 Old Reliance Road, (979) 778-9463, www.messinahof.com. Established with the release of its first vintage in 1983, Messina Hof boasts a 200-year heritage with the family traditions of winemaker Paul Bonarrigo going back six generations to Messina, Sicily. Winery tours and tastings attract tourists from all over the region. Messina Hof produces a variety of red, white, and blush wines as well as ports and champagne. At the inviting guest center, visitors can purchase wines as well as a number of other gourmet foods made with the local product, including Riesling raspberry hazelnut fudge. Yum! The Vintage House restaurant serves international cuisine and is open Wednesday through Saturday for lunch and dinner and Sunday for an extended lunch. For those planning a weekend trip to the area, the winery offers the Villa bed-and-breakfast.

Of course this area offers dozens of hotels and motels—where else would all those Aggie parents and supporters stay? Families like the reasonably priced Vineyard Court hotel, (979) 693-1220, www.vineyardcourt.com, at 1500 George Bush Drive East. The two-room suites include a small kitchen. For more luxury there's the College Station Hilton, (979) 693-7500, at 801 University Drive East.

There's no shortage of restaurants in this area either. From the diner-type college hangouts to more elegant surroundings, Bryan and College Station will not fail to provide sustenance. We've seen many Aggie parents and their college kids at the Oxford Street Restaurant & Pub, (979) 268-0792, www.oxfordstreetrestaurant.com. Dark wood, low lighting, and a Sherlock Holmes motif lend Oxford Street its British flair. The menu includes a full selection of appetizers as well as steaks, chicken, seafood, and prime rib. The restaurant, at 1710 Briarcrest Drive in Bryan, is open daily beginning at 11:00 a.m. The Deluxe Diner, (979) 846-7466, at 203 University Drive in College Station, is a great place for a variety of home-style burgers and sandwiches, salads, chicken-fried steak, and fried chicken. The Deluxe is open daily for breakfast, lunch, and dinner starting at 6:00 a.m. Save some change for the jukebox.

While you're in the area, you might consider making the drive to Brenham to tour the cool business that put this town on the map. The Blue Bell Creamery, (800) 327-8135, www.bluebell .com, offers tours and samples of its great ice cream Monday through Friday from 10:00 a.m. to 3:00 p.m. Reservations are recommended.

For more information about Bryan/College Station, call the Convention and Visitor Bureau at (800) 777-8292 or visit the Web site at www .visitaggieland.com.

OUT WEST

Johnson City/LBJ Ranch

No, Johnson City was not named after the 36th president of the United States, Lyndon Baines, but one of his ancestors. The young LBJ was raised in the town bearing his family name. Johnson City, 50 miles southwest of Austin, and the LBJ Ranch in Stonewall, about 13 miles farther west, combine to make a perfect day trip from Austin. As you might expect, attractions in these two locations center on the life of the late President Johnson. The LBJ National Historic Park (www.nps.gov/lyjo), in fact, includes both the ranch and LBJ's boyhood home as well as the nearby Johnson Settlement.

Start your visit in Johnson City with a tour of the visitor center, (830) 868-7684, www.johnson citytexaschamber.com, at 100 East Main Street.

Here you can pick up a map of the complex and a brochure on the park and also see the excellent exhibits, including scores of photographs, dedicated to LBJ's life and career. You can also listen to tape recordings of LBJ, Lady Bird Johnson, and other state and national leaders speaking on major issues of the 1960s, including poverty, health, civil rights, and the environment. This modern stone facility also includes a gift shop and bookstore. It's open daily.

Nearby is LBJ's Boyhood Home. This simple but comfortable Folk Victorian–style house was LBJ's home from the age of 5 in 1913 until he married Lady Bird in 1934. It was here, on the front porch, that Johnson made his first public speech in 1937, announcing his candidacy for the U.S. House of Representatives. National Park Service guides provide a brief introduction about the restored home and the career of LBJ every half hour throughout the day beginning at 9:00 a.m. A few items inside the home are original, but many are period pieces. An interesting collection of Johnson family photographs adorn the walls. Admission is free.

From here walk about 4 blocks along a cinder path through bucolic Hill Country terrain (you cannot drive it) to the Johnson Settlement. This exhibit hall is filled with displays detailing the selection of Johnson City as the site for the town in 1879 and features all kinds of fascinating stories about frontier life, including the cowboys, the cattle drives, the trails, and farming. The pleasant covered porch of this stone building is adorned with rocking chairs and has drinking fountains and restrooms. Another block down the path is the dogtrot cabin that once belonged to President Johnson's grandfather. The cabin, which has a shaded breezeway—through which a dog could easily trot—is typical of structures built during the 1800s.

This area also includes an authentic chuck wagon, used during cattle drives to haul food and supplies for the cowboys. There's also the James Polk Johnson Barn, built by the nephew of LBJ's grandfather in 1875, as well as a windmill, water tank, and cooler house. Across the field,

in a penned enclosure, you might spy a herd of longhorn cattle grazing in the field.

While you're in Johnson City, you might also want to check out two attractions not related to LBJ. Take F.M. 2766 about 8 miles to Pedernales Falls State Park. The 4,800-acre park features waterfalls, fishing, swimming, hiking, camping, and great places to picnic. Children will enjoy visiting the Exotic Resort Zoo, (830) 868-4357, www .zooexotics.com, on Highway 281, 4 miles north of Johnson City. The zoo's trams take visitors on one-hour guided tours of the 137-acre park that is filled with more than 500 exotic animals from around the world, many that will come right up and eat out of your hand. It's open daily 9:00 a.m. to 6:00 p.m. This is also a great place to bring a picnic lunch.

Now, it's time to head for Stonewall and the LBJ Ranch, also known as the Texas White House. On your way to Stonewall, however, you might want to make a quick stop at the Hye Post Office, (830) 644-2465, which is right on US 290 about halfway between Johnson City and Stonewall. The future president mailed his first letter here at the age of 4 and returned as president in 1965 to swear in Lawrence F. O'Brien as Postmaster General. This old post office and general store, built in 1904, is a Texas Historic Landmark.

Follow US 290 west a few more miles until you see the large signs indicating the entrance to the Lyndon B. Johnson National Historic Park, (830) 868-7128, www.nps.gov/lyjo. A 75-minute guided bus tour of the LBJ Ranch District is offered from 10:00 a.m. to 4:00 p.m. daily. There is no set schedule, as buses depart depending on demand. National Park Service guides will point out all the areas of interest in this historic spread, including LBJ's reconstructed birthplace, the site where Johnson was born August 27, 1908 (the

i The *Texas State Travel Guide* is an invaluable resource when planning a trip around the state. It is available free at www.traveltex.com. See our Media chapter for more about this publication.

house was rebuilt by President Johnson in 1964); the show barn, which is the center of present-day ranching operations; and the Johnson Family Cemetery where generations of Johnsons are buried, including the president and the former first lady, Lady Bird. You are allowed to get off the bus and look around at these three sites. The bus tour also takes you past the Junction School, where the future president learned to read at age 4, and the Grandparent's Farmhouse, where Johnson's paternal grandparents lived out their lives. The Ranch House, also known as the Texas White House, was added to the tour in 2008, following the death of the former First Lady who had long resided there. Adult admission is $6. Children ages 6 and younger are admitted free.

You can now retrace your path to Austin or head farther west to Fredericksburg.

Fredericksburg

This Hill Country town is so packed with things to do that it is easy to make a half dozen day trips or weekend getaways out of this destination. There is something here for history buffs, antiques lovers, foodies, outdoor enthusiasts, architectural historians, and military historians.

Fredericksburg, named for Prince Frederick of Prussia, is kin to New Braunfels (see our day trip under Down South), as both were founded by the Society for the Protection of German Immigrants—New Braunfels in 1845 and Fredericksburg in 1846. The settlers moved into the Comanche territory, and in 1847 their leader, Baron Ottfried Hans von Meusebach, negotiated a peace treaty with the Comanche that is commemorated every year with the Easter Fires Pageant, an event that involves hundreds of people in Easter Bunny suits, Comanches and pioneers, Easter eggs, and bonfires.

Fredericksburg has retained its German character in its architecture and cultural traditions. Indeed, many old-timers still speak what is called Old High German and can be heard talking among themselves on the streets and in stores. Local churches also offer German services and songs. The Vereins Kirche Museum (the People's

Church Museum) in Market Square, at the heart of the city, is a famous landmark. The octagonal building is now a museum of local history that is open Monday through Saturday from 10:00 a.m. to 2:00 p.m. There is a small admission charge.

The heart of the town is listed on the National Register of Historic Places. One very wide street cuts through the town, wide enough, it is said, for a team of oxen and a wagon to be turned around. Most of the sights are on Main Street or just a block or two off the thoroughfare. During the Gold Rush of 1849, Fredericksburg merchants made their fortunes as prospectors stocked up at the last Western outpost before embarking into the heart of Indian Territory. These days there is a similar feel to the town as tourists browse the antiques shops along Main Street, and the locals talk about the latest movie star who has bought a little piece of the picturesque Hill Country. Some Austinites own weekend homes in the town.

One of the first sights the visitor driving in from Austin sees is the Admiral Nimitz State Historical Park, 340 East Main Street, (830) 997-4379, www.tpwd.state.tx.us/park/nimitz. Chester Nimitz, who commanded the Pacific Fleet in World War II, grew up in landlocked Fredericksburg, and his grandfather once owned the Steamboat Hotel that now serves as the museum; the building looks remarkably nautical. The museum is open daily from 8:00 a.m. to 5:00 p.m. Admission is $3.00, $1.50 for students. Children age 6 and younger are admitted free.

A highlight of the museum is an exhibit featuring one of the tiny submarines used in the attack on Pearl Harbor. Other interactive and audiovisual exhibits illustrate the fierce battles in the Pacific. The George Bush Gallery of the Pacific War details the wartime experience of the 41st president, who was shot down in the Pacific. The Plaza of the Presidents consists of 10 monoliths detailing the wartime service of 10 presidents, beginning with President Franklin Roosevelt. In stark contrast to the exhibits, the museum is also home to a Japanese Garden of Peace, given by the people of Japan to the facility. There is a replica of the study and teahouse used by Admiral Togo, Nimitz's counterpart in the Imperial Japanese Navy.

Adding to the military flavor of the Fredericksburg area is the Hangar Hotel, a 2003 addition to the abundant lodging scene in town. This unique hotel, built in a hangar at the Gillespie County Airport, evokes a World War II Pacific Theater officer's club. The rooms are furnished with leather chairs and mahogany sleigh beds, and there is a '40s-era diner on-site. The hotel is located at 155 Airport Road, (830) 997-9990, www.hangarhotel .com. Military buffs also may want to visit nearby Fort Martin Scott, 1606 East Main Street, (830) 997-9895, www.fortmartinscott.com, a c. 1848 frontier fort that is now being restored. The only original building is the guardhouse, but replicas of original buildings are being constructed. Historical reenactments are periodically held here, and there is ongoing archaeological work at the site. During the summer the fort is open Wednesday through Saturday, and there is a small admission charge. After Labor Day and through March, the fort is open only on weekends.

Many visitors are drawn to Fredericksburg by the architecture and rich pioneer history. The Pioneer Museum, 309 West Main Street, is made up of several buildings, including a home and general store built in 1849, a barn and smokehouse, a firefighting museum, a pioneer log cabin, an 1855 church, and the Weber Sunday House. These tiny houses, sometimes just a single room, can be seen in both Fredericksburg and New Braunfels. They are called Sunday houses because they were built by farmers and ranchers as a place to bring the family on the weekend for Sunday church services. Many of them have been restored and are used as weekend homes by city dwellers. One of the best times of the year to see them is in spring when many of the tiny gardens are filled with wildflowers.

The Fredericksburg Chamber of Commerce, (830) 997-6523, www.fredericksburg-texas.com, provides walking tour maps and other pamphlets that give detailed information about the Sunday homes and other sights in the city. The maps and brochures also are available at many local businesses, including the German-style restaurants that dot Main Street. The Altdorf Restaurant, 301 West Main Street, has a beer garden and serves lunch and dinner daily, except Tuesday. The Old German Bakery and Restaurant, 225 West Main Street, (830) 997-9084, serves breakfast, lunch, and dinner and sells typical German baked goods, including rye bread, which often runs out early in the day. The bakery is closed on Tuesday and Wednesday.

The Fredericksburg Brewing Co., 245 East Main Street, (830) 997-1646, sells its own Pedernales Pilsner, a good choice after strolling through some of the 100 shops on Main Street, where many artisans and artists and collectors of antiques and Texana are located. Candle-making and glassblowing are just two of the crafts demonstrated here. One of the specialty shops is an outlet for Fredericksburg Herb Farms where shoppers can buy oils and vinegars flavored with herbs grown in the Hill Country. In addition to the Easter Fires and the herb festival, there are several other annual events that draw visitors throughout the year. In April there is a large antiques show; A Night in Old Fredericksburg is celebrated in July with food, dance, and song; the oldest county fair in Texas takes place in September with a traditional livestock show, horse races, a crafts and home-baked goods competition, plus evening dances; Oktoberfest celebrates the town's German heritage; and at Christmas there is the Candlelight Homes Tour, which offers wonderful views of some of the city's historical homes. Some are detailed in our Annual Events and Festivals chapter.

Fredericksburg is 85 miles west of Austin on US 290, so it is an easy day trip from the city and can be combined with a trip to the LBJ Ranch or Johnson City. (If you're traveling in June or July, be sure to stop along the way at one of the peach stands lining the highway.) But it is also a great weekend getaway location since the town has a wealth of bed-and-breakfast facilities and guest cottages. The latter are perfect for a romantic weekend since they are very private. Listings appear on the town's Web site, above. Lovers of the outdoors also head for Fredericksburg to visit Enchanted Rock State Park, just 18 miles north of the city, where a granite dome rises some 325 feet from the earth and offers wide views of the area (see our Parks and Recreation chapter). There are also several vineyards in the countryside around Fredericksburg, including Bell Mountain Vineyards, (830) 685-3297, on Highway 16 about 14 miles north of town. Two other wineries are about 10 miles east of town on US 290: Becker Vineyards, (830) 644-2681, www.beckervineyards.com, and Grape Creek Vineyards, (830) 644-2710, www.grapecreek.com. All offer tastings and tours.

Given the wealth of things to see and do in Fredericksburg, it is an ideal destination for a spur-of-the-moment day trip.

THE HIGHLAND LAKES

Perhaps you've already had the pleasure of making a trip out to Austin's beautiful Lake Travis, maybe even taken a swim in the refreshing waters or toured the lake from cove to inviting cove by boat. Possibly you've seen or boated up and down Lake Austin, that lovely stretch of Colorado River between West Austin's Tom Miller Dam and the Mansfield Dam. If so, you've seen two of Central Texas's six Highland Lakes. (Find out more about these two lakes in our chapter on Parks and Recreation.)

Make no mistake, however. Viewing Austin's two Highland Lakes definitely does not mean you've seen them all. Lake Buchanan, Inks Lake, Lake LBJ, and Lake Marble Falls all have their own distinct personality, and the only way to discover their wonders is to spend some time visiting them—one by one. Each lake is within 75 miles northwest of Austin, some closer, making visits to them either a perfect day trip or a wonderful weekend getaway.

The lakes, created by a series of six dams built on the Colorado River during the Depression of the 1930s and 1940s, vary immensely in size, shape, and degree of development. The dams were built and are managed by the Lower Colorado River Authority (LCRA), www.lcra.org, which aimed to control the flood-prone river while providing a dependable source of water

and electricity for the Texas Hill Country. For information about the lakes, the dams, or any number of the parks and campsites operated by the LCRA, call (800) PRO-LCRA or phone the Park Information Hot Line at (512) 473-4083. The common denominator that unites all these lakes is the focus on water activities: swimming, boating, and fishing. Camping, either in tents or RVs, is extremely popular around these lakes, although in most cases the campsites are either primitive or just a step above, meaning you'll find restrooms in some but hardly ever showers. In most cases you'll enjoy the offerings much more by either taking along a boat, renting a pontoon or personal watercraft (PWC), or taking a guided cruise. While there are a few trails, the Highland Lakes are not renowned for attracting large numbers of hikers or bikers. If you're determined to hike, we'll point out a couple of good spots.

Lake Buchanan

Let's start with the granddaddy of them all: Lake Buchanan, known as "Big Buc" to the locals and fishermen in these parts. While it's the oldest, largest, and northernmost (farthest from Austin) of all the Highland Lakes, Lake Buchanan is also one of the most undeveloped, retaining the feel of a laid-back fishing haven. (Although more boating enthusiasts from the "big cities" are beginning to discover the lake.) The eastern shoreline stands out for its rugged, hilly terrain and towering cliffs. (Drivers should take special precaution here.) The western shore is closer to lake level and offers plenty of spots to just stop off and get your feet wet or take a swim.

This immense water basin, which covers 23,060 acres (36 square miles), was created with the completion of the 2.08-mile-long Buchanan Dam in 1937. This lake is especially noted for its three scenic waterfalls—Fall Creek Falls, Deer

i The bridge that spanned Inks Lake for decades has been replaced by a modern structure, but the old one remains as a pedestrian bridge—and it offers great views of the lake and Buchanan Dam.

Creek Falls, and Post Oak Falls—as well as for the gorgeous cliffs and rock formations that line the shores. Birds, deer, and other wildlife are common sights all the way up from the dam to Colorado Bend State Park, (915) 628-3240, on the northernmost end of the lake. The park, filled with towering shade trees, is one of the nicest campsites on the lake. It has portable restrooms but no shower facilities or electrical hookups. This campsite, on the western shore, is accessible from the towns of Lampasas or Cherokee by car or by boat. Hikers and mountain bikers will be pleased to know this park also offers excellent choices for both.

Very important to know about boating on Lake Buchanan: This is not a deep lake even in times of abundant rainfall, so be sure to use your map, or better yet talk to the locals, and steer clear of sandbars and other hazards. Local experts warn that it is unsafe to try to boat upstream from Colorado Bend State Park, as you'll run into small but very rocky rapids. You'll find public boat ramps on both sides of the lake at the various parks, including Burnet County Park (Buchanan Dam), (512) 756-4297; Burnet County Park (White Bluff), same phone number, both on the eastern side of the lake; Llano County Park, (915) 247-4352, on the southwestern shore; and the Cedar Point Resource Area (LCRA Hotline) in the northwest. The various rental bungalows and cottages around the lake also feature boat ramps. You don't have to go way upstream to enjoy boating on the lake, however. The huge reservoir is perfect for sailing, speed boating, and bopping around on those ever-popular personal watercraft.

This lake also offers excellent scenic drives year-round but especially in springtime when the wildflowers are in bloom. Designated the

i Early summer is peach season in the Texas Hill Country. If you're heading to Johnson City, Stonewall, or Fredericksburg, be sure to stop at any one of a number of businesses along US 290 that sell fresh, ripe peaches, homegrown tomatoes, and other fruits. Some even have homemade peach ice cream!

"Bluebonnet Capital of Texas" by the state legislature, this area and neighboring Inks Lake attract scores of visitors to the Bluebonnet Trail each year during the spectacular wildflower season, which runs March through May depending on rainfall. The Lake Buchanan/Inks Lake Chamber of Commerce, (512) 793-2803, www.buchanan-inks.org, located at Buchanan Dam, offers an annual brochure and operates a hot line of the best viewing locations.

We suggest a stop off at the Buchanan Dam Museum and Visitor Center right off Highway 29 on the southeastern tip of the lake. It is open Monday through Friday 8:00 a.m. to 4:00 p.m. and 1:00 to 4:00 p.m. weekends and holidays. Here you'll find a fascinating pictorial history of the construction of the dam, comments from a few of the hundreds of workers who found highly coveted Depression-era jobs building the immense barrier, as well as information about the Kingsland Archaeological Center on Lake LBJ. The visitor center also features an 18-minute documentary about the dam itself. Also, this is where you'd come to take a free guided tour of the huge generating facility. Tours generally run from May to September. And don't miss out on the opportunity to take a stroll along the impressive pedestrian walkway that leads from the visitor center all the way out to the spillway. This is the best way to see for yourself what a huge undertaking this project was—and get a great view of Lake Buchanan at the same time. For those not interested in making the trek, there's an outdoor observation deck right off the parking lot.

From here you can choose to either head up the eastern side of the lake or follow the western shore. Both have their own attributes and attractions, and you will find rental cabins and bungalows as well as places to eat on both sides of the lake. Going up north on the eastern shoreline is the recreational development Canyon of the Eagles, (512) 756-8787 or (800) 977-0081, www.canyonoftheeagles.com. This 940-acre site includes a 64-room lodge, an RV park, camping facilities, a beach, general store, and, best of all, a nature preserve for wildlife such as the bald eagle and the golden-cheeked warbler. The Eagle Eye Observatory also is here, offering visitors a chance to peer through a 16-inch Ealing Cassegrain telescope and to chart the skies from a unique observing field. Stargazing parties are scheduled regularly. This is the place to catch the Vanishing Texas River Cruise on the Texas Eagle II, a 70-foot, 200-passenger boat with two observation decks.

Several tours are offered year-round, including the popular 2½ hour guided scenic wilderness cruise up the Colorado River Canyon. Bring your own picnic. Tours held November through March are especially fascinating because they take visitors upriver to see the winter habitat of the largest colony of American bald eagles in the state. Wildflower tours, vineyard tours, and sunset dinner cruises also are offered. You don't have to be a guest of the park to take a cruise. Call or check the Web site for a schedule and prices.

For the adventurous of spirit, Canyon of the Eagles also is home to Lake Buchanan Adventures, (512) 756-9912, www.lakebuchananadventures .com. This outfit offers 8-mile kayaking tours to Lake Creek Waterfalls, 3-hour hiking and kayaking excursions, boat rentals and more.

Inks Lake

Just a few miles west of the Buchanan Dam off Highway 29 is Inks Lake in what is known as the Central Texas Mineral Region. (Enter at Park Road 4 and travel south.) Only 4.2 miles long and just 0.6 mile at its widest points, Inks Lake is dwarfed by its gargantuan neighbor. Yet the lake is surrounded by such rugged natural beauty— highlighted by towering oak trees, wildflowers, scenic bluffs, and huge boulders of granite and pink gneiss—that it attracts nature lovers, campers, boaters, and fishing enthusiasts year-round. This lake was the second created on the Colorado River after the 1,548-foot Roy Inks Dam was completed in 1938.

Inks Lake features one of the most popular state parks in Texas. Inks Lake State Park, (512) 793-2223, is one of the most fully equipped parks in the region, offering both tent and RV sites, a few enclosed shelters, showers and restrooms,

picnicking, swimming, trails, a boat ramp, and even a public golf course. The 1,200-acre park extends along the entire eastern shoreline of the lake. Be sure to stop at the scenic overlook along Park Road 4 and check out the Devil's Waterhole, which has a beautiful waterfall. Teenagers just love to climb on the huge granite boulders that adorn this area.

From Inks Lake you might want to follow Park Road 4 south about 10 minutes to Longhorn Cavern State Park, (512) 756-4680. While not on a lake, this wonderful 637-acre state park is nevertheless a great place for picnicking and hiking. No overnight camping is permitted. Of course the major attraction here is the cavern itself. Located in Backbone Ridge, a huge piece of Ellenburge limestone formed by a shallow sea more than 450 million years ago, the cavern is open for daily tours year-round. The 1¼-mile round-trip walking tour takes about 85 minutes.

Lake LBJ

If Buchanan and Inks Lakes are the rugged members of the family, Lake LBJ is the refined cousin. The Colorado River meanders down from Inks Lake and branches out to skirt the town of Kingsland before it widens near the towns of Sunrise Beach on the western shore and Granite Shoals on the east. Once called Granite Shoals Lake, it was renamed in 1965 to recognize President Lyndon Johnson's efforts on behalf of the LCRA. At 6,200 acres, this gorgeous lake is the second largest of these four. Created by the Wirtz Dam, Lake LBJ offers plenty of wide-open waters for speedboats, sailboats, and personal watercraft. Unlike Inks and Buchanan, however, Lake LBJ stands out for the upscale homes and large manicured lawns that surround the basin. This

i Sadly, there is not one great map of the Highland Lakes area available for purchase. The closest we have found is the Texas Hill Country Tourist Guide map, although it covers an area much larger than the Lakes. Try www.texasoutside.com and click on the Highland Lakes.

lake is becoming increasingly developed and includes the resort community of Horseshoe Bay and others.

Because of its emphasis on residential development, this lake is not stocked with rental units, although there are a few. For real pampering, stay at the beautiful Horseshoe Bay Resort by Marriott, (800) 452-5330, at 200 Hi Circle North, www .horseshoebaymarriott.com. This luxury property not only offers divine guest rooms, it also has golf, tennis, a spa—and its own airport.

For other lodging options here and at the other lakes, we especially like the Web site www .lakesandhills.com.

If you're heading south on Highway 1431 from Kingsland, be sure to take a few moments to stop at Lookout Mountain, just a few miles south of State Road 2342. This scenic overlook provides an excellent overall view of the Colorado River valley. A few minutes farther south off this highway is the Kingsland Archaeological Site, (830) 598-5261, which is open by reservation only. The 10-acre site on the shores of Lake LBJ is a 5,000-year-old prehistoric campsite for hunter-gatherers along the Colorado River. Since it was discovered in 1988, archaeologists have uncovered more than 100,000 artifacts, including projectile points, grinding stones, and animal bone fragments. Photos of this site are on display at the Buchanan Dam Visitor Center.

Lake Marble Falls

Like Lake Austin, Lake Marble Falls is an inner-city lake that appears more like the river it is than a wide-open lake. Nevertheless, this 6-mile lake has grown so popular over the years that the community of Marble Falls and the huge Meadow Lake Country Club have grown up around it. The well-shaded 18-acre Johnson Park, (210) 693-3615, on the lake features a public boat ramp, a playscape for children, picnic area, overnight camping, and restrooms. Nearby is Lakeside Park (same phone), which also has a boat ramp but is designated for day use only. Entrance to both parks is free. RV campers will want to check out the Riverview RV Park, (830) 693-3910, on the shores of Lake Marble Falls at 200 River Road, www.touringtexas.com/riverview. This site offers full hookups as well as restrooms, showers, and laundry facilities. If you're ready for a good, inexpensive home-style meal while in Marble Falls, try the famous Blue Bonnet Cafe in town at 211 Highway 281 South, (830) 693-2344. You'll find everything from burgers to chicken-fried steak, pot roast, fried chicken livers, and fried catfish. The homemade biscuits melt in your mouth, as do the pies. The Blue Bonnet is open for breakfast, lunch, and dinner Monday through Saturday, and breakfast and lunch on Sunday. For lakeside dining, we like the River City Grille at 700 First Street, (830) 798-9909.

Once you've toured all the Highland Lakes, you'll know for yourself why they are the pride of the Texas Hill Country.

RELOCATION

Growth is many things to Austin-area residents. For some it means opportunity, broader horizons, and wider dreams, but for others it has come to mean the struggle to maintain the city's identity and quality of life that have been Austin hallmarks. The spirit of Austin is treasured by both longtime residents and newcomers. One key to the preservation of the city's unique character is the vitality of its neighborhoods.

Even the word *neighborhood* is loaded with meaning in Austin. Some neighborhood organizations have wielded considerable political clout at City Hall (see our Politics and Perspectives chapter), while others have created unique identities that act as a draw to both visitors and residents. In Austin, as in some of the smaller rural communities that have been absorbed by the city's growth, maintaining the neighborhood character, the particular sense of place, has been both a challenge and a goal. Many of the area's neighborhoods have succeeded; others have not. But with growth has come a dynamism that has revitalized some neighborhoods, created new ones, and, at a minimum, kept the quality-of-life issue on the front burner for every Central Texas resident.

OVERVIEW

The city has been leaping up the population list in record time in recent years. Beyond the city limits, the greater Austin metropolitan area has topped the million resident mark, and demographers are predicting the area will surpass two million residents in the early years of this century.

While downtown maintains some of the flavor of a midsize city, there has been a boom in downtown development that promises to give the heart of the city more of the feel of a busy, urban area. Highrise condo towers and loft developments are changing the downtown vibe and skyline. There is a symbiotic growth between the numerous condo/loft projects and new restaurants, shops, and cafes. Businesses, particularly high-tech companies, are eager to locate downtown, many of the older high-rises and warehouses are being converted to offices and living spaces, and the nightlife and restaurant scenes are even more vibrant. (See our Restaurants and Nightlife chapters.)

Growth is leaving its mark on Central Texas in many ways. On the plus side, growth has given the city a more cosmopolitan air. There is a greater diversity of restaurants, and more shops and theaters, and the city's increasingly multicultural population celebrates ethnic traditions and cultural differences. The largest Hindu temple in North America is not far from one of the area's most popular country barbecue joints, the Salt Lick (see our Restaurants chapter).

Growth brings choice and there are numerous choices for homeowners in terms of location and price. But growth also means traffic jams. Rush-hour commutes are now a factor for homebuyers, in addition to access to city services—police, fire, EMS, libraries, even parks.

A word about prices in the Austin-area real estate market: The median price of a home in Austin was $151,000 in June 2005, according to *Money* magazine, a 29 percent increase in five years. By the end of 2008 that had risen to $186,000 and values continue to rise, although some real estate professionals believe the Austin market is actually undervalued. That median price is about what a consumer will pay for a small "starter" home in the area, and it likely will be located on the fringes of Austin, perhaps even beyond. A good rule of thumb is the closer to downtown, the higher the price. Older neighborhoods, close to downtown, are now hot, and even a small cottage can cost upward of $350,000. For that same amount of money, a buyer can find a large, three-bedroom family home in one of the newer neighborhoods on the city's outskirts. A great way to get a visual picture of Austin real estate prices is to visit the real estate Web site, www.trulia.com, where urban "heat maps" displaying price in coded colors can be viewed. Because Austin has a significant young population—the highest number of 25 to 34 year olds in similar "creative class" cities—many of the older neighborhoods that once were the Austin suburbs are being revived by young homeowners with a flare for reinventing 50s-style.

Several significant trends in Austin's growth offer insight into what makes Austin neighborhoods tick. We begin with a look at some of these trends, followed by a geographic tour of some of the city's neighborhoods.

NEW URBANISM

It's a phrase that is much discussed in planning circles and in architecture schools across the country. For the uninitiated, "new urbanism" might be simply summed up as a return to the old neighborhoods of fond memory.

Hal Box, former dean of the University of Texas architecture school, has adopted a litmus test for examples of the new urbanism—it is the "five-minute Popsicle rule." Every child should be able to walk or ride a bike to the neighborhood store for a Popsicle and be home safely within five minutes. There are several "Popsicle rule" neighborhoods in Austin. Some of them are in upper-income neighborhoods, others in some of the city's older, working-class neighborhoods.

Austin has hosted several important conferences on New Urbanism and in 1997 launched an effort to draft a building and planning code that would embrace the spirit of the movement.

DOWNTOWN DISCOVERY

Another important trend in the growth of Austin has been the rediscovery of downtown as a place to live and work. Thanks to the presence of the Texas Capitol and the city's vibrant music scene, downtown Austin is alive both day and night and has not suffered the sort of blight some of America's cities have experienced. Within blocks of the city's main street, Congress Avenue, apartments and lofts offer residents a downtown lifestyle, although not at bargain-basement prices.

Ten blocks to the west of Congress Avenue is the hub of another downtown center that has become a magnet and a model for inner-city growth. Once the corner of Lamar Boulevard and West Sixth Street was an area dominated by car lots and automobile showrooms. Now, at the heart of this hub are the headquarters of two quintessential Austin companies. These local legends—Whole Foods Market, headquarters of a NASDAQ-traded gourmet/health food grocery store chain, and GSD&M, an award-winning national advertising agency—were founded by Texas baby boomers. Whole Foods Landmark Store and GSD&M's "Idea City" headquarters are at the heart of an urban neighborhood of bookstores, ice cream parlors, coffee shops, and bakeries, all within a stone's throw of several new loft and apartment developments. This is one of those Austin neighborhoods that locals love to visit.

The Second Street District just north of City Hall on Lady Bird Lake is another downtown neighborhood where high rises and lofts shade sidewalk cafes and shops. The urban boom along Fifth and Sixth Streets is fast bringing the Whole Foods hub and downtown into one vibrant neighborhood.

GENTRIFICATION

The downtown development trend is linked to two other Austin market characteristics: the gentrification of older, inner-city neighborhoods and what planners call "infilling." Eager to live closer to downtown, or in one of the city's colorful, older neighborhoods, buyers are looking for empty lots or run-down properties and then either building or moving older homes onto the property. Austin has grappled with the so-called

McMansion trend where older homes have been razed and bigger, sometimes intimidating homes have been built next door to small cottages. Critics say they spoil the flavor of the neighborhood and Austin has passed some building codes to address the problem.

Homes west of downtown have enjoyed prestige and market value for several decades. Now, that trend is beginning to occur south of Lady Bird Lake in older neighborhoods along South Congress Avenue, popularly called SoCo, and lately has spread east of the Capitol into what was once a depressed, primarily African-American neighborhood. Fortunately, the urban restoration has encouraged longtime businesses and homeowners to stay in the area. The East section of our Restaurants chapter is proof of the neighborhood's renewed vitality.

Many of the new residents are young, urban pioneers who are taking on the challenges of moving into older, run-down neighborhoods in areas north of the University of Texas campus and just west of Interstate 35 around the Hancock Center shopping plaza. Generally, neighborhoods close to downtown and west of the capitol have been the first to ride the gentrification boom and are now firmly established as prestigious neighborhoods, where a relatively small home can cost $350,000—if you are lucky.

Of course, the other side of the gentrification trend is a growing lack of affordable housing. The picture is getting tougher for average families, and there has been a growing concern that working people, particularly those providing vital services—police, firefighters, teachers, and city workers—are being priced out of the market.

The key to finding a bargain, particularly in an older neighborhood, is knowing which neighborhoods are being revived and which are suffering from the usual urban ills, including problems with crime and vandalism. That can be difficult for a newcomer, but Austin's active neighborhood association infrastructure can provide assistance. The City of Austin maintains a community registry, a reference guide to the approximately 300 active neighborhood associations in the city. It can be requested by contacting the planning department's neighborhood section at (512) 499-2648, www.ci.austin.tx .us/housing.

SUBURBAN EXPANSION

While some Austin residents are looking to the heart of the city for a home, others are looking to the hills. The major growth trend in the past two decades has been the expansion of the greater Austin area to the west. Back in the 1970s, the Austin City Council adopted a growth plan that called for expansion along the city's north-south corridor defined by I-35. The council was reflecting the concerns of environmentalists, who wanted to protect the vast underground Edwards Aquifer, the underground watershed that feeds Austin's icon and symbol of community environmental sensibilities, Barton Springs Pool in downtown Zilker Park (see our Close-up in the Parks and Recreation chapter).

But the lure of the Hill Country with its distinctive flora and scenic views proved more overwhelming. Much of the growth has occurred in the northwest, west, and southwest. In fact, the word *west* has something of a cachet in Austin real estate circles. The area's most prestigious neighborhoods are in West Austin; West Lake Hills, the incorporated community west of MoPac (Loop 1); and in western Travis County toward the Highland Lakes.

Austin is built on the border of two distinct geographic areas. I-35 roughly tracks the break between the Hill Country and the Blackland Prairie. To the west are rolling hills, live oak trees, and scrub dominated by so-called cedar trees (actually junipers) growing in the thin soil that barely dusts the limestone ridges. East of the interstate the land is flatter, covered with rich, black soil in which pecan trees flourish.

Both areas are picturesque, but the desire to live west may have more to do with age-old social patterns that have little to do with a modern, integrated Austin. Like so many other cities, the interstate highway also serves as a barrier between downtown and Austin's predominantly ethnic neighborhoods. Austin's neighborhoods are well integrated, particularly newer subdivisions, but like most American cities, Austin still has two distinct neighborhoods east of I-35 that historically have been primarily African American and Hispanic. These neighborhoods have strong identities. Neighborhood groups there have fought both to preserve community identity and to improve city services in their communities. Those lines are being blurred, particularly as young urban "pioneers" seek a home close to the city center.

The lure of living west has pushed development out beyond the Austin city limits, absorbing once small communities like Cedar Park, northwest of Austin in the next county. Just as the greater Austin area has pushed over the Travis County line into Williamson County in the northwest, in the southwest suburban developments have spilled over into Hays County. The small community of Dripping Springs, on U.S. Highway 290 West about 15 miles from the Austin city limits, is feeling the growth boom as homeowners eager for a spacious home on perhaps an acre or two of land are locating there. The search for the Hill Country life is now spreading out even farther west. Communities 60 miles or more from Austin are seeing home developments spring up in their communities. The growth also has spread east to some of the wonderful small, rural towns in the rolling farmland around communities like Smithville and Bastrop.

THE HIGH-PRICE BOOM

One of the hottest commodities in the Austin real estate market has been high-priced homes, those costing $1 million and up. Realtors attribute this trend to the impact of the city's growing high-tech sector. In 2000 the area had virtually full employment, as the experts define it, with the unemployment rate at 2 percent. In 2005 the jobless rate hovered just under 5 percent. The high-tech industry had produced a group of entrepreneurs and a large number of employees with valuable stock options.

Leading the pack, of course, was Michael Dell, founder of Dell Computer, who built a new home in West Lake Hills that has been compared to Bill Gates's mansion in Seattle. Dell's home was

appraised by tax authorities at $22.5 million—an appraisal he challenged—which was only half of what Gates's home allegedly cost. However, it did symbolize the high-price boom in Austin.

These high-priced homes are found in the city's most prestigious neighborhoods, some in close proximity to downtown, others out in the hills. An old ivy-clad mansion in the Enfield neighborhood close to downtown might sell for $2–3 million, while a sprawling lakeside home in the hills above Lake Austin might sell for $3 million. Some of the large homes in the hills reflect traditional Hill Country architecture with limestone walls, Mexican tile floors, and rustic timbers, while others are mock Tudor or French chateau–style.

We'll take a look at the city by geographic area.

NEIGHBORHOODS

Central

The geographic center of the City of Austin lies somewhere around Highland Mall at the intersection of I-35 and US 290 East, several miles north of the capitol. But most Austin area residents consider the center of the city to be the downtown area, along the shores of Lady Bird Lake and around the Texas Capitol. For the purposes of this book, we will define Central Austin as the area east of MoPac (Loop 1); south of R.M. 2222, known as Koenig Lane as it crosses the central section of the city; west of I-35; and north of Lady Bird Lake.

The central area embraces some of the city's most prestigious addresses and some of its more run-down, older neighborhoods. It also contains one of the most quintessential neighborhoods, Hyde Park, defined by advocates of new urbanism as a perfect "Popsicle rule" community.

Hyde Park was the city's first planned suburb. In 1889 Colonel Monroe Martin Shipe, a businessman from Abilene, Kansas, came to Austin and purchased a 206-acre plot of land in what was then far north Austin. The new suburb had its own electric streetcar system, dance pavilion, and walking paths. Shipe first built large Victorian homes for some of Austin's leading citizens. Later, smaller Craftsman-style bungalows were added to the neighborhood.

Today, Hyde Park is not only a much-sought-after address but also a popular spot for lunch or coffee with friends from across the city. It's located north of the University of Texas campus and bounded by Guadalupe Street on the west and 38th Street on the south.

Several miles southwest of Hyde Park is the Enfield neighborhood, east of MoPac (Loop 1) and west of Shoal Creek, which wends its way south through Central Austin to Lady Bird Lake, running alongside Lamar Boulevard for much of its course. As it crosses Shoal Creek, 15th Street becomes Enfield Road, running west through this affluent old neighborhood.

You can still find a few small apartments tucked away over old garages and in some of the smaller houses of the area, and even a small c. 1960s apartment complex or two along the major thoroughfare, Enfield Road. But the area is best known for its large homes with hefty price tags, set back on wooded lots lining the area's curving streets.

Another central neighborhood with a unique character is Clarksville, just south of Enfield Park. Sometimes described as part of West Austin (a reflection of the days when the city was much smaller), Clarksville is bordered on the west by MoPac, on the south by 10th Street, and north by Waterston Avenue. The property was originally owned by Texas Governor E. M. Pease, who gave the land to his former slaves in 1863 as an effort to keep them as workers on his plantation.

The neighborhood is named for Charles Griffin, who changed his last name to Clark after he was freed. Clark bought a two-acre plot on 10th Street in 1871. Some of the current residents are descendants of the founders, but the neighborhood has changed over the years. Originally, according to local historians, Clarksville was home to about 250 African Americans. That number has diminished as the demographics of the neighborhood have changed.

Clarksville remains a mix of comfortable, modest homes and some gentrified houses with high price tags. Within the neighborhood are several shops (see our Shopping chapter), bakeries, a pottery store, and restaurants, including one of Austin's top dining spots, Jeffrey's (see our Restaurants chapter).

Central and South Austinites have an affection for changing the names of streets and rivers as their paths cross the city. In fact, rivers even become lakes—Lady Bird Lake (formerly Town Lake), the portion of the Colorado River that runs through the heart of Austin, once represented a dividing line for some in the city. *Austin American–Statesman* humor columnist John Kelso helped engender the myth of North-South differences in the mid-'80s. North Austin, the mythology went, was the land of the yuppies while south of the river was occupied by "bubbas," laid-back old hippies, and assorted free spirits.

Those distinctions have faded somewhat, but South Austin is still viewed by some as a haven for free spirits. The distinctions have faded, perhaps, because the older neighborhoods south of the river are being eyed as fertile territory for downtown living. Prices in neighborhoods south of the river have escalated. One of the most popular neighborhoods is Travis Heights, an area east of South Congress Avenue, south of Riverside Drive, and west of I-35 where homes sell for $500,000 and up.

The South Congress Avenue corridor is undergoing rapid change. Once known for its X-rated movie theaters, streetwalkers, and even an old feed store (now Güero's restaurant), the wide avenue is now alive with restaurants, antiques shops, bakeries, boutiques, and a software store. The changes have affected the Bouldin Creek neighborhood, located west of South Congress Avenue, north of Oltorf Street. Older homes in this area are being snapped up by buyers eager to live near downtown. The neighborhood remains a mix of run-down houses, fixer-uppers, and newly renovated homes. The southern portion of this

i The Austin Neighborhood Council serves as a clearinghouse for Austin's diverse neighborhoods (www.ancweb.org).

area has a distinct Hispanic flavor, with popular Mexican bakeries and restaurants occupying the corner lots. (For more information on dining in this neighborhood, see our Restaurants chapter.)

The area south of Lady Bird Lake, west of Lamar Boulevard, and east of MoPac is one of Austin's most popular, older neighborhoods. Zilker Park wraps around the northern end of the area, while the Barton Creek Greenbelt winds around its western perimeter. Older homes in the Zilker neighborhood are much sought after. Farther south is the Barton Hills neighborhood where homes built 30 years ago are getting top dollar. The area has two critically acclaimed elementary schools, Zilker and Barton Hills, and enjoys quick access to downtown.

South Austin has continued to march southward, and neighborhoods age much like tree rings as the visitor drives south along the area's three major north-south streets—South Congress Avenue, South First Street, and Manchaca Road.

Much of the area between Oltorf and US 290 West is a mixture of older homes in working-class neighborhoods, some of them with a strong Hispanic flavor; others are home to free-spirit Austinites who frequent the area's ethnic restaurants. South of US 290 West, low- and middle-income homes, many of them built in the 1970s, give way to newer subdivisions. South of William Cannon Drive, neighborhoods like Cherry Creek, Southwest Oaks, Buckingham Estates, and Texas Oaks offer low- to midpriced homes, many of them dubbed "starter homes." These are traditional subdivisions with duplexes or apartments on the outer flanks of the neighborhood, single-family homes on the inner streets, and shopping facilities at nearby major intersections. Like most new homes in Austin, yards are enclosed with 6-foot privacy fencing, and most homes are constructed with at least the front wall faced in the local limestone or brick.

It is clear to anyone driving on I-35 south of the city that growth is pushing the Austin suburbs farther and farther south. Small communities like Buda are now the focus of new home developments, some aimed at offering a country lifestyle, others targeted at middle-income families who

i One of the attractions of living in the hills west of Austin is the beauty of the natural surroundings. In addition to the flora—the wildflowers, the live oaks, redbud trees, and cactus flowers—there is the fauna. There are many species of birds, and in late summer the monarch butterflies pass through on their way to Mexico. And then there are the deer. Some Austinites feed the neighborhood deer; others complain about them. Nurseries sell deer-resistant plants, and neighbors swap stories of how to keep the deer out of their roses (human hair clippings).

are having a difficult time finding comfortable, larger homes at affordable prices.

Southwest

In 1980 the intersection of South Lamar Boulevard and US 290 West was bordered by a sheep farm. Now it is home on all four sides to shopping centers, and a major highway construction project has created a whirligig of flyovers and underpasses to speed traffic in all directions. A Neiman-Marcus outlet store now stands where the sheep once grazed.

Southwest Austin, roughly defined as the area south of US 290 West and west of Brodie Lane, is one of the fastest-growing areas of the city, despite efforts to slow growth through restrictive city planning ordinances (see our Politics and Perspectives chapter). Much of the area sits above the recharge zone for the southern portion of the Edwards Aquifer, in the Barton Creek watershed. But the area's pleasant topography and easy access to downtown via MoPac have proved too much of a lure.

The Austin city limits do encompass much of this area, but a tiny island of real estate called the City of Sunset Valley marks the entrance to Southwest Austin. This area has few homes but has fast become a shopping mecca for residents in this part of Austin. Two large farm homesteads occupied much of the small community for years but now have been sold to retail developers.

Since Sunset Valley has a lower sales tax than the City of Austin, the shops here enjoy an advantage over other area merchants.

West of Sunset Valley, US 290 West passes through a community called Oak Hill. This area was settled in the 1840s and has long been a part of Austin, but it has clung to its name and some of its identity as a small community in the escarpment above the city. It was known by a variety of names until the locals settled on Oak Hill around the turn of the last century. The name is appropriate since the land here rises above the city and is shaded by hundreds, if not thousands of live oaks.

The massive US 290 West construction project has stripped the Oak Hill area of some its personality. One wag erected a sign when construction began asking WILL IT STILL BE OAK HILL WHEN THERE ARE NO OAKS AND NO HILL ANYMORE? The old highway was lined with a few small strip centers erected in pseudo Old West–style that gave Oak Hill its country character. One symbol of the old Oak Hill remains, the Rock Store, now a pizza restaurant, built by pioneer James Patton. It took Patton 19 years to build the store; he finished in 1898. The local elementary school is named in his honor.

Oak Hill is also the site of Convict Hill—a neighborhood is named in its honor. Here, from 1882 to 1886, convict labor was used to quarry limestone for the construction of the Texas Capitol. The stone was used in the capitol's basement. During the operation, eight convicts died and are buried somewhere in the neighborhood on the hill in unmarked graves. The hill stands above the highway just as it splits with US 290 West heading toward Johnson City and Highway 71 heading northwest to the Highland Lakes. The split is called the "Y" by Austin residents.

Oak Hill is now surrounded by several new neighborhoods and a large Motorola plant close to the Y. The neighborhoods here are popular because of the proliferation of oak trees and the relatively easy commute into town. A non-rush-hour ride from the Y to downtown is about 15 minutes, and even a rush-hour commute is faster than a ride into the city from northwest suburbs.

Neighborhoods in this area include Westcreek, Maple Run, Legend Oaks, and The Village at Western Oaks. Homes are priced for middle-income residents. Southwest of the Y and south of Slaughter Lane is the Circle C Ranch development, named for the ranch that once operated in this area. This development was built under the auspices of a Municipal Utility District, a MUD, a device created by the legislature and much used in the Houston area by developers who sold bonds to support the infrastructure in nonincorporated areas. In early 1998 Circle C was annexed into Austin but not without protest from some of the homeowners.

Environmentalists had opposed the Circle C construction, but developers and residents boast of its attractive assets, including a large greenbelt, golf course, swim center, and community building. There are plans to add more amenities, including recreational and business centers. The developer, Gary Bradley, also donated Circle C land to house the nearby Lady Bird Johnson National Wildflower Research Center (see our Attractions chapter). Land also was donated for a veloway and nature trail for bicycle riders and walkers. Homes are in the mid- to upper mid-range pricewise. Development does not stop at the Austin southwest city limits. There are a growing number of housing developments along F.M. 1826, known as Camp Ben McCullough Road, which runs southwest off US 290 West, just west of the Y. Other developments can be found farther along US 290 West toward the Hays County line and Dripping Springs. Most of these homes are on larger lots, over an acre or two, and attract homebuyers who want a little rural atmosphere but a short commute into the city.

West

As noted earlier, the area known as Clarksville, just east of MoPac (Loop 1), once was a half mile outside the city limits. Today the Austin city limits do not extend much beyond that, but the hills above the city are home to people who consider themselves Austinites. For our purposes, West Austin is the area west of MoPac and north of

US 290 West and south of Lake Austin and R.M. 2222.

Within the city limits, West Austin means two of the city's most prestigious neighborhoods. West of MoPac, between Enfield Road in the south and West 35th Street in the north, are Tarrytown and Brykerwoods.

In the last century this part of Austin was home to several large estates. After World War II, the landowners began to subdivide the land. The neighborhoods have been built out over a period of 50 years by a variety of builders, and homes vary in size and personality. Price is consistent— it's high. The tiniest cottage in this area can cost as much as a large four-bedroom home in the hills west of Austin, while large homes can sell for several million dollars. But the sheer variety of homes, the old trees, and beautifully landscaped gardens make this a favorite location.

The same amount of money can buy a whole lot more house in other parts of the city, but the Tarrytown or Brykerwoods address is still sought after. Many of the city's business and political leaders live in this area. Its proximity to downtown, the two highly rated elementary schools in the area, Casis and Brykerwood, plus the neighborhood's "village" atmosphere attracts homebuyers.

In addition to several small European-style shopping centers with cafes and shops, there are neighborhood churches, several parks, and the nearby Lions Municipal Golf Course. One of the city's popular swimming pools, Deep Eddy, is in this area.

Another of Austin's prestigious addresses is not in Austin at all. West Lake Hills is an incorporated city that overlooks downtown from the western hills, west of MoPac and east of Loop 360 (Capital of Texas Highway). A major attraction for homeowners in this area is the highly rated Eanes Independent School District, which encompasses West Lake Hills and much of the surrounding area. (See our Schools and Child Care chapter for more information.)

West Lake has its own city government, newspaper, the *West Lake Picayune*, and personality. Many of the homes are on steep, curved roads that have wonderful views of the downtown skyline. Homes in West Lake are varied in price, size, and style but generally are more expensive than most areas in Austin.

Tucked in between the southeast corner of West Lake Hills and MoPac is the small incorporated community of Rollingwood. Home prices here are generally upscale and expensive. Several large mansions line the cliffs above Lady Bird Lake in the Rollingwood area.

The major thoroughfare in West Lake Hills is R.M. 2244, popularly known as Bee Caves Road. This winding, hilly road is lined with several shopping centers that serve the West Lake community. Growth has been a hot issue for West Lake residents, also, particularly the proliferation of large retail centers at the intersection of Bee Caves Road and Loop 360 (Capital of Texas Highway).

The development along Loop 360 is an indication of the boom in the hills west of Austin. The highway was originally planned as a scenic loop with few traffic lights. It has maintained its scenic quality, but there are now several major intersections along the roadway, many leading to new upscale subdivisions. Just west of Loop 360 and south of Bee Caves Road is Lost Creek, a neighborhood of large family homes on generously sized lots carved out of the hillsides on the eastern edge of Barton Creek. The creek, which feeds Barton Springs Pool, runs through the Lost Creek Country Club. On the western banks of the creek is the Lost Creek Estates development, and a little farther north is The Estates of Barton Creek, home of the Barton Creek Country Club. The development of the Barton Creek club was hard fought by environmentalists, but the developers have won recognition for their environmentally sensitive golf course design and landscaping methods.

The hills south of Lake Austin and north and west of West Lake Hills are home to an ever-increasing number of developments of large, comfortable homes. Among them are Rob Roy, Davenport Ranch, West Rim, and The Preserve. They remain outside the Austin city limits, but some are likely to be targeted for annexation by the City of Austin. West of Austin, out toward

Lake Travis, are several new developments and one well-known, longtime incorporated resort area called Lakeway. The latter offers a variety of homes and condominiums that are popular as retirement and weekend homes since Lakeway offers a golf course, boating and tennis facilities, even a small airfield. Newer developments "out at the lake," as Austinites call it, like the Steiner Ranch, offer large family homes in the upper mid-range of Austin prices.

Northwest

On the north bank of Lake Austin, prices are not quite as steep as those developments west and south of the river. These new, comfortable family neighborhoods feature large family homes.

Northwest Austin is particularly attractive to employees working for the major high-tech companies, many located along U.S. Highway 183 North, dubbed Research Boulevard as it flows through Northwest Austin. South of Research are several neighborhoods built around the private Balcones Country Club.

The northwest corridor has seen the area's most explosive growth, and Austin has spilled over the Travis County line and into Williamson County. Children living in this area attend schools in the Round Rock Independent School District. While Austin has annexed a corridor of land along Research Boulevard, into Williamson County and to the Cedar Park city limits, beyond that strip fire, police, and EMS services are the responsibility of Williamson County authorities.

The residential area to the east and west of Research beyond Anderson Mill Road has seen home prices become static as market diversity increased. The growth along the Research Boulevard corridor also has led to long commute times for residents who have jobs in other areas of the city, a factor that may have contributed to static home prices.

North

The area north of R.M. 2222, known as Koenig Lane between MoPac and I-35, is a mixture of older, middle-class neighborhoods and some

run-down areas. There has been periodic talk of turning Koenig Lane into a major east-west boulevard—the debate over east-west traffic flow is a perennial political topic—but it remains a four-lane urban road (see our Politics and Perspectives chapter).

Generally to the west of Burnet Road, particularly in the Allandale neighborhood along Shoal Creek, there are many spacious 1960s-era, ranch-style homes that are now attracting young would-be homeowners who want a fixer-upper within the city. The advice of a knowledgeable Realtor is well advised in shopping North Austin. There are pockets of wonderful older homes that have survived the urban onslaught of strip shopping centers and suburban flight, but there are also run-down neighborhoods. Just as in South Austin, the farther a visitor drives toward the city limits the newer the homes become. Many of the northern subdivisions are touted as ripe territory for "starter homes."

Adjacent to the northern city limits is a planned community, Wells Branch, developed as a Municipal Utility District (MUD). Wells Branch has a variety of homes, apartments, and condominiums that attract singles and young families. The MUD is well designed and landscaped. Shops and gas stations have inconspicuous signs that give the area a well-groomed look.

Northeast

Throughout the 1990s boom, the area east of I-35 and north of US 290 East escaped much of the growth frenzy found in other parts of the city. But the location of a large Samsung facility in the area just outside the city, plus the relocation of several government office buildings to light industrial parks in the northeast, has prompted suburban development. The new developments are, for the most part, targeted at middle-income families. A few developments farther out toward the small town of Manor list at lower prices.

Meanwhile, the older neighborhoods within the northeast sector of the city are being eyed as gentrification targets, particularly since the old airport has closed.

East

Roughly defined as east of I-35, south of US 290 East, and north of Lady Bird Lake, this large area of Austin is destined for change. Just east of the interstate in the northwest quadrant of this section is the old Robert Mueller Municipal Airport. The city has developed a community discussion process to decide what will be done with the facility. Since it adjoins a municipal golf course in the south, many community leaders called for a mixed-use development of housing, shops, and recreational facilities and the new Mueller town center will include research facilities, film studios, homes, townhomes, parks, restaurants, and cafes, visit www.mulerraustin.com. The airport closing already has had an impact on prices of homes formerly in the flight path of the old facility.

Immediately to the north of the airport and to the southwest are two older neighborhoods that are beginning to attract the attention of homebuyers who want to live closer to the city center. Again, this is an area where the advice of a real estate agent is invaluable. It is also a good idea to talk to neighbors and check with city planners about the future of the area.

The interstate has served as a dividing line in the city, particularly separating the predominantly older African-American and Hispanic neighborhoods that lie south of the airport. Efforts have been under way, with some success, to bring affordable housing and home ownership to this area of the city.

Austin neighborhoods are integrated, but like most other large cities, there are neighborhoods where there is an ethnic concentration. Generally, the area south of Rosewood Avenue

and north of Lady Bird Lake has a distinctive Hispanic cultural flavor. Many popular Mexican restaurants are located here, as well as ethnic groceries and tortilla factories. Neighborhood associations in East Austin have fought to maintain their communities' identity and have resisted powerful forces, including the expanding University of Texas, which forged a compromise with area residents over condemnation rights. But the neighborhoods are attracting young Austinites of all ethnic backgrounds.

Southeast

Just as the northeast has not matched Northwest Austin in growth, so Southeast Austin has not seen the boom experienced by Southwest and Northwest Austin, but that is slowly changing. There are many apartment complexes east of I-35 along the East Oltorf Street corridor, and there have been several entry-level subdivisions built in far Southeast Austin. At the southernmost point of the Austin city limits, on the east side of I-35, is one of Austin's well-known golf communities. Onion Creek was, for many years, home to the Legends of Golf tournament. The secluded country club has a variety of homes and condominiums that attract retirees.

Round Rock

For many of their Austin neighbors, Round Rock is viewed as a booming bedroom community on their northern border, a place to avoid during rush hour if you are headed north on I-35 to Dallas. But for Round Rock residents, their fast-growing town is home, and they are turning to historic preservation and neighborhood planning to keep it that way.

Round Rock gets its name from a round rock. The large rock is located in the middle of Brushy Creek, which flows through what is now a city. Brushy Creek was the name of the village that sprang up here in 1852. Many of the Victorian-era homes in the town center now enjoy protective historic status.

Sam Bass, the infamous Texas outlaw, is buried in the Old Round Rock Cemetery. Until

20 years ago, the shoot-out between Sam Bass and Texas Rangers, sheriff's deputies, and local citizens was the liveliest thing that had ever happened in Round Rock. But with the growth boom in Central Texas, things have been humming in Round Rock for the past two decades. (Demographers predict the population of Williamson County could quadruple from 176,000 to 736,000 by 2030.)

Round Rock offers a variety of new homes, ranging from small homes suitable for a young family or empty-nest couple at starter-home prices to large homes with five bedrooms and three living areas priced less than the same home would cost in West Austin. Some of the area neighborhoods are west of the city limits—several are in the tree-shaded countryside near Brushy Creek. The city's historic homes also are prized. Major employers, including Dell Computer, have located in Round Rock, but many residents do commute to nearby Austin, making rush-hour traffic on I-35 a headache. There are plans to build a second north-south toll road along the right-of-way owned by the Missouri Kansas Railroad, east of the interstate. It will be known as Texas Highway 130 or MoKan, just as the major north-south highway in Austin built along the Missouri-Pacific right-of-way is called MoPac by the locals.

Round Rock does have a reputation as a good place to raise a family. The community's conservative values are touted by city boosters, and comparisons are made with the much more liberal politics and lifestyles favored in Austin. These are clichéd images, of course, but voting patterns and jury decisions tend to reinforce the two communities' respective images.

Williamson County also touts its lower crime rates compared with the more urban Austin in Travis County.

Pflugerville

Ten years ago, about 4,000 people lived in Pflugerville, the small community southeast of Round Rock and northeast of Austin. In the last three months of 1997, the same number moved into the community. This small farming community is the

i The Austin Convention and Visitors Bureau, in cooperation with the Historic Landmark Commission, produces an excellent walking tour guide to the Hyde Park neighborhood, one of several historic walking-tour brochures available at the bureau. The Visitor Information Center is at 209 East Sixth Street, (512) 478-0098 or (800) GOAUSTIN.

latest home hot spot in Central Texas, particularly for homeowners who feel priced out of the Austin market. Like Round Rock, a dollar goes a little further in the home-buying marketplace here. Plus Pflugerville has maintained its small-town aura, locally run schools, and low crime rate.

The area is experiencing some growing pains, and the city council has been forced to raise taxes and annex new areas to support city services. But the city is also putting taxes into city facilities like a recreation center and town library, hoping to add to the city's attractiveness as a good place to find an affordable home in which to raise a family. The new north-south MoKan highway will pass through the area.

Cedar Park

The old-timers in Cedar Park remember how this community got its name. Cedar posts were the town's main business until a few years ago. The small community on US 183, northwest of Austin, was home to several cedar yards where fence posts were stacked before being shipped to ranches all over the West.

Every June, the town's history is celebrated at the Annual Cedar Chopper Festival. Before 1990 most of the festivalgoers came from out of town to enjoy the parade, sample the down-home cooking, and take a carnival ride. Now, many of the town's 13,000 new residents join in the community festival.

Cedar Park is trying to hold on to its history, but it is also attempting to attract high-tech companies and other businesses to help boost the local tax rolls and make Cedar Park something more than a bedroom community by developing a pedestrian-friendly downtown center. Homes in the area, which includes the neighboring community of Leander, offer homebuyers a variety of homes at more affordable prices than they will find closer downtown Austin. Developers are intent on creating neighborhoods, not just suburbs.

The area also features rural homes popularly known as "ranchettes," large country homes on three- or four-acre lots with enough room for a small horse stable or a kennel run.

APARTMENTS

Finding affordable housing in the rental category also is a challenge in Austin. The area's low unemployment rate is one factor in the expensive market, according to analysts. Another factor is the city's attraction to young college graduates, many of whom are attracted to Austin by the lifestyle and high salaries paid by high-tech industries. But the booming economy has put some working Austinites in crisis. The Austin Tenant's Council, (512) 474-1961, a nonprofit social service agency, tries to help apartment renters who cannot afford rent increases.

Those who can afford the rents and are able to find a vacancy enjoy a lot of amenities. Most new apartment complexes are gated and provide residents with increased security. Many have security cameras in each unit that offer residents a view of the main gate and allow them to buzz visitors through after verifying their identities. Garages are an added feature, plus whole-home

i Central Texas enjoys a balmy climate for the most part, but heavy rainstorms can turn those picturesque Hill Country creeks into deadly torrents within minutes. Creeks, many of them dry creekbeds for much of the year, are part of the landscape tapestry in the region. When buying a home near a creek, check its location in relation to the floodplain. And if you are driving in a sudden rainstorm, never try to cross a water-filled creekbed.

music systems. Most have recreational facilities, including workout rooms, swimming pools, and tennis courts. Others offer business centers. The extras offered by the newest apartment homes include gizmos like T1 lines for Internet access, cybercafes, and built-in computer desks. Want to get away from the high-tech world? Take a book to the "reading grotto" or stroll through the rose garden. One new development in Austin also offers a potting shed, an organic fruit orchard, and herb and flower-cutting gardens. Many of the new developments are located along the MoPac corridor, Loop 360 (Capital of Texas Highway), and in Southwest and Northwest Austin, but there also has been some development along south Congress Avenue and north of the University in Central Austin.

Apartments for Rent is a monthly magazine that offers an overview of the area rental market, including some of the newest developments and older apartment facilities. The magazine is available at many grocery stores and can be ordered at (512) 326-1133. The guide is published in 24 states and the District of Columbia. Out-of-town residents can order a complimentary copy of the Austin magazine by calling (900) 420-0040. There is a $4 charge for the call. There are numerous apartment search sites online.

REAL ESTATE RESOURCES

There are more than 4,000 real estate agents and Realtors in the greater Austin area, some operating as individuals, others as members of large, long-established firms. Most offer relocation and custom-building services. For a complete list of agencies, contact the Austin Board of Realtors at (512) 454-7636, www.abor.org, or consult the Yellow Pages.

The Austin Board of Realtors (512-454-7636, www.abor.org) lists more than 5,500 area properties using a new computer system dubbed Stellar. This Multiple Listing Service gives potential homebuyers an opportunity to take a tour of Central Texas and see what the home market is like in various parts of the area.

THE SENIOR SCENE

What can you say about a city where one of the leading senior citizens is Willie Nelson? The graying ponytail may be one symbol of Austin's senior scene; another may be a subtle shift in attention to senior issues as more and more boomers slip into their 60s. Not all are famous, of course, but like so many other aging Americans they have a wealth of lifetime experience and energy to offer. Austin's active lifestyle and activist attitudes offer many outlets for that energy and experience.

POPULATION TRENDS

Austin's population is aging, but the percentage of people over the age of 65 in the Austin area is below the national average—7 percent in Travis and Williamson Counties, compared with 12 percent in the United States. When it comes to the number of residents 65 or older, among the 77 U.S. cities with populations of more than 200,000, Austin ranks 71st.

The 1990 and 2000 U.S. censuses revealed some interesting information about demographic trends in Texas. The fastest-growing segment of the state population is persons ages 25 to 44, representing around 40 percent of the Texas population, compared with about 30 percent nationally. The average age of an Austin city resident is 28.9 years.

However, as a Sunbelt state, retirees do come to Texas. They go particularly to the Rio Grande Valley near the Mexican border, where many retired Midwesterners spend their winters; San Antonio, whose extensive military infrastructure makes it attractive to retired military personnel; and the Hill Country to which many affluent retirees are attracted by the climate and lifestyle. In Central Texas the small communities of Wimberly, southwest of Austin; Fredericksburg, west of Austin; and San Marcos, particularly along the Guadalupe River south of Austin, are attracting retirees.

In the Austin area the older-than-65 population is spread out across many neighborhoods. Austin's older neighborhoods, such as Hyde Park, Allandale, and Travis Heights, have their longtime residents. Many newcomers are attracted to the Highland Lakes area, where the many recreational facilities (see our Parks and Recreation and Golf chapters) offer amenities many seek. Two areas noted for their concentration of senior citizens are Lakeway and Lago Vista, both on Lake Travis, but these communities are by no means restricted to senior citizens.

In Round Rock and the Williamson County area, the percentage of persons older than 65 matches Travis County, 7 percent, but the number of residents younger than 18 is higher—24 percent in Travis, 31 percent in Williamson County.

Developers of retirement homes are finding Williamson County attractive because of its low crime rate, its small-town feel combined with nearby big-city health services, and, perhaps for some, its more conservative lifestyle. One major development is Del Webb's Sun City Georgetown in northern Williamson County.

Sun City is the latest manifestation of a fairly recent trend in Central Texas that has seen the development of housing alternatives for retirees. Compared with some other regions of the state and other Sunbelt communities, there is not an abundance of retirement communities in the area, but the numbers are growing. However, there already have been some tensions between retired residents and the local tax districts over increasing property taxes to support the booming public school systems in Williamson County. Another trend has been the relocation of empty-nesters from the suburbs to bustling downtown Austin.

SENIOR RESOURCES

In response to the aging of America, local businesses are beginning to recognize a market and, in true American fashion, responding to a need. One local Austin real estate company with long-time experience in the marketplace has created a new service to help people find a new, smaller house or a home in a retirement community.

Several agencies and organizations offer information, advice, and research on community housing and nursing homes. These are a good starting point before embarking on tours or visits to facilities aimed at attracting and serving seniors. All the experts emphasize that research and careful consideration are vital before making a move to a new home, a residential facility, or a nursing home.

The attorney general offers two publications for consumers: the *Rights of the Elderly* and *Selecting a Nursing Home*. For copies write to the Texas Attorney General, Attn: Brochure Division, P.O. Box 12548, Austin, TX 78711, or call (512) 936-1737, or check the agency's Web site www.oag.state.tx.us.

AMELIA BULLOCK RELOCATION SERVICES
8008 Spicewood Lane
(512) 345-2100
www.ameliabullock.com
The company has been an Austin presence since 1969. In addition to its services for employees relocating to Austin, the company now offers Timely Solutions, a program to help seniors move to new homes, perhaps smaller homes or homes in communities geared to the senior lifestyle.

AMERICAN ASSOCIATION OF RETIRED PERSONS (AARP)
98 San Jacinto Boulevard
(866) 227-7443
www.aarp.org
This downtown office serves as the state headquarters of the influential national group for 50-plus Americans. Well-known for its advocacy, the AARP also offers information on a variety of topics of interest to seniors. Members receive travel discounts, access to a mail-order pharmacy service, and insurance coverage. Many local chapters hold their meetings at the city's senior activity centers, listed later in this chapter.

AREA AGENCY ON AGING OF THE CAPITAL AREA
2512 West Interstate 35, Suite 340
(512) 916-6062
TTY 916-6016, (888) 622-9111
www.capcog.com
This is a clearinghouse and ombudsman service agency for the 10 counties of Central Texas. It is a good resource for information on nutrition, transportation, home help, health screening, and legal services. The agency's Web site also lists a variety of links to other agencies and programs including the following:

ADULT PROTECTIVE SERVICES, ADULT ABUSE AND FINANCIAL EXPLOITATION HOT LINE
(800) 252-5400
www.dfps.state.tx.us

ALZHEIMER'S ASSOCIATION
(800) 272-3900
www.alz-tex.org

LEGAL HOT LINE FOR OLDER TEXANS
(800) 622-2520
www.tlsc.org

LOCAL SENIOR SERVICES
dial 211

MEDICAID HOT LINE
(800) 252-8263

MEDICARE HOT LINE
(800) MEDICARE (633-4227)

NURSING FACILITY INFORMATION HELPLINE
(800) 252-8016

TEXAS ATTORNEY GENERAL CONSUMER HELPLINE
(800) 621-0508

TEXAS DEPARTMENT OF HUMAN SERVICES
Nursing home complaints
(800) 458-9858

TEXAS DEPARTMENT ON AGING AND DIS-ABILITY SERVICES
Ombudsman Hot Line
(800) 252-2412

VETERANS ADMINISTRATION BENEFITS INFORMATION AND ASSISTANCE
(800) 827-1000
www.va.gov

AUSTIN GROUPS FOR THE ELDERLY (AGE)
3710 Cedar Street
(512) 451-4611
www.ageofaustin.org
Housed in a wonderful Central Austin historic building, c. 1902, AGE is an umbrella agency for more than a dozen nonprofit agencies. It is worth visiting the center both to enjoy the architecture and pick up information on a variety of services—adult day care, respite care, emergency residence for abused and neglected elders, family counseling, information, referral, mental health care,

Austin Senior's Guide is published annually and gives tips on senior living in the Austin area, plus information on discounts and products of interest to seniors, (512) 257-7607, www.seniorsguide.net.

and adult education. Seniors here also will find a newspaper, the *Senior Advocate,* (512) 451-7433, www.senioradvocatenews.com, aimed at what one national radio host calls "seasoned" citizens, and the SeniorNet Computer Learning Center, aimed at helping seniors become computer savvy, (512) 451-1932, www.seniornet.com.

FAMILY ELDERCARE
2210 Hancock Drive
(512) 450-0844
www.familyeldercare.org
Located in Central Austin, this nonprofit organization offers a wide variety of services for seniors. Eldercare receives some funds from the United Way. Programs include The Gatekeeper, a training program for social service workers and volunteers, plus business owners and members of community groups who interact with the elderly. The program trains them to identify and assist seniors who are suffering from abuse or neglect or who are being exploited. Another Eldercare program is In Home Care and Respite Services, which provides care for home-bound adults. There is also an Alzheimer's program as part of this service. Volunteers are trained in the guardianship and money management program, and then they are matched with seniors who need legal guardians, representative payees, or money managers.

THE SENIOR ADVOCATE
3710 Cedar Street
(512) 451-7433
www.senioradvocatenews.com
The *Senior Advocate* has grown from a newsletter to a newspaper in the past 20 years and now has an online presence in addition to its paper format. The goal is to provide "interesting, accurate, and vital information on issues and resources important to seniors," according to its publishers, Dave and Dana Smith. The paper has won several awards for editorial excellence and community service. In 1999 the paper won the National Mature Media Awards, ahead of such publications as *Parade* and *Essence* magazines.

The paper was also honored with an Outstanding Media Coverage award from the City of Austin in 1999 for publishing employment opportunities for seniors each month at no cost to the city. The job listings are a partnership effort between Austin's Senior Programs division and Experience Unlimited, a placement agency for individuals who are 50 years of age or older.

SENIOR HEALTH CARE CENTERS: PRIVATE SECTOR

Austin's two major health care providers run medical centers aimed specifically at the needs of seniors. St. David's Healthcare Partnership (www .stdavids.com) has two clinics, both in north Austin, one at 3300 West Anderson Lane, Suite 308, (512) 901-8250; the other at 5222 Burnet Road, Suite 200 (512) 420-9775. The Seton Healthcare Network (www.seton.net) operates a senior clinic in the Lakeway area in far West Austin at 1602 Lohman's Crossing Road, (512) 261-1758.

TEXAS DEPARTMENT ON AGING AND DISABILITY SERVICES (DADS)
701 West 51st Street
(512) 438-3011, (800) 458-9858
www.dads.state.tx.us
This is a state agency designed to assist seniors. The hot line, at the 800 number listed above, offers information and referrals on senior services. In Texas, consumers can simply dial 211 and ask for DADS information.

TEXAS ATTORNEY GENERAL
(512) 463-2100, (800) 252-8011
www.oag.state.tx.us
Consumers may request two detailed brochures from the Texas Attorney General, the state's chief law enforcement officer who is empowered to bring suit against offending facilities, including nursing homes and residential homes for the

ℹ **Many Austin businesses offer discounts to so-called senior citizens. Order a guide to deals in Austin from www .seniorsguides.net.**

disabled and the mentally handicapped. Both the current and previous attorneys general have filed suit to close down offending facilities. However, some consumer and advocacy groups have criticized the state legislature for allowing the nursing home industry to influence regulation. In 1997 legislation was passed aimed at responding to those criticisms. Write to: Research and Legal Support Division, Office of the Attorney General, Attn: Brochure Division, P.O. Box 12548, Austin, TX 78711.

TEXAS DEPARTMENT OF HUMAN SERVICES (TDHS)
(512) 438-3011, (800) 458-9858
www.dhs.state.tx.us
This state agency can provide consumers with the last two years of compliance history of any facility. The agency says consumers should expect to see some compliance failures on any report, since even the most minor are listed by state inspectors. TDHS can answer four questions: How many complaints have there been in the last year? How many quality-of-care violations have there been in the past two years? When was the last visit by TDHS and why? Has the owner had other facilities recommended for closure?

TEXAS DEPARTMENT OF INSURANCE (TDI)
(512) 463-6169, (800) 578-4677
www.tdi.state.tx.us
The state agency charged with oversight of the insurance industry in Texas provides consumers free of charge and on request with *A Shopper's Guide to Long-term Care*. This brochure is published by the National Association of Insurance Commissioners. The agency also offers a great variety of insurance publications on all kinds of policies and state regulations, many of which are helpful to newcomers.

RESIDENTIAL OPTIONS

Making a move is a major step at any age, and certainly a step that is not be taken lightly. Experts recommend carefully weighing needs, both current and future; lifestyle habits and patterns; location; and, of course, cost. Another important part of the process is to visit the community and spend time there. Apply some of the same rules experts recommend in choosing a day care center for children—visit at different times; talk to the residents and the staff; compare notes with others (important for children helping their parents find a place to live); and read the fine print.

The number of retirement communities and facilities is increasing in Central Texas, and there also are attempts to build affordable housing in Austin, a growing need as housing prices soar. We've offered a sampling. The Area Agency on Aging of the Capital Area (above) offers an extensive list, www.aaacp.org.

BUCKNER VILLAS
11110 Tom Adams Drive
(512) 836-1515
www.bucknerretirement.org
This is a North Austin nonprofit rental community offering a variety of residential options in a Christian environment. The facility offers the flexibility for residents to change their environment as needs change, from independent and assisted living to nursing home care. Apartments have two bedrooms and full kitchens. The facility also has an Alzheimer's program.

BROOKDALE LIVING
The Heritage at Gaines Ranch
4409 Gaines Ranch Loop
(512) 899-8400
www.brookdaleliving.com
Brookdale is a national rcompany with several independent and assisted living facilities in Austin. The highrise Heritage is in Southwest Austin and is set amid landscaped gardens. The community has both independent living apartments and an assisted-living program. There is an on-site health clinic, fitness and exercise programs, dining services, and 24-hour concierge, housekeeping, and transportation services. Brookdale operates these "Summit" facilities for both independent and assisted living in the area:

THE SUMMIT AT WESTLAKE HILLS
1034 Liberty Park Drive
(512) 328-3775

THE SUMMIT AT LAKEWAY
1915 Lohmans Crossing Road
(512) 261-7146

THE SUMMIT AT NORTHWEST HILLS
5715 Mesa Drive
(512) 454-5900
The three retirement communities at West Lake Hills west of Austin have been dubbed "retirement living for those who aren't the retiring type." The luxury rental communities have a variety of apartments, 24-hour security, transportation, catering, an on-site health care center, and recreational activities.

HOLIDAY CORPORATION:
THE CLAIRMONT
12463 Los Indios Trail
(512) 331-7195

THE CONTINENTAL
4604 South Lamar Boulevard
(512) 892-5995

ENGLEWOOD ESTATES
2603 Jones Road
(512) 892-7226

RENAISSANCE-AUSTIN
11279 Taylor Draper Lane
(512) 338-0995
www.holidaytouch.com
This national company operates four facilities in Austin. Each offers month-to-month rentals, catering of three meals a day, weekly housekeeping, paid utilities, planned activities, and on-site resident managers. Some have beauty shop and barber facilities and transportation services.

THE ISLAND ON LAKE TRAVIS
3404 American Drive
(512) 267-7107, (800) 422-4753
www.islandonlaketravis.com
Literally on an island connected by causeway to

the mainland, this independent living community is designed for active seniors. Rental apartments in this Lago Vista–area facility, northwest of Austin, have 24-hour security, indoor parking, an on-site restaurant, weekly housekeeping, and recreational facilities.

THE PARK AT BECKETT MEADOWS
7709 Beckett Road
(512) 891-9544
www.emeritus.com

The suburban assisted living facility in Southwest Austin is in a neighborhood favored by families, making it a good choice for elder family members who may need special care for Alzheimers or dementia.

WESTMINSTER MANOR
RETIREMENT COMMUNITY
4100 Jackson Avenue
(512) 454-4711
www.wmanor.com

This facility in Central Austin, near Seton Medical Center, has what it calls a Life Care Program, which allows residents to buy their apartments and a care program. Up to 90 percent of the entrance fee is returned to the buyer's estate, and a portion of the fee is deductible as a prepaid medical expense.

ADVOCACY

GRAY PANTHERS OF AUSTIN
3710 Cedar Street
(512) 458-3738

Located in Central Austin in the same facility as Eldercare, this senior citizen advocacy group has a national reputation for its organizational skills and education workshops. The group produces several handy publications, among them *A Caregivers Manual*.

TRANSPORTATION

Austin Capital Metro, (512) 389-7400, www.cap metro.org, the area public transportation service,

i In a booming area as property values grow, taxes can become burdensome for seniors on a fixed income. Check with the local tax assessor's office to learn of all the tax breaks and freezes afforded to seniors, for an overview check the Texas State Comptroller's Office, www.cpa.state.tx.us/.

has several programs designed for seniors. In a city some call an elephant's graveyard for hippies, the free bus pass for seniors is called an EasyRider. These passes are free to citizens 65 and older and can be obtained by showing your Medicare card, driver's license, or Capital Metro senior ID. An ID may be purchased for $3.00 at the downtown Metro office, 106 East Eighth Street, which is open from 7:30 a.m. to 5:30 p.m. weekdays. It just takes a few minutes to process the ID.

Groups of 20 seniors or more can request free transportation from 10:00 a.m. to 2:00 p.m. weekdays, 6:00 a.m. to 10:00 p.m. on weekends. Advanced reservations are required; call (512) 389-7583.

Capital Metro also offers curb-to-curb service and connections to medical services in some areas of the city. There is also a special transit service for the disabled. (See our Getting Here, Getting Around chapter.)

For general schedule information, call (512) 474-1200. Many grocery stores also stock bus schedules at their customer service counters.

MEDI WHEELS
(512) 476-6325
www.mealsonwheelsandmore.org

This service offers rides to medical appointments to people 55 or older. Please call a week in advance of your appointment.

SUPPORT SERVICES
(512) 480-3012
www.ci.asutin.tx.us/parks/seniors

This PARD program offers nonemergency medical transportation for seniors 60 and older. Reservations are required, with 24-hour notice.

Reservations can be made for medical, personal, and group travel.

LIFETIME LEARNING

AUSTIN COMMUNITY COLLEGE
5930 Middle Fiskville Road
(512) 223-7000
www.austin.cc.tx.us
The city's community college has several campuses around the area (see our Higher Education chapter). In addition to a full curriculum of credit courses, ACC offers a variety of enrichment programs, some of them aimed at topics of particular concern to the elderly, including family care-giving, retirement and recreation, and aging classes.

ELDERHOSTEL
The University of Texas
(512) 471-3500
www.utexas.edu/ce/personal/elderhostel/
The University of Texas offers five-day noncredit programs in the liberal arts at seven Elderhostel sites. They are at University of Texas in Austin, Big Bend National Park in far Southwest Texas, San Antonio, Galveston, El Paso, and Fort Worth. Art, music, and literature are the themes of the various programs. Lodging, meals, and field trips are included in the tuition fee. The program also is a clearinghouse for Elderhostel programs around the state at other schools and cultural institutions.

LIFETIME LEARNING INSTITUTE
Concordia Lutheran College, 3400 I-35
(512) 486-2000
www.concordia.edu
In fall and spring, Concordia offers several eight-week courses for people 50 and older on a variety of topics such as art appreciation, foreign languages, Texas history, financial planning, and social and political history. Tuition is $15 per course, and classes are held at a variety of locations around the city.

SENIORNET
www.seniornet.com
This Web-based site provides a wide variety of information for seniors, with links to local services. In conjunction with the site there is a computer training program in Austin located at Austin Groups for the Elderly (see earlier in this chapter).

UNIVERSITY OF TEXAS CONTINUING EDUCATION
The Thompson Conference Center
26th and Red River Streets
(512) 471-4652
www.utexas.edu/cee
This facility is near the LBJ Presidential Library on the eastern edge of the campus. Two community outreach programs offer classes for seniors. There is an annual membership program, Learning Activities for Mature People, featuring a series lecture and classes in fall, winter, and spring for $125. Three six-week programs, titled Seminars for Adult Growth and Enrichment, are offered annually in fall, winter, and spring. The cost is $195.

COMMUNITY ACTIVITIES

A wide variety of recreational activities are aimed at area seniors, and many of them can be found at a network of senior activity centers. These community facilities offer a place to meet for recreation, networking, and nutrition. Most city-run centers offer a hot lunch for a nominal fee, around $1.

The centers are operated by the Senior Program, which has numerous brochures and newsletters detailing programs and locations. Activities at the centers range from arts and crafts to health and fitness classes, line dancing, mah-jongg, poetry clubs and investment clubs, pool tournaments, stamp collectors' gatherings, and outings.

Austin

SENIOR PROGRAMS AND SERVICE CENTERS MAIN OFFICE
4201 Ed Bluestein Boulevard
(512) 974-1460
www.ci.austin.tx.us/parks/sractivity.htm

There are senior activities at all the city's recreation centers and several smaller senior centers at various locations throughout the city. There are also three designated Senior Activity Centers in the city, listed below. All have extensive senior programs and support services, and all serve a hot lunch for a small charge. Transportation is provided on request.

CONLEY-GUERRERO SENIOR ACTIVITY CENTER
808 Nile Street
(512) 478-7695
The daily programs here are designed to enhance the quality of life for seniors in East Austin. Seniors gather at the senior center daily to exercise. Domino sessions are a popular pastime, as are the ceramics classes. The center also arranges out-of-town trips for shopping and recreation, and there are popular regular events like Blue Jean Day and Over the Rainbow Social Evenings.

LAMAR SENIOR ACTIVITY CENTER
2874 Shoal Crest Avenue
(512) 474-5921
The seniors at this Central Austin center are avid tripsters, heading off on theater and museum outings to Houston and Dallas, and visiting historic Texas sites, including the Bush Presidential Library in College Station. Ballroom dancing is a popular activity and dances are held usually three times a week. There is also an array of classes offered in games and arts and crafts. In addition, a driving safety class is offered that grants graduates a cut in their insurance premiums.

SOUTH AUSTIN SENIOR ACTIVITY CENTER
3911 Manchaca Road
(512) 448-0787
Bridge, dominos, and mah-jongg are popular pastimes at this South Austin center. Students in the ceramics classes can fire their creations in the on-site kiln. Oil painting classes are also offered. The center also organizes day trips to country music

concerts, shopping trips to the outlet malls, and visits to major art exhibits in Dallas and Houston.

Round Rock
ROUND ROCK SENIOR CENTER
301 West Bagdad Avenue
(512) 255-4970
www.roundrocktexas.gov
This senior activity center is open from 8:00 a.m. to 3:00 p.m. daily and offers a wide variety of senior services and recreational pursuits. The center also serves meals.

Pflugerville
AUSTIN/TRAVIS COUNTY HEALTH AND HUMAN SERVICES
15803 Windermere Drive
(512) 972-5460
This is a senior citizen activity center that offers opportunities for recreation and interaction, plus support services and meals.

NUTRITION

Maintaining a healthy diet can be difficult for some seniors, particularly those on a tight budget or those who find themselves suddenly alone or unable to cook and shop for groceries. The programs listed below can lend a helping hand.

MEALS ON WHEELS AND MORE
3227 East Fifth Street
(512) 476-6325
www.mealsonwheelsandmore.org
This network of volunteers delivers hot, nutritious meals to the homes of more than 2,000 people who can no longer prepare food for themselves or leave their homes. The program also offers other services including:

- Groceries to Go—volunteers shop for participants who are unable to make a trip to the grocery store, and deliver vital groceries to their homes.

- Medi Wheels—volunteers provide transportation to and from medical appointments for more than 400 older people.
- Care Calls—volunteers brighten someone's day with a friendly telephone call, giving lonely seniors a chance to hear a friendly voice and talk to someone who will listen.
- Handy Wheels—volunteers perform minor home safety repairs such as installing smoke alarms, bathroom safety bars, house numbers, and replacing lightbulbs, to the residences of the homebound.

All of these programs welcome volunteers. If you want to make a donation, check out the Web site, where you can buy Stubb's Gospel CD, music from the city's legendary barbecue joint.

SENIOR SUPPORT SERVICES
(512) 480-3005
This program provides lunches every weekday to senior citizens at 18 locations in Travis County, including the city's PARD Senior Activity Centers (see previous listing). To be eligible you must be 60 or the spouse of someone enrolled in the meals program. The cost of the hot lunch is minimal, as low as 50 cents, a little more in some locations. Additional activities include shopping, field trips, educational programs, and holiday events. Free transportation also is provided with 24 hours notice. Call (512)- 974-1464.

WILLIAMSON-BURNET COUNTY OPPORTUNITIES INC.
(512) 930-9011
www.wbco.net
This two-county service nutrition program offers meals-on-wheels and other nutrition services for seniors in Williamson and Burnet Counties.

CAREGIVERS:
FAR NORTHWEST CAREGIVERS
(512) 250-5021

LAKEWAY SERVICE LEAGUE
(512) 261-3514

NORTH CENTRAL CAREGIVERS
(512) 453-2273

NORTHEAST AUSTIN CAREGIVERS
(512) 459-1122

SOUTH AUSTIN CAREGIVERS
(512) 445-5552

SOUTHEAST AUSTIN CAREGIVERS
(512) 472-0997

WEST AUSTIN CAREGIVERS
(512) 472-6339

ROUND ROCK CAREGIVERS
(512) 310-1060
This national program relies on local churches, synagogues, and mosques to set up their own grassroots organization to reach out to needy members of the community in a variety of ways. Caregivers is a network of volunteers who help those seniors who want to remain in their homes maintain their independence. Volunteers do small but meaningful tasks for the seniors, including driving them to appointments or grocery shopping for them.

TELEPHONE REASSURANCE PROGRAM
United Austin for the Elderly
(512) 476-6325
This service offers a daily contact program for seniors who live alone. Volunteers also have Phone-A-Friend, a program aimed at contacting lonely seniors.

JOB OPPORTUNITIES

The high-tech field gets a lot of attention for its youthful workforce, but there are opportunities for talented, skilled workers of all ages in Austin. One good place to find information on job availability for seniors is at the Austin PARD Web site, www.ci.austin.tx.us/parks/seniors.

AUSTIN SENIOR AIDES
(512) 480-3006
This PARD program matches seniors with non-profit agencies for part-time work. On-the-job

training is offered. To participate, a person must be 55 or older and have a low income.

EXPERIENCE UNLIMITED
(512) 480-3013
This PARD program encourages individuals 50 or older to register with the program's job referral bank. One of the program's innovative programs offered lifeguard jobs to seniors at the city's swimming pools.

OLD BAKERY AND EMPORIUM
1006 Congress Avenue
(512) 477-5961
A PARD program provides a showcase at the Old Bakery and Emporium for talented seniors to display and sell their crafts at this downtown attraction. (See our Attractions chapter.)

TEXAS WORKFORCE COMMISSION
South Austin Office,
4175 Friedrich Lane, Suite 200
(512) 381-1695

North Austin Office,
825 East Rundberg Lane
(512) 719-4145

East Austin Office,
3401 Webberville Road
(512) 223-5400

Round Rock Office,
1609 Chisholm Trail
(512) 244-2207
www.twc.state.tx.us

ℹ️ The Texas Silver-Haired Legislature is a nonprofit, nonpartisan group that works with the state legislature on senior issues. Delegates serve two-year terms. For participation information contact the Area Agency on Aging of the Capital Area at (512) 916-6062.

Formerly known as the Texas Employment Commission, this state agency offers employment counseling and referrals to Texas residents. The department also has a Mature Worker Services program that conducts seminars to help workers hone their interview and resume-writing skills.

VOLUNTEER OPPORTUNITIES

Opportunities abound for those with a lifetime of skills to help others in the community. From local museums to the police department, rape-crisis centers to literacy programs, the possibilities for meaningful activity are enormous. We have listed several volunteer clearinghouse organizations and groups who seek out seniors. Each year, around Christmas, the *Austin American–Statesman* publishes a comprehensive wish list from various community groups seeking either volunteers or donations.

VOLUNTEER SOLUTIONS
www.volunteersolutions.com
In 1997 a group of MIT students was searching for a way to make the Web work for America's needy. They came up with this Web site that tries to match volunteers with nonprofit agencies. The Web site has grown and now includes several cities across the United States, including an Austin site where more than 200 local nonprofits are listed. A great resource for anyone searching for a way to serve the community.

Following is a list of groups that use volunteers:

AMERICAN RED CROSS
Central Texas Office,
2218 Pershing Drive
(512) 928-4271

Williamson County Office
1106 South Mays Street, Round Rock
(512) 930-1700
www.redcross.org

CARE CALLS
(512) 476-6325

**COURT APPOINTED SPECIAL ADVOCATES
(CASA)**
(512) 443-2272
www.casatravis.org

FOSTER GRANDPARENTS
(512) 424-6130

**RETIRED AND SENIOR VOLUNTEER
PROGRAM (RSVP), (512) 854-RSVP (7787)**
www.rsvpaustin.org

UNITED WAY
(512)-472-6267
www.unitedwaycapitalarea.org

HEALTH CARE AND WELLNESS

The first hint that Austin is a city that values wellness is the constant reminder over the airport public address system: Austin is a Clean Air City. Smoking is strictly verboten in most public places, although a recent battle over smoking in nightclubs suggests there is a backlash to political correctness among some Austinites. Perhaps that is an indication of another much-valued community trait—tolerance. That tolerance combined with a willingness to try new approaches also means Austin is a place where alternative therapies and health care options are widely available. Even Austin pets get to choose between traditional and alternative medical care here; one of our pets has been treated with acupuncture and Chinese herbal therapy—at the suggestion, we might add, of our "regular" vet.

Health food stores, including the flagship store of the now international and publicly traded Whole Foods Market chain (see our Shopping chapter), are not only evidence of Austin's concerns about wellness but also serve as conduits for alternative therapy information. More and more mainstream stores stock organic foods, offer herbal supplements, and sometimes have on-site massage.

In addition to concerns about diet and health care, Austin residents place a great deal of emphasis on exercise. Running, jogging, walking, swimming, and bicycling are important activities, and visitors can see daily evidence of this around Lady Bird Lake and at Barton Springs Pool (see our Parks and Recreation chapter).

Austin is consistently included on top-10 lists of great places to live in the United States, and one of the criteria is the quality of health care available in a community. There is little doubt that Austin has a wide variety of health care options and an extensive support system that relies on both experts and grassroots networks. There is also little doubt that the city's health care system has been evolving and will continue to expand and change in the years ahead. The U.S. health care system has been undergoing some radical and profound changes in the past few decades; this, combined with Austin's growth, has created a fluid picture of the Central Texas health care infrastructure.

In the past couple of years, consolidations, expansions, and new developments have changed the medical scene. These changes are particularly apparent when reviewing the hospital and clinic scene in Austin and surrounding areas. There are two major players in Austin—the Seton Good Health Network (www.seton.net) and the St. David's Healthcare Partnership (www.stdavids.com). Seton has expanded with clinic facilities in the suburbs as the city has grown. There are several health research facilities in Austin focused on drug and therapy trials. These research facilities frequently advertise in the local media for volunteers (sometimes with pay) to participate in drug trials.

FINDING A PHYSICIAN

This can be a difficult task for newcomers to any city. Both Seton and Columbia/St. David's operate physician referral services on their Web sites. Seton's Physician Referral number is (512) 324-4444. For information about the St. David's system, call (512) 482-4100; for physician referral call (512) 478-DOCS (3627). There are also several professional organizations that offer referrals to their members. They include the Austin Travis

County Chiropractic Society Referral Service, (512) 263-3434; Capital Area Psychological Association, (512) 454-3706; Texas Chiropractic Association, (512) 477-9292; Texas Psychological Association, (512) 280-4099; and the Travis County Medical Society, (512) 206-1249.

HOSPITALS

Central

BRACKENRIDGE HOSPITAL
601 East 15th Street
(512) 324-7000
www.seton.net

The city-owned hospital serves as the regional trauma center for the Central Texas area and is served by STARflight medical helicopter services. The hospital also has a children's emergency room facility that offers state-of-the-art crisis care. After grappling with deficits, the city turned operation of the downtown hospital over to the capable hands of the Daughters of Charity, who also run the Seton Healthcare Network, which includes other hospitals and clinics in the Austin area. The 360-year-old Catholic order has gained a reputation for providing quality health care for both insured and needy patients while managing to retain profitability in a volatile marketplace.

Brackenridge is an acute-care hospital that, in addition to the trauma center, provides maternity, critical care, surgery, orthopedics, and nephrology services.

DELL CHILDREN'S MEDICAL CENTER OF CENTRAL TEXAS
4900 Mueller Boulevard
(512) 324-0000
www.dellchildrens.net

Thanks to generous donations by Austin entrepreneur Michael Dell and others, this Seton Network children's hospital is a showcase that serves a 46-county central Texas area. Rather than treat children like "little adults," the hospital is focused on children's needs and family-centered solutions. The award-winning building is located on the site of the old Austin airport and is at the heart of a proposed healthcare campus amid a town center development (www.muelleraustin .com). The green building uses art and nature to make children feel comfortable and the grounds are landscaped to remind them of the various flora in their hometown, be it a farm in the Blackland Prairie to the east or a town in the Hill Country. Inside, the surroundings are designed to be kid-friendly and not intimidating to youngsters who may be experiencing difficulties. Of course, the hospital also offers state-of-the-art pediatric medical care.

HEART HOSPITAL OF AUSTIN
3801 North Lamar Boulevard
(512) 407-7000
www.hearthospitalofaustin.com

This non-Seton, non-St David's entry on the Austin medical scene is situated at the southern end of a large swath of land sold by the state to private developers. The original Central Market sits on a portion of the land (see our Shopping chapter), and the hospital occupies a site to the south, just a few blocks east of the flagship Seton Medical Center Focused on heart health care, the facility also has a full-service emergency room.

ST. DAVID'S MEDICAL CENTER
919 East 32nd Street
(512) 476-7111
www.sdhcp.com

Part of the St. David's Healthcare Partnership, this downtown hospital is an acute-care facility. Medical services include a rehabilitation center, a psychiatric center for children, maternity and reproductive technology services, and cardiac and urodynamics programs.

SETON MEDICAL CENTER
1201 West 38th Street
(512) 323-1000
www.seton.net

The home base for the Daughters of Charity network of medical facilities in Austin, Seton Medical Center offers a wide range of medical and surgical services. It is in a "medical arts" area of Austin, where many of the city's physicians and medical support services are located. Offerings include a 24-hour emergency room, a neonatal center, a maternity facility, and cancer care services. It is also the headquarters for Seton's Good Health program, which focuses on wellness issues. For the families of patients, the hospital operates a nearby accommodations facility, Seton League House at 3207 Wabash Avenue, (512) 323-1999. The Seton system also includes home care programs, senior health centers, and several clinics throughout the greater Austin area.

SETON SHOAL CREEK HOSPITAL
3501 Mills Avenue
(512) 452-0361
www.seton.net
This private psychiatric hospital also managed by the Seton network serves patients of all ages and is situated along a pleasant stretch of Shoal Creek in the central medical arts area of the city around 35th Street.

South
SOUTH AUSTIN HOSPITAL
901 West Ben White Boulevard
(512) 447-2211
www.southaustinhospital.com
St. David's operates this acute-care facility in south Austin. The hospital has a 24-hour emergency room, a cardiovascular center, maternity services, and a neurological center. It also offers lithotripsy for noninvasive kidney stone removal.

Southwest
SETON SOUTHWEST MEDICAL CENTER
7900 F.M. 1826
(512) 324-9000
www.goodhealth.com
In response to the fast-growing Southwest section of the city, the Seton network opened a new medical center and emergency room in 2000 on F.M. 1826, known to the locals as Camp Ben McCullough Road. The facility is at the corner of F.M. 1826 and U.S. Highway 290 West.

Northwest
SETON NORTHWEST HOSPITAL
11113 Research Boulevard
(512) 324-6000
www.seton.net
This northwest branch of the Seton network has a minor emergency center, plus 24-hour emergency room, birthing units, and maternity services. Seton also offers Good Health School wellness programs on-site, and the facility houses the Seton Northwest Sports Medicine practice. A similar facility is planned for Southwest Austin.

North
NORTH AUSTIN MEDICAL CENTER
12221 MoPac Boulevard North
(512) 901-1000
www.stdavids.com
Part of the St. David's Healthcare Partnership, this north Austin hospital has acute-care medical and surgical units, a 24-hour emergency room, an outpatient surgery center, maternity facilities, a women's center, rehabilitation services, and oncology programs. The facility also houses the Austin Travel Clinic, where would-be world wanderers can receive the necessary shots and health information for travel to any part of the world.

Round Rock
ROUND ROCK MEDICAL CENTER
2400 Round Rock Avenue
(512) 341-1000
www.stdavids.com
Following a major $28 million expansion, this acute-care hospital serves the southern Williamson County area. Part of the St. David's Healthcare

i Hospice Austin, (512) 342-4700, www .hospiceaustin.org, serves both Travis and Williamson Counties, covering the Austin and Round Rock metropolitan area. Hospice offers medical, spiritual, and bereavement care for terminally ill patients and their families on an outpatient basis. Payment is on an ability-to-pay basis.

Partnership, the hospital has a 24-hour emergency room, family birthing center, medical-surgical unit, intensive-care unit, cardiopulmonary services center, plus an outpatient surgery facility.

PUBLIC HEALTH SERVICES

The Austin/Travis County Health and Human Services Department, (512) 329-5959, is a joint city and county tax supported service agency that oversees the operation of 13 community clinics in the city of Austin and the surrounding area. The agency also oversees immunization outreach programs that are held in local shopping malls. The clinics offer maternity care, well-child check-ups, dental services at some locations, and tests and treatment for tuberculosis, sexually transmitted diseases, and HIV. The Women, Infant and Children's Nutrition program, commonly known as the WIC program, is also administered by the health department. Fees are charged according to the ability of the patient to pay, but the agency says no one is turned away. Call (512) 972-4242 in Austin for locations (www. ci.austin.tx.us/health).

Community Clinics

PEOPLE'S COMMUNITY CLINIC
2909 North Interstate 35
(512) 478-8924
www.pcclinic.org
Payment is on a sliding scale at this community clinic. No one is refused treatment. The clinic offers adult outpatient and pediatric medical care, free immunizations, family-planning and prenatal services, treatment of sexually transmitted diseases, and women's health services. The clinic's Web site is an excellent guide to resources for the needy.

SETON MCCARTHY COMMUNITY HEALTH CENTER
2811 East Second Street
(512) 323-4930
www.seton.net
The Seton network provides medical care and social services for residents in the East Austin

area. No one is turned away, and fees are charged on a sliding scale. The center is named for the much-loved Bishop McCarthy, now retired.

SETON KOZMETSKY COMMUNITY HEALTH CENTER
3706 South First Street
(512) 323-4940
www.seton.net
The center provides similar services to those at the network's East Austin location, listed previously, including medical care and social services on a sliding-fee scale. No one is turned away.

VOLUNTEER HEALTH CARE CLINIC
4215 Medical Parkway
(512) 459-4939
This clinic serves patients who are not eligible for city or county support, Medicare, or Medicaid, and do not have their own insurance. The clinic treats only minor illness. Donations are welcome, but no one is turned away.

Round Rock

ROUND ROCK HEALTH CLINIC
2120 North Mays Street, Suite 430
(512) 255-5120
www.roundrockhealthclinic.org
Medicaid and Medicare patients are accepted at this outpatient clinic that offers well-child checkups, prenatal care, and family medicine.

WILLIAMSON COUNTY AND CITIES HEALTH DISTRICT CLINIC
100 West Third Street
(512) 943-3600
www.wcchd.org
Williamson County and cities in the area fund local public health clinics that provide medical services on a sliding-fee scale. Screenings for diabetes and blood pressure tests for seniors are among the services provided. The clinics also offer prenatal care, well-child checkups, and testing and counseling for tuberculosis, sexually transmitted diseases, and HIV.

Cedar Park

WILLIAMSON COUNTY AND CITIES HEALTH DISTRICT CLINIC
350 Discovery Boulevard
(512) 260-4240
www.wcchd.org
The clinic offers medical services on a sliding-fee scale, plus diabetes and blood pressure screenings for seniors and prenatal and well-child services. Counseling for those diagnosed with tuberculosis, sexually transmitted diseases, and HIV also is available.

AIDS SERVICES

The Austin area has an extensive network of services and programs to assist and support people with HIV and AIDS. For a complete listing of the services, call the AIDS information line, (512) 458-AIDS, or contact AIDS Services of Austin (www.asaustin.org).

AIDS SERVICES OF AUSTIN
P.O. Box 4874, Austin 78765
(512) 458-AIDS
www.asaustin.org
A clearinghouse for AIDS information in Central Texas, this agency serves HIV-positive individuals and their families. The agency also provides information on AIDS network services like the Animal Companions program, a volunteer group that provides grooming, veterinary care, in-home care, and a food bank for the pets of AIDS patients.

COMMUNITY AIDS RESOURCE & EDUCATION (CARE)
1633 East Second Street
(512) 473-2273
CARE provides legal referrals, counseling, transportation, screening, and other services for HIV-positive individuals.

DENTAL CLINIC
3000 Medical Arts Street
(512) 479-6633
Dental care for HIV and AIDS patients is offered on a sliding scale by this Central Austin clinic.

HIV WELLNESS CENTER
4301 North I-35
(512) 467-0088
The wellness center offers a holistic approach to care for people with HIV and AIDS. Among the therapies are nutritional counseling, acupuncture, massage, and other alternative approaches aimed at boosting the immune system.

Additional AIDS resources include the following:

- Austin/Travis County Health Department, HIV Services, (512) 708-3500
- Austin Area HIV Planning Council, (512) 499-2407
- David Powell Clinic (Austin–Travis County Health Department HIV clinic), (512) 380-4300
- HIV Study Group (experimental drug trials), (512) 450-1866
- Interfaith Care Alliance (AIDS care teams), (512) 477-3213
- National Aids Hot Line, (800) 342-AIDS
- People's Community Clinic (see above), (512) 478-8942
- Pediatric AIDS League, (512) 892-4776
- Project REACH (HIV education for people of color), (512) 476-4610
- Project Transitions (hospice, assisted living, and supportive housing), (512) 454-8646
- Texas Department of Health, HIV Division, (512) 490-2505
- Waterloo Counseling Center, (512) 444-9922

SUPPORT SERVICES

There is an extensive web of support groups in the Austin area for those with medical, psychological, or family problems. The Austin Area Mental Health Association, (512) 454- 3706, operates a clearinghouse to connect individuals to support groups. The listings maintained by the association are not limited to mental health care groups; they include information on medical recovery support groups and substance-abuse groups.

Support group information is also available from local chapters of national associations like the Arthritis Foundation, the American Cancer Society, and Overeaters Anonymous. These groups can be found in the Yellow Pages.

MENTAL HEALTH SERVICES

The Austin area has a wide array of mental health agencies and support services. The Austin area office of the Mental Health Association, (512) 454-3706, offers information and referral services. Following is a sampling of the major agencies and service groups.

THE ARC OF THE CAPITAL AREA
2818 San Gabriel Street
(512) 476-7044
www.arcofthecapitalarea.org
The Arc offers support services for families with developmentally disabled members. Those programs include the following: Pilot Parent, providing support groups and other assistance for families of children with disabilities such as spina bifida, autism, cerebral palsy, or mental retardation; Project Chance, working with developmentally disabled juveniles and adults who have been involved with the criminal justice program;

Community Advocacy Services, matching volunteers one on one with developmentally disabled adults living in the community or at Austin State School; and Community Living Assistance and Support Services, helping many individuals who might be forced by their disabilities to live in institutional settings.

AUSTIN CHILD GUIDANCE CENTER
810 West 45th Street
(512) 451-2242
www.austinchildguidance.org
Individual, family, and group therapy are offered at the center, which also provides counseling and testing services, child-abuse services, and parenting classes. Fees are charged on a sliding-scale basis.

AUSTIN RECOVERY CENTER INC.
8402 Cross Park Drive
(512) 697-8600
www.austinrecovery.org
The center operates a detoxification unit, plus outpatient and inpatient care for chemically dependent adults and teens.

Emergency Numbers

Emergency police, fire, and EMS Services in the Austin area	911
Police, nonemergency	311
Poison Center	(800) POISON-1
Crisis Intervention/Suicide Hot Line	(512) 472-HELP (4357) or TTY (512) 703-1395
Social Services Referral Hot Line operated by United Way	211 or (512)- 323-1899
Travis County Sheriff's Mental Health Unit	(512) 473-9734
Alcoholics Anonymous	(512) 444-0071, (512) 441-3369 (Spanish)
Safe Place for victims of rape, sexual abuse, and domestic violence	(512) 267-SAFE
Williamson County Crisis Center	(800) 460-SAFE

AUSTIN STATE HOSPITAL

4110 Guadalupe Street

(512) 452-0381

www.dshs.state.tx.us

The hospital is under the auspices of the Texas Department of State Health Services, which includes seven other state hospitals around Texas. The Austin facility serves the 37-county Central Texas area. Approximately 300 teens and adults receive care at the hospital.

AUSTIN-TRAVIS COUNTY MENTAL HEALTH MENTAL RETARDATION CENTER

1430 Collier Street

(512) 447-4141

www.atcmhmr.com

The center operates a 24-hour hot line, (512) 472-HELP, in addition to emergency psychiatric services and programs for mental illness, mental retardation, and substance abuse. Other services include psychiatric case management, vocational and educational services, diagnosis and evaluation, infant-parent training, child- abuse services, and homeless services. Fees are determined by the individual's ability to pay.

AUSTIN WOMEN'S ADDICTION REFERRAL AND EDUCATION CENTER (AWARE)

2015 South I-35, Suite 110

(512) 326-1222

www.ywcaaustin.org

This YWCA program offers chemical-dependency counseling, assessment, education, information, and referral.

PEOPLE'S COMMUNITY CLINIC

2909 North I-35

(512) 478- 4939

www.pcclinic.org

This community clinic (see above) also provides mental health services and links to other community services.

ST. DAVID'S PAVILION

1025 East 32nd Street

(512) 867-5800

www.stdavids.com

Pet Emergencies

Austin is a pet-friendly city, but accidents do happen to our treasured pets. Here are several important numbers to keep handy:

- ASPCA Animal Poison Control Center, toll-free (888) 426-4435
- Austin Animal Cruelty, (512) 974-5750 or 311
- Animal Control or report abuse and roadside animal sales, (512) 972-6060
- 24-hour animal emergency hospitals:

  Animal Emergency Hospital of Austin
  4106 North Lamar Boulevard
  (512) 459-4336

  Emergency Animal Clinic of Northwest Austin
  12034 Research Boulevard
  (512) 331-6121

  Emergency Animal Clinic of Northwest Austin, Southwest Branch
  4544 South Lamar, Suite 760
  (512) 899-0955

This clinic, part of the Columbia St. David's Healthcare Network, provides both in- and outpatient care for men, women, and children. The pavilion has a special program for those with eating disorders.

IMMEDIATE-CARE FACILITIES

In the trade they are sometimes called "doc-in-a-box," and immediate-care facilities are springing up in shopping centers and near busy intersections throughout the area. They provide nonemergency, outpatient care for weekend gardeners with battered green thumbs, Sunday jocks, and visitors who slip and fall while getting into the Austin spirit. Call ahead for hours and specific locations, and check your insurance before you check in.

South

PRO MED MEDICAL CARE CENTER
3801 South Lamar Boulevard
(512) 447-9661

Northwest

PRO MED MEDICAL CARE CENTER
13831 North Highway 183
(512)-335-6260

North

PRO MED MEDICAL CARE CENTER
2000 West Anderson Lane
(512) 459-4367

ST. DAVID'S MEDICENTER
810 West Braker Lane
(512) 339-8114

ALTERNATIVE MEDICINE

Austin is a hotbed of alternative therapies and wellness programs, and some practitioners of traditional medicine also include aspects of holistic healing in their own treatments. The area's hospitals offer wellness programs, plus several fitness centers formulate wellness programs for clients (see our Parks and Recreation chapter). There are consultants who work with employers to develop wellness and exercise programs for employees or individuals. All manner of therapies are available, including Chinese, homeopathic, ayurvedic, and Taoist tai chi. Check the Yellow Pages for alternative therapies—the acupuncture listings also include herbal and nutritional therapies.

Another good resource are the bulletin boards at local health food stores. The large outdoor bulletin board at the Whole Foods Market, Sixth Street and Lamar Boulevard, features a variety of alternative therapy providers. (See our Shopping chapter for information.)

Mark Blumenthal runs a nonprofit organization, headquartered in Austin, called the American Botanical Council. The council produces a magazine, *HerbalGram*, that focuses on herbal research and federal regulation of supplements. The council can be contacted at P.O. Box 201660, Austin, TX 78720, or (512) 331-8868, www.herbal gram.org.

A WORD ABOUT ALLERGIES

Allergies. Sooner or later you're gonna get 'em. At least that is what the experts predict for many newcomers to Austin. The abundance of flora has its downside for Central Texas residents. In the winter months—December, January, and February—the junipers in the Hill Country produce pollen that sets off the "cedar fever" season—the trees are colloquially known as cedars, but they are in fact junipers. Some opine that the purple haze produced by the pollen prompted Austin to be dubbed the City of the Violet Crown. Most sufferers are too busy sniffling and wiping their watery eyes to notice the violet glow.

In spring the live oak and elm pollens bring on misery for some, then in summer there are grasses and, of course, year-round attacks by mold spores and animal dander. Not everyone succumbs, but so many do that the local television stations broadcast allergy counts on their daily newscasts. In a classic case of market supply and demand, allergists do a booming business in Austin.

HIGHER EDUCATION

Back in the 1920s and 1930s, Austin's leaders billed our city as "The Athens of the West," both in tribute to, and promotion of, the element of culture bestowed by the area's colleges and universities. While we dropped that lofty title decades ago, Austin's distinction as an eminent educational center of the South remains. Our institutes of higher education add luster to the jewel that is Austin. For its sheer size and importance in the economic development of Austin, the University of Texas stands in a class by itself. But Austin's other fine colleges and universities are vitally linked to this city in countless ways as well. The symbiosis that exists between the Austin community and its various institutes of higher education is one of the defining characteristics of the region.

One need only walk through the campuses of our institutes to get a feel for Austin's educational traditions. The sprawling UT campus with its giant shade trees, sculptures, fountains, mammoth buildings, and the 27-story UT Tower, which has become as much an Austin landmark as a UT symbol, are enough to inspire a certain reverence. The Gothic Revival–style Main Building on the St. Edward's University campus stands as a stately landmark in South Austin, while Huston-Tillotson College's elevated site overlooking downtown from the east is a living legacy to Austin's education of African Americans during Reconstruction and ever since. Austin Community College's many modern campuses around the city serve as a reminder that there's always room for more centers of learning here. Texas State University south of us in San Marcos and Southwestern University north in Georgetown frame Austin with educational foundations dating back more than a century.

For cultural enrichment, we Austinites often turn to our colleges and universities. Art exhibits, lectures, theater, festivals, fairs, sporting events, symphonies, and jazz performances are just some of the many offerings we can enjoy on a regular basis.

The contribution these institutes have made to Austin's bright prospects for the 21st century is enormous. Austin's highly educated population was one of the attributes that attracted the high-tech industry to this area in the 1970s and one of the reasons its numbers continue to grow today. UT's outstanding research facilities act as a huge magnet for these industries, while the city's academic programs, many now aimed at training high-tech workers, continue to turn out qualified graduates.

It's impossible to imagine what life would be like in Austin without our colleges and universities. The University of Texas is not only the flagship of the state university system, it's one of the economic and cultural pillars of Austin. For decades, Austin's economy—and its reputation as an educational and political center—rested on UT and on state government. While UT's burden may be lightened now as new enterprises help drive Austin's economy, its significance to Austin will endure.

Nature endowed Austin with natural beauty—rolling wooded hills and peaceful rivers. Lawmakers, churches, and private citizens from all walks of life endowed Austin with its institutes of higher education. The Austin leaders who once envisioned "a university of the first class" could never have foreseen this.

THE COLLEGES AND UNIVERSITIES

Here, listed by size, are the colleges and universities that enrich our city.

THE UNIVERSITY OF TEXAS AT AUSTIN
24th and Guadalupe Streets
(512) 471-3434
www.utexas.edu

The 40 acres! This fond nickname for the University of Texas at Austin (UT) dates back to 1839, when city planners set aside a 40-acre plot called College Hill to be used for an institute of higher learning. UT didn't come along for another 44 years—and almost didn't come to Austin at all. The University officially opened on that 40-acre site on September 15, 1883. Today the University of Texas at Austin's main campus alone sits on more than 350 acres, while the university operates major research facilities on 915 additional acres around the city. UT owns the Marine Science Institute at Port Aransas, the McDonald Observatory near Fort Davis, the Winedale Historical Center near Round Top, the Bee Cave Research Center west of Austin, and writer J. Frank Dobie's ranch in Paisano. To top it off, the University of Texas at Austin is the flagship of the UT System's 15 campuses spread throughout the state. It's the city's largest employer, with 20,000 workers. And, with an average enrollment of about 48,000 students, is one of the nation's largest universities.

UT faculty members have won scores of prestigious awards, honors, and medals—Nobel Prizes, Pulitzer Prizes, the National Medal of Science, and the National Medal of Technology—and have been named to distinguished societies, institutes, and academies across the nation. Many alumni have gone on to leave their mark, both on Austin and on the world. Lady Bird Johnson, Walter Cronkite, Bill Moyers, Lloyd Bentsen, and First Lady Laura Bush all attended UT. UT's academic programs and professional schools often rank among the top programs and schools in the country. Seven UT doctoral programs rank in the top 10 in the nation, according to the National

Research Council. Civil engineering, computer sciences, aerospace engineering, classics, astrophysics/astronomy, chemical engineering, and the ecology, evolution, and behavior program all made the top-10 list.

The university's academic programs, made up of 15 colleges and schools, the Graduate School, and the Division of Continuing Education, offer more than 100 undergraduate degree programs and 170 graduate programs. Exceptional facilities abound, including the fifth-largest academic library in North America, with nearly eight million volumes (see our chapter on The Literary Scene), the Harry Ransom Humanities Research Center, an internationally recognized rare book and manuscript library, as well as state-of-the-art computer facilities.

UT is one of the reasons why so many people around the country get dreamy-eyed just hearing the name Austin. Before the high-tech industry came along to rocket Austin's name into the stratosphere, before the music scene crystallized to give Austin such a hip reputation, before big business discovered us, before the legions of filmmakers and tourists arrived, there was UT. While UT can't take credit for all the excitement surrounding Austin today, its contributions are enormous. Along with state government, the University of Texas has provided the foundation for much of what Austin has become. UT is noted for graduating so many students who've fallen in love with Austin's natural beauty and tolerant atmosphere that they can't bear to leave.

It's no wonder UT students and the public at large get along so well. Not only do these scholars, some of the nation's brightest, bring a palpable energy to this city (and make valuable contributions to its social consciousness—and

---

i Texas Box Office, (512) 477-6060 (charge-by-phone), www.texasboxoffice.com, is the place to go if you want tickets to UT athletics, performing arts, or any upcoming event at UT's Erwin Center. The box office also handles tickets for other Central Texas events.

ℹ️ The wacky "Hi, How Are You" frog mural on The Drag at 21st and Guadalupe Streets—a beloved symbol of Austin "weirdness"—was created by Austin singer-songwriter and artist Daniel Johnston in 1983. A feature-length documentary about him, *The Devil and Daniel Johnston,* premiered at the Sundance Film Festival in 2005.

conscience), having one of the nation's largest universities at our doorstep gives Austinites incredible opportunities for cultural and educational enhancement, for cutting-edge knowledge in an extraordinary range of professional fields—and for just plain fun. A stroll down The Drag, the part of Guadalupe Street that runs alongside UT, will have anyone feeling like a college student in minutes. This strip, with its bookstores, restaurants, coffeehouses, shops, and markets, is the melting pot of UT and the city.

One place on campus notorious for overcrowding is Darrel K Royal–Texas Memorial Stadium on a football Saturday. Texas Longhorns games are often the hottest ticket in town as the university and the city turn out to support their beloved team. (See our chapter on Spectator Sports.) Football isn't the only game in town, however. Many other Longhorns teams draw big crowds, including the UT women's basketball team. UT puts great emphasis on sports and goes all out to recruit some of the nation's top athletes. As a result, Longhorns teams have won more Southwest Conference championships in all sports than any other college or university. In accordance with tradition, the UT Tower glows orange many a night celebrating major UT athletic victories. In addition to intercollegiate sports, which involve less than 500 students, UT's recreational sports program attracts about 80 percent of the student body.

For both students and members of the general public interested in continuing education, culture, and entertainment, UT offers an enormous range of options. The Performing Arts Center's public performance spaces and backup facilities, including the Bass Concert Hall and the Bates Recital Hall, rank among the top five on any American campus. The Frank C. Erwin Jr. Special Events Center hosts more than 250 annual events. The Jack S. Blanton Museum of Art has an extensive permanent collection, and the Texas Memorial Museum holds extensive teaching and research collections and an exhibition space that includes the original Goddess of Liberty statue from atop the State Capitol. Of course UT also is home to the Lyndon Baines Johnson Library and Museum (see our Attractions and The Arts chapters).

UT sponsors two popular programs for the continuing education of Austin's adult community and for other nontraditional students. The University Extension program allows students to get college credit on a more flexible schedule. This nondegree evening program is aimed at filling students' educational gaps and continuing educational needs. University Extension offers more than 200 courses from anthropology to zoology and awards extension credit that could be applied to a degree program. The extension program also allows students to work toward a Business Foundations Certificate, classes that provide solid basics in business concepts and practices. Students don't have to be accepted to UT to enroll in any of these classes.

Much more casual is UT's Informal Classes program. This efficiently run program provides an amazing variety of workshops, short courses, and certificate programs for anyone interested. Here students can take short classes—from a couple of hours to several sessions—in hundreds of subjects, including such things as country dance, money management, creative writing, computers, and how to buy a house. Students can sign up over the phone with a credit card, and the university will mail a receipt and information on where the class is located, most often on the UT campus. (Parking can be a challenge.) UT students, senior citizens, and members of the alumni association get discounts on most classes. There are about six sessions per year, and schedules are available at distribution points around the city.

AUSTIN COMMUNITY COLLEGE
5930 Middle Fiskville Road
(512) 223-7000
www.austin.cc.tx.us

Austin Community College, which celebrated its 36th birthday in 2008, is the baby in the neighborhood when it comes to Austin's institutions of higher learning, most of which were born in the 1800s. Perhaps that's why we call it "junior" college. In fact, this public two-year undergraduate college is far from junior in size and in importance to the Austin area. ACC's enrollment has grown to more than 30,000 students on seven campuses around Austin, while thousands more take noncredit courses at ACC campuses and at various distance learning sites around the region.

The college is the second-largest institute of higher learning in the Austin area, after the University of Texas. That is certainly welcome news to those who fought to establish ACC back in the 1960s when, according to the prevailing conventional wisdom, Austin didn't need another college, what with UT and all the city's other fine colleges and universities. In fact, earlier efforts to establish a community college failed twice. At least some of ACC's success can be attributed to its achievement in taking higher education directly to the people it serves. The college's main campuses dot the Austin map from Oak Hill in the south to Cedar Park in the north, to the racially mixed, working-class area of East Austin. Each of these campuses demonstrates a strong commitment to provide education to all of Austin's residents.

Today, ACC offers two-year associate degrees and one-year certificates in 176 concentrations: 72 in applied sciences, 16 in the arts, 12 in science, and 76 certificates in technical programs. Students who graduate with an associate of arts or associate of science degree are prepared to transfer to a four-year college or university. The two-year associate of applied science degree prepares students to enter the local job market or transfer to select universities. For students studying for one-year certificates, ACC is a technical or vocational school, offering courses in such subjects as building construction, automotive technology, financial management, office administration, child development, surgical technology, and electronic technology.

As Austin's demand for high-tech workers skyrockets, ACC has established itself as one of the major learning centers focused on filling those jobs. It has invested in both technical infrastructure and in designing programs and courses of study aimed at preparing students for high-tech positions.

TEXAS STATE UNIVERSITY–SAN MARCOS
601 University Drive, San Marcos
(512) 245-2111
www.txstate.edu

This increasingly prestigious university about 35 miles south of Austin celebrated its centennial in 2003—with a name change! Southwest Texas State University is now Texas State University–San Marcos. It's the area's third-largest institution of higher education, with more than 26,000 students. More than half its students commute from outside San Marcos, including many from the Austin area.

Texas State—the alma mater of President Lyndon Johnson—gets national recognition in several areas: The Association of Teacher Educators calls it one of the top three teacher education programs in the country; the Association of American Geographers consistently ranks its geography department the best in the nation. Some faculty members in geography, speech communication, business, mathematics, and mass communication have been recognized as national leaders in their fields. Texas State is also proud of its record in recruiting ethnic minorities, which now make up 25 percent of the student body. The university, in fact, is among the top 20 producers of Hispanic undergraduate degrees in the country. Additionally, the university receives accolades for its enormous fund-raising efforts and steady increases in endowments. Its first capital campaign, concluded in 1999, raised $74.6 million on a goal of $60 million.

Texas State's geography department was the first to offer a doctoral program in 1996 and today offers two Ph.D. programs. In addition to its well-respected teaching program, the university

ⓘ UT's famous "Hook 'em Horns" hand signal was first introduced at a campus pep rally—in 1955!

is known for its business school. The university offers 114 undergraduate majors in education, applied arts, business, fine arts and communication, health professions, liberal arts, and science. The school also offers 81 master's and six doctoral programs. Texas State is the lead institution operating the Round Rock Higher Education Center just north of Austin.

Among the university's collections is the Southwestern Writers Collection, which includes J. Frank Dobie properties (see our chapter on The Literary Scene) as well as an extensive archive of written material that captures the literary and artistic spirit of the American Southwest. The Lonesome Dove archives in this collection include props and memorabilia from the film set of Texan Larry McMurtry's epic story about cattle driving.

Texas State first opened its doors in 1903 as a teacher training college called Southwest Texas State Normal School. Through the years it became a normal college, teachers college, and then college. TS became a university in 1969. Located on 427 acres and surrounded by magnificent cypress and pecan trees, the campus sits on the banks of the San Marcos River on the edge of the Texas Hill Country. TS athletes compete at the NCAA Division I level in eight men's and seven women's sports. The university also offers a wide range of programs for talented students in dance, band, choir, jazz, symphony orchestra, musical theater, and opera.

ⓘ The Texas Tomorrow Fund gives parents and grandparents the opportunity to pay for a future college student's tuition at today's prices. The fund, backed by the State of Texas, allows investors to buy college tuition in one lump sum or make regular payments. Contracts can be obtained for any public or private college or university in Texas or at www.texastomorrow fund.com.

ST. EDWARD'S UNIVERSITY
3001 South Congress Avenue
(512) 448-8400
www.stedwards.edu

A private Roman Catholic liberal arts university, St. Edward's offers undergraduate and graduate degrees to more than 4,000 students from across the United States and abroad.

Located in South Austin on 180 acres of rolling hills, the university was founded in 1885 as a college but got its start 12 years earlier when it opened as a school with just three farm boys enrolled the first year. As the school grew and began boarding students, Austin residents started referring to St. Edward's as the Catholic Farm due to the fact that it fed its faculty and staff by raising beef, grain, vegetables, and fruit on its own land. The Main Building, the imposing Gothic Revival–style building made of Texas white limestone, was dedicated in 1889—a grand structure for sure in the early Southwest. Rebuilt after a fire destroyed it in 1903, the Main Building was designated a Texas Historic Landmark in 1973.

Today, St. Edward's confers undergraduate degrees in more than 50 areas, as well as seven master's degrees in business administration, business administration in entrepreneurship, counseling, human services, computer information sciences, liberal arts, and organizational leadership and ethics. The undergraduate curriculum has been recognized by the Carnegie Foundation as among the most rigorous in the nation.

In addition to awarding degrees, the university is recognized for its tradition of producing graduates with strong values, both through required course work in ethics, philosophy, or religious studies and through its community outreach programs. It also gets high marks for its adult education program and for its efforts on behalf of Hispanic students, who make up 26 percent of the student body. St. Edward's is home to the nation's longest continuously running College Assistant Migrant Program (CAMP), a nationally recognized program that celebrated its 30th anniversary in 2003. CAMP provides freshman scholarships and financial aid to the children of migrant farmworkers. Many of the students who have taken advantage of this program over the years are first-generation college students in their families. St. Edward's has been repeatedly listed among *Hispanic* Magazine's "Best Schools for Hispanic Students." Additionally, the school has taken the lead role in the Austin ENLACE program, designed to improve higher education opportunities for Hispanic youth.

SOUTHWESTERN UNIVERSITY
1001 East University Avenue,
Georgetown
(512) 863-6511, (800) 252-3166
www.southwestern.edu

"Chartered as the state's first university in 1840, until the 1970s it was doing the conventional thing, providing the B.A. union card for its graduates' first jobs. Then with the catalysts of the new president's vision and the generosity of three Texas foundations, it was born again as a place to prepare for the 21st century." So writes Loren Pope in the book, *Colleges That Change Lives*. This book, subtitled *40 Schools You Should Know About Even If You're Not a Straight-A Student*, is one of several guides to colleges and universities that have taken note of Southwestern University in recent years. Called one of the best sleepers in the nation and one of the buried treasures among the nation's liberal arts colleges, Southwestern University may not remain one of Texas's hidden assets much longer.

Located 28 miles north of Austin in the seat of Williamson County government and even closer to our northern neighbors in Round Rock and Pflugerville, Southwestern University is a private Methodist four-year institute of higher learning that reflects the conservative values of Georgetown itself. Enrollment hovers around 1,250, a figure the university considers ideal.

Southwestern sits on a 100-acre campus filled with trees and dotted with beautiful Texas limestone buildings constructed in the stately Richardsonian Romanesque-style. The university also owns 525 more acres plus a 75-acre golf course. Consisting of the Brown College of Arts and Sciences and the Sarofim School of Fine Arts, Southwestern offers more than 35 bachelor's

degrees through its liberal arts curriculum and in preprofessional programs in medicine, law, business, theology, education, and engineering.

CONCORDIA UNIVERSITY–TEXAS
11400 Concordia University Drive
(512) 313-3000
www.concordia.edu

For more than 80 years, Concordia University sat on a relatively small 23-acre site on overcrowded and noisy I-35 in central Austin. That all changed in 2008, when Concordia moved to a new 389-acre campus and nature preserve in northwest Austin. And the six buildings currently on campus is just the beginning. Over the coming years, the Lutheran university plans to add a performing arts auditorium, science facilities, a chapel, and sports fields.

Concordia Lutheran College graduated to university status in 1995 when it became a member of the Concordia University System that spans the country. Founded as Concordia Academy in 1926 by pioneers who had Wendish and German ethnic backgrounds, the school originally trained young men for ministry in the Lutheran Church. Women were admitted for the first time in 1955, and in 1979 Concordia implemented a four-year liberal arts program for undergraduates. Concordia in 1998 took its first step toward becoming a graduate-level university when it instituted a master's degree program designed for working teachers. The university, which is owned and maintained by the Lutheran Church–Missouri Synod, has strong ties to the system's 12 other universities and seminaries. Students can transfer easily between schools and take classes offered at other campuses via the Concordia University Education Network, which uses video technology to transmit and receive courses. Concordia offers 16 majors in business, education and liberal arts, and sciences. The university also offers pre-professional programs in dentistry, law, medicine, and the seminary. The most popular majors at Concordia are in accounting and business administration. Education is another popular career pathway at the university, although students are enrolled in such diverse courses of study as behavioral sciences, church music, computer science, Mexican-American studies, and Spanish. In 2007, *U.S. News & World Report* magazine named Austin's Concordia University to its list of "America's Best Colleges."

Lutherans make up less than half of the 1,250-member student body at Concordia, which also attracts Roman Catholics, Baptists, and students from other Christian and non-Christian denominations.

Concordia has made great strides in serving the educational needs of Austin's working adults by offering evening classes and televised courses under its adult degree program. This centrally located university also opens its doors to the public for an extensive range of cultural and academic events, including art exhibits, lectures, theater, and music performances.

HUSTON-TILLOTSON UNIVERSITY
900 Chicon Street
(512) 505-3025
www.htc.edu

Huston-Tillotson University brings much more to Austin than merely its distinctions as the city's oldest institution of higher education and its only historically black college.

In East Austin on 23 acres of rolling hills that overlook downtown, Huston-Tillotson is a center of cultural and community involvement for Austin's East-side neighborhoods and one of Austin's largest minority businesses. The university is known locally for its participation in a number of cooperative relationships with the Austin Independent School District, the City of Austin, Austin Community College, and local business and community organizations.

This private four-year undergraduate university, affiliated with the United Methodist Church and the United Church of Christ, offers bachelor's degrees in arts and science to about 680 students from a variety of cultural and ethnic backgrounds. Within the college's five divisions—business, natural sciences, social sciences, humanities, and education—students can major in 20 areas of study, including the college's notable programs of chemistry, teacher preparations, sociology, and biology.

Huston-Tillotson University dates back to the 1870s, and one of its former buildings, Allen Hall, was, according to the college, the first building in Texas or anywhere west of the Mississippi constructed for the higher education of black students. Tillotson College was established by Congregationalists in 1875 (although it didn't open to students until 1881), and Samuel Huston College was founded by Methodists a year later. The two colleges merged in October 1952 to become the present-day Huston-Tillotson University, which changed its name from Huston-Tillotson College in 2005.

While the campus has modernized over the past century and a quarter, two of its historic buildings remain as splendid landmarks and fine examples of turn-of-the-20th-century architecture. The Evans Industrial Building, built circa 1912, was completely renovated in 1984 and designated as a Texas Historical Site. The Old Administration Building, completed in 1914, is one of the few remaining examples of the Modified Prairie Style popularized by Frank Lloyd Wright. This building was entered in the National Register of Historic Places in 1993 and is slowly being restored.

AUSTIN PRESBYTERIAN SEMINARY
100 East 27th Street
(512) 472-6736
www.austinseminary.edu

Known for its excellent preparation of leaders for the church, the Austin Presbyterian Seminary has graduates serving across the country and overseas. More than 300 students are enrolled in its various academic programs. Many live on campus in the seminary's housing units. The seminary opened in 1902 and has been at its current location, on about 12 acres along the wooded banks of Waller Creek, since 1908. Austin Presbyterian Seminary offers master's degrees in arts or divinity and doctor of ministry degrees. Additionally, the seminary offers classes for nondegree students as well as continuing education courses and a yearly series of lectures. An institution of the General Assembly of the Presbyterian Church (U.S.A.), the Austin seminary is one of 10 theological institutions related to the Presbyterian Church.

SCHOOLS AND CHILD CARE

Austin is a forward-looking place. That atmosphere, plus the city's worldwide reputation as a leader in the field of computer technology, has brought more and more high-tech industries to the area. And as employment soars, all of the Capital City area's 10 school districts have been affected by growth in student enrollment. This growth is sometimes due directly to industries within the districts, to employees searching for suitable housing nearby, or to families fleeing the big city for the more peaceful suburbs. In recent years bulging school districts have passed bond issues to build, enlarge, and improve schools at a pace never before witnessed. Some smaller districts have seen their student enrollment more than double over the past few years, and other districts are growing rapidly.

The question "Which came first, the chicken or the egg?" as it applies to education and technology has interesting implications for Austin. High-tech companies cite Austin's high education levels as one reason for locating here, and these same companies are competing with one another for well-trained, high-quality graduates at both the high school and college levels. As a result, many of the area's high-tech industries—and scores of other farsighted businesses and industries—are investing money, time, and expertise in local school districts to help propel education levels to new heights.

Texas as a whole faces considerable challenges in its huge public school system. Beginning in the 1980s state leaders from both political parties focused on improving the schools and, in response to lawsuits from poor school districts, changed the financing system. When then-Governor George W. Bush assumed the state's leadership, he proclaimed that education was his number one priority. Working with Democratic and Republican leaders in the state legislature, he embarked on major education reforms. Business leaders also have played a very important role in pressing for educational reforms, recognizing the need for a well-educated 21st-century workforce.

Accountability is a watchword of the educational system in Texas, and testing has become a vital tool. Although there are complaints that schools "teach to the test" or that too much weight is given to the results, parents and teachers generally support the rigorous testing regimen. This is the model that Bush took to Washington. Parents can access information about their child's school or district at www.tea.state.tx.us or by ordering a profile called a Snapshot.

SCHOOL FUNDING

One of the biggest issues facing the state's school system today is funding. In 1993—after nine years of court cases, public debate, and failed constitutional amendments—the Texas legislature passed a school finance-reform measure that included the so-called share-the-wealth provision. The plan, dubbed "Robin Hood" by critics, requires the state's wealthiest school districts to share their property taxes with poorer districts. The Eanes school district, for example, has consistently been classified a "rich" school district and has contributed to the pool. In the past few years, however, other districts in Central Texas, including Round Rock, Pflugerville, and Lago Vista, have also reached property tax levels that put them into the wealthy category. Surprisingly, the Austin Independent School District also falls

i The Literacy Coalition of Central Texas sponsors the Great Grown-up Spelling Bee for Literacy, a fun—but challenging—event in which teams of area professionals attempt to spell such words as *rhizoidal* and *poikilotherm*. The goal is to raise funds for the dozens of literacy providers in the region. Visit www.willread.org for information.

into this category—even though 60 percent of its students come from low-income families.

Area school district leaders agree that the plan has served poorer districts well. They argue, however, that the state's ever-growing reliance on local property taxes to pay for public education will not solve the basic problem: not enough state money being dedicated to the Texas school system. At the same time, individual schools' costs are growing as they struggle to meet Washington-mandated improvements. Revenues from the state lottery that go toward public education have not alleviated the pressure on school budgets, and the legislature is forced time and again to revisit the issue of school finance reform.

SCHOOLS

All the school districts in the Austin area operate special schools and/or programs for both physically and mentally handicapped students and those with behavioral or emotional problems.

Students who require more academic challenge are provided a number of opportunities, including honors programs, advanced-placement classes, programs for talented and gifted youth, and, in some cases,, magnet schools. The region's many Spanish-speaking students are offered bilingual classes or so-called ESL classes, where they study English as a second language.

The school year varies slightly in Central Texas but generally runs from mid-August to the third week in May, for a total of 176 school days. Children entering Austin-area schools must be 5 years old by September 1 to enroll in kindergarten. Texas also requires that all children receive immunizations to attend school.

Public School Districts

AUSTIN INDEPENDENT SCHOOL DISTRICT
Carruth Administration Center
1111 West Sixth Street
(512) 414-1700
www.austin.isd.tenet.edu

The Austin Independent School District puts great emphasis on providing high-quality education for children of all races, economic levels, and English-speaking proficiencies. The district offers a solid core curriculum that stresses math, science, reading, and writing as well as special opportunities for a full range of students, from academically superior to those with learning difficulties.

AISD provides educational opportunities for about 82,000 students on 110 campuses. The district's commitment to children is evidenced by the number of national honors and rankings it has received in recent years. Austin has achieved a higher than average number of National Merit Scholars and has outperformed other Texas schoolchildren on the Scholastic Aptitude Test (SAT). Sixty-one percent of the district's students are listed as economically disadvantaged, and 23 percent have limited English proficiency. The student population at individual schools within this huge district reflects the ethnic and economic makeup of the residents themselves. So within AISD, some schools have high concentrations of upper-income families while other schools have a higher concentration of economically disadvantaged families. AISD is proud of its record of regularly increasing enrollment of minority and economically disadvantaged students in honors programs and advanced-placement classes. But in a large urban district, the challenge to continue producing top-quality graduates is staggering.

i The Austin Independent School District offers a bus stop finder on its Web site, if you're new in town and need to know where your children will be picked up. It's at www.austin.isd.tenet.edu/schools/bus/busstop.phtml. Students must live at least 2 miles from the school in order to use bus service.

DEL VALLE INDEPENDENT SCHOOL DISTRICT

5301 Ross Road
Del Valle
(512) 386-3000
www.del-valle.K12.tx.us

Once a region primarily of farms and ranches, the Del Valle Independent School District has witnessed major changes of late as more and more high-tech industries, and Austin's new international airport, moved into the area. The district, located in the countryside of Southeast Austin and Travis County, serves the urban communities of Montopolis, Frontier Valley, Sunridge Park, and Pleasant Valley as well as the rural communities of Garfield, Creedmoor, Mustang Ridge, Elroy, Pilot Knob, Webberville, and Hornsby Bend.

Del Valle ISD students are spread out on seven elementary campuses, two junior highs, one high school, and an alternative learning center. Seventy percent of the district's students are listed as economically disadvantaged, and 17.5 percent have limited English proficiency. Del Valle offers an excellent range of courses from preschool through high school for students of all abilities and talents. Bilingual and English as a Second Language classes are in place throughout the district. Of special note is the district's technology program, which uses computers as an integral component of classroom instruction. Through its Adopt-A School program, Del Valle enjoys strong support of the area's business and technology community, which provides scholarships, grants, and awards.

DRIPPING SPRINGS INDEPENDENT SCHOOL DISTRICT

510 West Mercer Street
Dripping Springs
(512) 858-4905
www.dripping-springs.k12.tx.us

Located 19 miles west of Austin in Hays County, the Dripping Springs Independent School District saw explosive growth as a result of the 1990s economic boom in the Austin area. This small district of just five schools has nearly doubled in size since 1993. The suburban district always receives good ratings from the state. Dripping Springs Middle School is a National Blue Ribbon school. Students taking Scholastic Aptitude Tests score among the highest in an area that already beats the national average. The district sets high standards for its students and provides advanced placement and gifted and talented programs to its academically outstanding students. The needs of mentally and physically handicapped students are addressed within the schools themselves, with the assistance and guidance of the Hays County Co-op. To deal with the problem of overcapacity, the district has improved and expanded existing schools and built a new intermediate school. Eight percent of the district's students are listed as economically disadvantaged.

EANES INDEPENDENT SCHOOL DISTRICT

South Don Rogers Administration Building
601 Camp Craft Road
(512) 329-3600
www.eanes.k12.tx.us

Considered one of the finest school districts in Texas, the Eanes Independent School District has earned good ratings from the state. Eanes students taking the Scholastic Aptitude Test consistently score well above the national average. This district has about 7,350 students at six elementary schools, two middle schools, and one high school. The district is the largest in the state to have all schools and the district named Exemplary by the Texas Education Agency. Seven of its nine schools, including Westlake High School, are U.S. Blue Ribbon Schools.

Eanes is one of the wealthiest school districts in Texas, and 2.1 percent of its students are listed as economically disadvantaged. Just 2 percent have limited English proficiency. Eanes enjoys the benefits of having strong support from parents and the business community. In addition to its outstanding academic programs, the district is well known for its athletic programs for both boys and girls; the district has racked up state championships in golf, football, girls basketball, and girls swimming. The Eanes Independent School District encompasses 31.2 square miles in West Austin and in the municipalities of Rollingwood and West Lake Hills. In 1998 Eanes voters rejected a hotly contested proposal to build a second high school.

LAGO VISTA
Independent School District
8039 Bar-K, Lago Vista
(512) 267-8300
www.lagovista.txed.net
The smallest school district in the Capital City region, the Lago Vista Independent School District averages about 1,000 students in its three schools. It makes for small class sizes—and excellent schools. The district covers 35 square miles on north Lake Travis and serves the communities of Lago Vista, Point Venture, and South Jonestown Hills. Although its communities are known primarily for resort and retirement living, the district is changing as more and more families with children move into the area, many to take advantage of the high-quality education the district provides.

The district emphasizes college preparatory programs and lifelong sports. Schools provide a number of learning opportunities for children of all learning abilities, however, including special education and English as a Second Language. Students needing more challenge and enrichment are offered a Gifted and Talented program as well as a number of advanced placement and honors classes. Fourteen percent of the district's students are economically disadvantaged, compared with 50 percent statewide. Lago Vista ISD, like most others in this region, is growing. The district receives strong community support.

LAKE TRAVIS INDEPENDENT SCHOOL DISTRICT
3322 Rural Route 620 South
(512) 533-6000
www.laketravis.txed.net
The Lake Travis Independent School District, one of the smallest in this region with eight schools and about 5,550 students, is located west/northwest of Austin along Lake Travis's southwest shore. The district serves many nearby communities, including Apache Shores, Bee Cave,

Briarcliff, Homestead, Hudson Bend, Lake Pointe, Lakeway, The Hills, and Vineyard Bay. Once largely comprising resorts and retirement communities, the district is seeing its profile change as more families move into the area. The Lake Travis ISD offers excellent educational opportunities at all levels and provides classes and programs for both academically superior students and those requiring special help. Lake Travis High School is proud of its reputation for providing rigorous academic programs for high school students, who are required to earn credits in core subjects as well as foreign language, technology, fine arts, physical education, and health.

In addition to overall good ratings, several schools within the district have received top marks from the state. High school students taking the national Scholastic Aptitude Test have scored higher than the national average. The district also produces a steady number of National Merit Scholars annually. Lake Travis ISD, once a component of the Dripping Springs Independent School District, was formed in 1981 with just 541 students in its kindergarten through 12th grade classes. Today the district is growing rapidly and voters have approved a bond issue to renovate and expand the crowded high school.

LEANDER INDEPENDENT SCHOOL DISTRICT
401 South West Street, Leander
(512) 943-5000
www.leanderisd.org
The Leander Independent School District is northwest of Austin in Williamson and Travis Counties and educates students from the communities of Leander, Cedar Park, and a part of Austin. With about 25,000 students, Leander is now the third-largest district in this 10-district region. This district, which covers 200 square miles, much of it still undeveloped, is in another fast-growing area of Central Texas. Leander is building schools to keep up with huge enrollment increases and now has 19 elementary schools, six middles school and, with the opening of Rouse High School in the fall of 2008, four high schools.

Leander was among the pioneers in the state to develop an educational program aimed at better preparing high school students for college or the workforce by requiring them to take classes in a specific discipline. Leander ISD provides strong core curriculum classes and, for those requiring more challenge, an honors program. Individual schools within the district consistently receive Acceptable to Exemplary ratings by the state. The average SAT score in the district is above the state and national average. Twenty-one percent of the district's children are listed as economically disadvantaged, and 4.3 percent lack English proficiency.

MANOR INDEPENDENT SCHOOL DISTRICT
312 Murray Avenue
(512) 278-4000
www.manorisd.net

This small district in Northeast Austin and Travis County doubled in enrollment from 1993 to 2003, and it has almost doubled again since then, to about 6,000 students. One of the poorest districts in the state in 1985, it made great strides during the high-tech boom of the 1990s. Manor ISD is home to Applied Materials, the world's largest maker of computer-chip manufacturing equipment. Samsung is opening a $1.3 billion semiconductor factory in stages. Together the companies represent thousands of jobs and major tax revenue. A large industrial park in the district houses, among other businesses, Apple Computers.

What's happening in Manor demonstrates the benefits of having dynamic businesses that lend their support to schools. Among its many contributions, Applied Materials donated money to develop an up-to-date physics lab at Manor High School. Samsung and Applied Materials are working with Austin Community College to develop a curriculum in the district to begin training students interested in the technology field. That program could bring major opportunities for students in a district traditionally made up of working-class families, farmers, and ranchers that lists 60 percent of its students as economically disadvantaged. Manor has been working to improve its ratings and the SAT scores in the district. The district has five elementary schools, one

middle school and three high schools, including Manor New Tech, one of the country's innovative educational models that stresses project-based learning with an emphasis on math, science and technology.

PFLUGERVILLE INDEPENDENT SCHOOL DISTRICT
1401 West Pecan, Pflugerville
(512) 251-4159
www.pflugervilleisd.net

Located in Northeast Travis County, close to several of the area's largest high-tech industries, the Pflugerville Independent School District has seen its enrollment more than double over the past decade to about 20,000 students today. That enrollment makes Pflugerville the fourth-largest district in the region. While the major high-tech companies are not within the jurisdiction of the Pflugerville school system, residential communities are springing up throughout the district to provide homes for families moving into the area to be close to jobs in Round Rock and Austin. As a result, the district has backed an aggressive expansion campaign over the past several years that led to the construction of several new schools. Today the district comprises 25 campuses: three high schools, five middle schools, an alternative learning center, 15 elementary schools and a primary school.

High school students taking the national Scholastic Aptitude Test have scored above the national average, and several schools within the system have been given Good to Excellent ratings by the TEA. More than 40 percent of the district's students are listed as economically disadvantaged, and 13.5 percent have limited English proficiency. Pflugerville offers a Spanish bilingual program for kindergarten through third grade. High school students are offered foreign language courses in French, German, Spanish, Latin, and Russian in addition to a core curriculum that includes math, science, and language arts. High school students who desire can choose from among nine vocational programs, or they can choose from among advanced placement courses and honors classes.

ROUND ROCK INDEPENDENT SCHOOL DISTRICT

1311 Round Rock Avenue, Round Rock
(512) 464-5000
www.roundrockisd.org

The Round Rock Independent School District, just north of Austin in northern Travis and Williamson Counties, is a focal point of community involvement. Like several other districts in this area, Round Rock ISD has a fine reputation for offering excellent educational opportunities. The district has 42 campuses: 27 elementary schools, eight middle schools, four high schools, a ninth grade center and two alternative learning centers.

Students taking the Scholastic Aptitude Test in the district have outscored their fellow Texans and received marks above the national average. Additionally, Round Rock has a dozen national Blue Ribbon schools, including Westwood and McNeil High Schools. Several district schools have received the top ranking from the state, and the district regularly produces a number of National Merit Scholars.

About 24 percent of the district's students are listed as economically disadvantaged, compared with 50 percent statewide. Eight percent of Round Rock students are considered to have limited English proficiency.

Round Rock, the second-largest school district in this area, with more than 40,000 students, spans nearly 110 square miles in southwest Williamson County and northwest Travis County. Only the Austin school district has more students. Like some other districts in this area, Round Rock has experienced severe growing pains, and the district is increasing enrollment by about 1,000 students per year. In fall 2003 the district opened Round Rock Stadium, a $20.5 million, 11,000-seat football and soccer complex that is easily among the finest in the country.

Charter Schools

UNIVERSITY OF TEXAS ELEMENTARY SCHOOL

2200 East Sixth Street
(512) 495-9705
www.utexas.edu/provost/elementary/

> **i** Girls are encouraged to "Do the Math" at the Girlstart Technology Center, www.girlstart.org, an effort by leaders in the Austin technology sector to boost girls' interest in math and science. The center offers after-school classes, weekend camps, and summer day camps. Fees are on a sliding scale to encourage participation by low-income families.

A grand experiment in educating inner-city youth was launched in the fall of 2003 with the opening of UT's elementary charter school. The East Austin school, pre-K through fifth grade, offers students access to some of the university's most innovative teaching resources and aims to become a model for other schools throughout Texas. Students have a slightly longer school day and year, and students who do not achieve benchmarks are required to attend after-school and summer programs. The school also provides teaching experience for UT education majors. The charter school serves students living in the area east of Interstate 35, south of U.S. Highway 290, west of U.S. Highway 183, and north of Highway 71.

"This charter school will provide an unusual opportunity for the College of Education to determine what works in improving student performances and to share these findings with schools across the state of Texas," said Manuel Justiz, dean of UT's College of Education.

AMERICAN YOUTHWORKS

216 East Fourth Street
(512) 236-6100
www.americanyouthworks.org

In 1996 the State Board of Education approved its first applications for charter schools. Among the first six authorized statewide was Austin's American Institute for Learning, now called American Youthworks. The school, which now has two campuses, provides education and job training to students ages 16 to 21 who have dropped out of traditional schools or are considered high risk for dropping out.

Students work toward earning a General

Educational Development (GED) diploma. The cornerstone of the year-round open-enrollment school is the Certificate of Mastery, which guarantees that the student has acquired the skills necessary to succeed in the workplace or in college. Students receive training in computers, business, multimedia, and theater arts. Another aspect of the charter school is its involvement with the national AmeriCorps program. For persons ages 17 through 25, the Casa Verde Builders program teaches on-the-job construction skills, and the Environmental Corps program stresses education in water-quality testing, park maintenance, and other environmental areas.

PRIVATE SCHOOLS

Whether you're looking for a parochial school, alternative learning, a college-preparatory program, or a school that focuses on the visual and performing arts, the Austin area probably has a private school that fits the bill. If the city falls short in any category, it would be in the scarcity of high-quality boarding schools similar to those found in larger cities, especially in the East. Only St. Stephen's Episcopal School, an excellent educational institution, provides room and board for high school students. All the private schools in the area are coeducational.

In Austin many parents opt for private schools to round out their children's religious education, although the demand for all types of private schools is growing rapidly. In response, several schools in the Austin area are adding grade levels a year at a time or expanding existing facilities, although the pressure for space keeps mounting. Many schools have extensive waiting lists and require admissions tests and/or interviews. Some schools do not accept students based on a first-come, first-served system, choosing instead to accept students who meet their requirements. Some schools offer before- and after-school care and/or extracurricular activities; parents should check with the school if those extras are important.

One of the most important recommendations we can offer, based on our experience in researching the area's private schools, is that it is imperative to visit all schools under consideration before making a final decision. A particular school can sound wonderful over the phone or in writing but seem unsuitable for any number of reasons once you've seen the campus. The agony of choosing a private school can be lessened by determining your own list of requirements before beginning the search: Religious or nonreligious? Cost? Location? Extracurricular activities? Those are just a few of the factors that must be considered. Parents who do their research should be pleased with the range of educational styles, school sizes, and programs available. With few exceptions, they will find administrators who are eager to discuss their educational philosophy and more than willing to offer tours of their facilities. Again, space is not always available, so it's important to plan ahead. Just as the city's public schools have increased in number, so have the area's private schools. In the listings below, we've included most of Austin's largest private schools as well as a representative sampling of the area's other private schools.

Central

CONCORDIA ACADEMY AT AUSTIN
3407 Red River Street
(512) 248-2547
www.concordiaacademy.org
A Lutheran school, Concordia Academy opened in the fall of 2002 as a ninth grade and added a grade level each year until it became a full senior high school by the fall of 2005. Affiliated with the Lutheran Church Missouri Synod, the school is currently on the grounds of St. Paul Lutheran School, an elementary and middle school. Concordia offers a college-preparatory program that, in addition to the core subjects, includes religion, Spanish, art, choir, band, and athletics. Enrollment is about 40 students. The school is not affiliated with Austin's Concordia University.

THE GIRLS' SCHOOL OF AUSTIN
2007 McCall Road
(512) 478-7827
www.thegirlsschool.org

As its name implies, this is an all-girls' school that was founded on the philosophy that the male-based educational model does not fit the way girls learn. Since its opening in 2002, the Girls' School has grown to about 70 students from kindergarten through eighth grade, although class sizes are limited to 15 girls. The school offers all the core classes, as well as computer studies, public speaking, and a Writers' Workshop. Its mission "is to inspire girls to achieve personal excellence and go on to lead distinguished and fulfilling lives." The school is a member of the National Coalition of Girls' Schools.

HUNTINGTON-SURREY HIGH SCHOOL
4001 Speedway
(512) 478-4743
www.huntingtonsurrey.com
This alternative high school of about 75 students offers an academically stimulating environment for bright students who want a college-preparatory program, like to express themselves, and are willing to take on a great deal of responsibility. With a student-teacher ratio of 4 to 1, and sometimes 1 to 1, the school has no place for slackers to hide out. The educational focus is on writing, math, history, and science. Students sit around a table with the teacher to discuss lessons. The school has a morning session for freshmen and sophomores and an afternoon session for juniors and seniors. All students attend the school at midday to study foreign languages: French, Latin, Spanish, and German. The shorter-than-average school day allows students to work, perform volunteer services, or pursue outside interests such as music, dance, karate, swimming, and horseback riding for school credit. Huntington-Surrey is accredited by the Southern Association of Colleges and Schools.

HYDE PARK BAPTIST SCHOOL
3901 Speedway
(512) 465-8331
www.hpbs.org
Hyde Park Baptist School offers a Christ-centered educational program to more than 700 students on two campuses. The campus on Speedway is for students from kindergarten through high school; the school in Southwest Austin, called the Bannockburn campus, is for kindergarten through sixth grade. Hyde Park is a college-preparatory, honors school that stresses educational achievement. The school aims to produce Christian individuals who are responsible, productive members of society. Hyde Park, established in 1968, is accredited by the Southern Association of Colleges and Schools. In addition to daily Bible classes, the teachings of Christ are integrated daily into the basic curriculum. Additionally, students can choose from among three foreign languages: Latin, French, and Spanish. All elementary students are included in the schools' Excel program for gifted and talented youth. The school offers state-of-the-art computer labs for all students, a wide range of extracurricular sports activities, and more than a dozen other after-school activities. The nondenominational school is sponsored by the Hyde Park Baptist Church.

KIRBY HALL SCHOOL
306 West 29th Street
(512) 474-1770
www.kirbyhallschool.org
One of Austin's most academically superior schools, Kirby Hall is an accredited college-preparatory school for students from pre-K through 12th grade. One hundred percent of Kirby Hall graduates go on to college. Students rank three to four years above the national average on tests such as the Iowa Test of Basic Skills. In a historic brick building near the University of Texas campus, Kirby Hall is situated to allow students to walk to the university to audit classes and, with testing, achieve college credit. All the school's core curriculum classes for high school students are advanced placement classes, and many students graduate from Kirby Hall with college credit hours. This school is an independent, nondenominational Christian school for bright students who want to excel. It has no facilities for children with learning disabilities or for students with discipline problems. Entrance exams and uniforms are required. About 180 boys and girls attend Kirby Hall in classes that average 16 students in size.

THE AUSTIN INTERNATIONAL SCHOOL
12001 Oak Knoll Road
(512) 331-7806
www.austinape.org

Founded in 2001, the Austin International School aims to provide a quality French-American curriculum in a multicultural environment to students of all nationalities. Subjects are taught by native speakers in both French and English. Spanish also is taught at all grade levels. The French curriculum closely follows guidelines set by the French Ministry of National Education. The school offers classes to students age 3 through sixth grade. The school also offers a Summer Language Immersion Camp for children ages 3 to 8. The school is a local nonprofit association formed in response to demand by Austin's Francophone community.

ST. ANDREW'S EPISCOPAL SCHOOL
5901 Southwest Parkway—Upper School
(512) 452-5779
www.sasaustin.org

St. Andrew's was established in 1951, making it one of the area's oldest and best-known parochial schools. St. Andrew's serves about 700 students grades one through 12 on two campuses and offers a strong college-preparatory program. Along with a challenging core curriculum, the school offers fine arts, foreign languages, and physical education. Admission tests and interviews are required. Entrance is determined through an "applicant pool" instead of by date of application.

ST. AUSTIN'S SCHOOL
1911 San Antonio Street
(512) 477-3751
www.staustin.org

This Catholic parish school was established in 1917 and today educates about 245 students from kindergarten through eighth grade. Daily religious instruction is an integral part of the curriculum at all grades, and students are prepared for the sacraments of Holy Communion, Reconciliation, and Confirmation. For students in kindergarten and first grade, teachers use a modi-

i Mirabeau B. Lamar, the second president of the Republic of Texas, is known as the "Father of Education in Texas." Under his leadership the Republic set aside land for schools. During the Republic, however, most education was provided by private schools and churches.

fied Montessori approach stressing basic skills and concepts, designed to encourage students to progress at their own pace. The middle school program reinforces basic skills and emphasizes higher-order thinking skills. In addition to a strong core curriculum at all levels, students study Spanish, computers, art, music, health, and physical education. The music program for students in kindergarten through fifth grade is integrated with religious instruction through preparation for weekly Masses at St. Austin's Church.

SRI ATMANANDA MEMORIAL SCHOOL
4100 Red River Street
(512) 451-7044
www.samschool.org

The learning approach used at the Sri Atmananda Memorial School was developed in southern India and brought to Austin by the school's director, Patty Henderson. She had placed her 5-year-old son in the Indian school while the family was there on business and was impressed with the results. Students at Sri Atmananda are not assigned a classroom or a teacher but instead are allowed to select their own area of interest from among the many labs available to them: math-geography, computer, art, science, and others. All subject matter is thoroughly integrated, and teachers present material and offer structured activities, especially for older students. Children do not receive grades for their work, although the learning material presented is appropriate for each student's abilities. This small school offers classes for children from kindergarten through 12th grade. Sri Atmananda is the only school outside India to use this method, and several of the school's teachers have received their training in that country.

South Central

PARKSIDE COMMUNITY SCHOOL
1701 Toomey Road
(512) 472-2559
www.parksidecommunityschool.org

About 145 students attend this Montessori school for children from 3 years old through sixth grade. Parkside was established in 1991 and focuses on the teaching methods developed by Dr. Maria Montessori in Italy. The program allows children to express their maximum creativity and to work at their own pace under the guidance of the classroom teacher. The core classes of language arts, math, science, and social studies are covered in all classrooms along with art, drama, sewing, and others areas of study. Preschoolers can attend classes full or half days, depending on the desires of their parents. Parkside also has an after-school program for its students of all ages.

ST. IGNATIUS, MARTYR, CATHOLIC SCHOOL
120 West Oltorf Street
(512) 442-8547
www.st-ignatius.org/school/

For students in pre-kindergarten through eighth grade, St. Ignatius educates about 230 students, both members and nonmembers of St. Ignatius Church. The school provides a strong Christian education that includes daily scriptural readings and reflection. Children gather at Liturgy to listen to God's Word and to learn to apply it to their daily life. Additionally, St. Ignatius offers a strong core curriculum that includes literature and the language arts, science, math, physical education, and the fine arts. Upper-level students are introduced to hands-on learning in the science lab and on computers. The math program includes pre-algebra and algebra for seventh and eighth graders. Students receive instruction in preparation to receive the Sacraments of Holy Eucharist and Confirmation in second grade and Reconciliation in fourth grade. The school demands parent involvement and requires parents to spend a minimum of 20 hours each year in service to the school, either at the school or at any event sponsored by the Parent Teacher Organization.

St. Ignatius is accredited by the Texas Catholic Conference Department of Education.

North

AUSTIN MONTESSORI SCHOOL—GREAT NORTHERN CAMPUS
6817 Great Northern Boulevard
(512) 450-1940
www.austinmontessori.org

Great Northern, one of three Austin Montessori campuses, is for primary students through third grade. The classic Montessori classroom design displays all learning materials on shelves and allows students to act on their own initiative in order to maximize independent learning and exploration. The Montessori approach is hands-on. Children work individually and in small groups and participate in whole-class activities. Teachers, known as guides, are trained to recognize a child's particular developmental stage and offer the appropriate learning materials in social studies, math, reading, writing, art, and music as the child becomes ready to use them. Ethics, social skills, and practical life are emphasized, as the school focuses on developing the whole child. The Austin Montessori Schools are considered models for the Montessori approach, and the school has hosted observers from all over the world. The school is accredited by Association Montessori Internationale. There is a waiting list.

AUSTIN SEVENTH DAY ADVENTIST JUNIOR ACADEMY
301 West Anderson Lane
(512) 459-8976
www.austinjunioracademy.org

This Christian school, supported by four Seventh Day Adventist churches in the region, is on the grounds of the Austin First Seventh Day Adventist Church and accredited by the Seventh Day Adventist School System. Students from pre-K to high school attend multigrade classes and study from Christian and Seventh Day Adventist textbooks. Students take classes in language arts, science, social studies, and math as well as computer science and physical education. The school stresses academic achievement, and enrollment is open to anyone.

BRENTWOOD CHRISTIAN SCHOOL
11908 North Lamar Boulevard
(512) 835-5983
www.brentwoodchristian.org
About 760 students attend Brentwood Christian School, a pre-kindergarten through 12th grade college-preparatory school. The school provides a Christ-centered academic environment that gives high school students a choice of degrees to pursue: standard, advanced, or honors advanced. Brentwood students score above the 90th percentile compared with students nationwide on national achievement tests. The school has an extensive extracurricular sports program for boys and girls. Established in 1963, Brentwood welcomes students from all religious, ethnic, and national backgrounds if they are seeking a solid, Christian education. The school is affiliated with the Brentwood Oaks Church of Christ and is accredited by the National Christian Schools Association. Entrance exams are required.

PARAGON PREP
2001 West Koenig Lane
(512) 459-5040
www.paragonprep.com
Weekly academic competitions, cooperative projects, and an emphasis on technology are just a few of the aspects of this college-preparatory school for middle school students. Founded in 1997, Paragon Prep seeks bright, motivated students who are aiming for higher education. The independent school for students in sixth, seventh, and eighth grades uses renowned educational material, including the Chicago Math Series curriculum and the Junior Great Books program. Paragon calls itself "Internet intensive" and provides regular access to the World Wide Web through Internet classes that emphasize research and multimedia projects. The curriculum is designed so that students returning to public school for senior high will be exceptionally prepared. Paragon expects both student and parental commitments to excellence and offers

in exchange a dynamic, fun, and stimulating environment. The school aims to produce students who are well rounded, concerned for others, and knowledgeable about democratic and entrepreneurial principles. Admission is selective, based on student testing and interviews with the student and parents.

ST. LOUIS SCHOOL
2114 St. Joseph Boulevard
(512) 454-0384
www.st-louis.org
This Catholic school, located on an 18-acre campus across the street from St. Louis parish, was established in 1956 and today provides religious and secular education to more than 470 students from preschool through eighth grade. The school's well-rounded curriculum includes daily religion classes as well as language arts, math, science, health, computers, social studies, music, physical education, Spanish, and the arts. Children attend Mass weekly and are given weekly sacramental preparation to supplement the program at St. Louis parish. The school provides a stimulating and progressive academic program integrated with Catholic values and traditions. Extracurricular activities include liturgical and bell choirs, team sports, cheerleading, student council, and altar servers. St. Louis School admits students of all religious, racial, and ethnic backgrounds. The school, affiliated with the Catholic schools of the Diocese of Austin, is accredited by the Southern Association of Colleges and Schools.

South
STRICKLAND CHRISTIAN SCHOOL
7415 Manchaca Road
(512) 447-1447
www.stricklandschool.com
First graders at Strickland Christian School use the King James Version of the Bible as their basic reader. This religiously independent, non-denominational school was established in 1961 and today provides instruction for more than 250 students from pre-kindergarten through

eighth grade. The school strives to provide academic excellence and a Christian foundation. The school, developed by Texan Corine Strickland, was a leader in teaching children to read phonetically, starting in preschool, and still emphasizes developing strong readers. Its core curriculum also includes writing, spelling, and math. Children also take classes in science, social studies, and physical education.

East

AUSTIN PEACE ACADEMY
5110 Manor Road
Austin, TX 78723
(512) 926 1737
www.apacademy.org
Founded by Austin's Muslim community, the Peace Academy offers the full range of core classes such as math, science, history, etc., but the challenging curriculum also includes Islamic studies and the Arabic language. The East Austin school, which has about 135 students in pre-K to ninth grade, aims to help students preserve their Islamic identity, heritage, and practices. The school also boasts a state-of-the-art computer lab, language lab, and small class sizes designed to meet the needs of each student. Peace Academy is accredited by the Southern Association of Colleges and Schools.

West

AUSTIN CITY ACADEMY
9301 Highway 290 West
(512) 288-4883
www.austincityacademy.org
This pre-K to 12th grade Christian school takes biblically based learning a step further by stressing the arts as well as academics and God. Every student receives both vocal and instrumental instruction, as well as the core classes based on A Beka, Bob Jones and other Christian materials. The school, founded in 2002 and located about 16 miles west of downtown Austin, also plans to offer a full athletic program over the coming years. Small classes with a 1 to10 teacher/ student ratio allow for customized instruction.

As a member of the Texas Association of Private and Parochial Schools (TAPPS), the City Academy plans to participate in TAPPS fine arts, vocal and instrumental competitions.

AUSTIN MONTESSORI SCHOOL
MIDDLE SCHOOL CAMPUS
5677 Oak Boulevard
(512) 892-0826
www.austinmontessori.org
This is the only school in the Montessori system that provides classes for students aged 12 to 15. The school extends the Montessori curriculum developed for elementary students by Italian Maria Montessori. The program stresses individual development and hands-on learning. Teachers act as guides to help lead children along a path of learning appropriate for each child. The school was established in 1993 and is accredited by Association Montessori Internationale.

THE CHILDREN'S SCHOOL
2825 Hancock Drive
(512) 453-1126
www.thechildrensschool.org
This Montessori school for children in pre-K through fifth grade uses a progressive approach to learning that incorporates the classic Montessori curriculum with training in computer technology. For more than 20 years, computers have been an integral aspect of the Children's School, and today's youngsters are introduced to multimedia systems and language development through the use of computers. The technology training adds to the fundamental teaching methods of the Montessori system, which allows for the physical, emotional, and intellectual development of each child. The Montessori curriculum consists of hands-on learning in all the areas of study, including language arts, music, Spanish, art, science, physical education, and math. In addition to its complete academic program, the school offers a variety of extracurricular activities. The Children's School is accredited by the American Montessori Society. There is a waiting list to enter.

REGENTS SCHOOL OF AUSTIN
3230 Travis Country Circle
(512) 899-8095
www.regents-austin.com

Serving about 600 K–12 students, the Regents School is a nondenominational Christian school that integrates a college-preparatory liberal-arts program with a strong Christian education. The school looks for students who are college bound and want to be challenged. Students begin the study of Latin in third grade, which the school says helps them better understand English, science, and history. Students also study language arts, history, geography, math, logic, Spanish, and the arts. The Regents School of Austin opened in 1992 and is a founding member of the Association of Christian and Classical Schools. Admissions tests and interviews are required.

ST. MICHAEL'S CATHOLIC ACADEMY
3000 Barton Creek Boulevard
(512) 328-2323
www.smca.com

St. Michael's Catholic Academy offers a rigorous academic environment for about 400 college-bound students. The school, established in 1984 and located on 50 acres in Southwest Austin, challenges students to reach their full potential and helps them achieve that goal by offering a wide range of courses. Students desiring more academic challenge can pursue an Advanced Academic Diploma with Honors, which requires the completion of 10 semester hours of honors courses in addition to writing an honors thesis. The school's success in producing top-quality graduates is reflected in the number of students accepted to the nation's leading colleges and universities, in the amount of scholarships and awards seniors receive, and in the number of National Merit Scholars the school produces. The admissions process is competitive. The school is dedicated to serving a diverse student body and to that end offers a financial-aid program that allows students of all economic backgrounds the opportunity to attend. The school, which is owned and governed by a board of trustees,

is accredited by the Texas Catholic Conference Education Department.

ST. STEPHEN'S EPISCOPAL SCHOOL
2900 Bunny Run
(512) 327-1213
www.sstx.org

Austin's only boarding school for high school students, St. Stephen's also offers day classes for coed students in sixth through 12th grades. St. Stephen's is one of Austin's most academically superior schools. It regularly produces National Merit Scholars, its seniors score well above the national average on Scholastic Aptitude Test scores, and graduates are accepted to the world's most elite colleges and universities. The school stresses Christian and community values but welcomes students from all cultures, backgrounds, and religions. In fact, it was the first integrated boarding school in the South. Its range of academic offerings is outstanding and class sizes are small, both factors in its popularity. Additionally, St. Stephen's offers "Special Academies" in theater, soccer, and tennis. Admission is competitive and requires interviews, tests, and recommendations. On 428 acres, St. Stephen's has about 630 students, including 70 from 20 different countries. An observatory opened in fall 1998. St. Stephen's was established in 1950 and is affiliated with the National Association of Independent Schools and the Southern Association of Episcopal Schools.

ST. THERESA'S CATHOLIC SCHOOL
4311 Small Drive
(512) 451-7105
www.st-theresa.org/school

Four-year-olds through eighth graders attend this Catholic school in Northwest Austin. On the campus of St. Theresa's Catholic Church, the school offers a full, academically challenging curriculum designed to allow its 290 students to reach their full potential. St. Theresa's students score on average in the 90th percentile on national achievement tests. St. Theresa's also provides enrichment opportunities for each course of study. In addition to daily religion classes, lessons from the Bible are integrated throughout the basic core subjects. Specially trained instructors provide classes in library skills, physical education, and computer training. Students begin using computers in preschool, with a program that reinforces reading skills, and continue their technology training through middle school on the school's classroom computers and in two Internet-connected computer labs. St. Theresa's offers what it calls "mastery learning," which couples a well-trained faculty with the use of advanced technology and delivery systems.

Northwest

AUSTIN JEWISH ACADEMY
7300 Hart Lane
(512) 735-8350
www.austinjewishacademy.org
The only Jewish school in the Central Texas area, the Austin Jewish Academy opened in fall 1997. The independent school started with kindergarten through third grade and has expanded over the years to the eighth grade. The students at the school are motivated, creative self-starters who can work within varying degrees of structure. A strong Jewish education is part of the school's curriculum, but the school does not embrace any particular arm of Judaism or require that students be Jewish. Students study Hebrew daily and also take classes in Jewish history, prayer, Bible, and the study of Israel. The school also offers a sound core curriculum that includes language arts, math, and science as well as social studies, Spanish, art, music, physical education, geography, and world cultures. Judaic and secular studies are highly integrated. Strong parental involvement is one of the school's greatest attributes. The school is a member of the National Association for the Education of Young Children and the National Association for Supervision and Curriculum Development and is housed at the Jewish Community Center in North Austin.

HILL COUNTRY CHRISTIAN SCHOOL OF AUSTIN
12124 Ranch Road 620 North
(512) 331-7036
www.hccsa.org

Founded in 1996, Hill Country Christian School in North Austin provides a Christian and classical education to children from kindergarten through the 12th grade. The school's educational philosophy is linked to the belief that Jesus Christ is the true foundation of all knowledge and learning. The nondenominational school, affiliated with Hill Country Bible Church, is a college-preparatory institution. Teachings from the Bible are integrated into the school's basic curriculum, which includes language arts, math, science, history, art, music, and physical education. The Bible also is taught as a separate lesson or course, depending on the grade level. Students in the upper grades can participate in the school's extracurricular sports program. The school is pursuing accreditation through the Association of Christian Schools International.

REDEEMER LUTHERAN SCHOOL
1500 West Anderson Lane
(512) 451-6478
www.redeemerschool.net
Redeemer Lutheran School is Austin's largest Lutheran school and one of the largest of its kind in the country, with a program that encompasses preschool through eighth grade. Founded in 1955, the school aims to share the Christian faith by assisting parents in providing opportunities for spiritual, intellectual, physical, emotional, and social growth for children in a Christ-centered environment. The school follows the Texas Essential Knowledge and Skills curriculum program found in most public schools but incorporates Christ in the daily education process. Although a Lutheran school, children of all faiths are welcome to attend the school. In addition to the basic core curriculum, Redeemer Lutheran School offers music classes, Spanish, and physical education. Computers labs give students daily access to computer technology and to the Internet. The school also has an active extracurricular sports program and choirs for children of all ages. The school is affiliated with the Lutheran Church–Missouri Synod and accredited by the Lutheran School Accreditation Commission.

SUMMIT CHRISTIAN ACADEMY
2121 Cypress Creek Road (Pre-K to 12th)
1303 Leander Drive, Leander (Pre-K to 5th)
(512) 250-1369
www.summiteagles.org
Summit Christian Academy, serving pre-K through 12th grade students on two campuses, is an accredited college-preparatory school, Summit provides an academically challenging environment based on a Christian world view. The school offers a varied but rigorous curriculum designed to develop and encourage the creative, expressive, analytical, and critical-thinking skills necessary for college admission. Nearly 100 percent of the school's graduates go on to college, and a large percentage have received scholarships to prestigious universities. The school stresses a phonics-based approach to spelling and understanding of the language arts. Specially trained teachers introduce elementary students to computer programming skills. Middle school students who qualify can enter the advanced math track to begin earning high school credit in eighth grade. The school offers a nondenominational Bible program for all students. Bible classes are taught daily, and the study of religion is integrated throughout the school's programs.

Southwest

AUSTIN MONTESSORI SCHOOL—
SUNSET TRAIL
5014 Sunset Trail
(512) 892-0253
www.austinmontessori.org
Sunset Trail is the main campus of the Montessori system's largest school in Austin, providing education to students from age 14 months through upper elementary level. The school, founded in 1967, teaches children according to the method developed by Dr. Maria Montessori in Italy. She believed that children possess a natural and intense desire to learn about the world and that they can absorb knowledge effortlessly. The classroom is designed with all the learning material readily available on shelves in order to maximize independent learning and exploration.

The school does not use textbooks but allows children to explore concrete materials, using their hands and their minds. Teachers, known as guides, are trained to recognize a child's particular developmental stage and offer the appropriate learning materials. Children work individually or in small groups in learning science, social studies, math, reading, writing, art, and music. Ethics, social skills, and practical life are emphasized, as the school focuses on developing the whole child. In addition to regular classroom activities, students can choose to learn violin or piano using the Suzuki method, which is based on the concept that children can learn music the same way they learn to speak—by ear. There is a waiting list. Austin Montessori also has a campus for young students in North Austin and a middle school campus in West Austin.

AUSTIN WALDORF SCHOOL
8700 South View Road
(512) 288-5942
www.austinwaldorf.org
The Austin Waldorf School, the only certified Waldorf program in Texas, offers an educational program to students from age 4 through the 12th grade on 12 acres in the Oak Hill area of Austin. Waldorf schools, also known worldwide as Steiner schools, are based on the educational philosophy of Dr. Rudolf Steiner, an educator, artist, and philosopher who devised a method of instruction based on the idea that children pass through distinct developmental stages. The program is designed to engage each child's innate creativity and builds on a strong academic foundation by integrating art, instrumental music, song, stories, and crafts into the daily curriculum. The independent school teaches according to the phases of child development, offering lessons at each stage that are designed to nurture a child's imagination. Mastery of the academic disciplines is of utmost importance at the Waldorf School, where students are introduced to all major fields of human endeavor through the study of mathematics, sciences, and language arts. Students are given the opportunity to explore all aspects

of a subject matter and, with the guidance of their specially trained teacher, write and illustrate their own textbooks for each lesson. The school, founded in 1980, has grown to 370 students.

HYDE PARK BAPTIST SCHOOL— BANNOCKBURN
7100 Brodie Lane
(512) 892-0000
www.hpbs.org

This is the Southwest Austin campus of Austin's largest private school. The Bannockburn campus for students in kindergarten through sixth grade has about 165 students. Hyde Park's other school in Central Austin is a K–12 school with more than 700 students. Building on a solid Christian foundation, the school aims to produce educational achievement and offers its elementary students a wide range of opportunities, including introduction to computer technology, foreign languages, and a strong core curriculum that integrates Bible study with all areas of course work. All elementary students are included in both schools' Excel program for gifted and talented youth. Students entering the upper grades begin a college-preparatory honors program, and most go on to college. The nondenominational school is sponsored by the Hyde Park Baptist Church.

Cedar Park
TWIN LAKES CHRISTIAN SCHOOL
1150 South Bell Boulevard, Cedar Park
(512) 258-0080

Twin Lakes Christian School has revamped the educational format in its middle and upper schools in recent years and now offers individually structured classes for students, who work in "achievement centers." In other words, instruction is tailored to each student's educational needs. The school, on a 40-acre campus in Cedar Park, offers the traditional classroom structure for students in pre-kindergarten to fifth grade. The school integrates students' biblical education with strong academic instruction at all levels. Although the school is affiliated with Twin Lakes Christian

i Austin's Fund for Child Care Excellence honors "family-friendly" businesses and organizations that demonstrate leadership and innovation in creating family-supportive work environments. To see if your prospective employer has received this designation, check out the fund's Web site at www.fcce.org.

Church, the majority of students who attend are not from families that belong to the church.

Round Rock
ROUND ROCK CHRISTIAN ACADEMY
301 North Lake Creek Drive
Round Rock
(512) 255-4491
www.rrca-tx.org

Round Rock Christian Academy is a nondenominational school educating about 350 students from age 4 through high school. The school aims to cultivate a heart for God, develop the mind of Christ, and provide a distinctively Christian quality education. The school supports a Christian-based curriculum using primarily the Bob Jones and A Beka textbooks. Math is taught using the Saxon method. In addition to core curriculum classes of math, history, science, and language arts, classes in American sign language, drama, choir, Spanish, and logic are offered. The academy's Discovery Program, for students in first through fourth grades, is an after-school enrichment program providing more academic challenge to qualified students. Under the Aim program, students with learning disabilities or other special needs work with a staff educational therapist. The school is affiliated with and accredited by the Association of Christian Schools International.

THE AUSTIN SCHOOL FOR THE PERFORMING AND VISUAL ARTS
5700 North Pace Bend Road
Spicewood
(512) 773-3398
www.theaustinschool.org

With the opening of the Austin School for the

Performing and Visual Arts (ASPVA) in the fall of 2007, the Central Texas area got its first private educational institution for students in sixth through 12th grades who want to emphasize their artistic studies in the areas of dance, music, voice, visual arts and theater arts. The school, situated on a 450-acre campus on Lake Travis, about 35 miles northwest of downtown Austin, also provides a core curriculum in the language arts, history, math, sciences, geography and, of course, the fine arts. Its curriculum is in line with Texas Assessment of Knowledge and Skills (TAKS) requirements, so students should be able to move from ASPVA into "regular" schools without missing a beat. An audition is required in the application process and acceptance is based on "artistic promise," among other things.

CHILD CARE

For parents, few decisions arouse more angst than determining who will care for their preschool-age child while they're at work. As Austin grows, that concern intensifies as more and more parents compete for existing high-quality care. Area child care referral agencies insist that excellent care can be found, especially since more emphasis is placed these days on professional care, as opposed to just babysitting. Finding high-quality child care for infants seems to be the most difficult, according to the referral agencies. In fact, they say that people who are even thinking about having a child need to get on waiting lists at accredited child care centers. Parents often do not plan ahead for infant care, believing that because infants sleep so often, care shouldn't be difficult to find or cost too much. However, because state regulations require a higher ratio of providers to infants in licensed facilities than any other age group—4 to 1—it's often not profitable for a center to provide care for the very young, so they don't.

Finding care for toddlers is not as difficult, although in the fastest growing areas, especially in North Austin, Round Rock, and Cedar Park, the challenge to locate high-quality care increases. Child care in downtown Austin, with its high concentration of state office workers, also seems to be increasingly limited. Although after-school programs are offered at most schools in the capital area's 10 school districts, waiting lists can be long, so it's important to register early.

Another option is to have a child picked up by an after-school-care provider. Again, it's important to plan ahead, as these also tend to fill up in some areas.

Choosing a day care provider gets somewhat easier for parents once they know what to look for in a facility. The Texas Department of Protective and Regulatory Services (PRS), which oversees day care providers, lists three categories of service: licensed, registered, and listed. The agency's Web site, www.tdprs.state.tx.us, also offers histories of violations at facilities in Texas. Facilities that care for 13 or more children are considered day care centers and must be licensed by the state. Registered facilities are home care centers that accept 4 to 12 children. The standards vary somewhat for these two categories, although they both are subject to unannounced inspections by the PRS. In 1997 the Texas Legislature created the last category: listed. According to new regulations, persons who care for one to three children in their home must be listed by PRS and are subject to the same records investigations as other providers. These homes, however, are not inspected unless there is a report of child abuse or neglect.

Finding reliable and affordable child care, for regular daily care, occasional drop-in care, or in-home sitters, can be one of the first tasks a family faces on arrival in Austin. Some neighborhood associations provide residents with lists of babysitters in their areas, while parents in other areas have formed babysitting co-ops, in which parents take turns at sitting responsibilities. Be sure to check with your neighborhood association for information.

Several referral agencies around town can help by offering experienced guidance in the child care search and by providing parents with lists of providers from their databases. Following are some of the sitter services and referral agencies for child care that can help get you off to a good start.

FAMILYCONNECTIONS
825 East 53rd ½ Street, Building E-101
(512) 478-5725
www.familyconnectionsonline.org
FamilyConnections, a merger of Austin Families, Inc., and Connections Resource Center, offers customized child care searches by professionally trained specialists for individual or corporate clients. Its huge database includes child care centers, family day homes, parent's day out programs, school-age programs, and camps in Travis County and the surrounding counties. FamilyConnections says its mission is to improve the quality of early education and care for Central Texas children by providing information, education, and resources to those individuals who have the greatest influence on children during the critically important formative years—parents, caregivers, teachers, and community leaders. Payment for the service is based on a sliding scale of zero to $25. The fee covers up to six searches over a six-month period.

KID SPACE
13376 Research Boulevard
(512) 918-2562

1401 South I-35, Round Rock
(512) 244-7774
This center in the Galleria Oaks shopping center in Northwest Austin and its other facility in Round Rock accept children ages 1 to 12 for drop-in child care. Kid Space offers plenty of entertainment for children of all ages. They are open daily at 8:30 a.m. and offer service until 12:30 a.m. on Friday and Saturday nights. It's a good idea to make a reservation, but that can usually be done the day the service is required. Also call to find out about immunization requirements.

MOM'S BEST FRIEND
1101 Capital of Texas Highway South
Building H, Suite 200
(512) 346-2229
www.momsbestfriend.com
This popular business for the busy parent provides both sitters and nannies. A Mom's Best Friend can arrange for sitters to come to your home, hotel, or even your office for the amount of time you need. References and previous employers have been checked for all sitters, and a criminal background check has been conducted on all nannies. Clients looking for a certain age group in a sitter can, with enough advance notice, make a special request from among the staff, which ranges in age from mid-20s to mid-60s. Mom's Best Friend also offers a service it calls Mother's Helper, which includes light house maintenance as well as child care—great for the new mom. Separate housekeeping services can also be arranged.

STEPPING STONE SCHOOLS
13 locations around Austin
1910 Justin Lane
(512) 459-0258
www.steppingstoneschool.com
Consistently voted "Best Child Care" by readers of *Austin Family* magazine, the Stepping Stone School offers early-childhood education and an "enhancement" program for school-age kids. The schools offer a progressive curriculum and accept children from 18 months to 11 years. Some of the schools take infants also. The locally owned business has been in Austin since 1979. Check the Web site or call the administrative office, listed above, for a location near your home or work.

URBANBABY
www.urbanbaby.com
Austin is one of the original cities in the Urban-Baby network, which touts itself as a "network of comprehensive resource guides and interactive communities for urban parents in the top metropolitan cities." The online community was founded by Susan Maloney, a mom, former fashion editor, and stylist, who saw the Internet as a great meeting place and resource for busy moms and dads. In addition to online resources, the site also has message boards where Austin parents can offer tips and recommendations.

WORK SOURCE CHILD CARE SOLUTIONS
2538 South Congress Avenue
(512) 597-7191, (800) 825-1914
www.worksourceaustin.com
Managed by the City of Austin, this organization provides child care subsidies for eligible families in Travis County. Work Source also provides training for child care providers.

HOMESCHOOLING

Homeschools might as well have been called "underground schools" back in the 1970s and early 1980s because so many parents who chose to educate their own children guarded their secret as if they'd committed a crime. Indeed, many were prosecuted for failing to comply with compulsory attendance laws. A lot has changed. Today homeschooling is not only legal in all 50 states but the governor of Texas has also recognized the value of homeschooling by proclaiming a Home Education Week. In Austin parents can attend an annual book fair and convention for homeschoolers. The watershed occurred in 1987 when parents won a class-action suit against the state, which stripped the Texas Education Agency of its authority over homeschools. The Texas Supreme Court upheld the decision in 1994. Now attitudes toward homeschools in Texas are among the most liberal in the country. Here

the state asks only that parents pursue a course of study that includes math, reading, spelling, grammar, and a course in good citizenship. The curriculum, however, does not have to be filed with any government agency. An educational approach that was once largely the domain of Christian fundamentalists has spread to families of all kinds, and for many reasons. Certainly, many parents want to emphasize their children's religious education. Some choose to homeschool because they fear their children will be exposed to violence or the wrong influences in traditional schools. Others opt for homeschooling to give their children more flexibility to pursue outside interests. Many aim to ensure that their children achieve academic excellence.

The Texas Home School Coalition, based in Lubbock, is a nonprofit organization that supports parents in their efforts to educate their children at home. The organization operates a database of homeschool support groups around the state, where parents can go to get information about available curriculums for homeschools or about anything else they wish to know about educating their own children. Since 2001 the coalition has sponsored an annual state convention and family conference for homeschool families. For further information on homeschooling, contact the coalition at P.O. Box 6747, Lubbock, TX 79493, (806) 744-4441, www.thsc.org.

MEDIA

Austin's long and rich media history goes as far back as the Capital City itself. The *Austin City Gazette,* a four-page weekly, made its debut on October 30, 1839, the same year that Austin became the capital of the Republic of Texas. Published by Samuel Whiting, a journalist from Houston, the *City Gazette* carried local, national, and foreign news; letters to the editor; editorials; and an occasional work of fiction. By the time the *City Gazette* folded in 1842 (some say due to the threat of invasion from Mexico), the frontier town of Austin had other publications to take its place. Austinites, it seemed, were eager for news, although getting it to this remote outpost was never easy—and definitely not quick. During the Civil War, one local publisher debuted his one-page bulletin, the *Texas Almanac Extra,* which he rushed into print three times a week after waiting for Pony Express riders to hustle in with the latest editions of the Houston and Galveston newspapers.

Decades later, during the Depression of the 1930s, the dean of American television journalism, Walter Cronkite, got his start in Austin. "My first appearance before a microphone was during the college years at Austin," he writes in his book, *A Reporter's Life.* Cronkite admits that his daily sports report on Austin radio station KNOW consisted of scores he memorized from a Western Union sports ticker at a Sixth Street tobacco shop while pretending to read the newspaper. "Once out of sight of the smoke shop, I ran at breakneck speed back to the studio and typed out my daily sports intelligence before it fled my memory," Cronkite said. He then moved on to work in print journalism in Austin, covering Texas politics. "It was a vast and diverse state, and the fight for dominance and privilege in Austin was never ending," wrote Cronkite.

The Austin media landscape has changed a mite since Cronkite's days here. Today's residents are bombarded with choices over what publications to read, where to land on the radio dial for programming that serves their needs, and which television news program to select. Austin also has about as eclectic a selection of periodicals as one is likely to find in any city this size. Without a doubt, one of the pleasures of living in Austin, one of the qualities that define this city, is the abundance and diversity of reading material out there. It's not all award-winning stuff, but much of it is—and some of it deserves to be.

PRINT MEDIA

The list you'll find below represents a cross section of publications that make up the bedrock of the Austin print media. If your special interests lie elsewhere—in theater, business, technology, religion, public radio, or politics—take a look around; you're likely to find some publication that speaks to you.

Newspapers

AUSTIN AMERICAN–STATESMAN
305 South Congress Avenue
(512) 445-3500
www.statesman.com

As Austin's only daily newspaper, the *Austin American–Statesman* is in the unenviable position of trying to satisfy all the news demands of a complex society. Although its efforts haven't always been successful, former Editor Richard

Oppel helped improve the paper's scope of coverage in news, business, and editorials so much that the *Statesman* launched an advertising campaign using the slogan "It's Not Your Same Old Statesman." Indeed, the *Statesman* has come along nicely.

However, the paper's owner, Cox Enterprises, shocked the media world in 2008 when it announced its plan to sell all but three of its newspaper holdings—including, the *Statesman*—amid declining revenues for newspapers across the country. It is unknown how the sale will affect the *Statesman*'s future.

Meanwhile, one highlight of today's *Statesman* is the weekly "XLent" entertainment section. Published Thursday and available free at area distribution points, this tabloid insert captures the eyes of young-at-heart readers who want a viewpoint besides the *Chronicle*'s (see listing below) for entertainment news and features. Kudos also to longtime columnist John Kelso, whose wry comments on current issues and events appear regularly in the Metro section.

The *Statesman*'s main section features the top stories of the day, editorials, letters to the editor, and international news. Other daily news sections include Metro and State, Sports, Business, and Life & Arts. On Friday the Life & Movies section is published; Sunday delivers the Travel section as well as Insight, which includes coverage of local, national, and international issues, many written by the *Statesman*'s international staff.

AUSTIN BUSINESS JOURNAL
111 Congress Avenue, Suite 750
(512) 494-2500
www.austin.bizjournals.com
Published on Friday, the *Austin Business Journal* is the only newspaper in the area dedicated exclusively to business news and information. Founded locally in 1980, the tabloid-format newspaper covers developments affecting the growth of the region and monitors the progress of new businesses coming to the area. It also promotes networking by publishing a listing of weekly events and meetings of interest to the business community.

Of special interest to many businesspeople and newcomers are the *Journal*'s annual guides and directories, most notably the *Book of Lists*. This massive volume, issued in December, provides information on more than 1,500 companies of interest to the business community. The *Business Journal* is available for delivery or can be purchased at newsstands around the area.

THE AUSTIN CHRONICLE
4000 North Interstate 35
(512) 454-5766
www.austinchronicle.com
It's hard to plan an evening out on the town without first picking up a copy of the *Austin Chronicle*. The *Chronicle*, which celebrated its 27th anniversary in 2008, stresses coverage of music, entertainment, and the arts but also provides a vital alternative voice on local political and environmental issues. The *Chronicle*, a big, fat, free publication distributed Thursday around the greater Austin area, was founded by six local entrepreneurs, several of whom had worked on the *Daily Texan*, UT's student newspaper.

Although at times a little rough around the edges, the *Chronicle* easily disappears from newsstands within a couple of days of publication. Editor Louis Black, one of the original godfathers (as the founders like to call themselves), has become a dynamic voice on the issue of long-range city planning.

But let's not forget the *Chronicle*'s main focus: Entertainment, with a capital E! Movie reviews, book reviews, record reviews, features on the

i The much-anticipated results of the *Austin Chronicle*'s "Best of Austin" readers' poll highlight the best the city has to offer in dozens of categories, including arts and entertainment, dining, shopping, politics, high-tech, and so much more. Get the Austin Insiders' word in September or check back issues on *the Chronicle*'s Web site. *Chronicle* readers also choose winners for the Austin Music Awards, which honor the best of the best in ceremonies held in March.

fascinating figures that keep Austin interesting, art, theater and film listings, cartoons, and some insightful columns on everything from architecture to zydeco cram this 100-page-plus periodical. Of course the *Chronicle* knows the Austin club scene. You get the feeling that these writers don't just cover their beats, they live them.

THE DAILY TEXAN
(512) 471-4591
www.dailytexanonline.com
This award-winning student newspaper of the University of Texas is published Monday through Friday when school is in session. It covers largely campus news, but when the university is one of the largest in the nation, that's a big job. *The Daily Texan* is among the most recognized student newspapers in the country, and many of its graduates have gone on to win Pulitzer prizes with professional publications. *The Daily Texan* also provides some interesting local, state, and national news. Copies are distributed free in bright orange boxes on campus and at various locations around the downtown area.

Magazines

AUSTIN FAMILY
P.O. Box 7559, Austin 78683
(512) 733-0038
www.austinfamily.com
This free magazine, published monthly and available at about 500 distribution points throughout the greater Austin area, is an excellent resource for parents looking for news and information about summer camps, child care, schools, family-friendly events, and much more.

AUSTIN MONTHLY
P.O. Box 340927, Austin 78734
(512) 263-9133
www.austinmonthly.com
Started as a free publication in 1992 and dedicated to the positive aspects of city life, *Austin Monthly* has gone decidedly upscale the past few years. Now a slick four-color magazine, it is sold by subscription and at local newsstands around

the region. Yet it remains true to its origins. Good features on the region's interesting characters and on the events that make Austin such a happening city are combined with pictorial spreads, restaurant reviews, an events calendar, and much more.

THE GOOD LIFE
P.O. Box 4400, Austin 78765
www.goodlifemag.com
Award-winning Austin journalist Ken Martin and his wife, Rebecca Melancon, debuted this monthly magazine in 1997 as a publication for the 50+ crowd. Since then, the *Good Life* has morphed into a fine publication for just about anyone interested in reading "compelling community journalism," as its motto states. Published monthly, the *Good Life* prints a broad range of well-written news and feature articles for and about the people of Central Texas, with particular emphasis on Austin.

NEW TEXAS MAGAZINE
15121/2 South Congress Avenue
(512) 462-1990
Established in 1979, *New Texas* magazine is now Central Texas's oldest magazine—and it's still free at distribution points around Austin, San Antonio, and the Texas Hill Country. While it retains its "New Age" image, especially with advertisers, New Texas has branched out from its alternative lifestyle focus to include a broader spectrum of articles on life in and around Austin—and beyond.

TEXAS HIGHWAYS
150 East Riverside Drive
(512) 486-5858, (800) 839-4997
www.texashighways.com
Stunning color photographs and in-depth articles that celebrate the glory of Texas abound in this monthly magazine, published in Austin by the Texas Department of Transportation. This is the official travel magazine of Texas and provides current and accurate information on travel destinations throughout the state. It is a beautiful publication. *Texas Highways* started as an in-house

publication of the Department of Transportation but has been exclusively a travel magazine since May 1974. The magazine clearly stresses protection of the environment and of the state's cultural heritage and has won awards from such organizations as the San Antonio Conservation Society, the Texas Historical Commission, and the International Regional Magazines Association.

TEXAS HILL COUNTRY MAGAZINE
P.O. Box 429
Blanco, Texas 78606
(830) 833-0429
www.hillcountrymagazine.com
The more Austin expands, the more the interest grows in seeking Hill Country escapes. This full-color magazine, published quarterly, is an excellent guide to all things Hill Country, from features about the colorful people, places and things that make the Hill Country so unique, to information about upcoming events. The advertisements also are worth a look, as they tout local restaurants, shops, resorts, lodgings and other businesses that might appeal to visitors—or to those thinking of moving to the area.

TEXAS MONTHLY
701 Brazos Street
(512) 320-6900
www.texasmonthly.com
Winner of numerous National Magazine Awards, Texas Monthly is the state's showcase magazine. And it's published in Austin. This full-color glossy magazine offers lengthy news and feature articles and spicy true-crime stories of interest to its affluent, well-educated readers. It also provides frequently updated reviews of selected restaurants in Texas's major cities. Its regular column "Around the State" is a city-by-city guide to choice entertainment. The annual Bum Steer Awards, published in the January issue, take an irreverent look at the people and situations in Texas that the editors believe have been particularly weird or foolish over the past year; it's perennially one of the magazine's best-selling issues. The Best and Worst Legislators is another popular cover feature that comes out every other July

(as the Texas Legislature meets biennially). Look also for the annual Top Twenty issue, which lists the magazine's choice of the 20 most influential Texans of the year. Publisher Mike Levy, who started the magazine when he was 26 years old, has found a formula that satisfies the majority of Texas Monthly's readers.

TEXAS MUSIC
P.O. Box 50273, Austin 78763
(512) 472-6630
www.txmusic.com
This juicy, well-designed quarterly gets high marks for covering the Texas music scene. Insightful articles about contemporary bands and songwriters around the state combine with some interesting features on the state's long and varied history of music and music makers. Reviews of current CD releases and colorful photographs flesh out this glossy publication. There's also a great calendar of music-related events around Texas.

THE TEXAS OBSERVER
307 West Seventh Street
(512) 477-0746
www.texasobserver.org
Former Daily Texan writer Ronnie Dugger debuted the Texas Observer in 1954. Within six months the Observer established itself as a new voice in Texas media, becoming the first to report on lynchings in East Texas. For half a century this small biweekly magazine has struggled for survival while breaking the silence on story after story dealing with society's underdogs, the liberal movement, and Democratic causes. Dugger, who owned the paper until turning it over to the nonprofit Texas Democracy Foundation in 1994, called his magazine "A Journal of Free Voices," and wrote in the Observer's mission statement, "never will we overlook or misrepresent the truth to serve the interests of the powerful. . . ." Today the small Austin staff that runs the magazine and the freelance writers from around the state who contribute articles continue to bring to light liberal/progressive issues not treated in the mainstream media.

TEXAS PARKS & WILDLIFE
3000 South I–35, Suite 120
(512) 912-7000, (800) 937-9393
www.tpwmagazine.com

This visually enticing, well-written magazine highlights Texas's great outdoors. Published by the Texas Parks and Wildlife Department in Austin and distributed all over the state, *Texas Parks & Wildlife* is a great source of information for newcomers and residents alike who love the open air.

In and around Austin

HILL COUNTRY NEWS
103 Woods Lane, Cedar Park
(512) 259-4449

Published on Wednesday and Friday, the *Hill Country News* focuses on community news, business, and features in Cedar Park and northwest Austin. On Wednesday the *Hill Country News* is a free publication available in Cedar Park. Also published on Wednesday, *Hill Country News Northwest* is aimed at the Northwest Austin area.

LAKE TRAVIS VIEW
2300 Lohmans Spur, Suite 186
(512) 263-1100
www.laketravisview.com

Even if you don't live in the Lake Travis area, don't miss the *View* in April when it publishes the annual "Lake Travis Summer Guide," a special section that details fun things to do at the lake, including camping, recreational activities, and dining. The rest of the year, the *View* focuses on local government, the Lake Travis Independent School District, and on community news along Lake Travis's sprawling south shore.

OAK HILL GAZETTE
7200–B U.S. 71 West
(512) 301-0123
www.oakhillgazette.com

Residents of the Oak Hill region in south Austin have a wonderful local newspaper that covers just about everything there is to know in their growing neighborhood. News and sports from the local schools; columns from the district's county, state, and federal government leaders; a column aimed at senior citizens and another on lifestyle combine, of course, with area news and business coverage to make a fine neighborhood publication. Published by the Oak Hill husband-and-wife team of Will Atkins and Penny Levers, the *Gazette* has been in business since 1995. It's published on Friday and is available by subscription or at newsstands in the area.

PFLUGERVILLE PFLAG
200 West Main Street, Pflugerville
(512) 251-2220

Pfinding the *Pflag* isn't too hard in Pflugerville, the pfine community with the pfunny name. The *Pflag* is Pflugerville's pflourishing weekly newspaper. Published Thursday, it includes features of interest to local readers as well as community and business news about the town and the surrounding areas of Travis and Williamson Counties.

ROUND ROCK LEADER
105 South Blair Street, Round Rock
(512) 255-5827
www.rrleader.com

Established in 1877, just a few years after the city of Round Rock itself was formed, the Leader has grown significantly from the four-page, hand-set publication of the early days. The paper emphasizes community and school news, covers local and Williamson County politics, and also keep readers informed of the meteoric growth of the city.

WEST AUSTIN NEWS
5407 Parkcrest Drive
(512) 459-5474
www.westaustinnews.com

Serving the neighborhoods of West Austin, Northwest Austin, Rollingwood, and West Lake Hills, the *West Austin News* focuses on community, society, and school news. The weekly newspaper, published on Thursday, was started by local owner and publisher Bart Stephens in 1986. The paper publishes an annual sports guide in the fall and a shopping guide at Christmastime as well as biannual sections on Healthy Living and Home and Garden. In an effort to "Keep Austin Weird" (see the History chapter), newsroom execs say, the *News* sponsors an annual Art Car Parade in April. Artists(?) from all over Texas decorate their cars and show them off during the parade. The Art Car Ball precedes the event.

WESTLAKE PICAYUNE
3103 Bee Caves Road
(512) 327-2990
www.westlakepicayune.com
Serving the community of Westlake, the weekly *Picayune* covers community and local government news and the Eanes Independent School District as well as local arts and entertainment. While the newspaper is sold by subscription and at newsstands, a monthly special section called "Distinct" is mailed free to 10,000 homes in the area, those with the zip codes 78746 and 78733. "Distinct" is the *Picayune*'s lifestyle section and regularly features an article on an interesting local resident. Founded in 1976, the newspaper is now owned by Cox Enterprises, Inc., the Atlanta-based company that owns the *Austin American–Statesman*.

Ethnic Publications

ARRIBA ART & BUSINESS NEWS
1009 East Cesar Chavez Street
(512) 479-6397
Austin's oldest newspaper for the Mexican-American community, *Arriba* was founded in 1980. This eight- to 12-page tabloid, distributed free biweekly, is written in English and Spanish, highlights community and business news, and goes to great lengths to cover the Hispanic cultural scene. In addition to regular features on Hispanic artists, it publishes listings of gallery shows, museum exhibitions, and other events of interest to the community.

EL MUNDO
2116 East Cesar Chavez Street
(512) 476-8636
www.elmundonewspaper.com

An impressive weekly publication for the area's Spanish-speaking population, *El Mundo* includes local, national, and international news and features, as well as sports and entertainment of interest to the Hispanic community. Owned and operated locally by the Angulo family, this newspaper is a strong advocate for area Hispanics and does not shy away from taking issue with the mainstream press over its coverage of the community. The paper is published Thursday and is sold in area newsstands.

EL NORTE
1823 Fort View Road
(512) 448-1023
This Spanish-language monthly newspaper provides information relevant to Austin's Hispanic population, including changes in U.S. immigration policy, news on Hispanic and community leaders, community support organizations, and activities within the area's Catholic churches. The newspaper is distributed throughout the Austin area. Journalist Gloria Montelongo Aguilar and her husband, Miguel, started *El Norte* in May 1996 in the back room of their home with two used computers and a printer bought at a pawn shop.

NOKOA
The Observer
1154–B Angelina Street
(512) 499-8713
Working out of his home, publisher Akwasi Evans debuted *NOKOA* in 1987 with the goal of creating a newspaper that reflected the interests and views of progressive political activists of all ethnicities. For more than a decade, the free weekly paper has championed the rights of African Americans, Hispanics, Anglos, Asians, Native Americans, women, gays, lesbians, and the disabled communities. Evans calls the publication "a true progressive paper with an unabashed African-American perspective." The paper, published Thursday, covers Austin city government and the Texas Legislature when it is in session, as well as local, regional, national, and international news.

VILLAGER NEWSPAPER
1223 Rosewood Avenue
(512) 476-0082
www.austinvillager.com

This free weekly newspaper focuses on news of interest to Austin's African-American community. Owner T. L. Wyatt has been publishing the *Villager* since 1973 as a voice of advocacy with a focus on the positive events in the African-American community. Wyatt calls the *Villager* "the good news newspaper." The paper prints articles not often found in the mainstream press and analyzes news and events that pertain to its readers. Wyatt's weekly editorial column, "Rappin," appears on the front page. Newspapers are available on Friday at distribution points in East, South, and Central Austin.

Yearly Guides

AUSTIN NEWCOMER GUIDE
111 Congress Avenue
(512) 478-9383
www.austin-chamber.org

Published by the Greater Austin Chamber of Commerce, this annual guide provides information on housing, attractions, newcomer information, business, shopping and dining, arts and culture, retirement living, and other areas of interest to the recently arrived. It's sold online or at the chamber offices in downtown Austin. Also available are the chamber's other guides: *Relocation, Business Relocation,* and *Job Search.*

CELEBRATE AUSTIN
7514 North MoPac, Suite 200
(512) 346-6235
www.celebrateaustin.com

This four-color magazine has been giving visitors and newcomers the scoop on Austin for nearly 30 years. *Celebrate Austin,* found in 26,000 hotel rooms around the city, presents features on Austin personalities and places of interest and provides information on myriad topics: home buying, government, education, health care, recreation, shopping, the arts, and the high-tech industry, to name a few. Hardcover versions are placed for perma-

nent use in hotel rooms, but visitors can purchase the take-home softcover version either though the hotel or by mailing in a request card. The publication makes its annual debut in December.

TEXAS STATE TRAVEL GUIDE
150 East Riverside Drive
(800) 8888-TEX
www.traveltex.com

Published in Austin by the Texas Department of Transportation's Travel and Information Division, this hefty guide of nearly 300 pages features highlights of tourist attractions throughout the state. Seven special sections summarize attractions around Texas's major cities, including Austin and the Central Texas area. Among the guide's many attributes are listings and descriptions of nearly 150 Texas lakes. The guide also lists national and state forests as well as state parks. The publication is free and can be requested at the toll-free number above and can also be found at the Capitol Information Center on the grounds of the State Capitol.

TELEVISION

Austin's television industry provides a strong and vital link among residents of Central Texas. Live local news broadcasts relay information and flash the latest images of events and newsmakers around the Texas heartland and the world beyond. In times of tragedy and triumph, no other news medium rivals the awesome power of live television. None but television allows the faces and the voices of the participants themselves to illustrate the immediate events as a story unfolds.

i The locally produced *All Access Live* television show features backstage interviews and live concert performances by Austin and national bands. The show, hosted by VJ Brian "B-Doe" Bymark of the Austin Music Network, debuted October 4, 2003. It airs Saturday at 10:00 p.m. on KNVA, channel 54.

When it comes to television, Austin's national claim to fame is the long-running show *Austin City Limits*. The *Austin American-Statesman* has called this program "the city's cultural calling card to the world." And indeed it is! The program, which debuted in 1975—six years before MTV— is all about music. It showcases local talent as well as nationally and internationally known performers. Taped live on the University of Texas campus (until its new digs open about 2010) and featuring the illuminated Austin skyline as a backdrop, *Austin City Limits* can be seen on PBS stations around the country. The weekly one-hour program airs Saturday at 7:00 p.m. and the following Friday at 11:00 p.m. on the local PBS station, KLRU. While tapings are supposedly open to the public, tickets can be as hard to come by as a cool day in July (see our tips in The Music Scene chapter).

Not many residents of a town Austin's size can tune in to a bit of home while they're on the road. Besides *Austin City Limits* our city also claims *King of the Hill*. The Fox network's popular cartoon sitcom about a family of Texans headed by Hank Hill was created by Austinite Mike Judge, who also created MTV's wildly successful *Beavis and Butt-head*. *King of the Hill* airs on Sunday night at 7:30.

Local Stations

KTBC, Fox, channel 7 (cable 2)
KVUE, ABC, channel 24 (cable 3)
KXAN, NBC, channel 36 (cable 4)
KEYE, CBS, channel 42 (cable 5)
KNVA, CW affiliated, channel 54 (cable 12)
KLRU, PBS, channels 18 and 20 (cable 9 and 20)
KBEJ, UPN affiliated, channel 2 (cable 23)
KAKW, Univision, channel 62 (cable 99)

Cable Providers

Time Warner Cable, (512) 485-6800
Grande Communications, (512) 878-4000
Heartland Wireless, (800) 880-0292
Cox Communications, (512) 930-3085

RADIO

Just as Austin's live music performers inspire fierce loyalties among fans—and ardent debates over favorites—so, too, do the city's radio stations. Radio is a hot commodity here in Central Texas, and the stations that fail to deliver the mysterious programming formula that quickly captivates listeners soon fade into thin air.

On the other hand, a few stations have withstood the test of time. KVET-AM, now an all-sports station, dates back to the post–World War II era and was started by a group of veterans that included John Connally, who was later to become governor of Texas. KUT, Austin's public radio station, began broadcasting on November 10, 1958, and continues to get great ratings for a noncommercial venue. It offers National Public Radio and a wonderfully eclectic mix of music, local bands, and original programming. KGSR, at 107.1 on the FM dial, is another long-shining gem in Austin radio. KGSR plays more local bands than any other area station and offers some excellent original programming. Additionally, KGSR releases an annual CD, *Broadcasts,* that features a mix of local talent and national acts, most in live performances from the studio. Proceeds from sales go to charity.

Country music continues to be enormously popular around these parts, though it isn't the only sound in town—by far. Greater Austin radio serves up a 24-hour feast of music, news, talk, sports, and more music on an impressive number of stations. Rock, jazz, blues, urban, folk, Christian, and the increasingly popular Spanish/Latin beats are just some of the many musical offerings aired around the clock.

i Classical music station KFMA sponsors an annual violin contest for high school seniors in Central Texas, and the winner receives the loan of the station's $10,000 violin for use during his or her senior year. The violin is a replica of a 1742 Giuseppe Guarneri del Gesu violin handcrafted by Austin-based luthier (violin maker) William M. Townsend.

AM and FM Radio Stations

Alternative

KROX 101.5 FM (Rock alternative, mainstream rock)

Christian/Gospel

KFIT 1060 AM (Gospel)
KNLE 88.1 FM (Contemporary Christian)
KQJZ 92.1 FM (Gospel/Christian "positive" music)
KXPW 106.7 FM (Christian hits, dance, mainstream)

Classical/Easy Listening

KMFA 89.5 FM (Classical)

College Radio

KTSW 89.9 FM (College alternative)
KVRX 91.7 FM (Eclectic; 7:00 p.m. to 9:00 a.m. weekdays, 10:00 p.m. to 9:00 a.m. weekends)

Community

KOOP 91.7 (Community operated, eclectic music and talk; 9:00 a.m. to 7:00 p.m. weekdays, 9:00 a.m. to 10:00 p.m. weekends)

Contemporary Hits

KAMX 94.7 FM (Modern rock, Top 40)
KHFI 96.7 FM (Contemporary hits, Top 40)
KBPA 103.5 FM (Pop/rock, 1960s to present)

Country

KASE 100.7 FM (Country)
KVET 98.1 FM (Country, Texas music, Christian, news/talk)

In a Class by Itself

KGSR 107.1 FM (Local bands, blues, jazz, folk, reggae, rock, interviews, live studio performances)

Jazz

KQQT 106.3 FM (Smooth jazz)

News/Sports/Talk

KJCE 1370 AM (Talk, news)
KLBJ 590 AM (Talk, news, good local news)
KOKE 1660 AM (News, talk)
KZNX 1530 AM (ESPN)
KWNX 1260 AM (sports talk)
KVET 1300 AM (24-hour sports, UT sports)

Public Radio

KUT 90.5 FM (Eclectic music, local bands, NPR news)

Rock 'n' Roll/Oldies

KKMJ 95.5 FM (Soft rock)
KFMK 105.9 FM (Oldies, urban oldies, Top 40)
KLBJ 93.7 FM (Rock 'n' roll)
KPEZ 102.3 FM (Classic rock)

Spanish/Tejano

KHHL 98.9 FM (Tejano hits)
KINV 107.7 FM (Regional Mexican)
KKLB 92.5 FM (Tejano and dance)
KTXZ 1560 AM (Salsa, merengue, Spanish rock)

Urban/Rhythmic

KQBT 104.3 FM (Rap, R&B, hip-hop)
KDHT 93.3/99.7 FM (Top 40, R&B, hip-hop)

WORSHIP

When it comes to braggin' rights about whether Texas is God's Country, as many old-timers and newcomers will declare, the facts are clear: Texas has more churches than any other state in the Union. In 1997 the state had approximately 17,000 places of worship, according to that year's *Texas Almanac,* some 2,500 more than second-ranked California, and those numbers have grown. The state also boasts the largest number of church members, around 5.3 million, according to the almanac.

Among Protestants, the largest group belongs to the Southern Baptist Convention—4.5 million adherents. Roman Catholics make up the second largest group, with 4.3 million adherents. Survey data compiled by the almanac also suggests church attendance is higher in the rural areas of Texas than it is in the state's larger cities. In many of the state's smaller communities, the church or religious meeting place is the center of community activity.

When the Mexican flag flew over Texas, Roman Catholicism was the official state religion, and the parish church was the heart of the community. San Antonio's famous missions were established to bring Christianity to the Native Americans, and some of the mission sites were along creekbeds and riverbanks where Native Americans had gathered for centuries to celebrate their own sacred rituals. In the mid-19th century, Protestant preachers accompanied European settlers, although some groups, notably German, Czech, and Polish immigrants, were Catholic. No matter the denomination, church picnics and camp meetings were an important part of social life in 19th-century Texas.

Many of the smaller towns around Austin continue to hold annual church picnics where family members gather, some coming in from their new homes in the city, to renew their ties with their ancestral homes (see our Annual Events and Festivals chapter). A visit to the local church and its accompanying cemetery is a great way to explore Texas history and offers visitors insight into various ethnic customs that have been preserved by immigrant groups and settlers. For example, some of the small Czech communities east of Austin preserve the custom of decorating gravestones with pictures of their loved ones. (See our Attractions chapter for more on Austin's historic cemeteries.)

DIVERSITY

Religion played an important role in both Austin's early life and its development. The log cabin that served as the first state capitol building also was home to a Presbyterian church, but the Presbyterians were not the only denomination in town. From the beginning, Austin had a diverse religious community. In his book *Power, Money & The People: The Making of Modern Austin,* Anthony M. Orum (see our Politics and Perspectives chapter) cites the city's first census, taken in 1840, showing that of the 900 residents 73 were "professors of religion." There were Methodists, Presbyterians, Episcopalians, Baptists, and a large number of Roman Catholics.

In the second half of the century the city blossomed, as did the variety of religious groups. Several of the city's landmark churches were erected in the central city in the latter half of the 18th century. St. David's Episcopal Church, 304 East Seventh Street, was begun in 1854 and completed 16 years later. The Gothic Revival structure includes several genuine Tiffany stained-glass windows. Legend has it that gamblers helped fund the construction, hence its nickname, the "gamblers' church."

St. Mary's Cathedral, 203 East 10th Street, is the city's oldest Catholic church, designed by noted Texas architect Nicholas J. Clayton and built in 1874. The cathedral sits in the shadows of downtown high-rises, but, inside, the beauty of its stained glass, imported from France and Germany, remains vibrant.

Just north of the University of Texas campus in Central Austin is All Saints' Episcopal Chapel, 2629 Whitis Avenue, a Gothic landmark built by Bishop George Herbert Kinsolving in 1899.

The first Swedish Lutheran church in Austin stands at 1510 Congress Avenue. Gethsemane Lutheran Church was built in 1883 in the Gothic Revival–style, and builders utilized bricks from the state capitol building that burned down in 1881.

AUSTIN'S JEWISH COMMUNITY

Just two years after Gethsemane Lutheran Church was completed, the city's first synagogue opened. Congregation Beth Israel was serving the city's small, but very influential, Jewish community. Four of the city's leading businessmen and developers were members—brothers Phineas and Jacob De Cordova and German immigrants and brothers Henry and Morris Hirschfeld.

That tradition of civic leadership continues in the Jewish community. Austin's most famous business entrepreneur, Michael Dell, chairman of Dell Computer Corp., and his wife, Susan, have led the way in the development of the Dell Jewish Community Campus, a 40-acre development adjacent to the Northwest Hills neighborhood in Northwest Austin. The campus is home to several Jewish congregations. The campus also houses the Jewish Community Center and the Jewish Federation of Austin, plus cultural, social, and educational facilities.

The development of the campus did prompt debate and some opposition from neighbors who feared the complex would be too large and produce heavy traffic. The debate is not a new one in Austin. Several churches have experienced significant growth, prompting some neighbors

i The St. Elias Church Festival is held every October in downtown Austin at the stone church built at the height of the Depression by families who came to Austin from Lebanon and Syria in the late 1800s and early part of the 20th century. The festival is a celebration of Mediterranean food, dance, and family traditions. The Orthodox Christian church is located at 408 East 11th Street, (512) 476-2314, www.steliaschurch.org.

to voice concerns. There has been a long-running discussion over the growth of Hyde Park Baptist Church and the neighborhood in Central Austin.

On the positive side, the development of the Dell campus is evidence of Austin's flourishing Jewish population, now estimated at 8,000 members. Much of the growth has come as the city's high-tech center bring in professional workers from other locations around the country. Several local supermarkets have begun to offer kosher food handling and food products in response to the growth.

MULTICULTURAL TRADITIONS

Another impact of the high-tech boom has been the emergence of eastern religious temples in Austin. There are several Buddhist congregations in the city serving Chinese Americans, Japanese Americans, and other ethnic groups. There is also an Islamic center and several mosques in the city. While it is impossible to list every church in the Austin area, several religious organizations are listed at the end of this chapter. The *Austin American–Statesman* has a religion section on Saturday that lists local church and temple activities.

i A rare Gutenberg Bible is on display at the Harry Ransom Humanities Research Center, West 21st and Guadalupe Streets, on the University of Texas campus. One of only 48 extant copies, the Bible was printed in 1449 (see our Arts chapter for more on the center).

One of the most startling and beautiful sights in the Austin area is the Shree Raseshwari Radaha Rani Temple, the largest Hindu temple in North America, located on the outskirts of Southwest Austin. Built by Hindu artisans, this white-walled Indian-style temple with its colorful, intricate wooden decorations, sits near fields of golden marigolds on what once was a Texas cattle ranch. The temple, part of the Barsana Dham ashram, holds several important celebrations each year that evoke the spirituality of India. The Barsana Dham complex is approximately 5 miles south of U.S. Highway 290 West, on F.M. 1826 (Camp Ben McCullough Road).

Many of the city's diverse religious groups welcome visitors to their celebrations. Chinese and Vietnamese New Year, Hindu festivals, Buddhist observances, Roman Catholic feast days, Greek Orthodox festivals, are windows into the multicultural soul of Austin. (See our Annual Events and Festivals chapter for festival days.)

HISPANIC TRADITIONS

One popular Catholic festival is held December 12 in honor of Our Lady of Guadalupe, the dark-skinned Virgin who appeared to a poor Mexican peasant on a hill outside Mexico City. The day is celebrated with dancing and street processions by parishioners of Our Lady of Guadalupe Church, 1206 East Ninth Street. Built in 1907, the Catholic church is home to Austin's oldest Hispanic parish.

Several churches in the diocese offer services in Spanish and conduct Mariachi Masses throughout the year.

Another annual tradition that reflects the rich Hispanic heritage in this region is the Christmas Posada. In the days before Christmas, children dressed as Mary and Joseph go from door to door seeking a refuge as their namesakes did more than 2,000 years ago. Named for the Spanish word for "inn," the nightly treks can take place for one night or several, but they always end at the parish church (see our Annual Events chapter).

The Catholic Church is a vital part of Austin's Hispanic traditions, and it also serves as a focal point of community and a central point for social groups and political grassroots organizations.

AFRICAN-AMERICAN TRADITIONS

Among the first churches in Austin were those serving the city's African-American population. The Metropolitan African Methodist Episcopal Church, 1105 East 10th Street, in the heart of East Austin, was built in 1923 and is the oldest African-American church in Austin that remains active.

In a time when social inequalities were the norm, the African-American church served a vital role in Austin, as it did throughout the country. One of the first African-American church leaders in Austin was the Reverend Jacob Fontaine, who founded the Sweethome Baptist Church in Clarksville (see our Relocation chapter), the historic, once predominantly African-American neighborhood just west of downtown Austin and north of West Sixth Street. The original church is gone, but its name and spirit live on at the new church, built in 1935 at 1725 West 11th Street. A historic landmark, the building now stands at the heart of a popular gentrified neighborhood.

The Reverend Fontaine also was instrumental in founding other historic African-American congregations, according to Orum's *Power, Money & The People*. Fontaine founded the First Baptist Church, which once stood on the site now occupied by the city's downtown library. Another pioneering churchman in the African-American community was Francis Webber, an Anglo priest from Detroit who came to Austin in 1935. Orum credits Webber with reaching out to the African-American community from his parish headquarters, Holy Cross Church, particularly in providing health care for the city's Mexican-American and African-American communities.

Throughout the dark days of segregation, into the civil rights era, and now into the 21st century, the city's African-American churches have been involved in all aspects of the community's growth and survival. Greater Calvary Missionary Baptist Church operates a life training program for African-American male teens called Rites of

Passage. Once a week, boys ages 6 to 18 gather at the center to participate in the program. The program seeks to boost self-esteem and school grades and help participants learn the value of social consciousness, plus learn leadership and decision-making skills. The church members, many of whom are working poor, award small scholarships to the program graduates. The program, now being eyed by other churches in the area, receives no government funding.

SOCIAL ACTIVISM

Given the city's political life and history, it is natural that social activism has been a hallmark of several Austin churches for decades. Professor Orum cites the impact University of Texas campus church organizations and the Austin YMCA had on bringing students from diverse backgrounds together in the '30s and '40s.

Many Austin churches are committed to community causes, such as collecting food for the city's Food Bank or serving meals to the homeless. One young church member from an affluent and active West Austin church began a book drive for homeless men and women who pass through her church's soup kitchen. From the smallest effort to well-organized, major fund-raising campaigns, Austin's churches are engaged in serving the community. Some have taken their activism into the public-policy arena, representing both conservative and liberal thinking.

One of the most influential organizations, particularly on issues of education, is Austin Interfaith. Its membership is made up of church members from a diversity of congregations, many of them anchored in the city's working-class neighborhoods.

Interfaith was organized by Ernesto Cortes Jr., a legendary social activist who heads the Southwest office of a national grassroots political organization called the Industrial Areas Foundation, a network of mostly church-based coalitions aimed at community activism. The late Saul Alinsky, a community organizer from Chicago, created the foundation in 1940. Like Alinsky, his mentor, Cortes and his followers have been called radical by

i Several Austin churches celebrate October 4, feast day of St. Francis of Assisi, by holding blessing of the animals gatherings. Check the Religion listings in the Saturday edition of the *Austin American–Statesman.*

some, but there is no question the Austin Interfaith group has evolved into a potent force.

Like its sister organizations in Texas, Rio Grande Valley Interfaith and the very powerful Communities Organized for Public Service in San Antonio, the Austin group commands the attention of local politicians. City council members and school board officials are particularly attentive. Although the group does not endorse candidates, it does query them at intense, detailed "accountability sessions." Austin Interfaith has worked on several ballot initiatives and is credited with ensuring strong support in the minority communities, where it is particularly active.

POLITICAL CLOUT

Texas is a Bible Belt state. Generally speaking, north of Austin is considered staunch Bible Belt country, home to many of the state's most conservative churches and denominations. South of Austin is generally considered to be less conservative, more likely Catholic than Protestant.

Occasionally, a church in Austin will find itself at odds with a national church body over its stand on issues. Recently, one Baptist church was expelled from the Southern Baptist Convention because of its recognition of gay marriages. The incident is evidence of the city's liberalism, but other Baptist churches in the city are in step with their national leadership on such issues. Diversity is the keyword in Austin.

In general terms though, conservative religious views do manifest themselves north and east of Austin. In state elections on the lottery, for example, voters north and east of Austin tended to vote against gambling initiatives. The few dry counties in Texas are located north of Austin, also. In Travis County, home of the capital city, 48.4

percent of the churchgoers are Roman Catholic, according to the *Texas Almanac,* while immediately to the north in Williamson County, home of Round Rock, Southern Baptists make up 46.9 percent of the churchgoing public.

Williamson County politics, both at the school board and at city, county, and state levels, tend to be more conservative. Juries in Williamson County mete out harsher punishments, and the local newspapers are more conservative in tone. That same conservatism is reflected in community religious views.

PLACES TO WORSHIP

There are churches of all persuasions in Austin, some liberal, others conservative; some traditional, others decidedly New Age; some fundamentalist, some experimental. The *Austin American–Statesman* profiles a place of worship every Saturday.

A resource list of some of the religious organizations follows:

- Austin Baptist Association (1016 East 38th Street, 512-454-2558, www.austinbaptist.org) is an Austin umbrella group for Southern Baptist churches.
- Austin Area Interreligious Ministries (700 Tilery Street, Suite. 8, 512-386-9145, www.aaimaustin.org) is an interfaith group with 120 churches in its membership and works to coordinate community involvement in social issues.
- Hillel Foundation at UT Austin (2105 San Antonio Street, 512-476-0125, www.texashillel.org) is a Jewish center for university students that reaches out to convey aspects of Jewish culture to the community.

- Church of Jesus Christ of Latter-day Saints, Institute of Religion, 2020 San Antonio Street, (512) 478-8575, www.ldsces.org.
- Episcopal Diocese of Texas, 606 Rathervue Place, (512) 478-0580, www.epicenter.org.
- Friends Meeting of Austin, 3014 Washington Square, (512) 452–1841, www.austinquakers.org.
- International Buddhist Progress Society, 6720 North Capital of Texas Highway, (512) 386-6789.
- Islamic Center of Greater Austin, 1906 Nueces Street, (512) 476–2563, www.austinmosque.org.
- Jewish community Association of Austin, 7300 Hart Lane, (512) 735-8000, www.shalomaustin.org.
- Roman Catholic Diocese of Austin, 1600 North Congress Avenue, (512) 476–4888, www.austindiocese.org.
- Texas District Lutheran Church–Missouri Synod, 7900 US 290 East, (512) 926–4272, www.txdistlcms.org.
- Texas Conference of Churches (1033 La Posada Drive, 512-451–0991, www.txconfchurches.org) represents 51 religious governing bodies and is dedicated to promoting religious unity.
- United Methodist Church, Austin district, 1221 West Ben White Boulevard, Ste. 201-A, (512) 444–1983, www.umcad.org.

INDEX

ABOUT THE AUTHORS

CAM ROSSIE

Cam Rossie is a journalist and freelance writer who started her professional career while still a university student, working as a reporter, copy editor, and editor for daily and weekly newspapers in the Midwest. A former domestic and foreign correspondent for the Associated Press news service, her news and feature articles have appeared in newspapers throughout the United States and abroad. Her career with the AP began in Nebraska and later took her to New Mexico, Texas's Rio Grande Valley, and New York City. In 1984 she was chosen to open a new AP bureau in Northern Mexico. From her base of operations in Monterrey, Cam covered the U.S.–Mexico border from coast to coast, as well as other regions of Mexico and Central America. She is fluent in Spanish and is an accomplished public speaker who has lectured on journalism issues in the United States and Mexico.

An international journalism scholarship took her to Caracas, Venezuela, for nearly two years, sparking an interest in world cultures that remains to this day. In addition to living and working many years in Mexico and South America, Cam also lived for several years in Europe, where she wrote on education issues. While not at home in Austin, she travels throughout the United States and the world. Her passion for globe-trotting has taken her to more than 25 countries in Europe, Africa, the Middle East, and Central and South America. Her daughter, Quint Simon, was born in Mexico and has grown up as a third culture kid. This is Cam's sixth edition of *Insiders' Guide to Austin*.

HILARY HYLTON

Hilary Hylton is a freelance writer and author whose work covers a variety of topics, including business, social issues, personalities, government, politics, cuisine, and travel. Her work has been published in national, international, and regional publications.

Hilary has lived in Austin since 1977, watching it grow and change. She has written about many aspects of life in Austin—its food, politics, lifestyles, and business—for both Texas and national publications. Hilary is a freelance reporter for *TIME* magazine. Her magazine articles also have appeared in major city, business, lifestyle, and airline magazines—features on food, travel, business, and political personalities. Prior to freelancing, she worked as a journalist for several Florida and Texas newspapers. Her work was honored with a number of awards, including Texas Star Reporter by the Austin Headliners' Club. Hilary is also the author of a guidebook, *Texas Monthly's Mexico: A Completely Up-to-Date Guide to an Extraordinary Country*. Hilary is married to Peter Silva, an award-winning photographer represented by Zuma Press. They have two Australian shepherds, siblings Ben and Pepper, and several cats who serve as substitute livestock for the dogs. Hilary's personal interests include reading history, armchair travel, gardening, cooking, and collecting cookbooks—interests all nurtured by Austin's vibrant offerings.